Johnny Stephens
4th
Mt. Carmel School
942-2156

NEW HORIZONS
World Guide

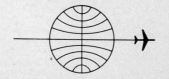

NEW

HORIZONS

World Guide

Pan American's
Travel Facts About 89 Countries

PAN AMERICAN WORLD AIRWAYS

EIGHTH REVISED EDITION: 1959–1960
FIRST PRINTING

ACKNOWLEDGMENT

This book was made possible through the cooperation
and assistance of our employees and agents in the countries and lands served by the Pan American. We also wish
to acknowledge the helpful assistance given by the tourist
offices and Consuls of the various countries represented.
Weather data were supplied by the United States Weather
Bureau and Ivan Ray Tannehill's *Weather Around the
World,* published by the Princeton University Press.

Inquiries and comments should be addressed to Pan American World Airways, P. O. Box 1790, New York 17, New
York.

NOTE: *While we have made every effort to provide current
and accurate information, there are frequent changes in immigration requirements, hotel rates and other facts relating
to travel abroad; and we can accept no responsibility for
inaccuracies and omissions.*

LIBRARY OF CONGRESS CATALOG CARD NUMBER: 54–5818
MANUFACTURED IN THE UNITED STATES OF AMERICA.
CLIPPER AND NEW HORIZONS, TRADE MARKS, REG. U.S. PAT. OFF.
TRADE DISTRIBUTION BY SIMON & SCHUSTER
630 FIFTH AVENUE, NEW YORK 20, N. Y.

FOREWORD

No one before has ever attempted to publish a book quite like this. It is not a "travel book" in the ordinary sense at all. It does not deal with "impressions"; but rather with useful facts, carefully gathered by Pan American from its stations in all parts of the world.

As you read these facts you will come to some interesting conclusions: You will see, for example, why summer is not necessarily the best time for a vacation. You will see how the airplane has made it possible to take advantage of the fact that the seasons are reversed south of the equator. December is June (weatherwise) in Rio de Janeiro. January is July in New Zealand; in Australia; in Santiago, Chile; in Buenos Aires and in South Africa. You will see that Mexico, Guatemala and the West Indies have an even better climate in "winter" than in summer. They're only minutes away from Miami, New Orleans, Houston and Los Angeles—or a few short hours away from any city in the United States. You will note that Europe is less than 7 hours by Jet Clipper, South America less than 12 hours.

You'll realize, too, that as in the United States, cities in Europe and elsewhere are often at their best in the winter when the theater, music and social season is in full swing; yet prices are considerably less.

You will discover that being unfamiliar with a foreign language is no longer any barrier to foreign travel. English, as you will note in country after country, has actually spread around the entire world.

As you thumb through the pages you'll probably get the urge to go somewhere. If you really need an excuse to do something about it, bear in mind that doctors all agree: vacations are a very necessary part of modern life. You owe it to your job, your health and your home life to take a vacation. There's no vacation like a trip, and no trip like a trip abroad.

TABLE OF

CONTENTS

HOW TO MAKE THE BEST USE
OF THIS BOOK

THE many countries covered in *New Horizons* are grouped into eight general areas taking in the entire world. Within each area, which is introduced by a regional relief map, the countries are arranged alphabetically. They are also listed in this order in the Table of Contents. (*See* Pages 6 and 7.) For your added convenience, there is an index in the back of the book that lists alphabetically more than a thousand places covered in the guide.

Each individual country is introduced by a map showing the principal points of interest for tourists, a weather chart (with which you can compare the weather of American cities you know on pages 18 and 19, and such background statistics as SIZE and POPULATION. In addition, there is a brief summary of CHARACTERISTICS, which will be useful in helping you make up your mind as to the type of place you want to visit. Following this, alphabetically arranged under paragraph headings, are more than three dozen subjects providing you with facts that you will need to know before you leave the United States and facts that will be helpful during your visit in specific countries. Concluding the data on each country, SOURCES OF FURTHER INFORMATION are given.

TIPS FOR YOUR
TRAVELING CONVENIENCE

1. To get a passport, you'll need your birth certificate (or a notarized affidavit of your birth which is vouched for by a relative or person who has known you a long time). You'll need two passport pictures (front view, 3″ x 3″ on a white background). A passport costs $10 for individuals or families traveling together. It is valid for two years and can be renewed for two more years for $5.

Apply in person at the Passport Division of the Department of State, or the Passport Agencies of the Department of State in Miami, New York and San Francisco—or in other cities apply at the office of the Clerk of a Federal Court.

Be sure to sign your passport and keep it on your person at all times (except, of course, when your hotel concierge in some countries needs to borrow it temporarily when you register)—*not in your baggage.* Specific papers required for entry by each country from United States citizens are listed with the countries on pages that follow.

2. Before you leave the United States, it's best to have visas and tourist cards (where required) for each country you think you *might* visit, because in some foreign countries it takes a long time to get them for other countries.

3. Some travelers realize a saving by exchanging some of their money into foreign currency before leaving the United States, where one may frequently get a better rate of exchange, but be careful to note the total amount of foreign currencies that may be taken into each country. The Clipper Passenger's Currency Converter lists currency for many countries with the United States equivalents.

4. It's handy to carry a few one-dollar bills with you so that it is not necessary to cash a traveler's check or exchange a large bill into local currency in order to make small purchases in those countries where you plan only a short stop-over between planes.

5. Just as the water in one section of the United States differs from that of another, the water of many foreign countries varies; and even though it may be safe to drink, i.e., sanitary, some people may contract diarrhea due to the *change* of water. This also applies to the ice in drinks. Consult your doctor as to what medicine to take along. A good rule to follow is—when in doubt, drink bottled water.

6. Specific health documents required for individual countries are listed under customs regulations in each chapter of this book. The general requirements are: for re-entry to the United States and for entry to most foreign countries you need a smallpox vaccination certificate. It's advisable to have this before you leave the U. S. Yellow fever and cholera certificates are required by most countries from passengers who have come from an infected area. Nearly all countries of the world have adopted the international sanitary regulations of the World Health Organization. These regulations establish the following periods of validity for vaccination certificates: smallpox—not less than 8 days nor more than 3 years old; yellow fever—not less than 10 days nor more than 6 years old; cholera—not less than 6 days nor more than 6 months old; typhus and typhoid-paratyphoid inoculation certificates are not required under the WHO sanitary regulations as a prerequisite for admission. They are recommended, however, for visits to some countries. The record of these inoculations must be entered by the health authority in the official WHO certificate of vaccination form. Passengers should obtain a copy of the form from the Pan American Ticket Office before obtaining their inoculations.

7. Tours—or pre-arranged travel plans—are often the answer to seeing the most and doing the most. Escorted tours are scheduled frequently; independent tours start any day you wish. All reservations are assured, you know the exact cost in advance, transportation is by the most direct and advisable routes with no timetable problems, hotels are carefully selected, meeting and transfer service and advice of a local representative are always available, and well-planned sightseeing leaves plenty of free time for personal activities. Often these established travel plans can be modified or extended to suit special interests and desires. You will find a wide choice of tours available.

8. In writing abroad from the United States, it's best to use International Air Mail. Rates per half-ounce are 10 cents to the Caribbean, Central and South America; 15 cents to Europe; 25 cents elsewhere. Air mail single postcards are 10 cents each to most countries, except Canada and Mexico, where they are 4 cents.

9. If you feel you can organize a group of friends or members of an organization for a trip abroad, you may want to check on Pan American's Tour Conductor Plan, by which you can obtain your own passage free of charge.

10. To avoid inconvenience and Customs in each country you visit, you may send gifts to the United States duty free without declaring them or paying duty or tax, providing the value of each parcel does not exceed $10 and does not include alcoholic beverages, perfume containing alcohol, or tobacco. *You don't have to deduct the value of these gifts from your duty exemptions* described on the next page. You may send as many gifts as you wish but not more than one parcel a day to the same person. International Air Parcel Post is convenient and fast. Mark "Gift" on the outside of each package.

11. If you don't want to disturb your savings, you can now budget part or practically all of your expenses including air fare, hotel accommodations, meals, sightseeing, etc., on the Pan Am Pay Later Plan. You can pay as little as 10 per cent down, then pay the balance in as many as 20 monthly installments. You can make the arrangements quickly and confidentially. No collateral needed.

12. 35mm Kodachrome slides in standard 2″ x 2″ frames covering travel areas all over the world are now available, should you want to augment your collection of travel pictures with some excellent shots taken by professional photographers.

13. Under Pan Am's Family Fare Plan families can travel together to many areas at extra savings during winter months. The savings are substantial.

14. If you are interested in foreign food, buy a copy of the de luxe *Complete Round the World Cookbook* of over 600 recipes gathered from famous hotels, restaurants and gourmets all over the world.

15. For the angler, *Fabulous Fishing in Latin America,* a guide to the 60 best fishing areas in Mexico, the Caribbean, Central and South America can be purchased.

16. For jet passengers and others who want to know details of jet travel, a booklet *Your Jet Clipper, New Way to a Magic World of Travel* is available.

Another Useful Travel Guide

The companion to this volume is NEW HORIZONS USA, Pan American's Guide to travel in the United States.

This 544-page book, which contains useful travel information, maps, and pictures, is available from the same sources as NEW HORIZONS WORLD GUIDE.

HOW TO CLEAR U.S. CUSTOMS
THE EASIEST WAY

INFORMATION FOR U.S. RESIDENTS

HALF THE fun of traveling is acquiring duty-free "bargains." Your purchases up to the value of $200, $300 or even $500—depending upon the circumstances—are exempt from duty if (1) they are for your personal or household use; (2) you declare them properly on your arrival in the United States; (3) your trip was not made just to buy them; (4) you didn't order them ahead of time. Bear this in mind when ordering from a representative of a foreign bootmaker or tailor, soliciting orders in the United States.

PURCHASES UP TO $500 DUTY FREE

Ordinarily, you have to be outside the country for at least 48 hours to qualify for the $200 exemption (allowed once in any 31-day period). You get an additional $300 exemption (total $500) if you have been abroad at least 12 days (allowed once each six months). Be sure to read about the important new regulation by which you can send gifts back to the United States without including them in these limitations. See Travel Tip No. 10 on Page 10.

Your exemptions may include the cost of alterations and of dutiable repairs on anything you took abroad—such as your car, radio, watch, etc. But remember this: Your exemptions are lost on any article which you fail to declare on your return from the trip on which you acquired it.

LIQUOR AND CIGARS

You can bring into the country the equivalent of 1 U.S. gallon of alcoholic beverages—but only if destined for a "wet" state; and not more than 100 cigars.

NO EXEMPTIONS ON SOME ITEMS

Be sure you know exactly what you can bring into the United States. There are some things which no one can bring into the country. Some other articles always require payment of duty or internal revenue tax.

Many fruits, vegetables, plants, seeds, flowers including corsages, meats and pets must meet Department of Agriculture or Public Health Service requirements. Any Pan American office can give you the latest requirements.

The advice of your customs officials is helpful when you want to bring back articles bearing a U.S. registered trade mark—especially watches, perfumes, and accordions.

Articles coming from Communist China or North Korea cannot be brought into the U.S. In addition, Chinese-type articles produced in other countries may require a Certificate of Origin. Consult the nearest U.S. Consul for the latest requirements before making purchases of this type.

WHAT'S ITS "VALUE"?

To the customs, the value of an article is its current sales price. Your sales slips or receipts can be your proof. If bringing back something that was given to you, put down as closely as you can its fair market value. But in any case, don't undervalue anything you acquired abroad! You'll find your customs officer an authority on all kinds of merchandise, including art objects and souvenirs.

CAN YOU PROVE PRIOR POSSESSION?

Naturally, you don't want to pay duty on personal possessions you took with you from this country. To be safe, register with Customs before beginning your trip any questionable article, such as a watch or camera of foreign manufacture.

SPECIAL RULES ON "SWING-BACK" TRIPS

A special situation exists along the United States borders. If you find your route through Latin America is going to involve a "swing-back" into the United States, including Puerto Rico, consult your nearest customs officer about its effect on your exemptions. If you fail to meet certain requirements at this "swing-back," you may lose your exemptions.

Can you declare orally? Under certain conditions you need only tell the Customs officer orally what articles you have to declare. Your purser aboard the Clipper will help you to determine if you qualify. In all cases, you will have to make a written declaration if duty or internal revenue tax is to be assessed or if articles are shipped to you.

MAKE FRIENDS WITH YOUR TRAVEL AGENT

THERE ARE few things in this world that are more fun than traveling. Yet there are a number of people who don't realize that one of the best ways to go about making the most of their travel time and money is to go first to a travel agent. A travel agent is an *expert* in the complicated details of arranging travel . . . figuring out routes and itineraries, reservations and costs. Experienced travelers use a travel agent's many services because he can get confirmed hotel accommodations and other reservations in advance—so important in countries where space is limited. Furthermore, it's such a *convenience* to have all your travel details handled for you.

And remember, it often saves you *time* and *money* when you utilize the services of a travel agent. Travel agents sell on a commission basis, paid by the companies they are authorized to represent. Since they represent a wide variety of transportation, hotel and tour organizations *in all price brackets,* they can give you unprejudiced advice on filling your individual needs and wishes. A travel agent knows best how to keep your travel costs down.

Often the travel agent can *save* you money by safeguarding you against mistakes and blunders that are not only embarrassing but costly. Also he often knows of travel, conducted and independent tours or sightseeing bargains that would otherwise not be known to you, or that are purchasable here, but not in the countries you plan to visit.

The trip you are making can be a high point in your life. Let your travel agent show you how.

PHOTOGRAPHY DATA
FOR AIR TRAVELERS

In the alphabetical listing of subject headings for each country in this book you will find a paragraph on photography that describes the local availability of film, camera equipment and developing facilities. As a general rule, however, it is best to take along with you supplies for your entire trip. In countries where specific import restrictions apply, these facts are included under customs regulations and documents required for united states citizens. Where there are no specific restrictions, the general rule should be to avoid bringing in quantities that would invite suspicion as to their use for other than personal reasons. Many persons carrying film in large quantities break the seals open and write their names and addresses on the packages, thus making it obvious that the film is being brought in for personal use. There are a few pointers about registering foreign cameras in the introductory section "How to Clear U. S. Customs the Easiest Way" on Page 11.

As noted, in several countries the photographing of military installations and evidences of poverty is forbidden. When in doubt, inquire first and be sure to obtain permission from local people before taking their picture.

You'll probably wish to take many pictures as a record of your trip and some from your Clipper window enroute, as well. Here are a few general suggestions and charts showing proper camera settings:

1. While flying, do not take movies or snapshots in either color or black and white when haze or smoke make it difficult to see the ground. A little blue haze doesn't matter much, although it's a good idea to use a haze filter.

2. To avoid possible reflection from the airplane window, hold your camera close to it without touching it. Let your body cushion the camera from small bumps. Take your pictures from the shady side of the plane, if possible. Most of the time this will be the left side when flying east, the right side when flying west.

3. When making aerial pictures, you should use, for stills, a shutter speed of at least 1/100 of a second or faster if your camera permits. Shoot movies at 32 frames per second.

4. Be completely familiar with your camera and its results. Keep it as cool and dry as possible when traveling in humid areas. Remember to take some pictures with human interest, not just postal card monuments (have your photo subjects *doing* something). Never hand-hold your camera when shooting at less than 1/25 of a second. Follow faithfully the exposure instructions which apply, but above all don't worry about it. Everyone misses a good shot occasionally.

5. Paragraph No. 12 on page 10 tells how you can purchase professional 35mm Kodachrome slides to augment your own collection.

Still Camera Settings for Kodacolor or Black-and-White Film in Sunlight
(Film with daylight speed of 50, such as Kodak Verichrome, or Ansco Plenachrome)

Landscapes	$\frac{1}{100}$ second at f/8 or $\frac{1}{200}$ second at f/5.6
Clouds (from above)	$\frac{1}{100}$ second at f/11–16 or $\frac{1}{200}$ second at f/8–11

Still Camera Settings for Kodachrome or Ansco Color Films at 1/100 Second
(For 1/200 second, use next larger lens opening)

Altitude	Bright Sun	Hazy Sun	Cloudy Bright
Below 2,000 ft.	Between 4 and 5.6	Between 2.8–4	Between 2–2.8
2,000 ft. to 4,000 ft.	f/5.6	f/4	f/2.8
4,000 ft. and up	Between 5.6–8	Between 4–5.6	Clouds from above, 8

NOTE: Always use a shutter speed of at least 1/100 second for aerial photographs.

Motion Picture Camera Settings for Kodachrome Film, Daylight Type 8 or 16 mm.
16 Frames per Second
(At 32 frames per second use next larger lens opening)

Altitude	Bright Sun	Hazy Sun	Cloudy Bright	Cloudy Dull
Below 2,000 ft.	f/8	5.6	4	2.8
2,000 ft. to 4,000 ft.	f/8–11	5.6–8	4–5.6	2.8–4
4,000 ft. and up	f/11	8	Clouds from above, f/11–16	Clouds from above, f/11–16

FACTS ABOUT
JET CLIPPER TRAVEL

IN THE fall of 1955, Pan American World Airways set the stage for the Jet Air Age by being the first U. S. airline to order a fleet of jets—44 in all. The first U. S.-built Jet Airliners were placed in service by Pan American October 26, 1958, although the prototype had been flying in tests and training flights for well over 2 years.

The planes are designed to cruise 575 miles an hour at 30,000 feet, or some 200 miles an hour more than the DC-7's, the previous top performer in Pan Am's international fleet. With favorable winds, they can reach ground speeds well above that figure.

The Boeing Stratoliner 707-121, first to be delivered, can carry from 90 to 165 passengers depending on the seating arrangement and space allotted to lounges, coatrooms and galleys. The larger (by over 25 tons) 707-321 Intercontinental can carry from 96 to 177 passengers. The Douglas DC-8's can carry from 88 to 159 passengers. All have a range of more than 4,000 miles.

The new Jet Clippers greatly reduce scheduled flight times throughout the world. For not only are they inherently much faster, but they operate with aids that minimize weather delays and permit seeking the most favorable wind conditions. Few cities of the world are more than a half day away from the U. S. by Pan Am Jet Clipper. The 707 Intercontinental could fly around the world in 40 hours flying time, needing only five stops for refueling. A 707 prototype set a passenger flight record of three hours and 48 minutes between Seattle and Baltimore—an average of 612 m.p.h., with ground speeds at times exceeding the speed of sound—658 m.p.h. at 31,000 feet. Jet Clippers set new transatlantic records during their first weeks of scheduled flights.

When they went into service, scheduled flying time from the United States to Paris (3,750 miles) dropped from 11 hours and 25 minutes to less than 7 hours, and other flights speeded up accordingly. Jet flying time from Chicago to London is only about 7 hours, 15 minutes; Tokyo to Seattle, 8 hours, 32 minutes; and New York to Buenos Aires, 11 hours, 15 minutes.

Pan American was the first U. S. airline to operate pure Jet Aircraft. Most planes previously operated by United States and worldwide airlines were piston-engine aircraft. Some airlines have turbo-prop-powered planes in service (primarily the British-built Viscount and Britannia). Turbo-propeller aircraft do have some speed advantage over piston-engine planes, but they are not jets.

Many of the larger pressurized piston-engine planes are capable of flying high enough to reach the so-called jet stream. In essence the jet stream is a huge circumpolar whirl of air, circling the globe from West to East. Its course varies from twenty-five to fifty thousand feet above Earth's surface; and when its extreme velocity is at the lower level, planes flying within it may add as much as 200 miles per hour to their normal cruising speeds. Pan Am Clippers frequently take advantage of the jet stream on Eastbound flights over the Atlantic and Pacific. However, the speed benefit of the jet stream is not consistent enough to allow reflection in published schedules. For the jet stream is apt to be erratic, on rare occasions even reversing itself with East-to-West winds up to 50 m.p.h.

WHAT WILL
THE WEATHER BE LIKE?

NATURALLY, the weather is one of your most practical concerns in planning your trip, because your comfort and much of your fun depend on having good weather.

That's why you'll find a chart showing average daily temperature highs and lows and average number of days with rainfall at the beginning of each section in this book, and a paragraph under the heading CLIMATE for each country.

Temperature figures in themselves mean little to most of us, but we do have a very definite *impression* of normal or average weather where we live or in locations we visit frequently.

The chart on pages 18–19, gives average temperatures in various cities in the United States, for each month of the year. By comparing these figures with the charts for the various countries, you can get a general impression of what kind of weather to expect.

First, a few general observations. Of course, in the Southern Hemisphere, the seasons are the reverse of ours, making our winter an ideal time to visit many of the countries below the equator. Most islands of the West Indies (where you'll find only a few degrees' variation between summer and winter temperatures) are ideal for vacationing almost any month of the year. Many of the cities you will visit in various parts of the world are either seaports or near large bodies of water, which tend to moderate the weather and reduce extremes between daily highs and lows or day and night temperatures. In very warm areas, such as Bolivia or Ecuador on the equator, however, inland cities in the mountains are the most comfortable places. It is about 5 degrees cooler for every 1,500 feet of altitude than it is at sea level. The altitude of principal cities is given in the weather chart for each country. In general, cities with daily variations of not more than 12 degrees are more comfortable than localities with abrupt changes between day and night readings.

Latitude, too, is an important determining factor in climate, and in the weather chart for each country you will find the latitude of the principal city given. In the following chart, next to each United States city, the latitude and altitude are given for comparison.

With allowances for altitude and proximity to the ocean, areas of similar latitude north or south have similar climates. Compare New Zealand and the West Coast of the United States, which are about the same distance from the equator. Note that Mexico City, on about the same latitude as Honolulu, is slightly cooler, with greater variation between lows and highs because of the altitude and distance from the ocean.

As another guidepost, keep in mind that climatologists consider 68 degrees the ideal temperature for human comfort, or 60 degrees if you are engaged in active sports.

Now, a look at the charts will show you, for example, that Cape Town in the Union of South Africa in June (the coolest month) is like Chicago in May, and that the summer weather there (December to February) is very near the ideal 68 degrees. The weather in western Europe is something like the weather in western United States; compare London and Seattle.

In the South Pacific, summer temperatures in Sydney, Australia (December to February), are similar to summer temperatures in Portland, Maine. Both summer and winter temperatures in the southern parts of Italy and Spain are about the same as in South Carolina.

A comparison of days of rainfall on the following chart with the rainfall figures for each country will also help give you a preview of your vacation weather. If there is as much as .01 of an inch of precipitation, the meterologists call it a day with rain. But if the rain occurs in a month when temperatures are warm, you can usually expect more showers in an otherwise pleasant, sunny day. If the rainy day occurs during a cold-weather month, however, the whole day is more likely to be gloomy. With temperatures below freezing, the precipitation is probably snow or sleet.

Even though weather is a logical sequence of natural causes, there's no foretelling unseasonable weather or record-setting temperatures, so don't expect the weather you experience on your vacation to conform with monthly averages every time. But wherever it's convenient, why not pack as much pleasure as possible into your trip and plan to visit a country when it's at its best, weather-wise? If you want to delve further into the fascinating subject of the weather, get a copy of *Weather Around the World,* by Ivan Ray Tannehill, chief forecaster of the United States Weather Bureau. It's published by Princeton University Press.

AVERAGE FAHRENHEIT TEMPERATURES

+ DAYS OF RAIN

FOR CITIES IN THE UNITED STATES

TO COMPARE WITH OTHER COUNTRIES

	JAN.	FEB.	MAR.	APR.	MAY	JUNE	JULY	AUG.	SEPT.	OCT.	NOV.	DEC.
EAST												
Boston	29°	29°	37°	47°	58°	67°	72°	70°	64°	54°	43°	32°
Lat. N42°21′—Alt. 21′	12*	10*	12*	11*	11	10	10	10	9	9	10*	11*
New York	31°	31°	39°	49°	60°	69°	74°	73°	67°	56°	45°	35°
Lat. N40°45′—Alt. 55′	12*	10*	11*	11	11	11	11	10	9	9	9	11*
Portland, Maine	20°	22°	33°	43°	53°	62°	68°	67°	59°	50°	38°	25°
Lat. N43°39′—Alt. 160′	12*	11*	13*	11*	12	12	11	10	10	10	11*	11*
Washington, D. C.	35°	36°	44°	54°	65°	73°	77°	75°	69°	57°	46°	37°
Lat. N38°53′—Alt. 25′	11*	10*	12*	11	12	11	11	11	8	8	9	10*
SOUTH												
Atlanta	43°	46°	53°	61°	70°	77°	79°	78°	73°	63°	52°	45°
Lat. N33°45′—Alt. 1050′	12	11	11	10	9	11	12	12	8	7	8	11
Asheville	39°	40°	47°	55°	63°	70°	73°	72°	67°	57°	46°	39°
Lat. N35°35′—Alt. 1985′	11	10	12	11	12	13	15	13	9	7	8	10
Charleston	51°	52°	58°	65°	73°	79°	82°	81°	77°	68°	58°	54°
Lat. N32°46′—Alt. 16′	10	9	9	8	8	11	13	13	10	6	7	9
Houston	53°	56°	63°	69°	75°	81°	83°	83°	79°	71°	62°	55°
Lat. N29°45′—Alt. 40′	10	9	8	7	7	8	10	9	9	6	8	10
Miami	68°	68°	71°	74°	77°	80°	82°	82°	81°	78°	72°	69°
Lat. N25°46′—Alt. 10′	8	6	7	7	11	13	16	15	18	15	10	8
Nashville	39°	41°	50°	59°	68°	76°	79°	78°	69°	61°	49°	41°
Lat. N36°09′—Alt. 500′	12*	11*	12*	11	10	10	11	9	8	7	9	11*
New Orleans	55°	57°	63°	69°	76°	81°	83°	83°	80°	72°	62°	56°
Lat. N29°56′—Alt. 5′	10	9	9	7	8	13	15	14	11	7	8	10

NOTE: All temperatures in this book are Fahrenheit. To reduce Fahrenheit to Centigrade subtract 32 and multiply by 5/9; to reduce Centigrade to Fahrenheit multiply by 9/5 and add 32.

* Includes days with snow.

	JAN.	FEB.	MAR.	APR.	MAY	JUNE	JULY	AUG.	SEPT.	OCT.	NOV.	DEC.

CENTRAL

Chicago
Lat. N41°52'—Alt. 595'

| 25° | 27° | 36° | 47° | 58° | 68° | 73° | 72° | 65° | 54° | 40° | 30° |
| 11* | 10* | 12* | 11 | 12 | 11 | 9 | 9 | 9 | 9 | 10* | 11* |

Cincinnati
Lat. N39°06'—Alt. 550'

| 33° | 34° | 43° | 54° | 64° | 73° | 77° | 75° | 69° | 57° | 45° | 35° |
| 13* | 12* | 13* | 12 | 12 | 11 | 10 | 9 | 8 | 8 | 10 | 12* |

Cleveland
Lat. N41°29'—Alt. 580'

| 25° | 26° | 35° | 46° | 58° | 68° | 72° | 70° | 64° | 53° | 39° | 29° |
| 17 | 15 | 15 | 13 | 13 | 11 | 10 | 9 | 10 | 11 | 14 | 16 |

Dallas
Lat. N32°47'—Alt. 435'

| 45° | 50° | 57° | 65° | 73° | 81° | 84° | 84° | 78° | 68° | 56° | 48° |
| 8* | 8* | 8* | 8* | 9 | 7 | 5 | 7 | 5 | 6 | 6 | 7* |

Detroit
Lat. N42°19'—Alt. 585'

| 25° | 25° | 34° | 46° | 58° | 68° | 73° | 71° | 64° | 53° | 40° | 29° |
| 13* | 12* | 13* | 11* | 13 | 11 | 9 | 9 | 10 | 10 | 12* | 13* |

Minneapolis
Lat. N44°58'—Alt. 815'

| 14° | 17° | 30° | 46° | 58° | 68° | 73° | 71° | 62° | 50° | 33° | 20° |
| 8* | 7* | 8* | 9* | 12 | 12 | 9 | 9 | 9 | 9 | 8* | 8* |

Memphis
Lat. N35°08'—Alt. 275'

| 41° | 44° | 53° | 62° | 70° | 78° | 81° | 80° | 74° | 64° | 52° | 44° |
| 11 | 10* | 11 | 10 | 10 | 9 | 9 | 8 | 7 | 7 | 9 | 11 |

Omaha
Lat. N41°15'—Alt. 1040'

| 22° | 26° | 38° | 52° | 62° | 72° | 78° | 75° | 67° | 55° | 39° | 28° |
| 6* | 6* | 8* | 10 | 12 | 11 | 9 | 9 | 8 | 7 | 5* | 6* |

Pittsburgh
Lat. N40°26'—Alt. 745'

| 31° | 31° | 40° | 51° | 62° | 70° | 74° | 72° | 67° | 55° | 43° | 34° |
| 16* | 14* | 15* | 13* | 13 | 12 | 12 | 10 | 9 | 10 | 12* | 14* |

St. Louis
Lat. N38°37'—Alt. 455'

| 32° | 35° | 45° | 56° | 66° | 75° | 80° | 78° | 71° | 59° | 46° | 36° |
| 9* | 9* | 11* | 11 | 12 | 11 | 8 | 8 | 8 | 8 | 8 | 9* |

ROCKIES

Denver
Lat. N39°44'—Alt. 5280

| 31° | 33° | 39° | 48° | 57° | 67° | 73° | 71° | 63° | 52° | 40° | 33° |
| 5* | 6* | 8* | 9* | 10 | 8 | 9 | 9 | 6 | 6* | 5* | 5* |

Salt Lake City
Lat. N40°45'—Alt. 4390'

| 29° | 34° | 42° | 50° | 59° | 68° | 77° | 75° | 65° | 53° | 41° | 32° |
| 10* | 10* | 10* | 9* | 8 | 5 | 4 | 6 | 5 | 7 | 7* | 13* |

SOUTH WEST

Albuquerque
Lat. N35°05'—Alt. 4950'

| 34° | 41° | 46° | 54° | 63° | 73° | 77° | 74° | 68° | 57° | 43° | 35° |
| 3* | 3* | 3* | 4 | 4 | 3 | 8 | 8 | 5 | 4 | 2* | 3* |

Phoenix
Lat. N33°27'—Alt. 1090'

| 52° | 56° | 61° | 68° | 76° | 85° | 91° | 89° | 86° | 71° | 60° | 53° |
| 4 | 4 | 4 | 2 | 1 | 1 | 5 | 6 | 3 | 2 | 2 | 4 |

WEST COAST

Los Angeles
Lat. N34°03'—Alt. 340'

| 56° | 56° | 58° | 60° | 63° | 67° | 71° | 72° | 70° | 66° | 62° | 57° |
| 6 | 6 | 6 | 4 | 2 | 1 | 0 | 0 | 1 | 2 | 3 | 6 |

Reno
Lat. N39°31'—Alt. 4490'

| 32° | 36° | 42° | 48° | 55° | 63° | 71° | 69° | 61° | 51° | 41° | 34° |
| 7* | 6* | 6* | 4 | 4 | 3 | 2 | 2 | 2 | 3 | 4 | 6* |

San Francisco
Lat. N37°46'—Alt. 65'

| 50° | 53° | 54° | 56° | 57° | 59° | 59° | 60° | 62° | 61° | 57° | 52° |
| 11 | 11 | 10 | 6 | 4 | 2 | 0 | 0 | 2 | 4 | 7 | 10 |

Seattle
Lat. N47°36'—Alt. 75'

| 40° | 42° | 46° | 50° | 56° | 60° | 64° | 64° | 60° | 53° | 46° | 42° |
| 18* | 16 | 19* | 16 | 12 | 9 | 5 | 5 | 8 | 13 | 17 | 16 |

COMPARATIVE TABLE OF CLOTHING SIZES

MEN'S

SHIRTS

American	European
13	33
13½	34
14	35–36
14½	37
15	38
15½	39
16	40
16½	41
17	42
17½	43

HATS

American	European
6½	52
6⅝	53
6¾	54
6⅞	55
7	56
7⅛	57
7¼	58
7⅜	59
7½	60
7⅝	61

SHOES

American	European
6	38
6½	39
7–7½	40
8	41
8½	42
9–9½	43
10–10½	44
11–11½	45
12–12½	46
13	47

SOCKS

American	European
9	23
9½	24½ (also *Cadet*)
10	25½ (also *Page 2*)
10½	26¾ (also *Homme 3*)
11	28 (also *Demi-Patron*)
11½	29¼ (also *Patron*)
12	30½

WOMEN'S

DRESSES

American	French	English
10	38	32
12	40	34
14	42	36
16	44	38
18	46	40
20	48	42
40	50	
42	52	
44	54	
46	56	

SHOES

American	English	European
4–4½	2–2½	34
5–5½	3–3½	35
6	4	36
6½	4½	37
7–7½	5–5½	38
8	6	38½
8½	6½	39
9	7	40
9½–10	7½–8	41
10½	8½	42
11–11½	9–9½	43
12	10	44

HATS

American	European
21	53
21¼	54
21½	55
22	56
22½	57
23	58
23¼	59
23½	60
24	61
24½	62

STOCKINGS

American	European
8	20¼ (size 0)
8½	21½ (size 1)
9	22¾ (size 2)
9½	24 (size 3)
10	25¼ (size 4)
10½	26½ (size 5)
11	27¾ (size 6)

AUSTRIA

WEATHER IN VIENNA—Lat. N48°20'—Alt. 550'

Temp.	JAN.	FEB.	MAR.	APR.	MAY	JUNE	JULY	AUG.	SEPT.	OCT.	NOV.	DEC.
Low	28°	29°	35°	41°	50°	55°	58°	57°	51°	43°	35°	31°
High	36°	38°	48°	56°	65°	70°	73°	72°	65°	55°	42°	38°
Average	32°	34°	42°	49°	58°	63°	66°	65°	58°	49°	39°	35°
Days of Rain	7	5	7	8	9	10	10	8	7	8	7	7

LOCATION ... Austria lies in central Europe to the south of Germany. Vienna, in the eastern part of the country, is 224 air miles east of Munich.

CHARACTERISTICS ... This beautiful country, which suffered so much during the war, is again ready to welcome tourists. There are many new hotels and restaurants and, of course, the same old beautiful scenery which has made Austria one of the famous tourist spots of the world. Here you will find the Salzburg Festival, famous the world over; Vienna with its cafés; Innsbruck with its marvelous skiing in the nearby Tyrol and Arlberg. The people are friendly and you can have a delightful time.

POPULATION ... Estimated 6,998,300, about a million less than the population of Chicago, Detroit and Los Angeles combined.

SIZE ... 83,849 square miles.

CAPITAL ... Vienna (or Wien), a city of 1,636,200, is almost as large as Detroit.

GOVERNMENT ... The State Treaty of 1955 re-established the sovereignty of democratic Austria. It is a federated republic of 9 provinces governed by a parliament which meets in Vienna.

HOW TO GET THERE ... By Pan American Clipper, 15 hours (elapsed time) to Vienna from New York via Frankfurt and Munich. By ship, 5 to 9 days to Le Havre, France, then about 28 hours by train to Vienna. Western Austria is most easily reached by PAA to Munich and thence a 2½-hour train ride to either Innsbruck or Salzburg. During the summer, there is also air service from Brussels, London and Amsterdam two or three times weekly direct to Salzburg.

ACCOMMODATIONS...The inn is a part of native Austrian life. Every village has at least one inn. Throughout Austria these accommodations are clean and comfortable. But there are first-class hotels in most places, which have private baths and excellent food. All large resorts have modern hotels and inns with modern conveniences. The best hotels in Austria generally charge around $7 a day for room, bath and three meals during the height of the season. Many Austrian hotels and inns have that ineffable quality termed "atmosphere." The historic *Goldener Adler* in Innsbruck has it, as does the *Goldener Hirsch* in Salzburg. Then there are the very modern hotels, like the *Europa* and the *Tyrol* in Innsbruck, the *Parkhotel Mirabell* in Salzburg. Other famous hotels include the *Schloss* in Velden on the Woerthersee, the *Bellevue*, the *Europa* in Bad Gastein, and the *Gruber* in Kindberg. In Vienna, the *Sacher*, the *Bristol*, the *Imperial* and *Krantz-Ambassador* are the best hotels; $6 to $10 single, plus about $3.60 for one meal. Among other good hotels are the *Astoria*, the *Kaiserin Elisabeth*, the *Erzherzog Rainer*, the *Park*, the *Prinz Eugen*, the *Stieglbraeu*, the *Regina, Europa* and *Kummer*. Rates at the latter are from $5 a day with bath.

ARTS...Vienna's reputation as an art center is due to its wonderful museums filled with collections by world-famous masters. One should visit the Albertina Museum, which houses a famous collection of the etchings of Raffael, Michelangelo, Titian, Rembrandt, and Italian and German primitives. Dürer's work housed in this museum is one of the world's outstanding collections. The National Museum of Fine Arts contains priceless collections. Here are represented all the great masters, such as Pieter Breughel and Dürer, the best Velasquez collection outside of Madrid, Rembrandt, Rubens, Holbein, Giorgione, Titian, Moretto, Raffael and Correggio. Don't miss the Belvedere Picture Gallery and the Vienna Museum of Natural History.

BALLET...Famous ballet of the Vienna Opera. The ballet, like the opera and symphony, does not perform in Vienna from the middle of July to the first of September, when they are on tour.

BANKS...The Creditanstalt-Bankverein and the Laenderbank are Austria's principal banks. Other banking institutions include the Hypotheken-und Creditinstitut, the Arbeiter and the Schoeller bank. The American Express Company will cash traveler's checks and so will the banks and most hotels.

CALENDAR OF HOLIDAYS...New Year's Day; January 6, Epiphany; Easter Sunday and Monday; May 1, State Holiday; 10 days before Whitsun Sunday, Ascension of Christ; Whitsun Sunday and Monday; 10 days after Whitsun, Corpus Christi; August 15, Ascension of Mary; November 1, All Saints' Day; December 8, Conception of the Holy Virgin; Christmas and December 26, St. Stephen.

CIGARETTES AND TOBACCO...All tobacco products, including U.S. cigarettes, are available and not so expensive as in the other capitals of Europe.

CLIMATE ... Of a temperate, sub-alpine climate, Austria has approximately the same seasons as New York. However, it rarely becomes either terribly hot or bitingly cold, and the seasons slip gradually into one another without abrupt temperature changes. From late October to mid-December the countryside has heavy rains, but Vienna is always agreeable. In the mountain regions snow begins to fall in mid-November. The air is crisp, clear and cold, but sunny. Spring climate in the mountains makes Austria a skiers' paradise.

CLUBS ... Austrian Press Club, P.E.N. Club, Jockey Club, Lions, Rotary. Clubs in the Anglo-American sense are unknown in Austria.

COMMON COURTESIES AND LOCAL CUSTOMS ... You may speak freely to the Austrians. The tempo of living in Austria is a bit slower than in the United States, so be patient when expecting personal service. The Austrians are very gracious. Many tourists take to native apparel upon arrival in Austria, but in Vienna the usual international city attire is recommended. Austrians enjoy going to their favorite sidewalk café for coffee and the newspaper.

COMMUNICATIONS ... Telephone, telegraph and cable facilities are fast and reliable in Austria. Airmail is available, although airmail postage is considerably higher than in the U.S.

CURRENCY ... The schilling is the principal monetary unit in Austria. At any bank about 25.65 schillings are given for the dollar, the Austrian schilling being worth about 4 cents.

CUSTOMS REGULATIONS AND DOCUMENTS REQUIRED FOR UNITED STATES CITIZENS ... Except for duty-free limit of 400 cigarettes or 80 cigars or 500 grams of tobacco, 1 bottle of wine, 1 bottle of hard liquor, you may take into Austria anything which is for your personal use. An unlimited amount of dollars may be brought into or taken out of Austria but not more than 10,000 Austrian schillings may be taken out. You need a passport but no visa. Vaccination certificate is necessary for re-entry to the United States.

DRUG STORES ... In some of the drug stores within the first Bezirk of Vienna, foreign products, including American, are available.

St. Wolfgang in Salzburg Province is typical of the charming villages that dot the Austrian countryside.

ELECTRIC CURRENT ... Almost entirely 220 volts, A.C., although there is still some D.C. current in a few unmodified sections of Vienna. Converters for round-prong plugs are also needed.

FAUNA ... The vast forest and rock districts of the provinces overflow with prize game. Chamois shooting is a special feature. Stag, marmot, roebuck, and mountain cock all abound. Hunting is good throughout the country, but the shoots of Styria, Tyrol, Vorarlberg, and the Danube are particularly renowned. All hunting equipment may be rented or brought into the country duty free. As for fishing, the mountain lakes and streams teem with brook, lake and rainbow trout, char, brook-char, pike, pike-perch, and many other fish.

FLORA ... The lower meadows of Oberinntal, near the Italian border, are rich in the multi-colored carpets of flowers for which the Alps are famous. Throughout the Alps the forests and flowers are strikingly beautiful, especially in the spring.

FOOD ... Most of the more-popular Austrian dishes are part of international cuisine everywhere—*Wiener Schnitzel, goulash,* and the various *strudels,* to name a few. There are numerous other less well-known specialties worth trying, especially dishes with small dumplings. And do not miss the Viennese pastry. Even in the small inns food is served in substantial quantities. A Continental breakfast of coffee and rolls is taken upon arising, with a heartier second breakfast at 10:00 A.M. In Vienna, large towns, and resorts, dinner is from 6:30 P.M., with a light supper after the theater. Afternoon tea, called *jause,* is served after 4:00 P.M. and consists of sandwiches, pastry, coffee and tea.

GAMBLING ... There are two large race tracks in the vicinity of Vienna. Casinos are also located in Salzburg, Bad Gastein, Velden, Kitzbuehel and Baden (15 miles from Vienna).

LANGUAGE ... German is the official language, but English is taught in the high schools. You will have no trouble getting information in English at your hotel or at other places you visit.

LAUNDRY AND DRY CLEANING ... You can have your laundry done quickly and thoroughly, and for little money, by the chambermaid at your hotel. Dry cleaning is fast and good in Vienna, but not so good in the provinces.

LIQUOR ... Austria is both a beer- and wine-drinking country. The beer is excellent and the wines are wonderful. *Vin ordinaire* is good and is cheap. The best red wine is Voeslauer, with Klosterneuburger a close second. But Austria is best known for its white wines, such as Duernsteiner, Gumpoldskirchner, Grinzinger, Nussberger, Riesling, and Veltliner. Austrian champagne is good. Schnaps, distilled liquors, obtainable in great and potent variety, are also good. Whisky is imported and expensive. Slivovitz, a South-Slav drink distilled from plum juice, is popular and strong. The famous Heurigenwine of new vintage is served by the wine growers in the backyards of their premises in all the wine-growing areas. Cocktails vary in price and quality, but are good at the large international bars.

MEDICAL FACILITIES... Austrian doctors are generally excellent. Ski resorts have first-aid centers with resident doctors. Inquire at your hotel. Hospital facilities in the larger cities are at prewar level.

MOTION PICTURES... Motion picture theaters are to be found in the larger cities. There are a good number in Vienna. Many of the films shown are American or English, but with German sound track.

MUSIC... There is music everywhere in Austria. Besides the famous Vienna Philharmonic Orchestra and the Vienna Symphony, there are the equally famous State Opera and the wonderful, gay, light Volksopera. These, however, like the ballet, do not play in Vienna from the middle of July to the first of September. In late July and August there is the world-renowned Salzburg Festival. In recent years, Vienna has come out with its own Spring Music Festival, called *Wiener Festwochen*, during the first three weeks of June. Also summer and fall peasant festivals are numerous, and most sizable villages have dances on Saturdays. Vienna has for centuries been considered the music capital of the world. From there burgeoned the works of Mozart, Beethoven, Schubert, Brahms, Gluck, Haydn, Bruckner, Wolf, Mahler, Lanner, the Strausses, and other great artists. The Vienna Philharmonic is world renowned. Herbert von Karajan, Dr. Karl Boehm, and Rafael Kubelik are the three leading conductors now, but there are many other famous ones. The Vienna State Opera is superb, and the gay Volksopera is not surpassed anywhere in the world. The Vienna Choir Boys are among the leading performers of religious music in the world and can be heard almost every Sunday at the Hofburg Chapel.

NIGHT CLUBS... Vienna has everything from swank night clubs with floor shows to fashionable little *tanz* bars where there is always wonderful music and good wine. However, don't expect the big shows of Paris. They just don't exist. The *Cobenzl Bar* in the Vienna hills is smartest of all. You can dine and dance with the city of Vienna and the Danube spread below you (open only in summer). The *Splendid, Eden, Moulin Rouge, Casanova Bar,* and *Maxim* are all good. Vienna specializes in *intime* small bars with piano players or orchestra. You'll find them everywhere within the Ring. If you like soul-stirring Gypsy violin music, *Kocze Antal's Monseigneur Bar* is a "must." Among the wine gardens, try *Hengl, Setzger, Kurtz-Manhart, Maly, Toni Karas.* The native inns in the smaller towns all have *bauernstube* rooms, handsomely decorated with folk art, where in the evenings there is dancing, singing and congenial company.

PHOTOGRAPHY... All equipment is available but expensive. Good developing everywhere, including color developing.

RELIGION... Austria is predominantly Roman Catholic. Cathedrals, abbeys and churches are numerous and beautiful throughout the country. There are Protestant services in the larger cities.

RESTAURANTS AND BARS... Vienna abounds in wonderful

restaurants, dance-bars and small, smart eating places. Coffee houses are a way of life here. You should dine once in the deep old cellars in the inner city. Try *Sacher, Mozart, Carlton*. The *Rathauskeller* is famous, also the *Lindenkeller*. Another famous keller is the *Hofkeller* where you can listen to zither music while you eat. The *Palais Auersperg*, a masterpiece of Baroque building with restaurant, beautiful winter garden, coffee shop and bar, is interesting to see. Best international restaurants are the *Drei Husaren, Stadtkrug, Franziskaner* and the restaurant of the *Sacher Hotel*. For Balkan food with the zip of music, try the *Pataky, Bosna* or the *Balkan Grill*. Other excellent restaurants include *St. Stephan, Kerzenstueberl, Deutsches Haus,* the *Weisser Rauchfangkehrer, Liesingerkeller* and *Schoener*. If, after dinner, you would like to drink wine (no food) in one of the oldest kellers in Vienna, visit the *Urbani Keller*. It's well worth it.

SHOPS AND STORES . . . Stores famous for their leather goods are Popp and Kretschmer, Nigst, Hiess and Foerster, as is the Lanz shop for native costumes. Antiques around Vienna's famous state-owned pawn-shop Dorotheum. Shooting, fishing and ski equipment may be purchased locally. For smart ready-made dresses try Elegance, Farnhammer, Stone & Blythe and Hoechsmann.

SPECTATOR SPORTS . . . From January to June there are international ski events at all the major alpine resorts. *See* SPORTS.

SPORTS . . . Skiing tops the list. It is the national sport of Austria, and her mountains and climate are perfect for it. Skiing huts and lodges dot the countryside, and many fine ski resorts may be found in Austria. Near Salzburg is the Bad Gastein resort with cable car, three ski lifts, jump, and skating rink. The Arlberg resorts west and Kitzbuehel east of Innsbruck are international favorites. The Obergurgl resort offers spring skiing. The St. Anton-am-Arlberg resort is known as "The Ski Capital of the World." Zuers and Lech have international competitions. Austrian ski schools, trails, runs, and incidental facilities cannot be surpassed. Austria contains over a thousand miles of perfect ski slopes. Hunting and fishing, mountaineering, bicycling and boating are also popular sports in Austria.

For golf the course at Dellach on the Woerthersee in Carinthia (Southern Austria) and Pertisau on the Achen Lake are well known. Tennis is popular; every sizable resort and all Austrian cities have good courts. There are sailing and rowing on all the larger lakes, and the Austrian rivers lend themselves exceptionally well to flat-boating. All the lake resorts offer swimming facilities. Opportunities for hiking and climbing are limitless. Trails are carefully marked, and the existence of the hut system and at least one clean, comfortable inn in every village makes it possible to range freely. All mountaineering equipment may be purchased on the spot and professional guides are available everywhere.

THEATERS . . . State Opera, Volksopera, Burgtheater, Volkstheater, Theater in der Josefstadt. All plays in German only.

TIME . . . Six hours later than United States Eastern Standard Time.

TIPPING ... Hotels and restaurants add a 10 per cent service charge to your bill, but tip an extra 10 per cent for special services. Tip 15 per cent in other cases; for luggage about 3 schillings per bag.

TOURIST TAXES ... All resorts in the provinces charge a small *kurtaxe*.

TRANSPORTATION ... There are taxis, streetcars, and buses in the larger cities, but taxis are not cheap. Chauffeur-driven and self-drive cars are available. Good train service is maintained within the country. The cable railways up and down and across mountains are remarkable and entirely safe.

WATER ... Water in Vienna is famous—it comes from mountain springs, coming on aqueducts. You can drink the water anywhere in Austria.

WHAT TO BUY ... Vienna has rapidly re-established itself as a shopping center. Knitwear, petit point, fine needlework along with the famous leather goods, antiques, crystal and porcelain and jewelry are worthwhile mentioning. Peasant costumes may be bought almost everywhere. Also hunting, fishing, and skiing equipment.

WHAT TO WEAR ... Take with you about the same clothes required for corresponding seasons in New York, but warm clothes are needed for the Alpine evenings, and good, strong shoes always. Even if you do not plan to ski, heavy slacks or ski trousers are suggested for the provinces in winter. You will also need galoshes or fur-lined boots for walking in the provinces in winter. Formal dress may be worn at the opera in Vienna and at the festival in Salzburg. Formal dress is also worn at the more fashionable resort hotels in the evening, but by no means is this a "must," particularly for men.

WHERE TO GO—SIGHTSEEING ...

Vienna ... Perhaps for the first sightseeing trip you make in Vienna it would be best to take a standard tour around the city. The buses are excellent and modern. Just ask your hotel porter for tickets. This would make it possible for you to plan from there on what you want to see most. Because there is so much of interest to see in Vienna, it is impossible to cover it all unless you plan to stay for some time. Vienna is divided into 23 districts. The inner town, the first district, is the most important. It is surrounded by the Ringstrasse. Each section of the Ringstrasse has a different name. The one in the very center of the city is the Opern Ring, the others are the Schotten, the Karl Lueger, the Dr. Karl Renner, the Burg, the Kaerntner, the Schubert, the Park, and the Stuben Ring. These take in two-thirds of the Old Vienna. The other third is bounded by the Franz Joseph Kai along the Danube Canal. The Opera House, a magnificent structure, is located where the Kaerntnerstrasse, the main shopping district, meets the Opern Ring. It was rebuilt after extensive war damages and reopened in November 1955. The building was designed by the famous Austrian architect van der Null, who after realizing that he had designed the Opera House at street level (the only one in the world at that time not raised above street level) committed suicide.

Austria offers skiing at its best and facilities are excellent. The group above is at Arlberg resort, an international favorite.

St. Stephen's Cathedral, affectionately called "der alte Steffl," is an impressive landmark dating from the twelfth century.

Heldenplatz is in the heart of Vienna and the location of the New Hofburg (Imperial Palace). Across the Ringstrasse is the domed National Museum.

Tickets for the symphonies and operas can be ordered through your hotel porter.

From the Opera House take a walk to St. Stephen's Cathedral, which was built in 1147 A.D. and partially remodeled from then to 1433, and also suffered much damage from bombs. However, the Gothic spire (448 feet) escaped damage. The Cathedral contains many beautiful pulpits, choirs, choir galleries, and a great organ. The catacombs connect with subterranean passageways which extend under the entire area around the Stefanplatz. Next on your list should be a visit to the Palace. The Hofburg Palace, whose oldest part was built in 1275 A.D. by Ottocar II, was the winter palace of the Habsburg emperors. It is now open to visitors who want to see the wonderful Habsburg collection. The renowned wrought-iron Michaeler Tor opens into the Michaeler rotunda. Off this are the imperial apartments and state suites, the private apartments of Franz Joseph, containing the personal furnishings of the Emperor, the suites of Empress Elizabeth, the gorgeous state apartments now used by the President of Austria and the rooms containing the imperial porcelain collection. Adjacent is the world famous Spanish Riding Academy which was founded in the 16th century. In the beautiful hall the famous Lipizzaner horses are put through the Spanish paces at regular performances. A main entrance leads from the rotunda to the central courtyard of In der Burg. Here too you should visit the Schweizerhof, from where you enter the unique collection of the crown jewels. You should also see the imperial chapel.

Another must is a visit to the National Library, one of the largest in the world. This contains a collection of papyri comprising 81,000 items, 1,200,000 printed books and a fabulous collection of manuscripts. The oldest known part of an illustrated Christian Bible is here too, as well as many other interesting early books and manuscripts. There is a music collection containing 19,000 volumes of printed music and 12,000 music manuscripts, a huge library and a collection of autographs.

Other places of interest to the tourist in Vienna are the Kapuziner church in whose crypt lie 144 Habsburgs (12 were emperors and 15 empresses), the House of Parliament and the University of Vienna. Nearby are the Minoriten Church, the Chancellery and the Votive Church.

In the 2nd Bezirk the Viennese Coney Island "Der Prater" is located with its well-known giant Ferris wheel.

The immense imperial summer palace and beautiful gardens of Schoenbrunn in the western outskirts of the city are an absolute must. Don't fail to walk through the interior of this palace.

If you want to look down on Vienna from the crests of the Vienna Woods include the Kahlenberg and Cobenzl in your sightseeing.

From Vienna there is good train service to the other fascinating tourist spots described below. Innsbruck can be reached in about 10½ hours on a route that takes you to Linz, Salzburg, Kitzbühel. Styria in the south is reached in about 4 hours.

Innsbruck...The ancient and impressive city of Innsbruck in Tyrol is known as the capital of "The Land of the Mountains." The best way to see Innsbruck is to walk around the city either in the early morning or early evening. In the blocks between the station and the Maria Theresienstrasse is the so-called new town, a section rich in sights, cafés and hotels. If you would like to know Innsbruck, take a tram to the point where the Maria Theresienstrasse becomes the Herzog Friedrichstrasse, a thoroughfare which bisects the old city, the part which was within the walls. There you will find the city moat used long ago, narrow Gothic houses, pointed arcades and wrought-iron signs. The Herzog Friedrichstrasse leads directly to a little cobbled square, the Stadtplatz, which contains the world-famous Goldenes Dachl. The Dachl, a small Gothic balcony three stories high with a steeply pitched gilded roof, is a rich, gleaming wonder. The entire neighborhood of the Dachl, containing several of those fountains for which Innsbruck is famous, is a must for sightseers. Try to visit the rococo parish church of Wilten, and be sure to make a journey on one of the two cable ascents from Innsbruck. One cable railway takes you to the Patscherkofel, the other to the Hafelekar. The entire Tyrol can be seen from there, outspread like a great relief map. Good hotels include the *Maria Theresia,* and the *Kaiserhof,* the new modern *Europa* and the *Tyrol,* and ancient inns such as the *Goldener Adler,* the *Goldene Rose* and the *Stiftskeller.* You should visit some of the night places where you will enjoy native singing and see native dancing. Tyroleans love life and celebrations and music.

Salzburg is the great festival city. Here the world-famous musical event takes place from the last week in July through the month of August. It's the world's leading summer musical festival. The city is jammed with musicians and music lovers. The works of the great musical masters, particularly Mozart, are to be heard day and night, played by several orchestras and chamber groups. But Salzburg does not offer music alone. It is one of Austria's most beautiful cities. Minor, but impressive, mountains surround the town. Riding in fiacres (one-horse open carriages) is a popular and charming feature of Salzburg life.

There are several organized sightseeing tours you can take such as the city-sightseeing and Salzkammergut tour, the tour to Gaisbergspitze via Gaisbergstrasse (4,218 feet), Grossglockner and Untersberg where Zeppezauer house is located at 5,471 feet.

Places of interest to the visitor are the famous Salzburg Cathedral which is the finest Italianate edifice in Austria. Attending the *Everyman* performance in front of the cathedral in the late afternoon is one of the most stirring experiences Europe can offer. It is theater at its most intense. You must see a performance of the Aicher marionettes, which have long toured Europe and won great acclaim. One of their best performances is *Faust* but their most outstanding is *Casperl,* the story of the gay befuddled peasant who drinks and has all sorts of improbable adventures. An interesting place is

Mozart's house which is near the Mozarteum, Europe's most distinguished summer music school, attended by many Americans. For a stay during the Salzburg Festival be sure to arrange your reservations well in advance. You can stop at the famous, charming *Goldener Hirsch*, the *Hotels Stein, Gastschloss Mönchstein, Muenchner Hof, Europa* or *Parkhotel Mirabell, Oesterreichischer Hof, Bristol;* or nearby at the *Salzburg Cobenzl*, the *Kaiserhof*, or the *Schlos Hotel* on the Fuschl lake. While in Salzburg, visit the charming *Til Eulenspiegel* restaurant, and the *Café Bazar*, where celebrities, tourists and natives mingle. Don't miss *Schloss Hellbrunn* with its water tricks.

Zell-am-See ... The best route at present from Salzburg is via Saalfelden. Just south of this town is the famous lake resort of Zell-am-See, an Alpine lake about 2¼ miles long, a mile wide and about 225 feet deep. The town, once a rather grand place, is now rather shabby, but there are still good and rather inexpensive hotels. So it is a good place to make your headquarters for trips to the places the High Tauern include. Castle Rosenberg in Zell-am-See on the main square is worth seeing, as is the thousand-year-old church tower. There is an excellent bathing beach, tennis courts and good shops. The main thing is to take a trip by cable railway up the Schmittenhoehe. It takes only fifteen minutes to reach the top of this mountain. Here there is a small chapel and a meteorological station. Zell-am-See is a winter resort, too. There are excellent accommodations and a good sparkling climate.

Bad Gastein ... High in the Alps, 47 miles south of Salzburg, is this famous old cure resort. In addition to being a summer place, it is also developing into one of Austria's excellent winter resorts. There are good shops, theaters, cinemas and, of course, the casino. Beautiful mountain walks abound. Go via cable car up to the tops of the Stubnerkogel for a breath-taking view of the Tauern. The radioactive springs of Bad Gastein are famous for their rejuvenating powers. The *Bellevue Hotel* and the *Hotel Europe* are excellent; the bar and orchestra of the Bellevue make the wintertime particularly gay. Above Bad Gastein, reached by chair-lift, is the *Bellevue Alm*— and if you have a longing to stay in a small Tyrolean lodge high up in the mountains with the world outside your balcony, make your reservations for the Alm early. It has a small swimming pool for summer—and in winter a roaring open fireplace in the bar.

Kitzbühel ... Situated between Zurich and Vienna on the main railway line is Kitzbühel, one of the best-known Austrian towns among tourists. In winter it is an outstanding skiing resort, considered second only to the Arlberg resorts by expert skiers. The town has every kind of a ski slope, a cable railway up the Hahnenkamm, ski lifts, any number of ski runs, including, of course, the famous Hahnenkamm run. There are excellent ski schools, with expert instructors and guides. For skaters there is an ice rink. First-class hockey matches are staged there frequently. Kitzbuehel is the scene of many important international winter sport competitions. There are a great many good hotels. The *Grand* is luxurious. Inns

Castle Orth at Gmunden, Traun Lake, in Salzkammergut lake region east of Salzburg. Traunstein Mountain is at left.

Kitzbühel is a typical Tyrolean village and famous international resort. Note the "onion" tower, typical of Byzantine influence.

and pensions abound. One of the best pensions is a castle where the paying guest may have every comfort. Some of the places of interest to see are the Church of St. Andreas and the Frauenkirche. You should take a side trip to the Kitzbuehler Horn and to Fieberbrunn, where there are a health spring and peasant festivals. The shops of Kitzbuehel are extremely interesting. It has been said of Kitzbuehel that despite its yearly influx of nobility and celebrities, the natives have remained unspoiled.

Styria . . . The southernmost province, of which Graz is the capital, is surnamed "the green state" for its beautiful wooded countryside. Here the peasants and the visitors wear the Styrian gray and green hunting suits and the Styrian version of the dirndl, most popular in Austria. Alt Aussee is the perfect place to stay. Bad Aussee, the larger center, is lovely with its white-faced, dark-timbered houses with balconies covered with beautiful flowers. Life here is lived and also ended with a great deal of ceremony. An Aussee wedding is a sight to see, as is a funeral with the glass and ebony, the plumes, and horses with their gleaming silver harnesses. There are well-known hotels here such as the *Post*. Go to Alt Aussee and take a room at the Hotel *Am See* with a balcony overlooking the lake. While having breakfast watch the Dachstein glacier with the strange glints of morning light. Go canoeing on the lake and watch it (you can almost taste the ice from the glacier). You should take a brine bath into which will have been dropped a few thimblefuls of strong pine oil for an exhilarating feeling. Near Aussee is Bad Ischl and the famous Salzkammergut lakes, easily reached from Salzburg.

Carinthia . . . Like Styria, the Province of Carinthia is also located in the southern part of Austria—to the west of Styria, bordering

Italy. Carinthia's Woerthersee is Austria's best-known summer resort. It is a country with beautiful lakes and mountains, and because of its location south of the main alpine region, spring comes earlier and fall lasts much longer. Lake bathing is possible from middle of May until middle of October. Carinthia has excellent winter-sport resorts also, such as Kanzelhoehe, famous for its perfect snow and many hours of sunshine. The highlight of Carinthia is Velden on Woerthersee, known all over Europe. It is a picturesque lake resort with first-class hotels (the *Schloss* is one of the best in Austria), an interesting program of social entertainment, including champion waterskiing. There are flower festivals, *corsos,* international dancing competitions, boat races, etc. At Velden, Poertschach or Klagenfurt you can swim, sail, water ski, play tennis or golf to your heart's content. One of the few golf courses in Austria is located in Dellach, a fifteen-minute drive from Velden. The many castles are another most interesting aspect of Carinthia. The ideal castle tour is from Klagenfurt via Hochosterwitz to the old walled town of Friesach and the ancient town of Gurk.

Sightseeing Along the Danube... During the summer months, the First Vienna Danube Steamship Company provides regular steamship service along the beautiful river Danube. The most beautiful stretch winds through the romantic "Wachau" valley, which is a famous attraction especially at blossomtime. However, due to the fast current, it is recommended to take this trip only downstream.

SOURCES OF FURTHER INFORMATION ... If you have time to visit more than the principal tourist spots described here, or if you wish to pursue any special interest, you would do well to contact the office of the Austrian State Tourist Department located at 277 Park Ave., New York 17, New York. There are also offices in London, Paris and Rome. Every city and resort in Austria has its *Fremdenverkehrsverein* (local tourist office) where all information, folders, maps, etc., may be procured. The hotels and travel agencies will also be helpful to tourists. Just ask your hotel porter for any tickets you may want for special events. You'll find he can even handle your ski-lift tickets so you won't have to wait in line on crowded week ends. Tourist information of all kinds as well as tickets for cultural and sports events, exhibitions, fairs and so forth are also available through the *Oesterreichisches Verkehrsbuero* Friedrichstrasse 7, Vienna 1, or through the Cosmos Travel Agency, Kaerntnerring 15, Vienna 1. Pan American's offices are at Kaerntnerring 5, Vienna 1 (Tel. 445631) and Makartplatz 1, Salzburg (Tel. 73281).

BELGIUM

WEATHER IN BRUSSELS—Lat. N50°50′—Alt. 190′

Temp.	JAN.	FEB.	MAR.	APR.	MAY	JUNE	JULY	AUG.	SEPT.	OCT.	NOV.	DEC.
Low	30°	33°	35°	40°	46°	52°	55°	55°	52°	44°	38°	33°
High	39°	43°	49°	57°	64°	70°	73°	72°	67°	56°	48°	42°
Average	35°	38°	42°	49°	55°	61°	64°	64°	60°	50°	43°	38°
Days of Rain	15	15	15	16	16	17	16	16	16	17	18	16

LOCATION ... Belgium is nestled among France, Germany, Luxembourg, and The Netherlands, with 43 miles of coast line. Its oldest and most important coastal city, Ostend, is only 55 miles from Dover. Brussels is only slightly over 1 hour's flying time by Clipper from London, and is within easy reach of most European countries.

CHARACTERISTICS ... This charming country with its wonderful museums, long stretches of beaches and gay cafés is a marvelous place to take a holiday. It is clean, modern, honest and very, very gay. You'll eat some of the finest food on the Continent.

POPULATION ... Estimated 9,000,000. Belgium is the most densely populated country in Europe. The population of Brussels and suburbs, the largest center, is 1,250,000.

SIZE ... A small compact country of 11,755 square miles, Belgium is approximately the size of Maryland. The distance between its farthest points is less than 200 miles.

CAPITAL ... Brussels. Not only the capital of Belgium, but the heart and center of the country, it's one of the largest and most beautiful cities in Europe. Brussels is also the center of the country's banking and commercial activity and is the Provisional Center of European Common Market Activities.

GOVERNMENT ... A constitutional monarchy with a parliament elected by universal suffrage.

HOW TO GET THERE ... By Pan American Clipper, from New

York to Brussels, 9 hours (elapsed time). By ship, 8 to 10 days to Antwerp, depending on the steamer.

ACCOMMODATIONS ... Among the principal hotels in Brussels are the *Metropole,* located on the Place de Brouckere in the center of town; the *Palace;* the *Plaza; Atlanta; Albert I; Central* and *Grand Hotel.* The *Hotel Amigo* is a new hotel located directly behind the Town Hall and adjoining the Grand'Place. The *Brussels Residence* offers luxurious duplex apartments on fashionable Avenue Louise. Rates at all of these hotels run about $5 to $8 single per day without meals.

ARTS ... Among the many museums and art galleries the tourist should see are the Museum of Ancient Art containing works of the fifteenth to eighteenth centuries, the Museum of Modern Art with works of the nineteenth and twentieth centuries.

BANKS ... Guaranty Trust Co. of New York, 27 avenue des Arts, Brussels; the American Express Co., 51 Cantersteen; Banque de la Société Générale de Belgique, 3 rue Montagne-au-Parc (agents for various banks); Banque de Bruxelles, 2 rue de la Régence (agents for various banks); Banque Lambert, 11 rue des Colonies; Kredietbank, Grand'Place; Société Belge de Banque, 61 Avenue Louise.

CALENDAR OF HOLIDAYS ... January 1, Easter Monday, May 1 (Labor Day), Ascension Day, Whit Monday, July 21 (National Holiday), August 15 (Assumption Day), November 1 (All Saints' Day), November 11 (Armistice Day), and Christmas Day are official holidays in Belgium. Processions and pageants take place all over the country. Ask at your hotel about these colorful events. Some of the interesting festivities include the Carnival at Binches on Shrove Tuesday with the procession of the Gilles; the procession of the Holy Blood at Bruges on Monday after May 2; the Combat of the Lumeçon, a local version of St. George and the Dragon, as well as the procession of the Golden Cart of Ste. Waudru, both taking place at Mons on Trinity Sunday; Procession of the Penitents at Furnes on last Sunday in July; historic cortege and St. Guidon procession at Anderlecht on September 16. Most beautiful and spectacular is the mystery called "Jeu du Saint Sang," played every 5 years in July-August on the open square at the foot of the belfry in Bruges, relating the story of the relic of the Holy Blood belonging to the city of Bruges.

CIGARETTES AND TOBACCO ... American cigarettes are expensive, but local brands are good and reasonably priced. Pipes of Belgian briar are excellent and inexpensive.

CLIMATE ... No extreme temperatures at any season. May through September is the best time to visit Belgium. (Brussels is also very worthwhile visiting from December 6 through the New Year, when the city is gaily decorated.)

CLUBS ... The American Chamber of Commerce, 21 rue du Commerce, Brussels, can advise you the meeting days of the American Club. Rotary, Lions and commercial clubs in every city.

COMMON COURTESIES AND LOCAL CUSTOMS ... Handshaking when you meet or leave anyone. Bring or send flowers when invited to dinner at a private home.

COMMUNICATIONS ... Cables; transatlantic telephone; airmail to the U.S.: postal card BF 5.50, letter BF 7.50 (for 5 grams).

CURRENCY ... The monetary unit is the Belgian Franc, worth about 2 cents ($1 equals 50 Belg. frs.). One franc is divided into 100 centimes.

CUSTOMS REGULATIONS AND DOCUMENTS REQUIRED FOR UNITED STATES CITIZENS ... Passport required. No visa needed. Vaccination certificate for re-entry into the United States. You can bring in 200 cigarettes, ½ lb. of tobacco or 50 cigars, 1 opened bottle of wine or liquor. Additional quantities can be left in transit on arrival.

DRUG STORES ... Pharmacies are the only type to be found in Belgium and usually carry only pharmaceuticals and a limited choice of cosmetics.

ELECTRIC CURRENT ... Both 220 volt and 110 volt A.C., so check first at your hotel. European plugs needed.

FAUNA ... Deer, wild boars, hares, wild fowl and game birds, wild ducks; hunting and shooting authorized only on private property; invitations to hunting and shooting parties can be obtained through hunting clubs or associations. Fishing is highly specialized, at sea, in rivers and streams; mostly private, however. Licenses for hunting and fishing are needed.

FLORA ... The Ardennes are beautifully wooded. Flanders abounds in pastures. The district of Ghent is renowned for its orchids and begonias and its azaleas are world famous. There are many beautiful public parks in most cities.

FOOD ... Most people think that Brussels ranks with Paris when it comes to food. Local specialties are *choesels à la Bruxelloise* (kidney), *waterzooi* (chicken in broth), lobster in whisky sauce, snipe cooked in brandy, chicken in sherry.

GAMBLING ... Casinos at Knocke-Le Zoute, Blankenberg, Ostend, Namur, Chaudfontaine, Spa and Dinant.

LANGUAGE ... French and Flemish are the official languages, but most people you contact will have a working knowledge of English.

LAUNDRY AND DRY CLEANING ... All the hotels have quick, expensive laundry and dry-cleaning service.

LIQUOR ... Good French wines and unlimited choice of other liquors. Whisky and cocktails about 80 cents each. Belgian beer is very good.

MEDICAL FACILITIES ... There are English-speaking doctors; ask at your hotel.

MOTION PICTURES ... All foreign pictures with subtitles in French, Flemish or the local language.

MUSIC ... There are excellent symphony concerts and occasional ballet at the *Palais des Beaux-Arts*. Also opera at *La Monnaie*. Ask your hotel concierge for details.

NIGHT CLUBS ... Night spots in Brussels are big and brassy and on the expensive side. You may have to pay around $2 for a highball and $20 for the bottle of champagne you're expected to buy, (unless you're at the bar) but there's no cover or minimum. Some require membership fees. Negro entertainers are popular here. Among the better-known and popular places are *Le Boeuf Sur le Toit; Parisiana; Gaité; Maxim's;* and the *Scotch Club*. *Le Moulin* and *Memling* are less expensive, more intimate. *La Nouvelle Equipe* is small but has the best dance music in Brussels.

PHOTOGRAPHY ... Black-and-white still and movie films are available in Belgium at about the same prices as in the U.S. Gevacolor negative or positive film costs BF.65.00 for 120 or 620 roll, developing (costs BF.40.00) of color film takes at least one month, of black and white 24 hours. *La Camera*, 47 rue de l'Ecuyer, Brussels, is recommended for photo purchases. Photogenic places in Brussels are: Grand'Place, Place de Brouckere (for night pictures), Cinquantenaire, Sablon church, Royal Palace, Royal Park, Palais de Justice, the Atomium on the site of the '58 World's Fair.

RELIGION ... While Belgium is a Roman Catholic country, there are churches of almost every denomination.

RESTAURANTS ... Some of the most famous restaurants in the world are in Brussels. Among them are: *La Couronne* on the Town Hall Square (Grand'Place); *Restaurant Chantraine* ("Epaule de Mouton") over 290 years old, *Les Ambassadeurs* ("Au Filet de Boeuf") just off the Grand'Place; *Rotisserie Ardennaise* on the Blvd. Adolphe Max; *Le Ravenstein; Rotisserie d'Alsace; Petit Louvain* and *Au Filet de Boeuf,* Rue des Harengs. There are many, many others. The *Carlton* is the smartest restaurant in town and offers dinner dancing. These are in addition to the hundreds of restaurants offering foods of many nations. On the grounds of the 1958 World's Fair, the restaurant atop the Atomium is still open.

SHOPS AND STORES ... Large department stores are open daily (except Sundays) from 9:00 A.M. to 6:00 P.M. Principal ones in Brussels include Au Bon Marché, A L'Innovation, Magasins de la Bourse, Galeries Anspach, and many excellent small luxury shops.

SPECTATOR SPORTS ... Soccer, tennis, bicycle races, horse races.

SPORTS ... Yachting, fishing, horseback riding, golf, tennis. You can go hiking, cycling or boating. There are Youth Hostels everywhere. The swimming is magnificent all along the coast.

THEATERS ... In Brussels plays in French at *Théâtre Royal du Parc, Théâtre du Palais des Beaux Arts, Théâtre des Galeries, Théâtre National, Théâtre de Poche.*

TIME ... Six hours later than United States Eastern Standard Time.

TIPPING ... Usually 15 per cent is added to your bill at hotels

The Grand'Place, Brussels' square, is the center of activity and historical interest with its fine cafés and shops.

The fifteenth-century Town Hall dominates the Grand'Place and is surrounded by guild halls representing characteristic trades.

and restaurants; if not, 15 per cent is about the usual amount to tip.

TRANSPORTATION... Good bus service. Taxis, chauffeur-driven cars and drive-yourself cars are plentiful but expensive. Train service is widespread and good.

TOURIST TAXES... BF.5.00 in Brussels and lesser amounts elsewhere.

WATER... may be drunk without danger in any major city.

WHAT TO BUY... Belgian lace from Flanders, linenware, Belgian porcelain, copperware, tapestry, diamonds cut in Antwerp, exquisite jewelry, Belgian crystal, rifles, shotguns and fine cutlery.

WHAT TO WEAR... You do not need evening clothes in this part of Europe. Both men and women should take along medium-weight clothes, with an overcoat for winter. Be sure to take a raincoat and walking shoes and in summer a swimming suit.

WHERE TO GO SIGHTSEEING...

Brussels... Brussels' architectural jewel is the Grand'Place with its lovely seventeenth-century buildings and the fifteenth-century Town Hall. Nearby is the well-known little statue of Manneken Pis, the most popular citizen of Brussels. The collegiate church of SS. Michel and Gudule (Gothic) with its sixteenth-century stained glass windows, the church of Our Lady of the Sablon (late Gothic) are magnificent monuments to be visited. Other points of interest are the House of Erasmus in Anderlecht, the seventeenth-century Cambre Abbey, the Royal Palace and Park, Parliament Buildings, the Archway of the Cinquantenaire and the nineteenth-century Palais de Justice (one of the largest buildings in the world). The battlefield of Waterloo, with its painted panorama of the famous battle and the Napoleonic relics, is a short distance from the capital, as is the Castle of Gasbeek, which belonged to Count d'Egmont.

Side Trips... Belgium is divided into two main sectors: Flanders, the Flemish-speaking flatland of the northwest, reaching to the coast, and Wallony, the French-speaking southeastern part.

Antwerp... a wealthy metropolis in the rich country of Flanders, is a cosmopolitan town and international business center, a wealthy artistic town and above all a port, the largest in Europe and third largest in the world. Here are some of the most famous Gothic and Renaissance buildings in all Europe. The Gothic Cathedral has an exceptional carillon and many magnificent masterpieces by Rubens, which are kept covered until noon every day. The Town Hall in Market Place has a fine Renaissance façade. In one corner of the square are several old guild houses. The Museum of Fine Arts contains sixteenth- and seventeenth-century paintings by such great artists as Rubens, Memling, Breughel, Van Dyck and Jordaens. In the Museum Mayer-Van den Bergh, you'll find other Flemish masters. Other places of interest are the Steen, tenth-century castle, Butcher's Hall, and Folklore Museum. The best hotel is the *Century*. Good restaurants are the *Criterium*, *La Belle Meunière* and *La Rade*.

Ardennes .. Wooded hills and valleys, steep rocks and winding streams abundant with fish, forests teeming with deer, ruins of ancient castles, watermills and hunting lodges—such is the scenery in Ardennes and Fagne. *La Roche, Ciney, Bouillon, Arlon* are worth a trip. The *Grottos of Han* on the Lesse river are worth seeing as is the Mardasson Memorial to American troops at Bastogne. There are many wonderful country inns in this area.

Beloeil Castle, residence of the Princes de Ligne. Rich museum, splendid French-style park with ornamental lakes.

Bruges ... One of the most beautiful medieval towns of Europe. A one-time harbor, it is now visited for its picturesque old buildings and dreamy canals. The thirteenth- and fourteenth-century *Halles* (market), with 310-foot belfry; thirteenth-century St. Sauveur cathedral; Gothic Notre Dame church; the Holy Blood Basilica; the thirteenth-century Beguinage and poetic *lac d'amour;* St. John's Hospital, where Memling lived and worked and where some of his best paintings are shown; and many other places are a delight. The *Duc de Bourgogne* (on a canal) is a good hotel.

Ghent ... Another place you won't want to miss. There is a beautiful view from St. Michael's Bridge. In one direction is the Enfilade des Monuments, consisting of St. Nicholas Church, Cloth Hall and adjoining Belfry, and the famous St. Bavon's Cathedral. In the other direction are several Romanesque houses and the Castle of the Counts. Other places to see are the Hotel de Ville, the Abbey de la Byloke, the Chateau of Gerard the Devil, ruins of St. Bavon Abbey.

Liege ... Wallony's intellectual and industrial center. Its architectural pride is the sixteenth-century Palace of the Bishop Princes. *Le Clou Doré* offers magnificent food and accommodations.

Ostend ... the famed coast resort has long been popular with tourists. There is the Casino, racing, tennis and golf and, of course, the Thermal baths. *Knocke-le-Zoute* farther up the coast is the newest and finest Belgian shore resort. Here they have the annual summer film festival. There is a casino, too, and a wonderful hotel, *La Réserve*.

SOURCES OF FURTHER INFORMATION ... Tourist offices in Town Hall and Central Station, Brussels; Pan American office is in the Shell Building, 55 Cantersteen (Tel. 11-64-05), Brussels.

DENMARK

WEATHER IN COPENHAGEN—Lat. N55°40'—Alt. 25'

Temp.	JAN.	FEB.	MAR.	APR.	MAY	JUNE	JULY	AUG.	SEPT.	OCT.	NOV.	DEC.
Low	29°	29°	31°	37°	45°	53°	56°	56°	51°	44°	37°	34°
High	35°	35°	39°	47°	57°	65°	68°	66°	60°	51°	43°	38°
Average	32°	32°	35°	42°	51°	59°	62°	61°	56°	48°	40°	36°
Days of Rain	15	14	15	12	13	12	15	16	14	17	16	17

LOCATION ... Denmark occupies the Jutland peninsula, protruding north from Germany between Norway and Sweden, and includes a group of nearby islands, of which Funen and Zealand, where Copenhagen is located, are the largest.

CHARACTERISTICS ... Denmark is one of the tidiest countries in Europe. Everything is bright and shining. The people are genial and gay, the food is wonderful and plentiful and the bars never close. Good hotels, night clubs, restaurants, shops and a palace at which the guard is changed at high noon when the King is in residence. Yachting and fishing are superb.

POPULATION ... Estimated 4,450,000, about twice the population of Philadelphia.

SIZE ... 16,575 square miles, about half the size of Maine. No part of the country is more than 40 miles from the open sea.

CAPITAL ... Copenhagen, a city of a million and a quarter inhabitants, about half the size of Philadelphia.

GOVERNMENT ... A constitutional monarchy, the crown holding power with the Rigsdag, or Parliament.

HOW TO GET THERE ... By Pan American Clipper about 11½ hours (elapsed time) from New York. By ship about 10 days.

ACCOMMODATIONS ... There are a number of fine hotels in Copenhagen. The *d'Angleterre* has long been famous for its distinguished service and delightful sidewalk café. Rates for a single room are about $6 to $9 per day. Other fine hotels are the *Palace* and

Imperial situated in the heart of town. Rates are $5 to $8 single. Newest and largest is the de luxe *Hotel 3 Falke* (3 Falcons), five minutes away. $5.50 to $6.50. Highly recommendable first-class hotels are *Alexandra, Astoria, Codan, Mercur, Europa, Richmond*, and *Terminus* which are near the Town Hall Square. Rates from $4 to $7. For those traveling on a small budget, comfortable accommodations are available at the various Mission Hotels for $1.25 to $1.50 a day. Despite the name, they are not religious organizations. There is a 15 per cent service charge added to the above prices. Between October and April some hotels reduce their prices 10 to 20 per cent.

ARTS... You could spend all your sightseeing time seeing the wonderful museums of Copenhagen alone. Here are a few of the most outstanding. The National Museum has outstanding collections from the time of the Vikings and other periods in Danish history. The Arsenal has a famous display of arms, armor and uniforms. In Rosenborg Palace you will enjoy seeing the regalia of the Danish kings. The Kunstindustrimuseet houses a fascinating collection of arts and crafts of Denmark and foreign countries from the Middle Ages to the present time. The world-famous Museum of Musical Instruments is in the same building. The Hirschsprung Collection of Danish art is an interesting and representative exhibit. The Thorvaldsen Museum contains the works, tomb and the personal effects of Thorvaldsen, one of Denmark's greatest masters. The State Museum of Art has fine paintings from the Danish Renaissance. The Ny Carlsberg Glyptotek contains an antique collection and a French collection.

BALLET... The Danish Royal Ballet Company is one of the finest in the world. Season at the Royal Theater in Copenhagen is September through May.

BANKS... The three leading banks in Copenhagen are: Landmandsbanken, Handelsbanken, Privatbanken, with branch offices all over the city. Banking hours are: 10:00 to 3:00; Saturdays, 10:00 to 1:00; Fridays also 5:00 to 6:00 P.M. American Express Office is located at Dagmarhus, H. C. Andersens Boulevard 12.

CALENDAR OF HOLIDAYS... New Year's Day; March 11, King's Birthday; five-day holiday from Maundy Thursday to Easter Monday; Store Bededag (public holiday fourth Friday after Easter); Ascension Day; June 5, Constitution Day; June 23, Midsummer Night; July 4, Celebration in the Danish-American National Park in Rebild; Christmas; December 26, Boxing Day.

CIGARETTES AND TOBACCO... American cigarettes are not available, so bring in the duty-free allowance. Danish cigarettes (55 cents per pack) and tobacco are similar to American brands.

CLIMATE... All of Denmark is warmer in the winter and cooler in the summer than the Northeastern section of the United States. The winter temperatures seldom go below 30 degrees and summer averages around 68 degrees. The Gulf Stream keeps the climate equable. Best time to visit Denmark is from the middle of April to November.

CLUBS ... There are many clubs of all kinds in Denmark. Ask the Personal Information Department of the National Travel Association óf Denmark for information about clubs which may interest you. Address in Copenhagen: 5-7 Banegaardspladsen (opposite the Central Station).

COMMON COURTESIES AND LOCAL CUSTOMS ... "Thank You" (*Tak*) is the most often heard phrase in Denmark. You shake hands when you meet people and when you leave. Bring flowers when invited to dinner at a private home or send them ahead.

Time is referred to as half of the next hour rather than half past an hour; for example, 6:30 is called "half-seven."

COMMUNICATIONS ... There are excellent telephone, cable and telegraph facilities all over Denmark.

CURRENCY ... The krone is the principal unit, worth 6.92 kroner to the dollar. (Buying rate 6.82.)

CUSTOMS REGULATIONS AND DOCUMENTS REQUIRED FOR UNITED STATES CITIZENS ... Your American passport is all you need to enter Denmark. No visa. Bring your international driver's license if you plan to hire a car. If you are not living at a hotel, you must register with the local police. You can bring in unlimited amounts of any currency, but take only 500 Danish kroner out unless more resulted from exchange. Other duty-free imports are: 400 cigarettes or 500 grams of cigars or tobacco, 2 bottles of liquor.

DRUG STORES ... Known as *Apothek*, Danish drug stores can supply all your drug needs with American or equivalent foreign products.

ELECTRIC CURRENT ... 220 volts, A.C., 50 cycle. The European standard type of transformer plugs are necessary in all hotels.

FAUNA ... Danish forests abound in deer, hare and wild fowl and game birds. Fishing in Danish lakes, streams and along the sea coast is excellent for both sportsmen and for the great fisheries that are one of the principal industries. Graceful swans are found in the parks and sea gulls are as common as pigeons in Copenhagen. Ducks waddle around among the people in Danish parks. Denmark is principally agricultural. There is a marvelous agricultural show the last week of June in Copenhagen.

FLORA ... Denmark is a land of beautiful flowers. The parks of Copenhagen are among the most beautifully landscaped in the world. Lilacs and roses are everywhere. The beech is the national tree of Denmark. There are impressive pine forests and lovely meadows and farmlands.

FOOD ... The Danes love to eat and eat well. They have done the most with the sandwich idea. There are over 200 varieties of delicious open-faced sandwiches available, the so-called *Smorrebrod*, which are the uniquely Danish variety of smorgasbord. The Danish dairy products, especially cheeses, are among the most outstanding in the world. The milk is marvelous. Seafood is a national specialty. Here, Danish pastries are deliciously different from the American variety. The variety is infinite. Boiled cod, fried eel (*stegt aal*), and a delicious soup made of rye bread and beer are Danish national dishes, too. The Danes are great consumers of coffee and enjoy tea. Cocktails are served, but not in all circles.

GAMBLING ... Gambling is prohibited except at Government-controlled race tracks and other sports events.

LANGUAGE ... The official language is Danish of course, but English is understood even by the man on the street in Copenhagen.

LAUNDRY AND DRY CLEANING ... Though service is not as fast as in American establishments, Danish laundries and dry-cleaning plants are excellent. Most hotels in Copenhagen have their own facilities.

LIQUOR ... Good, strong Danish beer and Danish *akvavit* (schnapps) are well known, as well as Cherry Heering. Good imported liquor and wines are also available.

MEDICAL FACILITIES ... Medical care is available to tourists at a very low cost at the Government health clinics. There are excellent doctors and dentists throughout the country.

MOTION PICTURES ... English and American pictures and other foreign films are shown in Copenhagen. Better motion picture theaters include the *Alexandra*, the *Palads*, the *Palladium, Dagmar, Kino Palaeet* and the *World Cinema*. See the local papers for time and program.

MUSIC ... Opera alternating with the Royal Ballet at the Royal Theater is one of the outstanding features of the winter in Copenhagen. There is an excellent symphony that performs at the Copenhagen Concert Hall and a visiting artist or musical group once a week during the winter. Also in the attractive Concert Hall of the Broadcasting House, the symphony orchestra of 90 musicians gives concerts weekly. During the summer, daily concerts are held in Tivoli Gardens.

NIGHT CLUBS AND CABARETS ... Night life in Copenhagen is gay and fairly inexpensive. The clubs, now called "night restaurants," no longer require memberships, are open from about 10:00 P.M. on. These and other restaurants with dancing and floor shows may stay open till 5:00 A.M. The *Adlon* and the *Stork Club* are the leading night restaurants with these hours. *Ambassadeur* and *Atlantic Palace* open at 9:00 P.M. Others include *Lorry,* the *New Look,* the *Valencia.* There is dancing at the *Wivex* and in the summer at the *Bellevue* and the *Nimb.* Most hotels have good orchestras and other entertainment. There are numerous sidewalk cafés and little bars.

PHOTOGRAPHY ... Copenhagen is fully supplied with all kinds of photographic equipment and supplies at prices almost equivalent to those in Germany. Black-and-white and color films are developed quickly and well in Denmark. Most photogenic parts of the city: old canals around fishmarket, flower market near the main street, stock-exchange and Nyhavn, also modern residential quarters around Grundtvig's Church and street scenes in the rush hours.

RELIGION ... The state religion is Lutheran. Other sects include Catholic, Episcopal, Methodist, Presbyterian and Jewish.

RESTAURANTS ... Eating being one of the Danish national pastimes, it's hard to find a poor restaurant in Copenhagen. You'll seldom go wrong just walking into the first place that appeals to you. The restaurants listed below are among the most widely known. There is excellent French food and a Parisian atmosphere at *Au Coq d'Or*. There are also excellent restaurants in the Tivoli Park area: the *Belle Terrace, Divan I* and *Divan II,* the *Nimb* and the *Wivex* which have lovely dining terraces. The *De 7 smaa Hjem* (7 small homes), the *7 Nations,* the *Hotel Imperial Restaurant,* the *Viking* in the Palace Hotel and the Roof Restaurant at *Hotel Codan* and the *Hotel Europa* are also very good. *Hotel Richmond* is excellent for both lunch and dinner. *Oscar Davidsen's* is the famous sandwich emporium. They list 175 different varieties, all delicious and reasonably priced. Davidsen's is also good for seafood. *Frascati* serves both Danish and Italian cuisine on their charming sidewalk terrace. The cafeteria at the Hotel Imperial is inexpensive and convenient, especially when you're in a hurry. The *KAR* restaurants (no liquor) are also good and moderate.

Dinner is served from 7:00 to 9:00, lunch at noon and breakfast from 8:00 A.M. in most restaurants. You can eat three very good meals a day in Copenhagen for about $4.

SHOPS AND STORES ... Copenhagen is one of the great shopping centers of the world. Department stores in Copenhagen which sell distinctive Danish souvenirs are: Magasin du Nord, Illum and Crome and Goldschmidt. The headquarters of Georg Jensen is here. Also good are A. Michelsen and Hans Hansen. The Permanent Exhibition of Danish Industrial Arts is a good place to pick up marvelous textiles, pewter, ceramics, china and toys. Silver and furs cost much less than at home. All shops close at 5:30 P.M. in the afternoon on weekdays and at 2:00 P.M. on Saturdays.

SPECTATOR SPORTS ... Soccer is the national sport in Denmark. Racing and trotting meets are also very popular. Bicycle racing and tennis matches are great seasonal favorites, too. See the local papers for more information on these events.

SPORTS ... There are golf courses at Aalborg, Aarhus, Asserbo, Esbjerg, Vesterhavsbad on the island of Fanø, Elsinore, Kolding, Copenhagen, Odense, and Rungsted. Tennis courts are plentiful. The local club will gladly arrange for you to use their courts. Riding clubs throughout the country will give you information about hiring horses. Kajak and canoeing are favorite holiday sports. There are lovely rivers, like Gudenna and Susaa, and the fjords. Freshwater fishing in some of the rivers may interest you, but if you prefer sea fishing, fishermen will be glad to take you out. There is great sport each year in tunny fishing in the Oresund off Elsinore. The season is from about August 15 to October 1. Sailing is ideal in Danish waters. You can hire a sailing boat at Svendborg or Skive.

THEATERS ... Copenhagen is a great theater town. The presentations of the *Royal Theater,* including ballet and opera, will interest those unfamiliar with the Danish language. During the summer there are open-air performances all over Denmark, including the Viking Festival at Frederikssund June 20 to July 5 with colorful pageantry. Consult the National Travel Association for information on current programs.

Tivoli and *Dyrehavsbakken* are great big amusement parks open from May to September. There are outdoor comedy theaters, side shows, animal circuses, band concerts and pantomime, to name but a few of the attractions at these mammoth fun fairs.

TIME ... Six hours later than United States Eastern Standard Time. Denmark uses the 24-hour clock (12:01 to 24:00 is P.M.). No daylight saving time.

TIPPING ... All hotels and restaurants add a 15 per cent service charge to your bill. This is sufficient. Tip 15 per cent if it is not added. The same rule applies to taxis, barbers, etc.

TRANSPORTATION ... Taxis, buses and trolley cars are plentiful in Copenhagen. There are good trains and cross-country buses for traveling in Denmark. Little steamers take you from island to island at reasonable rates. Cars for hire are readily available through all hotel porters and most travel agencies. Rates are reasonable. Apply to your Automobile Club.

WATER ... The water is safe to drink all over Denmark.

WHAT TO BUY ... Danish and Greenland furs and silver, which cost much less than at home; Royal Copenhagen and Bing and Grondahl porcelain; beautiful table and other linen; pewter and bronze ware; Danish toys; jewelry. *See also* SHOPS AND STORES.

WHAT TO WEAR ... As there are no extremes of heat or cold in Denmark, you'll need neither very heavy clothes nor your lightest cottons. Wool suits and dresses and a warm topcoat will be fine although it is recommended that women bring their furs for the winter months. Suits and a dressy black outfit will fill a woman's needs in Copenhagen. Formal attire is seldom worn except for Saturday evening dancing at the *Ambassadeur* or the *Wivex*. Business suits, a topcoat and tweeds in the country for men. Bring a raincoat, too. Conservative sports clothes are favored by the natives anywhere outside of Copenhagen. Wear conventional sport clothes for active sports.

WHERE TO GO—SIGHTSEEING ...

Copenhagen ... A wonderful way to get your first view of Copenhagen and environs is by the little motor boats that chug through the canals of the city and the surrounding coastline. Well-planned guided tours to various points of interest are available. Usually operating throughout the year, they range in price from $1 for the non-stop City Tour to $8 for the Copenhagen Night Tour. Others include all-day tours of South Zealand, all- or half-day tours of North Zealand, Deer Park, or historical areas. The "Lifeseeing" tours,

The "Little Mermaid," immortalized by Hans Christian Andersen, looks out to sea near Copenhagen's favorite promenade.

Only 22 miles from Copenhagen in Hilleröd stands historic Frederiksborg castle, which now houses the National Historical Museum.

such as the World of Tomorrow Social Tour and Industrial Arts Tour, offer opportunities for becoming acquainted with Danish life aside from their unique meeting service mentioned under SOURCES OF FURTHER INFORMATION.

Of course, it's fun to sightsee on your own, too. The King lives in the beautiful Amalienborg Palace. The Changing of the Guard takes place at noon when the King is in residence. The royal reception rooms in Christiansborg Palace are open to visitors Thursday through Sunday. Other sights are Grundtvig's Church, which is situated in the middle of the new residential quarter of Bispebjerg, and the Church of our Saviour, with a spiral staircase outside the spire. The Copenhagen Zoo is one of the most important zoos in Europe. Orstedsparken is one of the loveliest parks in Europe surrounding a charming little lake full of graceful swans.

Other sights of interest include the Rosenborg Castle, the University of Copenhagen, the Houses of Parliament and the Gefion Fountain at the entrance to Copenhagen's favorite promenade, Langelinie, where also the statue of the Little Mermaid can be seen. The Tivoli is a famous amusement park in the center of town, where you can dance, hear a symphony, dine or ride a ferris wheel. Side trips from Copenhagen can be made through the lovely surrounding countryside. You can go to Kronborg (Hamlet's) Castle 28 miles north. Bellevue Bathing Resort is only 8 miles from Copenhagen. The Deer Park is a beautiful wooded area where horses and carriages can be hired. At Lyngby there is an interesting Open-Air Museum, featuring old Danish farms (folk dances on Sundays in the summer). Fredensborg Castle is the lovely autumn residence of the Royal Family. Hornbaek Beach, 40 miles from Copenhagen, is worth visiting.

Now for sightseeing farther afield. There is a good four-day tour called "The Fairy Tale Tour," for approximately $80, which covers most of the places described below. You can have it adapted to suit your time and travel plans beyond Denmark. Or you can go on your own. The Danish Tourist Office or travel agencies will be glad to help you plan it.

Aarhus . . . Denmark's second largest city is Aarhus. Located on the Jutland peninsula, overnight by boat from Copenhagen or 6 hours by train. The Town Hall is striking, ultra-modern; the cathedral, part Romanesque, part Gothic. The University is beautifully situated in an extensive park. The open-air museum is very interesting. The deer parks and wood of Riiskov preserves are wonderful. The leading hotel in Aarhus is the *Royal*, but the *Ritz* and *Regina* are both up to date. Thirty-one miles from Aarhus is Silkeborg, resort center of the Jutland region. In the heart of the lake district, Silkeborg is a charming little town. The sailing is great, the beaches are lovely, and fishing is also very popular. Travel through the crystal lakes in shiny little lake steamers. The good hotel in Silkeborg is the *Dania*. Rates average around a dollar a day.

The Island of Funen is the second largest in Denmark. It is the

Town Hall Square in the cosmopolitan city of Copenhagen, often called the "city of spires."

fairy-tale Land of Hans Christian Andersen. You'll be enchanted by the quaint city of Odense, capital of the region. Andersen was born here and his house has become a museum, open to the public daily. The thirteenth-century Gothic church is one of the most delightful in Denmark. See the Funen Village, an open-air museum of Danish peasant life. It looks like something out of Andersen. The zoo is also very interesting. Excursions can be made among the lovely rolling hills. Quaint thatched farm houses and picture-book scenery abound. The *Grand Hotel* in Odense is superb.

Traveling to the south of Funen you'll come to the lovely old town of Svendborg. Twisting streets and old houses; many beautiful private castles in this region. Good swimming, boating, and fishing. The Travel Association here arranges tours to the small, beautiful islands of Aerö, Strynö, and Langeland, well worth the reasonable cost.

Aalborg ... is a very active city in the north of Jutland. Don't miss Jens Bang's House, a beautifully preserved Renaissance building. Night life here is very gay. The *Ambassador* and *Kilden* restaurants are known all over Denmark. There are a good golf course, fine fishing and other excellent sports facilities. Stay at the *Phonix*. Ribald National Park near Aalborg is the beautiful setting for the unique July 4 celebration. The de luxe *Rold Stor-Kro Inn* here is excellent.

SOURCES OF FURTHER INFORMATION ... To get the most out of your stay in Copenhagen and Denmark contact the Information Department of the National Travel Association. The office is near the Central Station and opposite the Terminus Hotel (Tel. Central 14.760 and 1946). The most wonderful part of this friendly organization is their introduction plan. They will arrange for you to meet anybody from brother butterfly collectors to diplomats. This meeting service is international friendship and hospitality at its best. They will also make arrangements for you to visit Danish institutions, concerts, circuses or even Danish homes. They will also provide information about restaurants, shopping, general sightseeing and special tours. The American Embassy is at Østerbrogade 14 (Tel. Tria 4505); Pan Am's office is at H. C. Andersen's, Boulevard 12 (Tel. By 10.000). In New York the Danish National Travel office is at 588 5th Avenue.

FINLAND

WEATHER IN HELSINKI—Lat. N60°12'—Alt. 25'

Temp.	JAN.	FEB.	MAR.	APR.	MAY	JUNE	JULY	AUG.	SEPT.	OCT.	NOV.	DEC.
Average	23°	22°	28°	37°	46°	55°	62°	59°	50°	41°	32°	28°
Days of Rain	18	16	14	12	12	13	12	16	16	17	19	19

LOCATION ... Finland lies northwest of Russia and east of Norway and Sweden. Helsinki in the south is about 250 air miles from Stockholm, 1,144 air miles from London.

CHARACTERISTICS ... Finland is a delightful and · vigorous country which is unspoiled by too many tourists despite the fact that it offers the traveler a great deal. This land, where the midnight sun shines through the summer, is a paradise of virgin forests, crystal lakes (about 60,000 of them), mountains and cascading rivers. As in all Scandinavian countries, its people are blond and blue-eyed, its cities clean, its food marvelous. The country is efficient, the people hospitable, and the rugged rather mystic quality of the country is reflected in the Finns themselves. For an unusual vacation, Finland is the answer.

POPULATION ... Estimated 4,400,000.

SIZE ... 130,165 square miles, the size of New Mexico plus Vermont.

CAPITAL ... Helsinki, with 440,000 inhabitants, is the size of San Antonio.

GOVERNMENT ... A republican form of government but more like the British parliamentary system than that of the United States.

HOW TO GET THERE ... By Pan American Clipper through-plane service from New York to Helsinki, about 20½ hours (elapsed time) via Keflavik, Oslo and Stockholm. Helsinki 's only 1½ hours flying time from Stockholm. By ship about 12 da s from New York to Helsinki.

ACCOMMODATIONS ... Among the luxury hotels in Helsinki are the *Palace* and *Vaakuna*. First-class hotels are *Helsinki, Kämp, Seurahuone, Klaus, Kurki,* and *Torni.* There are many less expensive but very good hotels there, too, such as the *Carlton* and *Andrea.* Rates in the top hotels run from $5 single and about $3 to $5 in the others.

ARTS ... There are many galleries and museums in Helsinki, and magnificent sculptures to be seen in the public squares. In the Ateneum, you will see collections of paintings by Akseli Gallen-Kallela, Albert Edelfelt, Eero Jarnefelt, Juho Rissanen and other famous Finnish artists. The National Museum houses a large collection of the works of these masters as does the Museum of the City of Helsinki, and the Traidehalli. The museums also contain sculpture by Finland's outstanding sculptor, Waino Aaltonen, by Jussi Mantynen, and others.

BALLET ... The Finnish Ballet Company, which includes the excellent prima ballerina Margaretha von Bahr, gives performances in the Opera House, except in summer.

BANKS ... The important banks with U.S. affiliations are: Pohjoismaiden Yhdyspankki, Helsingin Osakepankki, Kansallis-Osake-Pankki and Maatalous-Osake-Pankki. The banks and most hotels will cash traveler's checks.

CALENDAR HOLIDAYS ... New Year's Day; January 6, Twelfth Day; Good Friday through Easter Monday; May Day (student festival); March 25, Lady Annunciation Day; May 30, Ascension Day; Mid-Summer Eve and Day, another festive occasion; November 2, All Saints' Day; December 6, Independence Day; Christmas Day and the day after, St. Stephen's Day.

CIGARETTES ... American cigarettes are available at 50 cents a pack. Two similar local brands are the North State and Boston.

CLIMATE ... Similar to that of New England. July and August are the best times to visit Finland.

CLUBS ... Rotary Club, Lions, Zonta.

COMMON COURTESIES AND CUSTOMS ... The *sauna,* the famous Finnish bath, is a must when you visit Finland. Nearly every home has one, and almost every hotel. In Finland, both men and women always shake hands on meeting each other. Children should not be excluded from this ceremony. When introduced, you are also expected to mention your last name. When invited anywhere, you are expected to be prompt. This means you arrive between 7:30 and 7:35 for a dinner party scheduled for 7:30. Another Finnish social custom is that of observing the name day, as well as the birthday of friends and relatives.

COMMUNICATIONS ... Telephone, cables, radio and transatlantic telephones, airmail.

CURRENCY ... The monetary unit is the Finn mark, worth 321 to our dollar at official exchange.

CUSTOMS REGULATIONS AND DOCUMENTS REQUIRED FOR UNITED STATES CITIZENS ... Passport, no visa required. You may bring in 1 bottle of liquor, 2 of wine and 2 of beer; up to

20,000 Finnish marks and unlimited other currency. 20,000 Finnish marks and foreign currency to the amount imported may be taken out. You may bring in 100 cigarettes, or 25 cigars or ½ lb. of tobacco.

DRUG STORES . . . Chemists' shops and lots of them.

ELECTRIC CURRENT . . . 110 to 220 volts, 50 cycles, A.C. The plug-ins are the round, two-hole type requiring European-type transformer plugs.

FAUNA . . . Most numerous among Finland's mammalian fauna are the fox, squirrel, hare, moose. In the eastern and northern parts the bear, wolverine and lynx wolf are also found. For the game-bird hunter, Finland offers good opportunities. The capercailzie, the black grouse and the hazel-hen are rather common birds.

FLORA . . . The flora and vegetation of Finland resemble that of northern Minnesota. More than 70 per cent of Finland's land area is covered by forests. Predominant trees are pine, spruce and birch. In northern parts of the country there are large swamps which cover about one-third of the total land area.

FOOD . . . Some of the native foods are wonderful. Of course, try the *voileipäpöytä* (like smörgasbord), *piirakka* (Karelian rice pastry), Finnish pancakes served with lingonberry sauce. "Fish Cock" (kalakukko)—a strange but delicious blend of bacon and pork and fresh-water herring in a pastry loaf—reindeer steak or smoked reindeer, and in August, the crayfish. Attend a crayfish party, if you can.

GAMBLING . . . The National Lottery and playball machines. There is betting on horse trotting.

LANGUAGE . . . Finland is a bilingual country where approximately 91 per cent of the population speak Finnish, the rest speak Swedish. The tourist can easily get by in Helsinki and other big towns, as people very commonly speak English.

LAUNDRY AND DRY CLEANING . . . Laundries are plentiful. Dry-cleaning facilities are excellent but relatively slow.

LIQUOR . . . The Finns have two very rare liqueurs, Mesimarja (Arctic brambleberry) and Lakka (cloudberry or chamemorus). Scotch and American whiskies and cocktails are also available.

MEDICAL FACILITIES . . . The City of Helsinki Board of Health (near Market Square) arranges home calls by doctors any time of the day or night.

MOTION PICTURES . . . All languages, but mostly in English.

MUSIC . . . The Helsinki Symphony Orchestra gives concerts during the season at the University Hall. Opera at the Opera House. You should try to hear the Finnish opera, *The Maid of Pohjola*, by the Finnish composer, Oskar Merikanto. It has been more than fifty years since the First Symphony of Jean Sibelius was first heard. Sibelius was not only Finland's foremost composer, but was renowned the world over; a great musical event is the annual Sibelius Festival, which takes place in Helsinki during the first two weeks of June. The program consists mainly of Sibelius' music.

PHOTOGRAPHY ... Films and developing charges are reasonable in Finland. Color film is available as are black-and-white still and movie film. There is excellent service on developing as long as you make clear how many or how few days you can wait. An expert recommends the orange filter for lakes, islands and summer clouds, the dark green for full effect of the forest and landscape, and yellow for Lapland scenes. Sunsets in Finland are particularly strong and beautiful especially in July, August, and September. Recommended photo shops: Bögelund on the Esplanade, SVO on Keskuskatu and Nyblin at Mannerheimintic (Forum).

RELIGION ... Finland is 96 per cent Lutheran, but there are Methodist, Anglican and Roman Catholic churches, and synagogues.

RESTAURANTS ... There are dozens of restaurants in Helsinki besides the hotel dining rooms. Some of the better ones are the *Monte Carlo, Savoy, Palace, Theater Grill, Vaakuna, Torni, Motti* and *Walhalla.* There are also many restaurants where they have music for dancing; among these are the *Adlon, Kalastajatorppa, Casino, Kaivohuone* and *Fennia.* They have temperance restaurants, too, the *Kestikartano, Elanto, Primula* and *Pikapala.*

SHOPS AND STORES ... Stockmann's Department Store, Sokos, Renlund and Rake.

SPECTATOR SPORTS ... Racing, yachting regattas, auto and motorcycle races, track meets, Finnish baseball, which is called *pesapallo,* international canoeing competitions, cycling championships, tennis matches, soccer, the International Winter Games, skiing and ski-jumping competitions and reindeer races.

SPORTS ... Swimming, log rolling, tennis, football, golf (you can play at midnight in midsummer), sailing, skiing, fishing, hunting. The best fishing season is from the beginning of June to the end of August. The hunting season is in the autumn. The best skiing is in Lapland during March and April when days are long. (Ski resort hotels *Pallastunturi* and *Kilpisjarvi.*) Canoeing and hiking are favorites.

THEATERS ... Almost every town in Finland has its own theater where foreign as well as Finnish plays are produced. In Helsinki: the *National Theater* at Station Square, the *Swedish Theater.*

TIME ... Seven hours later than United States Eastern Standard Time.

TIPPING ... There is a 15 per cent service charge added to your hotel and 10 per cent on restaurant bills. The Finns do not encourage extra tipping. Taxi drivers and others are not tipped.

TRANSPORTATION ... Taxis are easy to get (chart in taxi translates meter reading); bus and train services excellent. Also water buses to take you to some of the outlying places. You can hire private cars with English-speaking guides. Taxi fares are twelve times the meter reading and are more after 11:00 P.M. Self-drive cars (mostly Volkswagens) are available for about $12.50 a day for the first 125 miles, then 6 cents a mile.

WATER ... Excellent.

WHAT TO BUY ... Famous Arabia rice china, pottery, Karhula-littala glass, ornaments of brass, wood carving, fabrics, hand-blocked linens, and articles made of woven birch bark, reeds, wickers.

WHAT TO WEAR ... Heavy clothes in winter months (fur coat, ski togs), and lightweight clothes for the summer months. Better have a coat even in summer. Fur hats in Lapland in winter season.

WHERE TO GO—SIGHTSEEING ...

Helsinki ... Whereas the city of Helsinki is over 400 years old, most of the present city was built after the turn of this century. This accounts for its modern architecture. There is a lot to be seen in Helsinki, which is called the White City of the North. You should take a walk through the beautiful parks and squares where some of Finland's most magnificent sculpture can be seen. In front of Stockmann's store on the Main Square is the famous statue of the Three Smiths. On the Market Square is the statue of The Maid of Helsinki Rising from the Sea, and on Observatory Hill one of their most famous symbolic statues, Shipwrecked. All of these have been done by outstanding Finnish sculptors. Visit the Olympic Stadium where the 1952 Olympics were held. Other places to see in Helsinki are the Parliament Building, the President's Palace, on the Market Square; the beautiful City Gardens at Eläintarha Park. Take a ferry from the foot of Aleksanterinkatu to Korkeasaari Island for a visit to Finland's only zoo. Also worth visiting are the Suomenlinna Islands just off Market Square.

Be sure to visit the great church of Suurkirkko, a magnificent white stone structure. At the Social Museum you will see an exhibition of Work Protection and Social Welfare work. From the Stadium tower you get a wonderful view of the entire city.

Turku ... Finland's former capital, Turku (45 minutes by air from Helsinki) was founded in the 13th century. It is Finland's oldest and third biggest city, with a population of 120,000. The Cathedral and the Castle from the 13th century, the Handicraft Museum and the Resurrection Chapel, a masterpiece of modern Finnish architecture, are some of the musts in this old city with an atmosphere of its own. Modern Turku ranks very prominently in the cultural life of the country and it is also one of the biggest ports. From Turku it is easy to make trips into the beautiful surrounding country.

Side Trips ... From Helsinki one of the most beautiful trips to take is to the city of Tampere. You may take a modern train, or go by motor bus and water bus. Tampere, with a population of 121,000 is clean, modern and Finland's second largest city. There is one excellent hotel, the *Tammer*. The Tammerkoski rapids flow through the town and many important industries are located here. Take a trip to the top of Pyynikki ridge where you will get a wonderful view of the city and its surrounding lakes. Other places to go to are the Cathedral with its famous fresco paintings and Näsilinna, the provincial museum, which is on the top of a hill where you get an excellent view of Lake Näsijärvi. There are two art museums here

The Helsinki Railway Station, Hotel Vaakuna to the right.

A View of the South Harbour in Helsinki. The Great Church in the background.

too, which house fine collections of modern Finnish art. If you are here in the summer, try the *Rosendal* summer restaurant.

From Tampere you go by water bus to Aulanko, the number-one tourist center of Finland. The water bus takes you through typical Finnish lake regions. Food and refreshments are served on these buses. Aulanko is on the shore of Lake Vanajavesi facing the town of Hämeenlinna. The *Aulanko Hotel* is one of the finest and most modern in the country and is surrounded by the Aulanko National

Helsinki Olympic Stadium, with statue of world-famous runner Paavo Nurmi in the foreground.

Park, one of the most beautiful in all Finland. The restaurant in the hotel has an orchestra and floor shows. There is a private bathing beach, tennis courts, golf course, and, of course, the traditional Finnish *sauna,* in addition to medical treatment and baths. One of the historic sights to see is the Hattula Church, which was built in 1250. The town of Hämeenlinna facing it is where Jean Sibelius was born and went to school. There's also a magnificent medieval castle built in the thirteenth century. From a tower high up in Aulanko National Park you get a wonderful view of the entire surrounding lakeland.

Lapland ... No visitor to Finland would miss a trip to Lapland, which is just as beautiful in the summer as it is in the winter. There are many legends about Lapland, one being that "it casts a spell on the visitor which compels him to return again and when he goes a second time he may stay, and if he does he'll turn into a reindeer." To reach Rovaniemi, the capital of Lapland, you may go by air in 4 hours or by train in 22 hours. Lapland was almost completely destroyed in the war, but has been entirely rebuilt. Rovaniemi is the gateway to the North. There is a good hotel here, the *Pohjanhovi,* and many tourists' inns and ski lodges.

Every tourist has heard of the midnight sun. There is daylight here continuously for two months, May to July. There are still about 2,000 native Lapps in existence and they are a particularly proud race. One thing a visitor MUST NOT do is stare at the Lapps in their native costumes or try to intrude on a Lapp *kota* (home). Lapland is rapidly becoming one of the most popular resorts in Finland. Transportation is excellent; buses will take you to the most far-away villages. In the winter it is a wonderful place to enjoy winter sports. Skiing on the treeless mountain slopes (practically unequalled anywhere else) continues far into spring. Reindeer-joring is an exclusive sport in Lapland. This is getting in a one-seated *pulkka,* following the leader (they say the driving is easy), and skimming over the snow. The annual Ounasvaara International Games held in Rovaniemi are one of the biggest winter tournaments in Northern Europe. During the short period of summer, Lapland is a splendid place for the fisherman, canoeist or hiker. Fish are plentiful in Lapland waters; trout, salmon and grayling are found in the streams, perch and pike in the lakes.

SOURCES OF FURTHER INFORMATION ... Local tourist offices in Helsinki are the Finnish Tourist Association, Mikonkatu 15 A, Helsinki; the Town Tourist Bureau, Linnankatu 14, Turku. Pan American's office is at Erottajankatu 15–17 (Tel. 19268). Other useful addresses in Helsinki are the American Legation, Itä Kaivopuisto 21; U. S. Information Center, Kaivokatu 10; Finnish Automobile Club, Fabianinkatu 14; Suomi Touring Club, Salomonkatu 17; Suomen Turistiauto Ltd., Lasipalatin. In New York the Finnish National Travel Office is at 10 East 40th Street, New York 16, N. Y. You may want to pick up a copy of the English-language magazine, *Finlandia Pictorial,* available in Helsinki.

FRANCE

WEATHER IN PARIS—Lat. N48°45′—Alt. 300′

Temp.	JAN.	FEB.	MAR.	APR.	MAY	JUNE	JULY	AUG.	SEPT.	OCT.	NOV.	DEC.
Low	32°	33°	36°	40°	46°	52°	55°	54°	50°	44°	37°	35°
High	42°	46°	52°	60°	67°	72°	76°	75°	69°	60°	49°	44°
Average	37°	40°	44°	50°	57°	62°	66°	65°	60°	52°	43°	40°
Days of Rain	14	14	14	13	14	12	12	12	11	15	15	15

LOCATION ... Although France is approximately on the same latitude as Montreal, the weather is usually somewhat warmer because of the Gulf Stream. The climate is similar to that of New York.

CHARACTERISTICS ... No one has to be told that Paris has everything for everyone. Its hotels are good, its restaurants, of course, out of this world. You can have a wonderful time in this famous, gay old city, not only during the summer season but also in winter and early spring when there are even greater attractions in theater, music and art. Other parts of France are awaiting you, too. The Riviera, with its long stretch of fashionable and magnificent beaches, its casinos, its luxurious hotels, is ready to help you to have a wonderful time, as are the Château country, Normandy and Brittany. The people are cultivated, witty, and charming. They are also worldly-wise and sensitive to criticism. Visitors from abroad are generally appreciated and treated with special courtesy. Devaluation of the franc offers the tourist a special advantage.

POPULATION ... 44,289,000, which approximates the population of New York, New Jersey, Pennsylvania and the New England states combined.

SIZE ... 212,821 square miles, about 20 per cent smaller than Texas.

CAPITAL ... Paris, with a population of 2,829,746, is the size of Philadelphia and San Francisco combined.

GOVERNMENT ... A republic, with a national assembly selected by all citizens of France, with participation of some of the French overseas territories.

HOW TO GET THERE ... By Pan American Jet Clipper, non-stop to Paris, about 7 hours from Boston, about 15¼ hours from Los Angeles via Jet connection in New York. Through-plane service to Nice on the Riviera via Lisbon and Barcelona about 16 hours from New York. Connections at Lisbon for Paris (4 hours). By ship, 5 to 9 days.

ACCOMMODATIONS ... There are countless hotels and pensions in Paris. You can find anything you want at any price. In the de luxe group are: the *Ritz, Plaza Athenée, George V, Meurice, Crillon, Prince de Galles, Royal Monceau, Raphaël,* and *Bristol.* Slightly less luxurious but very good are the *Claridge, Vendôme, Continental, Westminster, Napoléon-Bonaparte, Queen Elizabeth,* and others. Rates at official exchange run from about $10 a day and up single with no bath (no meals) at the top hotels. About $5 or $6 in the less swank group, and so on down from there. In the center of Paris, for businessmen, there are the *Scribe* and the *Ambassador.* Rates at official exchange run from about $8 a day up. Hotel space is hard to find in Paris from Easter until the end of October. This is the "on season" when the capital is thronged with visitors and prices rise accordingly. From December 20 to March 1 most hotels in Paris and on the Riviera reduce prices as much as 20 per cent.

ARTS ... Paris is the city for the art lover, the museum goer. Begin with the Louvre, of course. See the Venus de Milo, the Mona Lisa, the Winged Victory. Visit the Musée d'Art Moderne, the Rodin Museum, the Musée de l'Homme, the Jeu de Paume (impressionist painters), the Palais de Chaillot, Cluny, with sculptures, and exhibits of the Middle Ages, l'Ecole des Beaux Arts, Gobelins for tapestries, Musée de l'Armee for arms and armor. Museums are closed on Tuesdays.

BALLET ... The famed Paris Opera Ballet performs at the Opéra all year around except in August. Les Ballets de Paris, less classic but very good.

BANKS ... In Paris, National City Bank, 52 Avenue des Champs Elysées (8ème Arrt.), Tel. ELYsées 4542; American Express Co., 11 Rue Scribe (9ème Arrt.), Tel. OPEra 4290; Barclays Bank, Ltd., 33 Rue du 4 Septembre (2ème Arrt.), Tel. OPEra 4240; the Chase Bank, 39 Rue Cambon (1er Arrt.), Tel. OPEra 4430; Guaranty Trust of New York, 4 Place de la Concorde (8ème Arrt.), Tel. ANJou 1850; Morgan and Co., 14 Place Vendôme, Tel. OPEra 2420; Royal Bank of Canada, 3 Rue Scribe (9ème Arrt.), Tel. OPEra 0982; Thos. Cook & Son is at 2 Place de la Madeleine and 14 Boulevard des Capucines.

CALENDAR OF HOLIDAYS ... New Year's Day; Easter and Easter Monday; May 1, May Day; May 8, V-Day; Ascension Day, 40 days after Easter; Whitsunday (Pentecost) 10 days later and following Monday; July 14, Bastille Day; August 15, Assumption;

November 1, All Saints; November 11, Armistice Day; Christmas Day

CIGARETTES AND TOBACCO ... American cigarettes cost about $5 a carton. So take in as many as you are allowed and hang on to them. See CUSTOMS REGULATIONS below.

CLIMATE ... It never gets either very cold or very hot in Paris, although there are some exceptional days each season. Paris is interesting to visit in all seasons, but particularly so in winter and spring.

CLUBS ... In Paris: Jockey Club (very aristocratic—difficult to be admitted), International Club, Racing Club de France, Touring Club, Rotary Club, Lions International. Foreign members are admitted. In Nice and Marseilles: Propeller Club of the U. S.

COMMON COURTESIES AND LOCAL CUSTOMS ... You may find a number of customs in France new to you. Tickets are collected when you leave trains. All apartment houses have concierges who guard the door. Doors are locked at early hours each night. In small buildings the elevator will take you up but you are expected to walk down. It is customary to shake hands when you meet someone and when you say good-bye.

COMMUNICATIONS ... Excellent long-distance telephone and cable service. Local phone service is only adequate. The *pneumatique* is an inter-postoffice tube system which delivers a letter in about an hour, much faster than special delivery. Airmail to the United States costs 58 francs.

CURRENCY ... The monetary unit is the franc, worth about 4.937 to the dollar at official exchange rate. You can buy some French goods at a discount by paying in U. S. dollars or traveler's checks.

CUSTOMS REGULATIONS AND DOCUMENTS REQUIRED FOR UNITED STATES CITIZENS ... You may bring in 1,000 cigarettes, 250 cigars or 4 pounds of tobacco in your luggage, 2 bottles of liquor with seal broken, 2 pounds of any food stuffs, nylons and clothing for personal use. You need a passport but no visa unless you plan to stay more than three months. You will need a vaccination certificate to get back home.

One still camera and one movie camera with 20 rolls of color film or 10 rolls of black and white for each camera may be brought in. 20,000 francs may be taken out.

DRUG STORES ... There are many drug stores in Paris and several with English-speaking clerks which make a specialty of American trade.

ELECTRIC CURRENT ... United States electrical appliances can be used in France merely by buying locally a converting plug. This plug fits into the European-type electrical outlets and the United States-type cords can be plugged into the converter.

FAUNA ... In Paris, mostly poodles and sparrows.

FLORA ... In northern and central France, a wide variety of attractive wild flowers. In the south you will see vines, mimosa, orange trees and graceful cyprus.

FOOD . . . This is a volume in itself. French food is famous everywhere and Paris has some of the best restaurants in the world. You can find anything you want to eat in Paris at almost any price you wish to pay. Lunch is a two to three-hour affair involving several courses. The cheese is wonderful, hors d'oeuvres are usually superb, sauces are a national specialty, *Pâté de foie gras* is different from anything you've had in tins. Coffee is strong, but can be ordered to approximate the American taste. Try *purée de marrons*, chestnuts cooked with celery, spices and chicken consommé. Wonderful snails in garlic sauce and saddle of spring lamb done in white wine with chopped tarragon. There are hundreds of other magnificent dishes and regional favorites. The wines range from ordinary to superlative, depending upon price and taste. They are served with all meals. The French rarely drink water, but it is entirely potable. Pastries are famous, as are the *potages*, or thick soups. The French also do well by fish and salads. Milk is usually safe to drink, but make sure it's been pasteurized and purchased in a sealed bottle.

GAMBLING . . . Around Paris there is horse racing at *Auteuil, Chantilly, Longchamp, St. Cloud, Vincennes* and other nearby spots. The National Lottery has drawings every Wednesday. Nearest gambling casino in *Enghien,* 10 miles from Paris. Along the Riviera, and at Deauville, of course, the casinos are famous.

LANGUAGE . . . After two wars shared by the French with G.I.'s and "Tommies," almost every Frenchman not only can understand English but can now even understand an American trying to speak French.

LAUNDRY AND DRY CLEANING . . . Laundry is touch and go. In some hotels it's fine, in others it's very bad. In large hotels you can get your clothes cleaned in 48 hours.

LIQUOR . . . French wines, champagnes and brandies have no peer in the world. Liquor is now taxed in France, so drinks run higher than they used to be. Whisky is rather expensive. Brandy is really the national drink, but you can name your brand only in the best restaurants. But even the "bar brandy" in other spots is better than you often get at home. Vouvray and Mousseux are similar to Champagne, but cheaper. The Champagne name, of course, is patented and is applied only to wines from a certain district, just as Cognac applies only to the Cognac district. Best try a few wines and brandies and liqueurs for yourself and make up your own mind.

MEDICAL FACILITIES . . . The American Hospital at Neuilly is the favorite of Americans. But there are many English-speaking doctors. Ask at your hotel.

MOTION PICTURES . . . There are many cinema houses in Paris, many of them showing the same features you have seen or will see at home. The French movie industry is going strong and many French pictures are magnificent. Most Hollywood movies have French subtitles.

MUSIC . . . The Opéra, of course, is of great importance in Paris. Some of the world's greatest composers and conductors are French, so there is good music to be heard all the time. Good music can also be heard in celebrated concert halls such as: Salle Gaveau, Salle Pleyel and Palais de Chaillot.

NIGHT CLUBS AND CABARETS . . . Like food this would take a book in itself. But in Paris take a look at the *Lido* on the Champs Elysées, one of the most famous anywhere. There are floor shows. At most night clubs there will be a bucket of champagne on your table whether you order it or not. It is the equivalent of our cover charge, only more expensive. Look in at *Au Lapin Agile* in Montmartre, a spot with atmosphere. Drop in at *Schéhérazade, Novy,* and *Dinarzade* and let yourself be carried away by old Russian atmosphere, to the strains of gipsy violins. All famous, all good. For big brassiness, visit *Casino de Paris.* For formal elegance go to *Maxim's,* where on Fridays you must dress for dinner. Maxim's also offers piano and guitar in its informal and luxurious Midnight Room for after-dinner clientele. *Monseigneur, Le Drap d'Or, Jimmy's* and *l'Elephant Blanc* are elegant too. The *Nouvelle Eve* and *Moulin Rouge* are extremely popular and have floor shows. If you want to get real low-down, there is always the Place Pigalle in Montmartre with its many, many clubs of varying repute. If you hanker after a glimpse of the Existentialists, your best bet is the *Café de Flore* in St. Germain des Prés. Other spots where the prophets of this philosophy may be found are *Club St. Germain, Le Vieux-Colombier.* There's a night-club tour available from hotels.

PHOTOGRAPHY . . . Black-and-white and color still and movie films are available in Paris and other big cities; so are cameras. But prices are considerably higher than in the United States. Kodak-Pathé S.A. is located at 39 Avenue Montaigne, Paris.

RELIGION . . . France is a Catholic country and there are many magnificent Cathedrals which hold Mass. There are also many Protestant churches in Paris: American Church, British Embassy Church, Presbyterian Church, Eglise de L'Etoile; Eglise de Passy Eglise du Saint Esprit, Eglise de la Mission Etrangère, Methodist Church, Quakers, Russian Orthodox Church, Grande Synagogue. And in Nice, the beautiful Church of the Holy Spirit, the only American Protestant church in France, outside Paris.

RESTAURANTS . . . It is always possible to find a good little out-of-the-way spot undiscovered by tourists which has magnificent food and cheap prices. However, here are some of the better known in Paris: Maxim's (who is now preparing the meals for Pan American's crack Clipper flights between New York and the West Coast and Europe). *Lapérouse, La Tour d'Argent* and *Le Grand Véfour;* others such as *La Crémaillère, Lasserre, Taillevent, La Bourride, Laurent, Drouant,* are also very good. Food at the *Plaza Athenée* is excellent. *Chez Doucet* is a chain that is well known and one of the less expensive. For homesick Americans there are two *Pam-Pam,* which serve a club breakfast, American coffee and cheeseburgers. *Prunier* and *Méditerranée* specialize in seafood. *Pavillion d'Armenon-*

ville, *Pré Catelan* in the Bois de Boulogne have good food and delightful surroundings. Over on the left bank there are *La Coupole* and *Le Dôme*, both cafés beloved in the twenties and still doing business. *Harry's New York Bar*, famous among generations of Americans, is still at 5 Rue Daunou. The *Ritz Bar* is still the favorite meeting place of Americans. Montmartre is as cluttered with bars as New York's Fifty-Second Street. Some are clip joints; some are not. Use your head. Go to the *Café de la Paix*, of course. There are sidewalk cafés everywhere you turn where it is possible to sit for hours drinking very little or letting the saucers pile up.

SHOPS AND STORES ... *Aux Trois Quartiers* and *Samaritaine de Luxe* are two of the best department stores in Paris. There are also *Au Printemps* and *Galeries Lafayette*, either one a Frenchman's equivalent for Macy's. For linens there is *Grande Maison de Blanc*. The shops on the Rue de la Paix are magnificent. The Rue Royale, Avenue Matignon, Faubourg St. Honoré and its extensions across Rue Royale, the Rue St. Honoré have the smartest specialty shops. And now the big couturiers have opened what they call "boutiques" in which ready-to-wear merchandise and accessories are offered at far lower prices than in the custom salons. The *Bon Marché* is on the left bank. Don't miss the *Marché aux Puces*, the famous Flea Market of Paris, reached by Metro to the Porte of Clignancourt. It is open every Saturday through Monday.

The better shops and especially big stores (also hairdressers) are closed Mondays. Some shops close during August when many Parisians take their vacation.

SPECTATOR SPORTS ... Horse racing goes on almost all year at one track or another near Paris. Soccer is popular at the Parc des Princes and at Colombes Stadium. Tennis tournaments and championship matches take place at Stade Roland-Garros in the Bois. Boxing matches are frequent. Basketball games during the winter.

SPORTS ... Cycling is a favorite sport around Paris. There is a fine golf course at St. Cloud (card necessary), also at St. Germain, Chantilly, Mortefontaine, etc. Riding in the Bois. There is skiing in the French Alps and the Pyrenees in winter. Yachting, swimming, fishing, golf, riding all along the Riviera, Deauville, Biarritz, and good fishing in Brittany.

THEATERS ... In Paris: The *Comédie Française*, one of the most famous theaters in the world, is open all year except in July and August. Grand opera may be heard all year except during August at the *Opéra*. The *Opéra Comique* has light opera. The *Grand Guignol*, which features horror plays, is certainly worth a visit. The *Folies Bergère* is the mecca of many Americans and there are numerous music halls offering variety shows which you can enjoy without understanding French. Buy your seats from a broker; it saves wear and tear. Performances at 8:45 P.M. Matinees Thursday and Sunday at 3:00. *See* MUSIC for a listing of concert halls.

TIME ... Six hours later than United States Eastern Standard Time.

TIPPING...Hotels add a service charge to your bill, but still you must tip the bell boy, porter, chambermaid, waiter and anyone else who does anything for you. It is customary to tip movie-theater ushers. Cab drivers are tipped 20 per cent of the meter reading. There is a washroom attendant who must be tipped. The wine waiter gets a tip in addition to your regular waiter. The concierge should be tipped, too.

TOURIST TAXES...Port taxes of $6.50 1st class, $4.50 2nd class and $3 tourist class collected at all seaports. Embarkation taxes are 400 or 500 francs for European countries, 1500 francs for elsewhere.

TRANSPORTATION...There are plenty of taxis but somehow they are not always easy to get. It is advisable always to notice whether the taxi you hire has a meter. Unmetered cabs often charge exorbitant rates. It is wise to keep your cab waiting if you are shopping. Between twelve and two drivers won't take you anywhere except in the direction they are going. They are usually going to lunch. Taxi drivers are as volatile and excitable as ever and cabs are just as aged.

After 11:00 P.M. taxi rates are doubled. Consult your driver before you go anywhere, because at night clubs and theaters fixed-rate cabs are waiting. There are stands for cars for hire near most of the hotels. These are more expensive than ordinary cabs. Travel by Metro (subway) at least once. It is unlike any subway you have known. There are buses all over Paris too. You must queue up for these, and there are pads of numbers on posts near bus stops which you take, thus giving yourself an assured place in the line. Metro and bus operating hours, which vary, are posted on each station.

WATER...It's safe to drink. There are plenty of bottled waters, Perrier, Evian and Vittel, that are good and cheap.

WHAT TO BUY...Clothes, of course, from one of the great designers, if you can afford them. If you want the very latest, don't buy dresses anywhere but at top shops or couturiers. Fashions have a two-year patent in Paris. Shoes are not a good buy; they are apt not to be right for American feet. Paris hats are like no other hats anywhere. Lingerie, blouses, gloves, laces, china, Lalique glass, Daum crystal, cognac and champagne are all cheaper than at home. Made-to-order girdles are wonderful. Perfumes are amazingly inexpensive, for there is no middleman. Prices are standard in all stores. The handbags and umbrellas are excellent. Costume jewelry is low priced, too. Furs are better at home. Hermès' engagement and address book is a standard French gift for a man. For men there are also hand-rolled handkerchiefs, lisle socks, ties, wallets and fishing reels.

WHAT TO WEAR...Your newest, smartest clothes. The sort of thing you would wear in any large city at home. Don't wear white shoes on the street. You'll need a raincoat, a suit, walking shoes, evening clothes if you plan any gala night life. Men should dress as in any city. Dinner jacket is a necessity for a man. If you go to the Riviera, take your newest sports clothes, evening clothes and a fur jacket, beach clothes. Men need slacks, sport shirts, bathing trunks and robes. For skiing what you would wear at a good resort at home, or buy your ski things abroad.

WHERE TO GO—SIGHTSEEING ...

Paris ... There are various ways to see Paris. You can do it on your own and discover things or you can go on a guided tour which will probably save you time but won't give you the same feeling of working things out for yourself. You can hire a cab or walk and explore to your heart's content. Walk down the Champs Elysées from the Arc de Triomphe and you pass some famous restaurants and hotels. Midway is the Rond Point and from there to the Place de la Concorde you may walk down a tree-lined avenue to Avenue Gabriel, where you find public buildings, including the Presidential Palace and the American Embassy. At the Place de la Concorde you'll encounter the Crillon and the Marine Ministry. About two blocks away is the Church of the Madeleine which is a must, as are Notre Dame on the Ile de La Cité and the Sainte Chapelle located inside the Palais de Justice, and which has the most beautiful stained-glass window arrangement in Europe. There are lectures and tours through the Great Cathedral that are most interesting. See also the Tuileries Gardens along the Rue de Rivoli; you can't miss the Eiffel Tower or the Opéra.

Go to the Left Bank and take a look at the Boul' Mich, or, Boulevard St. Michel. The Sorbonne is nearby and the Pantheon. The Luxembourg Gardens and Palace are here, too. Of course, climb the hill to Montmartre, with its twisting streets and many restaurants and cafés. Sacré Coeur stands on top of the hill and you get a magnificent view of the city below. Back in the heart of Paris you will, of course, see the Place Vendôme, the Rue de la Paix. Take a stroll down the chain of Grands Boulevards: Boulevard de la Madeleine, Boulevard des Capucines, Boulevard des Italiens, Boulevard Poissonnière, Boulevard St. Denis, Boulevard St. Martin, which form a wide continuous avenue of shops and theaters.

Drive out through the Bois de Boulogne, with its lakes and fine restaurants and bridle paths. It's charming.

Browse at the open book stalls along the Seine. Take a trip on the Seine River, on the colorful "Bateau Mouche," and see all the familiar monuments from a different angle. Boat trips are 1 to 2 hours long, and some include lunch or dinner. Visit "Les Halles," Paris' central market at the end of a long night out, and have onion soup. Pay a visit to the Hôtel des Invalides and Napoleon's tomb. In fact, do anything that interests you. It is all fascinating.

Versailles—Fontainebleau ... There are many short trips out of Paris to the environs which are practically musts. Versailles is 12 miles away. Here are the gardens, the Palace of Louis XIV, the Grand Trianon and the Petit Trianon. You can see La Malmaison on this trip, too, the home of Napoleon and Josephine. Fontainebleau, with its Renaissance palace, its formal gardens, is fascinating. You can visit this on a standard tour or drive it in a cab. Fontainebleau, once a twelfth-century fortress, was reconstructed in the sixteenth century

Paris' famous Arc de Triomphe de l'Etoile is the final resting place of France's "Unknown Warrior."

The harbor and beach at Cannes is one of the most famous of the many delightful resorts on the French Riviera.

and eventually became the favorite residence of Napoleon. Drive through the 42,000-acre forest. During the summer in the gardens of Versailles and Fontainebleau there are fountain displays, Night Festivals with ancient dances, fireworks, etc. These nocturnal performances are a must, and tickets can easily be purchased in most of the travel agencies.

Go to St. Germain-en-Laye, just a short trip from Paris, to see the Royal Palace with its mile and a half long terrace. A trip to Chantilly-Compiègne is interesting. The latter is the spot of the German surrender in 1918 and the French surrender in 1940. There is a

Visitors to Montmartre, overlooking Paris, shouldn't miss the picturesque street cafes or white-domed Sacré Coeur seen here in the background.

Naturally, you can't miss visiting Paris' famous Notre Dame or browsing among the interesting bookstalls nearby.

large palace in the park with a collection of Gobelin tapestries.

At Chantilly there is a huge château set in a formal park. Chartres is about a day's trip from the city. Visit the Cathedral of Chartres, noted for its stained-glass windows.

The Château Country . . . No visit to France is really complete without a trip through the Château country, the center of which is Tours. The *Hotel Univers* or the *Métropole* are both good here. Make this city your headquarters and then take any of the standard trips to Blois, Amboise, Chaumont, Chenonceaux, Chambord, Loches, Luynes, Langeais, Villandry, Azay-le-Rideau, Chinon. During summer months Sound and Light Spectacles are given every night in most of these châteaux similar to those in Versailles. Night trips can be arranged from Paris or from Tours. Some of the châteaux are furnished in magnificent style; some are in ruins; others are visited for their architectural interest. Azay-le-Rideau contains a kitchen which is a rarity. It has, too, a Fontainebleau tapestry ordered by Charles I for the city of Rome. Villandry is famous for its Spanish Museum, its beautiful gardens. Chenonceaux is one of the most famous and is the castle given to Diane de Poitiers by Henry II. The gardens were ruined in 1944 by bombings but the château was unharmed.

Blois contains an ornate staircase in its inner court. Here, too, is the death chamber of Catherine de Médicis and her private chapel. Amboise is furnished with period pieces, Aubusson tapestries; there is an interesting collection of fifteenth- and sixteenth-century armors in the guardroom. Chambord is an enormous place with 365 rooms. There are innumerable turrets and spires, a wall surrounding the gardens and an estate which is the largest in France.

Visit Vouvray while in Tours. Here is where some of the finest wines in the world are made. Visit the vineyards with their acres and acres of grapes. While in Tours take a run down the Cognac country, if you are a brandy fancier. Here is the world-famous center for the Cognac which takes its name from the city and the region. A little farther on is Bordeaux, which is as famous for its wines as Cognac is for its brandy.

Pyrénées—Basque Region . . . In Southeast France the Pyrénées stretch from the Atlantic to the Mediterranean in a natural boundary line between France and Spain. On the coast of the Bay of Biscay is *Biarritz,* a famous beach resort made fashionable by the Empress Eugénie. There are luxurious hotels, a casino, excellent restaurants and a wonderful beach nearby. Not quite so fashionable but smart in its way is *St.-Jean-de-Luz* which is less expensive. *Biarritz* is expensive, about $25 per day American Plan, if it's the de luxe you want. There are also moderately priced accommodations. *Pelota* is a favorite local sport; or you can see a bullfight at Bayonne, nearby.

If you are heading eastward to the Mediterranean, you will go to *Lourdes,* home of the famous vision of Bernadette. There are many hotels and pensions here. The grotto is a national shrine and the Cathedral is composed of three churches, built one above the other with hundreds of memorial chapels donated by pilgrims to the shrine.

The tiny principality of Monaco lies near the French-Italian border on the Mediterranean Sea. Monte Carlo, the famous gambling resort here, is a short drive from Nice.

France — Chamonix with Mt. Blanc (15,781 feet), the highest mountain in Europe, in the background is a famous winter and summer resort easily accessible from Nice.

The baths are nearby where each year thousands of afflicted come to bathe in the holy waters. It is estimated that more than a million people make the pilgrimage to Lourdes each year. *Luchon* in the Pyrénées looks into Spain. It has excellent ski runs and thermal baths. There are dozens of hotels, best of which are the *Pyrénées Palace* and the *Sacaron*. Skiing is excellent on Superbagnères, a 6,000-foot peak with a wonderful hotel at its summit.

Pau is an interesting city with a fine bridge, public squares, a famous castle in which Henry IV was born, and a renowned boulevard with a gorgeous view facing the Pyrénées. It is a starting point for tours of the Pyrénées.

Nimes and *Arles*, old cities where Roman ruins may be seen, are on the route to *Marseilles* and the Riviera from the Pyrénées or *Carcassonne*.

The French Alps ... The French Alps extend south from Lake Geneva to the Riviera. Some of the best skiing in Europe is found here and some of the most breath-taking scenery. Mt. Blanc towers over the towns of Mégève and Chamonix. From here you may visit the Mer de Glace glacier, take the highest cable car in the world (12,605 feet) or go to Le Brevent with its astonishing view of the whole place. Grenoble is both a ski resort and glove center. Some of the most famous gloves are made there, and some of the best skis, those designed by Emile Allais. The French Alps contain nearly

30,000 guest houses and hotels from the ultra to the very simple.

Famous watering place is Aix-les-Bains in a valley in the heart of the French Alps. The spas here are famous. The *Splendide* is the top hotel. And here is the famous revolving solarium. Annecy, a little to the north, is equally pleasant.

The Riviera . . . Here is France's playground, the famous Côte d'Azur. The French Riviera stretches from Toulon to the Italian border and is dotted with famous spots: Nice, Cannes, Menton, Beaulieu, Cap d'Antibes, Eden Roc, Juan-les-Pins, St.-Tropez, and of course, Monte Carlo in the principality of Monaco.

Nice is the largest of the Riviera resorts. It has the Promenade des Anglais, a famous pre-Lenten Carnival, some fine hotels: the *Negresco,* the *Angleterre,* the *Royal,* the *Ruhl,* the *Plaza,* the *Splendid,* the *West End* and *Beau-Rivage.* Not so large, but smarter and more frequented by the International Set is Cannes, where Prince Ali Khan has a fantastic villa formerly occupied by Maxine Elliott. There are wonderful hotels, luxurious branches of Paris shops, wonderful beaches and two casinos. The beach boulevard La Croisette has the *Carlton,* the *Martinez* (the largest hotel on the Riviera), the *Majestic* and others. There are at least 35 hotels in the town. Between Cannes and Nice is Cap d'Antibes, which has the famous *Hotel du Cap;* the *Eden Roc,* with its famous pool and restaurant, and *Le Grand Hotel du Cap Estel,* a beautiful romantic spot with its own beach and lovely garden which is located on the low Corniche, one mile after Eze-sur-Mer. Also at Juan-les-Pins, the de luxe *Hotel Provençal,* built by Frank J. Gould.

There are, however, less swank and equally beautiful resorts along the Riviera. St.-Tropez, St. Raphael, Juan-les-Pins, all with wonderful beaches, many with fine hotels and small pensions. Or try some of the smaller fishing villages such as Villefranche, Cap Ferrat and Cap d'Ail. Many hotels reduce rates as much as 20 per cent in winter.

From Nice three roads lead to Monte Carlo and the Italian frontier. They are the Basse (low) Corniche, Moyenne (middle) Corniche, and Grande (high) Corniche. Each one runs on its different level out into the hills. From each you get that famous view of the Riviera.

At Monte Carlo there is the Casino, the most famous in the world. This is an enormous ornate building, marbled and mirrored with crystal chandeliers everywhere you turn. There are several hotels at Monte Carlo, most famous of which is the *Hotel de Paris.* There are the *Métropole,* the *Hermitage,* the *Mirabeau,* the *Monte-Carlo Beach,* any of which is first rate. Along the entire Riviera there is wonderful golf, fishing, swimming and boating. It is a yachtsman's paradise, but it is fun for small boatsmen, too; there are water skiing and underwater fishing. In the winter there is skiing about 25 miles inland from the beaches. There are fine restaurants along the Riviera. *La Bonne Auberge, La Réserve de Beaulieu* and *Château de Madrid* (on Middle Corniche) are the best restaurants on the coast. *Da Bouttau* in the old town of Nice (with a branch in Cannes) is an amusing restaurant for local and regional dishes. The *Réserve Montana* in La Napoule is really superb and relatively inexpensive, as is the *Château de la Chèvre d'Or* (with a splendid view) in Eze Village.

The Riviera is both a summer and winter resort these days. But the winter weather is not as warm as Florida. More like Southern California. You can take a delightful 7-day drive from Paris to Cannes by way of Avalon, St.-Seine-l'Abbaye, Vienne (home of the famous *La Pyramide* restaurant), Valence, Vaison-la-Romaine, Les Baux, Marseilles and along the coast to Cannes. There are marvelous restaurants, charming hotels along the way.

Normandy and Brittany . . . In Normandy you will want to visit the invasion beaches of Omaha, Arromanches and Utah. Rouen is the departure point for tours of both provinces. The city was heavily damaged by bombings but is still the museum city, the place where Joan of Arc was burned at the stake. Many towns in Normandy are still in ruins but rehabilitation is going on. Deauville, one of the most popular beach resorts in France, is back to normal and the season has been highly successful there. The *Normandy, Royal* and *Hotel du Golf* have been refurnished. There is a casino, horse racing, yachting, golf and polo. Paris shops have branches there.

Take a trip to Mont St. Michel at the junction of Normandy and Brittany, which is built on a small island with a single street that climbs to the abbey founded in the eighth century. It was a prison in Napoleon's time. The cobbled street is lined with shops and restaurants, most of which feature huge fluffy omelets made on an open fire before your eyes. Very good, too. In Brittany you'll find the women still wearing the white, starched coifs. You'll see the enclosed beds. Quimper is the tourist center. Market days, Wednesday and Saturday, are most picturesque. The square in front of the Cathedral is crowded with colored tents in which all sorts of things are sold. Dinard in northern Brittany is the largest seaside resort.

St.-Malo, across the harbor from Dinard, is a walled city full of charm. It is also a battlefield site now. There are many little fishing villages along the Britanny coast where traditions are preserved. The *Pardons,* religious pilgrimages, run from May to October.

There are tours of Normandy and Brittany from Paris.

SOURCES OF FURTHER INFORMATION . . . In Paris, contact the Direction Générale du Tourisme, 8, avenue de l'Opéra. Also, the Official Transportation and Tourist Information Office, 127, Champs Elysées. In other French cities, see the local Syndicat d'Initiative office. In New York the French Government Tourist Office is at 610 Fifth Avenue, with branches in other cities.

"Semaine de Paris," a weekly Paris entertainment guide in French and English. Price: 50 francs. The Guide Michelin is a must if you're touring France by car or are a serious gastronome.

Pan Am's offices in Paris are at 1, rue Scribe (Tel. BALzac 82.00 —Administrative office) and 138 Champs Elysées (Tel. BALzac 92.00 for reservations). In Nice, Hotel Negresco, (Tel. 839–52). In Bordeaux, 31 bis Cours Maréchal Foch (Tel. 48.31.93).

GERMANY

WEATHER IN FRANKFURT—Lat. N50°10'—Alt. 300'

Temp.	JAN.	FEB.	MAR.	APR.	MAY	JUNE	JULY	AUG.	SEPT.	OCT.	NOV.	DEC.
Low	26°	28°	31°	37°	46°	52°	55°	54°	49°	41°	34°	29°
High	35°	38°	45°	54°	65°	72°	74°	72°	66°	55°	44°	37°
Average	31°	33°	38°	46°	56°	62°	65°	63°	58°	48°	39°	33°
Days of Rain	15	15	15	13	13	13	15	14	13	14	14	15

LOCATION ... Germany is in the very heart of Europe, located between the Baltic Sea and the North Sea to the north and the Alps to the south. Frankfurt is about 400 air miles from London, less than 300 miles from Paris, and about 3,900 air miles from New York. The distance between Berlin, largest German city, and London is 700 air miles.

CHARACTERISTICS ... Nothing has changed the basic beauty of Germany: glorious scenery, art treasures, entertainment such as stage plays, music, gay folk festivals, and quaint ancient customs. In many ways, Germany is at present a most interesting part of Europe: the progress the country has made since 1945 in reconstruction is phenomenal. The German people have a true desire to make the tourist happy and comfortable.

POPULATION ... West Germany has a population of some 50,000,000, roughly one-third that of the United States, while in the entire country there are approximately 70,000,000 people.

SIZE ... The area of West Germany is about 94,254 square miles, about the size of New York and Pennsylvania combined. The entire country occupies about 182,000 square miles, an area not quite four times that of New York State.

CAPITAL ... Bonn, a city of 120,000, on the Rhine is the present capital of the Federal Republic of Germany—*Bundesrepublik Deutschland,* as West Germany is officially called. The former German capital, Berlin, largest city in the country, has a population of 3,300,000. Hamburg has a population of 1,800,000.

GOVERNMENT ... West Germany is a Federal Republic with a legislative body of two houses.

HOW TO GET THERE ... By Pan American Clipper, New York to Munich 13¼ hours; to Duesseldorf, 10½ hours; Hamburg, 16 hours; Stuttgart, 12 hours; Frankfurt, 12 hours. From Chicago via Detroit to Frankfurt, 18½ hours. Frequent local service via Pan American between Frankfurt and Berlin, Stuttgart, Hanover, Cologne, Duesseldorf, Munich and Vienna. By ship, about 9 days from New York to Hamburg or Bremen.

ACCOMMODATIONS ... In general throughout the country beds in hotels or inns, including mountain hotels, range in price from about $1 in plain houses to $6.00 in international de luxe hotels, without bath or meals. Meals are inexpensive by United States standards. For hotel listings look under individual cities below.

BANKS ... The Deutsche Bank and several others have offices in all major cities. Travelers' checks may be cashed at the banks, Thos. Cook, and American Express, at most airport terminals and at all hotels.

CALENDAR OF HOLIDAYS ... New Year's Day; Good Friday; Easter Sunday and Monday; Ascension Day; Whitsuntide, Sunday and Monday; May 1, Labor Day; June 17, Day of German Unity; Repentance Day, Wednesday before Sunday of the Dead, in November, a Protestant Holiday; December 25 and 26, Christmas. Roman Catholic holidays of Corpus Christi, All Saints Day and All Souls Day are also observed. There are also local and regional holidays.

CIGARETTES, CIGARS AND TOBACCO ... Many brands can now be purchased in tobacco stores and most hotels and restaurants.

CLIMATE ... With the exception of January, which is the coldest month, the winters are mild. There are long springs and agreeable summers; Indian summer until late October.

CLUBS ... Rotary and Lions among others.

COMMON COURTESIES AND LOCAL CUSTOMS ... Just about the same as at home.

COMMUNICATIONS ... Telegrams, cable, radiogram, telephone and airmal services to all parts of the world.

CURRENCY ... The monetary unit is the Deutsche Mark (DM), which is worth about 23.8 cents in United States currency.

CUSTOMS REGULATIONS AND DOCUMENTS REQUIRED FOR UNITED STATES CITIZENS ... Your American passport is all you need for entry into either West Germany or western sector of Berlin. Visa is no longer required. You may take in, duty free, 400 cigarettes or 75 cigars or 250 grams (8¾ oz.) of tobacco, 1 opened bottle of liquor, unlimited Deutsche Mark and other currency.

DRUG STORES ... There are two types of drug stores in Germany, neither of which have soda fountains nor serve food: the *Apotheke,* which sell only pharmaceuticals, and the *Drogerie,* which sell standard drugs, cosmetics, etc.

ELECTRIC CURRENT ... There is 220 voltage A.C. generally prevailing all over Germany. The plugs are the round, European type. But most of the leading hotels will provide an adapter on request.

FAUNA ... About the same as New York State with the exception of chipmunks, skunks, and such birds as tanagers and cardinals.

FLORA ... About the same as in New York State.

FOOD ... There are no food restrictions. Food is plentiful and of pre-war first-class quality. Frankfurters are called *Frankfurter Wuerstchen.* Some of the specialties in German foods are: dumplings and strudels in Bavaria; *Spaetzle* (a special type of noodle) in Swabia and Baden; Westphalian ham; Hamburg eel soup; New Year carp in Berlin and Northern Germany; Berlin doughnuts, Berlin potato-cakes; Helgoland lobster along the seashore; St. Martin's goose throughout Germany; Allgau district cheese; Bodensee *Felchen* (Lake Constance trout), Rhine salmon; Alpine cheese; and countless others.

GAMBLING ... There are many licensed casinos in the resort spots such as: Baden-Baden, Bad Duerkheim near Ludwigshafen in the Palatinate, Bad Homburg and Wiesbaden near Frankfurt, Garmisch-Partenkirchen just south of Munich, Bad Neuenahr not far from Bonn, Lindau and Constance on Lake Constance, Westerland on the Island of Sylt, and Travemuende near Luebeck on the Baltic Sea. There are Ecarte Clubs in Kassel and a casino in Hanover near the famous Kroepke · Café. The German Class Lottery, the football toto and numbers lottery, all under state regulation, are very popular.

LANGUAGE ... English is understood in all the tourist centers, hotels, railroad stations and better shops.

LAUNDRY AND DRY CLEANING ... Very good everywhere.

LIQUOR ... The Germans have famous wines (such as Rhine and Moselle and many others), Bavarian Beer, *Schwarzwaelder* (Black Forest) Kirsch (a great specialty), and Steinhaeger, a form of gin. You can also get all other kinds of liquor.

MEDICAL FACILITIES ... Excellent and available everywhere.

MOTION PICTURES ... The movie theaters in all larger cities in Germany show American and English films, as well as German and other foreign ones.

MUSIC ... Almost every German city has a philharmonic orchestra; 63 of them have standing opera companies with ballet. Among the most important annual events are the Wagner Festival Plays in Bayreuth in July and August, the Bavarian State Opera Festivals in Munich at about the same time, the Berlin Festival Weeks with international opera companies, chamber orchestras and ballet companies in September, the International Opera Festival in Wiesbaden during the entire month of May, the Mozart Festival in Wuerzburg, contemporary music festivals at the Kranichstein Institute in Darmstadt and at Donaueschingen, and the popular operetta performances on the floating stage in the Rhine at Koblenz, from the end of June till the middle of September. (For others, and exact dates, consult the Calendar of Events of German Tourist Information Office. See SOURCES OF FURTHER INFORMATION.)

NIGHT CLUBS AND CABARETS ... You will find many of them in all major cities. See listings under cities below.

PHOTOGRAPHY ... Black-and-white films, rolls and packs are available in all sizes; in color films AGFA and KODAK. Excellent work in developing (black-and-white) in all cities.

RELIGION ... There are churches of all denominations.

RESTAURANTS ... You'll find the restaurants excellent. Principal ones are listed under city descriptions below.

SHOPS AND STORES ... Stores are open from 9:00 A.M. to 6:30 P.M., close at 2:00 P.M. on Saturdays.

SPECTATOR SPORTS ... Almost every sport is practiced in Germany. Soccer is as popular with Germans as baseball is with Americans. In almost every city there is a big stadium, such as the *Olympia Stadion* in Berlin and the *Frankfurt Wald-* (Woodland) *Stadion.* The famous *Sports-Palace* and *Deutschland Halle* in Berlin, where ice shows, 6-day bicycle races and hockey contests take place, have been rebuilt; so has the huge *Westfalen-Halle* in Dortmund in the Ruhr District. Tennis courts, such as those at Bad Homburg, Berlin, Wiesbaden, and Frankfurt, present international stars; and the *Avus,* automobile race tracks in Berlin, as well as the *Nuerburg-Ring* in the Eifel Mountains, attract enthusiastic fans from all over. You can watch horse races, polo games, ice hockey, and even rugby.

SPORTS ... Golf, tennis, swimming, soccer, skiing, skating, rowing, fencing, sailing, boxing, sport fishing, hunting.

THEATERS ... Performances are given in all cities. In summer open-air music and drama performances are given in ancient cathedrals, monasteries and monastery ruins and medieval castles and castle ruins throughout West Germany. In West Berlin, the Municipal Opera, Schiller Theater, Schlosspark-Theater, Renaissance Theater, Theater am Kurfürstendamm, Komödie, Tribüne, Hebbel-Theater. 1960 is the year of the world-famous Passion Play of Oberammergau in the German Alps.

TIME ... Six hours later than U.S. Eastern Standard Time.

TIPPING ... There is usually 10 per cent added to restaurant bills and 15 per cent to hotel room bills. However, a small extra tip is usually given when you pay your bill either to a bartender or waiter. If tip is not included on bills, tip about the same as at home.

TOURIST TAXES ... Moderate and only in resort places.

TRANSPORTATION ... Modern trains, buses, taxis, and streetcars. Excellent through trains between all parts of Germany and the most important cities on the Continent. Excursion trains in scenic areas have glass domes and some have dancing and movie cars. Plane service to large cities is very good, too. Car rental service, with or without driver, is available through Metro and other Rent-a-Car systems at reasonable prices. Brochures can be obtained from any Pan Am office.

WATER . . . Excellent to drink. Sparkling and other table waters are available everywhere.

WHAT TO BUY . . . Some of the best things to buy are leather goods of all kinds, photographic articles (German cameras are among the best), optical goods, china, ceramics, jewelry, woodcarvings, cuckoo clocks, toys and watches.

WHAT TO WEAR . . . The same kind of clothes you would wear in New York City during the different seasons. No sports clothes in the theater.

WHERE TO GO—SIGHTSEEING . . .

Frankfurt . . . Frankfurt-on-Main, the first large city one encounters after landing at Rhein-Main airport, is the city where Goethe, creator of *Faust*, was born. The Goethe House and Goethe Museum are of sightseeing interest here. Coronation banquets of the emperors of the medieval German Empire were held in magnificent Roemer Hall in Frankfurt for centuries. Frankfurt is also a West German center of commerce and finance, and international fairs.

Among the leading hotels in Frankfurt: *Frankfurter Hof, Hessischer Hof* (de luxe), *Savigny Hotel.* First-class hotels are: *Savoy, Inselhotel, National, Monopol-Metropole, Basler Hof, Park, Carlton.* Good tourist-class hotels are: *Sued Hotel, Hotel Wiesbaden.* Rates are about $2 to $4 single and up, European Plan.

Worth visiting in Frankfurt are the many museums, which house magnificent art collections. Among them are: the Goethe Museum, Grosser Hirschgraben 42; the Staedel Institute of Art, Schaumainkai; City Gallery, Duererstrasse; the Frankfurt Society of Art, Eschenheimer Anlage 35; Frankfurt Cabinet of Art, Boersenstrasse; Zimmer Gallery Frank, Boehmerstrasse 7; Gallery Buchheim-Militon; Museum Senckenberg. There's great ballet at the Staedtische Opera, ballet groups also in the Circus Althoff-Bau in the Zoo.

Some of the best night clubs and cabarets in Frankfurt are *Astoria-Bar, Huettenbar, Pilotenbar, Parisianabar, Rheinland Pavillon, Koenigin-Bar, BB-Bar, Regina-Bar, the Ellis Elliott Bar, Tabu, Lippizaner Bar* (Hotel Frankfurt Hof), *Jimmy's Bar* (Hessischer Hof Hotel), *Tropicana.* Bavarian atmosphere in the large beerhall Maier Gustl's Oberbayern.

Principal restaurants are *Grillroom Frankfurter Hof, Restaurant zur Alten Post, Restaurant zum Kaiserkeller, Arnold Grill, Paulaner Keller* (City Betriebe) *Ratskeller, Pfaelzer Weinstube, Salzhaus, Brueckenkeller, Grillroom Park Hotel, Savarin, Heyland's Weinstube* and *Hamburger Hof.*

Shops and stores are open from 9:00 A.M. to 6:30 P.M. (Saturdays 9:00 to 2:00 except first Saturday each month). Best shopping area: Kaiserstrasse, Zeil, Hauptwache, Goethestrasse, Schillerstrasse.

Theaters include *Staedtische Buehnen, Kleines Theater im Zoo, Theater am Rossmarkt, Die Schmiere.*

Other cities in this area, each with its own features of interest, include Kassel, with its health resort, and Wilhelmshoehe.

Berlin . . . From Frankfurt, Berlin is 1⅔ hours by Clipper. The

Castle Neuschwanstein was built of marble (1869–86) by King Ludwig II of Bavaria, friend of Richard Wagner. It overlooks beautiful Alpsee.

This walled city, Rothenburg ob-der-Tauber, one of Germany's many medieval picture towns is annually the stage for a famous historical play.

airplane is the speediest and most comfortable means for foreigners to reach the former capital. A visit to the "Island City" is a worthwhile experience. Berlin has managed by almost superhuman effort to become an important industrial and cultural metropolis again. A variety of stage offerings, the Berlin Philharmonic Orchestra, and life along Kurfüerstendamm, the Berlin equivalent of Broadway, help make the city gay and interesting. Among the night clubs are *Remde's, St. Pauli, Cherchez la Femme, Old Fashioned Bar, Ciro Bar, Petit Palais, Bojar,* and the *Resi* with the famous water plays. In the Dahlem Museum are many of the paintings and sculptures of the former state museums. There are also many small galleries and exhibitions. Other places of interest: Charlottenburg Castle exhibitions; the new American Memorial Library; the Waldbuehne, a huge sylvan theater; the new Congress Hall, a present from the U.S.A.; and the new Hansa Quarter. The Berlin International Festival Weeks, usually in September, the Berlin International Film Festival, usually in June, a German Industries Exposition in the fall, the "Green Week," an agricultural show with equestrian, social and art events, and a number of important international sports events attract huge crowds from other countries. There are a number of luxury and good first- and second-class hotels, the best being: the brand-new *Berlin Hilton,* the *Bristol Hotel, Kempinski, Hotel am Zoo, Hotel Windsor, Hotel-am-Steinplatz, Savoy-Hotel* and *Hotel Berlin.* Restaurants with excellent cuisine are *Ritz, Aben, Schlichter, Rollenhagen, Mampe, Kurfürstenkeller, Kopenhagen, F. W. Borchardt* in Congress Hall, and *Wannsee-Terrassen.*

Mainz (Mayence) and **Wiesbaden** are only a few miles southwest of Frankfurt. 2,000-year-old "Golden Mainz," where Johann Gutenberg invented movable type and thereby became the father of modern printing, is a university town, also the center of German wine trade. This is where most Rhine River boat trips start and end. Wiesbaden, capital of Hesse, and a famous health resort, contains many art treasures. The *Hotel Nassauer Hof* and *Schwarzer Bock* here are excellent. Fifty miles south of Frankfurt are *Heidelberg,* alma mater of many Americans, city of the *Student Prince,* and the famous Heidelberg Castle, and *Mannheim,* Europe's second largest inland harbor, which has been restored in an astonishingly brief span of time. Not quite 40 miles farther south is *Karlsruhe,* on the Rhine. Its museum and collections are worth seeing. Karlsruhe is frequently used as the starting point for excursions into the Black Forest. Bruchsal Palace is nearby. Some 40 miles east is *Stuttgart,* capital of Baden-Wuerttemberg and of Swabia, charming metropolis among woods and vineyards, and West Germany's largest publishing center. Southeast less than 60 miles is *Ulm-on-Danube,* with its famous church spire rising 528 feet. The church took 500 years to build and contains art treasures accumulated during those five centuries. *Augsburg* is slightly over 50 miles in the same direction—city of the Fuggers and Welsers, merchant princes whose origin dates from the Middle Ages. (The Welser family once owned Venezuela.) The Fuggers established the world's first social settlement, the Fuggerei, a town within the city, in 1519 and restored it after the war. Augsburg is an important stopover on the "Romantic Road" which leads from Wuerzburg south via the medieval picture towns of Rothenburg-ob-der-Tauber, Dinkelsbuehl, Noerdlingen, and others, to Fuessen in the Bavarian Allgäu Alps. Augsburg is also Einstein's birthplace.

Munich, another 40 miles to the south, is a city of museums and art galleries, including the famous *Alte Pinakothek* and *Haus der Kunst,* of breweries and the Munich October Festival (last week of Sept. and first week of Oct.). Festival at the Bavarian State Opera in July and August, traditional international costume parade first Sunday of the October Festival. Among many theaters are the famous Cuvilliés-theater, rebuilt in 1958, the Kammerspiele, the Residenz-theater, the Kleine Komödie, and for operettas, the Gärtnerplatz Theater. The "Deutsches Museum" is the largest technology museum in Europe. Munich is also famous for its huge "Englischer Garten," which offers a very agreeable spot for a walk, and the Tierpark Hellabrunn, largest zoo in Germany.

A visit to Schwabing, the Montmartre of Munich, is very interesting. Here you find dozens of little restaurants and bars where students meet. *Bayerischer Hof, Vier Jahreszeiten* and *Königshof* are first class hotels. Night spots: *Bayerischer Hof Bar, Bei Heinz, Intermezzo, Lola Montez, Platzl* and *Hofbräuhaus, P 1, Gisela, Der Käfig* and *Studio 15* in München-Schwabing. Munich is the gateway to the Bavarian and Austrian Alps, with many scenic tours via the Lake District (Lake Starnberg, Tegernsee, Achensee and Walchensee).

One hundred and twenty-five miles to the north is *Nuremberg,* again an important toy center. It's also the town of Hans Sachs and the *Meistersinger,* of Peter Vischer and Veit Stoss, of the world's first pocket watch (the "Nuremberg egg"). A little over 60 miles to the northwest is *Wuerzburg,* where the annual Mozart Festival is held in the Residence Palace.

Hamburg . . . This important seaport and largest city in West

Germany dates from the time of Charlemagne. With its city built around the picturesque Alster basin, the town is located on the Elbe River. It is the center of much industry and is still the commercial artery of a wide hinterland. Besides its attraction as a great industrial and shipping center of tremendous reconstruction and development, the city offers theaters (the principal ones of which are *Deutsches Schauspielhaus; Kleine Komoedie; Rendezvous; Opernhaus; Thalia-Theater, Alstertor*), for concerts, drama, opera and operettas; important art collections, libraries, a planetarium and observatory, sports and all kinds of entertainment including the famed amusement center of St. Pauli. Among points of sightseeing interest are the Hagenbeck Animal Park, City Hall, Chile House and other characteristic business houses, the "fleete" (canals lined with quaint old buildings), fine churches, parks and gardens.

Hamburg's top art gallery is the Kunsthalle, Glockengiesserwall 1. A magnificent collection of North German folklore is housed in the Altona Museum, Museumstr. 21. Leading banks are Dresdner Bank, Jungfernstieg 22; Deutsche Bank, Jungfernstieg 22. Among the leading hotels in Hamburg: *Atlantic Hotel, Vier Jahreszeiten* (de luxe), *Hotel Reichshof*. First-class hotels are: *Alsterhof, Hotel "Berlin."* Good tourist-class hotels are: *Hotel Europaeischer Hof, Hotel Baseler Hospiz*. Rates are about $3 to $5 single, European plan. Among Hamburg night clubs are the popular Montmartre-like *Reeperbahn* in the St. Pauli district, and in the city itself are *Delhi-Palace, Tarantella, Die Insel*. Leading restaurants are *Vierjahreszeiten-Grill*, Schuemann's *Austernkeller, Fischereihafen-Restaurant* for seafood.

A 40-minute drive north leads to Luebeck, famous for its many medieval monuments. It is the birthplace of Thomas Mann. Here one may eat the delicious Luebeck marzipan pastry.

Northern Germany boasts of many spas and shore resorts ideal for pleasure as well as health and recreation. Among the spas on the Baltic shore is elegant Travemuende. In the North Sea are the Isle of Sylt linked to the mainland by dam and the unique rock-island of Heligoland, reachable by de-luxe boats from Hamburg or Cuxhaven.

Popular health resorts in the Harz mountains about 150 miles south of Hamburg are Harzburg, Braunlage and Hahnenklee. Nearby cities include Braunschweig (Brunswick), town of Henry the Lion, and Hanover, one of the important fair and exposition centers.

The third Hanseatic city, in addition to Hamburg and Luebeck, is *Bremen*, about 80 miles west of Hamburg, with its 11th century St. Petri dome, 15th century town-hall, market square and Roland statue, which combines medieval charm with outstanding examples of German reconstruction. You will enjoy visiting the old craftsmen's street "Boettcherstrasse," a variety of interesting museums, the harbor, colorful Rhododendron park and the Ratskeller, where Hauff wrote his tales and where you will find a variety of excellent wines.

Duesseldorf ... In this region you won't want to miss *Duesseldorf*, gay metropolis of art and fashion on the Rhine, a great business center known as the "Desk of the Ruhr." A walk through town will show the interesting contrast between old and new architecture, most striking. The Altstadt (Old City) harbors buildings and churches dating back to the 13th century, when West-German princes made Duesseldorf their residence. The city's main boulevard, Koenigsallee, is known continent-wide as a fashionable shopping center. Sidewalk cafés dot the pavement—their patisseries are magnificent. Fairs, exhibitions, museums, libraries, art collections, theater, opera and concerts attract visitors the year round. During Carnival, masquerades and the Rose Monday Pageant make the city one big playground. On St. Martin's Eve, tradition calls for thousands of children to parade through the streets carrying torches and lanterns. Duesseldorf has a number of luxury and first-class hotels, best of which are the *Breidenbacher* and *Parkhotel* (de luxe), and the *Atlantik, Esplanade, Eden, Fuerstenhof, Haus Münch, Savoy* (first-class). Night spots include: *Palette, Etoile, Carlton, Ciro, Kolibri, Melodie, Palladium, Tabaris* and the bohemian *Tabu* and *Fatty's Atelier.*

Cologne ... A short stretch up the Rhine River, southward, is Cologne, whose cathedral is one of the finest examples of Gothic architecture. Cologne dates back to long before the Roman era. You will see here remains of Roman fortifications, temples, invaluable mosiacs, and sculptures. International luxurious, first-class and good tourist-class hotels, include the *Excelsior Hotel Ernst, Dom-Hotel, Hotel Koelner Hof, Hotel Fuerstenhof am Dom, Touring-Hotel Bristol, Hotel Cologne.* (Bars: *Atelier, Capri, Charlott, Tabu.*) Another city more than 2,000 years old is *Aachen* (*Aix-la-Chapelle*), less than 30 miles west of Cologne. The city's hot springs have been used for curative purposes since before the Romans came. Charlemagne's throne of stone stands in the chapel he built here. The holy relics, including Christ's swaddling clothes, the gown the Holy Virgin wore the night Christ was born, and the crucified Savior's loin cloth are shown to the faithful every seven years in St. Mary's shrine. South of Aachen is *Trier* (*Treves*), once the capital of the west Roman empire, with magnificent remnants of Roman architecture: the imperial baths, an entire temple field, the mighty Porta Nigra (black gate), and the Roman circus.

The Rhine ... For a century and a half, a trip along the Rhine has been an essential part of the Continental "Grand Tour." The ancient cathedrals of Cologne, Mainz, Worms (city of the Nibelungs), Speyer, Xanten (the Siegfried city) and many others glide majestically by, their spires mirrored in the water. You see picturesque little wine towns nestled at the feet of vine-clad hills, and romantic medieval castles set off by terraced vineyards or steep crags.

Stuttgart ... beautifully situated about 120 miles south of Frankfurt, is an important city for exports. Among many museums are the Schiller Museum at Marbach and the Automotive Museum of Daimler-Benz. *Graf Zeppelin Hotel, Reichsbahn Hotel,* and *Park Hotel* are all good hotels here.

The Black Forest ... only 40 miles west of Stuttgart, is a charming, sunny cluster of secondary and high mountain ranges, named "black" because of the dark firs in the dense woods. Excellent roads traverse the entire region. The thatched-roof peasant architecture is found here, as are the colorful native costumes, particularly the women's headgear, differing in each valley. Baden-Baden is the doorway to the Black Forest and Lake Constance. The Black Forest is rich in curative thermal and mineral springs. In addition to the cure service, there is plenty of activity. You may gamble at the casino, play tennis and go trout fishing and horseback riding, and play golf on a lovely 18-hole course. During "Baden-Baden Week" at the end of August, international society assembles at Iffezheim Race Course to watch the most famous stables compete for the Grand Prize. Among the well-known hotels are *Brenner's Parkhotel, Badhotel Badischer Hof, Europaeischer Hof, Hotel Runkewitz,* and *Badhotel zum Hirsch.* The doorway to the southern Black Forest (Hochschwarzwald), is Frieburg (im Breisgau), where the magnificent "Muenster" stands. Before leaving the Black Forest, a stop might be made at Badenweiler, a charming spot where spring comes early, whose healing waters were used by the ancient Romans. Many Black Forest resorts are also fine for winter sports.

Hohenlohe and *Schwaebisch-Hall,* just an hour's drive from Stuttgart, are unchanged since the early Middle Ages. Castles and palaces in the Hohenlohe area are plentiful, and the ancient Free Imperial City of Schwaebisch-Hall (Swabian Hall) was already famous in the twelfth and thirteenth centuries. On the wide stairs of the city's cathedral a series of open-air festival plays is given every summer.

The German Alps . . . Another stretch of great scenery in Germany is this high mountain chain extending from Lake Constance in the west to the southeasternmost border of the country, some 150 miles. The quaint peasant architecture of the mountaineers, their picturesque garb and simple hospitality are enchanting. Throughout the area there are many mountain huts, hotels and shelters. While most of them are of the plain type the Alpinist would expect, there are also hotels which cater to more exacting tastes. The climb has been taken out of mountain climbing in Germany for those who do not wish to exert themselves. The almost 10,000-foot Zugspitze near Garmisch-Partenkirchen (*Golfhotel Sonnenbichl* and *Hotel Alpenhof*) and Mittenwald, the 8,904-foot Watzmann, the Nebelhorn near Oberstdorf, and all the other mountains are comfortably reached by mountain railroads, cogwheel railway and chair lift. In the German Alpine country there are many health and recreation resorts, including thermal spas. Of the gems in mountain settings, the Koenigssee National Park is considered the most beautiful. It is surrounded by natural rock walls 6,500 feet high. Of the many castles and palaces in Bavaria, best known abroad are the palaces built by King Ludwig II, the great friend and patron of Richard Wagner; Herrenchiemsee, Linderhof, and Neuschwanstein. The wealth of art treasures which these palaces and cathedrals such as Steingaden, Wieskirche, Rottenbuch, Oberammergau, and Ettal contain is astounding.

Eastern Bavaria . . . Two more recently discovered German tourist attractions are the Bavarian Forest (*Bayrischer Wald*) and Upper Palatinate Forest (*Oberpfaelzer Wald*), large wooded ranges interspersed with mountains, stretching along the southeastern border of the country. Passau, Regensburg, Weiden and Bayreuth lead to these areas. While the main characteristic of the Bavarian Forest is the vastness and magnificence of its woods, the Upper Palatinate Forest has a large number of medieval castles. Both areas have winter and summer sports facilities and climatic health resorts. Open-air plays are also performed in the region. There are, besides the cities mentioned, characteristic old Bavarian towns: Straubing, Amberg, Weiden. Abbeys and monasteries in the most beautiful Bavarian baroque and rococo are found on either side of the Danube. Romantic medieval castles stand in the valleys of the Oberpfalz, all easily reached by car.

Weser Hills Country . . . This is a most charming region in northern West Germany where all the characters in the Grimm Brothers' fairy tales and the Baron Muenchhausen tales are at home. Sleeping Beauty's castle, Sababurg, still stands in the woods. Baron Muenchhausen's hunting lodge is now a pilgrimage place for romantic souls. The tombstone of the much maligned Doctor Eisenbart is in Hannoversch Muenden, where the doctor's memory now is honored every year at a colorful folk festival. Many picturesque little towns line the Weser River banks, among them famous Corvey Abbey, founded A.D. 822, and Fuerstenberg, known for its porcelain. There are several health resorts, such as Pyrmont Springs, Oeynhausen and Wildungen.

Westphalia . . . Close to the Ruhr District lies the Westphalian Land characterized by brooks for trout fishing, climatic health resorts, winter sports centers, stalactite caves, castle ruins, and picturesque mountain towns. In the south are the Sauer, Sieg and Wittgenstein districts.

Fichtel Mountains and Luisenburg . . . Luisenburg Castle, immortalized by Goethe, is the stage every summer for the Luisenburg Festival Plays. In winter, guests come from all over for winter sports.

Many other places in various parts of West Germany worth visiting include: Kleve, Lohengrin's town; Nuerburgring; the Hunsrueck hills south of Trier; the various ranges of hills close to the right bank of the Rhine; Bergisches and Sauerland, Westerwald, Taunus and Vogelsberg, Odenwald, Swabian Forest and south German mountains.

SOURCES OF FURTHER INFORMATION . . . German Central Tourist Association in Frankfurt, New York (500 Fifth Avenue), Chicago and San Francisco. Also, consult the local tourist office, *Verkehrsverein*. For health resorts, see the *Kurverwaltung*. Pan American's office in Frankfurt is at Am Hauptbahnhof 12 (Tel. 333291); in Berlin Kurfürstendamm 227 (Tel. 66–5441); in Bonn, Wesselstrasse 16 (Tel. 52655); in Hamburg, Colonnaden 1 (Tel. 351101); in Duesseldorf, Königsalle 84 (Tel. 8711); in Munich, 3 Lenbachplatz (Tel. 558171); in Stuttgart, Hotel Graf Zeppelin (Tel. 93944); in Bremen, Bahnhofsplatz 5/6 (Tel. 302148); in Hanover, Luisenstrasse 1 (Tel. 25657); in Nuremberg, Flughafen (Tel. 32241).

GREAT BRITAIN
AND
NORTHERN IRELAND

WEATHER IN LONDON—Lat. 51°30′—Alt. 245′

Temp.	JAN.	FEB.	MAR.	APR.	MAY	JUNE	JULY	AUG.	SEPT.	OCT.	NOV.	DEC.
Low	35°	35°	36°	40°	45°	51°	54°	54°	49°	44°	39°	36°
High	43°	45°	49°	55°	62°	68°	71°	70°	65°	56°	49°	45°
Average	39°	40°	43°	48°	54°	60°	63°	62°	57°	50°	44°	41°

LOCATION . . . England, Scotland and Wales make up Great Britain, the largest island in Europe. Northern Ireland comprises the six northeastern counties of the island to the west.

CHARACTERISTICS . . . England, with all its differences, is the closest thing to home you'll find abroad. This is mainly because of the language. The English, though reserved, are friendly, and unfailingly courteous. It is one of the few remaining countries in which royalty is respected and that in itself breeds a tradition and dignity not found elsewhere. London has magnificence and the English countryside is utterly charming. There are places of historic and cultural interest from one end of the "tight little isle" to the other.

Scotland's charms are equally well worth visiting and very similar to those of England. Edinburgh, although conservative, is a lovely city, and of course the Scottish lochs and highlands are famous the world over.

POPULATION . . . The population of England and Wales is 43,757,880, which approximates that of France. Northern Ireland has a population of 1,380,000, Scotland, 5,095,969.

SIZE . . . The area of England is 50,327 square miles, about the size of Alabama. Wales, with 8,006 square miles, is the size of New Jersey. Northern Ireland, with 5,238 square miles, is a little larger than Connecticut. Scotland is about the size of South Carolina, with 30,411 square miles.

CAPITAL . . . Whereas London with a population of 8,346,137 is the capital of Great Britain, Edinburgh is the recognized and administrative capital of Scotland.

GOVERNMENT . . . The United Kingdom of Great Britain and Northern Ireland form a constitutional monarchy with executive power held by the cabinet and headed by the Prime Minister, who must be supported by a majority of the House of Commons. Parliament consists of two Chambers: the House of Commons, whose members are elected directly by the people, and the House of Lords, whose members sit for life, either by hereditary right, by appointment by the Queen, or by virtue of office.

HOW TO GET THERE . . . By Pan Am's Jet Clipper services of de luxe "President Special," or economy class Thrift fares less than 7 hours to London from New York and Boston. Via DC-7C Clipper 13 from Chicago via Detroit, 19 via Polar route from U.S. West Coast. From New York elapsed time to Glasgow (Prestwick Airport) 11 hours. By ship, about five days.

ACCOMMODATIONS . . . London hotels are world famous for their friendly service and pleasant atmosphere. Rates vary considerably with the average around $5.00 a night, including breakfast. Here are some of the best hotels in the various approximate price brackets. Prices quoted are for single rooms with bath. *Claridge's,* still the swankiest hostelry in town, is $18 and up. The rooms are large and gracious. You'll be treated royally. The *Savoy,* of course, is known the world over, as is the *Ritz.* The fashionable *Berkeley* is equally fine. Rooms are $13 per night. The *Dorchester* is very good. Rates here begin at $15. *Grosvenor House* is very popular and costs about $12 per night. *Brown's Hotel* hasn't changed in 100 years, chintz chairs, atmosphere, and quite moderate at $8.50. The *Westbury* in Mayfair is also very popular. The *Strand Palace,* the *Regent Palace* and the *Cumberland* are pleasant and inexpensive. Rates beginning at $5.50 to $6.50. Other good hotels include the *Hyde Park Hotel* beginning at $8.40, the *Mayfair Hotel* beginning at $10, the *Park Lane Hotel* beginning at $7.50 and the *Mount Royal* beginning at $8.

There are numerous hotels, private hotels and boarding houses in Edinburgh, but Americans will probably prefer the *Caledonian,* the *George,* the *Roxburghe* and the *North British.* Rates are reasonable. Don't expect lavishness, but you will be comfortable. Top rates about $6 per day, European Plan.

ARTS . . . London offers a wealth of museum and gallery-visiting experiences. There is the British Museum with its vast collection of the art of all ages, including some famous must-be-seens: Elgin Marbles from Greece, manuscripts of the Magna Carta, some of Shakespeare's First Folio, and important anthropological exhibits. The National Galley in Trafalgar Square is a must for all picture lovers. It has one of the world's most brilliant collections of French, Italian, Spanish, Flemish and English painting. The Tate Gallery, Millbank, offers an excellent collection of modern art from Turner on. The National Portrait Gallery in St. Martin's Place has portraits of Britain's great by artists of their times. The Victoria and Albert Museum of Art should also be seen.

Besides the large galleries and museums, London also has a number of charming, intimate museums that were the houses of great men of letters and public life. Visiting Carlyle House in Chelsea, Keats's House in Keats Grove, or Dickens' home in Doughty Street is like going back in time.

Galleries and museums in London are open usually from 10:00 A.M. to 5:00 P.M. daily and from 2:00 to 6:30 P.M. on Sundays. Admission is free most places.

Everyone interested in Scottish history will find plenty to fascinate him in Edinburgh. Visit the National Museum of Antiquities on Queen Street, the Scottish Naval and Military Museum at Edinburgh Castle, the old barracks which was turned into a National Repository in 1933. Here you will find flags, relics, historic uniforms and other objects devoted to each Scottish Regiment. Visit the Scottish National Gallery and the Royal Scottish Academy, both of which contain fine examples of past and contemporary Scottish Art. These galleries are on the "Mound." The Royal Scottish Museum is on Chambers Street.

When you go to Glasgow, be sure to see its Art Galleries situated in Kelvingrove Park, also the location of Glasgow University. This building, which is quite a work of art in itself, houses many treasures.

BALLET ... London's Royal Ballet Company has gained sensational success and reputation both at home and abroad. It may be seen at the Covent Garden Opera House. Many foreign ballet and dance groups may also be seen in the British Isles.

BANKS ... Guaranty Trust Company, Chase Manhattan Bank, and First National City Bank, all of New York, Bank of America; Royal Bank of Canada. English banks include Westminster Bank, Lloyd's Bank, Midland Bank, Barclay's Bank, and National Provincial Bank. American Express, 6 Haymarket; Thos. Cook & Son, Berkeley Street.

In Edinburgh: Clydesdale and North of Scotland Bank Ltd., Commercial Bank of Scotland, and Royal Bank of Scotland. *See* CURRENCY.

CALENDAR OF HOLIDAYS ... British national holidays include the Bank Holidays on Good Friday, Easter Monday, Whit Monday and the first Monday in August; Christmas Day; Boxing Day on the 26th of December and New Year's Day. The Queen's official birthday, celebrated in midsummer, is an occasion for pageantry but is not a public holiday.

CIGARETTES AND TOBACCO ... English cigarettes, cigars and tobacco are excellent, though expensive. Cigarettes cost about 55 cents for 20, cigars from 50 cents to $2.50 each, and pipe tobacco costs $1.25 for 2 ounces. American cigarettes are also expensive. If you are going to other parts of Europe, you may leave cigarettes in excess of duty-free limits with the customs office to be picked up when you depart.

CLIMATE . . . The British Isles enjoy a temperate climate. High summer temperatures are around 70 degrees; in winter the average low is about 35 degrees. The rainy months are November, January and February. Spring and fall are particularly delightful seasons; the winter months are apt to have fogs and mists. Northern Scotland is apt to be cool, like Maine.

CLUBS . . . Britain was the birthplace of the Social Club and many men belong to private clubs in London and Edinburgh. Some of these were founded long ago and they have a historic background, and entry to them is invariably confined to members and their guests. Rotary and Lions are both represented here.

COMMON COURTESIES AND LOCAL CUSTOMS . . . Though Britishers and Americans both speak a language called English there are many differences that can confuse you. Remember, cricket is as serious a matter as our baseball. In Scotland, asking what's worn under kilts is not funny any more. If you must know, the Scotsman wears "trews." Scotch jokes are out, too.

COMMUNICATIONS . . . Telephone, telegraph and cable service to all parts of the world. Local communication facilities are good. Airmail to the United States is 1s and 3d or 18 cents per ½ oz.

CURRENCY . . . The monetary unit is the pound, valued at $2.80. You may bring in unlimited amounts of all currencies. No more than declared on entry is allowed out.

CUSTOMS REGULATIONS AND DOCUMENTS REQUIRED FOR UNITED STATES CITIZENS . . . Duty-free import of 400 cigarettes (600 if in transit), 100 cigars, or 1 lb. of tobacco; 1 bottle spirits and 1 of wine or 2 of either if in use; ½ pint perfume; small quantity of food. You may take excesses and pay duty, of course.

Your American passport is all you'll need for identification purposes. If you plan to hire a car to drive yourself, bring your driver's license. A visitor's license may be obtained for 70 cents, from the Automobile Association or the Royal Automobile Club.

DRUG STORES . . . Drug stores, called chemists' shops, can supply you with everything you need in the way of medicine and toilet goods. They don't usually have soda fountains, although most department stores do.

ELECTRIC CURRENT . . . Voltage is generally 200–250 A.C., so you'll need a transformer for an electric razor. Converter plugs of the round-prong type are also needed. Many hotels will supply electric razor adaptors.

FAUNA . . . A great variety of animal and bird life abounds in the British Isles, mostly of the more domestic description. Notable among the birds is the nightingale. The forests contain deer and many species of small game and fowl.

FLORA . . . Mild climate and lots of rain make British gardens and countryside look like something out of a seed catalogue. The ardent English gardeners are well rewarded by beautiful colors and lush greenery. The various botanical gardens in England offer much to those interested in plants of other countries.

In Edinburgh the Princes Street Gardens are, of course, famous for their floral clock. Glasgow also has a most beautiful botanical garden, situated in the West End, in Great Western Road. The hot-houses contain the most beautiful blooms and flora of all countries.

FOOD . . . Despite the generally unspectacular reputation of British cooking, there are some world-famous restaurants in Britain that have superb food. Roast beef and Yorkshire pudding are traditional British dishes. Tea is a universal meal. It can mean anything from bread and butter to a spread of cooked dishes, followed by cakes. Don't miss having hot scones. *Haggis,* a traditional Scottish dish, is a pudding of liver, onion, spices and oatmeal boiled in the lining of a sheep's stomach. Then too, there is Scotch broth. Simpler dishes are scones, shortbreads, and the inevitable porridge.

GAMBLING . . . Most of the gambling is betting on horses or dogs. There is some form of racing every day and every night except Sundays. Bets are handled by legalized bookmakers.

LAUNDRY AND DRY CLEANING . . . Most hotels have good cleaning and laundry services available.

LIQUOR . . . Beer and whisky are the Britishers favorite drinks. Gin is a popular drink also, as gin and tonic, gin and bitters, gin and It (short for Italian vermouth) or gin and lime. If you order whisky you'll get Scotch. You will be able to get Irish whisky. Rye can be obtained, but Bourbon is less readily available. Scotch whisky in Scotland is one of the most expensive. Some of the lesser-known pot still whiskies may be a mixture of Scotch and Irish whisky. There are an unlimited number of malt beverages to be had. As com-pared with the American three—ale, beer and dark beer—the British assortment includes lager, bitter beer, mild ale, old ale and stout, to name but a few. They are served at room temperature.

MEDICAL FACILITIES . . . Your hotel will direct you to the nearest private physician. If you become ill or meet with an accident in Britain, you may obtain medical care, free of charge if necessary, under the National Health Scheme.

The medical facilities in Scotland are among the best in the world. The University of Edinburgh Medical College has few equals. Hospitals are numerous and their facilities are available to all visitors.

MOTION PICTURES . . . Known here as "the pictures" or the cinema, motion picture theaters usually open at noon. There are many of them which show the best of American films and other foreign films as well as all kinds of British movies.

MUSIC . . . In England, opera at Covent Garden and Sadler's Wells Theater. The English were the first to try operas sung in English on a large scale. The reception has been most enthusiastic. Modern opera, especially that of Benjamin Britten, is an integral part of the Covent Garden repertoire. The performances of the Royal Philharmonic are among the highlights of the symphony sea-son. There are also many chamber-music groups and visiting artists from the Continent. There are concerts at the Royal Festival Hall and Royal Albert Hall.

In Scotland, the Edinburgh Festival of Music and Drama, held in late August and early September, is known the world over. World-famous conductors, orchestras, singers and opera companies appear by invitation. The Scottish National Orchestra has a concert season in Edinburgh and Glasgow during the winter season, November to April. Edinburgh Castle is the headquarters for the Army School of Bagpipe playing, so it is possible to hear that haunting sad music in the city. The Highlands, of course, are the best setting to hear this unforgettable music.

NIGHT CLUBS ... The British phenomenon, the pub, can mean a wide variety of establishments from London's ultra-swank West End bars, whose snack bars serve some of the best food in town, to the smoky little neighborhood pubs, with their inevitable game of darts, that are the working-class Englishman's club.

The gay night life of London centers in such places as *Churchills Club* in Bond Street. The younger set likes to relax here. Admission and membership fee is $6 per person. Dinner and wine costs approximately $10 per person and whisky is approximately $12 a bottle. The *"400 Club"* is one of the plushiest night spots in town. Also very gala and less expensive is the *Embassy*. There are floor shows and dancing at all these places. Other clubs include the *River Club* on the Embankment, the *Empress Club* in Berkeley Street, *Siegi's* in Charles Street, Berkeley Square, *Les Ambassadeurs* and *Milroy*. Membership, where necessary, can be arranged by a telephone call to the manager. Membership fees are nominal. The following London restaurants also have dance orchestras and entertainment: quite moderate in price are the *Astor, Pigalle* Restaurant and *Edmundo Ros' Club*. More expensive but very good is *Quaglino's* in Bury Street. London clubs change name quite frequently, so check at your hotel before you set out for an evening.

PHOTOGRAPHY ... Good supplies of cameras and equipment, black-and-white still and movie film and color film are now available. Prices are higher than in the United States. Film developing services are good with a 48-hour service at most shops.

RELIGION ... The official religion is Protestant Episcopal; its members are often known as Anglicans. There are many other churches in Britain, including Catholic, Presbyterian and Lutheran, and Jewish synagogues.

RESTAURANTS ... Some of the best eating in London can be done in the dining rooms of the *Dorchester, Berkeley, Grosvenor House,* the *Savoy* and other fine hotels. There is usually music for dancing and the service is distinguished. Leoni's *Quo Vadis, Manetta's, Mirabelle, L'Epicure, Coqd'Or, Quaglino's, Hatchett's, Hungaria* and Cunningham's *Oyster Bar* are among London's many good restaurants, and *Simpson's* in the Strand is world famous. Excellent food is found in the Soho section of town, London's Greenwich Village. Here excellent French, Italian, Chinese, Greek, Hungarian and

Jewish cookery can be found. Try *Au Jardin des Gourmets,* and the *White Tower.* A booklet, "Good Food Guide," avaliable locally, is a good source for restaurants.

In Edinburgh, *Café Royal, Albyn Rooms, l'Aperitif* and leading hotels are all good. In Glasgow try the *Whitehall,* the *101 Club,* the *Grosvenor,* the *Royal, Rogano* and *Copacabana,* to name only a few.

SHOPS AND STORES . . . Harrod's, Dickins and Jones, Robinson and Cleaver's, Fortnum and Mason's and Simpson's are among London's top department stores. Marvelous tailors along Saville Row. Wonderful shops along Regent and Bond Streets. British designers include Digby Morton, Hartnell, Worth, and Charles Creed. Liberty's for silk prints. Shops are closed Saturday afternoons.

In Edinburgh Anderson's, George Street, for tweeds, tartans and Highland outfits. Hamilton and Inches for Scottish Silver Craft. Tensfeldt, Princes Street, for souvenirs. George Cockburn, Shadwick Place, for antique jewelry and silver. McCalls, Lothian Road, for Celtic silverware and tartan souvenirs. City Glass Co., for old glass. Romanes and Paterson for tweeds, tartans, cashmeres, and ladies' knitwear. Jenners is the largest department store.

SPECTATOR SPORTS . . . Horse racing goes on all year in England. The flat racing season lasts from March to December when the steeplechasing and hurdle racing begin. The first week in June is Derby Week. People come from miles around to see this great world-famous race, and gypsies camp on Epsom Downs, giving the whole event a carnival air. It is one of the most interesting events in the world and one of the gayest.

A visit to Lord's Cricket Ground in London is interesting. Rugby is mainly a university sport, not so popular as soccer. The biggest soccer event in England is the Cup Final, played at Wembley in April or early May. Other major sports events in England are the world-championship tennis matches at Wimbledon in London during June and July, the British Amateur and British Open Golf tournaments in May and July, respectively, and the Oxford-Cambridge boat race on the Thames in March or early April.

In Scotland, at the Highland games, which bring the clans together and are well worth seeing, you see hurling contests, wrestling, Scottish dances. Other spectator sports include golf tournaments, national and international; squash matches, association football, rugby, fencing, yachting regattas, bowling matches, horse racing.

SPORTS . . . There is a great variety of interests for the sportsman in Great Britain. There are some of the world's best golf courses. Near London is the famous Sunningdale course. Westward Ho! in Devon, Hoylake near Liverpool and the courses at Sandwich in Kent, to mention a few, are all excellent. In Scotland are St. Andrew's, Gleneagles, near Stirling, and the Old Prestwick course. Some other very fine courses in Scotland within 40 miles of Edinburgh include: North Berwick, Haddington, Mortonhall in Midlothian, and Muirfield, one of the oldest and most illustrious courses. An open letter from your golf club secretary at home will get you temporary membership.

You'll find tennis all over Great Britain. The grass courts are all good. A week-end visit is almost sure to include some tennis; the sport is nationally popular. Britain is also fine for fishing. Streams such as the Itchen, Frome and Axe have made English trout fishing famous. The dry-fly fishing here ranks with the best in the world. The moor country in western England offers the wet-fly fisherman excellent casting for salmon and trout. Fishing is also marvelous all over Scotland. The salmon fishing is world famous, but most of the salmon rivers are privately owned. It is possible to rent a boat for a month or a season. Salmon fishing is excellent in the Highlands and on the east coast. For brown-trout fishing there are innumerable hotels which own fishing streams for their guests. There are boats and guides available and the hotels cater mainly to the fishermen. In southern Scotland there are many streams in which you may fish by purchasing a ticket.

There's good hunting in Britain for deer, hare and many kinds of game, including pheasant, partridge, wild geese and duck. Game licenses cost $8.50 a season for as many guns as you wish and a hunting permit, or $5.60 and $2.80 for shorter periods. Most of the shooting in Scotland is done on private preserves. However, it is possible for the visitor to hire a moor for his very own, or, more modestly, to make arrangements for shooting through C. W. Ingram Esq., 90 Princes Street; or Walker, Fraser and Steel, 58 Castle Street, Edinburgh. Pheasant, October-February; wild duck, August-February; grouse, August-December, partridge, September-February.

Britain is wonderful for the hiker and bicycling enthusiast. There is a wide variety of landscape and terrain that can be covered in a short time. The Youth Hostel movement is very popular in the British Isles. There are more than 500 hostels offering low-cost accommodations for hikers and cyclists.

THEATERS ... First of all, try to see the famous Old Vic Company at the reconditioned *Old Vic* on the South Bank, London. It has a great tradition of fine acting and offers some of the best theatrical entertainment found anywhere. You'll want to check what's playing in the famous West End theaters. London offers a great variety of plays and musical comedies throughout the year. Besides new plays, there are always revivals of Shakespeare and the classics. You buy your program, but tickets are cheap, ranging from 42 cents to $3.08 for the best seats in the house. It is best to decide when you first arrive what you are going to see and get seats in advance. You'll want to spend a few evenings at the music halls, too. The *Palladium* is the home of vaudeville. See also Page 85 under MUSIC. Theater time is 7:30 or 8:00.

In Edinburgh there are two theaters for excellent touring companies and occasional premières, but it is at the time of the International Music and Drama Festival that the most interesting plays are given. It is here that Bernard Shaw's *Apple Cart* received its first performance and more recently T. S. Eliot's *Cocktail Party* and the *Confidential Clerk,* both of which were later presented in New York.

TIME... Five hours later than U.S. Eastern Standard Time.

TIPPING... The 10 to 15 per cent rule applies at restaurants. At hotels divide 10 to 15 per cent among those giving personal service. In all cases bellboys, doormen and taximen are tipped extra. Tip only for extra service such as delivery of tickets, etc. Tip cab drivers 6d (7 cents) for a fare of 2/6d (35 cents), plus 6d for each 1/6d of fare above 2/6d. Don't overtip.

TRANSPORTATION... London is a spread-out city. It will be worth your while to study the train and subway systems to various parts of it. They are good and not expensive. In both England and Scotland there are plenty of buses and trams. Taxis are available at all times and they are reasonable. There is excellent train and plane service all over Britain. Self-drive cars are also available at an average charge of $7.70 per day, allowing 80 miles. Excess mileage is charged at the rate of 2 cents per mile. Chauffeur-driven services are available in most towns for 21 cents per mile upwards, according to the type of car.

WATER... The water is safe to drink throughout the British Isles.

WHAT TO BUY... There's no purchasing tax for visitors on purchases worth £5 ($14) or more if they're delivered to the ship or plane or shipped home direct.

London is the Paris of men's clothing. British tailors are the best in the world. Custom-made clothes are much cheaper than in American shops. A beautiful Scotch tweed suit costs about $100, compared with $250 in New York. Wonderfully soft camel's hair coats can be bought for about the same price. Though some British tailors don't do as good a job on women's suits, you may wish to buy a length of tweed or woolen material to have made up at home. Handmade shoes cost around $25 a pair. They wear forever, too. The British make wonderful raincoats, including the famous Burberrys that are popular with both men and women. Sweaters, socks and scarfs in lovely soft wool and cashmere are also relatively inexpensive. Fine umbrellas, long a British specialty, are for sale at very reasonable prices. Fine old English silver is selling at a fraction of its price in America. Buy Belfast linen and lace-like porcelain from Northern Ireland. Fine China and glass are a good buy, but fragile to ship.

In Scotland, buy tweeds of course, tartans, woolens and cotton goods, silver jewelry, the kilt if you insist. But mostly Harris and Shetland tweeds. Cashmeres, too, are wonderful. English pipes are good buys.

WHAT TO WEAR... Even in the middle of summer the nights in England and Scotland can get as cold as October weather. Eighty degrees is considered an unusually warm day in London. Don't crowd your luggage with light cotton or tropical worsted clothes, unless you are going to warmer climates. A simple wool suit and lightweight wool dresses will fill a woman's daytime needs in the cities. Black cocktail dresses or dressy suits are best after five. The British wear

London's famous Piccadilly Circus is a center of business activity. Eros fountain is shown in the background.

evening clothes much more than we do, so if you plan to go at all gala bring along your formal clothes. A lightweight topcoat and a warm evening wrap are musts. So are comfortable shoes for sight-seeing and hiking. Casual sportswear, but not slacks, are correct in the country.

Lightweight flannel and worsted suits are fine for men in London and Edinburgh. Odd tweed jackets worn with gray flannel slacks are good in the country. A raincoat is definitely a must all year round in England and Scotland for both men and women. These suggestions are primarily for a summer wardrobe. If you are going in the winter, plan to wear heavier indoor and lighter outdoor clothes than you would in the United States.

WHERE TO GO—SIGHTSEEING ...

London ... What you see in London is largely up to you. You

The pleasant rolling countryside of Southwest England is the setting for this Inn at Yarcombe, a village in Devon near Exeter.

can do the museums and art galleries, you can wander around the various neighborhoods which make up the largest city in the world, you can go down to the "City," you can poke around Soho and Chelsea. But here are a few musts on anyone's list. Westminster Abbey, of course. This old English building is England itself. Here is where the sovereigns of Great Britain have been crowned for centuries. Here is where royalty is wed, and many of the great of England are buried in the Abbey. The history of the English people can be read in these graves.

You can't miss Big Ben at Westminster or Eros on his Piccadilly stand. The British Museum is a must even if you aren't a museum-goer. The Houses of Parliament are near the Abbey. Built in 1840, they are pseudo-Gothic with Victorian overtones. History is made here and you may be in on its making by obtaining passes to the debates in the House of Commons (by application to the Admission order office). There are guided tours available on Saturdays only, 10 A.M.–4 P.M., for which it is not necessary to make advance booking arrangements.

Go to the Tower of London, scene of some of the darkest chapters in English history. It is now a museum and holds the Crown Jewels and other treasures. Within its walls is the beautiful little chapel of St. John, one of the perfect examples of Norman architecture. Take a day to see this vast building which has stood since the time of William the Conqueror. And don't miss St. Paul's Cathedral, which was built by Christopher Wren. The graceful Renaissance dome has been a landmark for more than two centuries.

Take a bus to the "City," the financial heart of England. Here you will find "The Old Lady of Threadneedle Street" (Bank of England), Lloyd's, the Temple, Lincoln's Inn and Gray's Inn. This is where you'll find the Cheshire Cheese in Fleet Street.

Go to Marble Arch on Sundays and hear soapbox orators. Watch the riders along Rotten Row, go to the world-famous London Zoo in Regent's Park. Take a look at Mme. Tussaud's Waxworks. Make a point of seeing the changing of the guard at Buckingham or St. James' Palaces. Take a look at one of the most charming churches to be seen anywhere, St. Martin-in-the-Fields in Trafalgar Square; go to St. James' Park off the Mall and watch the ducks. You can do all this by sightseeing bus or just by meandering by yourself. A wonderful way to see London is to take the No. 11 bus, which wanders over a huge territory. Travel by Underground (subway). It is an interesting experience.

A half hour by suburban electric from the center of London is beautiful Hampton Court on the Thames, a great palace built by Cardinal Wolsey as a private residence. The palace contains a wonderful art gallery and an interesting collection of historic English furniture. Its hundreds of square feet of windows look out on the most glorious gardens in England. There are geometric boxwood mazes for you to wander through, quaint walled Elizabethan flower beds and graceful groupings of beautiful trees and shrubs. Hampton

Court is another all-day sight. From April to September you may take a daily river boat up the Thames between Westminster and Hampton Court through Richmond.

Windsor Castle definitely deserves a day of your time in and around London. It is an hour from Paddington or Waterloo Stations by train and a little longer by bus. William the Conqueror started it and Henry III and Edward III both made additions to the huge building. Windsor is a royal residence. Each monarch has left the mark of his era on the interiors. There are some fine foreign paintings by Rubens, Rembrandt and others and a wealth of British portraits. State apartments are interesting and also the Queen's Doll House. (There is a shilling admission charge to the former and sixpence to the latter.) Proceeds go to charity. Climb the 220 steps of the Round Tower and you will be rewarded by a marvelous view of the surrounding countryside that has changed very little since Chaucer stood on the same ramparts. The best way to see the lovely Great Park that surrounds this fairyland castle is in an open carriage. The things to do and see outside of London are numerous and fascinating. In the following short description of some of the major highlights, England has been roughly divided into seven sections. The English countryside is dotted with enchanting little inns and the food is comparable with that in the large cities.

The South of England . . . English history began here in the south. Probably the most important place to visit in England, outside of London, is the ancient town of Canterbury, 65 miles to the southeast. The magnificent Canterbury Cathedral is the seat of the Church of England. This imposing Gothic church was built during four centuries. The first church was consecrated on its site in 597 A.D. The grounds around the cathedral are lovely. If you plan to go to Canterbury, make your reservations before you leave the United States. It is one of England's most popular tourist spots and the inns are booked months in advance.

Knole, outside of Sevenoaks in Kent, 20 miles south of London, is one of the show places of England. The house has endless corridors of gracious rooms and the park and gardens are superb. The whole countryside in Kent, Surrey and Sussex is dotted with quaint villages and the scenery is very beautiful. (There is a motel, *Royal Oak,* near Lympne, Kent.) For contrast, hire a car and drive along the rolling Downs by the sea.

Winchester, Salisbury, and the New Forest . . . The New Forest is so called because it was man-made. William I created this Royal Hunting Ground. Herds of cattle and very tame "wild ponies" roam through it. Right in the center of this giant woodland is the *Parkhill* hotel. There's also a New Forest Motel. Staying here, you have a wonderful base of operations for seeing Winchester and Salisbury. Winchester was the capital of pre-Norman England. Things to see include the ruins of Winchester Castle and the cathedral, a lovely church containing an amazing mixture of architectural styles that blend together very happily. Salisbury is a charming town full of quaint, lovely old houses. Salisbury Cathedral has one of the most graceful spires in the world. Near by is Old Sarum, a fascinating hodgepodge of Roman, Saxon and Norman ruins. A wonderful place for a picnic. The weird prehistoric ruins of Stonehenge stand on the Salisbury Plain a few miles away. Scholars date them about 1,700 B.C.

The West Country . . . The town of Bath, first built by the Romans as a resort spot, is the outstanding place to visit in the west of England. Today, the architecture is late Georgian, built in the eighteenth century when Bath was the most fashionable town in England. Stroll through the Pump and Assembly Rooms. The ruins of the Roman baths are interesting, too. There are quite a few good hotels in Bath. The enchanting little town of Wells is near by and very much worth visiting. Go to Gloucester to see the magnificent, Perpendicular-Norman cathedral and a charming rural English city. The Cloisters have an interesting collection of old manuscripts.

England's southwest, Somerset, Devon, and Cornwall, has a Gulf Stream-warmed climate making it mild even in winter, with beaches, exciting villages, and a cove-dotted coast, where spring comes early. You might stop at Exeter, in Devon, for a look at its Cathedral (there's a *Devon Motel* at Alphington), or at fashionable Torquay. Here you will be surprised by subtropical plants, even some palms. See lush green Plymouth, from whose harbor both Drake and the Pilgrims sailed to make history. The last, most western and southern end of the island is Cornwall, with Land's End. Along its north coast with its quaint little hamlets lies Tintagel, with its memories of King Arthur. Don't miss the Cornish pasties.

Oxford and Stratford-on-Avon . . . There is a tremendous amount of territory to cover at Oxford. The famous university is surrounded by ancient traditions and scholarly atmosphere. See Magdalen, New and Christ Church colleges. The Sheldonian Theater is another must. From the Tower of St. Mary's Church you have a fine view of the town. The gardens are particularly lovely. Plan to stay at least two days in Oxford. There are some quite good inns. Confirm reservations in advance.

Stratford-on-Avon has been wonderfully preserved as a shrine to England's greatest poet. You may see the house where Shakespeare was born and Anne Hathaway's quaint little cottage. The town is typically Tudor England. The Shakespeare Memorial Theater has performances of the Bard's great works from April through November. Stay at the *Welcombe Hotel* or the *Falcon Inn*. The food is good at both places. There are other good restaurants in Stratford. Make reservations in advance, especially during the theater season. Shakespeare's grave is in the Church of the Holy Trinity.

Warwick Castle is near by. It is an interesting mixture of many styles of architecture, has a lavish interior.

Tewkesbury Abbey is the great church of the region. Tewkesbury is the scene of a major battle of the Wars of the Roses and the Abbey is a fine example of Norman architecture.

The Midlands and the Lake District . . . Nottingham is the most

The Houses of Parliament on the River Thames, with the clock tower which houses Big Ben, are one of London's famous landmarks.

Stratford-on-Avon—The Great Bard himself must have strolled the banks of the gentle Avon composing sonnets on a summer afternoon. Shakespeare Memorial Theater.

historic town in this region. See Nottingham Castle. See the quaint old "Trip to Jerusalem" Inn, near the dungeons of the Castle. It was a meeting place for Richard Coeur de Lion's crusaders. Nine miles from Nottingham is Newstead Abbey, the home of Lord Byron. It has been beautifully preserved by the town of Nottingham. The gardens and grounds are gorgeous.

Haddon Hall is a medieval house of great beauty. It is the property of the Duke of Rutland and is associated with the romantic Dorothy Vernon, who eloped with Sir John Manners in the sixteenth century. Chatsworth, the stately home of the Duke of Devonshire, is of interest not only for its fine collections of pictures but also as having been for short periods the house of detention of the unhappy Mary Queen of Scots. Both are well worth seeing.

The Lake District is a hiker's paradise. Often called "Little Switzerland," it is beautiful, full of charming little lakes, rolling hills and rugged open country. It was also the haven of great English poets, notably Wordsworth. Ambleside, Windermere (the largest lake is here), Grasmere and Keswick are all quaint little towns with good inns and restaurants. Any one of them would make a good base for seeing the Lake District.

Cambridge and East Anglia . . . Cambridge is the other great university town in England. Cromwell, Wordsworth and Darwin all studied here. See King's, Trinity and St. John's College. Don't overlook the lovely chapel of St. John and King's College chapel. The gardens are beautiful. Punting on the Cam is an experience you won't want to miss. The Round Church in the town of Cambridge is an interesting relic of Norman architecture.

East Anglia is the territory of English painters. Here in this strangely beautiful, flat moorlike country Constable and Turner produced their lovely canvases. There are many charming towns and villages. Ely is probably the most interesting from the point of view of sights to see, principally for its ancient and beautiful cathedral.

Other Cities . . . Two of the most interesting towns in all England for any tourist are York in the north, and Chester about 3 hours by train from London. Chester is a live, busy town, York a quiet cathedral town; but for an American sightseer, both have the charm that only great age brings. Both have Roman ruins, both have their ancient walls. Those in Chester are still standing so that the visitor may walk completely around them. York Minster is to many the most glorious church in all England, surely the most interesting cathedral with the most beautiful stained glass. Whoever sees the famed "Five Sisters" window or some of the simpler war memorials can never forget them. Like York, Chester is an old Roman town, but busier and gayer. You can shop in the medieval Rows, the delightful two-storied arcades, shops full of antique silver, jewelry and furniture, and almost touch and feel the fourteenth century. Either of these cities can be used as a base for a two- or three-day tour of the surrounding countryside. (In Chester, the *Blossoms* and, in York, *Royal Station*.)

The Tower Bridge, spanning the Thames. Not far from here, the Romans erected the first bridge in the first century A.D.

Quaint Lower Slaughter in the Cotswolds adds charm to the English countryside.

Wales ... It is easy to go to Wales from Chester. You should try to get to Wales, which has a hundred old castles, even if you don't make Chester. North Wales is the best. The cities of the south are grim, bleak coal-mining centers not unlike our own. Go to Llangollen for the annual Eisteddfod, which is a festival for musicians and dancers from all over the world. But it is the magnificent Welsh singing such as you heard in "How Green Was My Valley" which rules the occasion. Llangollen is in Denbighshire, where flows the River Dee. Go to Betws-y-Coed in Caernarvonshire. Visit Colwyn Bay, and Llandudno, modern resorts with good hotels and fine beaches. Try the *Imperial, St. George's* or *Craigside Hydro*.

Caernarvon Castle is where the first Prince of Wales was presented by his father, Edward I. The castle is forbidding and majestic. North of Caernarvon are the resort towns of Llanfairfechan, Penmaenmawr and Bangor. The highest mountain in England and Wales, Snowdon, is in this county which is famous for its steep mountain ranges and its mountain climbing. South of Caernarvon is Montgomeryshire, which is in Central Wales where the Wye and the Severn Rivers start their course. There are some charming towns and excellent fishing in the streams of Vyrnwy and Wye.

Westward on the coast is Cardiganshire with some delightful resort towns. At Aberystwyth is a college of the University of Wales. Still going south you come to Pembrokeshire with its many Norman castles. This is the oldest county in South Wales and full of historical interest. The stones at Stonehenge are believed to have come from here. And who could resist a lighthouse named Strumble Head? Cardiff is the capital and chief city in Wales.

Northern Ireland . . . Belfast, the pleasant and prosperous capital of Northern Ireland, may be reached by either air or steamer from England or Scotland. The city is surrounded by beautiful country that has that soft and green quality which characterizes so much of Northern Ireland. Stay at the *Grand Central* or the *Midland*. Make trips along the coast road and through the famous Glens of Antrim, their steep, wooded valleys, or take a bus or train to County Down, "where the Mountains of Mourne sweep down to the sea."

Spend a few days in Portrush, County Antrim, a famous seaside resort with long stretches of sandy beach and a championship golf course. Hotels: *Northern Counties* and *Skerry Bhan*. Visit the Giant's Causeway near by, myriad columns of bright red and yellow volcanic stone. County Fermanagh is one of the great beauty spots of Europe. Upper and Lower Lough Erne, two lakes which divide the county, are studded with islands on which are the ruins of castles, shrines and monasteries. Stay in the island city of Enniskillen at the *Hotel Imperial*. Visit some of the lovely rose gardens of County Armagh. The city of Armagh has been the ecclesiastical center of all of Ireland for more than fifteen centuries. St. Patrick founded his church there.

Edinburgh . . . Edinburgh, located on the Firth of Forth, is the Scottish capital. It is a beautiful city dominated by historic Edinburgh Castle, which sits on a rock some 270 feet high. The rock falls sharply on three sides to the gardens below it. The Castle has a long and bloody history. Here are the apartments occupied by Mary Queen of Scots when she gave birth to the child who became James I of England. See the National War Shrine here, too. The view from the Castle rock is spectacular—you look down on Princes Street, that famous and beautiful thoroughfare, which is lined with shops on one side and beautiful gardens on the other. This is the "New Town." You also see the Royal Mile (Old Town), which leads from the Castle to the Palace of Holyroodhouse, the Royal Residence that Her Majesty uses when in Edinburgh. Here Prince Charlie held the historic ball while at the Castle they were still fighting him. Here, too, are other apartments of Mary Queen of Scots and those of Lord Darnley, connected by an inner stairway. Next to the Palace are the ruins of Holyrood Abbey. Darnley is buried here. Parliament House, the famous St. Giles Cathedral, the Law Courts all have marked and made Scottish history. Be sure to visit the National Gallery of Scotland.

Old Town straggles down the side of the rock. Until the middle of the eighteenth century, Edinburgh consisted of this narrow, crowded ridge. Here were built the first tall flats; the first tenements. In the latter part of that century began the expansion which is now New Town. Princes Street is the dividing line. In the middle of the Gardens is the "Mound," an artificial hill constructed in the middle of the city. Visit the Zoological Park on the slope of Corstophine Hill; it is one of the largest in Europe. Visit also Craigmillar Castle, about 3 miles from the city. Greyfriars Churchyard you must see, also the Sir Walter Scott Monument, the Royal Scottish Academy and Arthur's Seat, in King's Park. This is a hill some 800 feet high. There are daily tours around the city.

Prestwick... Prestwick Airport, at which you land, is situated in one of the most historic parts of Scotland. It abounds with tradition, and is near the home of Burns. Visit his birthplace in Alloway and the memorial where many treasures dear to the heart of Burns lovers are on display, set in a most picturesque spot on the banks of the river Doon, with that most famous of bridges, the "Brig O'Doon" taking a prominent place in the picture.

The Auld Kirk of Alloway is the scene of Tam O'Shanter's run-in with the witches, as described in the famous poem. The scenery leaves little to be desired, and numerous hotels are situated near the airport, which, while not offering the best in everything, retain a complete charm of their own. Around the airport, there are 16 golf courses capable of testing the skill of the best. All are open to visitors.

Near Alloway lies Ayr, the center of the Robert Burns country. Ayr is a modern seaside resort and is filled with things to interest the Burns lover. Hotels are the *Station,* the *County,* the *Ayrshire & Galloway.* From Ayr it is possible to make a "Burns" tour of Dumfries (in the south near England), Thornhill, Cumnock and other points of interest.

Border Country... South of Edinburgh is the Border country, the country of Sir Walter Scott. His home at Abbotsford is worth seeing. The ruins of Melrose and Dryburgh Abbeys are nearby. Peebles on the River Tweed is the center of the Border country, a famed holiday area. There is good fishing here. North Berwick, 22 miles east of Edinburgh in East Lothian, has three golf courses and top hotels for the golfer. The *Marine* Hotel is excellent.

The Island of Arran, picturesque and colorful, lies off the coast of Ayrshire in the Firth of Clyde, southwest of Glasgow. It is about 20 miles long and is the quintessence of all Scotland.

Glasgow... Coming north from Ayr or Arran, you reach Glasgow, the most important seaport in Scotland. The Glasgow Art Galleries are famous; *see* ARTS. There's a good zoo at Calderpark. Hotels include the *North British,* the *Central, St. Enoch* and *More's.* Glasgow is an excellent shopping center, with stores offering high quality goods. Recommended are: Copland & Lye, R. W. Forsyth, MacDonalds, Wylie Lochhead, and Pettigrew & Stephen, to name only a few.

The Trossachs... On the way to the Highlands you come to the Trossachs, a strip of land in Western Perthshire. Tours through this region are by bus or a combination of train, bus and steamer. Gateway to this lake region is Stirling (36 miles northwest of Edinburgh), a historic town with a castle on a high rock which views the spot where Robert the Bruce defeated the English at Bannockburn. Stay at the *Golden Lion Hotel.*

Members of the police band in Edinburgh, Scotland, take time off for a skirl on the pipes outside the city's historical castle.

Dunvegan Castle on the Isle of Skye is the oldest inhabited castle in Great Britain, the ancestral home of the chiefs of the clan MacLeod for 800 years.

From Stirling you go to Callander. Here you take a bus to Trossachs Pier and stay at the *Trossachs Hotel*. Then on to Loch Katrine, Stronachlachar, and Loch Lomond, famed in song and verse. Loch Katrine is the scene of Scott's "Lady of the Lake" and is revered as such.

Loch Lomond is the queen of the Scottish lochs and is surrounded by mountains. There is an interesting trip, too, from Callander to Loch Tay to the northeast. Here you see thatched cottages. picturesque villages, mountains sloping to the loch shores. It is very old, very beautiful.

The Highlands ... The imaginary line of demarcation between the Lowlands and the Highlands of Scotland is drawn between the Firth of Clyde on the west and the Firth of Tay on the east. Above this line lies the rugged, beautiful but often dour country of the Scottish Highlands. Here is where you will find Balmoral Castle. Here also is the Isle of Skye with Dunvegan Castle, the oldest inhabited castle in Britain, and the ancestral home of the Clan MacLeod.

From the west coast start your tour of the Highlands at Oban (*Great Western, Alexandra* Hotels). This is a fine Scottish resort town, the chief yachting center of the North, and the base for those who wish to visit the Hebrides, and also take the steamer ride around the Island of Mull.

From Oban go northward on the road running beside Loch Linnhe to Ballachulish, at the foot of Glencoe, scene of the sinister murder of Clan MacDonald in 1692. Nearby is Fort William and Ben Nevis, highest spot in the British Isles. The road runs beside the canal and series of lochs (including Loch Ness of sea serpent fame) that runs right across the country, from Fort William to Inverness. This modern looking little city on the banks of the River Ness is considered the capital of the romantic Highlands, and like so many other Scottish cities was the scene of much fighting. (Hotel *Caledonian*.)

Macbeth's castle once stood in the midst of Inverness, the scene of a stormy past. Nearby is the battlefield of Culloden, where the Highlanders made their last stand against the English in 1746. You may see the names of the clans on some of the gravestones of these gallant dead. To the west from Inverness, the country is wild, the scenery more rugged and the Highlands more sparsely inhabited.

From Inverness eastward, some 15 miles, lies the town of Nairn and Cawdor Castle, still approached by a drawbridge over its moat. Farther to the east along the coast is Elgin, with its ruined cathedral, and farther yet we come to the mouth of the River Spey. This is the center of the finest salmon fishing in all Scotland. The counties of Ross and Cromarty are the heart of the best deer forests in Scotland.

There are two roads to Aberdeen—one through the resorts and seaside villages of Lossiemouth, Banff; and the other through the inland route of Keith, Huntley and Inverurie. All of these places have their own particular items of interest.

Aberdeen is the most Scottish of the cities of Scotland. It is a fine holiday resort, with a pleasant climate. There are numerous good hotels, including the *Caledonian* and the *Douglas*. Aberdeen abounds in tradition and beautiful buildings.

Leaving Aberdeen for the south, one should travel along the road through what is known as Royal Deeside, through Ballater and Balmoral, where the Scottish home of the Queen at Balmoral Castle can be seen. Nearby is Royal Braemar, where the famous Royal Highland Gathering of the Clans and Highland Games are held each September. This is the chief social event of the Royal Highland Season. Following the road over the watershed at Devil's Elbow down Glen Shee, you reach Perth (32 miles northwest of Edinburgh) on the River Tay. Perth is a beautiful country town immortalized by Sir Walter Scott.

This almost completes the circle to Stirling and is near the Gleneagles golf course, with its excellent hotel. A tour of the Highlands can be done by motor coach or by car. If you want to see more rugged country and the red deer and the lonely Scottish moors, go up over the Grampians way north to John O'Groats and on to the Shetland and Orkney Islands off the north coast.

SOURCES OF FURTHER INFORMATION ... The British Travel Association, 64 St. James's Street in London. Pan American's London office is at 193/4 Piccadilly, W 1 (Tel. Regent 7292).

The Scottish Tourist Information Center, Rutland Place, West End, Edinburgh 1. Pan American is at Prestwick Airport, and at 130 St. Vincent Street, Glasgow, C.1.

In New York, information and excellent literature on all of Great Britain are available through the British Travel Association, 680 Fifth Avenue. Other offices are in Chicago, Los Angeles and Toronto.

GREECE

WEATHER IN ATHENS—Lat. N37°59'

Temp.	JAN.	FEB.	MAR.	APR.	MAY	JUNE	JULY	AUG.	SEPT.	OCT.	NOV.	DEC.
Low	42°	42°	46°	51°	60°	67°	72°	72°	66°	60°	52°	46°
High	53°	56°	60°	68°	77°	85°	90°	90°	83°	74°	64°	57°
Average	48°	49°	53°	60°	69°	76°	81°	81°	75°	67°	58°	52°
Days of Rain	12	11	11	9	7	4	3	3	4	9	12	13

LOCATION ... Greece occupies the southern tip of the Balkan Peninsula in the Eastern Mediterranean Sea. The Athens airport is on the crossroads from Europe to Egypt, Africa, Asia and the Near East.

CHARACTERISTICS ... "Cradle of civilization and birthplace of the gods, land of legend and beauty which has inspired centuries of art and the essence of philosophy, Greece welcomes the world." These long-suffering, courageous people have an economic need for foreign tourists. Since Greeks are naturally unselfish and friendly, they give visitors a warm welcome. They offer a sunny country of great natural beauty and magnificent monuments straight out of your old schoolbooks.

Apart from its world-famed historical and archaeological relics, modern Greece provides many attractions to the traveler. The many islands and indented coastline, so characteristic of Greece, provide ideal beaches, yachting harbors and fishing places. For those who prefer the mountains and the inlands to the sea, for the huntsman, the mountain-climber, the hiker, the camper and the motorist, there is a vast wealth and variety of beautiful scenery richly scattered with relics of the Golden Age.

In organized resorts, such as the beautiful islands of Rhodes and Corfu, the gay social summer life provides a different type of holiday. For those who wish to combine a cure with their vacation, there is a large choice of famous spas rich in curative waters of every kind.

POPULATION . . . 7,602,000 (1951 census).

SIZE . . . 51,182 miles, a slightly smaller area than Florida.

CAPITAL . . . Athens, with a population of 1,100,000.

GOVERNMENT . . . Greece is a Royal Republic with a Parliament elected by universal suffrage.

HOW TO GET THERE . . . By Pan Am Jet Clipper to Rome, then by Olympic Airways or other connecting airline, only 3 hours to Athens. By ship from New York, 15 to 18 days.

ACCOMMODATIONS . . . There are many good hotels in Athens. In the de luxe group are: the *Grande-Bretagne,* the *Athénée Palace* and the *King George.* First class: *National, Acropole Palace, Alex.* Rates at official exchange, about $4 single with bath, European Plan, at the best hotels; about $2.50 in the first class hotels.

Reservations should be made as far in advance as practicable for the period of April 15 to November 30.

ARTS . . . Athens is renowned for its classical remains dating back to the fourth century, B.C., and earlier. The main sights are: the Acropolis with the Parthenon, Temple of Nike, Proplaea, Erechteion, Temple of Theseus, Theater of Dionysos, Odeon of Herodes Atticus, Temple of Olympus Zeus, the Stadium, Stoa of Attalos, Byzantine Churches: Saints Theodores, Kapnikarea and Saint Eleftherios. Museums: Archaeological, Byzantine, Benaki (collection of national costumes). Zappeion Building (modern Gree kart) and Zappeion Gardens.

BANKS . . . Bank of Greece, National and Athens Bank, Commercial Ionian Bank. The American Express Company is on Constitution Square. Traveler's checks and letters of credit may be cashed at any bank. Banknotes may be exchanged only at the Bank of Greece or the American Express Company. Top hotels, restaurants and night clubs are authorized to exchange small amounts of foreign currency.

CALENDAR OF HOLIDAYS . . . Greek national holidays include: January 1—January 6; March 25, Independence Day; Good Friday; Easter and Monday following; August 15, Feast of Virgin Mary; October 28, Anniversary of entrance in World War II; December 25, December 26. Good Friday and Easter Sunday religious processions are typical of the Greek Orthodox Church.

CIGARETTES AND TOBACCO . . . Good, mild cigarettes of local brands, American and British cigarettes are also available, but expensive.

CLIMATE . . . Mild Mediterranean climate. Spring and autumn are by far the best seasons to visit Greece. However, there are many pleasant sunny days in the winter, and even in the middle of summer the heat is often tempered by fresh breezes from the sea and mountains. The nights are invariably cool and pleasant even after the hottest days of summer.

CLUBS . . . Rotary, Lions, Propeller, riding, tennis, yachting, touring and automobile clubs.

COMMON COURTESIES, LOCAL CUSTOMS . . . Handshaking is almost *de rigueur* in Greece when you meet or leave someone.

Greeks are not too punctual, especially during the hot summer months. The summer siesta is an institution (2:00 P.M.–5:00 P.M.).

COMMUNICATIONS... Telephones: urban good, otherwise average. Cables, transatlantic telephone, airmail and teletype.

CURRENCY... The monetary unit is the Greek drachma. $1 equals 30 drachmae. The devaluation from drs. 15 to 30 in 1953 has made Greece a very inexpensive country for tourists.

CUSTOMS REGULATIONS AND DOCUMENTS REQUIRED FOR UNITED STATES CITIZENS... Passport. No visa required. Sojourn and exit permit needed after a two months' stay. You can bring in 200 cigarettes, equivalent weight of tobacco, or 30 cigars. Articles for personal use and small gifts, as well as a reasonable supply of food are duty free. Furs, typewriters, radios, cameras and films are registered on the passport upon entry and can be re-exported without trouble. Customs people, especially at airports, are courteous and efficient.

DRUG STORES... Local drug stores can supply most of your needs for United States or equivalent foreign products.

ELECTRIC CURRENT... 220 volts, 50 cycles, A.C.

FAUNA... Aquatic birds, partridges and rabbits are found here and may be hunted. Fish are also plentiful. *See* SPORTS.

FLORA... Pine trees on Mount Parnes at 30 minutes from Athens by car. A great variety of wild flowers are found in the surrounding area.

FOOD... The majority of tourist restaurants serve Continental food of good quality. There are also a number of typically Greek dishes like *mousaka* (alternate layers of eggplant, ground meat and white flour and milk sauce agreeably spiced), *souvlakia* (meat on small spits) and *dolmadakia* (rolled vine leaves containing rice, ground meat and spices). A great variety of excellent fish; a variety of good local wines, and excellent honey from nearby Mount Hymettus are available.

GAMBLING... There is betting on the horse races at the Phaleron Delta, 3 miles from Athens near the sea.

LANGUAGE... Greek is the local language. English and French are largely understood and spoken.

LAUNDRY AND DRY CLEANING... Modern laundries are available but a little slow even in good hotels.

LIQUOR... Excellent bottled wines: *Achaia, Santa-Helena, Cambas, Dekelia, Demestika, Marco, Tour-la-Reine*. Sweet wines: *Robola, Mavrodaphni, Samos, Santorini*. Local liquors: *Ouzo, Coriandolino of Rhodes*. All Continental wines and liquors are also available.

MEDICAL FACILITIES... There are English-speaking doctors. Ask at your hotel for information. Medical Association: Venizelos Ave. Number 20 (Tel. 32–143); first aid service (Tel. 525555).

MOTION PICTURES... Italian, Greek, French and U.S. films. Foreign pictures are usually shown with the original sound track.

MUSIC... The Athens State Symphony Orchestra plays on Sunday mornings at the Orpheus Hall in Athens, very often conducted by brilliant foreign conductors. During August and September, the Athens Festival is in full swing at the ancient open-air Odeon of Herodes Atticus. Performances include classical Greek drama, operas, concerts, dance recitals . . . all with internationally known Greek artists and other nationals.

NIGHT CLUBS . . . Athens is one of the most cosmopolitan and socially alive centers of the Mediterranean. Night clubs with floor shows: *Argentina, Athinea, Mocambo, Seventeen, Golden Horse Shoe, Asteria* and *Chez Lapin.* For local color, however, the *tavernas* are heartily recommended. Ask your porter for guidance.

RELIGION . . . Greek Orthodox. Churches of other denominations; Catholic, Protestant and Jewish in the center of Athens.

RESTAURANTS . . . The large hotels usually have first-class restaurants where meals à la carte are served. The best restaurants in Athens are: *Zonars, Floca, Averoff, Pantheon* and *Costis.*

SHOPS AND STORES . . . Stores are open daily, except Sundays. In winter: from 8:30 A.M. to 1:00 P.M., and 3:30 to 7:00 P.M. In summer 8:00 A.M. to 1:00 P.M. and 5:00 to 8:00 P.M., except Wednesdays. *See* WHAT TO BUY.

SPORTS . . . All the athletic sports and games practiced in other countries are to be found in Greece. *Hunting:* Visitors may hunt almost everywhere in Greece from Sept. 1 to May 15. Aquatic birds are numerous at Marathon and Souli, near Athens. Passage birds are to be found at Lake Carla, near Volos, Halkis and Limni in Central Greece. The hunting season on aquatic birds and on spring turtledoves begins March 15 and ends May 15. Partridges and rabbits may be hunted from the end of August to the middle of January. For information and hunting permits, apply to the Hellenic Hunting Association, 30 Kolokotroni Street, Athens. *Fishing:* Fish are plentiful in Greek waters. Amateur fishermen will find a warm welcome at the Association of Amateur Fishermen. For information apply to Mr. Petrovikis, Commercial Bank, 15a, Aristotelous Street, Athens.

Sailing and canoeing: Enthusiasts should get in touch with the Hellenic Royal Yachting Club at the Bay of Munichia. Yacht owners will want to take advantage of the facilities offered to members of the club, where they may be admitted through a member. Regattas are organized during the summer in many ports and islands. *Swimming:* is particularly pleasant in the limpid, blue sea during the spring and fall seasons. There are good beaches all along the coast near Athens. Bathing facilities, however, are rather primitive, except for the new beach development of "Astir" at Glyfada, 30-minute drive from Athens. The waters of the Cyclades Islands, also those of Corfu and Rhodes, are ideal for spear fishing.

Climbing and hiking: There are several mountains in Greece for hiking and camping. Mount Parnes, near Athens, is particularly popular for week-end and holiday excursions. Excellent climbing is to be enjoyed on Mount Taygetos in the Peloponnes, Kithairon, Parnassus in central Greece and Mount Olympus in northern Greece. Contact the Hellenic Alpine Club (Tel. 614510).

TIME ... Seven hours later than United States Eastern Standard Time.

TIPPING ... A service charge is included in hotels (15 per cent) and restaurant bills (10 per cent). In addition you usually tip an extra 10 to 15 per cent.

TRANSPORTATION ... While plenty of buses, street cars and trolley buses are available in Athens, visitors who desire faster and more flexible transportation may obtain taxis or hire cars (5 to 7 seats) for trips both in and around Athens. The rates for a car range from 3 drs. per kilometer (about 10 cents per ⅔ miles), provided the car is used for return. One-way fares cost about 5 drs. per kilometer out of town.

WATER ... In Athens it is safe to drink. A variety of good mineral waters are also available.

WHAT TO BUY ... Dolls, in miniature national costumes; embroideries, in modern Greek and Byzantine designs; handwoven silk, linen and cotton fabrics, rugs from Soufli, Crete, Kastoria, Arachova and the islands of Myconos and Spetsae; handwoven striped skirts, bags and sandals; laces from Aegina, Hydra and Spetsae, small islands near Athens; earthenware with classic or modern designs from Keramikos, Akel, Icaros (Rhodes), Kioutahia, Rhodios. Also Cretan pottery with Minoan designs. Peasant jewelry, silver and gilded, a variety of silver and copper items from Jannina (Yaniotika); silver and gold ornaments from Rhodes; lapel woolen ornaments from Evzones and Tsarouhia.

All these articles are to be found in shops around Athen's Constitution Square. Antiques in Pandrossu, Argentine Republic, Kriezotou and Philhellinon Streets. Turkish sweetmeats stuffed with almonds or pistachios; Hymettus honey; dried raisins, white or black; sweet wines (Mavrodaphni is an excellent Greek port wine).

WHAT TO WEAR ... Greek women are very chic and beautifully dressed, so bring something smart for dinner and evening wear, but also plenty of lightweight cottons, because in summer it gets quite hot. Sports clothing and swim suit for the island resorts.

WHERE TO GO—SIGHTSEEING ...

Athens ... Whether you want to take motorcoach tours available through travel agencies or go sightseeing on your own, here is a brief checklist of principal places in Athens and the logical sequence of side trips according to the length of your visit. Most important, of course, is the fabulous Parthenon (448–437 B.C.), which stands like a crown on the rocky hill of the Acropolis, dominating the city. Also here is the famous Erechtheum with the Caryatids supporting the porch, the Temple of Niki (Wingless Victory), and the Acropolis Museum. North of the Acropolis is the Temple of Theseus (believed to be 437–432 B.C.), best-preserved temple of Athens' classic period. Other places of interest include the Temple of Zeus, the Chapel of St. George on Lycavittos Hill, the National Museum, the Benaki Museum (noted for its fine collection of Greek costumes), the Byzantine Museum and the Stadium. Also the Stoa of Attalos.

The ancient Theater of Epidavros (fourth century, B.C.) offers an interesting one-day tour from Athens through many ancient sites.

Delphi...About 100 miles northwest of Athens, is reached by motorcoach or train and car. Beautifully situated on the slopes of Mount Parnassus at an altitude of 2,000 feet, Delphi is world famous as the site of the Oracle of Pythia and contains excavated ruins of many ancient monuments, including the Temple of Apollo, the open-air theater, the Stadium, the Temple of Athena, and masterpieces of sculpture. Stop at the *Apollo*, *Castalia* or new *Tourist Hotel*.

Epidavrous...About 92 miles southwest of Athens; is noted for its Sanctuary of Asclepios, ancient health resort. During July, the "Epidavros Festival" takes place with excellent productions of classical Greek drama in this ancient theater. Also of interest are the Tholos, the Stadium and a well-preserved, open-air theater with remarkable acoustics. Hotels include the newly built *Amphitryon* and the *Bourtzi*.

Sounion...Is an hour and a half south from Athens through beautiful countryside. This is the site of the Temple of Poseidon set on a hill overlooking the Aegean Sea. There is a tourist pavillion and restaurant here.

Olympia...Is reached by diesel train or car about 200 miles west of Athens. Located in a beautiful serene area, it is an ancient religious center with the Stadium where the Olympic Games were held. The Hermes of Praxiteles is among the beautiful pieces of sculpture found in the local museum. The hotel is the *Spap*.

Rhodes...Praised by poets as the "Island of Roses" and "Bride of the Sun," Rhodes is the largest and most beautiful of the Dodecanese islands, about 1½ hours by air southeast of Athens. Immaculately clean with its blue-trimmed, white-plaster houses, imposing public buildings and pleasant parks, Rhodes offers for contrast in the old city, ruins and buildings covering the Hellenic, Roman and Byzantine periods. Most notable is the remarkably well-preserved medieval walled city of the Knights Hospitalers of St. John of Jerusalem, with fascinating castles and palaces, buildings of Byzantine and Turkish architecture. Of interest too, are the glowing municipal flower gardens and the Museum of Rhodes, which contains, among other interesting items, the famous Venus of Rhodes. Short excursions from the city take you to the ancient cities of Lindos, with its temple of Athena on its acropolis overlooking the sea; the Kamiros, whose excavations reveal life in ancient times in the same detail as Pompeii does of a later period; the valley of butterflies; and the Monastery of Philerimos, among other points of interest. Vacation facilities are excellent in Rhodes. The de luxe *Hotel des Roses* on the beach, the *Miramare* and the *Hotel Thermae* in an attractive setting are the best and most convenient. Prices are very moderate.

Corfu ... In beauty is second only to Rhodes among the many islands of Greece. Located in the Ionian Sea, Corfu is northwest of Athens less than 2 hours by air. It's a pitcuresque place with lots of charm and facilities for sports; ideal for sightseeing. The *Astir* and *Corfu Palace* are among several good hotels.

Corinth ... Locale of St. Paul's sermons and epistles to the Corinthians, is situated on the isthmus about two hours by road or train west of Athens. Here are remains of ancient Greek, Roman and Byzantine periods. Chief points of interest are the temple of Apollo, fountain of Peirene, the Agora, Odeum, Theater and Museum. Hotels *Belle Vue* and *Corinth*.

Mykonos ... Is reached by boat from Piraeus, the port of Athens, in about 8 hours. It is a beautiful island noted for its picturesque windmills, gleaming white, modest houses, and good bathing. One of the most fashionable Aegean Sea islands, it is a meeting place for artists in summer. Stay at the newly built *Leto Hotel*.

Crete ... Is an hour by air south of Athens, the mythical birthplace of Zeus and site of extensive remains of early Minoan civilization, including the beautiful Palace of Knossos (2nd millenium B.C.)

Delos ... An hour by caigue (or small native motor boat) from Mykonos, is believed to be Apollo's birthplace. The excavated former religious and commercial center reveals interesting temples, clubs, markets, a theater, and private homes with beautiful mosaics.

Mount Athos ... A peninsula in Northern Greece not easily accessible, is religious territory dotted with beautiful fourteenth-century monasteries, where thousands of monks live in medieval seclusion. No women visitors are allowed on Athos.

SOURCES OF FURTHER INFORMATION ... The National Tourist Office, 6 Venizelos Avenue, Athens, publishes maps and folders. Pan Am is in the same building (Tel. 612695). The Greek Tourist Office is at 505 Fifth Avenue, New York 17, N. Y.

ICELAND

This green island (9 hours by Pan Am from New York) offers an unusual and interesting experience for the traveler who will stop for even a few days. Nearly half the size (40,000 square miles) of the British Isles, Iceland is a land of frost and fire with numerous volcanoes, hot springs and glaciers, beautiful mountains and fjords. Most of the population of 166,831 is concentrated in a small area near Reykjavik, the capital city of 67,589 population. These highly literate people, direct descendants of the Vikings, are friendly and hospitable. English is taught in the schools, and readily understood.

The climate is warmer than you'd expect because of the gulf stream. Mean temperature is 52° in summer, 32° in winter, similar to Quebec. Best time to visit Iceland is June to September when you can enjoy the Midnight Sun and in late August, the Aurora Borealis or Northern Lights.

To visit Iceland you will need a passport and visa. Duty-free customs allowances include one bottle of liquor and 200 cigarettes. The krona is the monetary unit; 25.20 kronur equals $1, each krona being worth about 4 cents. Suggested shopping items are sheepskins, Icelandic handmade silver, ceramics and other handicrafts.

There are two good hotels in Reykjavik, the *Hotel Borg* and the *Hotel Gardur*. Rates are about $4.50 to $6 double. Hotels add a 15 per cent service charge and there is no tipping. Local food specialties include *hangikjot* (smoked lamb), and various forms of dried fish. *Brennivin,* something like aquavit, is the local drink.

Sightseeing in Reykjavik should include a visit to the University, the hot springs reservoirs from which the city is heated, and the Museums. Thirty-five miles from the capital is Thingvellir, where the parliament (Althing), the oldest in the world, was founded in 930.

Main attractions for visitors are the Gullfoss or "Golden Fall," the beautiful waterfall (about 70 miles from Reykjavik) and the Great Geyser, the famous hot springs which spouts a jet of boiling water nearly 200 feet in the air (one of the largest in the world).

The Iceland Tourist Bureau in Reykjavik arranges tours and taxis; buses and car hires are available. For the mountain climber there are several 6,000-foot ranges in addition to the widely known Mt. Hekla, still an active volcano with impressive views. Icelandic streams offer excellent fishing for trout and salmon.

Pan Am's office is at the Keflavik Airport (Tel. 5170). The Icelandic Consulate General is at 551 Fifth Avenue, New York 17, N. Y.

IRELAND

WEATHER IN DUBLIN—Lat. N53°20'—Alt. 30'

Temp.	JAN.	FEB.	MAR.	APR.	MAY	JUNE	JULY	AUG.	SEPT.	OCT.	NOV.	DEC.
Low	35°	34°	35°	37°	42°	47°	51°	50°	46°	41°	38°	35°
High	46°	47°	49°	53°	58°	64°	66°	65°	62°	55°	50°	47°
Average	41°	41°	42°	45°	50°	56°	59°	58°	54°	48°	44°	41°
Days of Rain	21	18	19	17	16	15	18	19	16	19	19	21

LOCATION ... The Republic of Ireland is situated to the west of Great Britain. The six northeastern counties of the island which form Northern Ireland are covered under **GREAT BRITAIN.**

CHARACTERISTICS ... Ireland, with its castles, lakes, greenness, and soft-voiced people will delight you. Dublin is a charming city, full of interesting things to see. And who can resist the thought of seeing Donegal, the Yeats country, Connemara, Killarney and the River Shannon? The people are hospitable, the food good. It's a perfect place for a quiet vacation with some good fishing, inexpensive hunting, wonderful golf, and fine motoring.

POPULATION ... The total population of the island is 4,311,000, a few thousand greater than the population of Philadelphia and Los Angeles combined.

SIZE ... 32,585 square miles, about the size of Maine. It is said that no part of Ireland is more than 70 miles from the sea.

CAPITAL ... Dublin is the capital with a population of 522,183; it is almost as large as Indianapolis.

GOVERNMENT ... The southern twenty-six counties of the island have an independent, republican type of government.

HOW TO GET THERE ... By Clipper, through-plane service to Shannon, about 11 hours from New York, 9 hours from Boston, 13 hours from Chicago via Detroit. Shuttle service from Shannon airport to Dublin. By ship, about 5 days.

ACCOMMODATIONS ... Top hotel space is very limited, particularly in July-August. True, also at other times, as when the races are nearby, or at Christmas, Easter or Whitsuntide. Make reservations well in advance. Rooms with private bath are found only in the best areas. Their rates are about $6.50 single during peak season. Usually rates include room and a full Irish breakfast. Among the best (all $6.40) are the *Royal Hibernian;* the smart up-to-date *Gresham;* the *Shelbourne,* fine, old-fashioned atmosphere; the *Russell;* and the *Central, Clarence, Jury's,* and the *Wicklow* are slightly less expensive. There are many comfortable guest houses at slightly lower rates. Irish tourist offices have complete lists of hotels.

ARTS ... The National Museum, on Kildare Street, with its collections of Irish antiquities from Stone Age onward is world famous. See the museum's unique hoard of Bronze Age gold ornaments and priceless treasures of Early Christian metalwork. Nearby, the National Gallery in Leinster Lawn, facing Merrion Square, within easy reach of all parts of town, has as fine a collection of old masters as can be found anywhere outside of London. Also fine works by Rembrandt, Rubens, good examples of Italian school, a wonderful Goya, "Spanish Woman"; also the Hogarth works and many famous Irish painters: Barry, O'Connor, Orpen, and two Hones, among others. National Portrait Gallery is under same roof. Open every day, free. The Municipal Gallery of Modern Art, in a fine old Georgian mansion on Parnell Square, is a must. Fine works of Continental painters, English and especially Irish, such as Hone, Orpen, G. F. Kelly, Shannon, Fisher, Yeats and George Russell. Important works by the great Irish sculptor, Andrew O'Connor. The Heraldic Museum in Dublin Castle where family trees are traced is the only one of its kind.

BALLET ... British repertory companies, International and Royal Ballet Companies, grand opera and musical comedy companies. Season: all year round.

BANKS ... American Express Company, 116 Grafton Street, Thomas Cook & Son, 118 Grafton Street; Bank of Ireland; the Hibernian Bank; the National Bank; Munster and Leinster Bank and the Royal Bank are the principal banks in Dublin. All have sub-offices throughout the city; all have their head offices in College Green or Dame Street.

CALENDAR OF HOLIDAYS ... Good Friday, Easter, Whitsuntide, St. Patrick's Day, August Monday, Christmas Day and December 26. Local towns may be closed on afternoon of big local race-days. Bank holidays. *An Tostal* is a two-week period following the Dublin Spring Show in late spring, a time of splendid pageantry depicting the cultural, social and industrial life of the young Republic including the Dublin International Festival and Cork Film Week. The Wexford Festival is in October.

CIGARETTES AND TOBACCO ... Irish and American tobacco and cigarettes are available. Of course, Irish pipes (especially good, Peterson's Dublin). Good cigars are expensive.

CLIMATE ... Green Ireland has no extremes of temperature.

Gulf stream makes for mild weather, but with some rain. Best months to visit Ireland are April to September.

CLUBS...P.E.N. Club, Rotary Club, Lions Club, Variety Club, Skal Club, Publicity Club, Royal Dublin Society, and sundry commercial clubs.

COMMON COURTESIES AND LOCAL CUSTOMS...Same courtesies prevail as in America with regard to sending and acknowledgment of gifts, invitations, etc. Christmas is the biggest religious and civic festival of the year; on March 17 the Shamrock is worn and sent to friends in other countries to commemorate the feast of Ireland's patron, Saint Patrick.

COMMUNICATIONS...Cables, transatlantic phones.

CURRENCY...The monetary unit is the pound, worth $2.80. The dollar is usually accepted across the counter.

CUSTOMS REGULATIONS AND DOCUMENTS REQUIRED FOR UNITED STATES CITIZENS...An American needs his passport, but no visa. You may bring in, duty free 1,000 cigarettes, 200 cigars or 2½ lbs. of tobacco, ½ pint of perfume, $56 worth of gifts, only £10, United Kingdom notes (unless coming from Britain), any amount of dollars and Irish currency. You may take no more money out than you bring in. There are no camera or film restrictions.

DRUG STORES...Same as at home, except no meals.

ELECTRIC CURRENTS...220 volts, 50 cycles, A.C. Voltage of 110 is also available at first-class hotels.

FAUNA...Thoroughbred race horses and stud horses and dogs are famous; also all types of sporting and domestic animals indigenous to Western European countries.

FLORA...Plant life, vegetation, trees, shrubs and flowers indigenous to the British Isles, rose, lily, chrysanthemum, nasturtium, etc. Sub-tropical plants in the west.

FOOD...Irish food, plentiful in supply, is probably closest to American food to be found anywhere outside the United States. The milk is fine, but not pasteurized everywhere. As in Argentina, roast beef and steaks are famous and inexpensive. Hams and bacon, traditionally famous, and rich cream, eggs and all kinds of vegetables are readily available. Specialties include Dublin Bay prawns, pheasant and grouse. Game and local cheese are a feature in rural towns.

GAMBLING...More than 100 race meets, many of two- or three-day duration, greyhound night racing plentiful. Famous Irish sweepstakes, several times each year, based on big English classic races, prizes running to thousands of dollars.

LANGUAGE...English is spoken all over Ireland and accepted as the language of the country. In some outlying rural and coastal areas, however, there are districts where the Irish language (Gaelic) is spoken.

LAUNDRY AND DRY CLEANING...Laundry service is fast, clean. Two-day service. One day on dry cleaning.

LIQUOR...There is excellent Irish whisky. Old-fashioned, pot distilled with a barley base, it is not so smoky as Scotch. After dinner have an Irish Mist—Ireland's legendary liqueur—or an Irish Coffee. Dublin's famous Guinness stout, as you know, is darker, stronger, than Continental beers. For residents, the liquor restrictions are slightly complicated, but foreign visitors registered at hotels may buy a drink at any reasonable time. Prices are lower than at home, about 30 cents a drink, including Scotch.

MEDICAL FACILITIES ... Excellent.

MOTION PICTURES ... The Irish are among the greatest Hollywood fans in all Europe; cinemas with good pictures abound. In Dublin some of the leading cinemas, the *Savoy, Carlton, Capital, Metropole* and *Adelphi,* are all on O'Connell Street, the *Grafton* on Grafton Street, and the *Regal Rooms Cinema* and *Theater Royal* on Hawkins Street.

MUSIC ... Since the day in 1742 that saw the first performance anywhere of Handel's *Messiah* (at Dublin's Music Hall in Fishamble Street), the town has had a high standard of musical taste. There is the Trinity College Choral Society, the Royal Irish Academy of Music, and the *Feis Ceoil* (Music Festival which first produced John McCormack), along with the Palestrina Choir in the Pro-Cathedral; and the Hibernian Catch Club, oldest male-voice choral society anywhere, founded in 1680. Concerts with famous conductors and Radio Eireann Symphony Orchestra concerts during the winter in Dublin.

NIGHT CLUBS AND CABARETS ... Night clubs and cabarets are missing here. Ballrooms are found in the better hotels, but the Irish wit, gaiety and conversation are at their best in such world-famous pubs as the *Davey Byrnes, The Pearl* and *The Palace.* Irish coffee, a wineglass of black coffee with Irish liqueur whisky, plus fresh thick cream, makes listening at such places as *Neary's* (off Grafton Street) a treat not easily forgotten. Other good places, but more of the exclusive lounge bar type, are *The Shelbourne, The Buttery, Gresham, Dolphin, Russell, Red Bank* and *Wicklow.*

PHOTOGRAPHY ... Tourists can buy black-and-white still and movie film in Dublin, Cork, Galway, etc.; also color film, cameras and all photo equipment. Prices, particularly of cameras, are the most inexpensive in Europe. Principal still-camera and movie-camera equipment and film-developing dealers in Dublin are: Dixon and Hempenstall, Grafton Street; Roche's, O'Connell Street; Sight and Sound Equipments, Lower Abbey Street; Slattery's, Upper O'Connell Street at Parnell Street.

RELIGION ... Catholic: the Pro-Cathedral, Marlborough Street; Catholic University, St. Stephen's Green; Augustinian Church, Thomas Street; Carmelite Church, Whitefriars Street; Dominican Church, Lower Dominick Street; Franciscan Church, Church Street; Jesuit Church, Upper Gardiner Street; Passionist Church, Mount Argus, Harold's Cross; St. Patrick's Cathedral; Christ Church Cathedral; Dublin University Chapel; St. Andrews, St. Andrew Street; St. Georges, Temple Street. Church of Ireland (Episcopal). There are several Presbyterian churches, one being Abbey Church in Parnell Square, and several churches of Methodist and other Protestant denominations. Synagogue, Dolphin's Barn, South Circular Road.

RESTAURANTS ... Among the best Dublin restaurants you will find the *Moira,* the *Wicklow,* the celebrated *Jammet's,* considered an expensive city eating place but even here the moderate prices will astonish you; try the *Dolphin,* Essex Street, where fine steaks and chops are under a dollar. Leading hotel restaurants, such as the *Russell, Royal Hibernian* and *Gresham,* all have excellent service and food. So has the *Red Bank,* D'Olier Street, with a good oyster and seafood bar.

SHOPS AND STORES ... Most of the city's smart shops are in the Grafton Street area. For the ladies Sybil Connolly's, Brown Thomas and Company, Clodagh's, Irene Gilbert's, Switzer's, Walpole's. For the men, Kevin and Howlin for tweeds, Horton and Kelly's for tailoring. At Shannon, the customs-free airport, there is an international trading market, a well stocked souvenir shop with extremely low prices.

SPECTATOR SPORTS ... More than sixty racecourses in the country. Phoenix Park, Curragh, national stud headquarters, Punchestown and Leopardstown are a few that are near Dublin. Greyhound racing six nights a week from March to October. Hockey, cricket, soccer, Gaelic football, hurling, bicycle racing, tennis matches, automobile and motor-car racing, polo, all can be seen in and around Dublin. The Horse Show held in August draws visitors from all over the world. The All-Ireland Hurling and Football finals at Croke Park draw huge local crowds every September. Hurdle racing and steeplechases all winter. Big Irish Grand National in spring, usually Easter Monday, at nearby Fairyhouse course. Go out and see one of the famous Hunt Meets, such as the Meath or the South County Dublin Harriers, even if you don't ride. There are boxing matches which have a big local following, stadium matches, basketball, billiard matches. The annual yacht regatta, at Dun Loaghaire, is a great event. Girls hurling (Camogie, twelve to a side) play in Phoenix Park. Watch or join the players at old-fashioned bowls, at one of the many park greens.

SPORTS ... There are more than twenty golf courses in the neighborhood of Dublin, some with world-wide reputations, other courses all over Ireland. Golf is almost as popular here as in Scotland. Among the best, adjacent to Dublin: Royal Dublin (Dollymount and Portmarnock, both 18-hole championship ocurses), seaside, very scenic; Woodbrook, another 18-hole course (seaside), licensed clubhouse, professional instructors available. Special Dublin trains stop right at the course. Some of the better-known inland courses are Castle, Clontarf, the Hermitage and Milltown.

As for fishing, a license for salmon or sea trout for single line and rod costs $5.60, slightly more if used in more than one district. No license for brown trout. The River Liffey has good game fishing right near Dublin, open season from mid-February to mid-October. All over Ireland there is good sport; pike, brown and sea trout and off-coast sea fishing. It's very good in August and September, when mackerel fishing is also at its best. Best sea-trout fisheries are along the west coast, Connemara, Donegal, and Kerry. Fishing is free on the three lakes of Killarney, excellent for both salmon and trout. There are 23 fishery districts in Eire. Licenses can be obtained from the clerk in the respective district, also from local hotel proprietors and tackle agents. Consult Irish Tourist Association on fishing. Dun Laoghaire, near Dublin, is headquarters for Irish yachtsmen; the Wicklow Regatta in August is the big annual event for Irish boating enthusiasts.

THEATERS ... Dublin is the home of the famous Abbey Players. There are the Gate, Gaiety, Olympia and several smaller theaters.

TIME ... Five hours later than United States Eastern Standard Time.

TIPPING ... There is a service charge added to some hotel bills of about 10 to 15 per cent. Tip about 15 per cent in restaurants if the bill is under 10 shillings, a shilling for a bell boy, a doorman. For taxi men, a shilling, or say about 15 per cent of the fare.

TRANSPORTATION ... Train service good. Taxis cheap. One should tip well. Bus service everywhere is clean and cheap. Drive-yourself cars are available in larger towns.

WATER ... Water is good to drink.

WHAT TO BUY ... Hand-woven tweeds for both men and women, suits, topcoats, skirts, lace, linen, fine whisky, Peterson pipes, walking sticks. For antiques, fine old Irish Waterford glass, old silver, a great deal of which is superior to English of the same period. You may do better to bring your tweed goods home with you to be tailored. Good handmade shoes for men in Dublin. Wonderful fisherman sweaters from County Donegal.

WHAT TO WEAR ... Medium-weight clothes and sports clothes are fine for daytime wear. Good walking shoes are essential. You really don't need evening clothes. You'll need a warm topcoat for winter touring, or buy one there. Sportsmen will need golf and fishing togs. You'll need a raincoat, but you can buy fine ones there.

WHERE TO GO SIGHTSEEING ...

Dublin ... Dublin is the natural headquarters for all visitors to Ireland. It is the capital of the Republic of Ireland and the biggest port. It is a city of wide streets, lovely squares and parks, and wonderful examples of eighteenth-century Georgian architecture. There are houses and buildings by Gandon, Cassels and Johnston, who were among the greatest of eighteenth-century architects. Ceilings by Angelica Kauffmann and mantlepieces by Bossi are famous features of some of these magnificent old buildings. See Mansion House (Dawson Street), the Merrion Square home of Daniel O'Connell. Visit Ely Place, Fitzwilliam Place and St. Stephen's Green. Robert Emmett's house is on the western side and the church of the Catholic University erected by Cardinal Newman faces the square too. Visit Grafton Street; Percy Bysshe Shelley lived at No. 17, Richard Brinsley Sheridan stayed at No. 79, and Tom Moore and the Duke of Wellington attended Samuel Shyte's famous school. The provost's house in the grounds of Trinity College is impressive. O'Connell Street, the finest

Ross Castle is one of the famous landmarks in Killarney, 100 miles from Cork in southwest Ireland.

thoroughfare in Dublin, runs north from the river. See the Nelson Pillar, the O'Connell Monument. The General Post Office near the Pillar was headquarters of the Irish Volunteers during their Easter Rising. Parnell Square has the Municipal Gallery of Modern Art, the Gaelic League and the Rotunda. Here, too, are the Gate Theater, the Rotunda Hospital. See the birthplace of George Bernard Shaw at 33 Synge Street, and that of James Joyce at No. 41. Visit St. Patrick's and Christ Church Cathedral. The latter dates back to Norman times; the former to 1213 A.D. The Guinness brewery, one of the world's largest, is worth a visit. Take a look at Trinity College, the Custom House, the National Library. Spend some time in Phoenix Park, one of the finest in the world, containing a race course, zoo, sports grounds, the official residence of the President, the American Embassy, flower gardens, a lake and the tallest obelisk in the world—the Wellington Monument.

Seven miles south of the city is Dun Laoghaire, with a fine harbor and steamer service to Holyhead. It is a marine playground for all of Dublin with good swimming. The old village of Dalkey, a mile or so beyond, affords a magnificent view of the bay. Bray, 4 miles farther south, is a seaside resort with a promenade and all other resort features. To the north there are picturesque seaside villages of Howth, Skerries, Rush, Lusk, and others.

Basic Side Tours ... There are daily coach tours to other interesting and picturesque spots within a 30-mile radius of Dublin. From Shannon airport there are 3-day all inclusive luxury coach tours to Killarney and/or Connemara. You can arrange 6- and 9-day tours out of Dublin before you leave home. Or make your decision in Dublin. You may also hire a car with or without driver. A drive-yourself tour of 600 miles in, say, 7 days, is about $50, not including petrol. Bicycling is another fascinating way to cover Ireland. There are Youth Hostels and inns everywhere. A clockwise tour of the island is one of the best ways to see everything there is. On the way from Dublin to Cork you see the famous round towers, the Vale of Avoca, made famous by Thomas Moore. The *Fountain Hotel,* here, is good. The next county is Wexford, where you will see Johnstown Castle. The Saltee Islands, famous bird sanctuary, are off the coast. Waterford comes next, then the resort of Tramore, where there is a race meet every August. In Tipperary County, known to everyone, is the great rock of Cashel. In Cashel, the royal city of Ancient Ireland, stands the remains of King Cormac's Chapel, a must for all visitors.

Cork ... the third city in Ireland, on the river Lee, has excellent modern hotels. Five miles away is Blarney Castle with the famous stone. Down the river about 16 miles is Cobh (formerly Queenstown), the country's main port. Visit St. Colman's Cathedral. When you get to Killarney, the lakes, the mountains and the charm of it all will make you want to stay a few days. The *Great Southern Hotel* and *Lake Hotel* are good. Take some jaunting-car trips and boat trips up the lakes. Visit Ross Castle.

Galway ... is the springboard for sightseeing in western Ireland. Here you'll find rugged coast, mountains and fine salmon fishing. Centered about Galway City are dozens of old castles. shooting lodges and country houses which have been converted into hotels and inns. One of the finest is Ashford Castle, Cong.

A 30-mile steamer trip to the Aran Islands, where only Gaelic is spoken, is most rewarding. Allow a full day for this.

Westport ... is to the north, where you'll see Croagh Patrick, the Holy Mountain of St. Patrick, which is climbed by thousands on the last Sunday of July. The entire west of Ireland is the fisherman's delight. Lough Corrib in Connemara, Leenane, Ballinahinch, Kylemore and Recess are known to fishermen the world over. In County Mayo are many lakes in which fish abound. At certain hotels fishing privileges are available to guests. Continuing past Sligo and Donegal into Northern Ireland, visit Derry on the river Foyle. Nearby is Castlerock with its championship golf course.

NOTE: Northern Ireland is a part of Great Britain and is completely separate from the Republic of Ireland described here. Such facts as Customs Regulations and Calendar of Holidays for Northern Ireland coincide closely with those of GREAT BRITAIN, *see* page 85. For sightseeing in Northern Ireland, *see* page 97.

SOURCES OF FURTHER INFORMATION ... The Irish Tourist Association has offices in London, Paris, Chicago, New York (33 East 50th Street), and principal cities in Ireland. The address in Dublin is 15 Upper O'Connell Street. The American Embassy is at 15 Merrion Square. Information also at Pan American's office, 35 Westmoreland Street (Tel. 79011/2).

ITALY

WEATHER IN ROME—Lat. N41°54′—Alt. 95′

Temp.	JAN.	FEB.	MAR.	APR.	MAY	JUNE	JULY	AUG.	SEPT.	OCT.	NOV.	DEC.
Low	38°	40°	44°	49°	54°	61°	66°	65°	61°	54°	46°	40°
High	52°	55°	59°	66°	73°	81°	87°	86°	80°	70°	60°	53°
Average	44°	48°	52°	58°	64°	71°	77°	76°	71°	62°	53°	47°
Days of Rain	10	10	9	9	8	5	2	3	6	11	12	12

LOCATION . . . Italy occupies the familiar boot-shaped peninsula extending from the Alps into the Mediterranean Sea.

CHARACTERISTICS . . . Italy has never been so gay, so full of visitors. You can play in Rome or Florence or Capri, or relax in Sicily and in some of the charming little towns along the Italian Riviera. The wonders of Rome are well known. The history of the modern world has roots here. You will have missed something if you don't wander around the Colosseum, or see the Sistine Chapel. Rome is noisy, Latin, and very smart these days. The tourist receives wonderful treatment from everybody; in the hotels, in the shops, in the streets; even policemen are English-speaking.

POPULATION . . . Nearly 49,000,000, a few million more than France.

SIZE . . . 760 miles long and 100 to 150 miles wide, Italy's area is 116,319 square miles, roughly the size of New Mexico.

CAPITAL . . . Rome, estimated population 2,000,000, about the size of Detroit.

GOVERNMENT . . . Italy is a Republic in which all major political parties participate.

HOW TO GET THERE . . . By Pan American Jet Clipper via Paris to Rome, about 11 hours from New York; 18 hours via Lisbon, Barcelona and Nice. By ship to Naples or Genoa, 8 to 14 days.

ACCOMMODATIONS . . . The large Italian cities offer hotels for every taste and purse. During most of the year advance reservations are a must as demand far exceeds capacity. In Rome de luxe hotels are the *Ambassador, Bernini Bristol, Excelsior, Flora, Grand,* and the *Hassler*. Rate for single room with bath about $17 American plan, including service and taxes. Without meals, about $9. First class hotels include the *Continentale, De la Ville, Eden, Eliseo, Majestic, Massimo D'Azeglio, Mediterraneo, Quirinale, Residence Palace, Savoy* and others. A single room runs about $12.50 with meals; $6.50 without. Second-class hotels charge about $9 and $4.50 respectively. Rooms without private bath are much more reasonable, usually have hot and cold running water. An extra daily charge is made for heating from about Nov. 15 through Mar. 15. Categories for hotels are fixed each year by law and approved rates are posted or available on request. During the thrift season (Nov. 1-Mar. 1) a 25% discount from maximum rates is allowed. Not to be overlooked, especially for a stay of 3 days or longer, are the many pleasant and inexpensive *pensioni,* or private lodging houses. There is no exact U.S. counterpart for the *pensioni,* some of which offer service and facilities equal to hotels, plus a congenial and less impersonal atmosphere. The *Bellavista Milton, Roxy, Santa Caterina, Tea, Texas, Villa Borghese* and *Villa Waldorf* are among those centrally located. Rates for full *pensione,* taxes, service and all meals included, range between $5.50 and $9; it is usually possible to arrange for half *pensione:* breakfast and one other meal if preferred. Outside the main cities, new hotels are gradually beginning to appear in places of tourist interest. Foremost is the *Jolly Hotel* chain, with about 40 well-equipped reasonable new hotels scattered through Italy, Sicily and Sardinia.

ARTS ... Italy is the art lover's paradise. Museum after museum is filled with famous paintings and sculpture, tapestries, gold and jewels, ceramics. In the churches and palaces where Raphael, Michelangelo, Titian and the other great artists actually worked, you'll see their masterpieces in the original settings. Statues, mosaics and other treasures of the ancient Greeks and Romans are superbly displayed in the Lateran Museums, the National Museum (Baths of Diocletian), and the Capitoline Museums where "The Dying Gaul" and the famous Capitoline Venus are to be found. The Vatican Museums house a vast collection of the art of many ages and many peoples, the Sistine Chapel with Michelangelo's magnificent painting of the Creation, the Borgia Apartments and the frescoed Rooms of Raphael. The fascinating art of the Etruscans fills Rome's stately Villa Giulia and the Etruscan Museum in Florence. From the Pompeiian Rooms in the Naples Museum to the world-renowned painting of the Last Supper by Leonardo in Milan, there is hardly a town in all of Italy that cannot boast at least one priceless work of art.

The Uffizi Gallery in Florence, said to be the world's greatest, the Pitti Palace, the town hall-museums of Sienna and Perugia, the Doge's Palace and Academy Gallery in Venice are among the sights not to be missed.

BALLET ... The Rome Opera House has its own ballet company, as does La Scala in Milan, appearing in Florence, too. Foreign companies appear occasionally. The International Ballet Festival, held in July at Nervi on the Riviera very near Genoa, features outdoor performances by leading companies in a superb setting.

BANKS...In Rome, the Banca del Lavoro, near PAA's office, represents the major U.S. banks. Others are the Bank of America and Italy, Largo Tritone; American Express, Piazza di Spagna 38; Thos. Cook, Via Veneto 9–11. Banks and most hotel cashiers cash travelers checks at the official rate minus bank charges.

CALENDAR OF HOLIDAYS...National holidays are January 1, April 25, May 1, June 2, November 4; religious holidays January 6, March 19, Easter Monday, Ascension Day and Corpus Domini, June 29, August 15, November 1, December 8, 25 and 26. Detailed lists of events are available. See SOURCES OF FURTHER INFORMATION.

CIGARETTES AND TOBACCO...American cigarettes cost about 56 cents per pack. Take in as many as you are allowed. (*See* CUSTOMS REGULATIONS.)

CLIMATE...Rome is pleasant the year round, but there is a rainy season during the winter months. April to November are months usually filled with sunny, warm days, which by midsummer turn quite hot. Climate in the rest of Italy varies from very warm to freezing. So it depends on where you go and at which time of the year.

CLUBS...Lions Club and Rotary International.

COMMON COURTESIES AND LOCAL CUSTOMS...Dinner hour is late and so are opera and theater performances. The chaperone is still in good standing. When visiting churches, men wear coats; women should have a head covering, wear stockings and dresses with sleeves. Never go to a church in slacks. For an audience with the Pope, women must wear dark, long-sleeved, high-neck dresses or a suit, a hat or veil. Men should wear dark suits. If you are not a Catholic, you need not genuflect or kiss the Pope's ring, behavior which is mandatory for Catholics. Business closes down at 1:00 P.M., reopens about 4:00. Offices are open until 7:00.

COMMUNICATIONS...Telephone service is not as good as in America; for a long-distance call, one must make a reservation in advance. Telephone, cable, radio and mailing services are available in every hotel and in the various phone and post offices. Airmail rates for letters to the United States are lire 120, for postal cards lire 95. It saves time to let the porter or concierge send your cables.

CURRENCY...The monetary unit of Italy is the lira, worth about 625 to the dollar. For exchange, consult banks or your concierge and avoid sidewalk money changers. Italy has legalized operation of the *cambio* or authorized private exchange office.

CUSTOMS REGULATIONS AND DOCUMENTS NEEDED FOR UNITED STATES CITIZENS...You'll need a passport, no visa. Vaccination certificate for re-entry to the United States. You may bring unlimited dollars and lire. About 400 cigarettes, or 500 grams tobacco, 2 open bottles of liquor. No restriction on food or liquor when leaving. But you may take out no more than 30,000 lire.

One still camera with 5 rolls of film, and one movie camera with two rolls duty free. No restriction on portable radios if for temporary import only.

DRUG STORES ... Most American products are available in the bigger *farmacie,* which are roughly similar to the American drug stores. The *profumerie,* or perfume shops, carry familiar cosmetics and toiletries as well as perfume and souvenirs.

ELECTRIC CURRENT ... Italy is in the process of standardizing its current. Large areas already have 110–120 volts, A.C., others have 150–155 volts or some other current. However, American-made electric appliances are very popular in Italy, and everywhere one is able to purchase small transformers or rectifiers good for the local type of current. Plugs have prongs that are round, not flat. Therefore a converter plug is needed.

FOOD ... *Pasta,* of course, is the national staple; and this means not only spaghetti and ravioli but *pasta* of all sorts in an amazing variety of sizes and shapes. Despite everything you've heard, you won't find much garlic in typical Italian food. There are innumerable *risotto,* or rice, dishes mixed with peppers, chicken, meat, fish, onions and spices. *Pizza,* of course, is famous. This is a baked cheese and tomato open-faced pie. *Antipasto,* the Italian hors d'oeuvres, is much the same in Rome as at home. Veal is a favorite meat and *scaloppine* is familiar to everyone. The fruits, vegetables and salads are excellent. Beef is generally good. *Polenta,* a favorite in northern Italy, is worth trying. This is a porridgey dish of corn meal served most in native restaurants in the country. The northern Italians cook in butter. In the south they prefer oil. Italian cooking is rich, saucy and spicy and infinitely varied, so take it easy the first few days. Romans eat far more than Americans, especially at lunch.

Caffè espresso is the bitter, strong coffee especially brewed in *espresso* machines, Rube Goldberg contraptions which use forced, compressed steam to make the coffee. Milk is available in any milk shop, hotel, restaurant.

GAMBLING ... There are Casinos at Venice, San Remo, St. Vincent (Aosta Valley) and at Campione near Como. Pari-mutuel betting at horse racing, trotting and dog tracks. Weekly Government-run lotteries, too.

LANGUAGE ... You won't need to know Italian to get around easily in Rome or in the other principal tourist centers.

LAUNDRY AND DRY CLEANING ... Laundry is wonderful and fast; Italian laundresses do careful pressing on lingerie and shirts. It is advisable to select your dry cleaner carefully. Dry-cleaning facilities are available in all hotels or in dry-cleaning shops. The prices are somewhat higher than in the States. Be sure to inquire about the available delivery time before leaving your things.

LIQUOR ... Italian wines are famous and good. Best known are Chianti, Frascati and Soave. Valpolicella wine is also good. There are many brands of each kind. Gin and brandy are favorite hard liquors. But one must acquire a taste for Italian brandy. Best are

Buton Vecchia Romagna and Sarti. Strega is a native cordial which has quite a bite. The average price for a bottle of good wine is about $1 in a shop. In a restaurant or hotel, of course, one must add the service. Any popular American drink is available in all bars, restaurants and first-class hotels. You can get excellent Martinis in Rome. American whisky and Scotch are available at New York prices.

MEDICAL FACILITIES ... There are many English-speaking doctors and good hospitals. Rome has the Salvator Mundi International Hospital with American-trained staff.

MOTION PICTURES ... Most are in Italian but the *Fiammetta* and the *Acrobaleno* in Rome show exclusively English or French films in their original versions.

Rome has become a second Hollywood. In the street and in famous restaurants and night clubs you'll run across many American actors and actresses.

MUSIC ... In this land of Verdi, Puccini, Rossini and Mascagni, opera is a gala occasion: you'll hear wonderful music and see elegant audiences at their gayest during the winter season at Naples' San Carlo, in Rome, or at famed La Scala in Milan. In Rome there is open-air opera during July and August in the matchless setting of the Baths of Caracalla and frequent concerts in the Basilica of Massenzio, right in the heart of the Roman Forum. Also of interest are Musical May in Florence, the International Music Festival in Venice in September, outdoor opera seasons at the Campi Flegrei near Naples and in the Amphitheater at Verona, and the excellent orchestral and chamber concerts and recitals by world-famous soloists in principal cities during the fall and winter season.

NIGHT CLUBS AND CABARETS ... From October until the beginning of June, Rome's smartest clubs are the *Cabala* (*Hostaria dell'Orso*), the *Open Gate, Scheherazade, Bricktop's* and the *Jicky Club*. In summer nightlife goes outdoors, to the *Belvedere delle Rose* out on the Via Cassia, the *Villa dei Cesari*, the *Casina delle Rose* in the Borghese Gardens, or to dine and dance on the rooftops of the Eliseo, Ambassadors or Residence Palace hotels.

PHOTOGRAPHY ... Any photographic material is available in every big town. Prices are expensive. Film-developing facilities are available everywhere. Time for developing is reasonable, quality good. Don't mail your films from Italy. Take them out with you or go to Kodak S.p.A., Via Nazionale, 26–27, Rome; in Milan, Via Vittor Pisani, 16; or in Naples, 6–7 Via Marritima.

RELIGION ... Rome, needless to say, is Catholic and is filled with magnificent churches. The church set aside for American Catholics is Santa Susanna, near the Grand Hotel. Other churches are the American Church (Episcopal) on Via Nazionale, the English Church on Via Babuino, other Protestant churches, and synagogues.

RESTAURANTS ... No two Romans, much less visitors, will agree on restaurants. However, one should try *Passetto's*, the *Biblioteca del Valle, Capriccio's, George's* and for the unique experience of dining in an authentic ancient Roman setting—*Da Pancrazio,*

Taverna Ulpia or Pompeiian-decorated *Apuleius* on the Aventine Hill. Don't miss the *Hostaria dell'Orso*. It's reputed to have been the hotel where Dante stayed in the 13th Century; the food is epicurean. Try all three *Alfredo's*. There are countless little restaurants and *trattorias*, especially in the old parts of Rome, that are well worth exploring.

Hamburgers, ham and eggs and other American fare can be found in American style luncheonettes and restaurants such as *Jerry's*, the *California*, the *Colony* and the *New Madison House* in the PAA building.

Outdoor cafes are all over, since the Roman drinks innumerable small cups of *expresso* coffee. Try *Doney's* and *Rosati's* on Via Veneto for a coffee, ice cream or cocktails, and watch the people stream by.

In summer you'll dine outdoors on the Hassler Roof, at *La Cisterna*, *Romolo* or *Galeassi* in Trastevere, at *Tre Scalini* on Piazza Navona, the most beautiful square in Rome, and at *Palazzi*, the magnificent villa of Mussolini's mistress, Clara Petacci, about 20 minutes from the center by taxi and overlooking all of Rome.

In Rome and in all of Italy eating is a fine art and not to be hurried, so plan to take it leisurely and enjoy yourself. The price for a meal in a restaurant goes from a minimum of $1.50 to a maximum of about $6. Service is usually included in the check.

SHOPS AND STORES . . . The main shopping center is formed by Via Condotti, Rome's Bond Street, Via Frattina, Piazza di Spagna and Via Sistina. Specialty shops in this area disply a mouth-watering array of original, beautifully made gifts, clothing, accessories and household articles (*See* WHAT TO BUY). English is spoken everywhere. Stores close at 1.00 P.M., reopen at 4:00 until 7:30 P.M.

The closest thing to the American kind of department stores in Rome are the Rinascente, Piazza Colonna, and CIM, Via XX Settembre, but they are far smaller than those in America. Prices are reasonable. Rome is a fairly expensive European city but always less so than Paris.

SPECTATOR SPORTS . . . Horse shows, football, yacht races, speedboats tests, motorcycle races, golf, tennis tourneys, water polo. There are several race tracks near Rome for both flat racing and trotting races.

SPORTS . . . There are fine beaches for swimming throughout Italy. Best beach resort near Rome is Fregene. There is skiing at Terminillo, 1½ hour drive from Rome. (Also in Taormina, Sicily, and of course in the Dolomites.) You can fish at Rieti, near Terminillo, in the small resort near Naples, throughout the Apennines and Dolomites, and all along the Italian Riviera. Marvelous swimming and skin diving there, too. There are many good golf courses and tennis courts wherever you go in Italy. The Rome Golf Course at Acquasanta is open the year round and may be reached by streetcar. There is a bar and restaurant on the grounds.

THEATERS . . . Many theaters in Rome and Milan. Plays are all in Italian. Performance time is at 9:00 P.M. The prices are from

$2 to $5 per ticket. Occasionally foreign theater companies, performing in English or French, visit Rome and Milan, Florence and Naples.

TIME ... Six hours later than U.S. Eastern Standard Time. No daylight saving time observed.

TIPPING ... The normal tip is 10 per cent. Everybody gets tipped—from waiter and porter to taxi driver and usher, even though a service charge is included on your bill.

TRANSPORTATION ... There are streetcars and buses in Rome, and many taxis. You pay exactly what the meter reads, plus a small tip. Until 10:00 P.M. after which there is a supplementary charge of 150 lire—over the meter reading. Motor buses are modern and excellent. Auto rentals are available at about $12 a day. Trains are good first and second class, especially first- and second-class sleepers.

WATER ... Safe to drink in all important towns of Italy. All kinds of bottled mineral waters are available.

WHAT TO BUY ... Tortoise shell, amber, cameos, silver, handbags, men's ties, Florentine leather, straw and embroidery, olivewood boxes, gloves. Borsalino hats, Italian silks, custom-made shirts for men and blouses for women. Italian tailors are wonderful, too. Rosaries, crosses and religious statuary abound in Rome and some of them are beautiful. Perfumes and liquor are not good buys in Italy. Don't buy fountain pens from street vendors. Avoid the antique and old painting racket. You'll get hooked.

High fashion for women has become very important in Italy. There are lots of fashion houses which are comparable to those in France, also boutiques featuring original accessories and sportswear.

WHAT TO WEAR ... In spring, summer or fall in Rome wear lightweight clothes such as you would at home. Prints, dark sheers are acceptable. Rome is a dressy city, so don't appear in slacks. You'll need evening clothes in the winter and a couple of pairs of good walking shoes. You are bound to walk a lot in Rome. Men need sports jackets and slacks, lightweight suits and a dinner jacket in the winter. During the winter you'll need heavier clothing and a fur jacket. Men will want a topcoat or something heavier.

WHERE TO GO—SIGHTSEEING ...

Rome ... Volumes have been written about what to see in Rome so consider this merely as a check list. There are several guided tours to the museums and art galleries and other points of historical interest. Sightseeing tours are available at any tourist office and can be booked through the concierge of the hotel. The average price for a full-day tour in town is lire 3,000 ($4.50). If you prefer to do it on your own, see: the Borghese Gallery, the Capitoline Museum, the Gallery of Modern Art, of course the Vatican Museum (see VATICAN CITY), Hadrian's Tomb, a short walk along the River Tiber; you don't need to be reminded of St. Peter's, the Colosseum, the forums; take a ride out the Old Appian Way, see the Catacombs; gaze upward at the Palazzo Venezia, where Mussolini held forth on the balcony; the three Basilicas: S. Maria Maggiore, St. John Lateran and St. Paul's-Outside-the Walls.

See the Holy Child in the Church of Ara Coeli. Look at the Quirinal Palace, former home of the popes and kings; the Holy Steps (*Scala Santa*), the grave of the poet Keats, the Pantheon, relic of the Roman Empire, built in 27 B.C., the Circus Maximus, where the first chariot races were run; the Roman Capitol; the statue of Moses by Michelangelo in the Church of St. Peter in Chains on the Via Cavour.

See the famous Roman baths of Caracalla; the Spanish steps at the old church of the Holy Trinity of the Hills which lead to the Piazza di Spagna; the Capuchin Chapel on Via Veneto; the old bridges over the Tiber, and you can't miss seeing the enormous white-and-gold monument to Victor Emmanuel II. You can take it in from here and spend days and weeks and still not see it all.

Vatican City . . . is a state within a state ruled by the Pope. Each year thousands of pilgrims from all over the world throng to Italy for religious events here. The Vatican has its own railway station, power lines, radio station and printing plant. Here stands St. Peter's, largest church in Christendom. The treasures, the works of art are innumerable and breathtaking. Over the entrance is the famed Gotto mosaic. Inside the size will awe you; the nave is 151 feet high. The Treasury of St. Peter's contains the Cross of the Emperor Justinius, Charlemagne's robes, jewels and other treasures. The vaulted dome is by Michelangelo, and there are tombs of the Popes by Bernini and Canova. Take the elevator and climb 700 steps to the peak of the dome and survey all of Rome.

The Vatican itself is next, the residence of the Pope. The famous bronze doors are guarded by the equally famous, brilliantly uniformed Swiss guards. The Vatican museum may be visited from 9:00 to 2:00 Monday through Saturday. Most beautiful of all its treasures is the Sistine Chapel with Michelangelo's great masterpieces. Visit the rooms filled with magnificent painting, statuary, robes and tapestries. You need more than one visit to savor it all. Properly accredited visitors may attend group audiences with the Pope by calling the North American College (Tel. 672.256).

Side Trips . . . Half-an-hour's drive from Rome are the vast picturesque ruins of the Emperor Hadrian's Villa. A little farther on, the Villa D'Este with its world-famous fountains. Half-day tours to both places run daily, cost $3.20. Sixty miles north along the seacoast road are the painted Etruscan tombs of Tarquinia, unique in all the world, dating back to the 5th and 6th centuries B.C. 155 miles south of Rome is Cassino, the American battlefield, and 37 miles south is the beach of Anzio. North of Rome you come to Assisi, the birthplace of St. Francis, and the Basilica with frescoes of Giotto which honor him. There are excellent guided tours in tourist buses which swing on circle itineraries. These buses have sliding roofs, radios and public address systems, hostesses who speak English, bars, desks, reading lights. The circle takes in Milan, Genoa, Florence, Rome, Naples, Cassino, Perugia, Bologna, Verona and Venice. You can start anywhere and go as far as you like. See the Etruscan Gate in Perugia, the National Picture Gallery in Siena.

Florence . . . This city—"the cradle of the Renaissance"—(146 miles north of Rome) is one of the most visited in Italy. Stay at the *Excelsior, Grand, Anglo-Americano, Astoria, Majestic, Roma, Savoy* or at one of the city's many comfortable *pensioni*. Dine at the *Baglioni Roof, Oliviero, Buca Lapi, Buca di San Ruffillo, Da Zi'rosa, Giovacchino, Paoli* and *Sabatini* restaurants. Visit the Palazzo Vecchio, the Loggia dei Lanzi, under which is Cellini's "Perseus." See the Cathedral, or *Duomo* of colored marble, housing Michelangelo's last statue. You'll see the Campanile (bell tower) and the great art galleries containing astonishing examples of Renaissance painting and sculpture; the Uffizi and the Palazzo Pitti. Here you will see Flemish, Spanish and German masterpieces, as well as Italian.

Visit the Church of Santa Croce, with the tombs of Machiavelli and Michelangelo; the Church of Orsanmichele with its Donatello statues; the Palazzo Riccardi, residence of the Medici, with the Medici

Menaggio, an hour's ride from Milan, is one of the picturesque towns on Lake Como, most famous of the Italian lakes with the Alps in the background.

Eighteen centuries ago the "castle" in the background was built as the Emperor Hadrian's Tomb—is now part of the Castel Sant' Angelo in Rome.

The beautiful, rugged coast, the perfect climate and the relaxed atmosphere make the island of Capri near Naples a favorite vacation spot.

Famous St. Mark's Square, with the cathedral and the Ducal Palace, is one of the principal points of interest in Venice.

chapel containing fabulous frescoes of the Nativity by Benozzo Gozzoli, the Ponte Vecchio, the bridge across the Arno lined with shops. It was spared in the war but everything around it suffered. The area has now been almost completely rebuilt. Visit the Boboli Gardens, which have inspired murals in Italian restaurants the world over. Save energy by hiring an English-speaking guide if your time is short. You'll need two or three days or more to do justice to the city. There is a service called "Information Please" at Via Tornabuoni 10, which provides baby sitters, nurses and guides and also gives free shopping advice.

Naples ... The Bay of Naples dominated by Vesuvius is famous on postal cards all over the world. Naples suffered great damage in the war, and the city and its people still show the effects. The best hotels are the *Excelsior, Vesuvio* and *Royal*.

The main reason for going to Naples these days is to go on its side trips. Pompeii, with its fabulous ruins, is only a half hour away. Two hours away from Pompeii are Sorrento and Positano and the famous Amalfi Drive, which is cut into the side of the hills. From the drive you see spread out the tiny fishing villages and the bay. You can visit the summit of Vesuvius with a guide.

Capri ... Most famous resort near Naples is the Island of Capri, celebrated in song and verse. Here is the well-known Blue Grotto, the flower-laden villas, the small beaches, the walks along the cliffs. Drive to Anacapri, a charming village with a picturesque square. There is a good hotel here, the *Caesar Augustus*. In Capri try the *Quisisana* or *Morgano Tiberio*. Buy rope-soled shoes, scarves, cotton skirts and fishing shirts. Take the funicular to Marina Grande, the fishing village where you get a boat for a sail into the Blue Grotto. Lie in the sun on the beach at Marina Piccola. Relax and enjoy the beauty. You'll see lots of famous people here. It's a gathering spot for the international set.

Venice ... (2 hours from Rome by air) is the stuff of dreams. It is romance, beauty, an idyl. The Mecca of tourists for more than a hundred years, Venice is built on a series of small islands at the head of the Adriatic Sea. Its main "streets" are lagoons and canals on which float the romantic gondolas, the motor launches, the canal barges, the ferry boats. There are, however, streets and bridges on which pedestrians may stroll.

Venice was in her glory during the Middle Ages when her ships controlled the richest trade routes in the world. Her decline began in the sixteenth century, but her renown as a romantic, beautiful spot continues. You'll want to see the Basilica of St. Mark in famous St. Mark's Square, where everyone feeds the pigeons. St. Mark's was finished in 1500 and is a magnificent example of Byzantine architecture. The interior is lined with fine mosaics. St. Mark's Square also has the famous Clock Tower, which tells not only the hours but the daily position of the sun and moon. See the Palace of the Doges with its wonderful rooms decorated by sixteenth-century artists. Pay special attention to the Tintorettos. See the dungeons. The Campanile, or bell tower, dominates the Square. You can't miss it.

Other important churches in Venice include Frari and Sts. Giovanni and Paolo. Visit the privately owned San Gregario Cloisters; Palazzo Rezzonico, with its magnificent eighteenth-century rooms; Ca d'Oro, one of Venice's oldest houses. You will want to take a gondola through the Grand Canal, lined with historical palaces. You will pass under the Rialto, the Bridge of Sighs.

Stay at the *Gritti,* the *Danieli,* the *Grand,* the *Europa,* the *Bauer Grünwald,* the *Park,* the *Luna* or *Cipriani* on the Island of Giudecca. Dine at *La Taverna Fenice,* which is tops; world-famous *Harry's Bar; Florian's* on St. Mark's Square, which is very popular; *La Colomba,* or *Al Graspo de UA,* famous for seafood; the *Locanda* on the island of Torcello. If you have time, visit Murano and the Venetian glass factories. Cross the Lagoon by motor launch to the Lido, the famed beach resort, with its excellent hotels: the *Exelsior,* the *Grand Hotel des Bains,* the *Lido Palace.* Everyone rents a cabaña and lazes in the sun. There is a casino, too. The Feast of the Redeemer, held on the third Sunday in July, is a great festival with fireworks, song and color.

In the area there are several cities off the beaten tourist path which will interest particularly lovers of Shakespeare. Padua, for instance, and Verona, which was the setting of *Romeo and Juliet* and home of those *Two Gentlemen of Verona.* Nearby is Vicenza, with magnificent Palladian villas and theater.

Milan . . . This is the city of the famous Milan Cathedral with its pinnacles and statues. "The Last Supper," by Leonardo da Vinci, may be seen in the convent of the Church of Santa Maria delle Grazie. Milan is the home of the world-famous La Scala Opera, which holds forth from December to May. Make a point to see the museum, which is devoted entirely to relics of the opera. The Brera Gallery and Castle Sforzesco house works of many of the great masters.

Italian Riviera . . . The stretch of Ligurian coast from Savona to Ventimiglia is now officially called the Riviera dei Fiori (Coast of Flowers). Most important resort in this region is San Remo, which has luxurious hotels, a casino, and all the attributes of a fashionable playground. Here, as on the French Riviera, you may ski just a few miles from the Mediterranean, at Mt. Bignone, which is reached by cableway. There is a golf course halfway up the mountain, too. Genoa, about 4 hours away, is the birthplace of Columbus, whose house can be visited. Visit also Staglieno, the monumental cemetery. Beyond are famous Rapallo, Santa Margherita Ligure and Portofino, an international-set favorite, famous for its seafood. There are hotels and pensions. Excellent fishing, swimming. Continuing south (3½ hours by car) you come to Pisa with the leaning tower, fragments of an Etruscan wall, bridges over the Arno and a citadel.

The Italian Lakes . . . Most famous of the Italian lakes which have the Alps as their background is Lake Como, about an hour away from Milan. Bellagio is the best-known resort among the many villages which line its shores. Launches may be rented to visit spots of interest. At Cernobbio you'll find *Villa d'Este,* a luxurious hotel.

Lake Lugano is partly in Italy, partly in Switzerland. The town of Lugano, which is in Ticino across the Swiss border, has a casino. Lake Maggiore is another resort that is partially Swiss. Here is the town of Stresa, the center of the district, which has good hotels: the *Grand-Hotel et des Iles Borromees, Regina Palace* and *Milan.*

You'll find Lake Garda, a few hours from Lake Como, worth seeing. This is the largest of the Lakes. It is here that d'Annunzio lived. Pay special attention to the steep road bordering the lake.

The Dolomites . . . Cortina d'Ampezzo, the key resort of the Dolomites, was the site of the Winter Olympic games in 1956. There are excellent ski slopes, a bobsled track, toboggan runs, ski jumps and skating rinks. There are instructors who are multilingual, cableways and ski tows. There are numerous hotels and pensions. Try the *Hotel Cristallo* or the *Majestic Miramonti.* Best ski season is December to March. Other villages nearby are San Martino di Castrozza, Misurina, Ortisei. Cortina is famous also as a summer resort. Cervinia (Matterhorn-Cervin Massive) and Sestriere in the Western Alps also offer excellent skiing. Sestriere is also nice during the summer and has a new golf course. To the west is Bolzano, from which you may drive into Austria or Switzerland. The road to Switzerland is one of the dizziest mountain trips on the Continent, but magnificent.

Sicily . . . Way to the south, off the toe of the boot, is Sicily, which Americans know more about since the war than they did before. Taormina is the beauty spot, a delightful resort with unspoiled charm. You can ski on Mt. Etna and swim in the Mediterranean. There is a fine hotel, *San Domenico Palace,* with low rates. The best season is early spring. Summer is hot, but pleasantly so.

Some of the most magnificent and best preserved Greek temples and ruins are in Sicily, at Agrigento and Syracuse. Other towns of interest are Enna, Palermo, Segesta and Selinunte. Sicily is being modernized; new hotels are opening. For something different, it's worth a visit, and is less than 3 hours by air from Rome.

SOURCES OF FURTHER INFORMATION . . . The official Italian tourist office is ENIT (Ente Nazionale Industrie Turistiche) with offices in New York (333 6th Ave.), Chicago, New Orleans, San Francisco, and in Italy at major points of entry. In addition, each province and many of the larger towns have their own Tourist office (EPT—Ente Provinciale Turismo). Folders in English, maps, lists of local events, hotels and restaurants are available. One can also get this information in most hotels. (Inquire about the Italian Tourist Economy Plan by which tourists get special discounts during the winter months.) At the PAA office in Rome, pick up a copy of the PAA city map. Pan American has offices in Rome, Via Bissolati, 46 (Tel. 474841); and in Milan, Piazza San Babila 46, (Tel. 794444).

LUXEMBOURG

WEATHER IN BRUSSELS—Lat. N50°50' (110 miles NW of Luxembourg)—Alt. 1200'

Temp.	JAN.	FEB.	MAR.	APR.	MAY	JUNE	JULY	AUG.	SEPT.	OCT.	NOV.	DEC.
Low	30°	33°	35°	40°	46°	52°	55°	55°	52°	44°	38°	33°
High	39°	43°	49°	57°	64°	70°	73°	72°	67°	56°	48°	42°
Average	35°	38°	42°	49°	55°	61°	64°	64°	60°	50°	43°	38°
Days of Rain	15	15	15	16	16	17	16	16	16	17	18	16

LOCATION ... Crowded between Belgium and Germany, Luxembourg on the south borders France. The city of Luxembourg is about 175 air miles northeast of Paris, 110 air miles southeast of Brussels.

CHARACTERISTICS ... This tiny duchy is a mixture of Graustark and all the Lehar operettas you ever saw, and offers some of the loveliest scenery in western Europe. So all in all it is well worth a visit.

POPULATION ... Estimated 300,000, most of whom speak French, although there is a local language.

SIZE ... 999 square miles, five-sixths the size of Rhode Island.

CAPITAL ... Luxembourg City with a population of approximately 63,000 is the seat of the Government and the country's largest city. It is also the headquarters for the European Coal and Steel Community.

GOVERNMENT ... An independent Grand Duchy, governed by a Chamber of Deputies, elected by universal suffrage.

HOW TO GET THERE ... By Pan Am from New York to Brussels, 13 hours. Then only a short ride by train or car or connecting air services; from Brussels, electric train service every 2 hours; from Paris, 4 fast trains on the Paris-Germany line.

ACCOMMODATIONS ... In the city of Luxembourg there are some good hotels, including the *Grand Brasseur*, the *Cravat*, the *Alfa* and the *Kons*. Rates about $5 to $7 double with bath.

The city itself is fascinating with ruined fortresses and cathedrals in Gothic and Renaissance periods. General George Patton is buried at the nearby Hamme Cemetery.

FOOD . . . is excellent in Luxembourg. Try the *Rotisserie Ardennaise, Le Gourmet* or the *Cordial*. A few miles outside of town *La Cabane* is pleasant and cozy. The *Hotel Heinz* at Vianden also has an excellent restaurant in an attractive setting. Along the Moselle River the best food is at the *Hotel Simmer* at Ehnen. Coffee and cigarettes are high here, but everything else is reasonable. Specialties in the food line include Ardennes ham, jellied suckling pig, veal glacé in piecrust, crawfish, trout and magnificent pastries which are known all over the Continent. The wines are fine, too, particularly a native sparkling Moselle. Black currant wine is native, too. Absinthe, oddly enough, is legal here. Beer is good and cheap.

There aren't many night clubs in the Duchy, but in the city of Luxembourg try the *Plaza, Charlie's* or *Chez Nous*. One of the best bars in Europe is the one at the *Grand Brasseur*. Taxis are plentiful but come high. Laundry is good.

Wild-boar hunting and deer stalking are two popular winter sports. Hiking is a delight. The rivers are a paradise for canoers. There is an 18-hole golf course near the capital. The monetary unit is the Belgian and Luxembourg franc which is worth about two cents. Belgian francs are accepted in the Duchy, but Luxembourg francs are not accepted in Belgium. Best time of year to visit Luxembourg is May through September.

WHERE TO GO—SIGHTSEEING . . .

The northern section of Luxembourg is wild and rugged. Ruins of fortresses and castles brood on crags. There are wide rivers in which fish abound, and deep ravines. The middle section is farm land, rolling and smiling. To the east is the vineyard country. There are mines and steel mills in the southwest.

When sightseeing in Luxembourg City, take a look at the cathedral built in 1618, the Pont du Château, the Three Towers and the Pont Adolphe Bridge, which has one of the most famous stone arches in all Europe. The Passerelas viaduct connects the modern section of the city near the railroad terminal with the center of the city, which is built on rocks. In the inner part of the upper town is the Grand Ducal Palace, a Spanish Renaissance building.

Trips outside of the city of Luxembourg should include Moselle valley, Clervaux and Vianden (with its famous castle), Mondorf les Bains, the spa of the Duchy. The wine cellars in the town of Remich are interesting, and if you are around at Easter time the local wine fair at Grevenmacher is worth seeing. Visit the town of Echternach and see the old Benedictine Abbey founded by St. Willibrod. Here on Whit Tuesday there is an annual dancing procession which is a tourist attraction for all the Continent. For one of the loveliest sights in Western Europe, drive through the Sûre Valley.

MAJORCA

(BALEARIC ISLANDS)

WEATHER IN MAJORCA—Lat. 39°35′—Alt. max.: 4740, min.: sea level

Temp.	JAN.	FEB.	MAR.	APR.	MAY	JUNE	JULY	AUG.	SEPT.	OCT.	NOV.	DEC.
Low	36°	36°	42°	46°	54°	59°	61°	65°	62°	54°	48°	47°
High	56°	66°	62°	68°	78°	81°	85°	89°	84°	75°	68°	64°
Average	46°	51°	52°	57°	66°	70°	73°	77°	73°	65°	58°	55°
Days of Rain	11	7	10	7	2	9	6	3	8	13	8	10

LOCATION ... Largest of the Balearic group of islands, Majorca lies 135 miles south of Barcelona in the Mediterranean.

CHARACTERISTICS ... Set in the blue waters of the Mediterranean, Majorca is a land of eternal spring where medieval architectural splendor rubs shoulders with the modern. Because of its temperate climate, its picturesque scenery, and its separation from the mainland, the inland has been for many years the haunt of artists, poets and writers. People from many lands make it their permanent home, and tourists visit there in increasing numbers. Its recorded history began with the Romans, who were followed by the Vandals, the Arabs, the Moors and, lastly, by European Christians who contributed much to its artistic charm.

POPULATION ... Estimated at 415,000 in 1952, slightly smaller than Indianapolis.

SIZE ... 1,405 square miles, a little larger than the state of Rhode Island.

CAPITAL ... Palma, a city of about 200,000, compares with Jacksonville, Florida.

GOVERNMENT ... Spanish provincial.

HOW TO GET THERE ... By Pan American Clipper, elapsed time from New York, about 14 hours to Barcelona. Then by connecting plane, 55 minutes from Barcelona to Palma. By boat from Barcelona, overnight. By ship from New York, 8 to 10 days.

ACCOMMODATIONS . . . Hotel accommodations in Palma are excellent. Many fine comfortable pensions and inns may be found in the interior. De luxe hotels in Palma include the *Bahia Palace Hotel* and *Nixe Palace* $12 up American Plan, and the *Maricel* and *Mediterraneo* where prices for a single room, American Plan, range between $7 and $9. Class A hostelries include the *Alcina, Principe Alfonso* and the *Victoria,* where rooms are available for $5.50 to $6.50 a day. Accommodations on the European Plan (without meals) are also available. Another recommended hotel is the de luxe *Hotel Formentor,* uniquely situated among the pines near the beach about 1½ hours from Palma by hotel car. Rates, $10 American Plan.

CIGARETTES AND TOBACCO . . . Tobacco is unrationed; American cigarettes are available at prices similar to those in the United States.

CURRENCY . . . The standard of currency is the Spanish peseta, 60 to the United States dollar.

RESTAURANTS . . . Restaurants are numerous and reasonable—meals run from $1.50 and up. One of the best restaurants in Palma is the *Latz* run by Americans. There are several sandwich shops and snack bars. Night clubs, many of which have floor shows, include the *Villa Rosa, Trocadero, Casablanca, Tito's, Jack El Negro, El Patio* and *Virginia Club.*

SPORTS . . . The Majorcans, although by nature slow-moving, enjoy a variety of sports: bullfights, boxing, wrestling, the Basque sport of *pelota,* tennis, cycle racing, yachting and trotting. Racing meetings are held in the spring and fall. Palma has a modern roller-skating rink. Public swimming may be enjoyed at many of the adjacent beaches or in the municipal swimming pool.

TRANSPORTATION . . . All parts of the island are accessible either by train, bus or motor car.

WHERE TO GO—SIGHTSEEING . . .

Palma . . . Although much of its attractiveness lies in its ancient architecture and art treasures, Palma has kept up with the times. Smart shops, excellent hotels, good restaurants, and a fine system of roads and transportation enable the tourist to enjoy the comforts of modern living. Palma combines the old and the modern. Its magnificent thirteenth-century cathedral, erected on the site of a Moslem mosque, rises in golden splendor above the bay. Nearby, in the narrow streets and winding lanes of the older city, palaces of medieval noblemen stand beside the simple homes of modern workers. Convents, quaint patios and ivy-covered churches combine to transport the visitor back in time to the Middle Ages. A visit to Bellver Castle is also recommended.

SOURCES OF FURTHER INFORMATION . . . Complete information on Majorca and its neighboring islands of Minorca and Ibiza may be obtained at the Spanish Information Bureau, Paseo del Generalisimo, 38–40, Palma. In New York, contact the Spanish Tourist Office, 485 Madison Avenue.

A visit to the Carthusian monastery at Valldemosa, where
Chopin and George Sand lived
in 1838, is worth while.

Formentor on Majorca is the
best known of many fine
beaches in the Balearic Islands
which offer quiet relaxation
amidst beautiful scenery.

Majorca is dominated in part by mountains with rugged outcroppings
from the sea. Excursions to the hinterland reveal quaint villages,
groves of oranges and pomegranates, and places of historic interest.

NETHERLANDS (HOLLAND)

WEATHER IN AMSTERDAM—Lat. N52°20′—Alt. 16′

Temp.	JAN.	FEB.	MAR.	APR.	MAY	JUNE	JULY	AUG.	SEPT.	OCT.	NOV.	DEC.
Low	31°	31°	35°	39°	45°	51°	54°	54°	49°	43°	37°	33°
High	41°	42°	47°	54°	62°	68°	70°	70°	65°	57°	47°	42°
Average	36°	37°	41°	47°	54°	60°	62°	62°	57°	50°	42°	38°
Days of Rain	10	8	11	8	9	9	11	11	10	13	11	13

LOCATION ... Across the North Sea from England, The Netherlands (or Holland) is located between Belgium and Germany. Amsterdam is only 100 air miles north of Brussels and 230 air miles northeast of London.

CHARACTERISTICS. ... Crisp and clean and hospitable sums up the land of tulips and canals. You'll enjoy seeing all the things you've read about; the windmills, the wooden shoes, the colorful native costumes. And you will enjoy, too, the modern hotels and good restaurants where food is prodigious and inexpensive. The Netherlands is a flat country with plenty of lakes, rivers and canals and a charm and beauty rewarding to the person who spends more than a couple of days seeing the "musts." You'll feel at home with the Dutch, and they speak English with determination. The southeastern part of the country is made up of beautiful rolling hills dotted with castles, some of which are now hotels.

POPULATION ... 11,000,000, which approximates the populations of New York and Detroit.

SIZE ... 12,529 square miles, the size of Connecticut and Massachusetts.

CAPITAL ... Amsterdam, with a population of 875,000, slightly larger than Washington, D. C. The seat of the Government, however, is The Hague; the royal family lives at Soestdijk Palace near Baarn, 28 miles southeast of Amsterdam.

GOVERNMENT . . . A constitutional monarchy ruled by a Queen and Parliament of two chambers.

HOW TO GET THERE . . . By Clipper, through-plane flights to Amsterdam from New York, 13 hours (elapsed time); 1¼ hours from London. By boat from New York 8 to 11 days.

ACCOMMODATIONS . . . There are many fine hotels in Amsterdam, among them: the renowned *Amstel,* overlooking the river of the same name, the *de l'Europe* with its excellent "Excelsior" restaurant, the *Doelen,* the *Carlton* and the *Victoria,* all with good food and excellent bars. The *American,* a favorite of Americans, the *Schiller,* the *Park* and Grand Hotel *Krasnapolsky* are all very reasonable. Rates are from $3 to $6.50 per day, excluding a 15 per cent service charge, and, in some hotels, breakfast is included.

ARTS . . . See the Rijksmuseum (the State Museum) in Amsterdam with its collection of Rembrandt's paintings, including his famous "Night Watch"; Willet Holthuysen Museum, a seventeenth-century residence with a collection of porcelain, furniture, and library on the history of art; the Stedelijk Museum (Municipal Museum); Rembrandt House; Royal Palace on the Damsquare, built in 1648 by Jacob van Campen; Allard Pierson Museum, which houses a collection of Egyptian, Greek and Roman antiquities.

BALLET . . . There are two permanent Amsterdam ballet groups considered to be good. Outstanding troupes visit during the famous midsummer Holland Festival.

BANKS . . . The principal banks in Amsterdam are: the Nederlandsche Bank, which is the National Bank; Nederlandsche Handelmaatschapij, N.V.; the Amsterdamsche Bank; The Twentsche Bank; the Rotterdamsche Bank Vereniging. Most have affiliations with New York banks. Traveler's checks cashed in American Express, Thos. Cook & Son, stores and restaurants and some hotels.

CALENDAR OF HOLIDAYS . . . New Year's Day; April 30, Queen's birthday; May 5, Liberation Day; Good Friday; Easter Monday; Ascension Day; Whitsuntide Day; Christmas; December 26.

CIGARETTES AND TOBACCO . . . Dutch tobacco is reasonably good. American cigarettes are scarce and expensive. Bring your own and pay the duty. Dutch cigars are excellent and inexpensive.

CLIMATE . . . Very moderate, mild winters, cool summers, same as in England. April to October is the ideal time to visit.

CLUBS . . . The American Businessman's Club in Amsterdam, other private clubs through introduction by a member only. The Netherlands is not a very club-conscious country, but U. S. visitors should have no trouble when they want to visit one. There are Rotary and Lions Clubs here. For women tourists there are private organizations, sort of hostess clubs, which help with shopping, meeting Dutch families, etc., all free of charge. Check with the local tourist office.

COMMON COURTESIES AND LOCAL CUSTOMS . . . Not much different from home. Coffee is served in all offices at 11:00 A.M. The luncheon hour usually lasts from 12:30 to 2:00 and dinner is early, not later than 7:00 P.M. There's more handshaking here than in the States, but less than in the more southern countries, such as Belgium and France. The Netherlands is noted for its fine candy. Also try a *Koekje* (cookie). Meal servings are large and it's better not to overorder than leave wasted food on your plate. You may have trouble learning some Dutch because it's difficult, not always pleasantly translatable and the people would rather show you their English.

COMMUNICATIONS ... Telephone, cables, radio and airmail to the United States. (Commercial Cables, Western Union.) Telephone call to New York costs around $10, a cable about $5. Airmail letters up to 5 grams cost 50 Dutch cents, 20 cents for each additional 5 grams. Airmail postal cards are 40 cents. You can buy stamps at a coin machine near street mailboxes and mail your letter in the back of a streetcar for quick service.

CURRENCY ... The monetary unit of the Netherlands is the guilder or florin, which is divided into 100 cents. It is worth about 26 cents in our currency, and likewise, one U. S. dollar is approximately fl. 3.80.

CUSTOMS REGULATIONS AND DOCUMENTS REQUIRED FOR UNITED STATES CITIZENS ... Passport, but no visa required. Adults may take in duty free 400 cigarettes or 100 cigars or 14 ounces of tobacco; 2 bottles of liquor or wine, 1 small bottle of perfume, camera and 12 rolls of film, up to 1000 florins in cash; any other tourist items for personal use.

DRUG STORES ... Only real pharmacies. Some are open 24 hours a day. Not in the drug stores but readily available are snack bars, lunch counters and cafeterias. American soft drinks are available everywhere and a favorite with visitors is *Chocomel*, a cold chocolate-milk drink.

ELECTRIC CURRENT ... Voltage is 220 in Amsterdam and most other places except in some sections of The Hague, where it is 110. Plugs are the two-prong, round type. The 50 cycles (rather than 60 as in the U. S.) does not affect razors or radios.

FAUNA ... There is not much hunting in Holland ... small stuff only, like rabbits, foxes, pheasants, pigeons and partridges. Boars and deer live in reservations. Dutch cattle are world famous. There are fine horses, too, and plenty of pigs and sheep. There are bird sanctuaries at the Naarder Meer near Amsterdam and at many other places throughout the country.

FLORA ... Plenty of flowers ... the bulb fields near Haarlem ... season is from about April 15 till May 15. Aalsmeer is the center of the flower "industry" ... roses, lilacs, etc. A visit to one of the flower auctions is recommended (the one at Aalsmeer is the world's largest) as well as the annual spring open-air exhibition at *De Keukenhof* between Hillegom and Sassenheim near the bulb district.

FOOD ... Dutch food is world famous. Some typical Dutch dishes are *Rolpens* (minced beef, usually served with fried apples), herring, smoked eels, oysters, *poffertjes* (small salted fritters). Throughout Holland there are many Indonesian restaurants which you should try. The food is exotic, but delicious. Some of the specialties are *nasi goreng, bami goreng, sambal goreng, sate* and *kroepoek*. They taste something like Chinese food. And, of course, the Dutch cheeses are known the world over as being among the finest.

GAMBLING ... The totalisator is the only legal manner of betting. This pari-mutuel apparatus is in operation at the race courses (main ones are Duindigt, near The Hague, and the Sports Stadium at Hilversum, near Amsterdam).

LANGUAGE ... English is understood and spoken everywhere. Dutch, of course, is the official language.

LAUNDRY AND DRY CLEANING ... Available everywhere. Service is, on the whole, slower than in hotels in the States. Quality is good, prices are reasonable. Call room service and state your wishes.

LIQUOR ... All kinds of liquor are available in the better bars and hotels. A specialty is *jenever* (Dutch gin). The Dutch drink this straight and chilled, just as we do Martinis and Manhattans. Try the famous Holland beer as well as *Advocaat*, an unusual egg drink.

MEDICAL FACILITIES ... No American hospitals, but facilities are excellent and available everywhere. Ask your hotel clerk.

MOTION PICTURES ... All types of pictures are shown, but most are American with Dutch subtitles.

MUSIC ... Amsterdam Concertgebouw Orchestra is the third largest in the world and holds regular concerts. Most other large cities have municipal orchestras. Orchestral music as well as opera, drama and ballet is featured at the annual Holland Festival held June 15 to July 15 in Amsterdam, The Hague and Scheveningen, the well-known seaside resort.

NIGHT CLUBS AND CABARETS ... There are innumerable night clubs in Amsterdam. Some of the gayer and better ones are *Extase, Caramella, Villa d'Este, De Vliegende Hollander,* and *La Cubana*. Most of these places close promptly at 2:00 A.M. (1:00 A.M. on Sunday), but there are fashionable spots operated on a membership basis where you can go after that. A card may be obtained. (Inquire of Pan American or your hotel). There are several large clubs with floor shows, such as *Femina* and the *Casino*.

PHOTOGRAPHY ... All sorts of photographic equipment can be purchased in The Netherlands. Developing and printing are good and quite fast for black-and-white; color takes about two weeks. Best store in Amsterdam is Capi, Kalverstraat (main shopping street). Tourists usually shoot all sorts of street scenes, bikes, the canals, Royal Palace at the Dam Square, the harbor, the various museums. If you have an eye for it, "typical" and interesting photos can be made all over town. There are even a couple of windmills left right inside Amsterdam.

RELIGION ... The royal family belongs to The Netherlands Reformed Church (Presbyterian), but there are all sects. The two English churches in Amsterdam are Church of England, 42, Groenburgwal, and the English Reformed Church, in the ancient and very picturesque Begijnhof, right in the heart of the city.

RESTAURANTS ... Dutch cooking is first class. Fine restaurants serving excellent food can be found everywhere. A Dutch specialty is Indonesian food (*rijsttafel,* rice table). There are many outstanding Indonesian restaurants in the big cities. Also French, Swiss, Italian and Chinese. In Amsterdam the best places are the *Excelsior,* the dining room of the Hotel de l'Europe, and *Dikker and Thys.* Other excellent restaurants are the *Stuyvesant,* dining room of the Hotel Victoria, and the *Five Flies,* Old World restaurant in Spuistraat. The *Chalet Petite Suisse,* the *Black Sheep,* the *Boerderij* ("farmhouse"), and the *Lido* (overlooking a canal) are also very good. Best Indonesian place in town is the *Bali,* Leidsestraat. Chinese food is also very popular in The Netherlands, and you will find good Chinese restaurants in all the main cities. In all those places mentioned, $3 (approximately 12 guilders) will buy you a fine meal. *See* DRUG STORES for sandwich places.

SHOPS AND STORES . . . Shops and stores are open from 9:00 to 6:00, including Saturday. Service is friendly and good; most attendants speak English well. Main shopping streets in Amsterdam are Leidsestraat and Kalverstraat. There are also several department stores, including the Bijenkorf (beehive), that have branches in The Hague and Rotterdam. The American tourist will find prices in Holland very reasonable. Typical souvenirs (Delft blue) are sold in a great many shops. Many shops and stores accept foreign currency and traveler's checks.

SPECTATOR SPORTS . . . The most popular sport is soccer. Also tennis, hockey matches, cycling, swimming and sailing. Check locally on exact dates for important sport events such as "Head of the River" and varsity student rowing matches in the spring; Internal Tulip Rallye for automobiles in May; T.T. Motor Races in June; 4-day walking contest in July; international tennis matches in July; Grand Prix car races at Zandvoort; Amsterdam Olympic Day, sailing, horse races, cycle racing and baseball games. Some of these events are at resorts outside Amsterdam. The capital also has an 18-hole golf course.

SPORTS . . . The many fine lakes, such as Loosdrecht near Amsterdam and De Kaag near The Hague, offer excellent facilities, and Dutch beaches are sandy and free from stones. Aside from sailing, fishing and swimming, there's horseback riding, golfing, shooting and tennis. Very little polo or squash. Ice skating, of course, in winter. Remember Hans Brinker! There are some fine golf courses in Holland, especially Wassenaar near The Hague, Hilversum in Hilversum; De Pan near Utrecht and Kennemer in Zandvoort.

THEATERS . . . Practically everything is in Dutch, including current Broadway hits, with evening performances around 8:00 P.M. and matinees, including Sundays. No formal dress necessary. Cost per seat averages $1.50. Ask your hotel clerk about current performances.

TIME . . . Six hours later than Eastern Standard Time.

TIPPING . . . Usually 15 per cent. If a service charge is not included in the hotel bill, tip 15 per cent of the whole bill. Ask your waiter whether the bill is "inclusive" of tip.

TRANSPORTATION . . . Because of the flat country, bicycles are used by everyone, from the Queen down, and often dominate the road. Trains between Amsterdam, The Hague and Rotterdam run about every half hour. Taxis are not hard to get. Rates increase between 1:00 and 6:00 A.M. The trolleys are fun and cheap. You can hire a car from Universal Self-Drive Service, Westeinde 1 (Tel. 34435) and Avis Rent-a-car System c/o N. V. Amsterdamsche Rijtuig Mij., Keizersgracht 485 (Tel. 34834–43950). You buy "benzine" by the liter.

WATER ... Excellent everywhere, but bottled water is available.

WHAT TO BUY ... Silverware, china, chocolates and a Dutch specialty, *hopjes* (a coffee candy), leatherwear, diamonds, cigars, cheese, gin or liquors. Clothes are also cheap. Tourist favorites are old etchings, maps, prints and old Delft tiles, which cost 2 to 10 guilders each (about 50 cents to $2.50). Don't buy flower bulbs to take home, without a certificate of health. The growers and shop keepers will send them on to you. Fresh flowers can also be airmailed to the States. Feather hats are the big buy in Volendam.

WHAT TO WEAR ... Same type of clothing you would wear in the different seasons at home. In the summer be sure to have a raincoat and lightweight topcoat for cool evenings.

WHERE TO GO—SIGHTSEEING ...

Amsterdam ... Naturally you'll want to take a trip to the wonderfully colorful tulip fields. Holland has a million acres planted with tulip bulbs which are famous throughout the world. It is one of the most beautiful sights you can imagine. Since canals are the main thoroughfares in Holland, whatever you do, don't miss taking a trip through Amsterdam in one of the glass-topped motor launches. The boats go through all the important canals as well as the smaller ones. Amsterdam is a city combining the old with the new. Many of the housing projects and public buildings are magnificent examples of modern architecture. You'll find it especially interesting to visit some of the diamond-cutting factories such as Asscher's Diamant Co. Ltd. and the A. van Moppes and Zoon plant where there are daily tours during the summer. (Amsterdam is the world's headquarters for diamond cutting.) Other places of interest to the tourist are the Botanical Gardens, the Artis Zoological Gardens, and the almshouses, which are all pretty little houses surrounded by lovely gardens. You should see the New Church, which contains the tombs of Admirals de Ruyter, Van Galen, Van Kinsbergen and Van Speyk, and also see the Old Church, built in 1300, with sculptures by A. Quellijn.

Side Trips ... While in Amsterdam you can make excursions to picturesque Volendam and the island of Marken, popular with tourists. Here, perhaps more than any place in Holland, you will see the natives dressed in traditional Holland costumes. Also take a trip to Edam and Alkmaar, the world-famous cheese markets, on Fridays.

Schiphol, Amsterdam's great airport, is just a few miles outside of the city. It was opened in 1920 and completely destroyed during the war; now rebuilt, it is one of the leading airports in Europe. The village of Aalsmeer near Schiphol consists of little green islands completely covered with flowers, which are gathered in the morning and are taken to the auction. Later most of the flowers are dispatched by air to cities in and beyond Europe. Leiden nearby is the birthplace of Rembrandt and the home of the Pilgrim Fathers for eleven years before they left for America in 1620. John Robinson, their spiritual leader, is buried in the baptistery of St. Peter's Church here. Only a few miles east of Amsterdam, there is an unusual stretch of sandy country with delightful woods and two old fortress towns, as well as some new and modern villages. Het Gooi, within 20 minutes of the city, is known for its architecture and natural beauty. The Town Hall of Hilversum, designed by the famous Dutch architect W. Dudok is outstanding, and there is a wonderful 18-hole golf course. Artists will certainly want to go to Laren to see the permanent exhibition of works of modern Dutch artists. And while there see the Muiderslot, a medieval castle, in the same district. Several very fine hotels are the *Grand Hotel Gooiland* at Hilversum, the *Hamdorff* at Laren and the *Kasteel de Hooge Vuursche* at Baarn, in the vicinity of the Royal Palace. Further east, near Arnhem, in the center of the 15,000-acre national park Hooge Veluwe, stands the Kröller Muller museum, which contains the greatest collection of Van Gogh paintings found anywhere.

The Hague...Whereas Amsterdam is the capital, The Hague is the seat of the Government and has been since 1247 when Count Willem II built his castle there near the sea. All various Government departments are located there, including all foreign embassies. As in Amsterdam there are many interesting buildings both old and new to be seen in The Hague. Among the first places on your list to see should be the Knight's Hall, new addition to the Palace (built in 1280), where, the third Tuesday in September, the Queen opens the combined Chambers of Parliament in a colorful and solemn session; the Mauritshuis Museum houses a collection of famous Dutch paintings, among them 18 by Rembrandt. The Mauritshuis is the old palace of Prince Johan Maurits van Nassau, once Governor of the Dutch possessions in Brazil. The Palace is open daily to visitors. Modern art will be found in the Gemeente Museum (municipal museum).

There are excellent hotels and restaurants in The Hague. Among the better hotels are the *Des Indes, Wittebrug, Central* and *Terminus.* The restaurants in The Hague are superb. The *Warong Djawa* is one of the best-known Javanese rice-table restaurants. The *Beukenhof* in Oegstgeest, near The Hague, is one of the most famous restaurants in Holland, and *Saur* is wonderful for seafood. You can go to the *Royal* for French cuisine and to the *Jachthuis* for game. The *Old Dutch Restaurant* in The Hague has very excellent food and is inexpensive. While there you will want to attend a concert by the famous *Residentie Orchestra* with outstanding guest conductors and artists.

Within fifteen minutes by trolley you can get to Scheveningen, which is a wonderful seaside resort. This is divided into two parts, one the old fishing village where the women still wear the traditional costumes and wooden shoes (though not very colorful, more on the somber side) and the other part which is a fashionable resort, with many good hotels such as the *Kurhaus* (open all year) and the *Palace*, and many restaurants and all bathing facilities. It has a wonderful broad beach. You will have plenty of activity to choose from here; there are tennis courts, riding schools and a famous race-track at Duindigt. North of The Hague is the tree-shaded village of Wassenaar (there's a fine 18-hole golf course here) and to the south one of the best-known horticultural regions, which extends as far back as the Hook of Holland and Rotterdam. The glass hothouses here are famous for their grapes, tomatoes, peaches and flowers.

Rotterdam . . . Partly destroyed during the Second World War, Rotterdam is now on its way to becoming Holland's most modern and dynamic city. Two-thirds of an ambitious reconstruction plan has been carried out and it makes Rotterdam an open-air museum of modern architecture.

The harbor of Rotterdam, is actually Europe's largest seaport, and a sightseeing tour by luxury launch of the Spido Co. (departure from Willemsplein) showing the dry docks, shipyards, etc., is highly recommended. Also well worth seeing is *The Maastunnel*, first Dutch river tunnel, 7/10 of a mile long, 45 feet under low water level, which connects the city of Rotterdam with the harbor district.

In addition to the modern center of Rotterdam with its excellent shopping facilities and entertainment, there are various museums and galleries containing unique art treasures and modern sculpture, among which is the *Boymans Museum* with its large collection of old and modern painting from Hieronymus Bosch to Vincent van Gogh.

Hotels are the *Atlanta Hotel, Park Hotel* and the unique *Delta Hotel* situated in Vlaardingen (6 miles from Rotterdam) overlooking the channel connecting Rotterdam with the North Sea (Hook of Holland). Good places to dine include *Coq d'Or, Erasmus, Old Dutch* and *Witte Paard*.

SOURCES OF FURTHER INFORMATION . . . The Tourist Information office in Amsterdam is at 5 Rokin; in The Hague at 38 Parkstraat and Buitenhof (Kiosk). These and others in the larger cities have a variety of maps, folders and information in English, but make no reservations. Local travel agencies arrange sightseeing tours. Pan American's office is in the Hirsch Building, Leidseplein, Amsterdam C. opposite the American Hotel (Tel. 34760); Schiphol Airport (Tel. 722989). The U. S. Consulate General office (Tel. 790321) is at Museumplein, Amsterdam. In The Hague the USIS (Tel. 112015) is at Lange Voorhout, the United States Embassy (Tel. 184140) at Esso Building. Benoordenhoutseweg. Copies of the New York *Herald Tribune* and *The New York Times* (International Air Edition is printed in Amsterdam) are available in the larger hotels. In New York, the Netherlands Information Service is at 711 3rd Ave.

NORWAY

WEATHER IN OSLO—Lat. N59°55′—Alt. 40′

Temp.	JAN.	FEB.	MAR.	APR.	MAY	JUNE	JULY	AUG.	SEPT.	OCT.	NOV.	DEC.
Low	21°	21°	26°	34°	43°	50°	56°	53°	46°	37°	30°	24°
High	28°	30°	38°	48°	59°	65°	71°	66°	59°	46°	36°	29°
Average	25°	26°	32°	41°	51°	58°	64°	60°	53°	42°	33°	27°
Days of Rain	12	12	13	10	11	10	12	15	11	12	12	15

LOCATION ... Norway extends along the western part of the Scandinavian peninsula from a latitude the same as that of Scotland to well above the Arctic Circle. Oslo is the same distance by air from London as Chicago is from New York.

CHARACTERISTICS ... Norway is a long, rangy country with terrific distances. The population is almost all pure Aryan. They have a zest for life that will exhaust the average American. It is the land of the fjords, mountains, valleys and plains. Up north it has the midnight sun, so that it has almost constant daylight from April to mid-September. The scenery is magnificent, the people cordial, friendly and scrupulously honest. It is a rugged country, but the cities are cosmopolitan. Hotels are very good. A great number of new ones offering excellent facilities have been built since the war in the cities as well as in the rural districts. Food is plentiful.

POPULATION ... Estimated 3,200,000, Norway has fewer people than Chicago.

SIZE ... Although the total area is 125,182 square miles, about the same as that of New Mexico, Norway is shaped like a spoon, extending the distance from New York to San Juan.

CAPITAL ... Oslo, a city of 455,000, is the size of Kansas City.

GOVERNMENT ... A constitutional monarchy with a King and a parliament known as the Storting, but thoroughly liberal and democratic.

HOW TO GET THERE ... Through-plane service by Pan American Clipper to Oslo, about 13½ hours (elapsed time) from New York. By ship, 7 days to Bergen, 8 days to Oslo.

ACCOMMODATIONS ... Norway's hotels are crowded, so make your reservations well in advance. The beautiful *Grand* is completely redecorated. It's located in the middle of Oslo on the Karl Johans Gate; the rates are from $5.50 a day for single room and bath. Quiet and gracious service is the keynote at the *Bristol*. Rates begin at $5.00 at this excellent hotel. Other first-class hotels in the same price bracket are the *Continental*, the modern comfortable *Carlton Hotel*, the "*KNA*" (Royal Norwegian Motor Club), the *Hotel Norum* and on the Holmenkollen Hill overlooking Oslo and the harbor, the *Hollmenkollen Hotel*. The large new *Viking Hotel* with all modern conveniences has rates starting as low as $2.40. The Mission hotels are a good bet all over Scandinavia for those with limited budgets and a taste for simple comfort.

ARTS ... Oslo has a large variety of museums and galleries. The Viking Ship Museum is unique. Ships and other objects of old Viking culture are on display. The Ski Museum has exhibits tracing 2,500 years in the history of this sport and method of transportation. The National Open Air Museum is a restored village of medieval Norwegian times. The Vigeland Museum contains the work of Vigeland, Norway's greatest sculptor. The Historical Museum is devoted to ethnological and artistic exhibitis of Norwegian culture. The Museum of the Polar Ship *Fram* has interesting exhibits concerning this ship's famous arctic expedition and other polar explorations. The *Kon-Tiki* raft is also on view. Also of interest are the National Galleries, the Museum of Industrial Art, the Theater Museum and the beautifully decorated new Town Hall. Most museums open at noon.

BANKS ... Den Norske Creditbank, Christiana Bank og Kreditkasse, Bergens Privatbank. Most hotels, large restaurants and stores and the American Express Company will also cash traveler's checks.

CALENDAR OF HOLIDAYS ... Jan. 1, May 1, May 17 (Independence Day), Whitsun, Christmas Day, Boxing Day, Maundy Thursday, Good Friday, Easter Sunday and Easter Monday.

CIGARETTES, CIGARS AND TOBACCO ... Take all you are allowed under customs regulations. Duty on additional quantities is very high. However, local brands of American-blended cigarettes are good and plentiful. *See* CUSTOMS REGULATIONS.

CLIMATE ... The sunlit nights are a wonderful feature of the summer in Norway. From April to September the nights are very short, and around midsummer you can read a newspaper out of doors at midnight. Above the Arctic Circle, the sun shines 24 hours a day. Thanks to the Gulf Stream, the climate in Norway is temperate, never very hot or very cold. (See temperature chart.) For winter sports, January, February, March and April are ideal.

CLUBS ... Lions and Rotary Clubs in most large centers.

COMMON COURTESIES AND LOCAL CUSTOMS ... Eiderdowns take the place of top sheets even in the hotels, although you can get blankets and top sheet at good hotels. Dress is informal. At the best resort hotels dinner jackets are expected only in winter season.

COMMUNICATIONS . . . Telephone, telegraph, and cable facilities are available.

CURRENCY . . . The krone is the principal monetary unit. There are 7.15 kroner to the dollar.

CUSTOMS REGULATIONS AND DOCUMENTS REQUIRED FOR UNITED STATES CITIZENS . . . Unlimited dollars, 2 bottles of liquor, 400 cigarettes or 80 cigars or 500 grams of tobacco may be brought into Norway duty free. Also 300 kroner in and 99 kroner out, no larger than 50 kroner denominations. You need no visa to enter Norway, only your United States passport. Bring your driver's license if you wish to hire a car.

DRUG STORES . . . Norwegian drug stores carry many American products or their European equivalents.

ELECTRIC CURRENT . . . The voltage in Norway is 220 A.C., except for Stavanger, with 110 A.C. and Trondheim with 150 A.C.

FAUNA . . . Norwegian waters abound with many species of fish. Both salt-water and fresh-water fishing are excellent. Big-game animals include bear, moose and reindeer. Many small wild animals are found in Norwegian forests, including wolf, fox, lynx, otter and beaver. There are also game birds, grouse being the most abundant.

FLORA . . . The beautiful forests of Norway are mainly spruce, fir and pine trees. Birch trees are everywhere. The vegetation of the valleys of southern Norway is very beautiful. Wild berries are plentiful and flowers are profuse in the gorgeous spring season.

FOOD . . . Breakfast is a large meal with a cold buffet. Fish is served in great variety. Dinner is apt to be at 4:30. Tea and sandwiches at 9:00 P.M. Tourists don't have to eat at these hours, however. Good à la carte meals are available at all times.

LANGUAGE . . . English is spoken everywhere. It's taught in the schools.

LAUNDRY AND DRY CLEANING . . . There are good cleaning and laundry services in all principal towns. Inquire at your hotel.

LIQUOR . . . Beer and aquavit are very popular. The liquor stores (*Vinmonopolet*) carry all varieties of wine and liquor.

MEDICAL FACILITIES . . . Modern hospitals and excellent doctors are available. Ski centers have well-equipped first-aid centers with resident doctors. Inquire at your hotel if you need a doctor.

MOTION PICTURES . . . The latest American and English pictures are shown in Oslo with Norwegian subtitles. Be on time for performances, because late-comers may not remain at the end of a program to catch the beginning. Good cinema houses include the *Saga, Klingenberg, Colosseum,* and the *Gimle.* See local papers for time and features.

MUSIC . . . The Oslo Symphony Orchestra is outstanding. Norwegian folk music is very beautiful and an important part of the life of the people, having inspired Edvard Grieg and other composers. The International Festival of Music is in Bergen May 30 to June 15.

NIGHT CLUBS AND CABARETS . . . In Oslo *Telle Cabaret* has fine entertainment and serves all sorts of drinks. *Telle Grill* is small, exclusive and smart. The *Rainbow Room* is the biggest night club in Oslo, with a large orchestra and floor show. The Hotel Bristol has the formal *Moorish Hall. George's* is also very pleasant.

PHOTOGRAPHY ... Camera equipment, black-and-white and color, still and movie film are available at reasonable prices. Developing facilities are available and the quality of work is good. Developing takes from 2 to 7 days. Special service will be given to tourists. Recommended for photo purchases and services: J. L. Nerlien A/S., N. Slottsgate 13, Oslo. Some of the more interesting subjects for photographs are: the magnificent new Town Hall, the harbor with Akershus Castle, Holmenkollen, Frognerseteren and the Frogner Park with the Vigeland sculptures. Take plenty of film to the fjord region.

RELIGION ... Norway is a Lutheran country. Churches of other sects in Oslo include Catholic, Episcopal, Presbyterian, and a synagogue. Catholic churches in other larger cities.

RESTAURANTS. .. In Oslo you will find a large number of fine places to dine and dance. The *Frognerseter* Restaurant up in the Holmenkollen Hills overlooking Oslo and the harbor has a fine dining room. *Speilen* at the Grand Hotel is very attractive and serves good food. *La Belle Sole* is outstanding. *Blom,* which belongs to the Artists' Association, is a good restaurant. The *Hotel Bristol* and *George's Grill* next to it serve excellent food. The *Queen* (Royal Norwegian Yacht Club), and the *King* (Oslo Rowing Club) both have large restaurants with dance floors (May through September). *Wimpy's,* with an excellent American style short-order counter, is new.

SHOPS AND STORES ... Steen and Strom in Oslo is Norway's biggest department store. Maja Jensen is good for tinware, ceramics and toys; David Andersen and Tostrup for silver. Gresvig for sporting goods; Heimen for wood carvings and native craft products; Hjordis Egelund for souvenirs; Husfliden (Association of Home Arts and Crafts) for tapestries, sweaters and all sorts of woolens. A must is William Schmidt on Karl Johans Street. A/S Arild, next to PAA's office, has a nice line of sports clothes and hand-knitted sweaters.

SPECTATOR SPORTS ... Championship ski competitions are the greatest spectator attraction during the winter and soccer during the summer. Skating races also draw crowds. The Holmenkollen ski competition near Oslo is the first week of March.

SPORTS ... Most Norwegians who can walk can ski. This is the national sport and Norway is one of the ski capitals of the world. Ski-touring is very popular. Huts and lodges dot the routes of cross-country runs. Norway is full of all kinds of slopes and jumps, lifts, instructors and cheerful ski lodges. Renting your skis is wiser than bringing them. They are the best in the world and insured against damage. Tobogganing, skating and bob-sledding are also popular.

The fishing in Norway is excellent too. You fish for trout and pike in any of the streams or lakes. Salmon fishing is magnificent. You can even lease your own river for about $600 a month or just go where the salmon fishing is. Preliminary arrangements aren't necessary at many hotels that own rights. The equipment and boats are available at reasonable cost. Sailing and swimming also rank high. The Oslo Golf Club's course at Bogstad is ideal. There are also golf courses in Bergen, Stavanger and Trondheim. Tourists are welcome.

Norwegian alps are a mountain climber's delight. Cyclists and hikers will find pleasant rolling countryside beneath the snow-capped peaks. Winter ski lodges become hostels for the hikers and climbers in the summer months. The hunting is wonderful. Deer and moose abound for the big-game hunter. A license is inexpensive. Rabbit, fox, hare and game birds are abundant. All in all, Norway is a year-round sportsman's paradise.

THEATERS ... In Oslo the National Theater stages classical drama, modern literary plays and light comedy. There is an annual Ibsen cycle. The *New Theater* devotes itself to light plays, the *Central* to light opera. *Chat Noir* is the oldest music hall with up-to-date revues.

TIME ... Six hours later than U.S. Eastern Standard Time.

TIPPING ... Hotels add 10 or 15 per cent service charge to your bill. Don't tip more except to the baggage porters and for special services. Follow the 10 to 15 per cent rule in your other tipping. The krone is worth about 15 cents in U.S. currency.

TRANSPORTATION ... Taxis and bus service are available in Oslo. Good train and air service is maintained to other parts of the country, especially the big tourist resorts. Drive-yourself cars are available for hire at very reasonable rates.

WATER ... Excellent.

WHAT TO BUY ... Norwegian enamelware and silver are your best buys. Native craft products are beautiful. They include textiles, glassware, embroideries, brassware and leather goods. Furs are marvelous and Norwegian skis are the finest in the world. Prices are a good deal lower than they are at home, but our duty is high.

WHAT TO WEAR ... Warm heavy clothing is a must for Norway in the winter. The Norwegian concept of heating makes for much cooler homes than our own, so bring dressy wool clothes for evening. Black suits and dresses are formal enough for Oslo night life. Business and sports suits for men. Sweaters and raincoats for both sexes. Medium-weight clothes for summer wear will be most suitable. Leave lightweight cottons and silks at home. Warm clothes are needed for sailing, skiing, hiking and climbing. Norwegian winds are cold.

WHERE TO GO—SIGHTSEEING ...

Oslo ... The 900-year-old city of Oslo is full of fascinating things to see. The town is surrounded by wooded hills and distant snow-capped peaks. You'll want to see the changing of the guards at the Royal Palace, the beautiful buildings of the University of Oslo, the National Theater with its statues of Bjornson and Ibsen, and the Nobel Institute where the prizes are awarded. Stroll through beautiful Karl Johans Gate Park. There are band concerts and outdoor cafés here. The medieval castle, Akershus, built by Haakon the Fifth is a must. A trip up the Holmenkollen behind the city offers

The fjord country in western Norway offers magnificent scenery from your excursion steamer. This scene is near Bergen, about 300 miles northwest of Oslo.

a wonderful view. Oslo was the site of the 1952 Winter Olympics. There's the Holmenkollen Recreation Center here too. A visit to the harbor with its bustling market places will give you a good idea of native life. Just wandering around the medieval part of the city will be like going back over 500 years in the life of the country. Plan to see the Vigeland Sculpture Park, the *Kon-Tiki* balsa raft from the famous expedition, the Open Air Museum and the Viking Ships Museum at Bygdoy, in the outskirts of Oslo and the other museums mentioned under ARTS. These are just a few of the marvelous things to do in the interesting city of Oslo. There are also regular sight-seeing tours by boat down the Oslo Fjord. They start from the Town Hall.

Bergen ... is Norway's second largest city (12 hours by train from Oslo or 1¼ hours by air). The town has wonderfully harmonious examples of medieval, Renaissance and strikingly modern architecture. See the Mariakirken Church. Built in the twelfth century, it is the oldest building in Bergen. The Hanseatic Museum gives an excellent idea of the culture of old Norway. There is a fine art gallery and ethnological collection in the Bergen University, another interesting sight. Other things to see include the harbor and market places, the home of Edvard Grieg, the great Norwegian composer, and the old Norwegian Stave churches. Leading hotels in Bergen include the *Bristol,* the *Norge,* the *Grand Hotel Terminus* and the brand new *Orion.* Single rooms begin about $3 with bath. Side trips may be made to the beautiful fjords around Bergen. It's also the starting point for the famous coastal express steamers to the Land of the Midnight Sun.

Stavanger ... Norway's third largest city is the new gateway to the Norwegian fjords. (11 hours by train or 1 hour by air from Oslo.) The hotel facilities here are excellent. The *Alstor Hotel, Atlantic Hotel* and *Hotel Victoria* all have fine accommodations. The Atlantic Hotel is the newest and one of the finest in northern Europe. In the vicinity of Stavanger you have the *Sola Hotel* and the *Viste Hotel,* well-known sea resorts.

Trondheim ... is the principal city in north-central Norway (12 hours by train from Oslo, 1½ hours by air). There is a fabulously lovely cathedral begun in the eleventh century and still being built today. Norway's great Technical School is here. The River Nid runs through the town and can be crossed by four graceful bridges. Sailing, fishing and skiing are all wonderful near Trondheim. Cozy and cheerful ski lodges offer simple accommodations. The *Britannia, Astoria* and the *Bristol* are the good hotels in the town itself.

Lillehammer ... The charming village of Lillehammer is the center of the greatest skiing in Norway (4 hours by train from Oslo). Champions from all over the world come here to ski. The slopes are wonderful. Good mountain-lodge accommodations are available. The *Victoria* is the best hotel in town.

There are several circular motor-coach tours out of Oslo which take from 5 to 10 days. These tours take in all the points of interest. Remember that Norway is an enormous country; distances are great and there is lots to see. But whatever itinerary you decide to follow, be sure to include the fjords.

The Fjords ... To go to Norway without seeing some of the great fjords is like going to Paris without seeing the Louvre. The fjords are in the western part of the country and are often a mile deep and as high. Most famous are Hardangerfjord, Sognefjord, Romsdalfjord, Geirangerfjord and Lyngenfjord. The most comfortable way to see the fjords is on one of the coastal steamers which run along the rugged west coast. It is also possible to go by car or regular bus service, and take some of the local ferries. There are for instance several ferry trips to be made and you see some magnificent fjord scenery. The steamers make stops which allow for half-day inland excursions. In the early summer there is perpetual sunlight, so if you are touring the fjords at this time it is almost impossible to tear yourself away from the scenery to sleep.

North Norway ... About one-third of Norway lies north of the Arctic Circle and with modern means of transportation even this part of the country is now easily available for visitors with little time at their disposal. It is, however, essential to book in advance since distances are so enormous that good planning is necessary. There are special cruises out of Bergen and also round trips of 12 days by the regular coastal express steamers. Other prearranged tours are available from Oslo with a combination of air and sea transportation. The North Cape Certificate, which is given only to those who have visited this northernmost point in Europe, is a rare and prized document.

SOURCES OF FURTHER INFORMATION ... All leading travel bureaus and the Oslo Information Office, Roald Amundsenget 2, have folders in English, city and country maps, lists of local events, hotels and restaurants. For guides and tours, contact the travel bureaus. Pan American's office is at Kronprinsesse Marthasplass 1 (Tel. 410280). English-language newspapers, magazines and periodicals are available at newspaper stalls. In New York the Norwegian National Travel Office is at 290 Madison Avenue, Tel. MU 3-8933.

PORTUGAL

WEATHER IN LISBON—Lat. N38°43'—Alt. 285'

Temp.	JAN.	FEB.	MAR.	APR.	MAY	JUNE	JULY	AUG.	SEPT.	OCT.	NOV.	DEC.
Low	46°	47°	51°	54°	58°	63°	65°	67°	64°	58°	53°	47°
High	54°	56°	59°	63°	66°	77°	75°	76°	73°	68°	61°	58°
Average	50°	52°	55°	59°	62°	70°	70°	72°	69°	63°	57°	53°
Days of Rain	13	12	14	12	9	5	2	2	6	11	13	14

LOCATION ... Portugal lies between Spain and the Atlantic Ocean, a small rectangle in the southwest corner of the Iberian Peninsula. Lisbon, the capital, is 895 air miles from Paris and 319 air miles from Madrid. Among other places, the Azores, about 800 miles to the west, and Madeira Islands are an insular part of Portugal.

CHARACTERISTICS ... Lisbon is one of the pleasantest cities in Europe. Its hotels are fine and its restaurants famous. Portugal is like a picture postal card. The climate is ideal, the drives and the scenery utterly beautiful. For something different, plan a trip to Portugal, where Americans are very welcome and there are not too many of them. Discover this country for yourself.

POPULATION ... Estimated 9,000,000, the population slightly exceeds that of New York City and Baltimore combined.

SIZE ... 380 miles long and 140 miles wide—about the size of Indiana.

CAPITAL ... Lisbon, with an estimated population of 1,000,000; a city larger than Baltimore.

GOVERNMENT ... A unitary and corporative Republic, the Portuguese constitution having been approved by plebiscite in March 1933. President of the Republic elected through universal suffrage every seven years. Congressmen of National Assembly numbering 120, elected every four years.

HOW TO GET THERE ... By Pan American Clipper only about

10¼ hours (nonstop) from New York to Lisbon, 3½ hours from Paris, 1½ hours from Madrid. By ship, about 8 to 9 days.

ACCOMMODATIONS ... Lisbon has very good hotels to fit every taste and budget. The most luxurious hostelry in town is the swank *Aviz.* Minimum rate is $8.50 single, European Plan. First class and more moderately priced are the *Tivoli, Mundial, Imperio, Embaixador, Eduardo VII, Condestavel, Infante Santo* and *Florida;* single rooms, European Plan, range from $4 to $6. These are only a few of Lisbon's many hotels. Accommodations can be had for as low as $2.80 a day with all meals in the little native hotels seldom frequented by tourists, but full of native atmosphere. Rates based on official exchange are the same year round, and can be arranged on European Plan. Throughout the country there are a number of Government-owned *pousadas,* or guest houses, and privately owned *estalagens* (inns) which offer tourists comfortable and interesting if not luxurious accommodations.

ARTS ... There are Roman, Visigothic, Romanesque, Gothic, Renaissance, baroque and neo-classic style examples in Portugal, as well as some of modern architecture. A peculiar Portuguese style, the *Manuelino,* dating from the fifteenth and sixteenth centuries, will draw your attention, as it is exuberantly decorated with nautical and maritime motifs. It is essentially the style of the maritime discoveries period. The *Mosteiro dos Jeronimos* and *Torre de Belem* in Lisbon are very represenative of that art.

There is a Portuguese school of painting (fifteenth and sixteenth centuries) with its own characteristics, of which a very important collection can be seen at the Ancient Art Museum in Lisbon. Besides those Portuguese ancient paintings, beautiful examples of Spanish, Flemish, Italian, German, etc., painters can be admired, too. There is also a precious collection of goldsmith art, ceramics, tapestry, etc., in this museum. The Contemporary Art Museum in Lisbon, the Soares dos Reis Museum in Oporto, the Machado de Castro Museum in Coimbra and the Grão Vasco Museum in Viseu display the most characteristic Portuguese paintings and sculptures of the nineteenth and twentieth centuries. Remarkable are the Coaches Museum in Lisbon, with a very singular and rich collection of royal coaches, unique in the world, and the Popular Art Museum, also in Lisbon, marvelous synthesis of the Portuguese people's life.

BALLET ... Portugal has a national ballet group called Verde Gaio, which features mainly folk motifs. Foreign ballets can be seen during the winter season.

BANKS ... Banco de Portugal, Banco Nacional Ultramarino, Bank of London and South America, Banco Espirito Santo e Comercial de Lisboa, Banco Lisboa e Acores with airport branch.

CALENDAR OF HOLIDAYS ... New Year's Day; Mardi Gras, just before Lent; Easter (Good Friday); June 10, Day of Camões, national poet; Corpus Christi (in June, but date variable); June 13, St. Anthony, Municipal Holiday (only in Lisbon); August 15, Assumption; October 5, Proclamation of Republic; November 1, All

Saints Day; December 1, Independence Day; December 8, the Feast of the Immaculate Conception; Christmas Day.

CIGARETTES AND TOBACCO... American cigarettes and tobacco are available. The most popular of the local brands of cigarettes are *Tagus, High-Life, Aviz, Portuguese Suave, Paris, 20–20–20* (Three Twenties), *Unic,* and *Tip-Top.* Principal tobaccos are *Frances, Superior* and *Virginia.*

COMMON COURTESIES AND LOCAL CUSTOMS... A kind, warm greeting expressed by the handshake is a very important part of everyday life in Portugal and, in a way, an aid to understanding. The boss in an office shakes hands with his employees every morning. When Portuguese ladies go out in the evening, they are accompanied by some member of the family.

CLUBS... Rotary Club, Lions Club, Turf Club, Royal British Club and Circulo Eca de Queiroz in Lisbon. Club de Golf Estoril in Estoril; Sporting Club de Cascais.

COMMUNICATIONS... There are telephone, telegraph and cable facilities in all major centers. Airmail.

CURRENCY... The Portuguese monetary unit is the escudo, divided into 100 centavos. For example 85 escudos, 50 centavos is written Esc. 85$50. The escudo is worth about 3½ cents or 28$80 to the dollar. Unlimited dollars, escudos or other currencies importable and exportable.

CUSTOMS REGULATIONS AND DOCUMENTS REQUIRED FOR UNITED STATES CITIZENS... Your luggage is subject to inspection by the customs authorities, the regulations about inspection being similar to those in force in all European countries. 400 cigarettes or 500 grams of tobacco may be imported free of duty. There are no special fees on the import of holiday purchases to a total value not exceeding $400. The vsitor can bring into the country any amount of camera film he can prove to be for his own use, up to 500 Portuguese escudos. United States citizens need a passport, but no visa. For stopovers in the Azores, however, you need a visa. For return to the United States, you will need vaccination certificate.

DRUG STORES... No American-type drug stores, but pharmaceuticals at the pharmacies, and toiletries at the perfumists. American brands are readily available.

ELECTRIC CURRENT... Power is 210–220 volts 50 cycles, A.C. in the most important cities, 110–120 D.C. in a few places. Standard European round-pronged converter plugs, available locally, are needed for Portuguese outlets.

FAUNA... No special birds or animals of outstanding interest for the tourist are to be found in Portugal. The Lisbon Zoo at Parque das Larangeiras, Estrada de Benfica, has one of the finest collections of live animals in Europe, and beautiful gardens.

FLORA... Visit the Botanical Garden, Rua da Escola Politécnica, Lisbon, with exotic local flora, and the Greenhouse at Parque Eduardo VII, one of the best in Europe. The Forest of Monsanto is one of Lisbon's many attractions, with the belvedere of

Montes Claros overlooking the Tagus River.

FOOD ... Portuguese cuisine is delicious. *Bacalhau à Gomes de Sá*, a very special dish prepared with codfish, is worth trying. At the *Nicola*, one of the many cafés in Lisbon, you can try the tasty *bacalhau à Nicola*, a dish that is served on Fridays. For those who like a good steak, the *bife na frigideira*, which is served in all restaurants, is a delicious dish. *Caldo verde* is a soup made with mashed potatoes and thinly sliced cabbage, unbelievably good. *Iscas com elas* is another national dish made with thin slices of liver very specially seasoned and served with French-fried potatoes.

Almost every restaurant in Portugal has its own special dish. Cheese-making is one of the Portuguese specialties. The visitor will find delicious cheeses everywhere in the country. Cheeses from Serra, Azeitão, Serpa, Rabaçal, Ponte de Sôr and the small, fresh, white cheese made of goats' milk, will be a new taste sensation for cheese lovers. Portuguese pastry is also delicious. Almost every town in Portugal has its own specialty: *Ovos Moles* in Aveiro; *Doces d'Ovos* in Viseu; *Trouxas d'Ovos* and *Cavacas* in Caldas da Rainha; *Toucinho do Ceu* in Portalegre; *Queijadas* in Sintra; *Pasteis de Feijão* in Torres Vedras; *Arrufadas* and *Manjar Branco* in Coimbra; *Celestes* in Santarem; *Pão de Ló in Alfeizerão*. These are just a few of the many kinds of pastry, almost all of them also available in Lisbon.

Milk is good and safe to drink.

GAMBLING ... Casinos with roulette at resort towns, such as at Estoril (all year), Figueira da Foz, Povoa do Varzim and Espinho (during summer period only).

LANGUAGE ... The official language is Portuguese. In Lisbon Oporto, Coimbra and in all other big cities, it will be easy to find someone who speaks English. Some useful Portuguese expressions are: *bom dia* (good morning), *obrigado* (thank you), *onde é* (where is ...) and *quanto custa* (how much is ...).

LAUNDRY AND DRY CLEANING ... about the same in quality, price and speed as in the United States.

LIQUOR ... Port wine, the famous wine which comes from the Douro Valley, and Madeira wine from Madeira, are world renowned. Good sparkling and table wines are served at hotels and restaurants throughout the country. The most famous wines come from Bairrada, Ribatejo and Estremadura, where the large vineyards are. You may taste the best port wines at the Solar do Velho Porto in Lisbon and in Oporto at the cellars of the old concerns which for centuries have dealt with Port. Cointreau, Benedictine, Peppermint, Aniz, and many other liqueurs are available, as well as good brandies. American and English whiskies are available in most Portuguese bars.

MEDICAL FACILITIES ... Good modern hospitals in the large towns and small first-aid stations throughout the country. Ask at your hotel if you need a doctor or telephone Lisbon 775171.

MOTION PICTURES ... There are a number of motion picture theaters in Lisbon showing Portuguese and foreign films, including the best American pictures. Among the well-known ones are *St.*

Jorge, Tivoli, S. Luiz, Politeama, Eden and *Condes,* as well as two new ones, the *Monumental* and *Imperio.* Theaters open at 3:15 P.M. and shows are available also at 6:15 and 9:30 P.M.

MUSIC ... You can hear fine concerts with famous maestros at the *Teatro Nacional de S. Carlos* in Lisbon during the winter, played by the National Symphony Orchestra. Every year there is an opera season featuring famous artists. Military bands in summer play concerts in the main public gardens. *Fado,* the typical Portuguese song of Lisbon, can be heard every night in the typical restaurants of Bairro Alto. This is an approximation of the American blues and torch songs.

NIGHT LIFE AND CAFÉS ... You'll get the best in native atmosphere in the little cafés that are mainly frequented by Portuguese. Here, amid smoke and wine, the eerie *fados* are sung by entertainers and customers alike. These haunts are found mainly in Bairro Alto, one of the best of them being the *Luso.* Gayer and more conventional night clubbing at *Tagide, Negresco, Nina,* the *Wonder Bar* in Estoril. There is dancing at all these places. Other gay night clubs are the *Maxime, Montes Claros, Bico Dourado,* in Lisbon; *Choupana, Ronda, Palm Beach* in Estoril. Good bars include the *Rex, Americano,* the *English Bar,* the *Iberia.* Dining at the *Aviz Hotel* is very chic. *See also* RESTAURANTS.

PHOTOGRAPHY ... Color and black-and-white film for still and movie cameras is available in Lisbon, as well as all makes of cameras and equipment and developing facilities for black-and-white film; 8-hour service. All camera stores do reliable work.

RELIGION ... The principal local religion is Roman Catholic. However, there are a few Protestant churches and two Jewish synagogues.

RESTAURANTS ... Besides flavorful Portuguese cuisine, excellent French, Italian and Austrian cooking can be had in Lisbon. The most elegant places to eat in Lisbon are *Tavares, Gondola* (Italian cooking), *Irmãos Unidos, Macau* (Chinese cooking), *Vera Cruz, Alvalade* and *Negresco.* The food is superb, at about $4 including wine. The *Aquàro, Chave d'Ouro* (both with dancing), *Imperio, Gambrinus* and *Iberia,* in the center of Lisbon's business district, are very popular and moderately priced. For Austrian food the *Chave d'Ouro* is among the best. The *Gondola* serves fine Italian food. Typically native spots include the *Machado,* where you can hear the *fado* and national songs, *Mesquita Viela* and *Faia.* Among the plushiest tea rooms in town are *Caravela, Benard, Alvalade, Riviera, Imperio* and *Chave d'Ouro* mentioned above.

SHOPS AND STORES ... The two big and important stores in Lisbon are Grandela and Chiado. All best Lisbon shops are situated along the Rua Garrett (Chiado), Rua do Ouro, Rua Augusta and Rua da Prata. Shops open every day at 9:00 A.M., close at 1:00 P.M., reopen at 3:00 P.M. and close for the day at 7:00 P.M.

SPECTATOR SPORTS ... No one going to Portugal should miss seeing at least one bullfight. The bull isn't killed and the fight is not so gory as the Spanish version. The Amateur Fights held in summer in

Lisbon (*Campo Pequeno*) are full of color.

Soccer is the most popular sport in Portugal. Roller-skating hockey is also a national sport. The most important soccer games are played in the beautiful National Stadium every Sunday near Lisbon and throughout the country from the fall until late in spring. The roller-skating hockey matches are followed by an enthusiastic public. The Portuguese are world champions in this kind of hockey.

SPORTS ... The deep-sea fishing enthusiast will find exciting big-game fishing in Portuguese waters. Though there are all kinds of fish, the biggest is the tuna. Boats and equipment are for hire at reasonable prices. Golfing is mainly a tourist sport; there are good courses in resort towns. Tennis courts are also available. Horses may be hired in many large towns. Mountain climbing and skiing are both new in Portugal, but rapidly growing in popularity.

THEATERS ... Lisbon's most important theater is the *Teatro Nacional de S. Carlos,* intended for opera, ballet, symphony music. Other good theaters which present musicals and plays in Portuguese are the *Teatri Nacional D. Maria II, Teatro Avenida, Maria Vitoria, Variedades,* and the new *Monumental.*

TIME ... Five hours later than United States Eastern Standard Time. This is Greenwich Mean Time. Daylight Saving Time is observed from about the end of April until November.

TIPPING ... Ten per cent service charge is added to hotel and restaurant bills, but an extra 5 per cent tip is expected. Tip cab drivers 20 per cent because fares are very low.

TOURIST TAXES ... If you are traveling by water, entry tax 15 escudos, exit tax, 8 per cent of passage. If you are traveling by air, no entry or exit tax, except for air passage purchased in Portugal.

TRANSPORTATION ... Taxis, trolley cars and splendid buses are available in Lisbon. Good trains to principal cities, and a few excellent highways. Cars with chauffeurs are available for trips at Esc. 2$00 to 2$80 per kilometer depending on the seating capacity.

WATER ... Water is safe to drink everywhere in Portugal. However, bottled waters are available.

WHAT TO BUY ... Shopping in Lisbon, your best buys are cork products. Native craftsmen do amazing things with this material. Also exceptionally fine gold and silver jewelry, made in delicate filigree patterns, and flat silver can be found. Interesting native figurines and ceramics are available. Rope-soled sports shoes. Also fine embroideries and laces.

WHAT TO WEAR ... Lightweight street cottons are your best bet, from June to September. Warm clothing is needed for the winter months, especially if you are going to mountain areas. Generally, informal sports clothes and more formal street-length wear for evening will do. Evening clothes are worn only at the plushiest resort hotels and casinos. As in Spain, the typical costume for the women of fashion is the little black dress. If you wear sports clothes in the city, keep them conservative. Men need linen or tropical worsted suits, a light topcoat, dinner clothes, slacks and sports jackets.

WHERE TO GO—SIGHTSEEING . . .

Lisbon . . . Lisbon is a picturesque city, built, like Rome, on seven hills. The buildings are painted various pastel shades. The green hills and the blue sea make a wonderful backdrop for this colorful town. The Belem Tower, built in the early sixteenth century, is a wonderful specimen of the Manueline style with some Moorish influence, as its architect (Arruda) was one of the chief builders of the Portuguese fortresses in Morocco. The view from the ramparts is breathtaking.

The churches of Lisbon represent every conceivable style of architecture. Seeing them all would be impractical. Among the most beautiful and historically important are the Jeronimos Monastery and Church. In Manueline style, its cloisters of two pavements are regarded as among the most remarkable in the world. The cathedral blends Romanesque and Gothic styles and contains wonderful tomb sculptures of the fourteenth century. The city of Lisbon is crowned by a picturesque Moorish castle of the tenth century. The broad and beautiful Avenida da Liberdade runs through one of the most fashionable parts of Lisbon. Be sure and see the fabulous greenhouses of the Estufa Fria (cool garden) in Edward the Seventh Park nearby.

A visit to the harbor and the native fish market will give you an excellent chance to see the natives in their tartan-plaid costumes, reminiscent of the Scottish dress. The botanical and zoological gardens are among Europe's finest. Black Horse Square in the lower part of the city that was rebuilt after an earthquake in 1755 is surrounded by fine classical buildings. You will find that Lisbon's hills would be rough going if it weren't for the *ascensores,* out-door elevators that lift you up the hills for less than half a cent. Eiffel designed a number of these unique structures. These are just a very few of the things to see in Lisbon. The tourist could wander for days through the quaint narrow streets or along the wide modern boulevards and never cease to be interested by the unique and varied sights.

Estoril . . . Only 15 miles from Lisbon is Estoril, Portugal's fabulous seaside resort town. The beaches are magnificent and the climate is good all year round. The *Palace Hotel* is first class. Its facilities include fine golf links, swimming pool, private beaches, tennis courts, casino and splendid restaurants. Rates at this luxurious hotel are from $5 but can be much higher, single with meals. The *Atlantico* is more moderately priced, rates beginning at $4. A lovely swimming pool is now opened to customers and special guests. It is a very good place to stay. There are stables in Estoril and beautiful bridle paths along the beach and up in the hills. It is one of Europe's loveliest and gayest resorts.

A short drive from Estoril is the town of Sintra, called a little Eden by Lord Byron, who lived there for five years. An ancient Moorish castle stands in stern grandeur high above the town. The view is glorious. Visit also the Palacio de Sintra, with its beautiful Moorish tile mosaics and lovely fountains and gardens. But the most enchanting thing about this little town is the scenic beauty of the landscape. There are good hotels in Sintra, including the *Hotel*

Lawrence, Central and the Costa. Rates are reasonable. The Urca is the best restaurant in Sintra. You must not leave Sintra without visiting the unique Hotel Palacio Seteais. It has recently been con verted from an old castle in an exquisite setting of typical Portuguese scenery.

Setubal . . . Surrounded by orange groves, the lively town of Setubal is situated at the mouth of the Sado River. It is Portugal's main fishing port. The Church of Jesus is a masterpiece of Manueline architecture. The painted panels are excellent examples of the Portuguese Renaissance school of painting. The ruins of Cetobriga, destroyed in the fifth century, are fascinating and so is the old fortress of St. Philip, built in the sixteenth century. The medieval fortress of Palmela is a characteristic example of its era and the view from the towers encompasses all of Sintra, Setubal and Lisbon. The native market places are colorful and intriguing. There are very fine little restaurants with the best in native cooking and atmosphere. Hotels in Setubal include the Club Naval Setubalense, a fairly good hotel with very moderate prices. Near Setubal lies one of the most beautiful Portuguese beaches, the Portinho de Arrabida. Azeitao is an interesting little town, a center for famous wines and cheeses, with a nice rest house called Quinta das Torres. Another is Praia da Rocha on the southern coast. Evora, 68 miles from Lisbon, is rich in artwork.

Coimbra . . . Coimbra is Portugal's university city. The school is one of the oldest in Europe. This beautiful town is built on a series of fanned-out hills like an amphitheater. The University stands on the site of the former royal palace. The library and the lovely little chapel are well worth seeing. The Church of Santa Cruz is one of the most beautiful in all of Portugal. The tombs of the first two kings of Portugal are here. The gardens of the old monastery are still as they were seven centuries ago. There are good hotels and restaurants in Coimbra. Hotel Astoria and the Bragança are the best, rooms from $4 a day with meals. Moderately priced hotels are the Avenida, Central, International. Good places to dine include the Cardosa, Nicola, Café Santa Cruz, and for native food and pastry the Jardim da Manga. Coimbra is a fascinating mixture of many civilizations that have all left their mark on the city.

Oporto . . . Oporto is Portugal's second largest city and the center of the wine trade and export business. Situated about 200 miles north of Lisbon, the drive up along the coast is well worth the cost of hiring a car. Things to do and see in Oporto include a visit to the Roman, Gothic and Baroque Cathedral, with an exquisite silver altar; the little Roman Chapel of Cedofeita; the Gothic S. Francisco Church and the Soares dos Reis Museum in the ancient royal palace of Carrancas, where there is a magnificent collection of masterpieces dating from the Middle Ages. In the Palacio de Cristal gardens, one of the most beautiful Portuguese parks, you can enjoy a beautiful panorama of the Douro River. The Praça da Ribeira is a typical native market in Oporto's oldest quarter. There are many fine goldsmith shops in Oporto. Best hotels are Infante Sagres and Grande Hotel do Imperio, where rates begin at $3.50. Other comfortable hotels, moderately priced, are the *Grande Hotel do Porto, Peninsular, Batalha.* The *Escondidinho, Belo Horizonte, Caravela, Le Chien qui Fume, Marisqueira, Gambrinus* are among the better restaurants.

Fatima . . . Portugal's outstanding site of devotion is situated 105 miles northeast of Lisbon (169 Km.). A beautiful church has been erected to the Holy Mary on the spot of the apparitions. Hundreds of thousands of pilgrims worship there every year. Many cures have been claimed by pilgrims to the shrine. The shrine of Fatima has been recognized and dedicated by the present Pope and is exceeded in attendance only by Lourdes and Lisieux. Aside from two big pilgrimages—May 13 and October 13—Fatima is observed on the thirteenth of each month.

Madeira . . . Called the Pearl of the Atlantic, the beautiful island of Madeira is situated 625 miles southwest of Lisbon. The climate is perfect. It is seldom hotter than 75 degrees and never gets very cold. The scenic beauty of the island ranks with that anywhere. Funchal, the port town, is a gay city with good night clubs, hotels and gambling casinos. Beautiful beaches provide all water sports. There is good mountain climbing on the island. Madeira wine and embroideries are the chief industries. The dazzling New Year's celebrations have drawn tourists here for many years. The hotels in Funchal include the ultra chic *Reid's Palace Hotel,* the *Savoy* and the *Atlantic.* Good eating at the *Ritz,* the *Standard* and the *Golden Gate.*

The Azores . . . This Portuguese archipelago, 4 hours by air west of Lisbon, is interesting for its gorgeous unspoiled scenery and quaint old customs; an ideal place for the person interested in discovering vacation spots on his own. Santa Maria is a regular stop on flights via the southern route between the United States and Europe. São Miguel nearby is the biggest and most important island and provides the best tourist attractions. There are two principal tours: one of the Sete Cidades ("seven cities") and one of the Furnas Valley resort with mineral waters, attractive park and swimming pool, golf course, beautiful lake filled with carp and yellow perch. Interesting volcanic phenomena including a volcanic crater are seen on the Sete Cidades tour. Everywhere there are interesting aspects of island life—windmills, oxcarts, women in traditional regional clothes, colorful religious processions, pineapple plantations. There are two hotels on São Miguel, both named the *Terra Nostra;* one in the capital, Ponta Delgada ($2.50 to $4 American Plan) and the other in the Furnas Valley ($3.50 to $10.50 American Plan). The climate is semi-tropical, around 70 degrees in summer, 50 degrees in winter. Visa required.

SOURCES OF FURTHER INFORMATION . . . In Lisbon the Secretariado Nacional da Informação Praça dos Restauradores (or at the airport) has folders, maps and information. Sightseeing information also at the better travel agencies and at Pan American's office in Lisbon at Praça dos Restauradores 46 (Tel. 32181) and at the Portela Airport (Tel. 721101). In New York contact Casa de Portugal, 447 Madison Ave., for information on both Portugal and the Azores.

RUSSIA (U.S.S.R.)

WEATHER IN MOSCOW—Lat. N55°45'—Alt. 625'

Temp.	JAN.	FEB.	MAR.	APR.	MAY	JUNE	JULY	AUG.	SEPT.	OCT.	NOV.	DEC.
Low	5°	8°	15°	29°	42°	50°	54°	51°	42°	33°	21°	10°
High	14°	19°	29°	43°	60°	67°	71°	68°	56°	44°	28°	17°
Average	10°	13°	22°	36°	51°	58°	62°	54°	49°	36°	24°	13°

LOCATION ... Russia occupies one-sixth of the earth's land surface, stretching across two continents from the North Pacific Ocean to the Gulf of Finland.

POPULATION ... Estimated at slightly over 204,000,000.

SIZE ... 7,877,598 sq. miles, three times that of the United States.

CAPITAL ... Moscow, with a population of about 5,000,000.

GOVERNMENT ... The U.S.S.R. is made up of 15 republics or states with representatives in the Supreme Soviet, the highest legislative authority. The Supreme Court is the highest judicial organ, members being elected by the Supreme Soviet. Highest executive and administrative organ of state is the Council of Ministers (Premier, Ministers and their deputies) appointed by the Supreme Soviet.

HOW TO GET THERE ... Pan American Clippers connect with the Russian airline, Aeroflot, in Paris, Copenhagen, Brussels, Helsinki, Berlin, Vienna and New Delhi. Elapsed time New York to Moscow 15 hours, to Leningrad 20¼ hours, to Kiev 24¼ hours.

ACCOMMODATIONS ... Moscow's better hotels are the *National, Metropol, Savoy, Sovietskaya, Ukraine,* and the skyscraper *Leningrad Hotel.* Accommodations should be obtained through an *Intourist* tour. See under WHERE TO GO—SIGHTSEEING.

ARTS AND BALLET ... Two musts are the Tretyakov Art Gallery, and the Pushkin Museum of Fine Arts. World famous Russian Ballet can be seen at the Bolshoi Theatre.

CALENDAR OF HOLIDAYS ... Four holidays are observed with no work; Revolution Anniversary, November 7; Constitution Day, December 5; May Day, May 1; and New Years.

CIGARETTES ... Only local brands at about 40 cents a pack.

CLIMATE ... As varied as her scenery, Russian climate can mean waist-high Siberian snow and arctic blizzards with the temperature falling to 80 degrees below zero, or bathing in the Black Sea on Christmas Day. Most of the country has sharp seasonal changes. Summer is the best time to visit Moscow.

COMMON COURTESIES AND LOCAL CUSTOMS ... The average Russian has a keen sense of humor and an instinctive liking for foreigners. He can laugh at himself and has a gift for nicknames and ridiculing pomposity. He works and plays hard, and is very proud of his cultural ancestry. Your respect of these traits will increase the enjoyment of your visit.

COMMUNICATIONS ... Service to the United States: Cablegrams, 1 ruble per word; telephone, 48 rubles per 3 minutes; airmail letter, 1.60 rubles; airmail post card, 1.40 rubles.

CURRENCY ... The monetary unit is the ruble, valued at 25 cents; but upon entry, you can exchange 10 rubles to the U.S. dollar.

CUSTOMS REGULATIONS AND DOCUMENTS REQUIRED FOR UNITED STATES CITIZENS ... Passport and visa (available through *Intourist*). Allow plenty of time for a visa. Smallpox vaccination certificate. Typhoid and typhus vaccination are recommended. No limit on U.S. currency. No Russian currency. Keep your currency exchange slips. Reasonably quantities of liquor, cigarettes and food for personal use may be taken in and out duty free.

ELECTRIC CURRENT ... Both 120- and 220-volt current. Standard European type plugs are used.

FOOD ... You may find the food on the heavy side, but good. Meats, including "Bifshtek," and vegetables are cooked long. *Cotleka pojarski* (chicken cutlets), *koulebîaka* (meat or fish pie) and *Zharenny carps kashoi* (roast carp with porridge) are a few dishes to try. Soups such as Schchi (sauerkraut soup), ice cream and of course, caviar, are excellent. Tea and some wines are good, coffee poor. If you wish, bring instant coffee and ask for *kipyatok* (hot water).

LAUNDRY AND DRY CLEANING ... Laundry is no problem. Dry cleaning is not good, and service slow.

MEDICAL FACILITIES ... Chemist shops offer a variety of pharmaceuticals. Hospitals give free treatment even to the tourist, if he is unable to pay for it. 78% of the nation's doctors are women.

MOTION PICTURES ... The Russians are extremely fond of films. Some American films are shown, but with Russian dialogue.

MUSIC ... There's a variety of concerts to choose from. Principal concert halls are the Grand Hall of the Tchaikovsky Conservatoire, the Hall of Columns and Hall of the Palace of Sport.

PHOTOGRAPHY ... Don't take pictures in Art Galleries, museums, customs places, airports or railway stations without permission.

RELIGION ... Moscow has fifty-two churches of various denominations. Greek Orthodox is the most common.

RESTAURANTS ... Meals are expensive in Moscow, although for $5 to $10 you can get a meal for two in one of the national restaurants. Some restaurants have entertainment.

SHOPS AND STORES ... Most of the shops are open from 8:00 A.M. to 8:00 P.M., some much later. The famous department store, *Gum,* is an experience in itself. Interesting items to buy are: Chess sets, books, records, fur hats, and some gold items.

SPORTS ... Sports are popular, especially track and gymnastics. There are many stadiums, ski centers, swimming pools and boating stations; tennis, volleyball, basketball grounds and recreation parks. International competitions are held at the Luzhniki Stadium.

THEATERS ... Repertory companies offer a wide variety of shows. Get tickets through *Intourist.* Theaters include the Bolshoi Theatre, Moscow Art Theatre, Bolshoi Filial Theatre and the Maly Theatre.

TIME ... When it is noon in New York, it is 7:00 P.M. in Moscow.

TIPPING ... It is not necessary to tip in most places although a 10% tip is expected in restaurants.

TRANSPORTATION ... In Moscow and Leningrad the Metro, or subway, is famous for its clean, mural-covered stations. There are also buses, trams and taxis.

WATER ... Outside Moscow, drink *narzan,* bottled water.

WHERE TO GO—SIGHTSEEING ...

An *Intourist* itinerary, available through U.S. travel agencies, costs from $10 ($7 to groups) to $30 a day. The $30 plan includes conveyance by car to and from the airport or rail stations, de luxe accommodations in hotels, four meals daily, sightseeing in car with guide-interpreter. Tours can be arranged to include Moscow, Leningrad, Kiev, Minsk, Odessa, Yalta, Tashkent, Irkutsk, Riga, Uzhgorod, Lvov and Chernovtsy. You will also receive a better than official currency exchange rate from *Intourist.*

Moscow ... The Kremlin (1462–1505), the center of town, contains within its massive 65-foot walls the Grand Kremlin Palace, home of the Supreme Soviet; and the Lenin-Stalin Mausoleum with the preserved bodies of these former premiers. Just outside the Kremlin walls is Red Square, famous for military parades and exhibitions. Places to see include the Cathedral of Vasily Blazhenny (1554–60), the Minin and Pozharsky monument, the U.S.S.R. History Museum, the Museum of Lenin, the Obelisk of Revolutionary Thinkers, the U.S.S.R. Agricultural and Industrial Exhibit with many beautiful fountains and botanical gardens and some 300 buildings, and Sokolniki Park, site of the 1959 American National Exhibition.

Other places of interest include *Stalingrad* (more huge industry than sightseeing), *Leningrad,* with remnants of Czarist days atmosphere, *Kiev,* capital of the Ukraine with a gaiety about it, *Yalta,* site of Czar's winter palace and Big Three Conference, *Sochi,* on the Russian Riviera, and the ports of *Odessa* and *Sukhumi* on the Black Sea.

SOURCES OF FURTHER INFORMATION ... "Intourist," the U.S.S.R. Company is at 355 Lexington Ave., New York.

SPAIN

WEATHER IN MADRID—Lat. N40°25'—Alt. 2,150'

Temp.	JAN.	FEB.	MAR.	APR.	MAY	JUNE	JULY	AUG.	SEPT.	OCT.	NOV.	DEC.
Low	33°	35°	38°	42°	50°	56°	61°	62°	55°	47°	40°	35°
High	48°	52°	57°	63°	72°	79°	86°	87°	76°	65°	54°	48°
Average	41°	44°	48°	53°	61°	68°	74°	75°	66°	56°	47°	42°
Days of Rain	9	10	10	10	10	6	3	3	7	9	10	10

LOCATION . . . Spain along with Portugal occupies the Iberian Peninsula, from the Pyrenees at the French border to Gibraltar. Madrid is about halfway between Lisbon and Barcelona.

CHARACTERISTICS . . . The land of the bullfight is a land of color with skies and waters of brilliant blue. The architecture reflects the many influences that have shaped the country. Art galleries and museums filled with treasures abound. Food is wonderful, the top hotels are good, the tempo restful. There is music and gaiety in Spain, and a color that is not duplicated anywhere else in the world. Spaniards are unfailingly courteous to strangers, and while they may not always understand you, they will at least make the effort. It's a wonderful spot to rest. They won't let you hurry.

POPULATION . . . Estimated 30,000,000. The population density is similar to that of Illinois.

SIZE . . . 194,396 square miles, 3½ times the size of Illinois.

CAPITAL . . . Madrid. Population 2,000,000.

GOVERNMENT . . . A state, with Generalissimo Franco granted a life tenure as chief-of-state.

HOW TO GET THERE . . . By Pan American Clipper, elapsed time from New York, about 14 hours to Barcelona; Madrid is 1½ hours by air from Lisbon, 3¼ hours from Rome, and 1¾ hours from Barcelona. By ship, about 7 days to Lisbon, 6 to 8 days to Gibraltar.

ACCOMMODATIONS . . . In Madrid, the *Ritz* ($7–$16.50), Plaza de la Lealtad, fine food, summer garden restaurant. Other de luxe hotels ($4.75–$12): *Palace Hotel*, Plaza de las Cortes, good grill and popular bar, partly air-conditioned, the *Castellana Hilton,* Paseo de la Castellana, air-conditioned, offers modern luxury in the American manner, popular bar and night club; *Fenix Hotel,* Paseo de la Castellana, good food, summer garden; *Hotel Plaza,* Plaza de España, center of business area, penthouse grill and swimming pool; *Hotel Wellington,* Velazquez, 8, partly air-conditioned, good bar; *Hotel Savoy,* swimming pool; *Hotel Menfis,* downtown location, popular bar; *Emperador,* in downtown Madrid, swimming pool on the roof. Hotels classified as first class ($2.50): *Avenida; Carlos V; Gran Via; Lope de Vega; Montesol; Princesa; Principe Pio; Rex.* Meals are about $3 at most de luxe hotels, $1.50 at first class hotels. Rates given above are European Plan single. Add a 15 per cent service charge to hotel and restaurant prices given. An additional 10 per cent is charged as luxury tax for food served in luxury hotels.

In Barcelona are *Hotel Arycasa, Colón, Avenida Palace* and the *Ritz,* all in the de luxe category ($3.50–$6.00). First class hotels ($2.50) are the *Astoria, Condado, Emperatriz, Roma, Manila* and *Majestic.* On the famous hill, Tibidabo, overlooking Barcelona city and the Mediterranean, is *Hotel Florida* (de luxe), but it is closed in winter. There is a 15 per cent service charge at all hotels and restaurants.

There are also 26 Government-sponsored inns, 15 called *paradores* (converted castles) and 11 *albergues* (much like our motels), plain, clean, practical, in areas not served by hotels, at halfway points on main highways. Some, as those in Ireland, are remodeled castles. Basic rates, with meals, about $3.75 a day. Local and Continental cooking—local architectural features in them all.

ARTS... Outstanding is the Prado National Museum (not to be confused with El Pardo, residence of the Chief of State) with Spain's famous art collection to which several days should be devoted; open from 10 A.M. to 6 P.M. The Royal Palace, now open to the public mornings and afternoons 10 to 1 and 3 to 6, contains fine examples of tapestries, paintings and furnishings. Part of the Royal Palace contains one of the world's finest collections of armor. Also worth seeing are various other museums, such as the Museum of Modern Art, the Army Museum, and the Decorative Arts Museum.

In Barcelona one has the choice of 12 museums covering all periods. Especially recommended are the Municipal Museum of Archaeology (excavations from Roman and Gothic periods) and the Archive of the Crown of Aragon (one of the most important libraries in Spain). Also see the unique Museum of Catalan Art. There are several medieval monasteries in Poblet, Santa-Creus, Montserrat and Barcelona.

BALLET... Many prominent European and American ballet stars appear in Madrid and Barcelona during the spring. Fine Italian and French opera companies appear in both cities. There are several local ballet companies in Barcelona, most of them performing in winter.

BANKS... Both Barcelona and Madrid have branches of Banco Hispano-Americano (which has connections with several important U.S. banks), London and South America Bank, etc.

CALENDAR OF HOLIDAYS ... New Year's; March 19th (St. Joseph); April 1, Victory Day (official ending of the civil war); Holy Thursday; Good Friday; July 18, Labor Day; July 25, Apostle Santiago; October 12, *Fiesta de la Raza* (Columbus Day); November 1, Feast of All Saints; December 8, Our Lady of the Conception; Christmas; and in different localities many feast days, besides those big fairs, such as Barcelona's famous *verbenas of* San Juan and San Pedro, June 24 and 29, celebrated on the eve of these days. There is Seville's Holy Week and the popular *Feria* during the months of April and May; Pamplona's Patron Saint Day, *San Fermin,* July 7; Valencia's Patron Saint Day, *San José,* March 19, when the *Fallas* are celebrated; Madrid's festival of *San Isidro,* May 15, very typical and gay, and San Sebastian's, August 15, a festival starting on August 13 and lasting the whole week. Try to visit where you can on the big days.

CIGARETTES, CIGARS, TOBACCO ... Imported American and other foreign brands of cigarettes are plentiful. Spanish cigarettes are black, strong, inexpensive as are American type and Cuban cigars. You may bring in enough cigarettes for your personal use, about 1 carton.

CLIMATE ... Madrid has a 2,000-foot elevation and it is fairly cold in the winter and hot in the summer, but due to its dry climate, it isn't bad. It receives the fresh breeze from the nearby Sierra de Guadarrama which, it is said, makes it the most healthful capital of Europe. Best months are May, June, September and October.

Barcelona, situated on the Mediterranean coast, offers an ideal holiday climate. It is hot in the summer, mild in winter. Best seasons are spring, which starts as early as March, and autumn; winter does not start until November. Barcelona's hottest months are July and August, but the beautiful nearby mountains and coast are an excellent and comforting refuge.

CLUBS ... Many exclusive, smart clubs in both cities. In Madrid, Real Club Puerta de Hierro and Club de Campo. In Barcelona there's the Polo Club, Real Club de Golf el Prat, Real Club Nautico. For visits, contact the club secretary.

COMMON COURTESIES AND LOCAL CUSTOMS ... Spaniards are not too punctual, sometimes a little late for appointments. Luncheon is late, *aperitivo* (cocktail hour) may run as late as 9:00 or 9:30; with dinner served from 10:00 P.M. on to midnight, when the town really becomes alive.

After having made friends with a Spaniard and when separating after the first conversation with him, tell him your name and address, thus offering your house. This is a common Spanish courtesy.

COMMUNICATIONS ... International Cable and Radio. Telephone service is slow. Airmail postage to U.S. is pesetas 7.00 for letters, 6.00 for cards.

CURRENCY ... The monetary unit is the peseta, worth 60 pesetas to the dollar at the official rate of exchange. Money can be changed in hotels, travel agencies and banks. When changing money, the amount should be registered in the Foreign Currency Certificate which you will receive upon entry into Spain and show to Customs on leaving.

CUSTOMS REGULATIONS AND DOCUMENTS REQUIRED FOR UNITED STATES CITIZENS ... United States citizens need a passport but no visa for visits up to six months. One or 2 opened bottles of liquor and about 1 carton of cigarettes for personal use may be brought in duty free. You will need to declare your currency when entering Spain. You may take 10,000 pesetas into and up to 2,000 pesetas out of Spain. You may not take out a larger sum of foreign money than you took in. Cameras and films permitted. Purchases up to 25,000 pesetas may be taken out of the country by visitors without permit, but show receipts for purchases to Customs.

DRUG STORES ... In both Madrid and Barcelona you will find drug stores where English is spoken, with certain American products available at high prices; consult hotel clerk.

ELECTRIC CURRENT ... 110 volts D.C. or 125 volts A.C., 50 cycles. You will need an adapter for European plugs.

FOOD ... Spanish food is hearty, the variety is prodigious, and the cooking almost without exception wonderful. You need never fear any of the great variety of fruits: melons, grapes, figs, oranges, and many kinds you don't get commonly at home, all very fine. Watch for the tiny wild strawberries, the splendid seafood. Try the local specialties in the different parts of the country as you go about the countryside. There are delicate little cakes made with fruits and nuts. Spanish sweets are famous (particularly the excellent *turrones*) and suggest their Moorish ancestry. Pasteurized milk is available in Madrid and Barcelona, but not always in the smaller places. Milk should always be boiled for safety unless it is pasteurized.

GAMBLING ... Madrid has a fine race course, as does San Sebastian, where there is good horse racing over the Lasarte course each July, August, September. Greyhound racing in Madrid and Barcelona. Lotteries. There are no casinos for gambling, but betting on football games in winter and big betting on the *frontón* (or *jai alai*) games, but you had best just watch it, unless you know something about it. It's faster than light, and twice as exciting.

LANGUAGE ... The official language is Spanish, of course. English is understood in large cities and tourist centers only.

LAUNDRY AND DRY CLEANING ... Fine one- or two-day laundry service almost anywhere. Service is good and quick in the larger hotels. Prices are reasonable. Dry cleaning is not good and generally takes about a week.

LIQUOR ... You can drink sherry all through Spain, varying the type as often as you change cities, and if you choose, have it light (*manzanilla*), as well. As with the food, you might well enjoy one of the dozens of wines you find featured in its native province. Those of Málaga are delicious, always popular with Americans. There are many local liqueurs, such as anis, and several Spanish brandies usually a little grapier than the same French grade, but very good. And they have the additional charm of being cheap, as are all Spanish distilled liquors in comparison to the price charged for Scotch and other foreign beverages. You will enjoy experimenting with the dozens of Spanish wines, until you find the ones you will want to stick to. Popular American drinks are available in hotels and street bars. According to the place, prices vary from 15 to 25 pesetas, always more for Scotch and bourbon. Hotel bars are open usually until 11:00 P.M., other bars until 2:00 or 3:00 A.M.

MEDICAL FACILITIES ... English-speaking doctors and dentists are available in Madrid and Barcelona, with English-speaking staff in some of the better hospitals—consult your hotel clerk.

MOTION PICTURES ... British, French and American are shown at almost all theaters in both Madrid and Barcelona, usually with Spanish sound tracks. The *Savoy* in Barcelona and the *Voy* in Madrid feature films in original versions.

MUSIC ... The famous Spanish symphonic orchestras, the Sinfónica, Filarmónica and Nacional, as well as the Cuarteto de Música de Cámara and the Orquesta Sinfónica de Barcelona, give concerts all fall, winter and spring. San Sebastian has fine music each summer, especially during "Grand Week" in August as do Granada and Seville during their spring festivals. Barcelona's winter opera season ranks very high, about third in all Europe. Concerts and chamber music at the Palacio de la Música Catalana, opera at Teatro del Liceo. Best choirboy singing in Spain is at Monasterio de Montserrat, Barcelona. Barcelona is famous for its flamenco dancing in many small cafés and *boites,* also for the dancing in the streets of the native *sardanas,* usually in summer. Theatrical revues are well done and easy for foreigners to understand.

NIGHT CLUBS AND CABARETS ... Try the Castellana Hilton's *Rendezvous Room.* Dine and dance to good music; also *Rex, Pasapoga,* floor show, good music (closed during July and August); *Casablanca,* floor show, entertainment; *Micheleta, Parrilla Alcázar Flamingo, El Biombo Chino,* all with floor show, entertainment. For typical Spanish Andalucian-style dancing (flamenco) and decoration, try *Zambra* and *La Taberna Gitana.* During summer the *Villa Rosa,* on the outskirts of Madrid, is a popular night spot, open practically all night. Good music and floor show. Also the *Florida* and the *Pavillon,* good food, dancing, in the middle of the Retiro Park. *Club Riscal,* summer roof garden, has good food (*paella,* the Spanish rice dish, is their specialty).

In Barcelona some of the smartest places are *El Cortijo* (summer only), *La Masia, Sacha.* For good music and floor shows without food try *Bikini* in summer or the *Bolero, Emporium, Rigat; Rio* in winter.

PHOTOGRAPHY ... Color as well as black-and-white film is available. Also cameras. Other photo equipment is fairly expensive. There are Kodak shops in both Madrid and Barcelona with good-quality developing taking two or three days.

RELIGION ... Roman Catholicism is the state religion. Madrid has three Protestant churches, Barcelona, two. Both cities have Jewish synagogues.

RESTAURANTS . . . Both Madrid and Barcelona have plenty of really good eating places. In fact, the cooking is genuinely good almost everywhere, with a variety that is bewildering. Delicacies from every part of Europe superimposed on dozens of native dishes, game and seafood. Both Madrid and Barcelona have an abundance of 3-star restaurants, besides the leading hotels, which are, of course, excellent.

About the most famous of them all, in a land known for good food, are Madrid's *Jockey Club, Commodore* and *Horcher's.* Each is a de luxe, exclusive gourmet's delight with a superlative cuisine and a fine setting. Best French and Continental restaurants in Barcelona are: *Finisterre, Glaciar, Ecuestre, Reno, Hostal del Sol, Mesón Pollo al Ast, Parellada.* Near the waterfront and famous for seafood are *Caracoles* and *Solé, Cantábrico* and *Siete Puertas.* Both cities will serve you their own famous specialties along with dishes each province claims for its own: Valencia's *paella*—yellow rice, with chicken, seafood, lobster or snails; *zarzuela de mariscos* (a wonderful shellfish dish) and *butifarra a la Catalana*—an excellent Spanish sausage—come from Barcelona. The Bilbao and San Sebastian locale offers three famous seafood dishes: *chipirones en su tinta; angulas,* baby eels, which you'll like; and *bacalao a la Vizcaina,* sophisticated version of codfish. Both Madrid and Barcelona offer *cochinillo asado*—savory suckling roast—said to be best in Segovia. *Casa Candido* is a world-famous restaurant. Another superlative place to have a real Spanish meal while in Madrid is the small, charming *El Pulpito,* above the former hideout of Luís Candelas, the Castilian Robin Hood, where you see wonderful food cooked right before you. It has been operating in the same little spot since the Declaration was signed in Philadelphia. Also typical and very good are *Hostería del Laurel, La Barraca* (with *paella* the specialty), *Hogar Gallego* (seafood), *Casa Botín* (suckling pig), *Edelweiss* (German-style food), and *Casa Valentin, Hosteria Piamontesa, La Hoja* (with *paella* a specialty). At the better restaurants telephone for a reservation.

SHOPS AND STORES . . . Shops are open from 9:00 until 1:30. Everywhere throughout the country they close at 1:30, reopen about 4:00 P.M. (4:30 in summer). Closing time is usually about 7:30 P.M. Besides on local festivals and feast days, which vary, they close on major Holy Days of the Roman Catholic Church, such as Good Friday, November 1, *Todos Santos* (All Saints Day).

SPECTATOR SPORTS . . . The bullfight, of course, is the greatest national Spanish spectacle. Seeing at least one is a tourist must. All the bigger towns have their bull rings, most have their favorite matador. The pomp and color, the pageantry, the crowds, all add up to a fabulous show. Madrid, Barcelona, Cartagena, Malaga, Seville and Toledo, among others, have important rings. The season starts at Valencia during the festivities of the *Fallas* on March 19, the feast of San José, and ends in June at the fair there, and at Saragossa the second and third weeks in October. There are important ones at both Madrid and Barcelona every Sunday and feast day during the season, and often on Thursdays, as well.

Madrid's fine race track, the *Zarzuela,* one of Europe's best, has good racing each spring and fall, perhaps the best on Sundays and feast days in October. Seville's Pineda course is open both spring and September, October. Spain's best racing is perhaps at the magnificent Lasarte course at San Sebastian. There are many big races run off here during August and September, some of international importance.

Frontón (or *jai alai*), is extremely popular the year round. The world's greatest professionals appear on courts in at least 8 or 10 cities, including both Madrid and Barcelona, with matches daily. San Sebastian has first-rank matches during the summer. The Football (Soccer) season runs from September until June, with every town of any size having its own team. The Spanish League is large, divided into three divisions, with the usual finals and important cup play.

SPORTS . . . Winter sports will be good in Spain from December until April and are centered in La Molina, Puigcerda, in Gerona near Barcelona at Candanchu (Huesca), the Guadarrama near Madrid, and Sierra Nevada, near Granada. There are good skiing, races and contests in all these winter centers. Fishing and hunting in Spain are among the best in Europe: mountain streams with trout, splendid salmon fishing (so much so, it is said that 5,000 natives make their living fishing salmon, all with lines—no netting allowed in Spain). Sea fishing is good all along the coasts, with tuna taken from several centers. There's good hunting in the mountains, for deer, chamois, wild boar, and splendid duck shooting along the Guadalquivir River, famous everywhere. There are pigeon shoots all over Spain, spring, summer and fall. Madrid and Barcelona both have an excellent 18-hole golf course, tennis is played everywhere. Public bathing pools in all the big cities, wonderful surf bathing at San Sebastian and all along Spain's extensive coast.

THEATERS . . . Madrid's theaters and those all over the country start very late, by our standards. 10:30 P.M. and sometimes even a half-hour later. Everything's in Spanish, of course.

TIME . . . Six hours later than Eastern Standard Time.

TIPPING . . . About 10 per cent, for taximen. You are expected to give the movie and theater ushers as well as the doorman who procures your taxi and the boy who delivers your messages a peseta. Leave small change at restaurants in addition to the tip added to your check.

TRANSPORTATION . . . Taxis are likely to be hard to find, especially at bullfight time or when people are coming out of theaters; however, the number of modern taxis being put on the road in the largest cities is increasing every day. As a rule they cost less than the European average. In Spain the general rule is to stay off the trains and the local buses, both of which are usually crowded and somewhat antiquated. Important changes for the better include the *"Talgo,"* smart Irun-Madrid, stainless-steel Diesel train, and also the electro-Diesel "TAF" trains, which run regular schedules between Madrid and the more important cities, such as Barcelona. It is suggested that visitors to Spain make use of the services of Spain's airline, Iberia.

For shorter distances hired cars are easy to arrange and reasonable in price. Modern sightseeing buses are also available in the largest cities.

WATER . . . Water in Madrid and Barcelona is fine. In small towns better stick to bottled water. Best (natural) are Solares and Fournier.

WHAT TO BUY . . . Jewelry and Toledo ware; Talavera porcelains; mantillas; linens, gloves, lace and leather goods of every kind are superior; perfume is good, cheaper than French; and plenty of good pottery, glassware. Dozens of rare sherries or vintage brandies. Women's dresses made by the best Spanish couturiers are available in Madrid, Barcelona and San Sebastian at very reasonable prices, from Balenciaga (called *Eisa* in Spain), Pedro Rodriguez, Asunción Bastida, Pertegaz, and others. Men's suits custom-made at between $60 and $70 can be ordered in Barcelona at Rabat Rambla, Cataluña 112 or in Madrid at González y García, Peñalver, Montero and many others. Made-to-order shoes cost between $16 and $23.

WHAT TO WEAR . . . Spaniards are a well-dressed people and somewhat conservative in their attire, therefore ladies' slacks are not worn. Evening clothes are not necessary for tourists. Sports and beachwear will be needed for seaside resorts; however, "bikinis" and abbreviated men's trunks, French style, are not tolerated. It is suggested that ladies include a fur cape, which they will find handy after sundown during fall and spring months. Flat-heeled walking shoes should also be included if tourist haunts such as Toledo and the Escorial are to be visited. Lightweight suits for men for city wear, sports clothes elsewhere. It is customary to wear a jacket and tie in cities even in summer, though, strangely enough, hats are rarely seen either on men or women. When entering a church, however, women wear hats or cover their heads with mantillas.

WHERE TO GO—SIGHTSEEING . . .

Madrid . . . Buses are available in Madrid, Barcelona and other large cities. The bus lines also have well-organized and comfortable all-inclusive tours throughout the country. Top on your list for sightseeing in Madrid will be the famous Prado National Museum and other museums mentioned under ARTS. Also, by all means visit University City. With one of the finest campuses of its type in Europe, it embraces all the arts and sciences, was completely destroyed during the civil war, and completely rebuilt since 1939. A stroll through the Retiro Park, with its beautiful gardens, statues, fountains and artificial lakes, is well worth while.

Toledo . . . is a short drive from Madrid, the home of El Greco, and famous for its tempered steel as well as for its gold Damascene works. Visit the Cathedral, the Church of Santo Tomé, and the Jewish synagogue. A splendid view of the city may be had from the hill just beyond. *El Escorial* is famous for its monastery-palace, built by Phillip II, which houses the tombs of the Kings of Spain as well as other great persons. *Avila,* the medieval walled city, is the home of the famous Spanish mystic, Santa Teresa. *Segovia* is famous for the castle known as the Alcázar and for the unsurpassed magnificence of its Roman aqueduct.

Barcelona, ancient and modern city (1½ million inhabitants), founded in the second century B.C., 2nd largest city in the country, lies within a hilly amphitheater facing the Mediterranean (2 hours by air from Madrid). Barcelona, besides being the most cosmopolitan city in Spain and one of the most historic seaports of the Mediterranean, is rich in fine churches, in its Gothic Quarter, in its great avenues. It is Spain's most industrial and practical manufacturing city.

Be sure to visit the Gothic Cathedral, built almost directly over the site of the original Roman Temple of Jupiter. Do not miss the fine Monastery of Montserrat, with its wonderful boy choir, and its Black Virgin. Barcelona abounds in monuments, religious and civic, ancient ruins, modern architecture, and has at least a dozen museums. Do not forget that Pablo Casals, Nonell, Salvador Dali, Fortuny, Xavier Cugat and many other well-known artists come from this part of Spain. Barcelona is the place, above all, to eat seafood, best of the entire Mediterranean. It has music in its restaurants which is famous throughout the country and superlative bullfights.

Costa Brava, known as the Spanish Riviera, stretches north to the French frontier. Charming, beautiful and unspoiled. Few large de luxe hotels, but many small inns where comfort and food are supreme. Small night clubs, wonderful food, bathing, etc., and a type of personal service that you don't find, for example, on the French Riviera. Good hotels on the Costa Brava are *Hostal de la Gavina* in S'Agaro, the *Rigat Park, Carabela* and *Rosamar,* Lloret de Mar, and *Ancora,* Tossa de Mar.

For tours of the Costa Brava, or Andorra, the tiny independent state in the Pyrenees between France and Spain (can be reached only in summer), apply to any travel agency. All-inclusive excursions lasting four or five days cost $20 to $60.

Valencia . . . Ancient, beautiful Valencia, rich in historical interest, lies in the heart of the "Huerta de Valencia," the rich plain that has Spain's choicest orange and lemon groves. *Hotel Excelsior, Hotel Reina Victoria.* The climate is dry and very mild, the lush land produces several crops each season; there are flowers in profusion everywhere. There are the imported relics of old Greece. The province was once the independent Moorish kingdom of Valencia (1021 A.D.); it was retaken by Spain's national hero, El Cid, and then lost again to the Arabs. It belonged to Aragon, then to Castile. See the many white houses, showing the Moorish influence, the many monuments.

Valencia's lures are its gay fiestas, the smell of orange blossoms, its wonderful clear sky. The whole countryside is a garden, and it is almost always spring. The fig, pomegranate, and palm trees add to the riot of color, with hundreds of streams crossing the country everywhere. The almond trees and the olive add more green to the landscape. The Cathedral, built on a former mosque, has beautiful paintings by Goya. See the palatial Dos Aguas Palace, the Museo de Bellas Artes. Although it is wonderfully beautiful at any time of the year, try to visit Valencia in March for its greatest feast day, March 19.

Málaga is farther south along the coast. This Andalusian city is the center of Spain's golden coast, wonderfully even, mild winters, beautiful park, fine harbor. Its museum, left to the city by the painter Muñoz Degrain, is famed for its Murillo and other more modern masterpieces. The National Golf Tournament is played here each winter, and there are tennis matches, yachting. There are horse races in February.

Seville (400,000 population) is of enormous importance, an artistic and archaeological center with one of all Europe's most luxurious hotels (*Hotel Alfonso XIII*), with museums of interest, great churches, monuments, works of art. The fine arts museum has the best Murillos, the archaeological museum has Roman and Arabic art. Under Moorish rule for over five hundred years, the city has Arabic architecture everywhere. See the Alcázar, and as part of the Cathedral, the famous Giralda Tower, twelfth-century minaret. The glorious Maria Luisa Park; the Palacio de las Dueñas, belonging to the Duke of Alba; the houses with their iron gates—all these and more will delight the tourist. Holy Week, and the fair which follows it with a full week of bullfights, is the time to see the great city at its glorious best.

Granada, with its Alhambra, is where our Washington Irving lived and wrote; *Córdoba* with its Mosque-Cathedral, its fairs, and its romerias or tours will interest you.

Getting back to central Spain (107 miles northwest of Madrid), you will like *Salamanca*, old university town on the banks of the River Tormes, its Plaza Mayor, with its fine Town Hall, its magnificent arcades, and the Baroque style Pabellón Real (Royal Pavilion).

San Sebastian, world-famous summer resort and capital of the province of Guipuzcoa, one of the three that form the Basque country, shouldn't be missed. Its beach, famed La Concha (called "the shell" because of its shape), is visited by both Spaniards and foreigners by the thousands each season. The best of sports car and yacht races, famous stake races for horses at Lasarte, the best Basque ball players anywhere, and the very best bullfighting all are seen during the summer. Stay at *María Cristina, Londres* or *Continental Palace Hotel*; get there if possible during the "Grand Week" in August, and make reservations in advance.

The Balearic Islands can be reached by air in 50 minutes from Barcelona. These delightful islands are fully described on page 125.

SOURCES OF FURTHER INFORMATION ... The Spanish Tourist Office in New York is at 485 Madison Avenue, and there are others in Chicago and San Francisco. Within Spain, folders in English, city and country maps, lists of shops, etc., are available at Municipal Tourist Information Offices, and State Tourist Information Office. Information on sightseeing tours is available at these offices or at the larger travel agencies. Tickets for local events are available through your hotel porter. Feel free also to call upon Pan American for information: in Barcelona, Calle Mallorca 250 (Tel. 37–00–03); in Madrid, Edifico España (Tel. 47–14–03) and Palace Hotel lobby.

*The Alhambra (built 1248–
1354) is one of the finest examples of Moorish architecture in all Spain. It is located
in Granada.*

*The thrilling spectacle of the
bullring is a panorama of color
and excitement. This scene is
near Madrid.*

*One of the charming views along
Spain's Costa Brava is the village of Tossa de Mar with its
fishing boats and nets spread out
along the shore.*

*Seville is an artistic and archae-
ological center full of interest
for the tourist. This view is of
the Giralda Tower.*

SWEDEN

WEATHER IN STOCKHOLM—Lat. N59°16'—Alt. 35'

Temp.	JAN.	FEB.	MAR.	APR.	MAY	JUNE	JULY	AUG.	SEPT.	OCT.	NOV.	DEC.
Low	22°	21°	24°	31°	40°	49°	54°	52°	46°	38°	31°	24°
High	31°	32°	36°	46°	57°	67°	71°	67°	59°	48°	39°	33°
Average	27°	27°	30°	39°	49°	58°	63°	60°	53°	43°	35°	29°
Days of Rain	15	13	14	11	12	12	15	16	14	16	15	17

LOCATION . . . Sweden occupies the eastern portion of the Scandinavian Peninsula. Stockholm, the principal city, is 258 air miles east of Oslo, Norway, about 875 miles northeast of London.

CHARACTERISTICS . . . Cleanliness and efficiency, neither one of them obtrusive, are the first things you notice in Sweden. One of the most progressive countries in the world, it likes tourists; its hotels make them welcome, its restaurants offer wonderful food and the scenery itself is an invitation. The Swedes are strong, happy, vigorous people whose zest for life communicates itself to you. Summer with the midnight sun is unforgettable. The sportsman will find fishing, skiing and sailing in abundance. It's the land of "Swedish modern" and social reforms.

POPULATION . . . 7,434,000, roughly equal to the populations of Chicago, Philadelphia, Baltimore and Dallas combined.

SIZE . . . 173,400 square miles, about 10 per cent bigger than California, which it resembles in shape.

CAPITAL . . . Stockholm, population 800,000, about thirty thousand less than Minneapolis and St. Paul combined.

GOVERNMENT . . . A constitutional monarchy with a King and a *Riksdag*, or Parliament, of two chambers.

HOW TO GET THERE . . . By Pan American's through-plane service from New York, about 18½ hours to Stockholm, via Oslo. By ship 8 to 10 days from New York to Gothenburg direct or via Bremerhaven or Copenhagen.

ACCOMMODATIONS ... Stockholm has a hotel or pension to suit every budget. No matter where you stay, you will find cleanliness and friendly service. Best known is the *Grand Hotel,* beautifully situated opposite the Royal Palace. Rates here begin at about $6.00 single,' $10 double with bath. Other first-class and very popular hotels with somewhat lower rates are *Stockholm, Gillet, Malmen, Carlton, Foresta, Apollonia, Strand, Palace* and *Bromma* and the resort hotel *Grand Hotel Saltsjöbaden.* Most hotels add a 15 per cent service charge, but prices are still lower than in the United States. You can get a very good single room for as little as $2 in many hotels. It is advisable to make your reservations in advance, especially during the summer months. Hotels in other areas are listed under WHERE TO GO.

ARTS ... Stockholm has so many fine museums and galleries that it is hard to decide what to see first. The National Museum has an excellent collection of Swedish and foreign paintings. The Stockholm City Museum contains exhibits illustrating the history of the town from the Stone Age until the present time. The unique Skansen, an outdoor museum, beautifully situated on a hilltop, has exhibits showing life and work in Sweden centuries ago, as well as houses and farms of that time. At Skansen you will find beautiful parks, excellent restaurants and a large zoo. You can also enjoy music of all kinds. The home of Carl Milles, the famous sculptor, beautifully situated on the Island of Lidingö near Stockholm, has been transformed into an outstanding museum, containing antique sculptures as well as Milles' own works. Waldemarsudde, formerly the home of the late Prince Eugen, contains a fine collection of the works of the "Painter Prince" and his contemporaries. Parts of the Royal Palace, the Drottningholm Palace and the Pavilion of Gustavus III at Haga are also shown to visitors.

Also well worth seeing are the Historical Museum, remarkable for its excellent display technique, the Nordic Museum with the Royal Armory, the National Maritime Museum and the Technological Museum and the Museum of Natural History.

BALLET ... The famous Royal Opera Ballet performs in the Royal Opera in Stockholm. In June, the Royal Opera Ballet gives performances as part of the Stockholm Festival.

BANKS ... Representatives for the larger American banks will be found in Stockholm and other principal cities. Traveler's checks may be cashed at all Swedish banks, American Express, Thos. Cook & Son, and other recognized travel bureaus.

CALENDAR OF HOLIDAYS ... Legal holidays are January 1 and 6; Good Friday; Easter Sunday; Easter Monday; May 1, Labor Day; Ascension Day (forty days after Easter Sunday); Whitsunday (fifty days after Easter Sunday), Whitmonday; Midsummer Day (Saturday nearest June 24); November 1, All Saints Day; December 25 and 26. Easter Eve, Whitsun Eve, Midsummer Eve and Christmas Eve are bank holidays. Shops are normally open between 9:00 A.M. and 6:00 P.M. on weekdays and between 9:00 A.M. and 5:00 P.M. on Saturday and bank holidays, though most of them close earlier on Saturdays during the summer. Particularly colorful are the Midsummer and Christmas celebrations. Other interesting events—which do not have the character of legal holidays—take place on April 30, Walpurgis Night; June 6, Swedish Flag Day—Sweden's National Commemoration Day; and December 13, Day of St. Lucia, the Queen of Light.

CIGARETTES AND TOBACCO ... All brands of American cigarettes and tobacco can be obtained in Sweden, though the prices are high due to heavy taxation. A package of 20 American cigarettes will cost about 65 cents. Local cigarette brands—the best of which compare favorably with American brands—begin at 50 cents a pack. Cigars—local as well as a rich selection of foreign brands—are available at about the same prices as in the United States. *See* CUSTOMS REGULATIONS.

CLIMATE ... Misconceptions about the climate in Sweden are common, perhaps due to the country's proximity to the Arctic Circle. However, the climate in southern and central Sweden is very much the same as in New England; the winter on Sweden's West Coast is milder than the New York winter. The summer is pleasantly warm and the discomforts of high humidity are unknown. The long hours of daylight during the late spring and summer add to the pleasure. The Midnight Sun can be seen north of the Arctic Circle from early June to the middle of July. Although the period from the first of June to the first of September is the time most tourists visit Sweden, May and particularly, September, which generally is sunny and dry, would also be excellent choices.

CLUBS ... Lions International Club (the European Host Club); Rotary International; the Royal Automobile Club and the Swedish Automobile Association; American Club of Stockholm.

COMMON COURTESIES AND LOCAL CUSTOMS ... If you are invited to dine at the home of Swedish friends, arrive promptly and ready to eat. There is no cocktail hour. A great deal of formal toasting goes on at a Swedish dinner party. Never toast your hostess, but toast the other ladies. If you are the guest of honor, make a toast of thanks at the end of the meal. In restaurants in the bigger cities you have to wear a tie, and when dancing formal dinner jackets are required at all first-class restaurants, except during the summer. You may have heard the Swedes described as rather formal in many respects, but there is a definite trend away from formal manners, and in some respects, e.g., clothing requirements for the beach, they are anything but formal. If you want detailed information on the subject, write to the Swedish National Travel Office for the booklet "How to Feel at Home in Sweden."

COMMUNICATIONS ... There are excellent and inexpensive local and long-distance phone services. Telegraph and cable facilities can be found everywhere and you can send your cables over the hotel telephone. Letters of 5 grams (.17 ounces) are sent via airmail for 65 öre (13 cents) to the United States, postcards for 25 öre; international airletters cost 40 öre (8 cents).

CURRENCY... The monetary unit is the krona (plural kronor), which is divided into 100 öre. There are banknotes for 5, 10, 50, 100 and 1,000 kronor. According to the official rate of exchange, you get approximately 5.15 kronor for your dollar. However, since the exchange rate does not adequately reflect the purchasing power of the two currencies, it actually favors the dollar traveler.

CUSTOMS REGULATIONS AND DOCUMENTS REQUIRED FOR UNITED STATES CITIZENS... Medicines for private use, 2 quart bottles of liquor or wine, reasonable quantities of film, 500 cigarettes or 100 cigars or one pound of pipe tobacco may be brought in duty free. Firearms cannot pass customs without special permission. You are allowed to bring in 1,000 kronor in denominations not exceeding 100 kronor. Your passport is all that is necessary to enter Sweden. If you wish to stay for more than three months, you will have to get a special permit from the alien authorities. However, this is a mere formality and the permit is very easy to obtain. Bring your driver's license if you wish to hire a car.

DRUG STORES... No drug stores exist, in the American sense of the word. However, there are restaurants of the cafeteria type (often called "milk bars") everywhere, and there are pastry shops, called *Konditori,* where you can have coffee, tea, sandwiches and delicious pastry. Cigarettes are bought in tobacco shops or from automats. Drugs and medicines can be had at pharmacies, called *Apotek.*

ELECTRIC CURRENT... The voltage in most places in Sweden, including Stockholm, is 220 A.C., although 110 voltage is also used, particularly in the provinces. Alternating current is the dominating type. The plugs and outlets used in Sweden are different from the ones in the United States so bring along an inset of the type that is screwed into a standard lamp socket (they are the same in Sweden).

FAUNA... Sweden stretches from the 55th Parallel in the south to the 69th in the north—as does Alaska. Sweden's fauna, therefore, is very much the same as that of Alaska and Canada. The zoo at the above-mentioned Skansen outdoor museum offers an excellent exhibit of Sweden's fauna. There are reindeer (domesticated by the Lapps), moose, bear, wolf, capercailzie, black cock, hazelhen, ptarmigan, woodcock, crane, wild goose.

FLORA... Birch, mountain birch, juniper tree, pine, "arctic" raspberry, wild strawberry and raspberry, cloudberry, bilberry, lingonberry.

FOOD... The great Smörgåsbord tables have even surpassed the level of their pre-war lavishness. There are delicious pressed meats, sausages served hot and cold, salads, fish dishes and innumerable vegetable dishes. Remember when you're eating it that this is merely a first course and the main meal is to follow. Schnapps is drunk with this part of the meal. The Swedish are famous for their dairy products and fine fish dishes. Be sure to eat crayfish in August. Swedish pastries are wonderfully gooey and delicious.

Morning coffee and rolls will be served in your room at the hotel—larger breakfasts can be had in the dining room. Food in self-sufficient Sweden is plentiful. Mealtimes are about like those at home. Dinner is served beginning at 5:00 P.M.

GAMBLING ... Gambling casinos are not allowed in Sweden. Horse racing every Saturday and Sunday. Racetracks in Stockholm and also in Gothenburg, Malmö, Karlstad and Östersund. Only pari-mutuel betting.

LANGUAGE ... Swedish is the official language. English is spoken and understood by most people, especially in the cities. How do you do and good-bye in Swedish are *goddag* and *adjö*. Thank you, which is used on every possible occasion, is *tack så mycket* or *tack, tack*.

LAUNDRY AND DRY CLEANING ... Cleaning and laundry facilities are good everywhere and of high quality; it is more expensive than in the States—a suit costs about $3.00 and generally takes a few days. If you want it quicker there will be an additional fee. You will find dry-cleaning shops everywhere.

LIQUOR ... All American drinks and cocktails are available. Cocktails cost about $1, Schnapps about 35 cents. Liquor is not served in restaurants before 12:00 noon.

MEDICAL FACILITIES ... Stockholm and most of Sweden have excellent doctors, dentists and modern medical facilities. All doctors speak English. Ask at your hotel, should you need a doctor.

MOTION PICTURES ... Stockholm has about 130 theaters. American pictures with their original sound track are the most popular. French, British and Swedish films are also shown. See the daily paper for times, programs and theaters.

MUSIC ... The Royal Opera in Stockholm, one of the oldest opera houses in the world, is famous for its high artistic standards. The season is from August to June. Concerts are given at the Stockholm Concert Hall from September to May. Permanent symphony orchestras outside of Stockholm are found in Gothenburg, Malmö, Hälsingborg, Norrköping and Gävle. The "Stockholm Festival" in June offers outstanding opera performances and concerts. The concert repertory in Sweden includes internationally known works as well as the works of modern and classic Swedish composers. Concert halls are closed in the summer, but there are open-air concerts given in the parks, notably the Skansen in Stockholm.

NIGHT CLUBS AND CABARETS ... There are, for the present, few night clubs in Sweden. However, some of the larger hotels and restaurants have dancing and floor shows. Sweden will offer much more to the tourist interested in good music, good theater and fine outdoor life than those looking for gay night life.

PHOTOGRAPHY ... Every kind of photo equipment is available. A color-movie film, 8 mm., costs about $5. Developing takes about a week for ordinary pictures, but can be rushed. The best-known shops, which do an excellent job, are: Hasselblads Fotografiska AB,

Hamngatan 16; Nerliens Foto AB, Kungsgatan 19; Frid, Fredsgatan 5, all in Stockholm.

RELIGION . . . Sweden is a Protestant country. The State Church, of which everyone is a member by birth, is Lutheran. There are Catholic, Methodist, Episcopal, Christian Science churches and Jewish synagogues in Stockholm and elsewhere.

RESTAURANTS . . . There is a lot of superb eating to be done in Stockholm. Everyone will soon find his favorite spot to eat, but here are some of the best and most famous restaurants: the *Bacchi Wapen,* serving primarily French food, is first class; Stallmästargården is a must. *Den Gyldene Freden* is typically Swedish and *Berns* is a big restaurant with floor shows and excellent French and Chinese cusines. *Riche, Trianon, Djurgårdsbrunns Wärdshus,* (in the summer season) *Maritim, La Ronde, Strand's Roof Terrace* and *Tre Remmare* are all first class. The dining rooms of most hotels have very fine food, especially the swank *Grand Hotel Restaurant.* You can eat elegantly and superbly for $10 a day in Stockholm, you can eat well for half that figure, and you can eat quite adequately for only $2.50 a day. Expensive dinners start at around $3, but a very satisfying meal can be had for as little as $1. Milk bars serve good, inexpensive, lunch-counter food.

SHOPS AND STORES . . . In Stockholm: K. A. Anderson for fine jewelry; Atelier Borgila for unique, modern silverware; Fritzes for books; try Svenskt Tenn for pottery and textiles; note Nordiska Kristallmagasinet and Svenskt Glas for glass; Williams, Leja, Sörmans and Robell are fine exclusive women's-apparel shops; Bastman's for sporting equipment; Palmgren's for luggage and exquisite leather goods; Nordiska Kompaniet (NK) is the largest department store (see their modern furniture); Morris and Ströms are excellent men's shops. There are numerous exhibitions and shops that specialize in ceramics, pottery, textiles and handicraft products; the main shopping district in Stockholm consists of Kungsgatan, Drottninggatan, Hamngatan and adjacent streets.

SPECTATOR SPORTS . . . Racing is very popular in and around Stockholm. The season begins in May and lasts through the summer. Ulriksdal is the principal track. Trotting races are popular at the Stockholm Trotting Club during most of the year. Soccer, field and track events are most popular. Athletic and gymnastic exhibitions are held all year around at Stockholm's many gymnasiums. Yachting races and tennis matches enjoy seasonal popularity.

SPORTS . . . Sweden is a sportsman's paradise. The Swedes are an athletic, outdoor people and the facilities are of the finest. The lakes and mountain streams offer excellent fishing. Salmon and salmon trout, pike and perch are in abundance. There is tuna and other big-game fishing on the West Coast. Golf is nationally popular. There are good courses throughout the country; Kevinge, Djursholm, Lidingö and Saltsjöbaden are the best near Stockholm. The courses and club houses are open to tourists. Good tennis courts are found all over Sweden. Stockholm has indoor courts for year around play.

Yachting is popular and fashionable in the Stockholm archipelago Sailing and swimming are favorite summer sports. Boats can be rented at Saltsjöbaden's *Grand Hotel.* There are numerous indoor pools connected with the Swedish baths in Stockholm. The beaches on the archipelago are lovely. The mountains in the north are a hiker's paradise; guides are available. The end of summer is the best time of year. As in all Scandinavian countries, nearly everybody skis in Sweden. Accommodations, skis and guides are available at moderate rates. Other winter sports include skating, tobogganing and curling. There are exhibition skating matches.

THEATERS...The Royal Dramatic Theater season is from September to June. As part of the Stockholm Festival, special performances are offered at the beginning of June. The *China Variety Revue Theater* has a Continental revue program from April to September. The *Drottningholm Court Theater,* established in the eighteenth century by King Gustav III and preserved exactly in its original form, is unique, charming and definitely worth seeing. Performances are given during the Stockholm Festival in the beginning of June, and also later during the summer. The *Skansens Friluftsteater* is a beautiful open-air theater in the Skansen, where Shakespearean plays are given during the summer months. Ticket prices at all these theaters are moderate, ranging from $1 to $3.

TIME...Six hours later than U. S. Eastern Standard Time.

TIPPING...The hotels have a service charge of approximately 15 per cent. Hat-check girls and washroom attendants get 50 öre. Follow the 10 per cent rule for cab drivers. Tip porters at least 50 öre a bag.

TRANSPORTATION...The transportation system in Stockholm includes buses, trams and a brand-new subway, all of them modern and efficient. Taxi fares are reasonable and cabs can be ordered by telephone. Longer trips may be made by bus, train, or by air. Cars for long trips may also be hired with or without a chauffeur. The Swedish State Railways trains are regarded as the best and the most modern in Europe. They offer two classes, but most people go second class, which offers the same standard as the American railroad coaches.

WATER...The water is safe to drink in every town in Sweden. Bottled water may be necessary on prolonged hiking trips and fishing expeditions. Inquire at the local village.

WHAT TO BUY...Glass and crystal are your best buys. Pottery, pewter and silverware are excellent. Cutlery made of famous Swedish steel and stainless tableware are quite reasonable and should be high on your list. English and Swedish textiles are of very fine quality. Modern furniture is tempting, too. Smaller pieces can be dismantled for shipping. There are many bargains to be had in various native handicrafts. An American citizen is allowed to take out 2,500 kronors' (approximately $500) worth of goods for his personal use or, as gifts, for some other person's personal use. Since prices are very low, according to American standards, this permits many purchases. Shipment of bulky articles can easily be arranged.

WHAT TO WEAR ... Stockholm winters are only a little cooler than in northeastern United States. Bring woolens and tweeds. Summer temperatures are normally very comfortable with averages around 70 degrees (even far north); high humidity is unknown in Sweden. Eight hours of sunshine per day is the average during the summer months. You can leave the lightest summer clothes at home, but bring your topcoat as the nights may be chilly. Raincoats are a must. Sports clothes in the country and for general sightseeing wear are correct. Simple black dresses or dressy suits will be all you need in Stockholm. Formal clothes are rarely worn except at gala openings and banquets and when dancing in first-class restaurants. Flannels and sports jackets during the day, and business suits in the evening are correct for men. Rugged, simple clothes are worn in the mountains. The Swedish are conservative about clothes, so wear conventional outfits for active sports.

WHERE TO GO—SIGHTSEEING ...

Stockholm ... Stockholm is one of the loveliest cities in the world. The architecture is a perfect blend of centuries of good taste. Beautiful, clean modern buildings are in perfect harmony with seventeenth century Baroque. It's a good idea to take a boat ride through the waterways and around the islands of the city for your first bout of sightseeing. You'll get a fine over-all impression of this charming city. The Town Hall is Stockholm's trademark and one of the most beautiful buildings in Europe. The medieval section of town is called the "City between the Bridges." Here you'll find quaintly twisting little streets lined with artists' studios and curious little shops; the old church of St. Gertrud chimes the hours. Riddarholm Church is the burial place of many of Sweden's kings and queens. See the wonderful art collection at the Waldemarsudde, mentioned under ARTS. Take a night boat ride to Djurgården. Beautiful parks and magnificent buildings are found in this region. A landau ride by moonlight is wonderfully romantic here. Take a day to see Drottningholm Palace, three-quarters of an hour from the center of town by a little lake steamer. There is a fine inn here with atmosphere and good food. The palace, breath-takingly lovely, has been called the Swedish Versailles. There are many excellently planned tours of various parts of the city; private guides are available. Millesgården on the island of Lidingö (25 minutes by tramway from the center of Stockholm) is the home of the famous sculptor Carl Milles. It is surrounded by a charming terraced garden and contains a rich and unique collection of antique sculptures and works by the artist.

Side Trips ... Recently a new tour has been started with special consideration for guests from America: the Sunlit Nights Land Cruise of the Swedish State Railways, 8 days aboard a special luxury train. It takes you to the fabulous region of the midnight sun. You travel north from Stockholm in easy stages, visiting the romantic province of Dalecarlia, to beyond the Arctic Circle and back, stopping to

Stockholm's Concert Hall with its busy flower market in the foreground is just one of the capital's many cultural centers.

visit the colorful, nomadic Lapps and their reindeer herds, waterfalls, open-pit iron mines. For 4 days of the trip you are under the midnight sun, and never see darkness.

Uppsala is about 40 miles north of Stockholm (50 minutes by train). In nearby Old Uppsala there are burial mounds of ancient chieftains. The University was founded in the fifteenth century. The Renaissance castle and cathedral are very lovely and interesting historically. Stay at the *Gillet,* from $3.50 a night, or at the *Stadshotellet* at the same price. Both hotels have excellent restaurants.

Inquire about the excellent Nils Holgersson trip all over Sweden.

Dalecarlia ... Heading northwest you come to the charming province of Dalecarlia. Rättvik on Lake Siljan is the central point for excursions in this region. Many of Sweden's outstanding artists and poets have come from Dalecarlia. It is a great ski center and world champions belong to its clubs. Good accommodations and instruction are available and the skiing is wonderful. Summer is equally lovely in this region. See "The Road to Heaven," an open-air allegorical play performed at the village of Leksand each July. Hiking and mountain climbing are popular. There are Youth Hostels throughout the region as well as quaint inns. Gay festivals full of native costumes and music are a feature of Dalecarlia.

Lapland ... The northern-most part of Sweden is the unspoiled arctic region of Lapland. Arctic flora, mountain peaks shimmering in the sun and dazzling mountain lakes make Lapland serenely and gloriously beautiful. This is truly the Land of the Midnight Sun. The northern lights are here in all their blazing glory. The Swedish Touring Club has done much to enable the tourist to see this province. Trails have been cut through the forests, bridges and paths have been made, and much money has gone into building railroads through the rugged terrain. Boating facilities are available on the mountain lakes, fishing is popular and hikers and climbers will find endless attractions here. The culture of the primitive Lapps is much as it has been for centuries. The Swedish government has done a great deal to protect these people against exploitation. Riksgränsen is the best

The neat little island of Rid-
darholmen in Stockholm shows
how inlets, bays and straits
form a network, setting off
each section of the city.

Near the seaport city of Kalmar
in the picturesque southeastern
section of Sweden stands historic
Kalmar Castle.

Only 45 minutes by little white steamer from Stockholm is Drottningholm, the King's summer palace. This view is of the elegant Palace
Gardens.

base of operations for seeing Lapland. Guides, accommodations and tourist information are available. The *Laplandia* is the best place to stay and to eat. Rates begin at $3.50.

Skåne ... Skåne, the southernmost part of Sweden, is a fertile farm area with rolling plains and beechwood-clad ridges. It is sometimes known as the Chateau Country; thanks to its hundreds of castles and fine mansions, among them Glimmingehus and Trolleholm. Malmö is the third largest town in the country. It is a busy modern port. The modern architecture in the city is of the best. Lund is an old university town, also the site of Scandinavia's finest Romanesque cathedral. Hälsingborg (opposite Denmark's Helsingør) is the main port of entry for motorists. Nearby Båstad is one of the best resorts. Malmö is two hours by air from Stockholm, six hours by train.

Gothenburg ... Sweden's second city is Gothenburg. It is a vital port town and under 2 hours by air from Stockholm. There are theaters, a fine shopping district, modern housing developments and beautiful parks. Fishing, sailing and boating are all popular. So are golf and tennis. The regattas at nearby Marstrand are very popular, too. From Gothenburg to Stockholm, or vice versa, one can travel via the famous Overland Waterway (Göta Kanal), a 3-day trip. The new *Park Avenue Hotel* is first class. Rates begin at $5 a day. The *Palace* and the *Eggers* are also recommended. Average rates are $4.

Visby ... The Isle of Gotland in the Baltic Sea should be a must on your list. Its capital, Visby, is the only walled city in northern Europe. In the Middle Ages it was a great trading center, and it contains many fine buildings of that era. There are more than 90 medieval country churches on the island, many of them exquisite. Stora Karlsö island, just off the coast of Gotland, is a bird sanctuary with interesting flora. Visby is one hour by air from Stockholm, or overnight by boat. These are only the highlights of one of Europe's most beautiful countries. A holiday in Sweden is a relaxing and leisurely experience. The loveliness of the country and its friendly people will be a cherished memory.

SOURCES OF FURTHER INFORMATION ... Svenska Turisttrafikföreningen (Swedish Tourist Traffic Assoc.), Klara v. Krykogata 3A, Stockholm (general information); Stockholms Stads och Läns Turisttrafikförening, Gustav Adolfs Torg 18, Stockholm (general information); KAK (Royal Automobile Club), Södra Blasieholmshamnen 6, Stockholm (motoring) and Hotell'tjänst, Vasagatan 7, Stockholm (Tel. 10 44 37) (hotel accommodations). Pan American's office is at Jakobstorg 1, Stockholm (Tel. 23 19 20), open weekdays 9:00–5:00, Saturdays 9:00–1:00. In the United States write for descriptive literature to Swedish National Travel Office, 630 Fifth Avenue, New York 20, New York.

English and American newspapers and magazines can be bought at most newspaper stands and shops, guide books in English at all bookshops. "What's On in Stockholm" is a fortnightly publication, available at most newsstands.

SWITZERLAND

WEATHER IN GENEVA—Lat. N46°12′—Alt. 1,237′

Temp.	JAN.	FEB.	MAR.	APR.	MAY	JUNE	JULY	AUG.	SEPT.	OCT.	NOV.	DEC.
Low	28°	28°	31°	41°	50°	57°	60°	59°	51°	42°	35°	29°
High	30°	37°	44°	52°	61°	66°	70°	69°	63°	53°	42°	35°
Average	29°	33°	38°	47°	56°	62°	65°	64°	57°	48°	39°	32°
Days of Rain	12	13	13	15	15	15	14	13	12	12	12	13

LOCATION ... Almost in the exact geographic center of Europe, Switzerland is next door to France, Italy, Austria and Germany. Geneva and Zurich are a little less than two hours by air from London, Paris, Brussels and Amsterdam.

CHARACTERISTICS ... A matchless variety of attractions. The Alps, the Swiss lakes, picturesque old villages, sparkling modern cities, rustic simplicity, swank resorts have attracted generations of vacationists, winter and summer, to this small but vital country. The Swiss treat the tourist with a cordiality and warmth he deserves. Swiss efficiency has not been exaggerated, nor have Swiss honesty and cleanliness, all traits which give industrious Switzerland an importance far out of proportion to her size.

POPULATION ... About 4,900,000, slightly more than half that of Greater New York City. Zurich, Switzerland's largest city, has a population of 420,000; Basel, Geneva and Berne, the next largest cities, have less than 200,000 inhabitants each.

SIZE ... Slightly under 16,000 square miles, about twice the area of New Jersey.

CAPITAL ... Berne.

GOVERNMENT ... A Federal Republic with a democratic constitution modeled after that of the United States. Each of Switzerland's 22 Cantons (states) sends representatives to legislative bodies corresponding to the U. S. Senate and House of Representatives. Switzerland, founded in 1291, is the oldest existing democracy.

HOW TO GET THERE . . . By Clipper from New York to Frankfurt with connections to Zurich, 15 hours. Or from the U. S. West Coast about 20 hours to Paris via Pan Am's polar route, then to Zurich. Zurich is 2 hours from Rome by air. By ship 5 to 9 days to West Atlantic or Mediterranean ports and then overnight by train. Switzerland is the crossroads of the European railway network; from London and Paris the Simplon Orient Express passes through Lausanne to Italy, and the Arlberg Orient Express passes through Basel, with connections to Klosters, Davos, Arosa and St. Moritz, on the way to Vienna. "Europabus" from Amsterdam goes to Basel, Lucerne, Interlaken and Montreux with connections to Milan or Nice. You can even go by Rhine boat from Rotterdam to Basel.

ACCOMMODATIONS . . . Although some are more elegant than others, there's no such thing as a bad Swiss hotel: as far as service, basic comfort, cleanliness, courtesy and honesty are concerned, all are first class. Rates in luxury hotels begin at $8.00 per day per person, meals included. If you can dispense with the trimmings, you can be just as comfortable in a more modest hotel for half the price. (These rates are based on stays of three days or longer; they're slightly higher for shorter stays.) Some resort hotels offer attractive off-season rates. For names of hotels in each city, see listing under individual cities.

ARTS . . . The city art museums of Zurich, Geneva and Basel have fine permanent collections. The best Holbeins on the Continent can be seen in Basel. Even the museums of the smaller cities often feature temporary exhibits of outstanding interest. Many private collections, such as the famed Reinhart collection of modern European masters in Winterthur, may be viewed with special permission.

BALLET . . . Although Switzerland has no National Ballet, major companies touring Europe almost invariably play the larger Swiss cities. The Paris Opera Ballet, the ANTA Ballet and the Marquis de Cuevas' Company usually visit Lausanne in June.

BANKS . . . American Express and Thos. Cook & Son have branches in all major Swiss cities. The Swiss Bank Corporation, the Union Bank of Switzerland, Banque Populaire Suisse and Credit Suisse have foreign departments that correspond with American banks. Traveler's checks may be cashed at banks, large hotels and stores.

CALENDAR OF HOLIDAYS . . . August 1, Swiss Independence Day, is celebrated everywhere with fireworks displays. Other national holidays are: Christmas, New Year's Day, Good Friday, Easter and Whitmonday, Ascension Day and Corpus Christi Day in predominately Catholic regions.

CIGARETTES AND TOBACCO . . . Popular U. S. brands may be found generally at about 35 cents a pack. Swiss and British (made in Switzerland) brands run from 20 cents to 30 cents a pack and are usually milder than American cigarettes, but quite good. Matches are not given free when you buy tobacco. Pipe tobacco and cigars are available in all price ranges.

CLIMATE . . . Seasons and temperature ranges are similar to those of the northern U. S. without the extremities of heat and cold. Nights are cool even in the hottest part of the summer. There's considerable rain in the low-lying larger cities; weather is best from May to September and from December through March. The clearness of the air and absence of wind makes it possible to get a good tan in December in the high mountain regions; sun glasses are a must in winter and summer. The *Tessin*—southern Switzerland—has palm trees and a balmy, California-like climate.

CLUBS ... Rotary and Lions meet regularly in larger cities. Switzerland's two major auto clubs, TCS and ACS, are affiliated with American clubs. Local U. S. Consulates give information concerning meetings of the Swiss Friends of the U. S. A. and the Swiss Society for Cultural Relations with America, as well as local American Women's Clubs and other organizations. Use of the facilities of private golf, tennis, yacht and sports clubs may usually be arranged through hotels, or upon presentation of membership cards of similar U. S. clubs.

COMMON COURTESIES AND LOCAL CUSTOMS ... The Swiss, although equally friendly, are a bit more reserved than Americans. Only members of the family and intimate friends are on a "first name" basis. Men not only tip their hats to ladies but to friends of the same sex, and there's a good deal more handshaking. But, in general, the forms of etiquette and good manners are the same as at home. Kady is a service in Zurich which can provide you with baby sitter, translator, shopping service, etc.

COMMUNICATIONS ... The super-efficient Swiss Post Office operates telephone and cable systems. Calls may be dialed anywhere within Switzerland. Transatlantic telephone and cable service is excellent. Basic airmail rate to the United States: letter, 65 centimes; postal card, 50 centimes.

CURRENCY ... The monetary unit is the Swiss franc divided into 100 centimes. Current rate of exchange is approximately 4.25 Swiss francs to the dollar. Switzerland has no currency restrictions and is the most advantageous country in Europe for buying the currency of other countries you are visiting.

CUSTOMS REGULATIONS AND DOCUMENTS REQUIRED FOR UNITED STATES CITIZENS ... No visa required, only a valid U. S. passport. Personal effects, including 2 cartons of cigarettes, 2 bottles of either wine or liquor and 1 pint of perfume (both in unsealed bottles), and amateur camera equipment and film are admitted duty free. Special permission must be obtained from the Swiss Consulate for unusual or professional photographic equipment. Regulations on Swiss watches are likely to vary with the make so check with the United States Customs before attempting to bring them back.

DRUG STORES ... Swiss drug stores carry all the pharmaceuticals you need, including many familiar U. S. brands, but no chocolate sodas (for ice cream and soft drinks, go to a "tea room"), cigarettes or household appliances. American products are available at most department stores and groceries.

ELECTRIC CURRENT ... Most of Switzerland is supplied with alternating current, 220 volts, 50 cycles; American plugs do not fit Swiss sockets. In some Alpine valleys, there is direct current or some unusual voltage like 125 or 150. Always ask hotel staff before using your own electric appliances to avoid damage.

FAUNA ... Good hunting and fishing, but cantonal licenses are necessary. Most streams and lakes are restocked annually with game fish (mainly trout and perch). If you are interested in wild life, the Swiss National Park in the Canton of the Grisons is well worth a visit.

FLORA ... Tremendous variety of wildflowers in the Alpine regions. Edelweiss, which grows only in almost inaccessible mountain areas, is more or less the national flower. The extravagantly flowered Alpine meadow, which bursts forth spontaneously in all its glory each spring, is as much a symbol of Switzerland as the tulip field is of Holland.

FOOD ... Cuisine in Switzerland is French, German or Italian according to the language spoken in the region. By U. S. standards, restaurant prices are extremely low. A first-class meal, without wine or coffee, in an ordinary restaurant costs less than $1.50, and a gastronomic treat, with fine wines, in a de luxe restaurant can be had for about $6.50. Servings are much larger than we are accustomed to at home. Each region has its specialties in food and wine: melted cheese dishes (*fondue* and *raclette*) in the French-speaking regions; roasts with rich sauces, wonderful sausages, and *rosti* (something like hash-brown potatoes, only better) in the German-speaking parts; delicious air-dried meats sliced paper-thin (*bindenfleisch*) in the Canton of Grisons and in the Valais. Don't hesitate to ask the restaurant proprietor to describe the local specialty—a little interest will often pay gastronomic dividends. Bread, butter, and water are usually served only upon request. Water is completely safe everywhere. Pasteurized milk is not generally available, but when it is, it is safe to drink. The Continental breakfast—rolls, butter, jam, coffee, tea or chocolate—is the rule in Switzerland, but you can always order your orange juice, bacon and eggs, and cereal. Coca Cola is on sale just about everywhere, but you should also sample the various Swiss wines.

GAMBLING ... Many resorts and resort cities have Casinos with gaming rooms. *Boule,* a modified form of roulette, is the only game. Don't expect to make a killing—the limit per bet is 5 francs. There is occasional horse racing in larger cities with pari-mutuel betting, and winter racing (on snow tracks) in Davos, Arosa, and St. Moritz. If you're really interested in losing money, there are also the national lotteries and football and soccer pools.

LANGUAGE ... French, German, and Italian are recognized by the Swiss Government as official languages. There's a fourth, Romansch, a mixture of these with a little Latin thrown in, spoken by about 40,000 people in the Canton of Grisons. English, however, is spoken and understood in most places where tourists are likely to go. It's best though, to speak slowly and clearly and to avoid slang expressions.

LAUNDRY AND DRY CLEANING . . . Available in large cities and resort hotels. Service is excellent, work beautiful, prices outrageous. Don't complain if you pay over $3 for a dry-cleaning job—your Swiss host pays the same price. Not all hotels are equipped to do your laundry overnight.

LIQUOR . . . Bar prices are slightly lower than in the States. Bottled goods—Scotch, bourbon, gin—cost about the same. Swiss wines are very good, but unlike French wines they are not aged. It pays to ask the head waiter or restaurant proprietor to recommend wines. Swiss liquors, *Marc, Kirsch, Pflumli*, are renowned—but potent.

MEDICAL FACILITIES . . . Swiss doctors and hospital facilities have a well-deserved high reputation. All hotels have house physicians. There is a Swiss spa or sanatorium for almost every ailment. The Swiss National Tourist Office (*see* end of this section for addresses) publishes a descriptive listing of these.

MOTION PICTURES . . . Current American and British films are shown with English sound track. German, French and Italian films carry subtitles in other languages, but not English. Movie performances are not continuous; often seats must be booked in advance as in American legitimate theaters.

MUSIC . . . Larger cities feature regular concerts with outstanding local and visiting talent. Zurich, Basel, Lucerne, and Berne have their own opera houses and companies as well as guest performances; traveling companies visit Geneva. Check with the Swiss National Tourist Office for program of events and information concerning International Music Festivals in Lucerne, Montreux, Zurich, Ascona, the Engadine and other places.

NIGHT CLUBS AND CABARETS . . . See listings for each city under WHERE TO GO.

PHOTOGRAPHY . . . Film is available everywhere in all sizes and film speeds, color and black-and-white, still and movie. Good black-and-white and Ektachrome processing in 24 hours at local photo shops; three weeks on Kodachrome. Tourists are exempt from Swiss taxes on domestic and imported camera equipment.

RELIGION . . . Although individual regions in Switzerland are predominantly either Catholic or Protestant, there are always churches of the other denominations. Synagogues and Christian Science churches are found only in larger cities, Protestant services in English in larger cities. Hotels and local tourist offices give information on services.

RESTAURANTS . . . Recommended ones for each city are listed under WHERE TO GO. Restaurants in the railroad stations, called *"Buffet de la Gare,"* are usually excellent. *Movenpick* is a popular snack bar chain in several cities. Most trains have dining cars serving snacks, drinks and fine meals.

SHOPS AND STORES ... In Zurich, be sure to visit the Heimatwerk, not only a shop but a landmark. Native Swiss handicrafts are featured here. Prices are high, but values superb. See others listed for each city under WHERE TO GO.

SPECTATOR SPORTS ... Typically European: soccer, football, cross-country bike racing. Swiss folklore sports: Wrestling, "Hornet."

SPORTS ... Follow the Swiss themselves if you're interested in active sports. Swimming, boating, mountain climbing, tennis, golf, horseback riding, rifle shooting, trap shooting—there are excellent facilities for practically every sport. The Swiss ski schools are government supervised and very moderate in price—the same is true of mountain-climbing schools. Before embarking on either of these sports, even if you're an expert, a short course is advisable—the Swiss themselves enter in them every year at the beginning of the season. If you can't bring your own ski equipment, excellent skis and ski boots may be rented at a nominal cost.

THEATERS ... Legitimate theaters in larger cities—plays in the language of the region: French, German or Italian. Performances generally begin at 8:15 P.M. Top price for tickets is around $3.

TIME ... European Standard, 6 hours later than United States Eastern Standard.

TIPPING ... 10 to 15 per cent is the general rule. When tip is included in your hotel bill or restaurant check, it is not necessary to give more unless you feel that the service has been exceptional.

TOURIST TAXES ... Hotels in resort areas usually add a nominal Tourist Tax to your bill.

TRANSPORTATION ... The Swiss Federal Railways adhere almost 100 per cent to schedule. First class is perfectly comfortable; second class is clean, but sometimes crowded. Be sure to ask your travel agent about special holiday tickets on Swiss Federal and private lines. You can save up to 50 per cent on rail fares if you do enough traveling. Out-of-the-way regions may be reached on the safe, comfortable Post Office buses. Local tram and motor-bus transportation is convenient, comfortable and rapid. Taxis are apt to be expensive; look for cabs marked *Klein Taxi* or *Petit Taxi*—the tariff is considerably lower. Car rental is best arranged in advance through your travel agent, or through the concierge of your hotel. Rates: Cadillac with English-speaking driver, about $40 per day, Dodge or Buick about $35, allowing you up to 70 miles a day, with a surcharge of about 40 cents for each additional mile. Drive-yourself rentals come to around $13 per day for light American cars, about $10 a day for European cars, with a surcharge of from 9 cents to 12 cents per mile above 70 miles per day. Deposit required: $200 for American cars, $100 for foreign—double this if you expect to take the car out of the country. These rates include "all-risk" insurance. You must have a U. S. or International driver's license.

WATER ... 100 per cent pure and safe everywhere, unless otherwise noted in large red letters. All Swiss bottled waters (Henniez, Passugger, etc.) are carbonated, but many restaurants sell imported waters that aren't.

WHAT TO BUY ... Best bargains are watches. Popular Swiss makes sell for about 40 per cent less here than in the States, and there are even better buys in lesser-known makes. Prices are strictly controlled and the same everywhere, but the larger shops usually have a better selection. If you buy a gold watch or jewelry, don't forget to ask for an export certificate—this will save you 10 per cent.

WHAT TO WEAR ... You'll be comfortable in the same clothing you'd be wearing in San Francisco, Chicago or New York at the same time of the year. Compulsory formal dress is unusual—you'll be safe with a dark suit.

WHERE TO GO—SIGHTSEEING ...

Zurich ... Best introduction to Switzerland's largest city is through one of the conducted sightseeing tours, sponsored by the Official Tourist Bureau. These leave the Central Station at ten each morning and three every afternoon. Zurich is one of the centers of international banking, finance and insurance; its University Medical School and Technological Institute have earned a high position in the world of education, and its hospitals and clinics are among the world's best. In fall and winter, and during the June Festival, first-rate productions, featuring internationally celebrated stars, may be seen at the Municipal Opera House, the Civic Theater (*Schauspielhaus*), and the Concert Hall (*Tonhalle*). Zurich's Art Museum is well worth a visit; its permanent collection is small but very strong in modern French and German schools. Summer sports: golf (Dolder Grand Hotel and private clubs), tennis (Dolder Grand and Baur au Lac Hotels, and private clubs), swimming (pool with artificial waves at the Dolder Grand, large indoor swimming pool, heated, for winter use, public beaches on the Lake of Zurich), sailing, rowing and pedal-boating on the Lake of Zurich. All of Europe shops on Zurich's Bahnhofstrasse. Grieder and Co. is an outstanding de luxe department store; Jelmoli's is more popularly priced. The Grossmunster Cathedral, the Fraumunster, Wasserkirche, and St. Peter's churches were centers of the Protestant Reformation and are well worth visiting. De luxe hotels: *Dolder Grand, Baur au Lac*. Very good, but less elegant: *Carlton-Elite, St. Gotthard, Ascot, Eicher, Savoy, Central, Sonnenberg* (magnificent view of city and lake), *Bellerive, Eden, Storchen*, among others. Some restaurants with local atmosphere: *Walliser Kanne, Veltliner Keller, Caribou, Huguenin, Kronenhalle, Astoria* and, especially, the *Zunfthauses*, or ancient guildhall restaurants. *La Rotisserie de la Côte d'Or* and *Terrasse* are excellent inexpensive restaurants. Both have dancing. If you are homesick for an American-style restaurant, try one of the *Movenpick's* (Paradeplatz, Sihlportplatz, Claridenhof). The *Hermitage* is an excellent lakeside restaurant just outside Zurich. Most popular night clubs are the *Terrasse, Perroquet, Embassy, Börse* and the *Odeon*— but don't expect too much. Midnight closing is the rule.

Geneva ... One of Europe's most cosmopolitan cities, Geneva is headquarters of dozens of international organizations, including the Red Cross, World Council of Churches, International YMCA, International Labor Office, World Health Organization, and the European Office of the United Nations, which now occupies the impressive "Peace Palace" that was built for the League of Nations. It is hard to imagine a city with a more romantic setting: at the junction of the flashing Rhone and Lac Leman in the shadows of mighty Mt. Blanc, the Alps' highest peak. Geneva's lack of museums and art galleries (she has them, but mostly of interest only to specialists) is more than compensated by exciting lake and river promenades, vast parks, and smart shopping streets. An early morning or late summer evening stroll along the Quai du Mt. Blanc, the Quai Wilson, and through the Parc Mon-Repos is fascinating, but the most exciting spectacle of the capital of *La Suisse Romande* (French-speaking Switzerland) is the Park of Ariana with its exquisitely landscaped gardens and monumental cream-colored buildings, now the European Headquarters of the United Nations. Visit the fourth-floor terrace of the U.N. restaurant for a stunning view of the whole Genevese countryside, Lac Leman, and (if it is a clear day) majestic Mt. Blanc. Geneva's de luxe hotels are the *Beau-Rivage, Les Bergues, De la Paix, Richemond*, and *d'Angleterre*—all facing the Lake—and the new streamlined *Du Rhône*, overlooking the river. There are many less expensive but equally comfortable hotels scattered throughout the city: the Hotel Bureau, located in the Cornavin Station, is most helpful when, as is often the case, rooms are scarce in Geneva. The *Fêtes de Geneve*, held annually in August, is one of the Continent's gayest celebrations. Other annual events of interest: International Horse show (November), Exposition of Watches and Jewelry (September), Automobile Show (February). The *Amphitrion* and *Le Béarn* are among Geneva's most elegant restaurants; for local atmosphere the *Auberge à la Mère Royaume, Le Mazot,* and *La Perle du Lac* are recommended. *Le Gentilhomme* in the Richemond Hotel is also good. *Café Landolt* is the meeting place of students, intellectuals, and Bohemians. Night clubs are a bit on the rowdy side and far too expensive for what you get: *Chez Maxim, Ba-Ta-Clan, Moulin Rouge, Monique, Cave à Bob, Piccadilly, Le Gentilhomme*. Hotel Richemond is thoroughly respectable and the best place to take a lady.

Basel ... Second to Zurich in size, this city is splendidly situated on the Rhine and is an entry point from both France and Germany. This city is the seat of the important Swiss chemical industry, the Bank of International Settlements, and is the home port of the ever-growing merchant fleet that has made the "Swiss Navy" a reality. The Cathedral, built in the eleventh century on the site of a church that was then 400 years old, is well worth visiting, if only to see the charming square and medieval houses that surround it. An outstanding collection of Holbeins (he did much of his best work in this city) is on exhibit at the Art Museum, along with interesting modern works: Picasso, Braque, Klee, Chagall, and others. People who know about zoos say that Basel's is one of the world's best—it's only a five-minute walk from the Central Station. The *Three Kings* is internationally famous and one of Switzerland's oldest hotels—its guest books date back almost a thousand years. Lunch on the terrace overlooking the Rhine is unforgettable. Somewhat less romantic, but equally comfortable is the *Hotel Euler*. The *St. Jakob* is Basel's most typical restaurant, and very good. Also recommended: *Schützenhaus, Walliser Kanne, Kunsthalle, Odeon Grill Room*. Basel goes wild each year during the *Fasnacht* (carnival) celebration in February. The Swiss Industries Fair (April) is one of Europe's most important industrial expositions.

Berne... Capital of the Swiss Confederation, Berne is probably the most picturesque of the larger cities, chiefly because of its arcaded streets and decorative medieval fountains. Berne's most heralded attractions are the celebrated Clock Tower, with its hourly display of mechanical figures, and the Bear Pit, which has been maintained by the municipality since the sixteenth century. When visiting Berne's "old city," you'll see the Town Hall, the lovely Gothic Cathedral, and the Rose Gardens. A short walk beyond the Federal Capitol brings you to the Kleine Schanze, which offers a magnificent panorama of the snow-capped peaks of the Bernese Alps. Leading hotels are the *Schweizerhof* and the *Bellevue Palace*. A restaurant with typical Bernese atmosphere is the *Kornhauskeller*. For daily guided tours, of varying duration, to Bernese Oberland points of interest, inquire at the Official Tourist Office or your hotel.

Lucerne... Less than an hour from Zurich by train, this is the storybook Swiss city and one of the country's principal tourist attractions. The city's chief landmarks are the fourteenth-century covered bridge that crosses the River Reuss, and the familiar Lion Monument commemorating the heroic attempt of a company of Swiss Guards to save the life of Marie Antoinette. Lucerne is the capital of Central Switzerland's vacationland and only a short distance from the Rigi, Pilatus, Burgenstock (an ideal spot for a longer stay—three fine hotels and every imaginable facility) and Engelberg, for winter and summer sports. A trip by boat on the Lake of the Four Forest Cantons is interesting. The Lucerne Music Festival begins in August. There is a brand new modern hotel, the *Hotel Luzernerhof*, with grill room, restaurant and bar. Other leading hotels are the *Carlton-Tivoli, National, Palace* and *Schweizerhof*. Most typical restaurants: *Zum Wilden Mann, Old Swiss House*, the *Stadthof*, the popular *Stadtkeller* and the widely known *Harry's Restaurant Dubeli*, run by Harry Schrämli. The *Aklin*, in nearby Zug, is the finest in Switzerland. For a pleasant meal on what seems to be the top of the world, take the mountain railway to the peak of Pilatus or of the Stanserhorn, both about 7,000 feet high.

Lausanne... A half hour by train or 3 hours by boat from Geneva, Lausanne is the cultural, educational and medical center of French-speaking Switzerland. In the romantic lakeside suburb of Ouchy, where Byron lived, is the palatial *Beau Rivage*, a favorite

Excursion boats such as this one on Lake Lugano, Switzerland, provide many short tours to points of interest along the lake.

of visiting European royalty and ex-royalty. In Lausanne proper the *Palace,* the *de la Paix* and the *Royal* are the leading hotels. Two typical restaurants are *Aux Trois Tonneaux* and *Café à la Pomme de Pin.* Visit Vevey, a charming village rich with memories of Rousseau, Victor Hugo, Thackeray, Courbet, Byron and others, fifteen minutes from Lausanne, and Montreux, to see the historical Château de Chillon and for side trips to Rochers de Naye, Les Avants, Château d'Oex and Gstaad. The restaurant *de la Rouvenaz* is good.

Interlaken ... Chief resort town of the Bernese Oberland, Interlaken is famed for its superb view of the Jungfrau. The fine Casino features performances of native Swiss folklore: dancing, yodeling, alphorn playing and flag throwing. Excellent connection to *Jungfraujoch* (Europe's highest railway station, almost 12,000 feet) for an incomparable Alpine and glacial panorama; *Grindelwald, Murren,* and *Wengen.* Leading hotel in Interlaken is the *Victoria-Jungfrau,* Switzerland's largest.

The Valais ... Here is the indescribably beautiful Rhone Valley, beginning at Martigny (starting point for excursions to the St. Bernard Pass and its famous Monastery and Kennels). It passes through Sierre and Sion with picturesque vineyards and ancient ruins, Visp (the junction for *Zermatt,* celebrated summer and winter resort near the Matterhorn), and ends at Brig, the beginning of the Simplon, Europe's longest railway tunnel, through which the Orient Express passes daily. Direct connections for Milan and Rome.

The Grisons ... From Chur, Grison's capital, there are direct connections for Switzerland's legendary resorts: *St. Moritz, Arosa, Davos, Klosters, Pontresina, Celerina* and *Sils Maria,* best known for winter sports, but equally exciting in the summer. The trip by Postal Bus from St. Moritz through the Maloja Pass, along Lake Como to Lugano offers some of the most exciting scenic splendors of Switzerland, with a bit of the Italian Lake Country thrown in as a bonus. Nature lovers should see the small but lovely Swiss National Park.

Northeast Switzerland ... Off-the-beaten-path Switzerland, largely ignored by American tourists, is rich in attractions: pleasant rolling green country, the Rhine, lazy and meandering here; friendly, unspoiled peasantry, rich in folklore; relaxation, quiet. *St. Gall,* Switzerland's textile and embroidery center, is the principal city of this region. Its Cathedral and Abbey are regarded as outstanding examples of rococo architecture, and the exquisite Abbey Library is one of the showplaces of Europe. Near Schaffhausen one may watch the spectacular Falls of the Rhine, while enjoying freshly caught trout or salmon at Schloss Laufen, and then proceed to the story-book village of Stein-am-Rhine, a perfectly preserved sixteenth-century town. Not far away is the lovely Lake of Constance. Tourists can see the Landsgemeinde: the citizenry meets in the town square to decide upon important municipal issues. Near Appenzell is the imposing Santis peak, with its breathtaking air-cable railway. From this 8,000-foot peak parts of Germany, Austria, and the Alpine range are visible. Throughout this region delightful country inns, very reasonably priced and serving delicious meals, may be found. Charming hotels in St. Gall are the *Im Portner,* the *Hecht* and the *Walhalla.*

The Tessin ... The Italian-speaking section of Switzerland officially begins at Airolo, the exit of the St. Gotthard Tunnel, but the region most attractive to vacationists is concentrated in the Lugano-Locarno area. These two cities share the fabulous lakes of Lugano and Maggiore with neighboring Italy. From March through November one may be reasonably sure of warm, sunny weather in the Tessin. Tennis, golf and water sports (including water skiing) predominate. In Lugano, see the impressive Bernardino Luini frescoes in the tiny church of Santa Maria degli Angioli. Funiculars take you to the heights of Monte Bre, Monte San Salvatore and Monte Generoso, each offering a superb panorama. Lugano's leading hotels are the *Splendide, Palace,* and *Parc au Lac.* Just outside Lugano is *La Romantica,* a restaurant that richly deserves its name. Housed in the former villa of an Italian nobleman, this restaurant is the last word in old-world elegance and its terraces offer a rare view of Lake Lugano. Locarno, on Lake Maggiore, is smaller and more resort-like than Lugano. Nearby Ascona is a favorite resort of European artists, writers and musicians—gay, informal. The delightfully primitive mountain village of Ronco is worth a day's excursion. The lake view from its churchyard is unforgettable. Also recommended is a visit to the Isle of Brissago. The Botanical Gardens are world famous.

SOURCES OF FURTHER INFORMATION ... The Swiss National Tourist Office, Bahnhofplatz 9, Zurich, with branches in New York (10 West 49th Street), San Francisco, and many European cities, has a wealth of material such as maps, hotel guides, programs of events (art exhibits, musical performances, etc.), and booklets on fishing and wildflowers. Local tourist offices are to be found in every city or resort throughout Switzerland (usually marked in German *"Verkehrsbüro"* and in French *"Bureau de Renseignements"*). American legation at Berne, Consulates General at Geneva and Zurich, Consulate at Basle. Pan American's office is at 46, Bahnhofstrasse, Zurich (Tel. 237704).

YUGOSLAVIA

This southern European country is similar in size to Oregon (93,201 square miles) and has a population of 17 million. 469,988 live in Belgrade, the capital. Yugoslavia is reached by Pan American to European cities such as Paris, Munich, Frankfurt, Vienna, Istanbul, Rome, then by JAT (Yugoslav Airlines) to Belgrade and all tourist centers.

With its beautiful mountain and coastal resorts, plenty of historic lore, low prices and hospitable people, Yugoslavia is popular with tourists. To enter the country U.S. citizens need a passport and visa. 3,000 dinars (in 100-dinar notes) and unlimited foreign currency may be brought in. Duty-free allowances: 200 cigarettes, 1 bottle of wine, ½ pint other spirits. Items like cameras and radios should be declared. The rate of exchange is 400 dinars to the dollar. The climate varies from subtropical to Alpine. Best time to go is April to October for the coast, December to April for winter sports. Wear light summer clothing in cities and resorts. Woolens for the mountains.

Belgrade . . . Though a modern metropolis, Belgrade is full of cultural and historical monuments from earliest times, parks, residential quarters with lovely villas, museums, art galleries, interesting architecture of many influences. Best hotels are the *Metropole, Majestic, Moskva,* and *Excelsior,* $7 to $10 American Plan. The *Balkan, Bristol, Kasina, Prag* and *Splendid* are $3 to $7. Similar rates at the resorts. Yugoslav food is most like Viennese.

Capitals of the various republics—*Zagreb, Ljubljana, Sarajevo, Skopje* and *Titograd*—are important economic centers rich in cultural and historical monuments, medieval castles, museums, art galleries. From them excursions can be made to picturesque villages where folk dances and national costumes are of special interest.

The Adriatic Coast with many bays, islands, sandy beaches and varieties of flora is ideal for vacationing. Among the many attractive resorts are *Portoros* and *Rovinj* on the west coast; *Lovran* and *Opatija* on the east Istrian coast; *Kraljevica* and *Crikvenica* on the Croation coast; *Zadar, Biograd na moru, Split* and *Dubrovnik* in Dalmatia; *Hercegnovi, Budva, Sveti Stefan, Bar* and *Ulcinj* on the Montenegrin coast, *Rab* and other islands. The cultural remains of ancient and medieval times give these places a special charm. Of interest in the lake regions are *Bled,* cosmopolitan summer resort; *Bohinj,* the *Plitvice National Park, Borucko Lake, Ohrid, Prespa* and *Dojran.*

SOURCES OF FURTHER INFORMATION . . . The Yugoslav State Tourist Office, 509 Madison Avenue, New York 22, N. Y.

The Middle East

EGYPT

WEATHER IN CAIRO—Lat. N30°3′

Temp.	JAN.	FEB.	MAR.	APR.	MAY	JUNE	JULY	AUG.	SEPT.	OCT.	NOV.	DEC.
Low	45°	47°	51°	56°	62°	67°	70°	71°	67°	63°	56°	49°
High	67°	70°	76°	83°	89°	94°	96°	94°	89°	86°	79°	70°
Average	56°	59°	64°	70°	76°	81°	83°	78°	78°	75°	68°	60°
Days of Rain	3	2	2	1	0	0	0	0	0	0	1	2

LOCATION ... Egypt, an important crossroads between East and West, occupies the northeastern corner of Africa, with the Mediterranean on the north and the Red Sea on the east. Libya and the Anglo-Egyptian Sudan are border countries on the west and south. Egypt's northwestern corner, the Sinai peninsula, is separated by the Gulf of Suez and the Canal.

CHARACTERISTICS ... The banks of the Nile have witnessed the passing of many civilizations, which tourists may observe in remains dating from the dawn of history to Pharaonic Egypt, in the Pyramids at Giza, the Sphinx, Luxor tombs and temples, and those of Sakkara, Kena, Edfu, Kom Ombo and Aswan. Alexandria has vestiges of the Greco-Roman period. Early relics of Christendom in the Nile valley may be seen in the Sinai peninsula and along the coast of the Red Sea.

POPULATION ... Egypt has a population of about 23 million, which approximates the population of the states of California, Pennsylvania and Maine, combined.

SIZE ... 386,101 square miles, the size of Texas and New Mexico combined.

CAPITAL ... Cairo, with a population of about 3,000,000, the size of Detroit's metropolitan area.

GOVERNMENT ... A part of the United Arab Republic known as the Southern Region.

HOW TO GET THERE ... By Pan American Jet Clipper to

Rome, about 11 hours from New York. Then by connecting airline, about 5 hours to Cairo. For travelers in the Middle East, Cairo is 1½ hours from Beirut, Lebanon, and may be included at no extra cost by passengers who purchase in advance a ticket covering their full itinerary. By ship to Alexandria 13 to 17 days from New York.

ACCOMMODATIONS ... There are many fine hotels in Cairo: The newly built *Nile Hilton Hotel,* overlooking the Nile, has 400 air-conditioned rooms. Rates are from $18 to $23, American Plan. The *Shepherds Hotel* has provision for 240 air-conditioned rooms but only 126 are operative. Of others, *Semiramis, Mena House, Continental Savoy, Cosmopolitan* are best. Their rates are from $6 to $8 American Plan, including service charge. Without meals about $3 to $4. Air-conditioned rooms at the Semiramis and the Continental Savoy are slightly higher. In Alexandria, *Hotel Beau Rivage, Cecil, San Stefano, Mediterranée, Windsor, Roy, Crillon, Deauville* and *La Tourelle.* Rates about $5 to $6. Without meals, about $2 to $3. At Luxor, *Winter Palace, Luxor Hotel* and *Savoy.* Rates about $7 to $13 including meals. At Aswan, *Cataract Hotel* and *Grand Hotel.* Rates about $4 to $14. Without meals, $3 to $10.

ARTS ... Continuous excavations supply plenty of antiquities for the many museums. In chronological order covering the various historical epochs beginning over 7,000 years ago they are: the Egyptian Museum, Roman Museum, Coptic Museum, and the Arab Museum. There are also an Agricultural Museum, Modern Civilization Museum, Civilization Museum, the Museum of Modern Arts, and the Cotton Museum.

BALLET ... Oriental ballet, as well as visiting troupes from France and India, give performances during the tourist season.

BANKS ... The following banks in Cairo have connections with the U. S. Banks: American Express Co., 15 Kasr El Nil St., Thomas Cook & Sons, 4, Champollion St., First National City Bank of New York, 56 Abdel Khaleh Sarwat Pasha St. among others. Only banks and the important hotels cash traveler's checks.

CALENDAR OF HOLIDAYS ... Sham El Nessim in late April or early May, Anniversary of the Revolution on July 23, the Flooding of the Nile at the second fortnight of August, the Hegira New Year, End of the Fasting Month (Ramadan), Bairam Feast, and the Commemoration of the Proclamation of the Republic on June 18.

CIGARETTES AND TOBACCO ... Egyptian cigarettes are made of the best qualities of Turkish and Greek tobaccos. American cigarettes are sold everywhere at moderate prices.

CLIMATE ... Generally speaking, the climate of Egypt is similar to that of the rest of the Mediterranean region. In Cairo, the weather is hot although dry sometimes during the day in summer, but the evening is cooler. In winter Egypt enjoys a warm temperature, although it can get as low as 40 degrees in Cairo. Port Said and Alexandria temperatures are similar to those in the chart on page 196 but with less variation between summer and winter.

CLUBS ... The important clubs in Egypt are: the Automobile

Club, Aviation Club, Cairo River Club, Cairo Yacht Club, Cavalry Club, Fishing and Shooting Club, Gezira Racing Club, Gezira Sporting Club, Heliopolis Racing Club, Maadi Sporting Club, Maadi Yacht Club, National Club, Rotary Club, Rowing Club, Tewfikieh Tennis Club, Touring Club, and the Army Forces River Club.

COMMUNICATIONS . . . Communications with America through cables and telephone by Overseas Telecommunications Organization and Telephone Offices. Airmail to the United States is 20 cents for postal cards, 25 cents for letters.

CURRENCY . . . The Egyptian unit is the Egyptian pound (L.E.), which is divided into 100 piastres (P.T. 100), or 1,000 milliemes (1,000 m/ms). The American dollar corresponds to about 35 piastres. Currency may be exchanged in all accredited banks and at airports on arrival.

CUSTOMS REGULATIONS AND DOCUMENTS REQUIRED FOR UNITED STATES CITIZENS . . . Passport and visa required, also smallpox certificates and others if coming from Eastern, yellow-fever or cholera areas. Check with Pan American. Personal effects are admitted duty free, although some need to be declared. 200 cigarettes or 25 cigars or ½ lb. tobacco and 1 opened pint of liquor allowed.

DRUG STORES . . . American pharmaceuticals can be found in all dispensaries and drug stores.

ELECTRIC CURRENT . . . In central Cairo it's 220 volts, D.C. Elsewhere it varies, but is usually 110–220 volts, A.C.

FAUNA . . . The camel, which can be ridden around the Pyramids and the Sphinx, but not in the streets of the towns. In the Egyptian deserts, the desert rabbits, the gazelle, and the fox. Hunting excursions can be organized through the Hunting and Fishing Club or the Touring Club of Egypt.

FOOD . . . Oriental food is liked by most foreigners, but the majority of hotels serve Occidental meals. Milk should be boiled. (Powdered milk, however, is available.) Every kind of poultry, meat and fish or vegetables and fruits are available in abundance.

GAMBLING . . . Betting on weekly horse races in winter in Cairo and in summer at Alexandria. Bets are also authorized at the Shooting Club.

LANGUAGE . . . The tourist can make himself understood in English in all parts of Egypt. Among the various expressions in Arabic, the most used are: *Salem Aleikum* (good day), *Ahlan wa sahlan* (welcome), *Mutashaker* (thank you) and *Baksheesh* (tip).

LAUNDRY AND DRY CLEANING . . . Dry cleaning in Cairo and Alexandria is done by many firms. Laundry service is available in the cities all over the country at moderate rates.

LIQUOR . . . Egypt produces a good quality of beer as well as some kinds of wine, also imports many. Available at bars, hotels and restaurants. Scotch whisky is sold at moderate prices.

MEDICAL FACILITIES . . . There are in Egypt private and Government hospitals where good doctors are in attendance. Egyptian

Ramses II, the great Egyptian ruler, built these colossal statues, which stand among the temple ruins at Luxor.

The Nile, a camel rider, and the famous Cheops Pyramid form a traditional view of the Cairo area of Egypt.

hospitals use American equipment and methods. All physicians speak English.

MOTION PICTURES ... There are many theaters which show American films. There are also American cinemas, like *Cinema Metro, Kasr el Nil Radio, Rivoli,* and others, which are among the finest anywhere. Many theaters are air conditioned.

MUSIC ... There are concerts of both Oriental and European music to be heard at concert halls, dancing places, and on the radio. The Opera House invites famous foreign troupes during the winter.

NIGHT CLUBS AND CABARETS ... The most renowned night clubs are: *Auberge des Pyramides* (cabaret, dancing), *Abdine Place, Casino Mokattam, Fontana, Arizona.* Supper clubs with dancing are found at *The Mena House Hotel, Semiramis, Khassed Kheir* (Ex-King Farouk's Yacht) and *Sindbad's Cave.*

PHOTOGRAPHY ... Egypt has branches of the leading firms dealing in photography and films of various kinds. Kodak has a shop in Alexandria and one in Cairo at Sharia Adly 20. Developing and printing are good and fast. Tourists are requested not to take pictures of military installations or views which may affect Egypt's prestige.

RELIGION ... The official religion is Islam. In addition to the mosques, there are churches of every sect, as well as synagogues.

RESTAURANTS ... The best are the *Kursaal, Ermitage, Regent, St. James,* and *Khumais,* as well as restaurants in the larger hotels. All serve Continental food except *Khumais,* with its Oriental Room where you sit on huge hassocks and eat from large brass trays.

SHOPS AND STORES ... In the main cities of Egypt there are stores selling most of the required commodities. All the tourist's requirements are found at Khan Khalil.

SPECTATOR SPORTS ... A great number of sporting events are held in Egypt, such as horse races at Cairo and Alexandria; football matches with foreign teams. Championship matches take place among the various teams in the Mediterranean as well as between the Arab nations in several sports such as wrestling, swimming, tennis and basketball. Regattas and sailing boat races are held on the Nile.

SPORTS ... The tourist can participate in tennis, golf, swimming at sporting clubs and at some hotels, such as Mena House. Egyptian clubs are considered among the most luxurious found anywhere.

THEATERS ... The Opera House gives performances by foreign troupes during the winter season. However, there are also plays in Arabic in the Opera House.

TIME ... 7 hours later than Eastern Standard Time.

TOURIST TAXES ... There is no tax for tourists except at Luxor and Aswan, where a tax of 5 per cent is added to hotel bills.

TRANSPORTATION ... You can hire cars from the travel bureaus or touring companies. Taxis are numerous and inexpensive.

WATER ... Most of the towns have reservoirs for disinfecting the water to make it fit for drinking. Egypt has sources of mineral water, famous all over the world, which are sold in bottles everywhere.

WHAT TO BUY ... Wooden objects encrusted with ivory and ebony, silver and gold wires; and copper plates encrusted with different metals; leather objects; camel saddle ottomans.

WHAT TO WEAR ... Lightweight, crease-resistant clothing in light colors is best both winter and summer; a jacket for cool evenings, sun glasses, of course, and a lightweight hat.

WHERE TO GO—SIGHTSEEING ...

Cairo ... To get the most out of your sightseeing in Cairo you will probably need a dragoman (guide-interpreter). A brief checklist of principal places of sightseeing interest includes, of course, a visit to the Pyramids and the Sphinx at Giza, by camel if you wish. The Great Pyramid of Cheops is 446 feet high, 740 feet long on each side of the base, covers 12 acres, contains well over two million blocks of stone averaging 2½ tons each in weight. King Cheops' tomb, composed of huge slabs of granite, is in the center. You can climb up on the inside, or to the top of the outside if you're a hardy climber. Other places of interest are: the Citadel, with a wonderful view of Cairo and the Nile, the historical dwellings and mosques (mosques of Sultan Hassan, Mohammed Ali, Ihn Tuhûn and El Azhar are most notable), the Museums, the Babylon Citadel, Churches Kasr el Shamh (ancient churches), the ex-king's palaces, the zoological gardens, Helwân, the Barrage, Sakkarah, the Step Pyramid, Tombs of the Old Dynasty, Tombs of the Apis Bulls.

Side Trips ... In Alexandria, 113 miles northwest by air from Cairo, are the ports, the Corniche, Kait Bay Fort, Antoniades Garden, the historical sights of Kom El Shogafa, the Catacombs, Pompey Pillar, the Greek Museum, Ras El Tin Palace and Montaza.

At Luxor, 316 miles by air south of Cairo in the heart of ancient Egypt, are the Luxor and Karnak temples, the Valley of the Kings and Queens, Queen Hatshepsut Temple, and Memnon Colossi, Aswan, too, has many historical monuments of interest.

SOURCES OF FURTHER INFORMATION ... The Egyptian State Tourist Administration, 1 Adly Pasha Str., Cairo, for information and for hire of Pan Am's official guide. Pan American's office: Continental Hotel, Cairo (Tel. 75037–75097). In New York the Egypt Consulate is at 900 Park Avenue.

IRAN

WEATHER IN TEHERAN—Lat. 35°41'N—Long. 51°25'E—Alt. 4000 ft.

Temp.	JAN.	FEB.	MAR.	APR.	MAY	JUNE	JULY	AUG.	SEPT.	OCT.	NOV.	DEC.
Low	27°	32°	39°	49°	58°	66°	72°	71°	64°	53°	43°	33°
High	45°	50°	59°	71°	82°	93°	99°	97°	90°	76°	63°	51°
Average	36°	41°	49°	60°	70°	80°	85°	84°	77°	64°	53°	42°
Days of Rain	3	3	6	3	1	–	1	–	–	–	4	3

LOCATION ... Iran, one of the world's oldest empires, lies in southwestern Asia, and is an important country in the Middle East.

CHARACTERISTICS ... Traditionally Iran, or Persia as it was formerly called, is the land of sunshine, roses, and poetry. In Teheran, the age-old way of life is fast giving way to the Westernization. Iranians are known for their hospitality and are delighted when visitors from abroad appreciate the artistic contributions of this ancient country.

POPULATION ... Estimated at 18,000,000.

SIZE ... 629,343 square miles, twice the size of France.

CAPITAL ... Teheran, with a population of 1,800,000.

GOVERNMENT ... Iran is a constitutional monarchy ruled by H.I.M. Mohammad Reza Shah Pahlevi and a Parliament.

HOW TO GET THERE ... Direct service by Clipper from New York, Paris, Rome, Beirut, and other major world centers, 23 hours from New York, 9 hours from Rome, 3½ hours from Beirut.

ACCOMMODATIONS ... First-class Teheran hotels: the *Park, Ambassador, Sepide, Excelsior* and the *Teheran Palace.* Also the *Claridge, Pacific, Atlantic, Jam, Naderi* and *Caravan.* A few minutes from the business area is the first-class *Keyhan* and the *Plaza.* Rates for a single room with bath in the better hotels start at about $9, in the others at about $7, including continental breakfast. The *Park* also includes lunch. The fashionable *Darband Hotel* 35 minutes from the city, is best in the summer. Book hotels far in advance.

ARTS... Iran has gained fame the world around for its fine rugs and delicate miniature paintings. Samples of the finest of these and other works of art are on display at the museums in Teheran.

BANKS... Bank Melli Iran, which has accounts with many foreign banks; also Bank Bazergani, Bank of Teheran, Sepah Bank, Export and Mining Bank.

CALENDAR OF HOLIDAYS... As in many other Moslem countries, the official holiday is Friday, at which time most places are closed. The Pan Am office is open on Friday until 1 P.M.

CIGARETTES AND TOBACCO... American cigarettes cost around 40 cents a pack. Local brands are considerably cheaper.

CLIMATE... Teheran, Isfahan and Shiraz have a climate similar to that of the southwestern part of the U.S. April and October are the pleasantest times of the year to visit Iran.

CLUBS... American Club, the American Officers Club, Teheran Club, Iran Club, Masonic Lodge, Rotary, Lions, Iran-American Society and the Gorgan Club.

COMMON COURTESIES AND LOCAL CUSTOMS... There is no limit to true Iranian hospitality. One is expected to join one's host for a cup of tea, which may be served at any time of day. An Iranian evening meal, which consists of endless courses, starts about 10 P.M. It can be very embarrassing to admire a particular object in an Iranian's home only to have your host present it to you.

COMMUNICATIONS... International telephone and telegraph. Airmail to the U.S. is approximately $.30.

CURRENCY... The monetary unit is the Rial, with a fluctuating exchange rate of about 75 Riats = $1. There are no restrictions on currency imported or exported. Travelers checks and currency can be exchanged at the Airport, hotels, or at the Bank Melli.

CUSTOMS REGULATIONS AND DOCUMENTS REQUIRED FOR UNITED STATES CITIZENS... Passport properly visaed and immunization certificates. An exit visa is required before leaving the country. Duty-free imports are limited to 100 cigarettes, 10 cigars, or ½ lb. of tobacco and one opened bottle of liquor. Permission must be secured to take pictures with movie cameras.

DRUG STORES... Better drug stores carry both European and American products. They sell only drugs and medical supplies.

ELECTRIC CURRENT... 220 volts—50 cycles A.C.

FOOD... Food is interesting here. Restaurants feature European and Middle Eastern food. The top ones are the *Coq d'or* (formerly *Chez Souren*), *La Residence, Belluguette, Leon's Grill, Sheherazade,* and *Mehrabad Airport Restaurant*. Dining rooms at the Park Hotel and the Darband Hotel are also good. For the national specialty "Chelow-Kebab" go to *Fards* in the Shemiran suburbs or the *Shamshri* at the covered bazaar entrance. Try the famous Iranian caviar.

LANGUAGE... The official language is Persian but English and French are usually understood by personnel in hotels.

LAUNDRY AND DRY CLEANING... Laundries, including those with dry-cleaning facilities, can be found and prices are low.

LIQUOR . . . Vodka, beer and wine are the most popular local drinks. Foreign liquors are available but expensive.

MOTION PICTURES . . . Films are shown in English, Italian or French with Persian subtitles. Best theaters are *Asia, Eiffel, Moulin Rouge, Niagara, Plaza, Radio City, Royal, Takhte Janshid.*

NIGHT CLUBS . . . The Palace Hotel offers the best floor show entertainment in Teheran. Other places of note include the *Sheherazade, Miami, Colbeh, Everest.* For native atmosphere try the *Shoukufé.* Several of the hotels have dancing.

RELIGION . . . The official religion is the Shia Sect of Islam.

SHOPS AND STORES . . . The main markets of Teheran are the covered bazaar and the more modern central shopping areas along Lalezar Avenue and Istanbul Avenue. Imported items are usually expensive, but bargains in Iranian copper and brassware can be found.

TRANSPORTATION . . . Taxis are plentiful and inexpensive.

WATER . . . Travelers are advised to drink only boiled water, tea, or sterilized bottled drinks. Pure bottled water is not available.

WHAT TO BUY . . . Rugs, jewelry miniatures, silverware and brassware, "geeveh" (Persian shoes), embroidery.

WHAT TO WEAR . . . Summer requires the lightest weight clothing, but should include suit coats for men and long sleeved apparel for women. A light jacket or wrap is usually needed in the evenings when dining outdoors. Overcoats for winter.

WHERE TO GO—SIGHTSEEING . . .

Teheran . . . The handsome range of bare rugged Alborz Mountains is a striking feature of the Teheran area. In the city itself, one should not fail to visit the royal palaces, interesting government buildings, the covered bazaar, Houses of Parliament, Sepah Salar Mosque, Shah-Abdol-Azim Mosque, Reza Shah's Mausoleum at the side of the ancient city of Rey, the Crown Jewels, the Golestan Palace Museum, Archaeological Museum, Ethnological Museum, Museum and School of Fine Arts, the National Library, and the University of Teheran.

Isfahan . . . is a tourist must. This city is exciting with its fabulous Blue Mosque and others. The old summer Palace of the Shahs of past dynasties contains interesting ancient paintings. Shopping is fun at the bazaar, one of the most lively, and there are good buys.

Shiraz . . . also a must, is known as the city of roses, the nightingales and the poets—Darius, Xerxes and Artaxerces, whose tombs are nearby. 35 miles from Shiraz are the most famous ruins of Persepolis (500 B.C.), and there is a good hotel.

Other points of interest: the resorts on the Caspian shore, the mammoth oil refinery at Abadan, the gold-domed Mosque in the shrine city of Meshed, and the 18,550 ft. peak of Mt. Damavand.

SOURCES OF FURTHER INFORMATION . . . Pan American office in Teheran on Hafez Avenue at Sha Reza Blvd. (Tel. 65991–2–3). Iranian Information Center 350 5th Avenue, New York, N. Y.

IRAQ

WEATHER IN BAGHDAD—Lat. N33°21'—Alt. 112'

	JAN.	FEB.	MAR.	APR.	MAY	JUNE	JULY	AUG.	SEPT.	OCT.	NOV.	DEC.
Average Temp.	49°	53°	60°	71°	82°	90°	94°	94°	88°	78°	61°	53°
Days of Rain	5	5	4	3	1	0	0	0	0	1	4	5

Twenty-five hours by Pan American from New York and 9¾ hours from Rome, Baghdad, the exotic city of the Arabian Nights is now a modern metropolis. Where Nebuchadnezzar marched some 2,500 years ago, new highways roll out across the desert. Shiny American cars and red double-decker buses inch through traffic. Modern apartments and the towers of oil refineries loom above adobe huts and Bedouin tents. Strong steel bridges span the old Tigris River, The climate is hot in summer but humidity is low and nights are cool.

To visit Iràq you'll need a visa in addition to your passport. One bottle of liquor and 200 cigarettes are allowed duty free. American cigarettes cost about 55 cents locally. The unit of currency is the Iraqi dinar divided into 1,000 fils and equal to $2.80. The electric current is 220 volts, 50 cycles, A.C. The retail shopping center is Rashid Street. The drug stores have American products; the leading department store is *Orosdi-Back*. Iraq goods are found in the bazaars.

Among the several hotels, the newest are the first class, air-conditioned *Baghdad Hotel* with rates of $11.20 to $12.60 European Plan, and the *Khayyam* with rates from $7 to $14 including breakfast. At hotel restaurants which feature European cuisine, a complete dinner costs about $3. Milk should be boiled. Arab meals often include excellent rice and lamb. One famous dish is *samak masgouf,* which literally means "roofed fish," Tigris river salmon seasoned with tomatoes, salt, onions, curry powder and oil. *Raki* or *araq* is the potent national drink. Foreign liquors are fairly high priced. Bars are plentiful and there are excellent night clubs with European floor shows.

Outstanding points of sightseeing interest are the various mosques, which may be seen only from the outside, the National Museum and the Hanging Gardens of Babylon, where considerable excavation has been done. Babylon is about 2½ hours by car from Baghdad and during the hot weather should be visited early in the day.

Pan American's office is on Sadoon Street. (Tel. 88300).

ISRAEL

WEATHER IN JERUSALEM—Lat. N31°46′—Alt. Approx. 2,500′

Temp.	JAN.	FEB.	MAR.	APR.	MAY	JUNE	JULY	AUG.	SEPT.	OCT.	NOV.	DEC.
Low	38°	41°	45°	51°	56°	62°	65°	64°	62°	59°	50°	43°
High	51°	55°	62°	70°	78°	84°	87°	88°	85°	80°	66°	56°
Average	45°	48°	54°	61°	67°	73°	76°	76°	74°	70°	58°	50°
Days of Rain	12	12	8	4	2	0	0	0	0	2	6	9

LOCATION . . . The new state of Israel lies on the southeast coast of the Mediterranean between Egypt and Trans-Jordan.

CHARACTERISTICS . . . Here you will have the thrill of seeing a nation in the making, where modern garden cities lie adjacent to ancient sites. The Holy Land, with all its wonderful scenery and Biblical sites, offers inspiration to people of all faiths. There are modern and even luxurious hotels. The climate is sunny and warm. You are assured of a pleasant welcome, for the Israelis are eager to let the world know what they are doing.

POPULATION . . . Estimated 2,000,000.

SIZE . . . About 7,992 square miles, smaller than Massachusetts.

CAPITAL . . . Jerusalem, a growing city of more than 140,000.

GOVERNMENT . . . An independent republic established in 1948, with a President and a Parliament.

HOW TO GET THERE . . . By Pan American Jet Clipper to London, Paris, Rome, or direct to Vienna or Istanbul. Then by connection with El Al Israel Airlines to Tel Aviv. Elapsed time from New York about 19½ hours. By ship about 15 days.

ACCOMMODATIONS . . . Are not difficult to secure, but it is advisable to book hotel reservations well in advance. In Tel Aviv the air conditioned *Dan Hotel* on the seashore is now tops. The *Ramat Aviv Hotel* offers similar comfort and has a delightful swimming pool. The *Sharon Hotel* and *Accadia Grand* at Herzlia-on-the-Sea, and the small new hotel *Tadmor* are also good. All have kosher kitchens.

The best hotels in Jerusalem are the *King David,* the *Eden,* the *Holyland,* the *President,* which has a fine swimming pool, and the *Kings Hotel.* Others are the *Orgil* and the Y.M.C.A. Single rates American Plan in better hotels are about $8.25 to $13.75, about $6.50 in others, about $10.00 at resorts. Rates are slightly higher in summer, lower in winter, so check for specific prices.

ARTS . . . Permanent and transient exhibitions of paintings appear in Tel Aviv, Haifa, and Jerusalem, as well as in the smaller cities.

BALLET . . . Several ballet groups present dances. Lubal, a Yemenite dance group, is famous.

BANKS . . . Banks are open from Sunday through Thursday from 8:30 A.M. to 12:30 P.M., and on Fridays from 8:30 A.M. to 12 noon. Banks include Bank Leumi Le Israel, Barclays Bank, Israel Discount Bank, Ellern's, Jacob Japhet and Feuchtwanger.

CALENDAR OF HOLIDAYS . . .

Jewish Holidays . . . (Rosh Hashanah) in September or October; Yom Kipper ten days later; Succoth four days later, culminating on the eighth day with Simhath Torah; the week of Hanukkah (The Feast of Lights) in late November or December; Purim, in early March, and in April, Passover. May and early June are crowded with religious and national celebrations, such as Lag B'Omer and Shavuoth. Independence Day celebration is held in the spring.

Christian Holidays . . . Christmas begins on the evening of December 24, the Eastern Christmas on January 6. Other celebrations of special interest are: the Pilgrimage to Cana in Galilee on the Second Sunday after Epiphany, the Easter (Western) services on Good Friday, Easter Sunday and Monday; the Feast of Our Lady of Carmel, on the Sunday after Easter on Mt. Carmel; Pentecost ceremonies in May; the Feast of St. John; the Feast of Elijah on Mt. Carmel in mid-July; the Feast of Transfiguration on Mt. Tabor.

CIGARETTES AND TOBACCO . . . American cigarettes are available in hotels. Local Virginia brands are 35 to 40 cents a pack.

CLIMATE . . . Israel possesses a Mediterranean climate with unbroken sunshine during most of the year and fair, sunny weather with short spells of rain from November to March.

CLUBS . . . There are 21 Rotary Clubs in Israel. Other clubs in Tel Aviv include Automobile Club & Touring Association of Israel, Citrus House, Tel. 67612; Commercial and Industrial Club, 32, Yavne Street, Tel. 2667 and in Jerusalem the Touring Club, Tel. 5783.

COMMON COURTESIES AND LOCAL CUSTOMS . . . Israelis are pleased if they hear you speak even one word of Hebrew. The most used word is *Shalom,* meaning "Peace," an all-purpose greeting.

COMMUNICATIONS . . . General post offices in Haifa, Jerusalem and Tel Aviv are open from 7:30 A.M. to 7:00 P.M., but branches in smaller cities are open from 8:00 A.M. to 1:00 P.M. and from 4:00 P.M. to 6:00 P.M. except on holidays and Saturdays. The Central Telegraph Offices never close. Air mail, telephone and radio-telegraph.

CURRENCY . . . is the Israel pound, which is divided into 1,000 prutot. The rate of exchange is IL. 1.800 to the $1.00.

CUSTOMS AND CURRENCY REGULATIONS FOR UNITED STATES CITIZENS . . . You may bring into Israel duty free all your personal effects, traveling accessories and gifts whose value does not exceed $30, but no Israel currency. Tourists need a passport and vaccination certificate but no visa.

Undeveloped film must be passed by the censor when you leave the country, so keep a record of scenes. Black-and-white film can be developed and printed. PLEASE NOTE that land entry can only be made through the Mandelbaum Gate in Jerusalem.

DRUG STORES . . . In the larger cities of Israel drug stores containing many American goods or their equivalent may be found.

ELECTRIC CURRENT . . . 220 volts, A.C. single phase, 50 cycles.

FAUNA . . . Wild pig and duck abound near the Jordan swamps, and in the wasteland of the Negev the gazelle is seen occasionally. Wild animals include the jackal, bear and wild boar. There is a variety of wild bird life among which the eagle, falcon, owl, stork and quail are abundant, also many colorful sub-tropical birds.

FLORA . . . Israel's variegated climate supports a wide range of plants and flowers which give the landscape a splash of color. Many of the country's barren hills have been planted with trees as part of an intensive reforestation program.

LANGUAGE . . . You will have no language problem.

LAUNDRY AND DRY CLEANING . . . Normal service isn't fast but for a 20 per cent surcharge you can cut the time in half.

LIQUOR . . . Whisky and soda is about 75 cents. There are some good local wines such as Adom Atic, a red dry wine, and Carmel Hock, a white dry wine; Chablis, Pommereau and Carmel Port, Rishon, Cognac and cherry brandy are also popular.

MEDICAL FACILITIES . . . Good, with English-speaking doctors.

MOTION PICTURES . . . American and European films. Most cinemas offer two evening performances and one matinee.

MUSIC . . . Israel's musical life is a rich one with many concerts throughout the year. The annual Music Festival during Passover is a major event. The Israel Philharmonic, the principal orchestra, serves under world-famous guest conductors. Chamber music is also popular. Israel National Opera performs regularly in Tel-Aviv.

NIGHT CLUBS AND CABARETS . . . The Casino *Bat Galim* in Haifa, the *Dan Hotel* in Tel-Aviv and Jerusalem's *King David* and *Eden* Hotels feature dance orchestras nightly. The *Israel Touring Club* holds regular dances. Some have floor shows.

PHOTOGRAPHY . . . Films and camera accessories are hard to get so bring your own. *See* CUSTOMS REGULATIONS.

RELIGION . . . Best time to visit synagogues is Friday nights and Saturday mornings. There are three main Christian communities: Roman Catholic, Greek and Russian Orthodox, and Protestant.

RESTAURANTS . . . Excellent eating places serving Central European and Oriental dishes. Hotels and night clubs also serve fine food.

SHOPS AND STORES . . . The Wizo Shops in Jerusalem, Tel Aviv, and Haifa for Oriental and modern gifts. Freund and Rivoli in Tel Aviv for practical and luxury items. Shops and stores are open from 8:00 A.M. to 1:00 P.M. and 3:00 P.M. to 7:00 P.M. Sunday through Thursday and from 8:00 A.M. to sundown on Fridays. Shops and stores are closed on Saturdays and holidays.

SPECTATOR SPORTS . . . Several stadia throughout the country offer football and basketball games. The Ramat Gan Stadium, near Tel Aviv, is the best known.

SPORTS . . . Football, basketball, swimming and tennis are the most popular sports. Yachting and boating are also popular among others.

THEATERS . . . There are four main theatrical companies in Israel: the internationally famous *Habimah;* the *Ohel,* the workers' theater; the new *Chamber* theater group; and the Israel opera.

TIME . . . 7 hours later than U.S. Eastern Standard Time

TIPPING . . . Not as prevalent as at home. Taxi drivers are not tipped, but barbers and employees in the better hotels are usually given moderate gratuities. At most hotels and restaurants tipping is covered with a 10 per cent surcharge on your bills.

TRANSPORTATION . . . Regular train, bus, and taxi services link the main town and cities. Cars can be hired with a driver or a driver-guide. Israel also has an internal airline, *Arkia.* Luxury air-conditioned coaches, equipped with buffets, leave Tel Aviv daily to tour various parts of the country. Typical prices are: 3-days' tour of Galilee, IL. 76.000; 2-day's tour of Jerusalem, IL 46.000 (both the above prices include board and lodging); 1-day's tour of the Negev IL. 15.000. In addition, numerous companies arrange regular tours throughout the country at reasonable rates.

WHAT TO BUY . . . Israel handicrafts and art work are recognized among connoisseurs. Yemenite and Persian filigree work, oriental tapestry and embroidery, metal-chasing, and ceramics are recommended. Religious articles and books are also expertly produced.

WHAT TO WEAR . . . Light clothing for summer days, and fairly warm clothing for the winter months. Jackets, boleros, and sweaters are useful for summer evenings. Do not forget your sunglasses. Bring raincoats, overcoats, robes and woolen garments if you are coming in winter. Bring rubber overshoes or galoshes for the rainy months.

WHERE TO GO—SIGHTSEEING . . .

Tel Aviv . . . This humming beehive of a city is constantly expanding. Ever since the first structures were erected some 50 years ago on bare sand dunes near the Yarkon River, building has been continuing.

Reminiscent of the Europe from which many of the early settlers emigrated are the sidewalk cafés, where people meet at all hours of the day and night. The cafés also stretch along the wide sea front, which provides a favorite haunt during the long summer months.

Inquire about the "Meet the Israeli" program for meeting local people of common interests. *See also* tours under TRANSPORTATION.

Sightseeing in Haifa . . . Haifa, "the Gateway to Israel," is one of the major ports in the eastern Mediterranean. Tourists should visit the waterfront-dock area in the early morning. Do not miss the Bahai Gardens and the beautiful Bahai Temple.

On the southeast slope of Mount Carmel one finds the "Place of Burning," which commemorates the triumph of Elijah over the priests of Baal. In the center of the Carmelite monastery is a domed church in the form of a Greek cross. A double stairway leads to the choir containing a magnificent altar on which stands a statue of Our Lady of Carmel, by the famous Genoese sculptor Caraventa. Below the monastery is the School of Prophets where Elijah is said to have taught his Disciples. Mount Carmel is beautiful as well as interesting.

Sightseeing in Jerusalem . . . Israel's gracious capital is an interesting blending of past and present; it is one of the country's most ancient cities, abounding with relics of a rich past. It is also a modern town complete with wide streets, and modern shopping facilities.

On Mt. Herzl, a hill overlooking Jerusalem, lies the tomb of Theodore Herzl, the founder of modern Zionism, while on Mt. Zion can be found the traditional site of the tomb of King David, the builder of a more ancient Jewish state. The New Hebrew University Campus and Hadassah Medical Center are of interest.

Churches of many denominations stand in Jerusalem, including Church and Abbey of the Dormition on Mt. Zion, the Church of St. John (at Ein Kerem), and the Russian Orthodox Church, whose graceful green domes can be seen for miles. Ein Kerem, the birthplace of St. John the Baptist, is now a picturesque village. Above David's tomb, Mt. Zion houses a room revered by Christians as the Chamber of the Last Supper and the Upper Room. Modern addition to the city include the Knesset (Israel's Parliament), the Israel Touring Club in Talbia, standing among lovely gardens, as well as the giant structure of the Y.M.C.A. On the outskirts is Ramat Rachel, famous battleground during the War of Independence in 1948, which has already been rebuilt. Mea Shearim (the ultra orthodox section), the Bokharian, and the Oriental quarters complete the picture of this city.

Holy Land Tour . . . Starting from Jerusalem, the tourist can spend his first days viewing the sights of the Holy City. Departing southward, he can proceed to the ancient Negev city of Beersheba (famed for its association with the Patriarchs, Abraham, Isaac and Jacob) which is not far away from the ruins of Philistine Ascalon, topped by a Crusader fortification.

Continuing southward along the new highway, blasted through the Negev rocks and leading past fascinating scenery, you reach Sodom and the Dead Sea, which lies at the lowest point in the world. Farther south is the Port of Elath on the Red Sea from which, in ancient times, boats of the known world traded with the rich empire of King Solomon. King Solomon's mines are being reworked today and are among the many new enterprises that are developing.

Returning northward, the traveler can cut through the Judean Hills to Ramleh, visit the White Tower and Crusader Church and continue to Lydda, famed birthplace of St. George, England's patron saint, arriving soon afterward at Tel Aviv. After touring the city, one can drive via the Plain of Sharon to Nathanya (modern seaside resort) and the Roman Hippodrome, aqueduct and port of Caesaria; thence via the Prehistoric Caves to Haifa. Here you tour the city and Mount Carmel, proceeding via Haifa Bay to Acre, location of the Crusader Fortress of Richard the Lion Hearted, the Mosque of Jessar Pasha and many Oriental bazaars. Continue to Upper Galilee, visiting Safad (ancient Kabbalist center); then go to the Holy Places of Mt. Beatitude (site of the Sermon on the Mount), Tabgha (where the multiplication of the loaves and fishes took place) and Capernaum, where stand the ruins of an ancient synagogue in which, according to tradition, Christ taught. On to Tiberias (famed health resort since Roman times, built on the banks of the beautiful Sea of Galilee) and from there to Degania, cooperative agricultural settlement near the River Jordan. Its museum is named after A. D. Gordon, one of the founders and thinkers of this famous settlement. Continue via the Horns of Hittin to Mt. Tabor (the Mount of the Transfiguration), Cana of Galilee (site of the miracle of the changing of water into wine) and Nazareth, visiting the Church of the Workshop of St. Joseph, the Table of Christ. Driving back to Tel Aviv you pass through the biblical Jezreel Valley.

SOURCES OF FURTHER INFORMATION ... Israel Government Tourist Centers: 574 Fifth Avenue, New York; others in Paris, London, Rome, Zurich. In Israel, Lydda Airport and principal cities. Pan Am's office in Tel Aviv is at 38 Achad Haam Street (Tel. 4422).

Cana of Galilee is the locale of the story of Jesus' miracle of turning water into wine at the marriage feast.

From historic Mount Carmel, which dominates the city, one can get an expansive view of Haifa, Israel's harbor city.

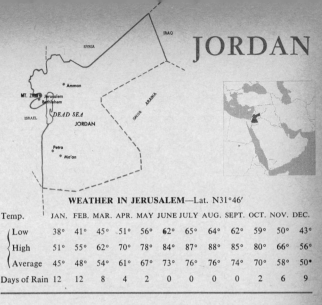

JORDAN

WEATHER IN JERUSALEM—Lat. N31°46'

Temp.	JAN.	FEB.	MAR.	APR.	MAY	JUNE	JULY	AUG.	SEPT.	OCT.	NOV.	DEC.
Low	38°	41°	45°	51°	56°	62°	65°	64°	62°	59°	50°	43°
High	51°	55°	62°	70°	78°	84°	87°	88°	85°	80°	66°	56°
Average	45°	48°	54°	61°	67°	73°	76°	76°	74°	70°	58°	50°
Days of Rain	12	12	8	4	2	0	0	0	0	2	6	9

LOCATION ... The Hashemite kingdom of Jordan is an Arab country and member of the Arab League. It is situated in the heart of the Arab world. On the north, it is bounded by Syria, on the northeast by Iraq, on the east and south by Saudi Arabia, and on the west by Israel.

CHARACTERISTICS ... Jordan comprises Trans-Jordan proper and Central Arab Palestine and includes some of the most sacred shrines of Islam and Christianity. Within its boundaries lie Bethlehem, the birthplace of Jesus; Jericho, the oldest walled city in the world; Hebron, where Abraham was buried; the River Jordan; the Dead Sea; the Mount of Olives and the ancient walled city of Jerusalem, the holiest city in Christendom. Tourism for years has been the main industry of this country and tourists are sure to receive a hearty welcome by all. Jordanians often seek to promote direct contact between groups of tourists and inhabitants through various social gatherings. There are comfortable hotels in Jordan and the climate in general is ideal.

POPULATION ... The population, which is preponderantly Moslem Arab, is estimated at 1,400,000, of whom about 12 per cent are Christians. Besides the Moslem and Christian Arabs, there are fair Circassians, swarthy Copts, Persian Bahais, Syriacs, Turcomans, White Russians, and 217 Samaritans who are descended from Biblical times.

SIZE ... The total area of the kingdom is 37,500 square miles.

CAPITAL . . . Amman, the ancient Philadelphia, is the busy and rapidly growing capital of Jordan.

GOVERNMENT . . . Jordan's Government is a constitutional monarchy with a bicameral legislature. The House of Representatives is elected by direct, secret ballot. The Senate is appointed by the King upon the recommendation of the Government. The King appoints the Prime Minister, who in turn appoints his Cabinet. The Cabinet is responsible to the House of Representatives. All men above 18 years have the right to vote.

HOW TO GET THERE . . . By Pan American Clipper to Beirut, Lebanon, 18¾ hours from New York; then by direct connection to Jerusalem or Amman. From Cairo it is 2½ hours flying time; from Beirut it is 1¼ hours. There is also an overland route by car from Beirut via Damascus to Amman or Jerusalem. Or go to Beirut, Alexandria or Port Said by ship, then by air.

ACCOMMODATIONS . . . Hotels in Jordan cannot for the present compare with luxury hotels in the United States, but they are clean and comfortable. There are good hotels in all the major towns and cities. Most of them have hot and cold running water; rooms with private baths are available. Many hotels have central heating. In Jerusalem, the *Ambassador,* the *Orient House,* the *American Colony Hostel,* and the *National.* In Ramallah (10 miles from Jerusalem and 4 miles from the airport) there is the *Grand Hotel.* In Amman are the *Amman Club* and the *Philadelphia.* Rates are $3.50 to $8.50, including meals with a 10 per cent service charge added. Be sure to reserve hotel space well in advance, especially at Christmas and Easter time.

BANKS . . . Foreign currency may be brought into the country without limit but must be declared to the customs authorities on arrival. Tourists are required to exchange foreign currency at authorized banks or money changers who must record amount cashed on the Exchange Contol Form used when you made your declaration. Only 10 Jordan Pounds (JD 10.000) may be taken into the country.

CALENDAR OF HOLIDAYS . . . National Holidays: March 22, commemoration of the signing of the charter of the Arab League; May 25, Independence Day; Sha'aban 9 (Hegira Calendar) commemoration of Arab revolt against Turkish rule; January 15, Arbor Day.

There are several Moslem feasts based on the lunar calendar. For Christians, Christmas and Easter are most important with ceremonial pageantry. Tourists will find it specially interesting also to attend the Samaritan Passover feast on Mount Gerizim near Nablus. This feast generally falls in April and is celebrated by slaughtering sheep as sacrifice according to ancient Samaritan tradition. Arab Legion Field Day in Amman on May 9 is a special event. Tourists will love this spectacular exhibition of outstanding horsemanship, swordsmanship and sportsmanship.

CIGARETTES AND TOBACCO . . . No American brands, but Virginia tobacco leaves are imported for local production of cigarettes. Local cigarette brands such as *Friends, Windsor, Gold Star* and *Select* are popular. Tourists may bring with them, duty free, 200 cigarettes or about 7 oz. of tobacco.

CLIMATE...The country offers a vast range and contrast of climate and scenery, from the temperate heights of the rugged, purple-hued mountains of Moab to the gently rolling hills of Judea, the deep tropical depression of the Jordan Valley and the Dead Sea and finally the dry, arid desert of the eastern plateau. Jericho, 845 feet below sea level, is an excellent winter resort. *See* WEATHER CHART on page 211.

CLUBS...The Y.M.C.A., the Lions Club, Rotary Club, Masonic Lodge. A tourist would have to be accompanied by a member to make use of the above-mentioned clubs.

COMMON COURTESIES AND LOCAL CUSTOMS...The Jordanians are extremely hospitable. A guest is considered a sacred trust.

COMMUNICATIONS...Telegraph service and airmail.

CURRENCY...The monetary unit in Jordan is the Jordan dinar (JD). This is divided into 1,000 fils. The dinar is equivalent to $2.80, or £ 1. No more than JD 10 allowed in or out of Jordan. *See* BANKS.

CUSTOMS REGULATIONS AND DOCUMENTS REQUIRED FOR UNITED STATES CITIZENS...Tourists may procure visas at Jordan consulates or at Jordan frontier-ports, if they arrive via a neighboring Arab country or hold a visa to an Arab country. A gratis visa is granted to tourists staying in Jordan for a week or more. As for travel between Jordan and Israel, only a one-way crossing is permitted. American visitors in Jordan wishing to cross over into Israel must contact their consulate three days in advance for arrangements to be made, but can not thereafter return to an Arab country. The visitor may bring duty-free into the country: personal effects, a pair of binoculars, one camera, one typewriter, one transformer, one projector, 200 cigarettes or 25 cigars or 200 grams of tobacco, one liter of wine or spirits. He may not bring in radios, phonographs or records unless willing to pay the duty on these.

DRUG STORES...Arab drug stores, called pharmacies, can supply you with everything you need in the way of medicine and toilet goods. They don't have soda fountains.

FAUNA...The mule, camel, Arabian horse and cattle in general, as well as poultry, migratory and local birds. Among wild animals Jordan has the jackal, hedgehog, gazelle, mole, bat, field mouse and the fox.

FLORA...Jordanian flora is similar to that of Southern Europe. Jordan is rich in all kinds of flowers.

FOOD...Food is excellent and plentiful in Jordan. All the hotels serve Continental food of good quality and variety. Tourists should try some of the delicious Arab dishes, such as barbecued lamb, rice and stuffed vine leaves.

LANGUAGE...Arabic is the common language in Jordan. The tourist, however, can get along with English or French. The majority of the people are bilingual and many speak more than two languages fluently.

LAUNDRY AND DRY CLEANING . . . Laundry is excellent and inexpensive.

LIQUOR . . . Arak is the native drink. It is made of grapes and may be taken straight or with water. Whisky is another favorite drink. If you order whisky you'll get Scotch. Bourbon is rare. Popular American drinks and cocktails are available in all hotels and bars. Prices are reasonable.

MEDICAL FACILITIES . . . Hospitals are available in all principal towns and cities in Jordan. Most doctors are graduates of American and British universities and speak English fluently.

MOTION PICTURES . . . The motion picture houses show American, European and Arabic films.

MUSIC . . . Jordan musical life is limited to Arabic music. Occasional concerts are held.

NIGHT CLUBS AND CABARETS . . . No night clubs exist in Jordan. Typical of Jordan are the attractive garden cafés that have orchestras and occasional floor shows.

PHOTOGRAPHY . . . Tourists may take photographs of sites of religious, historical or scenic interest but may not take pictures of scenes of squalor or of military installations. Travelers using colored film should bring a supply with them to Jerusalem. There are no facilities for processing Kodachrome.

RELIGION . . . There are churches of all denominations. The State religion is Islam. Various American Missions are established in Jordan, e.g., Quakers, Lutherans and Baptists.

RESTAURANTS . . . All hotels serve meals to residents and nonresidents. Among best restaurants in Jordan are the *National* in Jerusalem and the *Leon Dor* in Amman.

SHOPS AND STORES . . . Souvenir stores are to be found everywhere in Jordan offering a wide variety of local handicrafts.

SPORTS . . . Football, basketball, boxing, swimming and tennis are the most popular sports. Besides the Dead Sea, the Zarka Pool about 15 miles northeast of Amman offers good swimming.

TIME . . . 7 hours later than United States Eastern Standard Time.

TRANSPORTATION . . . Jordan has good roads. All the historical and religious sites are easily accessible by car. A network of autobuses connects all the major towns and cities, but the usual means of transport is the taxi. Cabs in Jordan are very comfortable and inexpensive. One can take a taxi for 10 miles for about $1.50. Cab companies have arrangements between all the major towns and cities whereby a person can hire a seat in a car and thus travel comfortably and very cheaply indeed.

WATER . . . Water is safe to drink throughout Jordan cities and well-established villages. Bottles of soda water can be bought everywhere.

WHAT TO BUY . . . Tourists will love the delicate bronze and silver work, the fascinating Oriental jewelry, the exquisite mother-of-pearl products, the rich cross-stitch embroidered linen work, the at-

In this general view of Jerusalem, as seen from the Mount of Olives, one can see the big dome of the Dome of the Rock (Mosque of Omar).

The great size of the fascinating buildings of Petra is emphasized by the man with his donkey shown at the entrance.

tractive Crusader jackets of Bethlehem, products of the famous olive-wood industries, and the colorful Palestine pottery. Also religious art. These goods can be bought very cheaply.

WHAT TO WEAR...Light clothing for summer and warm clothing for winter. Raincoats and overshoes for the rainy months, sun-glasses, wrap for cool evenings, comfortable sightseeing shoes.

WHERE TO GO—SIGHTSEEING...

Jerusalem...The city is bisected by the Armistice line resulting from the Palestine hostilities of 1948, leaving a big part of the New City in the hands of the Jews and the Old City in the hands of the Arabs. The Old City proper is enclosed by a 40-foot wall forming an irregular quadrangle about 2½ miles in circumference. The two principal streets intersect in the middle of the city and divide it into four quarters. The most impressive section is the Harem esh Sherif, or Place of the Temple, in the Moslem quarter. The vast majority of the Holy Places are in the Old City or its environs under Arab control. Many of them are sacred to all three faiths.

Church of the Holy Sepulchre...A collection of chapels housing the tomb in which Christ was laid to rest after the Crucifixion: the most venerated shrine in Christendom. *Via Dolorosa*...The way of the Cross along which Christ walked from the Court of Pilate to the hill of Golgotha, marked by 14 stations. *Garden of Gethsemane*...The retreat where the Savior passed his last hours of agony on the night before he was crucified, where he was betrayed by Judas. *Mount of Olives*...The grove of trees overlooking Jerusalem from which the Master ascended to Heaven within view of his disciples. *Tomb of the Virgin Mary*...The Church of the Assumption where Mary, mother of Jesus, was interred by the Apostles.

The Dome of the Rock...An octagonal mosque erected on the ancient site of the Temple of Solomon by Abdul Malik Ibn Mirwan in the seventh century to commemorate the ascension of Mohammed; second only to Mecca as an Islamic shrine. *Aqsa Mosque*...A Romanesque, churchlike structure built over the Stables of Solomon, to which God conveyed Mohammed from Mecca in one night. *Wailing Wall* ... A remnant of Herod's Temple where the Jews gathered for centuries to weep over the destruction of Jerusalem. *Citadel* ... A fourteenth-century group of towers erected on a massive substructure at the bottom of a moat, forming a fine example of the ancient wall towers of Jerusalem; sometimes called the Tower of David.

Palestine Archaeological Museum ... Constructed with a gift of $2,000,000 by the Rockefeller Foundation. Contains a priceless collection of antiquities. *Bethany* ... One and a half miles southeast of Jerusalem; home of Mary and Martha; Lazarus' tomb; excavation of fourth- and twelfth-century churches. *Bethlehem* ... About 10 miles south of Jerusalem; Church of Nativity of Christ; Milk Grotto; Shepherd's Fields; Fields of Boaz. *Nablus* ... About 41 miles north of Jerusalem; Jacob's well where Christ talked to the woman of Samaria; ancient Samaritan community. *Sebastia* ... About 50 miles north of Jerusalem; the Samaria of the Bible where St. John the Baptist is supposed to be buried; nearby is the Church of St. John, a Crusaders' edifice of the twelfth century.

Emmaus ... Thirteen miles northwest of Jerusalem; the Church of the Franciscan Monastery stands on the site where Christ appeared to his disciples after the Resurrection. *Hebron* ... South of Jerusalem, 27 miles; tombs of the Prophets Abraham, Isaac and Jacob; Oak of Mambre, where the angels appeared to Abraham. *Jericho* ... Twenty-four miles northeast of Jerusalem; ruins of the old Canaanite city brought down by Joshua; Elisha's Fountain; Mount of Temptation. *Jordan River* ... Northeast of Jerusalem 27 miles; the world's most famous river flowing from the Lake of Tiberias to the Dead Sea for 184 miles; Christ's Place of Baptism near Jericho; Allenby Bridge. *Dead Sea* ... Twenty-five miles east of Jerusalem; as the lowest spot on earth the shore of the Dead Sea is 1,290 feet below normal sea level and the bottom is 2,600 feet below; site of the destruction of Sodom and Gomorrah and the rescue of Lot. *Jerash* ... Thirty-six miles from Amman; built by the soldiers of Alexander the Great. It reached great heights under the Romans and even in ruins has a special grandeur.

Petra ... For those who have dreamed of an adventurous trip to Tibet or the other great Shangri-las of the world, the great southern desert plain of Jordan offers a spectacle forgotten for over 500 years. The secret city of Petra, carved from the red rocks of the hidden valley offers a unique opportunity.

SOURCES OF FURTHER INFORMATION ... The Jordan Government Tourist Department has information sections at the Jerusalem Airport, in Jerusalem itself and in Amman.

LEBANON

WEATHER IN BEIRUT—Lat. N33°55′—Alt. approx. sea level

	JAN.	FEB.	MAR.	APR.	MAY	JUNE	JULY	AUG.	SEPT.	OCT.	NOV.	DEC.
Average Temp.	56.5°	57.7°	61.2°	66°	71.8°	77.7°	82°	83.1°	80.8°	76.1°	67.3°	60.6°
In. of Rain	7.3	5.7	3.9	2.2	.8	.1	0	0	.3	2.1	5.3	7.5

LOCATION ... Lebanon occupies a small strip of land at the east end of the Mediterranean, bordered by Israel on the south and by Syria on the north and east.

CHARACTERISTICS ... This is a wonderful little country, which has within its boundaries some of the most magnificent ruins in the world, the famous Cedars of Lebanon, and modern cities and villages which turn the clock back hundreds of years. There are wonderful beaches; within a short distance there are high mountains on which skiing is excellent. It is the biblical "Land of Milk and Honey," with orange and olive groves, banana plantations, wonderful wild flowers and crystal-clear rivers gushing from grottos. It is a fascinating mingling of the old and the new.

POPULATION ... 1,600,000; the country has a slightly greater population than Detroit.

SIZE ... About 120 miles long and varying from 30 to 35 miles in width, total area is 4,015 square miles.

CAPITAL ... Beirut, with a population of about 600,000, which is somewhat larger than Cincinnati.

GOVERNMENT ... An independent republic.

HOW TO GET THERE ... By Pan American Clipper one-stop service from New York to Beirut, only 18¾ hours. By ship about 14 to 21 days depending on the steamship line.

ACCOMMODATIONS ... Check on the availability of the ultra-modern *Hotel Phoenicia-Intercontinental,* under the management of the Intercontinental Hotels Corporation of New York. It includes a swimming pool, American style coffee shop and all the other fine features for which these hotels have become popular, yet is designed to retain the atmosphere and local color of this legendary area which dates back to the ancient Phoenicians. Other hotels in Beirut are the air-conditioned *Bristol,* the *Excelsior,* the *Riviera* and the *St. George,* which has a private beach for bathing. Rates run about $8.50 per day single and $14 double the year round.

ARTS... The National Art Museum and the Museum of the American University in Beirut both house excellent collections of art and antiquities.

BALLET... Visiting French troupes.

BANKS... In Beirut Banque Nationale; Banque Zilkha; Banque de Syrie et du Liban, Bank of Iran and Middle East, Arab Bank, Ltd., Banco di Roma, First National City, Netherlands Trading Society, Chase Manhattan Bank, Bank of America.

CALENDAR OF HOLIDAYS... There are 23 legal holidays in the year. The principal ones are: January 1 and 2, New Year's; Easter; November 22, Independence Day; Christmas Day.

CIGARETTES AND TOBACCO... American brands are available at about double their cost at home. Local cigarettes are excellent. No actual duty-free allowance, but usually you may bring in 200 cigarettes or about ½ lb. of tobacco.

CLIMATE... The climate is almost as varied as ours. There are four distinct seasons, but it is almost always cold in the mountains and usually quite warm near the sea. April through November is the best time to visit Lebanon.

CLUBS... Lions, Masonic Lodge, Propellor, Rotary, St. George's and Skal. A tourist would have to be accompanied by a member to make use of any of these clubs in Beirut.

COMMON COURTESIES AND LOCAL CUSTOMS... The Lebanese are extremely hospitable. A guest is a sacred trust. Even in the poorest homes the Lebanese offer gifts and hospitality.

CURRENCY... The Lebanese pound is the monetary unit. The average rate is $1 United States equals £ 3.20 Lebanese. However, there is an open market for the exchange of money which fluctuates daily. Currency of any denomination is exchanged on this market openly and legally.

CUSTOMS REGULATIONS AND DOCUMENTS REQUIRED FOR UNITED STATES CITIZENS... Passport and visa required for entry. Vaccination certificate. Duty-free allowance: 1 carton of cigarettes or ½ lb. of tobacco; 1 quart of liquor.

DRUG STORES... The drug stores here do not have soda fountains as in the United States. The majority are chemists' shops. All chemists' shops are stocked with American brands of toilet articles and patent drugs.

ELECTRIC CURRENT... The current in Beirut is 110 volts, A.C. No transformer is necessary for radios, electric razors or American electrical appliances.

FAUNA . . . Principally the mule, Arab horse, and cattle in general, as well as poultry, migratory and local birds. Fish of various forms common to the Mediterranean.

FLORA . . . Lebanese flora is similar to that of Southern Europe. It is rich in flowers and the Cedars of Lebanon are outstanding.

FOOD . . . Barbecued meats; rice dishes and wonderful dishes cooked in grape leaves, similar to Syrian foods, are native here. A majority of tourist restaurants serve Continental food of good quality and variety. Milk is bottled and pasteurized; you can drink it with safety in the better restaurants and hotels (but ask for the bottle!).

GAMBLING . . . Gambling by government decree is presently not permitted.

LANGUAGE . . . French, Arabic and English. You should have no difficulty when using only English in Lebanon.

LAUNDRY AND DRY CLEANING . . . Laundry is good and inexpensive. Dry-cleaning establishments are modern.

LIQUOR   rack is the national drink, but drink it cautiously. At the better restaurants and hotels you can get cocktails and most of the European liquors. A great variety of American liquors is available at very reasonable prices.

MEDICAL FACILITIES . . . There are excellent hospitals, among them the Hospital of the American University; St. Joseph's Hospital; St. Charles Hospital with English-speaking doctors.

MOTION PICTURES . . . There are many motion picture theaters; mostly American films are shown. The theaters in Beirut include: *Radio City, Dunia, Roxy, Capitole, Rivoli, Al Hamra* and *Empire*.

MUSIC . . . There is no national symphony, but there are concerts presented by the Lebanese Academy of Arts.

NIGHT CLUBS . . . *Kit-Kat* is the most popular. There are several others including the *Lido, Eve*. Dinner and supper music at the *Black Elephant, Cave De Roy*, the *Rainbow Room* or the *Roof Garden* at the Capitole Hotel and *The Casbah* at the Commodore Hotel.

PHOTOGRAPHY . . . You can purchase all types of films in Beirut, color, black and white, both still and movie. Prices are about the same as in the United States. Kodak is at Place de l'Etoile, Beydoun Bldg., Beirut. There are many good subjects in and around Beirut. Pigeon Rock and, of course, Baalbek are favorites of amateur photographers.

RELIGION . . . There are churches of all denominations. Beirut has two resident Cardinals.

RESTAURANTS . . . In Beirut *St. George Grille* is outstanding. There's good food also at *Lucullus*, and Italian dishes at *Manera's*. Some of the best food is at the Hotels *Bristol* and *Commodore*.

SHOPS AND STORES . . . There are excellent shops in which you can find merchandise from both East and West. Some of the better known in Beirut are: Daoud, Asfar and Sarkis, Bachour and Barakat, Achkar et Cie. You may bargain in the bazaars, but feel your way in the better places.

SPECTATOR SPORTS . . . Horse racing, soccer, basketball (the latter is extremely popular), wrestling, boxing.

SPORTS . . . Tennis, swimming, skiing, golf, fishing, shooting. aquaplaning, water polo, volley ball, ping pong, ice skating at Bristol Hotel Rink.

THEATERS . . . No legitimate theaters.

TIME . . . Seven hours later than United States Eastern Standard Time.

TIPPING . . . In most hotels and restaurants there is a service charge of 12 per cent added to your bill. If not, tip about 15 per cent.

TRANSPORTATION . . . Taxis and private cars are the popular ways to get around. As Lebanon is such a small country, it doesn't cost very much to go from one place to another. You can take a taxi for 10 miles for about $2. There are buses, but you wouldn't want to use them.

WATER . . . In Beirut it is very good and you can drink it safely, but it's not recommended in the smaller villages.

WHAT TO BUY . . . The most popular things are the beautiful brocades (which can be bought for $8 per yard and cost $25 per yard in the United States), embroideries, rugs, brass objects, inlaid ivory furniture, hammered Persian silver, gold filigree jewelry, and leather goods.

WHAT TO WEAR . . . Take along your very best clothes and about the same weights as you would wear in New York City for the different seasons. Swimming suits are essential from April through September; the beaches are beautiful and the water excellent. Raincoats are necessary the rest of the year. The first rainfall occurs in October.

WHERE TO GO—SIGHTSEEING . . .

Beirut . . . Beirut is a harbor with docking space for huge ships. You should see the National Museum. Visit the American University, the largest American educational unit outside the United States; the Oriental Library of the French University; the Great Mosque built in the twelfth century; the Pigeon's Grotto. Take a tour of the residential (Ras Beirut) section and see the modern apartment houses.

Trips to the North . . . From Beirut take the beauiful coastal road to Tripoli, which is like going back through history. In Tripoli see the Crusaders' fortresses, the monastery of the dervishes, the ancient mosques and Turkish baths and towers built by the Mameluke Sultans in the fourteenth and fifteenth centuries. The good hotels here are: the *Hakim* and the *New Royal*. Going east from Tripoli you reach the world-famous Cedars of Lebanon, which certainly no one should miss seeing. Here, too, is a famous winter resort with wonderful skiing from January until April. There is "spring snow" which gives an ideal surface. Here you ski beneath and near the famed Cedars and stay at good hotels. There are high mountains, some of them 10,000 feet, so that expert skiers from everywhere come here. The Cedars of Lebanon, oldest in the world, date back to 4000 B.C.;

Pigeon Rock, one of the landmarks near Beirut, is one of many good subjects for the camera fan in sunny Lebanon.

Of the original 54 imposing columns which surrounded the Temple of Jupiter, six still stand among the ancient Roman ruins at Baalbek, 35 miles northeast of Beirut.

they were used in building Egyptian tombs and Roman ships.

From Tripoli you can take one of the most beautiful tours in Lebanon, through the "Sacred Valley" and the "Cedars of the Lord," which is the birthplace of the Maronite order of monks. The monasteries may be reached only by paths which are really steps cut into the steep rocks. Lakluk is another important winter resort in this area. The "Sacred Valley" is ringed with precipitous hills on whose slopes are crowded dozens of tiny villages.

If you have time you should go eastward from Tripoli to Baalbek and see the magnificent Roman ruins, including the Temple of Jupiter. The villages above Beirut are clustered together in the hills. A trip from Bikfaya to Souk el Gharib is an unforgettable sight.

Resorts in the South... Most of Lebanon's famous summer resorts are situated along the Beirut-Damascus highway. Best known are Aley and Bhamdoun. Here from July to October there is a gay social season. Tennis tournaments, battles of flowers, water sports, automobile and horse racing and other special activities take place. Aley's climate is mild and there are many things to do and see. There are night clubs, and three good hotels, the *Grand,* the *Montania* and *Tanios.* The Grand has a night club. Bhamdoun has a lot to offer, too, including a view of the valley of Hammana. The best hotel is the *Ambassador Palace.*

SOURCES OF FURTHER INFORMATION... The Pan American office in Riad-El-Solh Square, Beirut (Tel. 21934 and 20140).

SYRIA

WEATHER IN DAMASCUS—Lat. N33°31'—Alt. 700'

	JAN.	FEB.	MAR.	APR.	MAY	JUNE	JULY	AUG.	SEPT.	OCT.	NOV.	DEC.
Average Temp.	46°	49°	52°	61°	70°	75°	80°	82°	77°	68°	56°	47°
Days of Rain	4	5	3	6	0	1	0	0	0	5	5	5

LOCATION ... Syria is the Northern Region of the United Arab Republic, which also includes Egypt.

CHARACTERISTICS ... Syria is predominantly Arabic in character and culture, though the urban Arab is adopting Western dress and habits to an increasing extent. Syria is a country of considerable interest, with its ruins of ancient civilizations and its historical monuments, reflecting the imprint of a hundred conquerors. It's a fantastically old land of Biblical fame, and traces of its exotic past may still be seen behind the modern facades of its cities.

POPULATION ... 3,518,285.

SIZE ... 66,046 square miles, slightly smaller than the state of Washington.

CAPITAL ... Damascus, with a population of 374,700. The District of Damascus has 767,391.

GOVERNMENT ... A part of the United Arab Republic.

HOW TO GET THERE ... By Pan American Clipper Damascus is 23 hours elapsed time from New York, 1 hour from Beirut, 6½ hours from Rome. By ship 18 to 21 days.

ACCOMMODATIONS ... Among the better hotels in Damascus are the *New Omayad,* the *New Semiramis, Orient Palace, Cattan Hotel.* In Aleppo, the *Baron* and *Ambassador* are best. In Lattakia, try the *Casino Hotel;* in Palmyra, the *Zenobia Hotel.* In first-class hotels the maximum rate is $10, including meals and service.

ARTS... The principal museums in Syria are: the Museum of Damascus, with the Castle Alhir, which was carried from the desert to Damascus, and the new Azem Palace. These museums contain monuments of various origins: Aram, Assyrian, Chaldean, Palmyrene, as well as the archeological finds of Tell Ras Shamra, and figure groups dressed in traditional costumes. The Museum of Aleppo contains Assyrian and Hittite monuments.

BANKS... No American banks, but among the principal banks in Damascus are: Banque de Syrie et du Liban, Banque Misr-Syrie-Liban, Rafidain Bank, Arab Bank, British Bank for the Middle East, Arab National Bank, Ltd.; in Aleppo the Banque Albert Homsy; in Lattakia the Banque de Syrie et du Liban, Banque Misr-Syrie-Liban, Crédit foncier d'Algérie et de Tunisie, Banco di Roma.

CALENDAR OF HOLIDAYS... The chief religious holidays with the Moslems are: the 3-day feast, Al Fitr, which takes place immediately after the month of fasting (Ramadan), and the Feast of Sacrifice (Qurban) which lasts four days. Christian shops are closed on Sunday and Moslem shops on Friday.

CIGARETTES AND TOBACCO... American cigarettes are available for 35 to 40 cents a pack. Local brands (a mixture of Syrian and Turkish tobacco) *Al-Sayed, Jockey Club,* and *Extra Extra* are cheaper.

CLIMATE... Like other Mediterranean countries, the coastal area is warm and rainy in winter, relatively hot in summer. In the interior (Damascus, Aleppo, Homs, Hama) the winter is cold, the summer hot (*see* weather chart page 222). In the desert area (Palmyra) the extremes are even greater with sharp fluctuations of temperature between night and day. April is the best month to visit Palmyra.

CLUBS... The most important clubs in Damascus are the Orient Club (Al Shark) and the Families Club. There's also an Orient Club in Aleppo. Lions in both cities as well as Rotary.

COMMON COURTESIES AND LOCAL CUSTOMS... Arab hospitality is well known. It is considered only polite to accept a small cup of Arabic coffee when visiting friends or business houses. This custcm prevails to a great extent even in visiting the bazaars or *souks* particularly when one is actually doing more than window-shopping. The serving of coffee and tea (in the cold months) and a sort of lemonade-orangeade, *gazoz* (a carbonated local beverage), is a ritual which must be observed. Arab people are particularly generous, and it can be very embarrassing to admire greatly some object in an Arab's home only to have your host present it to you. Remember that Syria is 90 percent Moslem, and many of the strict Moslem rules laid down in the Koran are followed to the letter, even among modern business people. This particularly refers to their home life and the women of the family. Women are gradually emerging from behind the veils, although among orthodox Moslems, the womenfolk may still not make an appearance. It is customary to take a gift when visiting someone's home.

COMMUNICATIONS... Telephone, telegraph. Airmail postage

for letters to the United States costs 70 piasters (95 if registered), postal cards 60 piasters.

CURRENCY . . . The unit of currency in Syria is the Syrian pound, divided into 100 piasters. One U.S. dollar is equivalent to about 365 Syrian piasters. American currency can be changed with local banks or money-changer at the above-mentioned rate, which varies only slightly.

CUSTOMS REGULATIONS AND DOCUMENTS REQUIRED FOR UNITED STATES CITIZENS . . . Passport and visa required. There is no duty on personal effects to the value of 200 Syrian pounds (about $90). These regulations are subject to frequent change, so check with your local Pan American office and Syrian Consul for last-minute changes.

DRUG STORES . . . There are drug stores but they follow the French and English, rather than American system of filling prescriptions.

ELECTRIC CURRENT . . . 110 volts, A.C. 50 cycle transformer plugs for round prongs are needed but can be purchased locally.

FAUNA . . . Of interest to tourists are the partridge and the starling, the camel, the cows, sheep, goats and ever-present patient donkey of Damascus, Arab horses, and the gazelle, which can be found in the desert.

FLORA . . . Plants of interest are tarragon, safflower and caraway (which produces caraway seed). Trees include pistachio, apricot, nut, poplar, *platanus orientalis,* apple and cactus fruit. Several varieties of grape are also grown locally.

FOOD . . . Both European and Oriental foods are offered in restaurants. Usually, a meal costs $1.50, $3 if ordered à la carte, in the better places, such as Orient Club, New Omayad Hotel, the new Orient Restaurant on the International Fair Grounds. Milk is available everywhere, but should be drunk only after boiling, since it is not preserved and sterilized as in Europe and America. European brands of powdered milk are generally used.

GAMBLING . . . There is gambling in some night clubs. However, there are no horse or dog races.

LANGUAGE . . . The official language is Arabic, but English and French are easily understood. Many people have an excellent knowledge of English. The usual greeting is made by raising the hand while saying *marhaba* (hello).

LAUNDRIES AND DRY CLEANING . . . Laundries, including those with dry-cleaning facilities, can be found throughout the country. Hotels can also take care of your laundry.

LIQUOR . . . The better hotels and restaurants have bars where familiar brands of whisky, usually Scotch, are available, also wine, cognac and beer. Try the local arrack, made from grapes and flavored with anise.

MEDICAL FACILITIES . . . There are many Government hospitals and sanatoriums in both Damascus and Aleppo with English-speaking doctors. Inquire at your hotel or of Pan American.

MOTION PICTURES ... The principal theaters in Damascus which show mostly films in English or French with Arabic subtitles are: the *Dunia, Fardows, Balkis, Al Chark, Amir* and *Al Ahram*.

MUSIC ... The prevailing music is Oriental. There are no organized symphonic concerts in the country. However, some chamber music is played in the "Club of the Friends of Art" and other clubs.

NIGHT CLUBS AND CABARETS ... The *Orient Club* (*Al Chark*) on Najmeh Square, Damascus and the *Family Club*, Kassaa Street, have dancing, drinks and gambling. Others which also have restaurants include *Al Ghaza*, the *Syriana* on Omayad Square; *Karawan*, Saad 'Alloh Jobri; *Semiramis* on Parliament Street. *Ashbilia* in Doummar near Damascus is open only during the summer. The new Orient Restaurant also has a cabaret.

PHOTOGRAPHY ... Photograph equipment and supplies, including color films for movie cameras and developing service for black-and-white still pictures are available in Damascus and Aleppo. Boyajyan, Sport and Azad are three places in Damascus for buying and developing. Photographing military installations is prohibited.

RELIGION ... The religion of the greater part of the population is Islam. Other religions and sects are: Catholic, Protestant, Syriac, Greek Orthodox. There are no American churches in Syria.

RESTAURANTS ... The chief restaurants in Damascus are the *Normandie, Socrates, Tour d'Argent, Oasis, Airport Restaurant, Orient Restaurant* and *Restaurant International*. All serve both Western and Oriental meals.

SHOPS AND STORES ... The main markets of Damascus are: Souk Al Hamidieh, Souk Madhat Pasha, Bzourieh Street, Sanjakdar Street, Fouad the First Street, Hijaz Street. Working hours are from 8:00 A.M. to 7:00 P.M. (closed from 1:00 to 4:00 P.M. for lunch). Prices are moderate. Shops are closed on Friday, some on Sunday.

SPECTATOR SPORTS ... From time to time, basketball or football matches are held in Damascus. Tickets are sold in most markets.

THEATERS ... There are no big theaters for dramatic performances in Syria, the existing theaters being of the small and popular type. Shows are played in the evening; rates are quite moderate. There are two groups of foreign-colony residents that present amateur dramatics and oratorios.

TIME ... 7 hours later than U.S. Eastern Standard Time.

TRANSPORTATION ... Buses, taxis and, in Damascus and Aleppo, electric trolleys and cars for hire (with driver).

WATER ... Potable in Damascus. No bottled water available.

WHAT TO BUY ... Beautiful hand-worked copper and brass trays with silver inlay (from 8 inches to 4 feet in diameter); hand-loomed brocades which are famous, wood and mother-of-pearl inlay work, items from the glass blowing "factories," mosaics, and embroideries.

WHAT TO WEAR ... Light clothing for summer, warm clothing and raincoat for winter months.

WHERE TO GO—SIGHTSEEING . . .

Damascus . . . Damascus is the oldest continuously inhabited city in the world, dating back 6,000 years. The Great Oasis (or Ghouta) in which the city is situated, according to legend, may be the site of the Garden of Eden. The city abounds with local color, varied costumes, resulting from the influence of three great religions: Christianity, Islamism and Judaism. One of the chief places of interest is the Omayad Mosque, originally the church of John the Baptist, built by Theodosius in the fourth century and later converted into a Moslem basilica. The silence of its magnificent carpeted interior offers a startling contrast to the noise of the city outside.

Other places of interest include the Azem Palace, the home of Judas, the chapel and home of Ananias, the tomb of Saladin, the place at the city gate where Paul was lowered in a basket to escape the Roman soldiers, the Museum of Damascus, St. Paul's Church, the historical gates of the city, and the street of Biblical times called Straight, still one of Damascus's most important thoroughfares, running through the Grand Bazaar and connecting the old East and West Gates.

One of the largest bazaars in the world is located only a short walk from the center of the city. To wander through these crooked, narrow streets is to get the real atmosphere of the East, the smell of spices and garlic, exotic perfumes, the sight of beautiful brocades, Oriental rugs, brass and copper, inlaid ivory, and magnificent jewelry, along with American dime-store items. More fascinating still is the swarming mass of people representing every nationality imaginable—Arabs, Greeks, Persians, Druses, Kurds, French and the most out-of-place-looking American tourists.

Side Trip . . . In Aleppo, about 225 miles from Damascus, places of interest are: the Museum of Aleppo, the Citadel of Aleppo, the historical gates of Aleppo, the Great Mosque. Stay at the *Baron Hotel* or *Ambassador Hotel*. Worthwhile, too, is a trip to visit the historical monuments of Palmyra, which is best made by air. (Special trips can be arranged via Syrian Airways—one hour in each direction. *See* PAA office). In this town there are monuments of Roman and other ancient civilizations, especially the civilization of Palmyra during the prosperous reign of Queen Zenobia. Here one can also see the ancient cemeteries with their wonderful decorations, the Citadel of the Ma'anites and other places of interest. Stay at the *Zenobia Hotel*. Maloula, probably the only village left in the world where Armak, the tongue in which Jesus spoke, is still in normal usage, is an interesting hour's drive from Damascus and is worth a visit. The remarkable Crusader Castle, *Krak de Chevaliers*, oldest and best-preserved fortress of its kind in this area lies a four-hour drive to the northwest.

SOURCES OF FURTHER INFORMATION . . . There are a number of tourist agencies in Damascus that frequently organize trips for tourists and provide them with guides who speak English well. Pan American's office in Damascus is at Sharia El-Fardows (Tel. 12500).

TURKEY

WEATHER IN ISTANBUL—Lat. N41°10′—Alt. 30′

Temp.	JAN.	FEB.	MAR.	APR.	MAY	JUNE	JULY	AUG.	SEPT.	OCT.	NOV.	DEC.
Low	38°	36°	40°	46°	55°	62°	67°	68°	62°	57°	49°	43°
High	46°	45°	52°	60°	71°	78°	82°	82°	75°	68°	58°	51°
Average	42°	41°	46°	53°	63°	70°	75°	75°	69°	63°	54°	47°
Days of Rain	10	8	9	7	7	5	3	4	6	7	11	12

LOCATION ... Except for the area south of Bulgaria and east of Greece on the European continent, Turkey lies in Asia, occupying the peninsula of Asia Minor, across the Black Sea from Russia and across the Mediterranean from Egypt. Istanbul, divided by the Bosporus Strait, is astride two continents. It is 843 airmiles from Rome.

CHARACTERISTICS ... Turkey is a wonderful vacation spot which is rapidly growing more popular with cosmopolites who are discovering for themselves its wonderful scenery, splendid climate, classic examples of Byzantine architecture, and an atmosphere of sophistication. The Turkish people are extremely cordial and international-minded. If you are looking for something different with the exotic atmosphere of the East, you'll like Istanbul.

POPULATION ... 24,797,000 (1,240,000 in Istanbul).

SIZE ... 299,992 square miles, slightly larger than Texas.

CAPITAL ... Ankara, population 552,600.

GOVERNMENT ... A Republic with a National Assembly elected by universal suffrage. The President is elected by the Assembly.

HOW TO GET THERE ... By Clipper from New York to Istanbul, 15¼ hours, 1¼ more to Ankara—routings via London, Paris, Frankfurt, Vienna and Rome. By ship, about 15 days via Italy, Egypt and/or Greece.

ACCOMMODATIONS ... The new *Istanbul Hilton* overlooking the Bosporus, beautifully decorated in Turkish decor, has 300 rooms (some air-conditioned), each with bath and balcony, and everything from an American soda fountain to a glass-enclosed night club. The

Divan Hotel is also new and completely modern and comfortable, and in its dining room is served some of the best Turkish cooking in Istanbul. Next best are the *Park,* and the *Plaza,* just off Taksim Square. In Ankara there are the *Çelik Palas* and the *Ankara Palas* near the business center, *Barikan Otel, Moderne Palas* and *Bulvar Palas,* all near the American Embassy, and the *Turistik,* near Ulus Square. Rates run from $8.50 single and $10.50 double without meals.

ARTS ... The magnificent Archaeological Museum contains the sarcophagus of Alexander the Great. Nearby is the Museum of Oriental Antiquities containing an excellent collection from ancient Hittite, Assyrian and Egyptian civilizations. The Museum of Mehmet the Conqueror, the Çinili Kösk, is a jewel. Don't miss the Kariye Camiî where restoration of the Byzantine mosaics and frescoes makes it a major art museum. Other museums are the Naval Museum, Museum of Islamic and Turkish Art, Municipal Museum, and nearby the Mosque of Sultan Ahmet, a unique example of sixth century Byzantine mosaics, thought to be on the remnants of the passage of the Great Palace and unimaginatively called the Museum of Mosaics. At Besiktas see the Museum of Paintings and Sculpture.

BANKS ... The principal New York banks have representatives in both Istanbul and Ankara. Ottoman Bank, Iş Bank, Central Bank, Yapi ve Kredi Bank, Holland Bank, Bank of Rome, and Italian Commercial Bank all cash traveler's checks.

CALENDAR OF HOLIDAYS ... New Year's Day; April 23, Children's Day; May 1, Spring Day; May 19, Youth Day; August 30, Victory Day; and October 29, Republic Day—all stores close. Christmas and Easter are also celebrated by Christians in Turkey. Two Turkish religious (Moslem) holidays are kept: Seker Bayram and Kurban Bayram, the dates of which vary from year to year. The former is outstanding for beautiful illuminations of mosques and other public buildings.

CIGARETTES AND TOBACCO ... There are many varieties of excellent Turkish cigarettes and tobaccos processed in the American manner. Yeni Harman and Bafra are two popular cigarettes. Prices are 10 and 20 cents a pack. American cigarettes are not available.

CLIMATE ... Istanbul has much the same climate as New York. In summer the heat is tempered by cool breezes from the Bosporus by way of the Black Sea. Ankara, which has an elevation of 2,600 feet, has a drier climate with cool nights all summer long. Southern Turkey has a climate comparable to Florida. In general the best time of the year to visit Turkey is between June and December and the Indian summer, September to November is particularly delightful.

CLUBS ... Rotary.

COMMON COURTESIES AND LOCAL CUSTOMS ... The fez is outlawed now in Turkey and will be seen only as a purchasable curio in the bazaars. An occasional peasant woman will be seen veiled but this is not a true veil, merely a head scarf which can be partly drawn. The Turks are very sensitive on these questions, so tread lightly. Turks always shake hands on meeting both men and women.

COMMUNICATIONS... Cables, airmail, telephone to the United States. Postage for letters is 2.00 lira for 10 grams and for postal cards 1.75 lira. ,

CURRENCY... The monetary unit is the lira (which contains 100 kurus). United States $1 equals 9.00 Turkish lira. Money can be exchanged at any bank.

CUSTOMS REGULATIONS AND DOCUMENTS REQUIRED FOR UNITED STATES CITIZENS... Only a passport is required of U.S. citizens. No visa. Smallpox vaccination certificate required for return to the United States. You are allowed 50 cigarettes or 20 cigars; 1 opened bottle of liquor. Cholera inoculation certificate is required if coming from infected area. No United States currency, checks, etc. above the amount imported, only 99 Turkish lira, may be exported. Only 100 Turkish lira can be imported.

DRUG STORES... There are no American-type drug stores. Turkish drug stores carry pharmaceuticals, perfumes, cosmetics and toiletries. A very few American and European products are available, but are very expensive.

ELECTRIC CURRENT... The voltage is 110 A.C. in most sections on the European side, 220 A.C. on the Asiatic. Transformer plugs must have round prongs. Hilton Hotel: 220 A.C.

FAUNA... Wild boar, pheasants, hares, partridge, quail, woodcock, deer.

FLORA... Wonderful flowers—abundant roses, carnations, tulips, violets, chrysanthemums, brown orchids. gladioli, hydrangea and many other well-known varieties.

FOOD... Wonderful seafood and rice dishes. Try *börek*, a delicious thin pastry filled with white cheese, egg and parsley; *dolmas*, grape or cabbage leaves filled with ground beef and served with sour cream; chicken or turkey stuffed with *iç pilav*, rice cooked with currants, pine nuts and spices; *kiliç*, swordfish grilled on a spit with bay leaves, and of course, *şişkebap*. Pasteurized milk is available. Better hotels serve international food. Prices run $3.50 and up. Turkish beer is excellent, somewhat like German beer.

GAMBLING... Racing with pari-mutuels at Istanbul and Ankara. There is a monthly national lottery. No gambling in the night clubs.

LANGUAGE... English is spoken in hotels and principal shops and restaurants. Turkish is the official language. French is also spoken in most circles in Istanbul and Ankara.

LAUNDRY AND DRY CLEANING... Hotels can handle both laundry and dry cleaning. Avoid sending unusual materials or women's clothing with ornaments, sequins, etc. Prices are much the same as in the United States and service is reasonably good.

LIQUOR... Turkey makes some good red and white wines. Their liqueurs are comparatively good and varied. Roseleaf, banana, strawberry, tangerine, sour cherry are some of the flavors. Turkish vermouth, gin and brandy are fair; vodka is very good. Local liquors are inexpensive. *Rakı* is a native drink distilled from the grape. It is drunk only with *meze* (Turkish smorgasbord—marvelous!) and not as a highball. Popular American drinks are available at the Hilton, Divan and Park Hotel bar. The Screwdriver (orange juice and vodka) is a famous drink here. Also try a vodka martini.

MEDICAL FACILITIES ... The Admiral Bristol Hospital (more familiarly known as the American Hospital) in Istanbul is modern and staffed with English-speaking doctors. There are many English-speaking private doctors available. Consult your hotel.

MOTION PICTURES ... *Yeni Melek, Atlas, Ar* and *San* are central downtown theaters in Istanbul which show American and British films with English sound track and Turkish titles, as well as European films in various languages. Fairly new movies are shown.

MUSIC ... Istanbul has a symphony orchestra which gives concerts of the works of Turkish composers as well as the works of the great masters. There is opera and ballet too, although European companies rarely perform here. Radio Istanbul and Radio Ankara have symphony and philharmonic orchestras whose concerts are open to the public by invitation.

NIGHT CLUBS AND CABARETS ... In Istanbul you'll want to take in the entertainment and dancing at the new glass-enclosed *Sadırvan Supper Club* set in the garden of the new Hilton among the fountains for which it is named. They also have a *Marmara Roof* cocktail lounge and *Karagöz* (puppet decor) bar adjoining their Terrace Restaurant. Others include the *Taksim Casino* (outside in the summer), *Park Hotel, Kervansaray,* the new *Kordon Blö* (Cordon Bleu)—all near *Taksim Square*—the *Konak Hotel* with orchestras and floor shows of European and local entertainers, and the new *Club X*. In Ankara the top night club is *Süreyya's* (open in winter only), also the *Ankara Palas* and *Club 47* (where the doors are closed after the 47th person enters).

PHOTOGRAPHY ... Film is impossible to find now. Film developing is all right for black-and-white but color developing is not good. Foto Sabah for developing, usually in 24 hours.

RELIGION ... Turkey is a Moslem country, but there are many Christian churches, including Catholic, Greek Orthodox and Protestant, as well as Jewish synagogues. Most Americans attend the Dutch chapel, located just off the main street of Istanbul.

RESTAURANTS ... In Istanbul, the new Hilton offers the *Bosporus Terrace* with soda fountain and coffee shop, the more formal *Terrace Restaurant* with bar and the glamorous *Sadırvan Supper Club*. Wonderful food may be had at the *Divan Hotel* and at *Abdullah Efendi* on the main street; there is also *Ekrem Yeğen* and *Fisher's;* and it's *Pandelli's* for lunch in the famous *Misir Çarşisi* (Spice Bazaar) or *Liman Restaurant* near the docks; *Çinar* on the beach near the airport with American bar. While sightseeing up the Bosporus, stop at *Canlı Balık* or *Rex,* where the seafood is marvelous and the view delightful. *Divan Hotel, Lebon, Markiz* are all excellent for tea, ice cream and pastries. In Ankara the place is *Karpiç*. Eating out in Turkey is inexpensive.

SHOPS AND STORES ... The main shopping area is all along the main street in the European section of Istanbul. Most shops are open daily except Sunday from 9:00 A.M. to 7:00 P.M. For travelers the best and favorite shopping for all Turkish novelties is in the famous bazaars in the old section of Istanbul.

SPECTATOR SPORTS ... There is horse racing, soccer, wrestling, boxing, track meets, basketball, tennis and golf.

SPORTS ... Swimming, sailing and fishing are excellent in the waters of the Bosporus, Aegean Sea, the Black Sea, and the Sea of Marmara. Hunting wild boar is a favorite national sport. Horseback riding can be arranged. Winter sports include sledding, skiiing at the famous slopes of Bursa at the foot of Mount Olympus.

THEATERS ... There are several theaters in Istanbul and Ankara where plays in Turkish are produced. Companies visiting Turkey perform English and French plays. Tickets for matinees or evening performances can be purchased through your hotel at between $2 and $3.

TIME ... Seven hours later than U.S. Eastern Standard Time. Daylight saving is not observed.

TIPPING .. About the same as elsewhere in Europe, 10 to 15 per cent. Your baggage porter gets 50 kuruş per bag; minimum 1.00 lira.

TRANSPORTATION ... There are taxis, buses and trams in Istanbul, and a one-minute subway between Pera and Galata. Ferries link the European and Asiatic shores. The trip takes about 20 minutes. Taxis charge about Turkish Lira 5.00 within the new section of the city and Turkish Lira 7.50 from the new section to the old section (where the bazaars and mosques are). Bus tickets vary in price with the distance. Trams are 40 kuruş first class and 30 kuruş second class. Buses and trams are marked with origin and destination. Automobiles may be rented through your hotel for 2.00 lira a kilometer, minimum of 100 kilometers, i.e., about 25 cents per kilometer, for sightseeing outside the city. You may hire a car for sightseeing exclusively inside the city for about $22 per day. Taxis are comparatively inexpensive and the easiest mode of transport for tourists.

WATER ... Water is safe to drink, but there are many fine table and mineral waters if you prefer.

WHAT TO BUY ... Gold and silver hand embroidered handbags and exquisitely painted filmy scarfs, bed jackets of silky mohair, attar of roses and other perfumes, wonderful candies, silver and gold filigree, rugs and carpets, Bursa silks, ceramics, hand-carved meerschaum pipes, costume jewelry—handmade brass and copper ashtrays, şişkebab skewers and martini stirrers, Turkish slippers, Turkish "towels" beautifully embroidered in original designs, Kütahya titles and wonderful old copper. In the bazaars it is best to bargain.

WHAT TO WEAR ... In Istanbul dress as you would in New York or any other large city. You will need lightweight clothes in the summer, warm clothes in winter. Raincoats are essential in the rainy season as rain is very heavy and often quite sudden. Beach clothes are essential for both men and women. In Ankara you will need warmer clothes in winter than you do in New York or Istanbul. A light topcoat is a good idea. Men will need sports jackets and slacks, medium-weight suits for spring and winter and light suits for summer. Evening or dinner clothes are usually not necessary.

WHERE TO GO—SIGHTSEEING ...

Istanbul ... Türk Ekspres has a sightseeing bus service direct from the Hilton Hotel. American Express and Wagons-Lits/Cook (local agent of Thomas Cook) offer tours at $2.80 for a half day. Individual guides are available and charge about $11 for a full day. The Aya Sofia, a thousand years older than Saint Peter's Cathedral in Rome, is considered by architects to be one of the seven wonders of the world. Near it is Saint Irene, the oldest church in Istanbul; the fountain of Sultan Ahmed III, the Yerebatan Cisterns, built by the Emperor Justinian; Sultan Ahmed, called the Blue Mosque; the ancient Byzantine hippodrome and the Mosaic Museum, conveniently grouped for sightseeing. A short distance away are the marvelous Süleymaniye Mosque and the Mosque of Beyazit. In Istanbul there over 400 mosques some of which were originally churches; some are decorated with beautiful old tiles and all are interesting. See the Edirne Gate, the Kariye Camiî, containing some of the most glorious mosaics and frescoes from the Byzantine period, and by all means drive out along the old Byzantine Walls to the Castle of the Seven Towers. A whole day can be spent in the Topkapı Palace and the newly opened mysterious and fascinating Harem section. Don't miss the fabulous horde of treasure and precious stones in the Treasury or the porcelain collection, which is one of the finest and largest in the world. Go to the famous Kapalı Çarsı and be sure to take a ferry ride up the Bosporus and to the Princess Islands.

Other Trips ... From Istanbul you may go by ferry to the health resort of Yalova and on to Bursa at the foot of Mount Olympus. Turkey is rich with the history of Christianity. It was in the city of Iznik (39 miles northeast of Bursa) that the Iznik Council formulated the creed of Christianity. Mount Ararat is the spot where Noah's Ark came to rest.

Ankara ... You may fly from Istanbul to Ankara, seat of the Turkish Government, in 1 hour or make overnight trip by train. The *Ankara Palace Hotel* is fairly good as are the *Barikan Otel* and the *Bulvar Palas Otel*, which has an American-type bar. Be sure to take the trip to the fortress in time to watch the sunset at Akkale. See the Ahı Elvan Mosque, the Arslanhane Mosque, the Roman Aqueduct, the Orman Çiftliği (the model farm founded by Atatürk). You will see the Government buildings, the Presidential residence at Çankaya and other buildings and monuments of interest. Visit the Turkish National Theater, dine at Karpiç, where you should try the marvelous borsch and beef Stroganoff. Visit the tomb of Atatürk.

SOURCES OF FURTHER INFORMATION ... In Istanbul, Türk Ekspres, Wagons-Lits/Cook and American Express travel agencies; Pan American's office at Istanbul Hilton Hotel Arcade (Tel. 474530) and Ankara Palas Otel, (Tel. 13681/11032). In Ankara, Ministry of Press, Radio and Tourism. Turkish Information Bureau, 444 E. 52nd Street, New York, N.Y.

Bermuda, the Bahamas and the Caribbean

ANTIGUA

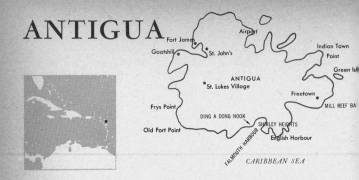

Fort James
Goatshill
Airport
St. John's
Indian Town Point
Green Isl
ANTIGUA
St. Lukes Village
Freetown
MILL REEF BA
Frys Point
DING A DONG NOOK
Old Fort Point
SHIRLEY HEIGHTS
English Harbour
FALMOUTH HARBOUR
CARIBBEAN SEA

WEATHER IN ST. JOHN'S—Lat. N17°03′—Alt. Approx. sea level

Temp.	JAN.	FEB.	MAR.	APR.	MAY	JUNE	JULY	AUG.	SEPT.	OCT.	NOV.	DEC.
Low	70°	70°	70°	71°	73°	74°	74°	75°	74°	73°	72°	71°
High	82°	83°	83°	85°	86°	86°	87°	87°	88°	87°	85°	84°
Average	76°	76°	77°	78°	79°	80°	80°	81°	81°	80°	79°	77°
Days of Rain	20	15	14	13	15	16	19	18	18	19	19	20

LOCATION ... Antigua is one of the Leeward Islands, the Lesser Antilles, southeast of Puerto Rico, 1,692 miles from New York.

CHARACTERISTICS ... Antigua, "Where There Is Sunshine Every Day of the Year," has some of the finest beaches in the West Indies, also three golf courses, fishing, tennis, sailing. An ideal spot for those seeking a quiet and restful holiday. There is no night life.

POPULATION ... 48,000, of which the majority are colored.

SIZE ... The island is 108 square miles, about 16 miles across at any point, with headlands extending out all around the island, forming bays and beautiful beaches.

CAPITAL ... St. John's, with about 18,000 population.

GOVERNMENT ... Antigua is a British Colony in the Leeward Islands. Along with the other Leeward Islands, Antigua is a member of the new Federation of British West Indies.

HOW TO GET THERE ... By Pan American Clipper, Antigua is 1½ hours from Pueto Rico; 8½ hours (elapsed time) from New York. From Miami 3¾ hours non-stop to San Juan, thence 1½ hours to Antigua. By ship the journey takes about a week from New York, Boston or Montreal.

ACCOMMODATIONS ... (All rates given are single, American Plan.) *Antigua Beach Hotel,* 5 miles from St. John's, with beach, tennis court, small golf course. Accommodates 50. Rates $12 to $18,

December 15th to April 30th. $7.25 to $10.50 other times. *White Sands Hotel,* 5 miles from St. John's with private beach and swimming pool. Accommodates 58. Rates $20 to $28—December 20th to April 30th. $14 to $18 other times. The new *Anchorage Hotel* on the beach with riding, fishing, sailing facilities. Rates $22 to $25—December 15th to April 30th, $15 to $18 other times. The new *Half Moon Bay Hotel,* 40 minutes from the city with excellent beach and swimming pool. Rates $30—December 15th to April 30th. $18 other times. The new *Trade Winds Hotel* offers cottage accommodations with central lounge and bar. Double rate $35. *Kensington Guest House* in St. John's accommodates 15. Rates $6 to $8, December 15th to May 31st. $5 to $7 other times. *Happy Acre Hotel,* one mile from St. John's. Accommodates 30. Rates $10, December 15th to May 31st, $8 other times. *Lord Nelson's Beach Club,* six miles from St. John's. Accommodates 20. Rate $12, December 15th to April 30th, $9 other times. *Jardines* in the city. Rate $5 to $6 year around. The *Mill Reef Club,* with tennis courts, fishing, boats, numerous beaches and small golf course, accepts only guests introduced by members. Closed September and October.

BANKS ... Barclays Bank (D.C. & O.), Royal Bank of Canada.

CALENDAR OF HOLIDAYS ... Usual English holidays are observed, including New Year's Day; Good Friday; Easter Monday; Whitmonday, first Monday in May; May 24, Empire Day; Queen's Birthday (in June); first Monday in August; November 14, birthday of heir to the throne; Christmas Day; Boxing Day. Early closing days, Thursday and Saturday.

CIGARETTES AND TOBACCO ... American cigarettes are scarce, so visitors should bring their own supply, paying duty ($1.95 B.W.I. per carton of 200). English cigarettes and tobacco are available; cigarettes cost from $2.88 to $3.80 B.W.I. per carton of 200.

CLIMATE ... The climate is delightful in both summer and winter. There need be no fear of excessive heat in the midsummer months. September and October have a relatively high humidity.

CLUBS ... The American Mill Reef Club and a number of social clubs in St. John's are open only to members or by invitation. The sports clubs which offer tennis, golf, etc., welcome visitors at all times.

COMMON COURTESIES AND LOCAL CUSTOMS ... Negroes are referred to as "colored people." Ladies do not wear shorts in St. John's while shopping. Men wear coats at dinner. Visitors should remember that there is no color bar in Antigua and that all hotels, bars and some clubs are interracial. Visitors should avoid the indiscriminate giving of alms, which encourages begging, a nuisance which tourist organizations are trying to check. Antigua is intensely British. Ill-informed criticism of British customs or traditions is resented.

COMMUNICATIONS ... Radio telephone to United States and Canada during working hours. Cable open 8:00 A.M. to 5:00 P.M. Sundays and holidays 8:00 A.M. to 10:00 A.M. and 7 P.M. to 8 P.M.

CURRENCY ... British West Indian dollar valued at 4 shillings and 2 pence (British currency) or about 58 cents. United States currency must be converted into West Indian or English currency.

CUSTOMS REGULATIONS AND DOCUMENTS REQUIRED FOR UNITED STATES CITIZENS... Only proof of nationality for visitors from the U.S. who hold return tickets. No visa is required. Yellow fever and cholera certificates required if coming from infected areas. Vaccination certificate is essential for return to U.S.

DRUG STORES... Miss O'Neal's and Harpers are well stocked with drugs, patent medicines and toilet preparations.

ELECTRIC CURRENT... At the Antigua Beach Hotel, 110 volts, A.C.; in St. John's 220 volts, A.C.

FAUNA... Dove, pigeon, some migratory duck, yellow breast, blackbirds, reef fish, tarpon and bonefish.

FLORA... Red lilies, roses, hibiscus, Bougainvillaea, poinsettia, mahogany, coconuts, royal palms, cabbage palm, palmetto, fig, banana, plantain, avocado, citrus, papaya, mangoes in season.

FOOD... West Indian cookery is excellent and Antigua is no exception. Local supplies of fresh milk are not abundant but are safe.

GAMBLING... Pari-mutuel betting at two race meets a year. No gambling casinos.

LANGUAGE... English.

LAUNDRY AND DRY CLEANING... Native labor always available for washing. Dry cleaning is limited.

LIQUOR... Gin, whisky, and rum are very reasonable.

MEDICAL FACILITIES... Hospital and English- and Canadian-trained doctors.

MOTION PICTURES... One movie house in St. John's, English and American films shown.

MUSIC... Steel bands playing calypso and local dance orchestras.

NIGHT CLUBS AND CABARETS... No night clubs or cabarets. Dancing at hotels.

PHOTOGRAPHY... Cameras and film available at José Anjo and Co. 53 High St., St. John's. Developing and printing (black-and-white only) done quickly and well.

RELIGION... Anglican (Church of England), Catholic, Methodist and Seventh Day Adventist churches.

RESTAURANTS... Luncheons and dinners served at hotels.

SHOPS AND STORES... Main shopping districts in center of St. John's. Prices reasonable. Open from 8:00 to 12:00 and from 1:00 P.M. to 4:00 P.M. Thursday early closing, open from 8:00 to 12:00.

SPECTATOR SPORTS... Cricket and football. Horse racing.

SPORTS... There are tennis and golf at the tennis and golf clubs and at Mill Reef Club. Fishing can be arranged by chartering of sloops from St. John's, English Harbor or Beach Hotel.

TIME... One hour later than Eastern Standard Time.

TRANSPORTATION... Automobiles are for hire with drivers or drive yourself, first obtaining a visitor's license by presenting your state license at police headquarters.

WATER... Dependent on rainfall for water supply. Drinking water is boiled. Soda water, tonic water, Coca-Cola are available.

Tourists stand on a hill in Shirley Heights overlooking Lord Nelson's Dock Yard beyond and the harbor.

Guests of the Mill Reef Club are served drinks on the sunlit terrace with its view of white sand beaches and blue-green water.

Hotel guests hold fish speared in the clear shallow waters near the reefs, which provide excellent fishing for spear and goggle enthusiasts.

WHAT TO WEAR ... Light clothes, summer suits, shorts. Evening clothes are not essential and rarely worn. Coats in evening.

WHERE TO GO—SIGHTSEEING ... Dockyard at English Harbor, where Nelson, Rodney and Hood were stationed in the Royal West Indian Squadron while pursuing the French and Spanish Fleets, is of unusual interest; also near English Harbor is Clarence House, the country house of the Governor, built in 1787 by the Duke of Clarence, who later became William IV. Fig Tree Drive in the mountainous tropical part of the island can be seen by automobile.

SOURCES OF FURTHER INFORMATION ... There is an Antigua Tourist Committee in St. John's. Pan America's office in St. John's is at 37 High Street (Tel. 241).

BARBADOS

ATLANTIC OCEAN

CARIBBEAN SEA

BATHSHEBA

Holetown

BARBADOS

St. Michael

Bridgetown

WEATHER IN BARBADOS—Lat. N13°4'—Alt. Approx. sea level

Temp.	JAN.	FEB.	MAR.	APR.	MAY	JUNE	JULY	AUG.	SEPT.	OCT.	NOV.	DEC.
Low	70°	69°	70°	71°	73°	74°	74°	74°	73°	73°	73°	71°
High	83°	83°	84°	85°	87°	87°	86°	86°	86°	86°	85°	84°
Average	77°	76°	77°	78°	80°	81°	80°	80°	80°	80°	79°	78°
Days of Rain	14	12	11	9	11	17	19	18	16	17	16	16

LOCATION ... Barbados is the most eastern of the West Indian islands.

CHARACTERISTICS ... The flying fish play around Barbados just as they do around Mandalay. It's one of the specialties of this colorful West Indian Island, where the natives speak with a British accent. Their rum is marvelous and so is their weather, which is summer the year round. It boasts some of the finest bathing beaches in the world. The perfect spot for a relaxing and unusual vacation.

POPULATION ... Estimated 228,243, roughly the population of Jacksonville, Florida.

SIZE ... Barbados is triangular in shape and is 21 miles long by 14 miles across the widest part.

CAPITAL ... Bridgetown and environs has an estimated population of 18,500.

GOVERNMENT ... Barbados is one of the 10 territories entering upon the Federation of the West Indies. It now has almost complete internal self-government but is still in the technical sense a Crown Colony.

HOW TO GET THERE ... By Pan American Clipper from New York (11¼ hours) or Miami to Puerto Rico, then by "island hopping" to Barbados. By ship, from New York or New Orleans to Trinidad for connection to Barbados.

ACCOMMODATIONS ... There are many fine hotels, residential clubs and guest houses in which you can stay in Barbados. Among

Excursions from Bridgetown take you through the rolling countryside and sugar-cane fields of Barbardos.

A native fisherman shows tourists his net on the beach. Most of the beaches have clubs which afford excellent ocean swimming, fine cuisine and bars.

those right on the beaches are the *Aquatic Club, Ocean View, Hastings, Royal-on-sea, Paradise Beach Club, Crane, Powell Spring, Bagshot House, St. Lawrence Hotel, Accra Beach Club, Super Mare, Sea View* and *Cacrabank;* others (across the street from the ocean) which are excellent are the *Marine, Windsor* and *Rockley Beach.* Rates are from about $8 per day up (including meals). Among the residential clubs with luxurious accommodations are the *Barbados Country Club, Colony, Coral Reef, Colleton House, Eastry House, Four Winds, Sam Lord's Castle,* and *Miramar.* Here rates are $30 to $50 American Plan per day.

CURRENCY ... The U.S. dollar is valued at $1.69 B.W.I. U.S. notes and travelers cheques are accepted by most hotels and large business houses.

CUSTOMS REGULATIONS AND DOCUMENTS REQUIRED BY UNITED STATES CITIZENS ... Proof of identity. While a birth certificate is *not* accepted as proof of identity in Barbados, it may be used as proof on returning to the United States. The official recommendation of proof of identity in Barbados is a passport, current or expired, but bona fide visitors returning within 6 months will encounter little difficulties in satisfying the Immigration Officials. Smallpox vaccination for return to the United States. One hundred cigarettes may be brought in duty-free.

RESTAURANTS ... The major restaurant in Broad Street is *Goddard's.* Some hotels, like the *Royal,* offer 24-hour service for persons who miss regular meal hours, and the *Bird and Bottle,* situated at the Marine Hotel, is popular with late diners. *Le Bistro* at Sunset

Gardens is popular, picturesque. Light snacks may be obtained at the *Flying Fish Club* in Bridgetown, the *Beau Brummel* in Hastings, among others. *John's* in St. James, the *Morgan* and the *Coconut Creek,* all of which are night clubs, also serve meals with drinks. The Crane Hotel has a *Fish Pot* restaurant, where a la carte dishes, especially sea food, are served.

SPORTS . . . 9-hole golf course, Rockley Golf and Country Club. Tennis at Savannah Club and The Royal Barbados Yacht Club. There is deep-sea fishing and boats may be rented for this purpose. Bring your own equipment.

WHERE TO GO—SIGHTSEEING . . .

Bridgetown . . . In Bridgetown, the capital, you must see St. Michael's, the Anglican cathedral, which was rebuilt of coral rock in 1780 after the original building had been blown down during a hurricane. George Washington and his half brother, Lawrence, went to church here when they visited Barbados in 1751. Other places of interest to the visitor are Codrington College on the Atlantic, the oldest university college standing in the British colonies; St. John's Church, which contains the tomb of Fernando Palaeologus, one of the last descendants of the Christian Emperors of Greece, who died in 1678. There is a fine view of the Bathsheba Coast from St. John's Church.

The Barbados Museum, an interesting place to see, is at St. Michael, 1½ miles from Bridgetown. Bathsheba, 14 miles from the town, is a beautiful seaside resort. It is here at Tent Bay that it is fun to watch the flying fish fleet come in daily. At Holetown, a short distance away, there is a monument commemorating the first landing of the British. Perhaps the best known of the historical sights is Sam Lord's Castle, on the southeast coast (now a hotel). It was built about 1820 by Samuel Lord, a planter whose one desire was to acquire enough money to build the finest home the island had ever seen. It is an imposing structure, having four entrances with steps of black-and-white marble. The interior of the building is by an Italian craftsman.

You should certainly see the pottery market in Bridgetown, on Trafalgar Square, and pay a visit to the Public Library. Some of the world's finest beaches are in Barbados. Safe, good swimming is one of the main pastimes. The average temperature of the water is 77 degrees. The Paradise Beach Club is one of the best. It's at St. Michael, close to Bridgetown. The Barbados Aquatic Club is also a fine beach where you can obtain excellent hotel accommodations. Other residential clubs of note include the Colony, Coral Reef, Four Winds, Accra Beach, Rockley Beach, Kingsley, Le Bistro and Miramar.

SOURCES OF FURTHER INFORMATION . . . Carib Publicity Co. Ltd., Room 210, K. R. Hunte's Building, Bridgetown, publish The Bajan Magazine (1st of each month) and The Barbados News (15th of each month) of special interest to tourists. The Barbados Tourist Board maintains an Information Bureau at Pier Head, Bridgetown, at Seawell Airport and at 750-3rd Ave., New York City. Da Costa & Co., Ltd., are General Agents for Pan American in Barbados.

BERMUDA

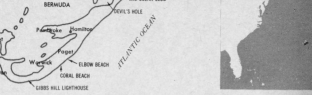

WEATHER IN BERMUDA—Lat. N32°20′—Alt. 50′

Temp.	JAN.	FEB.	MAR.	APR.	MAY	JUNE	JULY	AUG.	SEPT.	OCT.	NOV.	DEC.
Low	58°	57°	57°	59°	64°	69°	73°	74°	72°	69°	63°	60°
High	68°	68°	68°	71°	76°	81°	85°	86°	84°	79°	74°	70°
Average	63°	63°	63°	65°	70°	75°	79°	80°	78°	74°	69°	65°
Av. Daily Hrs. of Sun	5	5	6	8	9	10	9	8	6	6	6	5

LOCATION . . . Approximately 772 nautical miles southeast of New York, with the Gulf Stream running between Bermuda and the United States.

CHARACTERISTICS . . . Bermuda is a place for tourists to enjoy bicycling, tennis, golf, swimming, sailing, fishing and relaxing in an atmosphere of semi-tropical beauty. While one can dance after dinner at some of the hotels, there is no night-club life.

POPULATION . . . 37,254, according to the 1950 census, of which approximately 13,500 are white and 23,500 are colored.

SIZE . . . The total area of the more than 150 islands which make up "Bermuda" is about 20 square miles.

CAPITAL . . . Hamilton.

GOVERNMENT . . . The Government of Bermuda is a system analogous to that of Great Britain. Since 1685, the Governor has been appointed by the British Crown to represent the Queen. Politically, these islands hold a unique place among the possessions of the Crown. Bermuda has its own elected House of Assembly and a Legislative Council, and is officially designated as the oldest self-governing Colony in the British Commonwealth.

HOW TO GET THERE . . . By Pan American Clipper, flying time from New York, or Boston, 3 hours. By ship from New York; 40 hours.

ACCOMMODATIONS . . . One of the charms of Bermuda is that you can find almost any type of accommodation you wish, from luxurious hotels with swimming pools and tennis courts to charming quiet guest houses with limited number of guests. Rooms in private homes are also available. Rates given are double per person. Breakfast and dinner are included on Modified American Plan. Among the larger hotels: *Princess Hotel* and *Cottages* in Pembroke, between Hamilton Harbor and Pitt's Bay. One of the oldest and most famous hotels. All rooms have baths. Swimming pool, tennis courts, dancing. Accommodates 350. Rates $7 to $15 European Plan. *Belmont Manor* in Warwick Parish, opposite the city of Hamilton, overlooking the Great Sound. Tennis court, swimming pool, golf course, beachclub privileges. Rates $14 to $18, Modified American Plan. *Castle Harbour* in Tucker's Town. Modern and luxurious. Swimming pool, golf course, private beach, tennis court, fishing. Dancing nightly. Accommodates 500. Rates $16 to $24, Modified American Plan. *Elbow Beach Surf Club,* located on its own beautiful beach. Gay social spot with dancing nightly, social directors, group activity. Each room with bath. Accommodates 320. Rates $15 to $20, Modified American Plan. *St. George Hotel* in historical St. George's. Has special Family Plan and supervised children's program. Swimming pool, golf course, beach facilities, dancing. Accommodates 200. Rates $11 to $16, Modified American Plan. Among the smaller hotels: *Harmony Hall* in Paget. Accommodates 74 guests. Rates $13 to $18, Modified American Plan. *Inverurie* on the harbor in Paget. Accommodates 114 guests. Rates $12 to $17, Modified American Plan. Some cottage suites.

Bermuda abounds in guest houses which offer the same service as hotels but provide a quieter, more leisurely vacation. Most of them limit their guests to 50. Rates are about the same as at hotels. Most are American Plan. The following are typical: *Cambridge Beaches* in Somerset — small cottages and main house, private beaches. All rooms with bath. Rates $15 to $22, American Plan. *The Horizons* in Paget near Coral Beach. Main guest house and cottages. All rooms have baths. Rates $13 to $20, American Plan. *The Ledgelets* in Somerset — small cottages, and rooms in main house. All rooms with bath. Rates $15 to $20, Modified American Plan. *Lantana Cottage Colony* also in Somerset. Rates $17 to $20, Modified American Plan. *Pomander Gate* in Paget is an old Bermuda mansion with picturesque cottages (and magnificent flower garden), and swimming pool. Rates $13.50 to $20, Modified American Plan.

There are many others. Rates at hotels and guest houses may vary occasionally. Alternate plans such as the Bermuda Plan (room and breakfast) are often available. Residential accommodations, usually on the Bermuda Plan, are $3.50 to $6.

ARTS . . . The Bermuda Historical Museum in Hamilton under the Public Library and the museum attached to the Aquarium offer an excellent insight into Bermuda history.

BANKS . . . Bank of Bermuda; Bank of N. T. Butterfield and Son.

CALENDAR OF HOLIDAYS . . . New Year's Day; Good Friday; May 24, Empire Day; the Queen's Birthday (celebrated in June); July

28, Somers Day; Cup Match Day (day before Somers Day); Remembrance Day (Armistice Day); Christmas; December 26, Boxing Day.

CIGARETTES AND TOBACCO . . American cigarettes are available, same price as in United States. Tourists are allowed to bring in 100 duty free. English tobacco, pipes and cigarettes are available in good supply.

CLIMATE . . . Bermuda has pleasant summer weather from May to mid-November. Winter months have spring-like temperatures. There are few all-rainy days and there is no rainy season, but there are occasional quick unexpected showers.

CLUBS . . . American Legion, American Veterans of Foreign Wars, Bermuda Bridge Club (visitors may join for a small fee), English-Speaking Union, Garden Club, Lions Club, Rotary Club. For golf, tennis and yacht clubs, see SPORTS.

COMMON COURTESIES AND LOCAL CUSTOMS . . . Negroes are always referred to as colored people. Men must wear coats and ties in better restaurants, and golf hose must be worn with shorts in restaurants. When driving in Bermuda always keep to the left side of the road.

COMMUNICATIONS . . . Radio telephone to U. S., Canada, West Indies and England open 9:00 A.M. to midnight, every day. Twenty-four hour cable service. Airmail to U. S., Canada is 8d or 10 cents.

CURRENCY . . . American and Canadian money is accepted. Bermuda has its own money valued about the same as the English pound. No Bermuda money may leave the Island; English bank notes can be used by residents of the sterling area. The pound is now at $2.82.

CUSTOMS REGULATIONS AND DOCUMENTS REQUIRED FOR UNITED STATES CITIZENS . . . No passport or visa required but return ticket or onward transportation is essential and for U. S. Immigration authorities, proof of U. S. citizenship, such as an old passport, birth or baptismal certificate or voter's certificate. One hundred American cigarettes or 100 cigars or 1 lb. tobacco allowed duty free. On departure there is documentary tax of £1 or $2.85 on air and ship tickets.

DRUG STORES . . . Several drug stores in Hamilton and Somerset and more in St. George's that carry everything to be found in American drug stores. Larger hotels carry moderate supplies of toilet articles.

ELECTRIC CURRENT . . . 110 volts A.C., 60-cycle service, except at the Castle Harbour Hotel where the current is 220 volts A.C., 60-cycle. This hotel, however, will supply adaptors for standard electric shavers.

FAUNA . . . Eleven species of birds call Bermuda home. But each year fifty to a hundred different species seek shelter from ocean storms. Many varieties make the Islands a regular stopping-off place. Game fish abound in Bermuda's waters (see SPORTS).

FLORA . . . Plants from many parts of the world adorn the gardens of Bermuda. Probably the most outstanding plant is the Easter lily, in bloom during the months of February through May. This lily is grown commercially for cut flowers. There are many other well-known flowering plants such as the poinciana and the frangipani. Of the woody plants, the oleander and hibiscus are planted extensively as hedges, and bloom profusely from April to September. Other notable shrubs and climbers include the bougainvillea and passion vine.

FOOD . . . Almost everything is imported. There are few farms and only a handful of truck gardens. Milk is pasteurized. There is virtually no livestock because the cost of feed is high and land limited Bermuda lobster is a famous local dish. Cassava pie, a Christmas dish in which the root of the cassava plant is grated to make a flour or meal, is filled with chicken or pork and baked. Sweet-potato pudding is native, too. Meals at the hotels, however, are similar to those served in first-class hotels in the United States.

LANGUAGE . . . English.

LAUNDRY AND DRY CLEANING . . . Same as in the United States.

LIQUOR . . . The chief local drink is West Indian rum, ranging from 35 cents up per drink. Popular American drinks are available and range from 50 cents to $1. Bars in restaurants open on Sundays at noon, are closed from 2:30 to 6:00 P.M. Closing time on week days, and from 6:00 P.M. on Sundays, is midnight; 1:00 A.M. in hotels. Public bars open every day from 10:00 A.M. until 10:00 P.M. and are closed all day Sunday.

MEDICAL FACILITIES . . . The King Edward VII Memorial Hospital is well equipped. Hotels and guest houses have lists of English-, Canadian-, and American-trained doctors and dentists.

MOTION PICTURES . . . There are three motion picture theaters in Hamilton and many more dispersed throughout Bermuda.

MUSIC . . . Local bands excel at calypso and popular American music. There are American bands, too.

NIGHT CLUBS AND CABARETS . . . Bermuda exists without night clubs or cabarets, but there is dancing and entertainment nightly at nearly all the big hotels. Bars in restaurants close at midnight. Those in hotels at 1:00 A.M.

PHOTOGRAPHY . . . Bermuda offers a field day for photographers. Even the rankest amateur photographer will want to take along his camera. Black-and-white and color in still and movie film available at approximately the same price as in the U. S. Pictures (other than movie film) can be developed in Bermuda, overnight service on black and white and Ektachrome color film. Among the best photo subjects are Salt Kettle, Somerset, St. George's, the South Shore beaches and Gibb's Hill Lighthouse. The pastel houses and brilliant flowers lend themselves particularly well to color photography.

RELIGION . . . Bermuda is Protestant Episcopal (Church of England), but many other denominations have large congregations. In addition to these churches there are Presbyterian, Wesleyan-Methodist, Roman Catholic, Christian Science, and Seventh Day Adventist.

RESTAURANTS . . . Majority of hotel dining rooms are open to others than their own guests. Guest houses are the exception. There are excellent dining places almost anywhere on the Islands. *Tom Moore's Tavern* in Bailey's Bay is famous. *The Plantation* at Leamington Cave is noted for its lobster. *The Waterfront* on East Broadway, and *No. 1 Parliament Club* on Front Street in Hamilton are popular spots for lunch and dinner. *Waterlot Inn* in Southampton, recently renovated, and *The Breakers* overlooking the beach in Smith's Parish are excellent. Among the better bars (the first two of which serve no food) are: *Swizzle Inn*, which, as its name indicates, serves fine rum swizzles *"21"*, which bears no relation to the famous New York restaurant, but which somehow reminds you of it; and the *Penthouse Club* with its open-air terraces overlooking the harbor.

SHOPS AND STORES . . . There are many fine shops featuring English antiques and silver at prices lower than in the United States. Trimingham's and H. A. and E. Smith are famous for sweaters, tweeds and Bermuda doeskin. A. S. Cooper on Front Street sells Wedgwood and Jasper china and William Bluck and Company have many fine bargains in antiques. Most of the better stores are located in Hamilton and are open daily from 9 A.M. until 5 P.M., except during the lunch hour, Thursday, when they close at noon, and Sunday, when they are closed all day.

SPECTATOR SPORTS . . . Cricket is the "national sport"; matches are played Thursdays and Sundays. Soccer and rugby are played from October to April. Water carnivals at hotel swimming pools. Sailing races all year for small boats of all classes. The Newport, R. I.-Bermuda Race occurs every even-numbered year, the outstanding blue-water race in the world.

SPORTS . . . Golf, tennis, sailing (there are small boats for hire which you can sail yourself; larger craft with crew; charter sloops with boatmen). Sailing is year round and important in Island life. Many classes of smaller yachts are raced on Thursdays and Sundays throughout the year: International One-Designs, 5.5 metres, International 14-ft. dinghies, Luder 16's, snipes and fireflies.

The annual Bermuda Game Fishing Tournament, held from May through November, is well known and creates great rivalry among resident and visiting fishermen. A special Tournament is held in winter. World record amberjack, bonefish and wahoo have been taken from Bermuda waters, and eminently respectable catches of marlin, blue and white tuna, mackerel and dolphin are frequent. Boats, complete with tackle and bait, may be chartered for a day's deep-sea fishing for $60 for parties of six or less. Water skiing equipment may be rented. Golf clubs are excellent. Mid-Ocean Club is world famous, open to the public several days a week. Riddell's Bay Golf and Country Club, Belmont Manor Golf Club, Castle Harbour and St. George courses (both nine holes) are open to the public. Swimming in pools or at beaches. Equipment for golf, cycling, fishing may be rented.

TIME . . . Bermuda is an hour later than U. S. Eastern Standard Time. Daylight saving time is voted upon each year.

TRANSPORTATION . . . Bicycles, especially motor-assisted cycles with one-horsepower motors, are the most popular form of transportation. Everyone goes everywhere on them. They may be rented by the hour, day, or week. Prevailing rate is $5 a week for bicycles, $14 (for four days) for motor-assisted cycles. There are no automobiles for hire, but there are English taxis with very reasonable rates. Carriages may be hired by the hour or day with rates fixed by the Bermuda

Exploring Bermuda by bicycle is a leisurely and pleasant way to see the mid-Atlantic Colony's charming scenery.

Carriages may be hired by the hour or day and are fun for sightseeing about the island or for "taxi" service.

Government. Passenger ferries take you from one point to another. Buses traverse the Islands but are apt to be crowded and slow. There are no trains in Bermuda.

WATER . . . Bermuda is dependent on rainfall for its water supply. The water is excellent to drink. Bottled water is also available.

WHAT TO BUY . . . Tweeds, cashmere and shetland sweaters, British and Scotch woolens, English leather goods, perfume (much lower than in the States), English pipes and tobaccos, English china (Wedgwood, Spode), silver (great savings here), doeskin gloves and men's doeskin slacks. West Indian trinkets and gadgets, cedar boxes, calypso sports shirts.

WHAT TO WEAR . . . *Women*: for spring and summer — cottons, prints or pastel crepes. Shorts and slacks (Bermuda or knee-length shorts preferable). Don't go cycling in a halter bra; the Colony frowns on overexposure, so keep it conservative. Tweeds, sweaters and woolens in winter and late fall. Evening gowns of seasonal type. A lightweight raincoat is advisable in the winter months. You will find that a beach robe, two bathing suits, culottes or pedal pushers are handy. *Men*: Bermuda shorts and slacks in warm weather. Ties and coats are required in some restaurants. Lightweight jackets with shorts, slacks in summer, wool suits in winter. Black or white dinner jackets the year round. White in summer is more comfortable. Raincoat, swimming trunks, sport-shirts and a beach robe are essentials. Distinctive Bermuda shorts best purchased locally.

WHERE TO GO — SIGHTSEEING . . . Not to be missed are seventeenth-century St. George's with Fort St. Catherine, the Aquarium, Leamington and Crystal Caves. Gibb's Hill Light, Devil's Hole, and the south-shore beaches. A trip through the Marine Gardens in glass-bottom boats is interesting. Bermuda is a skin diver's paradise.

Most fun of all is to cycle around, exploring things for yourself, but there are organized tours arranged by Penboss Associates, American Express, Thomas Cook's, Bermuda Holiday House, Harnett and Richardson, John S. Darrell, Wm. E. Meyer and other local agents.

SOURCES OF FURTHER INFORMATION . . . In the U. S., Bermuda Trade Development Board, 620 Fifth Avenue, New York City (Tel. CI 6-6055), in Canada, 111 Richmond Street West, Toronto, Ontario and in England, 6 Lower Regent Street, London, S.W.1.

In Bermuda, Visitor's Service Bureau, Hamilton; and Bermuda Trade Development Board, Hamilton. "This Week in Bermuda" a weekly calendar of events, is available without charge. Pan American's office is at 61 Front Street, Hamilton (Tel. 1051).

CAYMAN ISLANDS

Grand Cayman, British West Indies, is 22 miles long and 8 miles wide, the largest of the three Cayman Islands. It is located south of Cuba, west of Jamaica and is reached by PAA affiliate LACSA airlines in about 2 hours from Miami or by connection with Pan American flights to Havana, San José, Costa Rica, or Panama City. All you need for entry is some form of identification such as birth certificate; smallpox vaccination certificate for reentry to the United States.

This delightful island is, more than many Caribbean islands, the place to get away from it all. There is no radio station, television reception or telephone; the local newspaper is a monthly. The natural aspects of the island and the attitude of the people (population about 5,000) are still unspoiled.

A low island of coral limestone, Grand Cayman is heavily covered with a luxuriant growth of mangroves, sea grape palms, hardwoods, breadfruit, mangoes and varieties of citrus: oranges, limes and grapefruit, and numerous tropical fruit trees including almonds. A spectacular crescent beach of flourlike white coral extends for six miles along the west end of the island. Wonderful for swimming. There are numerous other beaches and small coves bordering the irregular shore line. Fishing is excellent, also hunting in the ponds and swamps. A small yacht club is available to tourists. There's also a beach club with dancing to a native band.

Among the things to see and do: A drive to the east end of the island (by rented bicycle or car) which will show the visitor how people can live happily and peacefully by the land and sea with no poverty; the Turtle Kraal in North Sound; a picnic on Rum Point; "Hell," the forbidding coral formation on the north end of the island; the spectacular beauty of West Beach. There are many caves and "blow holes" along the ragged shore. Natives will tell you stories of buried treasure and the latest ship wrecks.

Hotels, all in or near Georgetown, the capital, all American Plan, are: *Galleon Beach Hotel,* new de luxe hotel, on the splendid unbroken sweep of West Bay Beach, open December 16 to April 16, has dancing, tennis court. Rooms, all with bath, are $25 single, $45 double. *Pageant Beach Hotel,* $25 to $32.50, double in winter, $14.50 to $22.50 in summer; *Sea View Lodge,* $8 to $12 per person in winter, $6 to $8 in summer; *Windsor House,* $10 single, $20 double in winter, $6 single, $10 double in summer; *Bay View Hotel,* $6 to $10 per person year around; *Buccaneer's Inn,* Cayman Brac, $20 to $22 double December 1 to April 15, $12 to $14 double in summer.

CUBA

WEATHER IN HAVANA—Lat. N23°08'—Alt. 30'

Temp.	JAN.	FEB.	MAR.	APR.	MAY	JUNE	JULY	AUG.	SEPT.	OCT.	NOV.	DEC.
Low	65°	65°	67°	69°	72°	74°	74°	75°	74°	73°	69°	67°
High	79°	79°	81°	84°	86°	88°	89°	89°	88°	85°	81°	80°
Average	72°	72°	74°	76°	84°	81°	82°	82°	81°	79°	75°	74°
Days of Rain	8	6	5	5	10	13	12	14	15	15	10	8

LOCATION ... Cuba lies in the West Indies about 100 miles from the Florida Keys and 130 miles from the Coast of Yucatan, Mexico.

CHARACTERISTICS ... Havana is the city of fun and frolic, of sunshine and sociability. Hotels are luxurious, beaches are fine, food and drink among the best in the world. The tourist is no novelty here and everything is done to make his vacation pleasant. If you want to try out your rumba, there is no better place than Havana.

POPULATION ... Estimated 6,500,000, roughly the combined population of Chicago and Detroit.

SIZE ... The largest island of the West Indies, Cuba is 760 miles long and ranges from 25 to 125 miles wide. The area of 44,218 square miles is slightly larger than the area of Tennessee.

CAPITAL ... Havana, population 1,000,000.

GOVERNMENT ... A republic, governed by a President, a Senate and a House of Representatives.

HOW TO GET THERE ... By Pan American Clipper, frequent daily service from Miami to Havana, about 1 hour flying time; to Camagüey, 1½ hours. Frequent flights within the country via Cia Cubana de Aviacion, S. A. (CUBANA).

ACCOMMODATIONS ... Among Havana's more than 25 hotels you will be able to choose one that will suit your taste and purse. They range from the ultra swank to the small and quiet native hostelries. Summer rates are often much less than the winter rates given here. The most luxurious hotel in Cuba is the famous *Nacional de Cuba* operated by Intercontinental Hotels Corporation, in the fashionable Vedado section. The decor is colorful, the food superb and it's newly air conditioned. It has a beautiful pool, and the famous Casino Internacional. Rates are $18 to $27 single, $25 to $28 European Plan. Lower rates prevail between April 16 and December 14.

Other hotels with minimum single rates, European Plan (add about $7.00 for meals) are: the *Comodoro*, $17, and *Copacabana*, $10, in Miramar, the *Vedado* $16 and *Presidente* (Cuban atmosphere) $10 in Vedado section, the *Sevilla-Biltmore* $10, *Caribbean* $8, and *Regis* $8, on the Prado; the *Lido* $8 near shopping district and *Royal Palm* $6 at Industria 354; the *Copacabana* $10; and *Saint John's* $12. Brand new hotels include the *Habana Hilton* with 640 rooms, *Habana Riviera* 360 rooms, $22 up, and the *Capri* 260 rooms, all air-conditioned. The *Chateau Miramar* has apartments by day ($16), week or month, as does the nearby *Rosita de Hornedo* nearby (suites from $22 daily). Many of the above have air-conditioned rooms and swimming pools.

ARTS . . . Cuba offers an interesting variety of native, European and modern art. Don't miss the National Museum's interesting collection of classic and modern Cuban paintings. There is also a rich collection of objects relating to the Cuban Wars for Independence. The museum is open daily from 9:00 A.M. to 5:00 P.M. Nominal admission charge. The Tobacco Museum of La Corona Company shows a complete history of Cuba's famous industry, cigars. There are also numerous works of art in El Templete Shrine, and in some of the Catholic churches. In the Presidential Palace there are valuable paintings by Cuban artists.

BALLET . . . There is a local ballet company under the direction of Alicia Alonso, the famous ballerina. Also the Sociedad de Pro Arte Musical has a ballet school. Visiting companies perform here.

BANKS . . . Trust Company of Cuba, Obispo 257; Chase Manhattan Bank, Aguiar 310; First National City Bank of New York, O'Reilly and Compostela Streets, First National Bank of Boston, and Royal Bank of Canada, Aguiar St. All have branch offices in Vedado.

CALENDAR OF HOLIDAYS . . . January 1, January 28, February 24, May 1, May 20, October 10, October 12, December 7, December 25. There is a fabulous carnival on each of the five week ends preceding Holy Week.

CIGARETTES AND TOBACCO . . . Cuba is famous for its marvelous cigars and tobaccos. The finest cigars in the world are made here. American cigarettes are available for about 40 cents a pack. Local brands are 10 cents per box.

CLIMATE . . . The constant trade winds make the Cuban climate one of the world's most delightful. Though located in the tropical zone, the temperatures range from 75 to 90 degrees in the summer months and average 70 degrees during the winter season. Cuba is ideal to visit the year around.

CLUBS . . . There are many clubs in Havana. The Havana Yacht Club, Havana Biltmore Yacht and Country Club ($6 greens fee), American Club, Rotary Club, Lions Club, Vedado Tennis Club, Rovers Club ($3 greens fee).

COMMON COURTESIES AND LOCAL CUSTOMS . . . There is a special division of the Havana police force to help tourists whenever they can. These men are required to speak English. The Cuban government has a passion for changing street names and the Cuban public is determined not to recognize these changes. If you are doing any sightseeing at all away from a guided tour, get a map with both traditional and most recent street names.

COMMUNICATIONS . . . Local and long-distance telephone service, All America Cables, Western Union, and for radiograms, RCA, Inalambrica and the Telephone Company.

CURRENCY . . . The monetary unit is the peso, which has the same value as the American dollar.

CUSTOMS REGULATIONS AND DOCUMENTS REQUIRED FOR UNITED STATES CITIZENS . . . No passport, vaccination certificate or visa is necessary but you must have proof of nationality. Cameras, portable radios, typewriters, cigarettes, and fishing and hunting equipment (no rifles) may be brought in duty free as part of your personal baggage. After a stay of 48 hours you may take out duty free 5 bottles of liquor and 100 cigars.

DRUG STORES . . . Drug stores in Cuba are different from those in the United States. They sell only medicine and prescriptions. Almost all the American and European products are available.

ELECTRIC CURRENT . . . 110 volts, 60 cycle, A.C.

FAUNA . . . There are more than 300 species of native birds in Cuba. Many of these may be seen at the Zoological Gardens in Havana. The variety and abundance of fish in Cuban waters is extraordinary: outstanding are red snapper, marlin, pompano, shark and dolphin. Quite a few types of big game inhabit the Cuban forests.

FLORA . . . The Cuban countryside is a panorama of luxurious tropical vegetation. One sees everywhere the beautiful royal palm, and there is an abundance of exotic flowers. The woods of the Cuban jungles are famous for their strength and durability.

FOOD . . . Cuban cooking is of Spanish origin modified by Creole innovations. French cuisine is popular. American dishes are served at restaurants catering to tourists. Seafood is very popular. Try *cangrejo moro*, made with succulent big Moorish crab and spicy rice; *langostino*, the giant fresh-water prawn best served cold; *congrí* (rice with black beans or, as it is cooked in the Oriente Province, with red navy beans); *arroz con pollo* (rice with chicken); roast suckling pig, superb in the Cuban manner; and *patas a la andaluza*, made of beeves' feet. Milk should be boiled unless it's pasteurized.

GAMBLING . . . has been one of the star attractions in Havana. Check on gambling at different night clubs. Tropicana, Montmartre and Sans Souci have gambling rooms as do the Comodoro and Sevilla-

Biltmore hotels. Visit the Casino Parisien at the Hotel Nacional. Oriental Park offers horse races and also has a gambling room, and the Greyhound Kennel Club has dog races every night. These clubs remain open only part of the year.

LANGUAGE... English is spoken fluently by those hired in public activities.

LAUNDRY AND DRY CLEANING... Almost all hotels have laundry and dry-cleaning service. Service is good, quick and reasonably priced.

LIQUOR... Rum is the classic Cuban drink. Cuba is the home of Bacardi rum, the Daiquiri and, of course, the Cuba Libre. A Daiquiri or Bacardi cocktail in Havana is a superior thing indeed. Rums are cheap and in great variety. Standard brands of whisky are available everywhere.

MEDICAL FACILITIES... The Anglo-American Hospital with a staff of English-speaking doctors and nurses. Centro Medico Quirurgico and Clínica Miramar. The principal hotels have doctors.

MOTION PICTURES... Several theaters show only Spanish language films; the rest feature American and English films. Most theaters in Havana are air conditioned and have the most modern equipment. Among the principal ones are: *Radiocentro*, 23rd and L Streets and *La Rampa*, 23rd and O Streets, Vedado; *América*, Galiano and Concordia Streets, Havana City; *Miramar*, 5th Avenue and 82nd Street, Miramar, *Rodi*, Linea and B Streets, Vedado, *Payret*, across from Central Park and *Arte y Cinema*, one block from the Nacional Hotel.

MUSIC... The Auditorium, Calzada and D Streets, Vedado, is the leading Cuban music center. The Philharmonic Orchestra of Havana and the National Cultural Institute Chamber Orchestra give concerts here during the winter season. The handsome outdoor Amphitheater on Belgica Avenue has free band concerts three or four times a week. All over Havana you will hear vigorous Latin American dance music at its very best. It's the home of the rumba and the conga.

NIGHT CLUBS AND CABARETS... Cuban night life is as gay as any in the world and as varied. The hundreds of little sidewalk cafés open before noon and close in the small hours of the morning. They are wonderful to sit at and watch Havana life go on around you.

The principal Havana night clubs are: *Sans Souci*, a very lovely night spot surrounded by palm trees. Two floor shows every night; gambling room and bar. *Tropicana* has two dance floors; one in the open surrounded by beautiful palm trees, and the other indoors, air conditioned, furnished in modern style with a luxurious bar; two floor shows every night featuring international and local stars. *Montmartre* is located on 23rd and P Streets, two blocks from the Nacional Hotel; air conditioned, gambling room, bar, two floor shows every night. The *Casino Parisien* at the Nacional Hotel presents excellent floor shows nightly. *Bambu Club* is located in the outskirts of Havana, typically Cuban with a very good floor show.

PHOTOGRAPHY .. All types of equipment and films are available. One-day developing service is available and good. Kodak Cubana Ltd. in Havana is at Calle 23, No 156, Vedado.

RELIGION ... Cuba is a Catholic country and there are cathedrals everywhere. Principal Catholic churches: Sacred Heart, La Merced, Santa Rita, San Agustín, San Antonio.

In Havana, churches of other denominations include: Episcopal Cathedral, 13th Street, corner 6th, Vedado. Baptist, Zulueta and Dragónes Streets; Methodist, Industria No. 82; Presbyterian, Salud 40; Jewish, G. Sy 502, Vedado. First Church of Christ Scientist, Alturas de Almendares, Marianao.

RESTAURANTS ... Meals are not cheap; however, there are excellent restaurants. Among them: *La Reguladora,* one of the oldest and the finest; *La Zaragozana;* the excellent *Tally-Ho* and *La Rue 19* in the Vedado section; *Monseigneur, La Roca, 21 Club* near the Nacional Hotel. *Rio Cristal* and *El Sitio* are a little way out of town but worth trying. The dining rooms in the *Nacional,* the *Sevilla-Biltmore* and the brand new hotels listed on page 250 serve international cuisine as well as native dishes. The *Florida* and the *Chez Merito* serve international food. Other excellent restaurants are the *Rancho Luna, Mandarin* (Chinese), the *Vendome* and *Centro Vasco* in the Vedado section, the *Palacio de Cristal* near the Central Park and the *Emperador* in the new F.O.C.S.A. building.

SHOPS AND STORES ... There's a Sears, Roebuck retail store in Havana. Other shops include *El Encanto, Fin de Siglo, Sanchez Mola, La Filosofia.* All of them are located on San Rafael and Galiano Streets, the shopping district.

SPECTATOR SPORTS ... Jai-alai, baseball and cockfighting are the three national favorites of Cuba. You can see cockfighting in the Jesus del Monte quarter almost any time of day or night. Horse racing is popular the year around at Oriental Park. Polo, swimming meets and football are seasonal favorites. The Havana Yacht Club stages an International Star Class Regatta in the last week of January. The St. Petersburg-Havana Sail-Cruiser Race takes place in March, and there are rowboat races on the bay during June and July. Annual tennis tournaments are held for the Havana Cup at the Vedado Tennis Club. National baseball championship from October to February each year. Golf tournaments at the Country Club of Havana, and the Havana Biltmore Yacht and Country Club. Basketball games, boxing fights every Saturday, wrestling matches.

SPORTS ... Most of the clubs in Havana are private, but in such hotels as Nacional, Comodoro and Vedado, tennis and swimming are available. (Only swimming at the Vedado.)

There are many good golf clubs, among them the Country Club of Havana and the Jaimanitas Club. Cards are needed. See also under CLUBS. La Concha, a splendid bathing establishment with tennis courts, too, is located at Marianao, about 10 minutes from Havana, Varadero is 40 minutes by plane (CUBANA—daily service) from the capital with 5 miles of white sandy beach. In Havana, there are fresh-water pools at the Country Club and the Casino Deportivo. Fishing is superb. You can catch big-game fish north and south of Havana. There are swordfish, marlin, tuna, snapper, barracuda, in fact, some 700 varieties of fish in Cuban waters. There are charter boats of all types available. Night fishing off Cojimar is an exciting experience. Boats, complete with bait, ice and manpower, can be hired.

There is good deer hunting around Candelaria in Pinar del Rio Province, and near Trinidad in Las Villas Province. Wild boar roam the Cayo Romano near Cabarien, and wild fowl and guinea hen are plentiful in Santiago. You may bring shotguns with you and get licenses on 3-weeks' notice at the Cuban Tourist Commission. The fee is $15.00. There are excellent hunting guides available.

THEATERS ... There are many theaters in Havana. The largest is the *National* at San Rafael and the *Central Park* which presents musicals, dramas and motion pictures. The Palace of Fine Arts shows Spanish plays. Vaudeville and Spanish plays can be seen at *Teatro Marti.*

TIME ... Same as United States Standard Time.

TIPPING ... Tipping is done on the same basis as at home.

TRANSPORTATION ... There are taxis and local buses for traveling around the city. Modern buses, some of them air conditioned, will take you all over the island at very reasonable fares. It is possible to rent a car for self-driving, rental rates depending on make of car and year.

WATER ... For drinking purposes mineral water should be bought or, if not, the regular water boiled. Mineral water can be obtained everywhere.

WHAT TO BUY ... Havana is a marvelous shopping center for luxury and novelty items. Don't believe all you hear about the bargains obtainable; the prices aren't substantially lower than those at home. Tops on the list are French perfumes, bottled locally and slightly lower in cost. Buy them only in reputable shops and be sure the bottles are sealed. Customs regulations vary according to brand. Cuban rums, liquors and cordials are among the best buys. Leather goods, alligator skin particularly, are very good and quite reasonable. The better skins are soft and pliable; cheaper varieties tend to be stiff and dry. You can get almost anything you want in Havana shops, but these are your best buys. *See also* CUSTOMS REGULATIONS and SHOPS AND STORES.

WHAT TO WEAR ... Remember, Havana is a cosmopolitan city. Slacks and shorts are *not* acceptable away from the beach and country clubs. Cool, dark cottons are best during the day. Black cocktail dresses after five. You can go as gala as you wish after dark. White jackets are correct formal attire for men. Lightweight casual sports clothes are good for men in the daytime, but leave the loud shirts at home. Most Cuban men wearing *"Guayaberas"* go without ties in the daytime, wear them at night. White and natural linen suits are

Cuba's climate is ideal for enjoying the outdoor facilities of Havana's luxury hotels such as this pool at the Nacional.

acceptable all the time. Bring a raincoat to Cuba between May and November. Comfort without too much informality is the keynote in Havana. Women shouldn't wear slacks on the golf course. Conservative shorts are all right for tennis. Modified for coolness, traditional riding clothes are required. Wear what you wish for hunting and fishing.

WHERE TO GO—SIGHTSEEING . . .

Havana . . . Morro Castle, the fort at the entrance to Havana harbor is the number-one sightseeing landmark. Take a launch trip across the bay to it. La Fuerza Castle, the second oldest fort in the hemisphere, is also worth seeing. Make a tour of the colonial quarter with a guide or a good map. There are many beautiful old buildings and colorful streets. Aldama Palace, facing the gardens of Fraternity Plaza, is an excellent example of early colonial architecture. The San Francisco Convent is a wonderful colonial structure which formerly housed the Post Office. And, of course, the Maine Monument is interesting to any North American. The Presidential Palace contains beautiful paintings by leading Cuban artists. The National Capitol is a modern, rather gaudy building which cost about $20,000,000. Paseo de Marti or Prado Boulevard is the center of Havana's social activities. It is called the Champs Elysées of Havana. Take a drive along Malecon Drive, which extends along the waterfront from the Prado, Vedado. Vedado, the swank residential section, is worth driving through. There are many beautiful homes and avenues. Miramar is another suburb worth seeing. There are drives and guided tours by the score. Or you may take a cab and go where you will. It's all worth seeing.

Matanzas . . . This old city is about 65 miles from Havana. Nearby are the Bellamar Caves, which are illuminated at night, and are astonishingly beautiful, and the beautiful Valley of the Yumurí. Farther down the coast is Varadero Beach, one of the most beautiful in the world. There is a large choice of hotels here as at other resorts. There's the luxurious *Oasis Motel,* operated by Intercontinental Hotels Corporation with single rates, December 16 to April 15, $15 and up (lower other times), and *Hotel Varadero Internacional,* a luxury resort with supper club, casino, pool, cabañas.

Santa Clara . . . Capital of the Las Villas Province, Santa Clara, is a charming inland town, an educational center with its Central University Art School and Teachers College. This progressive little city offers a mixture of quaint old colonial architecture and customs and fine modern parks. The old Carmen Church was built by the original founders when the town was called Villaclara. A central point for excursions to other parts of the Province, Santa Clara has good hotels. Hunting, especially for deer and wild fowl, is good. There are guides, cars and equipment for hire. Visits may be made to the large sugar plantations. There are several planes a week to Santa Clara from Havana.

Cienfuegos . . . Also in Las Villas Province 200 miles from Havana is Cienfuegos, "The Pearl of the South." This outstanding sports center with its excellent swimming, fishing and yachting facilities lies on magnificent Jagua Bay, one of the most beautiful of the Caribbean, where Hemingway in his more active days came to fish tarpon at the mouth of the Damuji River. Famous yachts often harbor here. It is a favorite with celebrities as well as convention delegates. Fifteen miles southeast are the beautiful Guamuhaya Mountains and the famous Hanabanilla Falls nearby. The narrow harbor entrance only 5 miles from town is flanked by the Pasa Caballos Touring Club, the Castle of Jagua (built before 1819 when the city was founded, for protection against pirates) and the Rancho Club. The Cayo Carenas, the Fishing Club and the Rancho Luna Beach are all nearby.

The city itself, with a population of about 95,000, is attractively laid out, with several good modern hotels with roof gardens. Covadonga's restaurant across from the Moorish-style Valle Castle and the Pan American Club both have excellent food, including their famous *paella.* There are three excellent yacht clubs with views of the bay and the fascinating surrounding countryside. There's a handsome new airport with frequent service from Havana in little over an hour. Cienfuegos even has its own version of Forest Lawn, a replica of the Parthenon built by Boston architect Pablo Donato, in a green pasture on top of a windswept hill.

Trinidad . . . On the south coast of the island facing the Caribbean is this old colonial city which retains its old-world charm. The Cuban Government declared it a National Monument in order to preserve its historical landmarks and wonderful old buildings. Here are the palaces of the Iznagas, Canteros and Borrells. There are magnificent collections of antique art owned by private families which may be seen upon request. Stay at the modern motel *Rancho Club* near the city.

Santiago de Cuba . . . Daily plane service, train from Terminal Station, Havana, and bus from Havana. It may also be reached by car along the modern highway that splits Cuba down the middle. The city was founded in 1514. Cortez, the great conqueror of Mexico, was the first mayor. There is an enchanting mixture of the old and the new in this busy Cuban city that was Cuba's first capital. There are narrow, twisting streets and romantic old houses. The country clubs and the yacht club offer transient memberships for tourists. The beaches around Santiago are magnificent. The facilities of the fashionable beach clubs are also open to tourists. Visits to San Juan Tower, the old cathedral and the fort in the harbor will all prove historically interesting. There is a traditional fiesta in the colorful Afro-American manner every August. The hunting and fishing around Santiago are excellent. The city is ringed by majestic mountains, a part of the Sierra Maestra range, often called the "Alps of the Tropics." Guides are available for hunting, fishing and sightseeing. There are many organized excursions and cars are available at reasonable prices.

Isle of Pines ... Seventy-six miles across peaceful and beautiful sea, the Isle of Pines, off Cuba's southern coast, is believed to be the setting of Stevenson's novel, *Treasure Island*. It may be reached by daily plane or a delightful steamer voyage that is enchanting by moonlight. In bygone times the island was a haven for pirates, and legends of buried treasure still exist. The island's climate is exceptionally healthful. There are wonderful beaches, huge citrus plantations; the sailing around these waters is the best. The medicinal springs around the Isle of Pines are reputedly excellent. Hotels include the *Rancho Rockyford* in Santa Barbara, *Hotel Santa Fe* and annexed motel units at Santa Fe and the *Bibijagua Hotel* at Bibijagua Beach.

Pinar del Río ... Westward from Havana about 109 miles, this province is one of the most beautiful on the island, and it is here that some of the finest tobacco in the world is grown. There are famous mineral springs at San Diego de los Baños, and there is also the port of Mariel, where the Cuban Naval Academy is located. In Los Organos mountains near Candelaria is the Soroa Tourist Center with a good restaurant and in the Valley of Viñales the modern *Hotel Rancho San Vicente*.

Camagüey ... This capital city of Camagüey province is on the Central Highway 354 miles from Havana and a busy international air junction. It is an important sugar industry center; a city of churches, the most notable of which are the Cathedral, San Francisco, Merced, Soledad, Carmen and La Caridad. It has an interesting colonial atmosphere preserved in the ancient houses of Moorish-influenced architecture. The Holy Week processions and Carnival Fiestas (in June) are popular here. There is good hunting. Hotels include the *Colón, Gran, Plaza* and *Residencial*.

SOURCES OF FURTHER INFORMATION ... The Cuban Tourist Commission has offices at Cárcel 109 (P. O. Box 1609), Havana; 336 East Flagler Street, Miami; and 610 Fifth Avenue, New York City. Pan American's office is at Calle 23, No. 105, Edificio Idal, Vedado, Havana (Tel. U-4921).

DOMINICAN REPUBLIC

ATLANTIC OCEAN

Santiago

Jarabacoa

HAITI   DOMINICAN REPUBLIC
Constanzia
San Juan

Ciudad Trujillo   Boca Chica

San Cristobal

CARIBBEAN SEA

WEATHER IN CIUDAD TRUJILLO—Lat. N18°28′—Alt. Approx. sea level

Temp.	JAN.	FEB.	MAR.	APR.	MAY	JUNE	JULY	AUG.	SEPT.	OCT.	NOV.	DEC.
Low	66°	66°	67°	69°	71°	72°	72°	73°	72°	72°	70°	67°
High	84°	85°	84°	85°	86°	87°	88°	88°	88°	87°	86°	85°
Average	75°	76°	76°	77°	79°	80°	80°	81°	80°	79°	78°	76°
Days of Rain	9	6	7	9	14	14	15	14	14	13	11	9

LOCATION... The Dominican Republic and Haiti occupy the island of Hispaniola about 50 miles southeast of Cuba and about the same distance west of Puerto Rico.

CHARACTERISTICS... This little country is the spot where Columbus landed and where he is buried. It is a curious combination of modern efficiency with contemporary buildings, spotless streets, supermarkets, luxurious hotels and centuries-old civilization. The hotels are the newest and most elaborate in the West Indies, the beaches are good, the fishing and hunting excellent. Tourists are welcome here. They are treated courteously and with the efficient service that marks this government. The highways are excellent. The climate is unvaryingly pleasant.

POPULATION... Estimated 2,250,000, approximately the population of Los Angeles.

SIZE... The area is 18,816 square miles, about the size of New Hampshire, Vermont and Rhode Island.

CAPITAL... Ciudad Trujillo, with about 250,000 population.

GOVERNMENT... A republic.

HOW TO GET THERE... By Pan American to Ciudad Trujillo, 4 hours from Miami, 5¾ hours nonstop from New York and about 1 hour from San Juan. By ship, about 6 days from New York. Good air service within the country by Dominican Airlines.

ACCOMMODATIONS... Several ultramodern luxury hotels have recently been built in Ciudad Trujillo. *El Embajador* (the Dominican Ambassador) overlooking the International Fairgrounds is completely air-conditioned and completely elegant, has a luxurious swimming pool, golf course, tennis courts, casino and *Embassy Club* night club. Rates about $20. The *Jaragua,* recently enlarged, is also luxurious, has a dining terrace, roof garden, Spanish patio, salt-water pool, clay tennis courts, massage room facilities, some air-conditioned rooms; offers floor shows, music for dancing, casino. Rates about $17. Both of these are now Intercontinental Hotels. Rates given are for double European Plan for winter (less after April 15). Add $9.00 per person for American Plan, $6.50 for Modified American (without lunch). Suites are also available. Other Ciudad Trujillo hotels include the attractive *Gazcué* on Bolivar Avenue, from $14, and the *Comercial* (downtown), from $12. Hotels in the interior are shown under WHERE TO GO—SIGHTSEEING.

ARTS... The magnificent new National Gallery of Fine Arts situated on Calle Máximo Gomez in the capital shows painting, sculpture and ceramics by Dominican and foreign artists. Paintings and sculptures are available for purchase.

BALLET... There is an Academy of Ballet which occasionally presents public shows at the local theaters.

BANKS... In Ciudad Trujillo the Royal Bank of Canada, Dominican Reserve Bank, Bank of Nova Scotia, Agricultural and Credit Bank of the Dominican Republic, the Central Bank, Bank of Credit and Savings. Working hours are from 8:00 to 12:30 Monday through Friday, except for one additional hour Friday afternoons.

CALENDAR OF HOLIDAYS ..January 1, New Year; January 6, Three Kings; January 21, La Altagracia's Day; January 26, Duarte Day; February 27, Independence Day; June 29, Saint Peter and Paul; March 19, Saint Joseph; May 1, Labor Day; August 15, Crowning of our Lady of Altagracia; August 16, Presidential Oath of Office; September 24, Our Lady of Las Mercedes; October 12, Columbus Day; October 24, United Nations Day; November 1, All Saints Day; December 8, Immaculate Conception Day; December 25, Nativity.

CIGARETTES ...Visitors are permitted to bring in 2 cartons of cigarettes duty free. Locally manufactured cigarettes are also available, the most popular being Hollywood, Cremas and Benefactor.

CLIMATE... Climate is warm and tropical, but seldom uncomfortable. The cool season between November and March is particularly pleasant with warm sunny days and cool evenings.

CLUBS... The Santo Domingo Country Club and La Voz Dominicana (luxuriously appointed and air-conditioned) offer facilities for tourists; Club #16 de Mayo, Casino del Caribe, Golfito Tennis Club. Also Rotary.

COMMON COURTESIES AND LOCAL CUSTOMS...It is customary for a jacket and tie to be worn in most of the hotels after 6:00 P.M. The wearing of shorts and beach-type wear is discouraged in the downtown area. When visiting local churches, women should wear a veil or hat. It is customary to shake hands when introduced and introductions are made formally. During the evenings the old Spanish custom of chaperoning still exists for young unmarried girls.

COMMUNICATIONS . . . International telephone and cable service; All America Cables, Inc. (Tel. 3117); RCA serves the Republic, too (Tel. 3722). The airmail rate for postal cards and letters to the United States is 11 cents per half ounce.

CURRENCY . . . The monetary unit is the Dominican peso on par with the U. S. dollar. U. S. bills are fully acceptable both in shops and hotels. There are no currency restrictions.

CUSTOMS REGULATIONS AND DOCUMENTS REQUIRED FOR UNITED STATES CITIZENS . . . No passport or visa required, only a Tourist Card for which a charge of $2.10 is made. This card, which may be purchased at certain Pan American sales offices or airports, entitles the visitor to remain in the country for 15 days and is extendable for a further 45 days upon application to the Immigration Department.

DRUG STORES . . . All very modern with United States products available.

ELECTRIC CURRENT . . . The voltage in local hotels is 100 volts, A.C., 60 cycles.

FAUNA . . . Colorful tropical birds, flamingos, parrots, etc. Deer were imported as an experiment and are said to be breeding in the mountainous section of the Republic.

FLORA . . . Beautiful tropical flowers of all varieties. Banana, palm and coffee trees in abundance. Pineapples, avocados, other fruits. Sugar cane, of course, and tobacco.

FOOD . . . The food is naturally Spanish; *salcocho,* for instance, is a soup containing 18 ingredients, such as pork, yams, Spanish sausage, onions, pumpkins and tomatoes. Very fine indeed. There is the inevitable *arroz con pollo; casabe* baked with cheese and boiled eggs; and *pastelitos*—pastries filled with chicken or other meat. The hotels and restaurants serve international food, too.

GAMBLING . . . Nightly at the *Jaragua, El Embajador* and *La Paz* hotels and *Voz Dominicana.* There are weekly lotteries with prizes ranging from $25,000 to $50,000. Pari-mutuel betting at the modern race track Perla de las Antillas.

LANGUAGE . . . The official language is Spanish but English is spoken and readily understood by almost everybody. The typical greeting is *¿Cómo estamos?* or *¿Que hay—Cómo estamos?*

LAUNDRY AND DRY CLEANING . . . Very good and available at several places in Ciudad Trujillo. Hotel Jaragua offers special services to guests. Prices vary depending on the type of clothing.

LIQUOR . . . The native drink is rum and can be obtained at very reasonable prices. Popular American drinks are also available at approximately the same prices as at home. The hotel bars are opened from 11:00 A.M. until 1:00 A.M. on Sunday through Friday and from 11:00 A.M. to 2:00 A.M. on Saturday, with unlimited extension during fiestas.

MEDICAL FACILITIES... Most hospitals have English-speaking doctors on their staffs. Doctors are very competent. Practically all of them speak English fluently. The hospitals in Ciudad Trujillo are among the most modern and best equipped of the Antillés. The Red Cross offers its services in case of emergencies.

MOTION PICTURES... In the capital, there are several motion picture theaters showing current American, Mexican and European films. The *Olimpia, Santome, Elite, La Voz Dominicana, Leonor* and *Rialto* are air-conditioned. English-language films carry Spanish subtitles.

MUSIC... There is the National Symphony Orchestra, which presents a series of concerts each year. Native music is lovely. The national dance is the *merengue.*

NIGHT CLUBS AND CABARETS... *El Embajador* and the *Jaragua* hotels both have night clubs with floor shows and music for dancing. The air-conditioned *Voz Dominicana* also offers good music for dancing.

PHOTOGRAPHY... Tourists can buy most any kind of film in Ciudad Trujillo, as well as cameras and photographic equipment. Prices are a little more expensive than at home. There are facilities for film developing. It takes around 3 days to do a good job. The Santo Domingo Gift Shop, Farmacía Esmeralda are among the places where photo equipment and films may be purchased. Good spots for taking pictures are the ruins, the Cathedral, the Altar de la Patria and the beaches.

RELIGION... The religion is Roman Catholic. There is, however, an Episcopal Church where English is spoken, located on Independence Avenue in Ciudad Trujillo. Catholic churches offer Mass each day from 5:30 through 7:30 A.M. On Sundays, Mass is said at the Convento Dominico from 6:30 A.M. through 8:30 A.M.; last Mass at 11:00 A.M. Cathedral services begin at 6:30 A.M. with High Mass celebrated at 9:00 A.M. Last Mass at 12:00 noon.

RESTAURANTS... Aside from the good, new hotel restaurants, there are many restaurants where European, American, Chinese and native food is served. Among the best known in Ciudad Trujillo are *Mario,* an air-conditioned Chinese restaurant; and the *Cremita. El Dragón* is a modern Chinese-American restaurant, air conditioned. Try the *Vesubio* for Italian specialties. All of these restaurants are located within five minutes' taxi ride from any of the hotels.

SHOPS AND STORES... The main shopping street in Ciudad Trujillo is Calle el Conde. Some of the principal stores are La Opera, Cerame, Miss America shop, El Palacio, La Pueñta del Sol-Lopez de Ars, Dragón de Oro (specializing in Chinese products), Artes Dominicanas handicraft shops at Arzobispo Nouel 16 and at the airport. There are two free port stores located on the International Fair Grounds. Tax and duty free prices on liquors, perfumes, cameras, watches, glass and chinaware, jewelry and miscellaneous wearing apparel. A visit to the Mercado Modelo (Model Market) should be included on shopping expeditions. This market, unlike many in Latin America, is an excellent example of modern design and cleanliness. Working hours are from 8:00 A.M. to 12:00 noon, and from 2:00 to 6:00 P.M., daily including Sunday.

SPECTATOR SPORTS . . . Horse racing at the Pearl of the Antilles track, baseball from April through September; cockfighting, polo from February through March. A new, modern baseball stadium is located within ten minutes' taxi ride from all the hotels. Dominicans are mad about baseball and have their own league that's outstanding.

SPORTS . . . The Santo Domingo Country Club and Ambassador Hotel each have an interesting golf course and a pool. Privileges are extended to visitors. Tennis courts are available at the Hotels Gazcué and Jaragua. Beach swimming is excellent at Boca Chica. Small sailing boats may be hired. Riding horses are available, too. The *Hotel Hamaca*, on the interesting island La Matica, has boats and water skis.

THEATERS . . . Stage shows and TV shows are shown at *La Voz Dominicana* Radio and Television theater from 5:00 to 10:00 P.M. daily including Sunday.

TIME . . . Same as United States Eastern Standard Time.

TIPPING . . . The usual 10 to 15 per cent.

TRANSPORTATION . . . There are cars for hire with chauffeurs. The highways are excellent. There are taxis.

WATER . . . With the emphasis on Public Health in this country, it is sure to be drinkable. Hotels serve bottled water on request.

WHAT TO BUY . . . Tortoise-shell boxes and accessories, embroideries, woven baskets. Handicrafts of local mahogany, green ebony, Dominican oak, etc., at Artes Dominicanas.

WHAT TO WEAR . . . Ciudad Trujillo and other coastal cities are warm. You will need summer clothes, beach things; dinner clothes at the top hotels. The mountain resorts of Constanza and Jarabacoa are much cooler, so take topcoats and a warm dress or two. Men will need linen or cotton suits, medium-weight jackets and slacks for the hills, beach clothes and summer dinner clothes.

WHERE TO GO—SIGHTSEEING . . .

Ciudad Trujillo . . . The first thing you notice is the cleanliness, the spotlessness of the city. This is due to the fact that the city has been almost completely rebuilt since the hurricane of 1930 which practically destroyed it, and partly because the government of Trujillo has concentrated on civic improvements. Don't miss the cathedral which is the Basilica of Santa Maria la Menor, which has some wonderful carvings, a treasure room and the Columbus Cross. In the heart of the original city of Santo Domingo are the ruins of Alcázar de Colón, built by Don Diego, Columbus' son, which are being reconstructed. The Tower of Homage, the oldest stone fortress in the Americas, is now a prison which may be seen only from the outside. Also on the outskirts of the capital on a brand new campus is the University of Santo Domingo, the oldest university in this hemisphere. It dates back to 1538. The new National Capitol cannot be

El Embajador, an Intercontinental hotel in Ciudad Trujillo, offers the ultimate in comfort.

missed. It is built of pink stone and stands in the western part of the city. Organized tours in modern limousines with English-speaking guides vary from $4.50 for the half-day city tour to $6.50 for tours to San Cristobal and Boca Chica.

San Cristobal is about 18 miles from the capital. It is reached by the Sánchez Highway, along which is the Santo Domingo Country Club. The city is the birthplace of President Trujillo, its primary claim to fame. Here is La Toma, the President's plantation. There are two wonderful bathing pools, one for the President and his guests and the other for the public. The *Hotel San Cristobal* is luxurious. Rates are about $11 double.

Boca Chica . . . Driving east along the coast highway, tourists may visit Boca Chica, an attractive beach resort about 45 minutes from the capital. A modern hotel, the *Hamaca,* has been opened. Superior swimming and sailing. Rates are $12 single and $20 double (A. P.).

The interior of the Dominican Republic is just beginning to be exploited as a tourists' paradise. Roads are good. The coffee and sugar plantations, the rice paddies and the tobacco farms are interesting to see. At Jarabacoa is the *Hotel Montaña,* high in the Cordillera Central. Rooms facing the valley have superlative views. American Plan rates are about $10 single to $17 double, lower off-season and for stays of a week or longer. There is a casino here, a dance floor, a children's playground. The *Hotel San Juan* is at San Juan, the center of the ancient Carib Indian civilization. American Plan rates are about $12 double. This is off the beaten track. The hill resorts are cool.

Santiago . . . 45 minutes by plane from Ciudad Trujillo or 3 hours by car is Santiago, the second city of the Republic and capital of the fertile valley of Cibao, in the heart of the Dominican agricultural region. The *Hotel Matum* (about $17 double American Plan) and the *Nueva Suiza* in the mountains at Constanza ($14) are both new.

SOURCES OF FURTHER INFORMATION . . . The Director General of Tourism, Ciudad Trujillo; The Pan American office at Edificio Copello, El Conde St. (Tel. 2515 and 3269). Other useful local telephone numbers are: U.S. Embassy, 9–4141; Immigration Department, 2487; In New York, the Dominican Republic Information Center is at 507 Fifth Ave.

GRENADA

WEATHER IN ST. GEORGE'S—Lat. N12°07'—Alt. Approx. sea level

Temp.	JAN.	FEB.	MAR.	APR.	MAY	JUNE	JULY	AUG.	SEPT.	OCT.	NOV.	DEC.
Low	72°	72°	72°	74°	75°	74°	74°	75°	75°	75°	74°	73°
High	82°	82°	83°	84°	85°	84°	84°	85°	85°	85°	84°	83°
Average	76°	76°	77°	78°	79°	78°	78°	79°	79°	79°	78°	77°
Days of Rain	14	8	8	7	10	17	20	21	18	16	17	16

LOCATION ... The most southerly of the Windward Islands group, Grenada is only 109 air miles from Trinidad.

CHARACTERISTICS ... This little British island is called the Spice Island because of the cocoa, nutmeg and clove that grow here. From end to end the island is only 21 miles long, but in this small area there is a great variety of scenery. St. George's lies on a point of land, and the streets rise rather sharply from the bay. Its red-roofed houses are pale pink and green; the effect is charming. There are mountains, valleys, and rockbound coasts where the surf thunders, a calm harbor where the water is deep-blue and quiet. And 2,000 feet above sea level is Grand Etang, a volcanic lake. This is a tropical isle, quiet and peaceful, with a rainy and a dry season. The hot days are tempered by trade winds; the swimming is superb, the whole place utterly beautiful and peaceful and just made for the traveler who wants to rest in sunshine. Some of the most beautiful white sand beaches you'll ever find are here.

POPULATION ... Estimated 90,586, mostly Negroes of African descent.

CAPITAL ... St. George's (population about 10,000) also serves as capital for the Windward Islands of Grenada, St. Lucia, St. Vincent, Dominica and the Grenadines.

GOVERNMENT ... Member of the Federation of the British West Indies, including the island of Carriacou.

HOW TO GET THERE ... Grenada is only 1 hour flying time

from St. Lucia; 3½ hours from Martinique, 5 hours from Antigua, and 55 minutes from Trinidad (all by British West Indian Airways connection with Pan American flights). From New York to Trinidad, 8¾ hours flying time. By ship about 14 days from Montreal.

ACCOMMODATIONS... The *Santa Maria Hotel* is the best on this charming little island. The hotel overlooks the bay and harbor of St. George's, which is the main and capital city. Rates run from about $10.50 per day with meals. The *Saint James Hotel* and *Sea View* guest house are in town, *Ross Point Guest House* 1 mile from town; rates about $6 per day with meals. The *Green Gables* runs about $5 per day. In addition to pleasant and inexpensive guest houses there are furnished beach bungalows. For recreation there are swimming, fishing, golf and tennis.

CURRENCY... The monetary unit is the British West Indies dollar, worth about 60 cents in United States currency.

CUSTOMS REGULATIONS AND DOCUMENTS REQUIRED FOR UNITED STATES CITIZENS... No passports or visas are necessary for genuine tourists. Smallpox certificate required for return to the United States. No duty on personal effects to the value of $2,130.18. No duty-free allowance on cigarettes or liquor.

WHERE TO GO—SIGHTSEEING...

St. George's... Drive along the wharf past the Botanic Gardens returning via Richmond Hill. Drive through the Sendall Tunnel, which connects the quay side of St. George's with the part that lies on the sea. A high ridge of land separates the two sections. Don't miss old Fort George with its view and ancient battlements. Take a trip to Grand Etang, a volcanic lake about 1,700 feet above sea level. Lake Antoine and Lake Levera are in the north of the island, reached through the town of Sauteurs. A good idea of the island may be had from the drive which goes through Grand Roy, Concord, Gouyave, Victoria, Sauteurs, Grenville and St. Davids, and back to St. George's. This takes about 3 hours. Visit also Grand Anse with its two miles of white sand fringed with coconut palms.

SOURCES OF FURTHER INFORMATION... Tourist Trade Development Board and Beewee Tours Information Bureau, both in Grenada.

Colorful schooners are a familiar sight in the lovely harbor of St. George's, capital of Grenada.

GUADELOUPE

WEATHER IN POINTE-A-PITRE—Lat. N16°—Alt. Approx. sea level

Temp.	JAN.	FEB.	MAR.	APR.	MAY	JUNE	JULY	AUG.	SEPT.	OCT.	NOV.	DEC.
Low	69°	69°	69°	71°	73°	74°	74°	74°	74°	73°	72°	70°
High	83°	84°	85°	86°	86°	86°	86°	87°	88°	87°	86°	84°
Average	76°	76°	77°	79°	80°	80°	80°	81°	81°	80°	79°	77°
Days of Rain	19	15	15	13	18	21	22	22	20	19	20	19

LOCATION ... The largest French possession in the West Indies, Guadeloupe consists of two islands which lie about 62 air miles south of Antigua and 120 miles northwest of Martinique.

CHARACTERISTICS ... In Guadeloupe, popularly called the Emerald Isle, you'll find the climate delightful, the atmosphere relaxed and informal, the scenery picturesque and the people friendly.

SIZE ... With an area of 583 square miles the two islands that make up Guadeloupe are about half the size of Rhode Island.

CAPITAL ... Basse-Terre, but Pointe-à-Pitre, 40 miles away, is the chief commercial town, with a population of 45,000.

GOVERNMENT ... A department of France similar in relationship to France as a state to the United States.

HOW TO GET THERE ... By Pan American Clipper 3 hours from San Juan, Puerto Rico, which in turn is 5¼ hours from New York. By ship from New York about 8 days.

ACCOMMODATIONS ... are limited during the winter, so it's best to reserve in advance. The *Grand Hotel* in Pointe-à-Pitre has 65 rooms with bath. European Plan rates are about $5 single and $8 double. *La Pergola du Gosier,* 5 miles from the airport in the southern part of Grande-Terre island with private beach, can accommodate five couples in individual cottages called "Pergolettes." The food is excellent here. American Plan rates are $20 double. Four miles farther is the *Cottage* (also called the *Grand Large*) which accommodates only four but has an excellent French restaurant and white sand beach. Three miles from Basse-Terre on a black sand beach is the *Rocroi Beach Hotel,* which accommodates 8 guests in bungalows, $6 double European Plan; and nearby at Gourbeyre, the *Dole Hotel.*

CUSTOMS REGULATIONS AND DOCUMENTS REQUIRED FOR UNITED STATES CITIZENS... Proof of citizenship and continuation or return ticket for a stay up to 10 days. Cholera and yellow fever certificates if coming from infected areas. Smallpox inoculation certificate for return to the U.S.

NOTE... Refer to Martinique, pages 281 and 282, for general facts such as Calendar of Holidays, Cigarettes, Currency, Food, Liquor, Music, Religion, Water and What to Wear.

RESTAURANTS... Aside from the hotels mentioned above, *Cercle Metropolitain* (European dishes), 8 miles from Pointe-á-Pitre, is about the best, and in the residential section of Vernou, *La Clairiere* has excellent tropical and European food and wines.

SHOPS AND STORES... Perfume and souvenirs can be purchased at reasonable prices. Stores are all open from 8:30 A.M. to 12:30 P.M. and 2:30 P.M. to 5:00 P.M., except Sundays and holidays.

SPORTS... Guadeloupe is an ideal place for spear and rod fishing, water skiing at the Yacht Club, riding, hunting, and hiking.

TRANSPORTATION... Buses to all areas of the island are available at very low cost. Drive-yourself cars are available for $9.00 a day at the following addresses: Vivies & Co., Assainissement, Henri Devarieux, 42 rue de Nozieres. Taxis for hire at La T.A.G. or Kancel.

WHERE TO GO—SIGHTSEEING... The roads are good on both islands, and there are a number of interesting things to see and do all within easy reach of Pointe-à-Pitre. Principal historic sights include Sainte-Marie de Capesterre, where Columbus landed in 1493, and Fort Richepanse at Basse-Terre as well as rock-engravings recalling early life at Trois-Rivières. The beaches are delightful. For white coral sands there's the limestone island of Gosier, Sainte-Anne, Sainte-François, Moule and Port-Louis, and for black ferruginous sand there's the beach of the Rocroi Beach Hotel, among others.

The thick tropical forests offer interesting areas for hiking, especially the Victor Hugo trail and Merwart trail. The volcanic peak of La Sonfrière offers an interesting climb. Other points of interest include the mountain lakes (the Grand-Etang, the Etang Lombi and the As de Pique) and the waterfalls such as the Saut de la Lézarde, the Carbet and the Coulisse. The island of Grande-Terre, which has a flat terrain, offers a picturesque coastline, especially between Pointe des Châteaux and Moule, a principal harbor town during the 18th century, and in the vicinity of Anse-Bertrand.

SIDE TRIPS... The nearby French islands of Marie Galante, Désirade, Saint Barthelmy and the French part of Saint Martin offer interesting trips by schooner or private air service.

SOURCES OF FURTHER INFORMATION... Information is available at Pan American World Airways' Agency, Camille Bunel & Co., Quai Lordenay, Pointe-à-Pitre (Tel. 140), or in New York at the French Government Tourist Office, 610 Fifth Avenue.

HAITI

WEATHER IN PORT-AU-PRINCE—Lat. N18°33'—Alt. 25'

Temp.	JAN.	FEB.	MAR.	APR.	MAY	JUNE	JULY	AUG.	SEPT.	OCT.	NOV.	DEC.
Low	68°	68°	69°	71°	72°	73°	74°	73°	73°	72°	71°	69°
High	87°	88°	89°	89°	90°	92°	94°	93°	91°	90°	88°	87°
Average	76°	77°	78°	79°	80°	82°	82°	82°	81°	80°	78°	77°
Days of Rain	5	7	10	14	16	9	9	13	16	14	9	5

LOCATION ... Haiti occupies the western third of the island of Hispaniola (next to the Dominican Republic) between Cuba and Puerto Rico.

CHARACTERISTICS ... Colorful Haiti with its voodoo drums, its fascinating capital and its twin wonders, La Citadelle and Sans Souci Palace, has a lot to offer the visitor in search of the exotic. The crowded, colorful streets of Port-au-Prince filled with Negro women carrying baskets on their heads contrast with modern automobiles, smart shops and excellent hotels to make a fascinating sight.

Haitians are a proud people because of their hard-won emancipation from slavery. Foreigners are welcomed as equals. There are no race or class prejudices. The Haitian peasant is invariably friendly and self-reliant. Theirs is a soft-spoken and gentle hospitality.

POPULATION ... About 4,000,000, mostly Negroes or mulattoes descended from the French settlers. There are about 3,000 white foreigners.

SIZE ... 10,714 square miles, approximately the size of Maryland.

CAPITAL ... Port-au-Prince with a population of 250,000.

GOVERNMENT ... An independent republic with a President and National Assembly of two houses.

HOW TO GET THERE ... By Pan American Clipper flights to Port-au-Prince direct from New York 7⅓ hours; 2¾ hours flying time from Miami; about 4 hours from Camagüey, Cuba; 1½ hours from Kingston, Jamaica. By ship about 5 days from New York.

ACCOMMODATIONS... There are a number of fine hotels in Petionville, up the mountain above Port-au-Prince, 10 to 15 minutes by car: *El Rancho, Ibo, Lele, Choucoune, Villa Creole, Montana* and still higher the *Dambala.* All have swimming pools; rates from $12 to $30 single, and $20 to 60 double. Less expensive hotels here include the *Majestic* and *Marabou.* First-class hotels in Port-au-Prince include the *Riviera, International Club* (Thorland), *Beau Rivage, Castel Haiti* and *Simbie Palace* with European modified and American plan rates. Older first-class hotels are *Sans Souci, Splendid* and the *Oloffson;* all have swimming pools. Fairly good second-class hotels, some with private bath, at rates from $5 to $10 a day with meals: *Plaza, Excelsior, Majestic, Mon Reve* and *Park* in Port-au-Prince. Six new pensions in Petionville: the *Clerveaux,* the *Star,* and *Villa Tropicana, Doux Sejour, Green Garden, Salvador.*

ARTS... The Centre d'Art has become an important art exhibition center. Here the primitive paintings and sculptures of native Haitians are displayed, and more and more Americans are buying them. This center was organized in 1944 and has become of great interest to the international art world. The Foyer des Arts Plastiques is another center for primitive art. The National Museum has exhibits depicting the history of Haiti. The Museum of Ethnology has an interesting voodoo section devoted to all props of the voodoo rites.

BALLET... No formal ballet, but plenty of native dances. It is possible to see voodoo dances in the hills near Port-au-Prince. You may not see the real religious ceremony but you will see enough to satisfy your curiosity.

BANKS... The National Bank of the Republic of Haiti; the Royal Bank of Canada; Banque Agricole et Industrielle; Banque Colombo-Haïtienne.

CALENDAR OF HOLIDAYS... New Year's Day (Independence Day); January 2, Forefathers Day; April 14, Pan American Day; May 1, Labor Day; May 18, Flag Day; Ascension Day; Corpus Christi; August 15, Assumption; October 17, Dessalines' Death Anniversary; October 24, UN Day; November 1, All Saints' Day; December 6, Anniversary of discovery of Haiti; Christmas.

CIGARETTES AND TOBACCO... Popular American brands of cigarettes are available for about 40 cents. Principal local brands are *Christophe, Creole, Tambour* and *Splendid.*

CLIMATE... Port-au-Prince has a sunny, dry climate, not unlike Arizona. The nights are cool the year round. The new hotels in suburban Petionville (4 miles from city, elevation 1,500 feet) are making this a popular summer resort.

CLUBS... The Petionville Club with foreign resident members; the Turgeau Club, the Cercle Bellevue, and Club Port-au-Princien are the exclusive Haitian clubs. For other clubs *see* SPORTS.

COMMON COURTESIES AND LOCAL CUSTOMS... Although Haiti became independent early in the nineteenth century (following more than a hundred years as a French possession), the Haitians are proud of their French heritage, and French remains the official language. You will find this French background pervading the atmosphere wherever you go. You are in a completely foreign land where the aristocracy is mostly mulatto. It is, in fact, one of the few Negro republics in the world.

COMMUNICATIONS... All America Cables and Radio, 70 Avenue du President Trujillo and RCA Communications, Inc., operate direct radio telegraph facilities, West Indians Telephone Co. provides telephone service to the United States. Airmail service.

CURRENCY... The monetary unit is the gourde, worth 20 cents. No exchange restrictions.

CUSTOMS REGULATIONS AND DOCUMENTS REQUIRED FOR UNITED STATES CITIZENS... For a stay of up to 30 days, only proof of identity is required. Tourist card is issued on arrival at a cost of $1. Smallpox vaccination certificates. Transportation ticket out of the country. One carton of cigarettes or 50 cigars, 1 bottle liquor allowed duty free.

DRUG STORES... At La Belle Creole Department Store there is a complete drug cosmetic section stocked with standard American products. There is a luncheonette just like at home, and you can have ice cream, called *crème à la glace,* if you like.

ELECTRIC CURRENT... 110 volts, 60 cycle, A.C.

FLORA... Palms, Bougainvillaea, hibiscus, frangipani, mimosa, mahogany trees and all the other tropical trees and flowers you might expect and some that you wouldn't.

FOOD... Rice and beans are the mainstay of Haitian cooking. They are served as a separate course at the main meal of the day. Native cooking makes excellent use of spices. Their fish is wonderful, particularly *langouste* (rock lobster). Avocados appear frequently at meals; sweet-potato pudding is a national dish. Mango pie is another national favorite. Coconut ice cream is popular. Fruits are plentiful, bananas, figs, mangoes, etc. Haitian coffee is famous.

GAMBLING... The Casino International is open all year.

LANGUAGE... French is the official language. However, most of the people speak Creole, a patois of French, African, Spanish and English origins. The tourist can get along easily with English.

LAUNDRY AND DRY CLEANING... Laundry is good and cheap. There are several good dry-cleaning establishments.

LIQUOR... Haitian rum is well known the world over. It is light and good. Champagnes are plentiful and quite cheap. Brandies and whiskies cost less than at home.

MEDICAL FACILITIES... New hospitals have been built: General Hospital; Asile Français. Canape Vert Hospital; Hospital Schweitzer. There is an American wing of St. Francis de Sales Hospital.

MOTION PICTURES... *Rex, Paramount,* and new drive-in theaters showing mostly French-language films.

MUSIC... There is a national orchestra, but the music of Haiti is in its drums; it fills the air each week end. At the hotels and night clubs there are small but good dance bands.

NIGHT CLUBS AND CABARETS... A man on his own can

find many night spots in and around Port-au-Prince, but in general night life is confined to the hotels. On Saturday evening everyone drives to the *Cabane Choucoune* at Petionville, a few miles up in the hills. This is a circular building with a thatched roof where the elite of Haiti and the foreign colony dance the meringue. *Club Bacoulou* has excellent Wednesday-night shows. The other important night club in Haiti is *Casino International* with dancing nightly to an excellent native orchestra. *Aux Calebasses* has typical Haitian music and atmosphere, is frequented by the uninhibited meringue lovers on Saturday night. The unusual open-air *Théatre de Verdure,* in the waterfront exposition section, has regular performances of folklore music and dancing.

PHOTOGRAPHY ... All supplies are readily available in local stores such as Don Mohr Sales Corp., 48 rue Roux, Port-au-Prince. Black-and-white film can be developed in 3 days.

RELIGION ... Catholicism is the dominant religion, but there are several Protestant churches.

RESTAURANTS ... Food at the hotels is good. *Aux Cosaques* is a true Haitian restaurant; Haitian seafood and beef specialties are superb and moderate in price. *Le Picardie* in Petionville has an excellent French cuisine, as does *Le Perchoir,* spectacular restaurant overlooking Port-au-Prince. Other good restaurants are *Savoy Vincent; Nobbe-Bondel; Rendez-Vous; Le Rond Point; La Tonelle; La Fregate; Le Pavillon Italien.*

SHOPS AND STORES ... There are some very fine shops. To mention only a few: Fisher's, Mme. Paquin's, Mme. Ewald's, Canape Vert, Tam-Tam, Carlos. For mahogany items visit Caribcraft, Cardozo's, Meinberg's and Deslandes'. La Belle Creole is good for perfumes, China, silver, and cashmeres at lower prices than at home. There are many book stores. Haiti now enjoys free port shopping prices on many imported items.

SPECTATOR SPORTS ... There are none really, unless you include watching a voodoo dance. There is cockfighting, of course. The national game is soccer.

SPORTS ... Tennis, golf, swimming, horseback riding, which is particularly fine, are available. At all hotels except pensions there are good swimming pools; some have several tennis courts. Spear fishing is a popular native sport and you can hire boats and an instructor if you wish. There is excellent duck shooting within a few hours of Port-au-Prince and pigeon and wild guinea hen shooting year around. Arrangements can be made with tour operators for guides and guns.

THEATERS ... Théatre de Verdure is the principal theater.

TIME ... Same as United States Eastern Standard Time.

TIPPING ... Ten per cent is ample. Many hotels have adopted the European practice of adding a straight 10 per cent to your bill to simplify this often-vexing problem.

TRANSPORTATION ... You can hire a car complete with chauffeur for about $20 a day. Or you can take your choice of the "personalized" ground tours offered. You may also fly except on Sundays and holidays to the Citadelle, about a 45-minute flight from the capital. Incidentally, if you hire a car, the chauffeur usually pays his own expenses. You can hire taxis on a point-to-point basis at reasonable rates. An official taxi tariff is available at the airport or at your hotel. Drive-yourself service is also available. Your U.S. driver's permit and tourist card will get you a temporary license.

WATER ... Generally safe in hotels and restaurants of principal cities. Use caution elsewhere especially when traveling in the country.

WHAT TO BUY ... Mahogany products, of course. There are beautiful bowls, figures and furniture. Sisal and straw products are native, too. Haitian rum is excellent and cheap. Pick up a voodoo trophy, of course, if you can find one that's authentic. Tortoise-shell combs and jewelry are fine here. Hand-made laces and embroideries are particularly beautiful.

WHAT TO WEAR ... Light summer clothing similar to that worn in Miami. For the hills you'll need a top-coat and a sweater or two. For men, cotton or linen suits, slacks and a sweater. Evening clothes only if you are entertained by the diplomatic set.

WHERE TO GO—SIGHTSEEING ...

Port-au-Prince ... Port-au-Prince, capital of one of the few Negro republics in the world, is unlike any capital city you have ever seen. It is a mixture of elegance and crudeness, of sophistication and primitiveness. The streets are jammed with automobiles and burros. Peasant women walk with huge baskets of vegetables on their heads; there are pseudo-châteaux and houses on stilts. But everywhere there is color, gaiety and charm. While in Port-au-Prince, visit the Iron Market, which is filled with an amazing variety of merchandise. The market extends for two blocks and is roofed over with iron, hence its name. Everything is for sale here: foods, clothes, leather goods, junk of all sorts and some fine things. Saturday is the biggest day, but the market is never closed.

Visit the Palais National, the Presidential palace, which is a dazzling white building against a backdrop of mountains. Visit also the museum which displays, among other things, the diamond crown of Emperor Soulouque, who ruled Haiti more than a century ago. See, too, the anchor of the Santa Maria, which allegedly was wrecked in Haiti. In the Museum of Ethnology there is a permanent exhibit of Indian and African relics. Be sure to see a typical woodwork shop where bowls and furniture are made of mahogany.

La Citadelle and Sans Souci ... To visit the fabulous Citadelle of the early nineteenth century and equally fabulous King Henri Christophe Sans Souci Palace, you must go to Cap-Haitien and Milot. You may drive to Cap-Haitien in about five hours or fly in about 45 minutes. At Cap-Haitien the *Hotel Mont Joli* has added a new wing and a large swimming pool overlooking the city, with rates starting at $8 single, American Plan. Two other first-class hotels are the immaculately clean *Beck Hotel* and the *Hostellerie du Roi Christophe*. There are two pensions, *André* and *Martin,* which are less expensive but without private baths.

Friendly village people show how corn is ground, one of the interesting ancient customs of the Haitians.

There are arranged tours to the Citadelle which, of course, is the one thing you must see while in Haiti. You go to Milot from Cap-Haitien, about a 15-minute drive, then make the ascent to the Citadelle on horseback through magnificent tropical mountain scenery. But before leaving Milot, you have a chance to see Sans Souci, the palace which is an exact copy of the Sans Souci Palace of Frederick II of Prussia at Potsdam. Sans Souci had marble floors, walls of native hardwood covered with rare tapestries and brocades. Although it is now in ruins, you can still see where Christophe fell beneath his horse while reviewing his troops and where he finally shot himself with a gold bullet he kept. It is about a 2 hours' climb to the Citadelle, but it is well worth it. You must remember that every stone, every bit of ammunition was brought up by hand. The Citadelle was built to be an impregnable fortress to which Christophe and the army might retreat and live indefinitely. Its huge cellars were filled with grain and rice.

If you drive from Port-au-Prince to Cap Haitien you will see the sisal fields which are the backbone of Haiti's principal handicraft industry; the valley of the River Artibonite; the town of Gonaives, from which you enter the mountain country. You go over the North Pass at Mt. Puilboreau into the Valley of Plaisance with its thatched-roofed huts, banana trees and pleasant coffee plantations (coffee is Haiti's principal export), then to the village of Limbe and thence to Cap Haitien. You may hire a car and chauffeur for $100 for 3 days. The driver pays his own expenses. There are several reliable tour operators who can help you with arrangements.

SOURCES OF FURTHER INFORMATION . . . There is a tourist information office at the site of the former exposition in Port-au-Prince, Pan American's office at Rue Dantés Destouches (Tel. 3451). In New York the Haiti Tourist Information Bureau is at 30 Rockefeller Plaza. There are others in Chicago and Miami.

JAMAICA

WEATHER IN KINGSTON—Lat. N18°—Alt. 25'

Temp.	JAN.	FEB.	MAR.	APR.	MAY	JUNE	JULY	AUG.	SEPT.	OCT.	NOV.	DEC.
Low	67°	67°	68°	70°	72°	74°	73°	73°	73°	73°	71°	69°
High	86°	86°	86°	87°	87°	89°	90°	90°	89°	88°	87°	87°
Average	77°	77°	77°	79°	80°	82°	82°	82°	81°	81°	79°	78°
Days of Rain	5	4	4	5	7	6	5	9	10	12	7	5

LOCATION . . . The island of Jamaica lies in the Caribbean Sea about 90 miles south of Cuba. Kingston is 589 air miles from Miami.

CHARACTERISTICS . . . Long famous as a resort, Jamaica has a great deal to offer the tourist. Kingston is colorful, with fine shops, wonderful drives and good hotels. The north coast, which includes such well-known resorts as Montego Bay and Ocho Rios, is where the international set are to be found during the season. There are super-luxurious hotels, white coral beaches lapped by cerulean blue waters which are always warm, golf courses, fishing, yacht clubs and all the other things that give glamour and luxury to a vacation.

POPULATION . . . Estimated at 1,340,000, of which about 15,000 are white.

SIZE . . . Largest of the British West Indies, Jamaica is 145 miles long, covers an area of 4,411 square miles, smaller than Connecticut.

CAPITAL . . . Kingston, with a population of approximately 120,000.

GOVERNMENT . . . A British colony with a Governor appointed by the Crown, Jamaica is a unit of the new Federation of the West Indies.

HOW TO GET THERE . . . By Pan American Clipper, from Miami to Montego Bay, 2¼ hours nonstop; total elapsed time to Kingston, 3 hours. New York to Kingston via Montego Bay, 7 hours, via Avianca. Steamship service from New Orleans, New York, and Miami.

ACCOMMODATIONS...Jamaica hotels operate on American Plan (including all meals). These rates are substantially lower during the summer. The *Myrtle Bank* is the largest hotel in Kingston, the capital of Jamaica. It has its own swimming pool. Rates about $15 to $22 per day. The *South Camp* and the *Melrose* are less expensive. In the Parish of St. Andrews, a suburb of Kingston (in the Blue Mountains), there is the *Manor House,* which has an adjoining golf course. Rates from about $15 to $18 per day. At the *Mona, Flamingo* and *Courtleigh Manor* rates are about $12 to $15. The *Mount Royal Hotel,* a converted colonial mansion, is four miles from Kingston. Other hotels are listed under WHERE TO GO.

ARTS...The Institute of Jamaica, which contains the Science Museum and Library, the History, Art and Exhibition Galleries. Principal art dealer is Hills Galleries.

BANKS...In Kingston: Barclay's Bank, King Street; Royal Bank of Canada, King Street; Canadian Bank of Commerce, Harbor Street, and Bank of Nova Scotia, King Street. Banking hours are 9:00 to 12:30 except Saturday 8:30 to 11:30.

CALENDAR OF HOLIDAYS...New Year's Day; Ash Wednesday; February 22, Federation Day; Good Friday; Easter Monday; May 24, Empire Day; the Queen's official birthday (in June); August 1, Emancipation Day; November 20, Constitution Day; Christmas Day; December 26, Boxing Day.

CIGARETTES AND CIGARS...The manufacture of cigars and cigarettes is one of the leading industries in Jamaica. American cigarettes are available at all hotels and stores.

CLIMATE...The "high season," mid-December to mid-April, is absolutely perfect. Sunshine every day and cool nights. The summer season—June to October—has recently been discovered by United States tourists, with the result that this season almost equals the winter season in popularity. The constant trade winds keep the island far cooler than any resort on the United States eastern seaboard.

CLUBS...The Royal Jamaica Yacht Club, many golf clubs. *See* SPORTS. Others are the Jamaica Club, St. Andrew's, Liguanea Club. There are a Y.M.C.A. and a Y.W.C.A.

COMMON COURTESIES AND LOCAL CUSTOMS...Being British, Jamaica is on the conservative and formal side.

COMMUNICATIONS...Telephone, cables, radio and airmail.

CURRENCY...The British pound, half crown, florin, shilling and pence. The pound is worth about $2.80.

CUSTOMS REGULATIONS AND DOCUMENTS REQUIRED FOR UNITED STATES CITIZENS...No passports or visas required for a stay up to six months, providing you have a return ticket. Visitors are given a special tourist card on arrival which must be handed back to immigration authorities on departure. No household pets are allowed. Allowed in duty free: 1 carton of cigarettes, 50 cigars or ½ lb. tobacco; 1 pint of liquor or 1 quart of wine. No foreign rums. Smallpox vaccination required for return to the United States. Also for return carry some sort of proof of U.S. citizenship such as birth certificate, naturalization papers or old passport.

DRUG STORES . . . Good.

FAUNA . . . Red-tailed buzzard, hawk, parakeet, Blue Mountain duck; in all there are about 52 species of birds in Jamaica.

FLORA . . . Jamaica produces a great variety of plant life, wonderful fruits obtainable at all seasons of the year, beautiful trees, shrubs, flowering plants, ferns and exquisite orchids, the silk-cotton tree, or *Ceiba,* the poinciana.

FOOD . . . Mutton is one of the popular meats on the island. There is a great variety of locally produced beef and pork and vegetables. The residents of the island eat large quantities of fish. Milk is produced in large quantities.

GAMBLING . . . There is horse racing at Knutsford Park Race Course, Kingston. Marley Race Course is at Old Harbour, 24 miles from Kingston. Thirty-six meets a year, including 3 sweepstakes.

LAUNDRY AND DRY CLEANING . . . Laundry is good. Hotels have 24-hour service. Numerous excellent dry-cleaning establishments with 24-hour service.

LIQUOR . . . Jamaica rum is world famous. There is no other rum like it. It is, of course, cheaper here. There are imported liquors available too, at the same prices as at home.

MEDICAL FACILITIES . . . Excellent doctors, dentists and hospitals. The Kingston Public Hospital is the largest and there are two large private hospitals (the Nuttall Memorial Hostel and St. Joseph's Sanitarium) in Kingston, too. There are 24 other hospitals throughout the island including the excellent Andrews Memorial Hospital. The University College of the West Indies operates an up-to-date hospital.

MOTION PICTURES . . . There are some fine motion picture theaters in Kingston and its suburbs. The *Carib* (air-conditioned), *State* (air cooled), *Odeon, Tropical, Palace, Majestic, Rialto* and *Queens* (all open air). The latest English and American films are shown.

MUSIC . . . Concerts at the *Ward Theater,* Sutton Street, Kingston.

NIGHT CLUBS AND CABARETS . . . The two principal night clubs are the famous *Glass Bucket* and the *Rainbow Club. La Ronde* is a new Montego Bay night club and there are a few others on the north coast.

PHOTOGRAPHY . . . Black-and-white and color, still and movie film are available as well as cameras and other photographic equipment. Prices are reasonable. Stanley Motta, Ltd., and Swiss Stores, Ltd., will sell German cameras in bond for delivery on departure from the island at savings of about ⅓ over United States retail prices. Other firms include Lambert's Camera Corner, McGregor's and, at St. Ann's Bay, Hunter Bros. First-class developing facilities are available with 24-hour delivery.

In your collection of photographs you'll want to include Hope Gardens, Castleton Gardens, Nelson's Quarter Deck, Port Royal, and on the north coast, Fern Gully, Ocho Rios, Dunn's River and Shaw Park.

RESTAURANTS ... The Myrtle Bank Hotel has one of the better restaurants in Kingston, and there are many other restaurants, ice-cream and soda fountains, milk bars, etc., in different parts of the city. *Jamaica Arms* is an air-conditioned cocktail lounge serving seafood and all kinds of other good dishes. The *Balcony Inn* in downtown Kingston is air-conditioned, specializes in old Jamaican dishes, such as steaks and chickens broiled over pimento logs. The old English-style *Blue Mountain Inn,* seven miles away, has a first-class cocktail lounge, good food and wine served amidst beautiful surroundings. The *Continental* in Half Way Tree is another popular restaurant.

SHOPS AND STORES ... The largest stores in Kingston are on King Street and Harbour Street. Shops are open from 8:00 A.M. to 4:00 P.M. except on Wednesdays, when they close at 2:00 P.M., unless a large cruise ship is expected that day; then they will keep open until later in the afternoon for tourists. Among some of the shops are the Swiss Stores, English Shop; Men's Shop; Topper; Antoine De Paris, and Dadlanie; Issa's; Nathan's; L. A. Henriques Co.; Stivens Colosseum, Ltd.; Andrew H. B. Aguilar. The "free port" shops in Kingston and Montego Bay sell all types of luxury articles at about 50 per cent savings. The two airports have similar shops for liquor.

SPECTATOR SPORTS ... Cricket and football, horse racing, polo, yachting regattas, tennis and golf tournaments, boxing, cycle racing.

SPORTS ... Golf at many clubs; cards can be arranged. (Inquire of Pan American.) Some of the best are the Liguanea Golf Course, 2½ miles from Kingston; Constant Spring Golf Club, Cayman's Golf Club, 10 miles from Kingston; the Manchester Club, oldest course in Jamaica; the Upton Country Club, beautifully situated near Ocho Rios, for golf, tennis, swimming, riding. Tennis clubs include the Manchester Club, among others. Polo, horseback riding. There are several stables where you can hire horses for any length of time, and there are many beautiful bridle paths. Yachting—the Royal Jamaica Yacht Club holds annual regattas. Swimming is a popular pastime. In addition to the lovely beaches, Kingston has several fine sea-water pools, including Morgan's Harbour Beach Club where water skiing is popular. *See* WHERE TO GO below. Rafting is an exciting sport and safe because you are always in the hands of a skillful native pilot. Mountain hiking, trap shooting, and of course fishing. There is some of the finest fishing, both deep-sea and river, to be had; Black River, on the south coast, and the mouth of the Martha Brae near Falmouth in the north are two excellent fishing spots. Here you can catch tarpon and kingfish. In the rivers, mountain mullet, hognose mullet are to be had. Fly-fishing is not too satisfactory. Visitors should bring tackle similar to that used in Florida. No fishing licenses are required.

THEATERS ... Plays at the *Ward Theater* in Kingston.

TIME ... Same as United States Eastern Standard Time.

TIPPING ... About the same as at home, 10 to 15 per cent.

TRANSPORTATION ... Taxicabs are all metered. Drive-yourself cars are available. Motor buses connect all towns and villages. The Government Railway operates a service between Kingston and Montego Bay and Kingston and Port Antonio.

WATER ... Most modern pipeline supply.

WHAT TO BUY ... Rum, Scotch, tweeds, English doeskin, Kent brushes, Rolls razors, Royal Doulton and Spode china, leather goods, woolens, French perfumes and toilet waters are among the best buys.

WHAT TO WEAR ... Light summer clothes are worn the year around. Light suits for men and women. No overcoats are needed. Better take evening clothes for the night life in Kingston and the resorts. Also several swim suits and lots of beach attire.

WHERE TO GO—SIGHTSEEING ...

Kingston ... Don't miss a trip to the Institute of Jamaica, which is located on East Street. There is everything there representing the past and present of the island, Arawak carvings, ancient almanacs and live Jamaican animals. There are also the Art, Natural History Galleries and the Lecture Hall. This museum contains some interesting relics of the early days of the islands. The Myrtle Bank Hotel's private motor launch will take you up the harbor to Port Royal, the historic stronghold.

The Hope Botanic Gardens are a sight well worth seeing; located 5½ miles from Kingston at an elevation of 600 to 700 feet, there are over 200 acres under cultivation. There is a magnificent collection of orchids, tropical trees, citrus, coffee, fruit and other tropical plants. Near Hope Gardens, nearly a mile above the sea, is Newcastle, the site of the military station in the famous Blue Mountains.

You'll be interested in visiting "Morgan's Harbor," on the site of the old naval dockyard at Port Royal across the harbor from Kingston. The old naval dockyard was originally known as King's Yard when Port Royal was the capital of Jamaica and was the site of King's House, which was the residence of the Governor in the time of Captain Morgan. It is a 10-acre site and has been completely fitted out with luxurious facilities for tourists, such as salt-water swimming pool, white sand beach, a restaurant specializing in seafood, beach cabañas, dancing to calypso bands. It also includes a complete yacht marina with power and sailing boats for hire and all facilities for repairing and reprovisioning yachts. Guests at all the main hotels will be given complimentary membership to the club.

North Shore Resorts—Montego Bay ... Of all the lovely Caribbean resorts, Montego Bay on the North Coast is by far the best known to travelers. It is the seaport and chief town of the Parish of St. James, about 113 miles from Kingston. One of its features is its unsurpassed sea bathing. The deep blue water, the temperatures of which range from 70 degrees to 80 degrees the year round, is delightful. Here the gentle, prevailing trade winds make the Bay ideal for sailing. The few remaining traces of the island's aboriginal Arawaks can be seen at kitchen middens in the areas of Tryall, Cali-

Evening sailing at Montego Bay. Sailboats are available at the pier in front of Doctor's Cave.

fornia and Williamsfield, while an Arawak rock carving is to be seen at Kempshot. The town derives its name from manteca (or lard) which the Spaniards shipped from this picturesque bay. The ancient British fort still stands and the town's courthouse has been called a model of colonial architecture.

Montego Bay offers a wide variety of sports, including tennis, sea bathing, horse racing, polo, golf, badminton, fishing and alligator shooting. It also has some of the most beautiful hotels in the island. Among the internationally known hostels on the "Gold Coast" hotel strip are *Montego Beach* and *Sunset Lodge,* two beach-side hotels favored by the international set. Nearby is the luxurious beach resort community of *Round Hill,* while in town the *Ethelhart* offers guests modern service, excellent food and an open-air dance floor. *Casa Blanca Hotel* is another of Montego Bay's fine hotels; it is right on the Caribbean and has its own bathing club and beach. *Gloucester House,* a modern, conservative but excellent hotel on the Bay, is within a hundred yards of *Doctor's Cave Beach Club.* Directly behind Doctor's Cave Beach facing the Caribbean is the *Casa Montego. Beach View* and *Hoctor House* are very good hotels facing the sea. *Montego Inn* is in the center of the town, while *Half Moon Bay* and the *Montego Bay Motel* are situated about four miles out along the coast as is the excellent *Royal Caribbean* on picturesque Maloe Bay.

Doctor's Cave Beach Club is world famous for its coral sands and crystal-clear water. There is an excellent reef, and much of the area's social life centers around its Riviera-like setting. Membership is available to guests at all Montego Bay hotels, and water-skiing, skin-diving and sailing are among the many aquatic activities it offers.

Ten miles inland from Falmouth, in neighboring Trelawny, is *Good Hope,* an eighteenth century great-house in the center of a 6,000-acre cattle ranch. It offers horses and good trails for riding, and the easy, gracious life on a plantation home set in the midst of tall, waving coconut palms. It has its own private Florida Beach.

Rates in the Montego Bay area range from $12 to $18 during the summer and $21 to $30 during the winter, American Plan.

Ocho Rios... About 65 miles east of Montego Bay is Ocho Rios, glorious resort area offering visitors full range of accommodation and resort activities. The town is about 7 miles east of St. Ann's Bay, where Columbus established Sevilla Nueva, the first community in the island, and it is rich in scenic beauty and historical lore. At St. Ann's Bay is the *Windsor Hotel,* and in the Ocho Rios area are six hotels and several guest houses. On the shore are the luxurious *Jamaica Inn; Silver Seas,* a seaside hotel favoured by sportsmen; the cottage-type *Sans Souci;* the big popular *Tower Isle Hotel,* a self-contained resort with its distinctive Island Tower, a quarter mile offshore; the 53-room *Falcon Dip Hotel* near the Tower Isle; and the *Plantation Inn,* a gracious, colonial-type building overlooking the sea. And at Mamee Bay is the completely air-conditioned *Arawak Hotel.*

In this area you will find the Dunn's River Falls, where a beautiful, tree-shaded mountain stream tumbles into the blue Caribbean. This is one of the island's best-known beauty and bathing spots, and you can alternate between the warm salt surf and the cool fresh water of the falls. *Shaw Park Hotel* is nearby, located in an attractive mountain setting and surrounded by beautiful gardens. Rates in the Ocho Rios area are approximately the same as at Montego Bay.

In the Parish of St. Mary at Port Maria, 12 miles east of Ocho Rios, many internationally known personalities have established summer homes, and here is the *Casa Maria,* small, but very good. It is perched on a hillside overlooking the bay, and has its own salt-water swimming pool as well as a private sea beach. Nearby is *Trade Winds,* a motel-type, low-cost resort built on a cliffside.

Port Antonio... Located in the eastern area of the island has long been celebrated as a tourist resort. Here are the beautiful Boston Beach, San San Bay and the unplumbed Blue Hole (sometimes called Blue Lagoon). Tourists can take a 2-hour rafting trip down the Rio Grande on bamboo rafts guided by experts. The rafts hold three passengers. It is a most thrilling experience and a must for your trip. *Titchfield Hotel* and *Bonnie View* offer excellent accommodations, cuisine, and resort activities.

SOURCES OF FURTHER INFORMATION... The local tourist board is located at 80 Harbour Street. In New York it is at 630 Fifth Avenue; in Chicago, 312 Champlain Building and in Miami, 901 Ainsley Building. Pan American is at 117 Harbour Street, Kingston, and at the airport in Montego Bay.

MARTINIQUE

WEATHER IN FORT-DE-FRANCE—Lat. N14°38′—Alt. Approx. sea level

Temp.	JAN.	FEB.	MAR.	APR.	MAY	JUNE	JULY	AUG.	SEPT.	OCT.	NOV.	DEC.
Low	69°	69°	69°	71°	73°	74°	74°	74°	74°	73°	72°	70°
High	83°	84°	85°	86°	86°	86°	86°	87°	88°	87°	86°	84°
Average	76°	76°	77°	79°	80°	80°	80°	81°	81°	80°	79°	77°
Days of Rain	19	15	15	13	18	21	22	22	20	19	20	19

LOCATION ... One of the largest islands in the lesser Antilles, Martinique is situated halfway between Puerto Rico and Trinidad. Fort-de-France is 278 air miles from Trinidad.

CHARACTERISTICS ... Martinique, "where it is always summer," is known in the Caribbean as Madinina, queen of the Antilles. It is a place for tourists to enjoy tennis, swimming, sailing, fishing, water skiing and relaxing in an atmosphere of tropical beauty. The natives are friendly toward tourists and will do their best to be helpful. There is practically no night life and by 10:00 P.M every place is quiet.

POPULATION ... About 250,000 which include a mixture of many nationalities and races.

SIZE ... Approximately 50 miles long and 19 miles wide, Martinique has an area of 425 square miles.

CAPITAL ... Fort-de-France, a city of 66,000.

GOVERNMENT ... The former colony of Martinique became a department of France in 1947.

HOW TO GET THERE ... By Pan American DC6B Clipper, 4 hours from San Juan, Puerto Rico (which in turn is 5¾ hours from New York) including 3 island stops; and 2 hours from Trinidad. By ship from New York about 8 days, and from Trinidad 2 days.

ACCOMMODATIONS ... Have been limited, particularly during the winter season. However, the situation has improved with the opening of the *Hotel L'Imperatrice,* and the new *Auberge de L'Anse Mitan,* which has an excellent sunbathing beach. The *Lido Hotel* and the *Berkeley,* situated 4 miles and 2 miles from town, respectively, continue to be popular. The hotels offer very good French cuisine and excellent French wines. Other hotel accommodations, offering more economical rates, are also available: the *Hotel du Vieux Moulin,* the *Bristol* and the *Madiana.* Rates run up to about $33 for American plan, double in air-conditioned rooms. Lower rates at *Hotel de l'Europe* in the heart of town. Single $7, double $9, American plan.

ARTS ... Museums and native crafts: Museum of Saint-Pierre, birthplace of Empress Josephine, at Trois-Ilets; native pottery, straw hats and baskets, Martinican dolls, woodcarving ... Museum of Fort Saint Louis.

BANKS ... Bank of Martinique, a private bank, represents the French-American Banking Corporation; Credit Martiniquais represents the Royal Bank of Canada and the National City Bank of New York; Banque Nationale pour le Commerce et l'Industrie (private bank).

CALENDAR OF HOLIDAYS ... All Catholic holidays, plus Bastille Day on July 14; November 11, Armistice Day; May 1, Labor Day; and the famous carnival on Mardi Gras; the funeral of Carnival King on Ash Wednesday, the only spectacle of its kind, with the entire population mourning. Stores are closed on all these days and usually every Saturday afternoon and Sunday.

CIGARETTES AND TOBACCO ... American and English cigarettes are available but expensive, about 45 cents a pack. French tobacco and cigarettes are available. No local brands.

CLIMATE ... The climate is summer like all the year round. Fort-de-France is rather hot but the nights are cool. See weather chart.

CLUBS ... There are four clubs in Fort-de-France, the Lido Club, the Cercle, the Fort Royal, and the Yacht Club, which are open to tourists without any special authorization.

COMMON COURTESIES AND LOCAL CUSTOMS ... Every time people meet or leave each other, they shake hands. There is no obligation for men to wear a coat and tie in restaurants. One can wear shorts, slacks, or beach dresses for shopping in town.

COMMUNICATIONS ... Telephone and cable services are available. Radio telephone with nearly all the world.

CURRENCY ... The monetary unit is the franc. American dollars can be exchanged at the present rate of 420 francs to $1.

CUSTOMS REGULATIONS AND DOCUMENTS REQUIRED FOR UNITED STATES CITIZENS ... Proof of citizenship, smallpox vaccination certificate, continuation or return ticket are the only documents required for a stay up to 3 months—cholera and yellow fever certificates if coming from infected areas. Duty free imports: 1,000 cigarettes, 1 bottle of liquor.

DRUG STORES ... French drug stores sell only drugs.

ELECTRIC CURRENT ... The voltage in hotels is 110–115 volts, 50 cycles, A.C. You need a converter plug for your electric appliances.

FAUNA... There are few species of birds and mongooses. Specimens of the local fauna can be seen at the museum of Fort Saint Louis. In certain villages, fights between snakes and mongooses are arranged as a tourist attraction, if you can take that sort of thing.

FLORA... There is a great variety of flowers in Martinique: hibiscus, wild orchids, Bougainvillaea, Chinese hats, antoriums, lauriers, ixoras, and many others. The vegetation is very dense and tropical (arborescent ferns). The main plantations raise sugar cane, bananas, pineapples, coffee and cocoa.

FOOD... Martinique has good native dishes, such as colombo, made with Indian seeds comparable to curry and saffron, peeled and cooked with pork or beef and eaten with rice. A delicious dish is crabs stuffed with rice. Crayfish are also very good, the size of a small lobster. Try calalou soup made from herbs, and gombos eaten with rice and fried codfish. A delightful dish is the yam baked in its own skin with cheese and butter. You must taste the wonderful salad of palm heart or coconut heart. Milk here is safe to drink.

GAMBLING... No gambling of any kind.

LANGUAGE... French is the official language, but you will have little difficulty when using only English.

LAUNDRY AND DRY CLEANING... Dry cleaning is not reliable.

LIQUOR... The chief native drink is the famous rum punch, which is inexpensive, as are American drinks—whiskies (no bourbon), beers, colas, and others. Daiquiri is now a popular drink. Hotel bars and others are open till 10:00 P.M.

MEDICAL FACILITIES... There are no American hospitals. The Clinics St. Paul and Roseau are about the best private clinics.

MOTION PICTURES... There are five motion picture theaters in Fort-de-France, including one modern air-conditioned theater, showing mostly French and American films with French sound track.

MUSIC... Martinique is renowned as being the home of the beguine. Native orchestras and dancers excel at this fascinating music and dance.

NIGHT CLUBS... There are dances from time to time at the members' club of the Lido Hotel. Dances in many places during Carnival season.

PHOTOGRAPHY... Cameras, movie films, black-and-white or color, and photo equipment are all available. Prices are about the same as in United States. Developing takes two days.

RELIGION... Martinique is almost entirely Roman Catholic; however, other denominations are represented.

RESTAURANTS... *Chez Etienne* and the *Hotel de l'Europe* both in town, are considered the best. *Manoir,* situated on a hill five minutes from town also has excellent food. Ask for snails, pâté de foie gras, and crayfish bouquet. The *Lido* and *Berkeley* Hotels are also very good. A good meal will cost $5, aperitif and wine included.

SHOPS AND STORES... The shopping district is close to PAA's office. At Roger Albert you can find perfumes very cheap, handicrafts, Martinican dolls, French silver, crystal. Beaufrand offers perfumes, china. Mad has native crafts, such as straw hats and baskets. Merlande and Marsan have nice materials, clothing, shoes, etc. La Regence and La Rotonde have champagne and other French wines. Le Foyer Modern, home furnishings. Bally, Survi and Clement will provide you with Martinican rum. These shops are not too expensive. They are open from 8:30 A.M. to 12:00, and from 2:30 P.M. to 5:00 P.M. La Malle des Indes sells antiques.

SPECTATOR SPORTS . . . Football every Sunday at the Stadium. Cock fighting is popular.

SPORTS . . . Only tennis and water skiing.

THEATERS . . . A troupe from France comes every year.

TIME . . . One hour later than U.S. Eastern Standard Time.

TRANSPORTATION . . . Buses are used mostly by the natives. Better take a taxi that will drive you for a very reasonable rate. Self-drive auto rentals are available at the rate of $9 per day.

WATER . . . Drinking local water is safe, and good, inexpensive locally-bottled mineral water is plentiful (Didier water).

WHAT TO BUY . . . See SHOPS AND STORES.

WHAT TO WEAR . . . Only washable summer clothes. Don't forget your swimming suit, dark glasses, raincoat, and a light jacket.

WHERE TO GO—SIGHTSEEING . . .

Martinique . . . Is world famous for the eruption of Mt. Pelée in 1902, which wiped out the entire population (40,000) of the former capital city of St. Pierre in three minutes. There was only one survivor, a prisoner held in an underground dungeon, who died soon after, it is said, from the effects of radioactivity. Ruins of the city, called the "Pompeii of the New World," afford an interesting climax to a trip along the spectacular west coast of the island, with its fishing villages, tropical beaches, cliffs and coves. The volcanic museum at the foot of Mt. Pelée vividly impresses the visitor with the violence of this catastrophe.

Martinique is also renowned as the birthplace of Napoleon's Empress Josephine, whose marble statue stands in the center of the Savanna, the public park in Fort-de-France. Across the beautiful Bay of Fort-de-France, at Trois-Ilets near a native pottery factory, a small museum commemorates Josephine's birthplace. In Fort-de-France, ancient Fort Royal (now Fort St. Louis) was the scene of fierce battles among the Dutch, French and English, as the island changed hands during the seventeenth and eighteenth centuries.

Off the southwest coast of the island rises the great Diamond Rock, which was commissioned as a ship by the British Navy in the eighteenth century. For over ten years, H.M.S. Diamond Rock held out against the French. This is also the location of the island's most beautiful beach, Diamond, facing Diamond Rock.

SOURCES OF FURTHER INFORMATION . . . Martinique Tourist Bureau, Fort-de-France. The Société de Commerce et de Representation Bord de Mer specializes in tours and sightseeing. Pan Am's agent here is L. de la Houssaye & Cie, 1 rue Liberte (Tel 25.94).

NASSAU
AND THE BAHAMAS

WEATHER IN NASSAU—Lat. N25°05'—Alt. Approx. sea level

Temp.	JAN.	FEB.	MAR.	APR.	MAY	JUNE	JULY	AUG.	SEPT.	OCT.	NOV.	DEC.
Low	67°	67°	68°	69°	72°	75°	76°	76°	76°	75°	71°	69°
High	76°	77°	78°	80°	83°	86°	88°	88°	87°	85°	80°	78°
Average	72°	72°	73°	75°	78°	81°	82°	82°	82°	80°	76°	74°
Days of Rain	3	4	2	4	9	10	15	12	13	15	7	6

LOCATION ... Scattered over more than 70,000 square miles of sea, the Bahamas are composed of nearly 700 islands and about 2,400 cays. The islands extend from a point 60 miles east of Palm Beach to the north of Haiti in a 760-mile arc stretching in a south-easterly direction. Important islands include New Providence, site of Nassau, Abaco, Andros, the Biminis, Berry Islands, Eleuthera, Exuma, Grand Bahama, Harbor Island, San Salvador, Spanish Wells, Inagua, Cat Island and Long Island.

CHARACTERISTICS ... The Bahamas form a chain of beautiful semi-tropical islands that have a charming atmosphere and some of the finest beaches and sea bathing anywhere. Nassau, the most sophisticated and modern of the resorts in the Bahamas, is quaintly British, decorous and utterly lovely. Spend your days basking on world-famous Paradise Beach. Spend the evening dancing under the Bahamian moon on the terrace of one of Nassau's famed resort hotels, later making the rounds of the native night clubs and cabarets. Nassau offers its visitors a royal welcome and goes all out to make them comfortable.

POPULATION ... Estimated at about 85,000, with Nassau and New Providence Island totaling about half that figure.

SIZE ... The total land area of the group is approximately 4,466 square miles, about half the area of Massachusetts.

CAPITAL ... Nassau, on the island of New Providence, which is 21 miles long and 7 miles wide at its widest point; population about 45,000.

GOVERNMENT... The Government of the Bahamas is a system analogous to Great Britain (not a Crown Colony). Since 1718, the Governor has been appointed by the British Crown.

HOW TO GET THERE... By Pan American Clipper, Nassau is only 50 minutes flying time from Miami, and 4 hours flying time direct from New York. By ship, overnight from Miami, 2½ days from New York.

ACCOMMODATIONS... Nassau has some of the most luxurious and beautiful hotels to be found anywhere. The five largest are the *British Colonial, Ft. Montagu Beach, Emerald Beach, Nassau Beach Lodge* and the *Royal Victoria*. Others are *Carlton House, Olympia Hotel, Royal Elizabeth, Lucerne Hotel, Parliament Hotel, Prince George Hotel, Windsor Hotel, Dolphin Hotel* and *Towne Hotel*.

Apartment houses, private homes with accommodation for rent, seaside villas and magnificent Bahamian homes can also be rented. Residential clubs are the *Balmoral Club, Coral Harbour* and the *Pilot House Club*. Guest houses include, *Buena Vista, Loft House, Van Zelan Guest House, Victoria Guest House* and *Harbour View*. The winter season is the most fashionable and formal time of year in Nassau. Winter rates vary widely. Typical are the *British Colonial Hotel*, $22 and $42 single, $37 to $52 double, Modified American Plan (breakfast and dinner); *Royal Victoria Hotel*, $23–$26 single, $38–$46 double, Modified American Plan; *Pilot House Club*, $12–$15 single, $18–$30 double, European Plan; *Carlton House*, $12 single, $16–$24 double, European Plan; *Buena Vista*, $10 single, $14 double, European Plan. *Grosvenor Close Apartments* from $65 per week for one-bedroom apartments, from $75 for two-bedroom apartments; *Harbour View*, $8–$12 single, $12–$16 double European Plan. All these rates are reduced substantially for the low-cost summer season from May 1 to December 15.

ARTS... Art exhibitions, usually staged as charity benefits, take place in the winter season. The Nassau Public Library has an interesting display of museum relics.

BANKS... Royal Bank of Canada; Barclay's Bank; Canadian Bank of Commerce; Bank of Nova Scotia. Banking hours: 9 to 1.

CALENDAR OF HOLIDAYS... New Year's Day; Good Friday; Easter Monday; Whitmonday (day following Whitsunday); May 24, Empire Day; the Queen's Birthday (celebrated by Proclamation); August Bank Holiday (first Monday); October 12, Columbus Day; Christmas Day; December 26, Boxing Day (called "Boxing Day" by the British because in the old days it was the custom to give Christmas "boxes" of food, clothing, etc., to one's servants and to the poor and needy).

CLIMATE... The weather is warm and sunny and ideal for visiting any time of the year, although by tradition the social season is Christmas to Easter. Some winter evenings are cool.

CLUBS... Bahamian Club; Bahamas Country Club; Balmoral Club; Nassau Yacht Club; Pilot House Club; Royal Nassau Sailing

Club; Porcupine Club; Racquets Club (residential club); Coral Harbour Club; Lions Club. For golf and tennis clubs, see SPORTS.

COMMON COURTESIES AND LOCAL CUSTOMS ... Abbreviated sun-dresses, very short shorts, and bra and halter ensembles are *not* worn on the public streets. As in Britain all traffic moves on the left-hand side of the road. Also, when walking along the sidewalk, keep to the left.

COMMUNICATIONS ... Calls to any part of the world are made by radio-telephone service and cables by radio-teletype. Radio station ZNS broadcasts on 1540 kc/s, and provides service to visiting yachtsmen by regularly scheduled bulletins. Airmail rate to U.S., 6d or 7 cents per half ounce.

CURRENCY ... The Bahamian pound based on the British sterling system is currently worth about $2.80 U.S., but American and Canadian dollars are acceptable generally.

CUSTOMS REGULATIONS AND DOCUMENTS REQUIRED FOR UNITED STATES CITIZENS ... No passports or visas are required, but you will need some proof of nationality. You may take in 200 cigarettes and 1 quart of liquor, unrestricted amounts of dollars, but not more than £ 5 in Bahamian, Bermudian, Jamaican or Bank of England notes.

DRUG STORES ... Plentiful and modern, similar to those in the United States, but without soda fountains.

ELECTRIC CURRENT ... 115 volts, 60 cycles, A.C. All plugs and electrical appliances are the same as standard United States equipment.

FAUNA ... Raccoon on New Providence; wild hogs, wild horses, donkeys, cattle on some of the islands; the iguana on Andros; many birds, including the flamingo, considered the national bird on Inagua Island. For fish, *see* SPORTS.

FLORA ... Many varieties with never a time when some flowers are not in bloom. Peak blossom time is early summer with royal poinciana trees, Easter lilies, passion flowers. Poinsettias at Christmas time. Radiant hibiscus, oleander, Bougainvillaea and other exotic flowers.

FOOD ... With the exception of vegetables and fish, most food is imported from other countries. Meat from the United States, Canada and Australia. Bahamian specialty dishes include turtle soup and turtle pie, conch chowder, fish chowder, baked Nassau grouper with peas and rice, broiled native crawfish, or fillets of any of the famous Bahamian food fish, such as kingfish and dolphin. Be sure to try soursop ice cream and mango ice cream. Other native deserts include coconut pie, pudding and ice cream, and guava duff.

GAMBLING ... During the winter season a Government-supervised Casino operates at the Bahamian Club.

LANGUAGE ... English, of course, with British undertones, which some find fascinating.

LAUNDRY AND DRY CLEANING ... Excellent, modern, speedy service.

LIQUOR ... All brands are available and prices are much lower than at home. Scotch for example is about $3.50 a fifth, rum $1.50.

MEDICAL FACILITIES ... There's a new modern hospital and excellent doctors.

MOTION PICTURES ... The *Savoy*, with first-run American pictures.

MUSIC ... There's a wealth of native music in the form of Bahamian folk songs and calypsos, heard nightly at the hotels, or in the night clubs and cabarets, or over the local radio stations. Also, during the winter season. well-known guest artists perform.

NIGHT CLUBS & CABARETS: Native spots include *Chez Paul Meres' Club, Blackbeard's Tavern, Dirty Dick's Bar, Captain Kidd's Inn, The Cat and Fiddle Club*, the *Pirate's Den, Junkanoo Club, The Club Crazee* and the *Silver Slipper Club*.

PHOTOGRAPHY ... Nassau is an excellent place to buy cameras and photo equipment. All types of film are available, also developing facilities. The quality of work is reasonably good. There is 24-hour service on developing. Lightbourne's Pharmacy is a particularly good place.

RELIGION ... Twenty-eight denominations are represented in Nassau.

RESTAURANTS ... There are few restaurants, as such, in Nassau. The hotel dining rooms have wonderful food, and even though you are not staying there, you should arrange to dine at Cumberland House or Buena Vista, famous for their Bahamian dishes. Places to try are the *Grand Central* and *City Garden Club; Shell Room; Golden Dragon*. Black's *Candy Kitchen* and the *El-Bo-Room*, two American-style soda fountains, also run a restaurant service.

SHOPS AND STORES ... Nassau has wonderful shops where you can buy almost anything. Specializing in fabrics are the Windsor Shop, the Nassau Shop, West of England Store, the Jaeger Shop, Solomon's Mines, Barry's, the Park Store, and W. J. Saunders. Women's resort fashions at Stewart's, Ambrosine, Mademoiselle, Sally and Vera's. Gifts at Treasure Traders, the City Gift Shop, the Island Bookshop and the Chinese Emporium. French perfumes at the Paris Shop, Vanito, the New Colonial Pharmacy and the City Pharmacy. Shops close at noon on Fridays, stay open late on Saturdays.

SPECTATOR SPORTS ... Yachting regattas, local and international; championship-caliber golf and tennis tournaments; Bahamas-wide fishing tournaments; horse racing every Tuesday and Friday in winter at Hobby Horse Hall; boxing and wrestling at Nassau Stadium; cricket; soccer; rugby football; basketball; softball; water-skiing exhibitions.

SPORTS ... Golf and tennis at the Bahamas County Club; tennis at Paradise Beach, Fort Montague Beach Hotel, British Colonial Hotel; badminton at the Nassau Stadium; spear-fishing; water-skiing; horseback riding; sailboats, bicycles, motor bikes and cars for hire.

FISHING . . . There are many different varieties of game fish in Bahamian waters, the principal fighting game fish being amberjack, African pompano, barracuda, bonefish, bonito, dolphin, grouper, jack, kingfish, mackerel, mako, blue marlin, permit, sailfish, shark, snapper, tarpon, albacore tuna, Allison tuna (the mighty bluefin tuna which run off Bimini and Cat Cay each May and June), and the fighting wahoo, a game fish which, pound for pound, puts up the scrappiest fight of any fish. There are also the crawfish and three different kinds of turtle. Throughout the year, visitors may compete in fishing tournaments.

TIME . . . Same as Eastern Standard Time.

TIPPING . . . Same as at home, about 10 to 15 per cent.

TOURIST TAXES . . . If you stay less than 48 hours, 85 cents; if you stay more than 48 hours, $1.70 on departure.

TRANSPORTATION . . . Taxis, 28 cents for the first mile and 14 cents each additional mile, per person; picturesque horse-drawn carriages, 18 cents per mile per passenger, or $1.40 an hour; bicycles, 35 cents an hour, $1.50 a day, $7 a week; motor bikes, $3 a day, $18 a week. You can hire English sports cars for about $10 a day.

WATER . . . Excellent, but if you prefer, hotels will serve you bottled water.

WHAT TO BUY . . . Woolens, tweeds, silver, doeskin gloves and doeskin fabric, English brushes, pipes and leather goods, French perfumes, cosmetics and lingerie, liquor, china and porcelain, tortoise-shell articles—and, of course, the colorful native straw and sisal bags, hats, mats, coasters, and native bracelets and necklaces of dyed fish scales or shells.

WHAT TO WEAR . . . Lightweight summer clothes. Sports shirts and shorts or slacks for men; washable spectator dresses or sundresses for women; shirt-type blouses and shorts are quite acceptable for women, but no abbreviated dress is worn on public thoroughfares in Nassau. Bring swimsuits of course. Formal dress is necessary for winter season from December 15 through Easter.

WHERE TO GO—SIGHTSEEING . . .

Nassau . . . There are many interesting places to see in Nassau. You can take sightseeing tours available locally or go around on your own. A trip to Nassau's forts should be included. Fort Charlotte, with its eerie dungeons, about one mile west of Rawson Square, is the largest. It commands the western entrance to the harbor. Nassau's streets are lined with historic old churches and beautiful colonial houses and there are some interesting public buildings on Bay Street.

Blackbeard's Tower, now the ruin of an old watch tower, overlooks Tower Heights Village, 4 miles east of Nassau. Queen's Staircase, Elizabeth Avenue, is a flight of 66 steps said to be hewn out of solid rock by hand, and it leads to Fort Fincastle. Nearby on Bennett's Hill is the Water Tower, 126 feet high. Visitors may go to the top by elevator, where they will get a wonderful view of the city and harbor. Paradise Beach, one of the world's most famous beaches, is a 10-minute boat ride from Prince George's Wharf. Here there are bath houses, cabañas, tennis courts, bar, restaurant, game rooms, everything you can possibly want. Visit the famous Sea Gardens, too.

Out Islands . . . Island settlements scattered throughout the Bahamian archipelago are rapidly emerging as miniature resorts in their own right. There are scheduled and chartered air services, as well as regular mail boats from Nassau to the Out Islands. Unless otherwise noted, all rates given are summer rates.

Abaco . . . Great and Little Abaco northernmost of the Bahama islands are growing in popularity with sportsmen. There are several fishing camps on these Cays which provide accommodations. The best known are Green Turtle Cay, Long Bay Estates, New Plymouth Inn and The Other Shore. All these camps operate on Modified American and European Plan during the winter season and prices range from $10.00 to $20.00 per day.

Andros . . . The largest Island of the Bahamas, 35 miles southwest of Nassau. Andros Town and Andros Yacht Club are two new resort ventures of the Island and accommodations are available at the smart *Lighthouse Club*. On Pot Cay, Andros, *Bang Bang Club* offers fine game fishing and comfortable accommodations. American Plan rates vary from $27 to $50 per day depending on season and fishing facilities.

Bimini . . . Bimini, the nearest Bahamian island to the U.S. mainland, is regarded as "the gateway to the Bahamas" by the thousands of yachtsmen who make it their port of entry. Bimini is also famous for its big-game fishing, notably the annual tuna and marlin fishing, for its splendid bonefishing and fighters. Additional information on fishing can be obtained from the Executive Secretary of the Bimini Big Game Fishing Club. Accommodations include *Anchors Aweigh Hotel*, $18 to $20 American Plan; the *Compleat Angler*, $8 European Plan; *Seacrest*, $14 American Plan, $6 to $8 European Plan; and *Brown's Hotel*, $13 American Plan.

Governor's Harbor, Eleuthera . . . This lovely Out Island resort was the site of the first attempt at permanent settlement of the Bahamas by the British around 1648. Today, Governor's Harbor here is one of the most progressive of Out Island resorts, and offers fine accommodations to year-round visitors. Accommodations, all American Plan, include *Belmont*, $15 per person; *Buccaneer Club*, open from December 15 to April at $15; and *French Leave*, $25 single, $44 double.

Harbor Island, Eleuthera . . . This historic old settlement, known for its Pink Beach of pink coral sand, is just off the northeast tip of Eleuthera, and offers modern facilities and excellent resort accommodations. Accommodations, all American Plan, include the *Little Boarding House*, $10 to $12 a day per person; *Picaroon Cove Club*, $22 double and up; *Pink Sands Lodge* and *Sea View Hotel* (jointly operated), $20 to $28 a day single, $12 to $16 double.

Nassau's Straw Market at Rawson Square is a popular spot.

Coconut palms cast patterns of shade on Nassau's charming beaches of white sand.

Rock Sound, Eleuthera ... An old settlement is the site of the modern *Rock Sound Club,* a tiny resort on its own. Here there is a salt-water swimming pool, golf course, tennis courts, guest cottages with private baths and fine food; open from November 15 to June 15 with American Plan rates of $10 per person, except from January to April when rates are $30 double.

SOURCES OF FURTHER INFORMATION ... The Nassau Development Board is on Bay Street, Nassau. Principal travel agents are on Bay, Frederick and Shirley Streets. Pan American's office is on Mathew Avenue. In New York write the Nassau Bahamas Information Bureau, 620 Fifth Ave., New York, N. Y.

NETHERLANDS ANTILLES

WEATHER IN CURAÇAO—Lat. N12°15'—Alt. Approx. sea level

Temp.	JAN.	FEB.	MAR.	APR.	MAY	JUNE	JULY	AUG.	SEPT.	OCT.	NOV.	DEC.
Low	74°	74°	75°	76°	78°	78°	78°	78°	78°	77°	76°	75°
High	84°	85°	85°	86°	88°	88°	88°	88°	90°	89°	88°	88°
Average	79°	80°	80°	81°	83°	83°	83°	83°	84°	83°	82°	82°

LOCATION ... The territory of the Netherlands Antilles (formerly Netherlands West Indies) consists of the islands of Curaçao, Aruba and Bonaire off the coast of Venezuela and a group of small islands at the north end of the Leeward Islands 500 miles away.

CHARACTERISTICS ... Curaçao has the quaint fairy-tale charm of The Netherlands itself. The gabled houses and bridges are all part of the illusion. This is a wonderful spot to buy perfumes and other luxury items. It is also a delightful place to relax.

POPULATION ... Approximately 184,000, of which 121,198 live on the island of Curaçao. Aruba has about 63,000 inhabitants.

SIZE ... Curaçao is 36 miles long and 2½ to 7 miles wide. Aruba is 19 miles long and about 5 miles wide.

CAPITAL ... Willemstad, population 46,899.

GOVERNMENT ... Formerly a Dutch colony, Curaçao since 1950 is an overseas territory, an integral part of the Kingdom of The Netherlands but with complete freedom in its internal affairs.

HOW TO GET THERE ... By Pan American Clipper, one-stop flights from New York, 8 hours; or service from Miami, about 6½ hours elapsed time. By ship about 4 days.

ACCOMMODATIONS ... Built over Curaçao's famous fortress with spectacular view is the fabulous brand new air-conditioned *Curaçao Intercontinental* in the center of Willemstad, with beautiful terraces, gardens, dining rooms and a split-level swimming pool with port holes for spectators. Rates are $16.50 up double without meals between mid-December and mid-April, about $2 less other times.

Other good hotels in the capital include the *Americano*, which faces the harbor, rates $8 and up, single; *Piscadera Bay Club*, which offers sea bathing, $16 and up single with three meals daily; *Hotel Avila*, with salt-water swimming pool, $11.50 and up; *Hotel Bellevue*, $4.50 and up; *Hotel San Marco* in the business center, rates $9.25 and up. Rates mentioned are modified European Plan which includes breakfast; some hotels also offer American Plan (all three meals).

ARTS ... The Curaçao Museum, housed in a restored building of old Dutch architecture, contains beautiful paintings, furniture, decorations and other antiques of past centuries, as well as exhibits of recent history of the island. Specimens of all trees and plants found on the island grow in its spacious gardens.

BANKS ... Maduro and Curiel's Bank, Hollandsche Bank Unie, Edwards, Henriquez and Co.'s Bank, and the Curaçao Bank, which is the Government-owned bank.

CIGARETTES AND TOBACCO ... Same as at home.

CLIMATE ... Curaçao is famed for its truly Caribbean climate. The sun shines almost continually and cool breezes prevail. The ideal time to visit Curaçao is the end of November to May. The rainfall is scant (22 inches per year), with short showers.

CLUBS ... Club de Gezelligheid, Van Engelen Club, Kwiek Club; Bellevue Country Club, Piscadera Bay Club with guest rooms. Cards may be arranged. (Inquire of the local Tourist Commission.) Lions and Rotary Clubs are here.

COMMUNICATIONS ... Telephone and telegraph to the United States. For further information apply to Landsradio and Telefoondienst: Postoffice building, Handelskade 18, Hato Airport and All America Cables and Radio, Inc., Handelskade 26.

CURRENCY ... The monetary unit is the guilder, worth about 53 cents. Most stores accept United States currency.

CUSTOMS REGULATIONS AND DOCUMENTS REQUIRED FOR UNITED STATES CITIZENS ... Birth certificate or naturalization papers. Re-entry permit for resident aliens. No passport, no visa. Smallpox vaccination and yellow fever certificate required if coming from a yellow fever area. Visitors who stay on the island 24 hours or less need no documents except some proof of nationality.

DRUG STORES ... Modern as at home. Soda fountains.

ELECTRIC CURRENT ... 120 volts, A.C., 50 cycles (60 in Aruba).

FOOD ... Creole food is the specialty of the island; you'll also have Dutch, Spanish, Oriental and American food.

GAMBLING ... There's a casino in the new Intercontinental Hotel.

LANGUAGE ... Dutch, Spanish and English. Also a dialect called *papiamento*.

LAUNDRY AND DRY CLEANING ... Modern in Willemstad.

LIQUOR ... Curaçao is the famous native liqueur. There are also Holland gin, Holland beer and imported whiskies to be had at more reasonable prices than at home.

MEDICAL FACILITIES ... The St. Elizabeth and the Green Cross Hospitals are excellent.

MOTION PICTURES ... Modern movie theaters.

NIGHT CLUBS AND CABARETS ... The *Kinikini Room* at the Hotel Curaçao Intercontinental, *Club Chobolobo,* Chobolobo Estate, Schottegat Road and *Piscadera Bay Club* and *Club Bahia.*

PHOTOGRAPHY ... All kinds of black-and-white and color still and movie film available at about the same prices as in the United States. Black-and-white developing and printing within 24 hours. Large choice of cameras and photo equipment (European and American) at prices lower than in the United States.

RELIGION ... Protestant, Roman Catholic churches and Jewish synagogues, one of which is the oldest in the Americas.

RESTAURANTS ... *Avila Hotel* for wonderful food. The *Lido* for quick lunches. The *Afro* restaurant, *Far East* and *Chunking* for Chinese and American dishes. *Piscadera Bay Club* for luncheon and dinner in a seabreeze, the *Old Dutch Tavern* for Dutch and Indonesian food in a seventeenth-century Dutch setting, the *Club Chobolobo* for cocktails and dinner dancing. Other good ones are the *Hotel Americano* and *Restaurant Hato Airport.* Check also on the new *Curaçao Intercontinental.*

SHOPS AND STORES ... Curaçao, because of its low import duty of 3.3 per cent on nearly all goods, is one of the greatest shopping centers. *See* WHAT TO BUY.

SPECTATOR SPORTS ... Tennis, basketball, softball and baseball. Soccer at Curaçao's Rif Stadium and many club fields.

SPORTS ... In Curaçao, golf at the Shell Golf Club, tennis and basketball at the Kwiek Club, Curaçao Sport and Van Engelen Club. Also fishing, horseback riding, soccer, baseball and sailing.

TIME ... One-half hour later than United States Eastern Standard Time.

TIPPING ... About the usual 10 to 15 per cent.

TRANSPORTATION ... Taxis are plentiful; before taking a taxi it is wise to know whether the driver is quoting the fare in American currency. Ask the driver for a copy of the official tariff. For all rides in town, taxi fares increase 50 per cent between 10:00 P.M. and 6:00 A.M. For all trips out of town, fares are 25 per cent higher between 10:00 P.M. and midnight and 50 per cent higher after that. Station-wagon fares are lower than taxi fares. But you should arrange the fare with the driver before starting off. There is good bus service, too.

WATER ... Drinking water is safe to drink right from the tap.

WHAT TO BUY ... European cameras and photographic accessories, jewelry, liquor and liqueurs (among them the locally made Curaçao Liqueur) are high on the list of articles bought by tourists. Swiss watches can be purchased here cheaper than any other place in the world, because of the low import duty. French perfumes (all the famous makes) are very cheap. Silk and carved ivory from the Orient, Brazilian and Argentine leather goods, Portuguese embroideries and laces, Spanish shawls, Irish linen, Panama hats. Delft Blue porcelain, silverware and brassware, Dutch dolls for souvenirs are among the "wonderful buys" on this island.

WHAT TO WEAR . . . Lightweight summer clothing, for every season. Take a raincoat along.

WHERE TO GO—SIGHTSEEING . . .

Curaçao . . . Willemstad, with its gabled roofs and narrow buildings, looks like The Netherlands. There are many ancient buildings to be seen in the city itself. You should go to see the oldest Protestant church on the Islands, built in 1769, located on the square right behind Government House. The synagogue dates back to 1732. You will be interested in seeing Franklin D. Roosevelt House, the mansion and offices of the American Consul, located on the top of Ararat Hill, from which you get a magnificent view of Willemstad and the Caribbean.

The business as well as the old residential section of the city have magnificent examples of Dutch colonial architecture; the suburbs of Willemstad and the housing projects adjacent to the oil refinery have strikingly modern residences amidst well-kept gardens.

Less than two miles from Willemstad's shopping center is the swank resort of Piscadera Bay. Here is beautiful *Piscadera Bay Club;* founded as a private club it has now added several pavilions with the most modern of resort hotel facilities, which are open to visitors. There is a beautiful sandy beach and tennis courts; guests have the privileges of the nearby Shell Golf Club.

Take a trip across the pontoon bridge called the Queen Emma to Punda, the oldest section of Willemstad, and see the floating market, small Caribbean schooners filled with fruits and vegetables from the neighboring Latin-American republics. Next you are in Fort Amsterdam, where the official residence of the Governor of The Netherlands Antilles is located. Fifteen minutes from town by car is the historical Jewish Cemetery, one of the oldest Caucasian cemeteries in the Western Hemisphere. You should take a trip (55 minutes by car) to the famous coral cavern of Boca Tabla.

Aruba . . . The island of Aruba, though smaller than Curaçao, is an important oil-refining center. The capital, Oranjestad, is typically Dutch. Aruba's Palm Beach is one of the finest in the West Indies. It is 3 miles long. Bathing and sailing here are excellent. This is also one of the great fishing centers of the island. Aruba, as well as Willemstad, has a wonderful shopping center and a beautiful residential section of modern homes, club buildings, etc., painted in the gayest of colors. Stay at the *Strand Hotel,* which faces the Caribbean. Other good ones are *Basi Ruti* on Palm Beach and the *Scala,* a commercial hotel in the center of Oranjestad. The *Trocadero* restaurant on the schooner harbor is excellent.

SOURCES OF FURTHER INFORMATION . . . The Curaçao Tourist Bureau at Kerkstraat 8a has maps, folders and information. S. E. L. Maduro and Sons, at Ruyterplein 4, are agents for Pan American in Willemstad. In New York the Netherlands West Indies Tourist Bureau is located at 475 Fifth Avenue.

PUERTO RICO

WEATHER IN SAN JUAN—Lat. N18°28′—Alt. 20′

Temp.	JAN.	FEB.	MAR.	APR.	MAY	JUNE	JULY	AUG.	SEPT.	OCT.	NOV.	DEC.
Low	70°	69°	70°	71°	73°	74°	75°	75°	75°	75°	73°	71°
High	80°	80°	81°	82°	84°	85°	85°	85°	86°	86°	84°	81°
Average	75°	75°	75°	77°	79°	80°	80°	81°	81°	80°	79°	76°

LOCATION ... Puerto Rico lies between the Atlantic Ocean and the Caribbean. Ciudad Trujillo is about 45 miles to the west, and St. Thomas, Virgin Islands, is 75 miles to the east of San Juan.

CHARACTERISTICS ... You really are "at home abroad" in Puerto Rico, for it is part of the United States, yet truly foreign in atmosphere. It has been called the most European of the Caribbean countries and with justice. The beaches are wonderful, the hotels among the most luxurious, the food familiar or exotic depending on your taste. Yet you have a wonderful feeling of being at home in Puerto Rico despite the fact that chaperones are still the fashion and that coffee and banana trees flourish before your eyes. Fishermen will be particularly happy there. The sun shines the year round.

POPULATION ... 2,210,703 (1950–51 census), about equal to the inhabitants of Los Angeles and Miami combined.

SIZE ... 95 miles long and 35 miles wide, Puerto Rico has an area of 3,435 square miles, about one and a half times the size of Delaware.

CAPITAL ... San Juan, with a population of 224,205, slightly larger than Syracuse, New York.

GOVERNMENT ... The island became a possession of the United States after the Spanish War of 1898. In 1948, the Hon. Luis Muñoz Marín became the first elected governor. Puerto Rico became a Commonwealth in July 1952, with a Constitution giving the island full autonomy. A Resident Commissioner in Washington has a voice but no vote in Congress.

HOW TO GET THERE ... By Pan American Clipper, direct non-stop flights from New York, about 5¼ hours flying time; from Miami nonstop, 3¾ hours. Otherwise only by 12-passenger freighter.

ACCOMMODATIONS ... The new *San Juan Intercontinental* in the Isla Verde section of San Juan is another fine example of what you can expect from the Intercontinental hotels—ultramodern structures and equipment, efficient service and colorful atmosphere that provide both the comfort and glamour that most travelers want. Completely air-conditioned, each room has a private balcony overlooking the ocean; and there's a pitch-and-putt golf course on the 15-acre grounds. Rates are $15 to $23 single, $19 to $27 double. Newest in Puerto Rico are the dramatic *La Concha* with shell-shaped night club, in the Condado section, $15 to $36 single, and $19 to $40 double and *Dorado Beach,* the Rockefeller-developed 1200-acre resort estate with outstanding golf course, 14 miles away (regular air service $9). Rates here are $35 up single, $45 up double including breakfast and dinner. Other fine oceanside hotels are the *Caribe Hilton,* each room with private balcony, $15 to $23 single, $19 to $27 double; and the *Condado Beach,* $13 to $21 single, $16 to $24 double. At the new luxurious *La Rada* rates are $12 to $18 single, $16 to $24 double (kitchenette studios here also). At the new villa-type *Coral Beach* on Isla Verde beach rates are $14 to $29 single, $21 to $39 double. These hotels are air-conditioned, have bars, restaurants, their own beaches, night clubs, swimming pools and cabañas as well as tennis and other recreation. At the new sound-proofed *International Airport Hotel* rates are $10 single, $14 double. *The Normandie,* a first-class hotel, has rates of $9 up single, $14 up double. Guest houses are also available.

ARTS ... In Rio Piedras, the University of Puerto Rico (with beautiful campus and fine buildings in a Baroque style) has a small museum on the main Quadrangle open from 8:00 A.M. to noon, Monday through Saturday, and 1:30 P.M. to 4:00 P.M. Monday through Friday. The Museum and Zoo in Muñoz Rivera Park have a display of industrial products and historical records, and a small zoo.

BANKS ... Besides several Stateside representatives, such as First National and Chase Manhattan, there are good local banks.

CALENDAR OF HOLIDAYS ... The same as ours, plus such celebrations as January 6, Three Kings Day; January 11, Hostos' Birthday; March 22, Abolition of Slavery; July 17, Muñoz Rivera's Birthday; July 25, Constitution Day; November 19, Discovery of Puerto Rico. The Christmas festivities are famous.

CIGARETTES AND TOBACCO ... Well-known brands are available, but prices are a little higher than at home.

CLIMATE ... There are no extremes of heat or cold. The hills and mountains are always several degrees cooler than San Juan. From November to May the coast is cooler. San Juan averages about 355 sunny days a year. Puerto Rico is ideal for vacationing the year round. December through May is especially recommended.

CLUBS ... Rotary, Lions, Elks, American Legion, Propeller Club,

Exchange Club, Knights of Columbus, Union Club, besides a large number of private clubs.

COMMON COURTESIES AND LOCAL CUSTOMS...Although it is part of the United States, Puerto Rico's newspapers are printed in Spanish. Also, there is no color line or segregation in the sense that we know them at home. "Out on the island" means anywhere outside San Juan and its environs.

COMMUNICATIONS...Telephone and All America Cables and RCA service to the United States and other countries. Airmail, 7 cents per ounce.

CURRENCY...Same as in the United States.

CUSTOMS REGULATIONS AND DOCUMENTS REQUIRED FOR UNITED STATES CITIZENS...You do not need passports or visa, but proof of nationality required for return home. Anything you buy in other Caribbean spots is declarable there as part of the United States. Vaccination certificate not required unless certain other areas are included in trip.

DRUG STORES...Same as at home.

ELECTRIC CURRENT...Same as in the United States.

FAUNA...Wonderful tropical birds, doves, mocking birds, cuckoos, flycatchers.

FLORA...All sorts of tropical flowers, orchids, Bougainvillaea, hibiscus, mahogany trees, pineapple and other tropical fruits.

FOOD...Puerto Rican food is definitely Spanish. Famous are *arroz con pollo; asopao,* a soupy dish of rice cooked with shrimp or chicken; *pasteles,* grated plantains with a meat filling wrapped in plantain leaves and boiled; *lechón asado,* a barbecued pig; *jueyes,* fresh land crabs, shelled and boiled; and *pastelillos,* thin dough filled with meat or cheese and deep-fat fried. Of course, you may find good plain American cooking in Puerto Rican restaurants. Good French, Chinese, Hungarian and Italian food, too.

GAMBLING...State lottery with drawings every Sunday; gambling casinos at the *Caribe Hilton,* the *Flamboyant,* the *San Juan Intercontinental, La Concha Hotel,* the *Condado Beach* and *Escambrón Club.* There is horse racing with pari-mutuels.

LANGUAGE...Although Spanish is the mother tongue, English is spoken and understood throughout the island.

LAUNDRY AND DRY CLEANING...Good at the hotels and in principal cities.

LIQUOR...Puerto Rico is the proud Rum Capital of the world, sending its fine, light-bodied rums to all parts of the globe. Among the best-known brands are Don Q, Ron Rico, Merito, Brugal and Carioca; brandies and whiskies are also available.

MEDICAL FACILITIES...There are good American and Puerto Rican doctors and hospitals.

MOTION PICTURES...There are many good theaters showing the latest Hollywood, European and Mexican pictures.

MUSIC . . . Puerto Rican music is distinctive and ear-catching. The *danza, plena,* and *aguinaldos* are the most representative. They are usually heard at religious festivals, home gatherings, private parties and sometimes at night clubs. Records of this music are easily obtainable at record shops. The work of Puerto Rican composers is known everywhere. There are a number of important musical events such as the Casals Festival and Opera Festival.

NIGHT CLUBS AND CABARETS . . . You can find almost any sort of night life you want in and around San Juan, from the lavish terraces and restaurants of the new luxury hotels to the native cabarets. Especially popular are the *Latin Lounge,* the *Escambrón Beach Club,* the *Piff Paff Pouff, El Morocco, Voodoo Room, Club 22* and the *Flamboyant,* among others.

PHOTOGRAPHY . . . Camera equipment and all types of film are available at prices slightly higher than in the United States. Developing facilities are also available for black-and-white film.

RELIGION . . . Although Puerto Rico is predominantly Roman Catholic, there are Episcopal, Methodist, Lutheran, Baptist and Presbyterian churches; also a synagogue and Christian Science reading room.

RESTAURANTS AND BARS . . . Most famous and oldest is *la Mallorquina* in old San Juan, noted for its delicious seafood and Spanish dishes. Be sure to have *asopao* here. Continental in atmosphere and food are the *Swiss Chalet, Las Guitarras* and *Le Rendezvous* in *Hotel La Rada. Mago's Saxony Steak House* for excellent charcoal steaks. You'll find Italian food at *La Estrella de Italia.* For an intimate luncheon or dinner (American food) tiny *El Burrito* in old San Juan is delightful. Hotels serve cosmopolitan as well as Puerto Rican cooking, but if you want native atmosphere and food drive to *Cecilia's Place,* or *Mario's* (both in Isla Verde), *Patio Español* downtown or *El Manolete* in Hato Rey. Other favorites: *Coamo Spring Hotel* in Coamo, Cobian's *Rancho Hotel* in Aguas Buenas, *Ladi's* in Salinas, *La Palma* in Mayaguez, *Hotel Meliá* in Ponce, *La Parguera* Guest House and *Doña Julia's* at La Parguera and *El Mediterráneo* in old San Juan.

SHOPS AND STORES . . . In addition to modern department stores and gift shops in the leading hotels, there's Martha Sleeper's, Mary Vela's, Triana's and other small stores that carry a variety of native-made sports clothes. Nancy Nance for needlework. Notre Dame Industrial School is especially good for fine embroidered linens. Imports are featured at Guisti Caribbean Shop and fine tropical furniture can be ordered for shipment from Humphrey Associates. Out on the island there's the Doll House in San Germán, and the famous Market in Ponce.

SPECTATOR SPORTS . . . Cockfighting is a national pastime. On Sunday, fights are held in San Juan and every little village. The Galleras (pits) Canta Gallo in Santurce are easily reached as is Tres Palmas Gallera on the Bayamon Road. Horse racing on Wednesday and Sunday afternoons at El Comandante; baseball is also very popular; games are played at Sixto Escobar Park; tennis tournaments are held at Rio Piedras Tennis Courts, *Caribe Hilton* and *Dorado Beach* Hotels. Boxing bouts are at Sixto Escobar Park.

SPORTS . . . There are two nine-hole golf courses in the capital area. Guest cards are available upon request. El Dorado Beach Hotel has a new 18-hole course. Out on the island there are nine-hole courses at some of the Sugar Centrals, where you may obtain permission to play. The big hotels have their own tennis courts, and guest privileges are accorded at some of the private clubs.

Swimming, of course, is wonderful. There are pools and beaches at the hotels. Escambrón Beach Club in San Juan has cabañas; Luquillo Beach, one hour's drive from San Juan, is magnificent. Skeet and trap shooting is available at the Club Metropolitano de Tiro. Horses may be hired for trips out on the island.

Fishing, as you might guess, is excellent. The annual winter and summer fishing tournaments are open to visitors. First-class deep-sea cruisers, equipped with finest fishing rig and captained by widely experienced fishermen, can be chartered for $65 a day, maximum of six persons. Rate includes bait, tackle, ice, crew and gasoline. You can try for tarpon, sailfish, marlin, tuna, dolphin and other deep-sea varieties. Four-passenger boats for tarpon fishing rent for $30 a day and skiffs with a "live well" for bonefishing at La Parguera are $9 a day.

THEATERS . . . Spanish operas and plays are staged at the old Tapia Theater in San Juan. Visiting companies perform here, too.

TIME . . . One hour later than Eastern Standard Time.

TIPPING . . . About the same scale as at home.

TRANSPORTATION . . . All taxis are metered with rates starting at 25 cents for the first quarter mile and 5 cents for each additional ¼ mile. There is good bus service within the metropolitan area, but it is wise to avoid buses during the rush hours. There is also bus service between San Juan and Mayaguez daily. *Público* cars provide inexpensive transportation throughout the island. They are similar to the jitneys which used to be found in many cities in the United States. Local tour agencies offer drive-yourself service.

WATER . . . It's perfectly safe throughout the island.

WHAT TO BUY . . . Hand-made and embroidered blouses, lingerie, mahogany bowls and souvenirs; men's linen suits. Don't forget there's an internal revenue tax on rum which must be paid at the airport upon departure on direct flights to the United States. Woven baskets are inexpensive and beautiful. Bamboo products and furniture made of native woods are good buys.

WHAT TO WEAR . . . You never need heavy clothes in San Juan. Bring summer cottons and silks. Some summer dinner and evening things for hotel wear. If you are going into the hills, take a topcoat and some medium-weight clothes. Men will need cotton or linen suits, sports jackets, slacks and beach attire. Black or white dinner jackets.

WHERE TO GO—SIGHTSEEING . . .

San Juan . . . Puerto Rico is as long and only twice as wide as

From the lighthouse at El Morro, tourists can view San Juan and the harbor, a panorama of brilliant color.

Puerto Rico has dozens of palm-fringed sunny beaches, and the water is ideal for swimming.

El Morro is one of the old-world fortifications and a site of historical interest near San Juan.

Long Island. You can see most of the island in two or three days. Variety is the thing to expect. Old San Juan itself is an islet, connected to the modern sections of Condado, Santurce, Hato Rey and Rio Piedras through a series of bridges. In San Juan visit El Morro (1539), one of the most interesting forts in the Western Hemisphere and actually an historic site; La Fortaleza (1533), built to protect the entrance of San Juan harbor and now used as the Governor's residence; the Cathedral of San Juan Bautista (1527), where the remains of Don Juan Ponce de León, the "Gran Conquistador," lie; the Submarine Gardens and San José Church. San Cristobal Fort ends the land protection of the walled city of San Juan.

Trips Near By ... You will want to go to Luquillo Beach, about 27 miles east of San Juan, and El Yunque, both of which can be done in a day. El Yunque is a Tropical Rain Forest which is utterly beautiful. Luquillo, a wonderful beach, nestles at its foot. There is excellent swimming here. A beautiful 45-minute drive to Aguas Buenas takes you into the mountains. Here you will find Cobian's *Rancho Hotel*. Rates are $12 double with living room, bedroom and bath.

A 3-day island tour (with driver-guide or by drive-yourself service) takes in most of the highlights of Puerto Rico. Aside from the variety of scenery, a trip around the island will turn up a lot of memorable incidents. They may not be more important than the glimpse of a large goat perched on top of a post in a pretty plaza or an unscheduled cockfight, initiated by the fowl themselves instead of their owners. These impromptu incidents will prove interesting. Overnight stops can be made in the larger cities of Ponce and Mayaguez.

In **Ponce** the *Meliá* is a good hotel, with air-conditioned bar and restaurant, good food, and pleasant modern rooms at rates from $5 single, European Plan. Actually a visit to Ponce is worthwhile, if only to see its famous fire station—red-and-black striped, with arched doorways outlined in colored lights. It has an opera bouffe quality that is almost unbelievable. Make a tour of the needlework center of Mayaguez, where the newly enlarged *La Palma Hotel* has modern rooms beginning at $6 single, European Plan. A visit to a rum distillery and a trip to a pineapple plantation should also be included while in this area. Nearby is historic San Germán.

Phosphorescent Bay, a short boat ride from La Parguera on the south coast, turns to liquid diamonds at night. It's a must for the sightseer. You could drive to La Parguera from San Germán for the evening or you might want to stay at the new and charming 12-room Guest House in the little village itself, $3 to $5 single.

Another popular resort is *Coamo Springs Hotel,* from $8, American Plan.

SOURCES OF FURTHER INFORMATION ... Guest house information and general information is available from the Puerto Rico Visitors Bureau in San Juan and at 666 Fifth Avenue, New York. Pan American's San Juan office is at Calle Recinto Sur, No. 307 (Tel. 2–5000).

PIGEON ISLAND Gros Islet

Vigie MORNE FORTUNE
• Castries

CARIBBEAN SEA

ATLANTIC OCEAN

ST. LUCIA

Soufrire
▲ PETIT PITON
▲ GROS PITON

Vieux Fort

ST. LUCIA

WEATHER IN ST. LUCIA—Lat. N13°55′—Alt. Approx. sea level

Temp.	JAN.	FEB.	MAR.	APR.	MAY	JUNE	JULY	AUG.	SEPT.	OCT.	NOV.	DEC.
Low	71°	71°	72°	73°	74°	75°	75°	74°	74°	74°	73°	73°
High	83°	83°	84°	86°	87°	86°	87°	88°	88°	87°	86°	84°
Average	77°	77°	78°	79°	80°	80°	81°	81°	81°	81°	80°	78°

LOCATION ... St. Lucia, the second largest of the Windward Islands, lies south of Martinique and is directly in the path of the trade winds on the route of the sailing clippers of long ago.

CHARACTERISTICS ... This delightful island, one of the Lesser Antilles, is French in heritage, British in character. The towns of Castries and Soufriere have a quiet charm which appeals to the visitor who wants to get away from regular tourist attractions. There is splendid bathing on uncluttered white sand beaches, excellent fishing, some magnificent scenery and a combination of mountains and sea which is irresistible. Winter months are dry and sunny but not excessively hot. An ideal spot for a different vacation.

POPULATION ... About 87,144, of which 24,300 live in Castries.

SIZE ... 27 miles long and about 14 miles wide, the island has an area of 233 square miles and a coastline of 150 miles.

CAPITAL ... Castries, one of the most beautiful harbors in the West Indies, with its beautiful green hills on each side covered with flamingo trees, alemada vines, hibiscus and other tropical shrubs. Hotels and residences are located on the sides of the hill overlooking the harbor.

GOVERNMENT ... A British colony.

HOW TO GET THERE ... By Pan American from New York to Guadeloupe, Martinique or Antigua, then via British West Indian Airways; or nonstop from New York or Miami to San Juan with short island hops through the West Indies to St. Lucia. Steamship lines make stops at principal Windward and Leeward Island ports and there is motor-vessel service available between the islands.

ACCOMMODATIONS... The *Hotel Antoine* is located high on a hill with a magnificent view of the capital and the harbor; quiet, charming West Indies atmosphere and excellent food, including native dishes. Rates $8.50 American Plan. The *Hotel Villa,* also on a hill, is newer and closer to town, also with excellent food. Rates $8 to $10. American Plan. About a half mile from Castries on the beach is the *Blue Waters Hotel.*

CLUBS... *Pigeon Island Beach Club* caters specially to tourists. It stands on a charming little bathing beach, has a good bar, and meals are served to order. The *Vigie Club* is private but cards may be arranged upon proper introduction. (Inquire at your hotel.) This is a beach club and night club too. *Lawn Tennis Club,* cards needed. *Luna Park Club, Palm Beach Club, Blue Danube.*

CURRENCY... British West Indies dollar, worth about 60 cents in United States currency.

CUSTOMS REGULATIONS AND DOCUMENTS REQUIRED FOR UNITED STATES CITIZENS... Regulations are the same as for other British West Indies islands. Proof of citizenship required.

DRUG STORES... There are modern chemists' shops in Castries.

WHAT TO WEAR... Washable summer clothes, cotton; slacks and shorts. Evening clothes not essential. Lightweight topcoats advisable.

WHERE TO GO—SIGHTSEEING...
Castries... Castries, the capital of this little British island of St. Lucia, one of the Lesser Antilles chain, is a good harbor flanked by the imposing hills of Vigie and Morne Fortuné. There are interesting drives, good beaches, splendid fishing. Drive to Gros Islet and take a launch to Pigeon Island. The drive to Soufriere is picturesque and includes a stop at Sulphur Springs, noted for their medicinal value.

Soufriere, the next largest town to Castries, is in the shadow of two peaks, Gros Piton and Petit Piton, which rise from the sea to more than 2,000 feet. The land rises behind the town to the live crater of the volcano for which the town is named. The Piton peaks may be climbed by experienced climbers. The view is magnificent and rewarding. Other things to see on this charming island include a drive to the top of Morne Fortuné, where a visit should be made to Fort Charlotte. Take a drive along Barre-de-l'Isle. There is wonderful scenery, beautiful tropical foliage, and a pervading charm which make a visit to this spot memorable.

SOURCES OF FURTHER INFORMATION... There is a St. Lucia Tourist Trade Development Board in Castries. Peter and Co., Ltd., are agents for Pan American there.

TRINIDAD
AND TOBAGO

WEATHER IN PORT-OF-SPAIN—Lat. N10°45′—Alt. 25′

Temp.	JAN.	FEB.	MAR.	APR.	MAY	JUNE	JULY	AUG.	SEPT.	OCT.	NOV.	DEC.
Low	71°	71°	71°	73°	74°	74°	72°	73°	73°	73°	73°	72°
High	85°	86°	87°	88°	88°	87°	87°	87°	88°	88°	87°	86°
Average	78°	78°	79°	80°	81°	80°	80°	80°	80°	80°	80°	79°
Days of Rain	14	8	8	7	10	17	20	21	18	16	17	16

LOCATION ... Most southerly of the West Indies, the island of Trinidad is only about 10 miles from the Paria peninsula of Venezuela. The tiny island of Tobago lies about 20 miles northeast of Trinidad.

CHARACTERISTICS ... Trinidad is the most colorful and polyglot of all the West Indian islands. Here you may see an East Indian woman in a sari with a ring in her nose, Hindus in traditional dress, calypso-singing Negroes, Portuguese, Spaniards and Chinese. There are Moslem mosques, Hindu temples and bazaars. There are wonderful roads, beautiful scenery and some fine bathing beaches. The climate is splendid and the nights are cool.

The island of Tobago, sometimes called Robinson Crusoe's Island, is where you will find the magnificent Bird of Paradise Sanctuary, a whole coastful of wonderful beaches, small but modern hotels and an unspoiled quality which exists in very few places elsewhere in the Caribbean. Tobago can be reached by plane or boat from Trinidad.

POPULATION ... Trinidad has a population of 729,300 of which about one-third are East Indians. Tobago has a population of about 35,600.

SIZE ... Trinidad, 50 miles long and 30 miles wide, is about the size and shape of Rhode Island. Tobago is 26 miles long and about 7 miles wide.

CAPITAL ... Port-of-Spain, with a population of 120,650.

GOVERNMENT . . . A British colony, Trinidad and Tobago are combined for administrative purposes. Trinidad is the site of the capital of the new Federation of the West Indies.

HOW TO GET THERE . . . By Pan American Clipper de luxe or tourist service, New York to Port-of-Spain, 8¾ hours flying time; frequent Clipper service from other British West Indies islands and the Virgin Islands. By ship, about 4½ days from New York.

ACCOMMODATIONS . . . The *Queen's Park Hotel* is located opposite the Savannah, which is 200 acres of green turf in Port-of-Spain. This is one of the main centers of the city's sports life. Rates from $10. A modern hotel, the *Bretton Hall,* is situated a few yards from the Queen's Park Savannah. Rates from $12.00. Two other modern hotels situated conveniently near the city are the *Bergerac* (rates on application) and the *Normandie* (some air-conditioned rooms). Rates from $22.00. Among other hotels are *Hotel Coblentz* ($7.50) and *Bagshot* ($18.00). These rates are European or Continental Plan per person in W.I. dollars. Discount 40 per cent to get approximate equivalents in United States dollars. There are many guest houses in Port-of-Spain and in the surrounding countryside. Most of them are charming, all of them reasonable. The *Mt. Saint Benedict Guest House* has a superb view. There is a PAA guest house with air-conditioned cocktail lounge and rooms near Piaro airport. Also the *Bel-Air Hotel* at the airport.

ARTS . . . Royal Victoria Institute Museum; Art Society; Trinidad Art Centre.

BANKS . . . Barclay's Bank, Canadian Bank of Commerce; Royal Bank of Canada; Gordon, Grant & Co., Ltd., Bank of Nova Scotia. Banking hours are 8:00 A.M. to noon, Monday through Friday; 8:00 A.M. to 11:00 A.M. on Saturday.

CALENDAR OF HOLIDAYS . . . New Year's Day; Federation Day; Good Friday; Easter Monday; Empire Day; Queen's Birthday; Corpus Christi; Whit Monday; First Monday in August; Christmas; December 26 (Boxing Day).

Two important events of interest to tourists are the calypso season and the Moslem Hosein Festival. Calypso begins in early January and the Festival of Hosein takes place on the 6th, 7th and 8th day after the Mohammedan New Year. Other events of interest are: agricultural and horticultural shows and the Roman Catholic Feast of La Divina Pastora (*Siparia Fête*). Carnival is celebrated on the two days preceding Lent. The streets are crowded with bands of costumed natives roaming from place to place. It is one of the gayest and most colorful carnivals in the world.

CIGARETTES . . . Most brands of American cigarettes are available. English cigarettes are plentiful as are locally made brands. 200 cigarettes or equivalent allowed in duty free.

CLIMATE . . . January to March is the ideal time in Trinidad. The weather is cooler then, but even in the hotter months the nights are cool. The rainy season is June to December, but although the rains are heavy they are of short duration.

CLUBS ... Trinidad Yacht Club, American Women's Club, Canadian Women's Club, Rotary Club, the Trinidad Country Club (cards may be arranged; inquire of Pan American), the Y.W.C.A., the Palm Beach Aquatic Club. *See also* SPORTS.

COMMON COURTESIES AND LOCAL CUSTOMS ... Since this is a British Crown Colony, afternoon tea is a ritual. Customs are standard European and American.

COMMUNICATIONS ... Airmail service to the United States. World-wide cable and radio telephone service also available.

CURRENCY ... Trinidad's monetary unit is the W.I. dollar, worth about 60 cents United States or $1.69 W.I. to the United States dollar.

The Bureau de Change, at King's Wharf Passenger Center, issues W.I. currency in special envelopes in exchange for United States and Canadian currency at the prevailing official rate of exchange. The Bureau reconverts unspent balances of W.I. currency into United States currency provided that (a) *the original exchange transaction was made at the Bureau* and (b) surplus W.I. currency does not exceed the amount originally issued. Original envelopes must be presented when reconverting.

CUSTOMS REGULATIONS AND DOCUMENTS REQUIRED FOR UNITED STATES CITIZENS ... No passports or visas, only proof of nationality. Yellow fever inoculation required for entry from some areas. Smallpox vaccination certificate for re-entry to the United States. You may bring in 1 quart of spirits or wine.

DRUG STORES ... There are chemists' shops in Port-of-Spain which carry well-known brands of merchandise, but they do not have soda fountains and other things we find in drug stores at home.

ELECTRIC CURRENT ... 115/230 volts, 60 cycles, A.C.

FAUNA ... Wonderful birds, including the famous *"Qu'est-ce-qu'il dit"* (What does he say?) bird which repeats the question several times. There are deer and small game, too. The many species of humming birds have caused the place to be called "Land of the Humming Bird." There is a small zoo situated in the Emperor Valley, Royal Botanic Gardens, Port-of-Spain.

FLORA ... The place is ablaze with flowers of all descriptions. In the wonderful Botanic Gardens there are cabbage palms, strychnine plants, flytrap flowers, orchids. All over the island there are lemon grass, bamboo trees, coconut palms, para rubber trees, Ceylon willows, century plants, red flowering immortelles which blaze all over the island during the early months of the year, *Poui* trees, which have golden and pink blossoms, and hundreds of brilliant tropical blooms. Anthurium lilies are beautiful here.

FOOD ... Creole cooking is most popular in Trinidad. But it's possible to have international fare as well. Specialties include *sancoche* and *callalloo,* excellent soups, both of them. *Pastelles,* made of meat and cornflour dough, are wonderful. Crabmeat served in shells and tiny oysters are famous. Excellent Chinese food is available, and because of the large East Indian population, curries are famous, as are *roti* and other Indian dishes which are very hot and spicy. Of course, fresh fruit abounds; avocado pear, sapodillas, mangoes.

GAMBLING ... Horse racing is very popular. Pari-mutuel and forecast betting and sweepstakes. There are eight meetings throughout the year; December-January: Five Days—Queen's Park Savannah Port-of-Spain. February-March: Two Days—Shirvan Park, Tobago. March-April (Easter): Five Days—New Union Park, San Fernando. May: Two Days—Arima. June-July: Five Days—Queen's Park Savannah, Port-of-Spain. August-September: Five Days—Santa Rosa, Arima. October: Two Days—New Union Park, San Fernando. October-November: Two Days—Shirvan Park, Tobago.

LANGUAGE ... English, of course, is the native tongue. But French, Spanish, Hindi, Chinese and other languages are heard here.

LAUNDRY AND DRY CLEANING ... Laundry is good. Dry cleaning good, with 8-hour service. Prices compare favorably with those in the United States. The Sanitary Laundry and the Trinidad Steam Laundry, both reliable, have branches throughout the island.

LIQUOR ... Rum is the national drink. Trinidad is the home of Angostura Bitters. Many rum drinks cost about 20 cents and they are wonderful. Whisky, brandies and gins are available at prices comparable to those in the United States. Gin is slightly less and the British gin flourishes here. But Planter's Punch is the thing. Bar hours —8:00 A.M. to 8:00 P.M. Hotel bar hours—8:00 A.M. to 11:00 P.M.

MEDICAL FACILITIES ... Excellent nursing homes are available. The General Hospital in Port-of-Spain is modern and the San Fernando hospital is one of the largest and most modern in the West Indies. Good English-trained doctors are available.

MOTION PICTURES ... There are five main cinemas: the *Astor;* the *de Luxe;* the *Globe;* the *Strand* and the *Starlite* (drive-in)—which show American and English films.

MUSIC ... Trinidad is the home of the calypso, and the more recent innovation, the steel band, which consists of steel drums of varying tones beaten to calypso rhythm. The calypso singer, as everyone knows, takes a topical theme and weaves it into an extemporaneous song. In January, calypso tents spring up all over the city and various calypso singers vie with each other in a "war."

NIGHT CLUBS AND CABARETS ... There are few night clubs as we know them, but there is dancing weekly at the *Trinidad Country Club*, the *Trinidad Yacht Club*, the *Lotus Restaurant*, *Tavern on the Green*, *Normandie* and *Bel-Air* hotels. The *Bombay Club* is a late spot.

PHOTOGRAPHY ... Photographic equipment is in good supply in Port-of-Spain. Special 24-hour service for film developing may be had in Port-of-Spain at Chan's Photographers, on Frederick Street; Pereira and Co., Ltd., 24 Frederick Street; W. C. Ross and Co., Ltd., 27 Frederick Street.

RELIGION ... Because of the polyglot nature of the population, one finds churches of almost all faiths here—Hindu temples, Moslem mosques, Jewish synagogues, Catholic and Protestant churches.

Trinidad and Tobago allow you to rest and relax. These tourists picnic amid Tobago's tropical beauty spots and excellent swimming conditions.

RESTAURANTS ... In the hotels, especially the *Normandie,* for French cuisine. *Trinidad Country Club* for dining and dancing. *Tavern on the Green* serves American-style food and local specialties. Downtown there are the *China Clipper, Kimling, Ying King,* and the *Lotus,* all serving Chinese dishes. *Belvedere* on Lady Chancellor Hill overlooking Port-of-Spain, *Angostura Lounge* and *La Ronde* are worth visiting.

SHOPS AND STORES ... Frederick Street is the main shopping thoroughfare, where you may buy British products quite cheaply. There are East Indian and Chinese bazaars with some fascinating goods, and two good East Indian shops on the Western Main Road.

SPECTATOR SPORTS ... Horse racing at four race tracks. Boxing and basketball. Also cricket, soccer, hockey, water polo.

SPORTS ... Golf at St. Andrew's Golf Club; tennis at the Tranquillity Square Lawn Tennis Club; swimming at the Trinidad Country Club. There is good deep-sea and underwater fishing and duck shooting in season.

TIME ... One hour later than our Eastern Standard Time.

TIPPING ... About what you would at home.

TRANSPORTATION ... There are motor buses and taxis, as well as drive-yourself car service.

WATER ... Water is safe to drink at hotels.

WHAT TO BUY ... Rum is cheap and very, very good. You can buy British woolens and other British merchandise far more reasonably than in the United States. Trinidad is best for silver jewelry.

WHAT TO WEAR ... Tropical clothes, cottons, beach wear. Take a raincoat in summer. Men will want summer light-weight suits, slacks, sports jackets, dinner jacket, and beach attire.

WHERE TO GO—SIGHTSEEING ...

Trinidad is one of the most colorful of the West Indies. Its population is a mixture of East Indian, British, Negro, Chinese, Spanish, French and Portuguese—which in itself makes the country fascinating. You will want to see the Pitch Lake (asphalt) which is said to be 285 feet deep. You can walk on the lake without sinking in.

Trinidad asphalt has paved some of the most famous streets in the world. Take a drive over the beautiful North Coast Road and swim at Maracas Bay. The return drive over "The Saddle" is famed for its bamboo groves. There are fascinating teak forests and thousands of scarlet ibis in the Caroni Bird Sanctuary from July to October.

At Couva near the shore of the Gulf of Paria is the largest sugar factory in the British Empire. There are good beaches in Trinidad, most of which are not within easy reach of Port-of-Spain. But the scenery everywhere is magnificent. Inland, the mountains rise to a height of 3,000 feet and afford wonderful views of the valleys and the sea. There are miniature waterfalls in the Diego Martin and Maracas Valleys.

Tobago ... The little island of Tobago is rapidly becoming a favorite tourist spot. Tobago may be reached only from Port-of-Spain by coastal boat or by plane. Allegedly the setting of the story of Robinson Crusoe, the island is famous for its tropical birds, particularly the bird of paradise, which is found on Ingram Island (Bird of Paradise Island) off the northern tip of Tobago.

There are six hotels, all American Plan. (Winter rates quoted are in W.I. dollars.) The *Arnos Vale Beach Hotel,* situated on a 450-acre estate is seven miles from Scarborough, the chief town on the island. It has a central house, cottages, and beach house. Riding horses for hire, cabin cruiser and sailboat for fishing or exploring the coast, a coral beach. Rates from $33.50 W.I. currency. *Bluehaven* also offers every comfort and convenience, first-class cuisine and wine cellar. There are a fishing launch and cruiser available to guests. The terms, inclusive of all room service, are from $20 per day W.I. The *Robinson Crusoe,* which is located on Rockley Bay, faces the sea and has its own beach, drive-yourself cars for rent. Rooms with bath are from $20 per day. *Bacolet Guest House* consists of small bungalows surrounding the main bulding. Rates from $12 up. The *Alma Guest House* at Mason Hall, twelve to fifteen miles from Scarborough, *Bird of Paradise Inn,* at Speyside, 26 miles from Scarborough, and *Crown Point Hotel,* a few yards from Crown Point Airport, are Tobago's latest additions.

You will want to drive to Man O'War Bay, a wonderful natural bay with hills reaching to the water's edge. Here is a wonderful sandy beach. Pigeon Point is one of the best bathing beaches in the West Indies. You may swim here at the *Aquatic Club.* There are cabañas, but cabañas thatched with palm leaves. It costs a shilling to swim here, on introduction by a member. (Inquire of Pan American.) Equipped with sea goggles, you may see fascinating marine life in the Coral Sea Gardens at Buccoo Reef and enjoy a swim in the cool water of the *Nylon Pool,* so named by American visitors to this spot.

SOURCES OF FURTHER INFORMATION ... Trinidad and Tobago Tourist Board at King's Wharf Passenger Center, Port-of-Spain; Administration Building, Scarborough, Tobago. New York office, 48 East 43rd Street, New York 17. Pan American's office is at 12 Abercromby Street, Port-of-Spain (Tel. 6161).

VIRGIN ISLANDS

Charlotte Amalie
ST. THOMAS I

CANEEL BAY
ST. JOHN I

SEA
VIRGIN ISLANDS

CARIBBEAN

ST. CROIX I
Frederiksted
Christiansted

WEATHER IN ST. THOMAS & ST. CROIX—Lat. 18°20′—Alt. Approx. sea level

Temp.	JAN.	FEB.	MAR.	APR.	MAY	JUNE	JULY	AUG.	SEPT.	OCT.	NOV.	DEC.
Low	69°	70°	70°	71°	74°	75°	76°	75°	74°	74°	73°	70°
High	84°	84°	84°	85°	86°	87°	88°	89°	88°	87°	85°	84°
Average	77°	77°	77°	78°	80°	81°	82°	82°	81°	81°	79°	77°
Days of Rain	20	16	16	14	20	16	15	16	14	19	20	19

LOCATION . . . The Virgin Islands of the United States consist of the islands of St. Thomas, St. Croix, St. John and about 50 nearby islets. St. Thomas is 75 miles east of San Juan, Puerto Rico, St. Croix is 40 miles south of St. Thomas and St. John.

CHARACTERISTICS . . . These perfectly delightful islands, which the United States acquired by purchase from Denmark, offer excellent vacation facilities. Since they are free of customs duty, it is possible to purchase all sorts of wonderful things at a fraction of their cost in the United States. There are new luxury hotels and the older ones are small but charming. The Virgin Islands have a delightful climate, and a charm all their own. It's hay-fever free too.

POPULATION . . . 28,000 inhabitants, 15,000 of whom live on St. Thomas, 12,000 on St. Croix and about 1,000 on St. John.

SIZE . . . St. Thomas has an area of 32 square miles, St. Croix, 82 square miles, and St. John, 20 square miles.

CAPITAL . . . Charlotte Amalie with 11,463 population is the capital of St. Thomas. Christiansted is the capital of St. Croix.

GOVERNMENT . . . The islands are governed by a legislative assembly made up of 11 locally elected senators and a governor appointed by the President of the United States.

HOW TO GET THERE . . . By Pan American Clipper only 40 minutes from Puerto Rico to St. Croix. About 8 hours (flying time) from New York with stopover in Puerto Rico. St. Croix is about 25 minutes by air from St. Thomas.

ACCOMMODATIONS . . . There are a number of excellent hotels on St. Thomas. Unless otherwise mentioned, rates given are minimum modified American Plan (breakfast and dinner) single and double, December through April. They're lower other times. *Bluebeard's Castle,* $23 and $40, overlooks the town and sea; the new *Virgin Isle Hotel,* $22 and $39, is the last word in luxury and has a beautiful pool, two cork tennis courts, dancing nightly, terrace for each room. New *Flamboyant Hotel,* $22 and $40 up, two miles east of town, overlooking the sea, has swimming pool. You can walk down to the beach. Downtown is the famous *Hotel 1829,* with excellent food, $12 and $24. The *Trade Winds,* $12 and $18, and *Caribbean,* $18 and $28, are near the airport, have walks down to the beach. *Grand Hotel* is in center of town, a commercial hotel on European Plan, $5 up single, $8 up double. The *Mountain Top Hotel* is situated on top of the highest peak, approximately 1,500 feet elevation, $25 single, $40 double, excellent food. There are also many excellent guest houses, such as *Smith's Fancy, The Gate, Estate Contant, Galleon House, Miller's Manor, Sea Horse Inn,* and the *Beachcomber,* which accommodate a limited number of guests, ranging from $8 European Plan and $12 American Plan, on up; *Adams 1799 Guest House, Harbor View, Van Dyck Plantation, Villa Santana* and *Water Isle Hotel.*

St. Croix, Christiansted Area: The *Buccaneer Hotel,* with beautiful beach and view of harbor, $21 and $28, *Hotel on the Cay* with main house and cottages, where guests are rowed in a boat from Christiansted wharf, $18 and $26; *Grapetree Bay Hotel & Villas* on a 750-acre resort, $28 and $38; *St. Croix by the Sea,* with beach and beautiful pool, $20 and $30; *Cruzana Club* manor house with new harbor $16 and $30; *Richmond Plantation,* guest house $14 and $28 double, American Plan.

Christiansted Town: *Club Comanche* $12 and $23; *Pink Fancy* Apartments $35 per week, European Plan. *Mahogany Inn* $36 doubles only. *King Christian* Apartments $18 and $24 European. $75 per week.

Frederiksted Area: *Estate Carlton Hotel* with private golf club, pool and beach $36 and $40. *Estate Good Hope,* with beach, $60 double in suites, American Plan; *Clover Crest Hotel,* with pool, $20 and $34, American Plan; *La Grange Guest House,* $34 double American Plan; *Sprat Hall* with beach, $18 and $32, American Plan. *Cane Bay Cottages,* $55 per week, European Plan.

The new *Caneel Bay Plantation* is the swankiest resort on St. John. There are several good guest houses and also housekeeping cottages: *Cruz Cottages, Gallows Point, Trunk Bay Estate.*

ARTS . . . St. Croix's collection of Pre-Columbian Arawak and Carib Indian in St. Croix Museum is one of the most complete in existence. St. Thomas has a museum which offers interesting displays pertinent to the islands' seven centuries of colorful history.

BANKS . . . In both St. Thomas and St. Croix, the Virgin Islands National Bank, and the West Indies Bank and Trust Company.

CALENDAR OF HOLIDAYS . . . Besides all the ones we observe at home, the Islands have a few of their own: March 31, Transfer

Day (the day the Islands were taken over from the Danes), Carnival—3 days of holiday (a real festival with street dancing, parades, floats, steel bands, calypso singers, crowning of king and queen). Carnival is usually celebrated during the last week in April. June 22, Organic Act Day; July 25, Supplication Day; two Thanksgivings, one the same as at home, the other October 25 in thanksgiving for the Islands' freedom from hurricanes (a hurricane has not been reported since 1926); November 1, Liberty Day; December 26, Christmas second day, beginning of Christmas Festival, Parades and Floats.

CIGARETTES ... American cigarettes are only 15 cents a pack.

CLIMATE ... Not the usual tropical rainy seasons, but occasional sun showers. The temperature averages about 80 degrees and varies little from day to night and season to season. Constant trade winds keep the humidity down.

COMMON COURTESIES AND LOCAL CUSTOMS ... Brief shorts are frowned upon. Walking shorts are accepted for men and women during day but ladies are more appreciated in female attire.

COMMUNICATIONS ... All America Cables and Radio, West Indian Cable and Wireless, Ltd. Telephone service to the States.

CURRENCY ... United States money is used.

CUSTOMS REGULATIONS AND DOCUMENTS REQUIRED FOR UNITED STATES CITIZENS ... Same as Puerto Rico.

DRUG STORES ... Several on both St. Thomas and St. Croix, well stocked with United States products.

FAUNA ... Wild deer, doves and mongooses.

FLORA ... Magnificently colored hibiscus, oleanders, Bougainvillaea and orchids grow here, also tropical trees: banana, mamee, cocoa, papaya, orange, tamarind, lemon, lime, sapodilla, mahogany, turpentine.

ELECTRIC CURRENT ... 110 and 120 volts, A.C.; no problem.

FOOD ... In some places they serve native Creole and Danish dishes, but for the most part the hotels and the restaurants specialize in typical American food, charcoal-broiled steaks, and seafood.

GAMBLING ... There is horse racing on certain holidays in St. Thomas and St. Croix. In St. Croix there are donkey races on Feb. 22 under the auspices of the St. Croix Jonkey Clubs. They also have cockfights at two arenas. The big event is the Great West Indian Steeplechase. There is a legal lottery with monthly drawing.

LANGUAGE ... English, of course. Some Spanish also spoken.

LAUNDRY AND DRY CLEANING ... There are several good laundries and dry-cleaning places on both St. Thomas and St. Croix.

LIQUOR ... Any brand of liquor you want at the lowest prices: Scotch for $2.25 a fifth and up, excellent cognac for $3, rum for about 70 cents a bottle. In the bars try a *Cruzan Morning* cocktail.

MEDICAL FACILITIES ... There is a Government-owned hospital with a capable staff on each of the three islands.

MOTION PICTURES ... In St. Thomas *Center Theater* is air-conditioned and shows American films. Both Christiansted (the new *Alexander*) and Frederiksted have movie theaters.

NIGHT CLUBS AND CABARETS... There are numerous night spots as well as the restaurants in the leading hotels. Some of the better known and most popular in St. Thomas are: the *Magic Lamp*, the *Seven Queens Quarters* (air-conditioned), the *Hideaway* and *Sebastian's* on the waterfront; the *Virgin Isle Hotel*, and *Bluebeard's* offer dancing nightly. *Smith's Fancy*, *The Gate*, *Galleon House*, *Yacht Haven*, *Estate Contant* and *Mountain Top Hotel* all have attractive bars. Night clubs include *Pink Barreee* and *Pilgrim's Terrace*. On St. Croix there's the *Morning Star Night Club* on north road four miles west of Christiansted. *King Christian, Unicorn, Calabash, Hamilton House* and *Jones Cocktail Lounge* in the city. *Victoria House Cocktail Lounge* and *Plantation Club* are night spots in Frederiksted.

PHOTOGRAPHY... Black-and-white and color film, as well as photo equipment, is available. Developing service is good and prices are reasonable.

MUSIC... Native scratch bands, steel bands and calypso.

RELIGION... While the Virgin Islands are predominantly Roman Catholic and Lutheran, there are churches of other denominations, including the Anglican Methodist, Baptist, and Presbyterian.

RESTAURANTS... In addition to the hotel dining rooms, there are several good places to eat. In St. Thomas, don't miss the *Mountain Top* for Sunday brunch, *Chateau Chinon* with Danish atmosphere. The *Grand Gallery, Seven Queens Quarters* and the *Magic Lamp* are on Main Street; *Sebastian's* on the waterfront; also *Yacht Haven, The Gate* and *Galleon House* on St. Croix. In Christiansted try *King Christian, Mahogany Inn, Hamilton House, Calabash, Big Brodies, Unicorn, Jones Cocktail Lounge* and *Morning Star*. In Frederiksted *Victoria House* and *Plantation Club*.

STORES AND SHOPS... In St. Thomas try Continental, Inc., Bolero, Spanish Main Shop, Amerindies, Patio, Cavanagh's, Elverhoj, Maison Danoise, the French Shop, Little Switzerland, Scandinavian Silver Center, A. H. Riise Gift Shop, Venegas, Sparky's among others.

In Christiansted go to International Shop for the Virgin Island Character Dolls. Try Continental Inc., Island Sport Shop, Danish House, Compass Rose, Ay Ay, Carib Cellars, Vickys, Cavanaugh, Island Imports. In Fredericksted, Florhall Gift Shop.

SPECTATOR SPORTS... There are not many spectator sports in either St. Thomas or St. Croix. There are baseball and basket ball. Horse racing in St. Thomas and St. Croix, donkey racing and cockfighting in St. Croix.

SPORTS... Deep-sea fishing, spear fishing; lobster diving; conch diving; sailing in yawls, sloops and schooners; motor cruises; yachting; horseback riding; tennis. In St. Thomas there's a nine-hole golf course, swimming at Brewer's Beach, Morning Star, Lindberg beach on the Caribbean, or Magen's Bay on the Atlantic. At St. Croix, swimming at Cramer's Park, Fort Louise Augusta and West End beaches, golf and tennis at Estate Carlton, tennis at the Hotel Buccaneer.

TIME... One hour later than U. S. Eastern Standard Time.

Watching the fruit boats come in is one of the interesting things to do in St. Thomas. Here tourists are sampling some coconuts.

Bluebeard's Hill provides a magnificent view of the harbor and colorful buildings of Charlotte Amalie, capital of St. Thomas.

TIPPING ... Same as at home.

TRANSPORTATION ... There are cars to hire with or without a chauffeur and conducted tours can be made by car; trips over some of the old plantations can be made by horseback.

WATER ... ALL water for drinking should be boiled.

WHAT TO BUY ... This is truly a shopper's paradise. Because it is a free port, you can buy things for much less than at home, such as: Danish American, English and Scandinavian silverware; Peruvian, Mexican, Danish and Guatemalan silver jewelry; Scandinavian crystal and ceramics; French perfumes; Florentine, Mexican and Guatemalan leather goods; English woolen goods; Haitian sisal footwear; mahogany, tortoise-shell, bead and sea jewelry; corals and cameos; liquors; bay rum; Italian linens and alabasters; knickknacks from Haiti, Puerto Rico and Tortola.

WHAT TO WEAR ... For women, light summer dresses, sports clothes, sweaters and maybe one cocktail dress; and if you are staying in one of the better hotels, a dinner dress. For men, sports clothes, lightweight suits (hats are seldom worn) a dinner coat. Men wear tropical shorts, brightly colored shirts on the beaches.

WHERE TO GO—SIGHTSEEING ...

St. Thomas ... It will not take more than possibly a day to explore the principal highlights on St. Thomas, even outside of the capital, Charlotte Amalie. You'll want to visit the French Village, where the people are descendants of the early French settlers. Here is the beautiful shrine of St. Anne, which overlooks the village. Drake's Seat is another place to see. It is reported that this is where Sir Francis Drake, the famous navigator, sat while he was charting the channels and passages of the Islands. Take a trip up the street of 99

Steps to Government Hill, where Government House, the official residence of the Governor, is located, also, the magnificent administration building. There is an ancient Danish cemetery; the tombs were built on conch shells cemented together and in most cases brightly painted. Some of them even have the faces of the people sculptured on them. The dungeons of Old Fort Christian, built in 1671, are another historic sight. See St. Peter and St. Paul's church with its magnificent altar, and All Saints Anglican Church, which has an organ over one hundred years old. The District Courthouse in Emancipation Park is where the proclamation was issued, freeing the slaves in 1848. There are many legends about Bluebeard's Hill and Castle. You can take a trip in a glass-bottomed boat that operates daily and get a wonderful view of marine life.

St. Croix . . . The island of St. Croix is the largest of the Virgin Islands but not so developed a tourist place as St. Thomas. This is an agricultural island deriving its revenue principally from sugar cane, cattle ranches, and rum distillation. Points of sightseeing interest on St. Croix are included on twice-daily tours visiting the following historical sites: the old Fort in Frederiksted dating back to 1760; the old Fort in Christiansted; the Steeple Building; the Lutheran Church with tombstones on the floor and in the walls (official Danish Government Church); Government House, seat of Danish Government; the newly furnished Reception Hall with replicas of original Danish Government furnishings; the interesting archways and decorative architecture; the Christiansted wharf and downtown business area; trading schooners at the wharf; the many donkey carts for local color; Alexander Hamilton Store where Alexander Hamilton worked as a boy; Rachael Levine Monument at Grange (mother of Alexander Hamilton); East End of Island, most easterly point in U. S.; the Bethlehem Sugar Factory; Cane Fields; windmills dotting the Island; old ruins of sugar estates; Salt River, where Columbus first landed in the Virgin Islands and had his first battle with Carib Indians. Go to Buck Island with its beautiful beaches, and Butler's Bay, which was made famous by Philip Freneau, the poet of the American Revolution, in "The Beauties of Santa Cruz." Sailing and fishing boats are available for a day's outing.

St. John . . . There are daily boats to the ᐧland of St. John. There you have *Cruz Bay* with guest cottages, *Gallow Point,* also located on Cruz Bay (accommodations, three housekeeping cottages) and *Trunk Bay Estate,* a delightful spot overlooking the Atlantic Ocean. Also *Caneel Bay Plantation,* a delightful modern beach colony recently renovated by Laurence Rockefeller, who has purchased large acreage for a national park. The island offers excellent swimming, fishing and exploring. Horses are available, with or without guides.

SOURCES OF FURTHER INFORMATION . . . The Chambers of Commerce and offices of the Department of Trade in St. Thomas and at Christiansted as well as at 750 3rd Avenue, New York, N. Y. The Virgin Island Tours Office, St. Thomas, for tours and for trips to St. John. Pan American offices and travel agencies on both islands.

Mexico and
Central America

COSTA RICA

WEATHER IN SAN JOSÉ—Lat. N9°56'—Alt. 3,700'

Temp.	JAN.	FEB.	MAR.	APR.	MAY	JUNE	JULY	AUG.	SEPT.	OCT.	NOV.	DEC.
Low	57°	57°	58°	60°	61°	62°	60°	60°	60°	60°	59°	58°
High	76°	78°	80°	81°	81°	80°	78°	79°	80°	79°	78°	77°
Average	67°	68°	69°	71°	71°	71°	69°	70°	70°	69°	68°	67°
Days of Rain	2	2	2	5	19	21	19	20	24	24	18	7

LOCATION ... Costa Rica lies between Nicaragua and Panamá, bordered on the east by the Caribbean and on the west by the Pacific Ocean.

CHARACTERISTICS ... Its cleanliness, ideal climate, beautiful scenery, restful atmosphere and hospitality offer special attractions to the tourist. Its cities are quaint and friendly. The charm of the country lies mainly in its colorful countryside. Costa Rica has the highest percentage of literacy in the Latin American republics. In fact, it has more school teachers than soldiers. The people are friendly and helpful.

POPULATION ... 941,977 inhabitants.

SIZE ... 23,000 square miles, or about the size of the state of West Virginia.

CAPITAL ... San José City, with 124,383 inhabitants.

GOVERNMENT ... A republic. Its President is elected by the people for a four-year period.

HOW TO GET THERE ... By PAA affiliate, LACSA Airline, 5¾ hours (elapsed time) to San José from Miami via Havana and/or Grand Cayman, B.W.I.: about 1 hour by Clipper from Managua, 1¾ hours from Panamá.

ACCOMMODATIONS ... San José has many good hotels; the largest is the *Gran Hotel Costa Rica* with 130 beautifully furnished rooms with private bath, located in the heart of the city. Rates begin at $7. The *Gran Hotel Europa*, recently rebuilt in modern design, has 86 rooms and is famous for its excellent cuisine. Rates start at $7. The newest hotel, the *Balmoral,* is located in the downtown section and has 83 modern, well-appointed rooms. Rates start at $7. The new *Royal Dutch Hotel* is conveniently located. Rates are $6 to $8. Other modern hotels in the downtown section are the *Metropoli, Fornos, San José Inn,* and the *Tala Inn.* Rates in these hotels range from $3 up.

ARTS ... The National Museum, located at the antique Bella Vista Fort in San José City, contains interesting collections of Indian relics in gold, pottery and stone from the ancient civilization which existed long before the Spaniards came to Costa Rica.

BALLET ... Foreign and local companies appear at the National Theater occasionally.

BANKS ... Banco Central de Costa Rica, Banco Nacional de Costa Rica, Banco de Costa Rica, Banco Anglo Costarricense, Banco Lyon, Banco Agrícola de Cartago, Instituto Nacional de Seguros. Traveler's checks may be cashed anywhere.

CALENDAR OF HOLIDAYS ... The public holidays are: January 1, New Year's Day; March 19, Feast of St. Joseph; Thursday and Friday, Easter festivals; April 11, Anniversary of the Battle of Rivas; May 1, Labor Day; Corpus Christi, a Thursday in June; June 29, Feast of St. Peter and St. Paul; August 2, Feast of Our Lady of the Angels; August 15, Feast of the Assumption; September 15, Independence Day; October 12, Columbus Day (*Día de la Raza*); December 8, Feast of the Immaculate Conception; Christmas Day.

CIGARETTES AND TOBACCO ... The best American cigarettes are available for about 55 cents (American currency) a pack. Various brands of good cigarettes are manufactured in Costa Rica.

CLIMATE ... One of the greatest attractions of this country is its wonderful climate. Costa Rica, like other Central American countries, has only two seasons, the rainy season and the dry one. The ideal time to visit is during the dry season from December to April, but the climate is agreeable all year around.

CLUBS ... Union Club, Costa Rica Country Club, San José Golf Club, Rotary Club, Lions Club, Junior Chamber of San José (Jaycees).

COMMUNICATIONS ... The Government postal system extends to practically all the centers of population, with airmail service to the principal cities and to foreign countries. Telephone and telegraph services are very well organized. All America Cables and Radio, Inc., the Tropical Radio Telegraph Co. and Compañia Radiográfica provide excellent radio telephone service to points all over the world.

CURRENCY ... The unit of currency is the colón. The rate of exchange in the free market is 6.63 colones per United States dollar.

CUSTOMS REGULATIONS AND DOCUMENTS REQUIRED FOR UNITED STATES CITIZENS ... Similar to those in effect throughout Central America. Baggage is inspected on arrival, but for tourists it is a simple, easy matter, quickly dispensed with. For travelers carrying only clothing and personal effects, no declarations are necessary. One bottle of liquor, about 1 pound of tobacco, 1 camera and six films, 1 used portable typewriter, 1 pair binoculars, used sporting articles, books and manuscripts, are considered as baggage and allowed duty free. Visitors who do not intend to remain in the country for more than 48 hours may enter with only some form of identification and continuing transportation. For longer stays you need a Tourist Card, available for $2 at airline offices or Costa Rican consulates, or a valid passport visaed (at no charge) by the Costa Rican Consul at the point of departure. The visa is valid for 4 years for U.S. citizens on a reciprocal and multiple-entry basis.

DRUG STORES ... The usual variety of medicines and drugs is available including practically all American products.

ELECTRIC CURRENT ... Electric current in San José is the same as in the United States, 110 volts, 60 cycles, A.C.

FAUNA ... There are special hunting zones with an interesting variety of wild life which includes: puma, deer, bear, wild pig, squirrel, monkey, wild turkey, alligator, rabbit, jaguar, fox, pigeon, etc.

FLORA ... Many varieties of beautiful tropical flowers are seen everywhere in Costa Rica. The Guaria Morada (*Cattleya skinerii*), Costa Rica's national flower, as well as many other kinds of orchid, grow in the mountains and in beautiful gardens near the cities.

FOOD ... *Tamales, tortillas* and *gallo pinto* are the favorite native food. In addition all kinds of Continental food are served in private homes and hotels.

GAMBLING ... All forms are prohibited with the exception of the Government lottery.

LANGUAGE ... Spanish is the official language, but a high percentage of people speak English fluently. At the airport, aviation companies, souvenir shops, hotels and better stores the tourist will find employees who speak English.

LAUNDRY ... There are many good dry-cleaning establishments in San José City.

LIQUOR ... Here you will find all kinds of American and European liquors. The National Liquor Factory is one of the best in Central America, and some of its products are comparable to those from abroad.

MEDICAL FACILITIES ... There are many English-speaking doctors. The principal hospitals in the capital city are: San Juan de Diós Hospital, Seguro Social Hospital, Clínica Bíblica, Clínica Mater.

MOTION PICTURES ... American and European pictures are shown at the *Palace, Raventós, Lux, Coliseo, Roxy, Ideal, Center City, Rex, Variedades, Moderno.*

MUSIC ... There is a Symphony Orchestra which gives concerts at the National Theater weekly. There are also performances in the same theater by visiting pianists and violinists. The Military Band offers concerts three times a week in Central Park.

NIGHT CLUBS AND CABARETS ... San José City has several night clubs: The new *Balmoral Supper Club; Chez Marcel,* French food and atmosphere; *Patio Tico,* American and native atmosphere; at the *Casino Central* you will find gay Spanish atmosphere with floor shows nightly.

PHOTOGRAPHY ... Black-and-white and color films are available in all photo stores in San José, as well as a complete line of cameras and equipment, both foreign and American made. Developing facilities are available and the work is of top quality. 24-hour service is available if desired.

RELIGION ... The official religion is Roman Catholic, but in accordance with the Constitution religious liberty prevails. There are other denominations represented in the capital city and elsewhere.

RESTAURANTS ... At the *Gran Hotel Costa Rica* and the *Gran Hotel Europa*, Continental food; the *Hispano*, Spanish food; *Patio Tico*, American food; *Chez Marcel*, French food; *Vesuvio* and *Ana's*, Italian food. Other good restaurants include the *Americano, El Balcón de Europa, Tixe's, Gina's, Holland House, Casino Central*, Drive-Inn *El Ranchito*.

SHOPS AND STORES ... The best stores are located along Central Avenue of San José City, and around the Central Market.

SPECTATOR SUORTS ... Soccer football, including games with foreign teams, is played on Sundays at the National Stadium. Basketball and baseball matches are played at the baseball stadium.

SPORTS ... Swimming, horseback riding, hunting, golf, tennis and ping-pong. There's wonderful big game fishing, marlin, black, Pacific sailfish, tuna, etc.

TIME ... Same as United States Central Standard Time.

TIPPING ... About the same as in the United States.

TRANSPORTATION ... San José is well equipped with taxis, for which the usual rate is about $1.30 per hour, for one to four persons. Excellent highways connect San José with all points of interest in the country. There are also bus services. Three international airlines serve Costa Rica, in addition to a local one. The Ferrocarril Eléctrico al Pacífico, owned by the Government, links San José with the port of

Oxen and carts are still an important means of transportation on the coffee fincas of Costa Rica.

Puntarenas. The Northern Railway Company is a private concern and connects San José with Port Limón. U-drive cars are available in San José.

WATER ... You will find good drinking water anywhere.

WHAT TO BUY ... Costa Rica has lovely leather, wooden and tortoise-shell articles.

WHAT TO WEAR ... In and around San José, the tourist ordinarily wears medium-weight clothes all year round. Evening dress is not essential in San José for the one-day visitor. To visit the volcanoes you need sweaters and coat, as it is very cold.

WHERE TO GO—SIGHTSEEING ...

San José ... When in San José, tourists should visit the National Theater, which has solid marble stairways, beautiful sculpture, beaten gold and bronze decorations, immense ceiling and wall paintings executed over sixty years ago. Other places worthwhile visiting in town are: the National Museum, with interesting collections of pre-Spanish relics; the National Congress on Avenida Central, where the Nation's laws are made; the Metropolitan Cathedral, principal church of the Roman Catholic faith; the National Stadium, where exciting international matches are frequently staged; the National University, University City, one of the most remarkable constructions of San José. One of the things which attracts tourists is the promenade of the young people around Central Park during the evenings.

Side Trips ... Near San José is the Costa Rica Country Club, which offers facilities for golf, tennis, bowling, and swimming. Ojo de Agua, on the highway to Alajuela about 30 minutes by bus or taxi from San José, is a very nice swimming pool with a special section for children. The water supply for the pool is from natural springs which look like an eye, hence its name.

La Catalina Summer Resort on a coffee plantation, is the beautiful vacation spot only 35 minutes from San José on the way to the Poas Volcano; it has facilities for swimming, tennis, golf, riding. One of the most interesting sightseeing points in Costa Rica is the active crater of the Irazú Volcano at an altitude of 11,322 feet. It is only 1½ hours from San José on a good paved road that reaches the summit. Another interesting trip is to Poas Volcano, which has the world's widest geyser, a boiling lake of sulphur that erupts to a height of 2,000 feet. In the Province of Cartago, a short distance from the Capital City, the beautiful valley of Orosi is well worth seeing, as are the Ruins of Ujarrás, an old church located in the same province. From San José you may take a morning trip to Escazú, Santa Ana, Villa Colón, returning to the hotel for lunch. Another place of interest to visit is Puntarenas, on the Pacific coast, a 4-hour scenic ride by electric railroad. Puerto Limón is on the Atlantic coast, a 5-hour train ride from San José through magnificent scenery.

SOURCES OF FURTHER INFORMATION ... National Tourist Board, P.O. Box 777, San José. Pan American office in San José is at Avenida 1a and Calle 1a (Tel. 4204). The LACSA office in San José is at Ave. Primera between Calle Alfredo Volio and Calle Primera.

EL SALVADOR

WEATHER IN SAN SALVADOR—Lat. N13°43'

Temp.	JAN.	FEB.	MAR.	APR.	MAY	JUNE	JULY	AUG.	SEPT.	OCT.	NOV.	DEC.
Low	59°	60°	61°	64°	65°	65°	65°	65°	65°	64°	62°	60°
High	86°	89°	90°	90°	87°	86°	86°	86°	85°	85°	84°	85°
Average	73°	75°	76°	77°	76°	76°	76°	76°	75°	75°	73°	73°
Days of Rain	1	1	2	4	12	19	20	20	17	16	5	2

LOCATION ... El Salvador, smallest and most densely populated of the Central American republics, lies along the Pacific next to Guatemala and Honduras.

CHARACTERISTICS ... A lot of sightseeing with a minimum of travel is in store for you in El Salvador. Active volcanoes, beautiful lakes, lush tropical scenery and inviting Pacific beaches all lie within a few miles of San Salvador, the tiny Republic's modern capital. The people are thrifty and industrious, welcome visitors to their fascinating country, which like the rest of Central America, is one of the most accessible but least-traveled vacation spots. El Salvador abounds in sights to see and things to do—ranging from visiting hinterland villages, which still bear the mark of Spanish colonial times, to hunting alligators.

POPULATION ... The inhabitants number approximately 2,500,-000, born of the fusion of Spaniard and Indian. The pure Indian strain has almost disappeared.

SIZE ... 7,772 square miles, about the size of New Jersey.

CAPITAL ... San Salvador, situated in the Valle de las Hamacas at the foot of the Volcano of San Salvador, was founded by order of Don Pedro de Alvarado in 1525. Its population numbers about 200,-000 inhabitants. It is 2,250 feet above sea level. San Salvador in the last few years has grown to the point where it is called the most progressive city in Central America.

GOVERNMENT ... A republic.

HOW TO GET THERE . . . By Pan American Clipper from New Orleans via Merida and Guatemala; from Houston and Dallas, via New Orleans or Mexico City; from Los Angeles via Guatemala or Mexico City. From New Orleans 6 hours; from Los Angeles, 10½ hours; from Mexico City, 4 hours; from Miami via Havana, 5 hours.

ACCOMMODATIONS . . . Check on the availability of the new *El Salvador-Intercontinental,* another fine hotel, managed by Intercontinental Hotels Corporation of New York. This new air-conditioned structure, only 10 minutes from the center of San Salvador, features an individual garden terrace or private balcony for every room, with a spectacular view of both the city and the famous volcano. There's an outdoor swimming pool too. Rates are about $11 and up single, European Plan. The *Hotel Astoria* and *Hotel Nuevo Mundo* are two modern hotels in the heart of the city. Rates $10 to $12 per day, American Plan. There are various smaller hotels and pensions with rates of $4 to $6, American Plan, among them *Hotel Internacional, Boarding House* and *Casa Clark.*

ARTS . . . For Indian relics the National Museum, the Mayan ruins of San Andres 20 miles from the capital, with ruins dating from the sixth century, the temple ruins of Tazumal.

BANKS . . . Bank of London and Montreal, Ltd.; Banco Salvadoreño; Banco Central de Reserva, Banco de Comercio, Banco Hipotecario. Traveler's checks may be cashed at any of these banks, also at hotels and transportation companies.

CALENDAR OF HOLIDAYS . . . New Year's Day; Holy Week; May 1, Labor Day; August 4, 5, and 6, Fiesta of the Patron of San Salvador; September 15, Independence Day; October 12, Columbus Day; December 12, Indian's Day; Christmas Day.

CIGARETTES . . . American cigarettes of popular brands are available at United States 50 cents a package. Local cigarettes of good quality cost 14 cents.

CLIMATE . . . El Salvador has a rainy season and a dry season. (See weather chart.) Climate is warm but not everywhere nor at all hours. Evenings are usually cool.

CLUBS . . . The Country Club boasts excellent tennis courts, swimming pool and golf course. The Circulo Deportivo Internacional is a favorite resort for swimming, tennis, volley ball. The Club Salvadoreño has good bowling alleys, billiards and excellent cocktail lounge. It also has a beautiful night club, for members and guests only. There are Lions and Rotary clubs here, too.

COMMUNICATIONS . . . Tropical Radio and All America Cables for telegraph and long-distance telephone calls. Local telephone service is of modern standard. Airmail to the United States.

CURRENCY . . . The local monetary unit is the colón. The official rate of exchange is ¢2.50 for $1 United States.

CUSTOMS REGULATIONS AND DOCUMENTS REQUIRED FOR UNITED STATES CITIZENS . . . Tourist cards are issued by consulates at no cost to all citizens of Western Hemisphere countries. Vaccination certificate. Firearms require permits. One kilogram of tobacco in any form (5 cartons of cigarettes, or 330 cigars or about 2 lbs. of tobacco), and 2 bottles of liquor allowed duty free.

DRUG STORES . . . American and European products available.

ELECTRIC CURRENT . . . 110 volts, 60 cycles, A.C.

FAUNA . . . Deer, wild pig, jaguar, and other tropical animals.

FLORA . . . Orchid, carnation, rose, gardenia, among others.

FOOD . . . Salvadorean food is less spicy than that of most Latin countries, but chile and other hot sauces are served if requested. Try *Gallo en Chicha.* Tamales, *tortillas, enchiladas,* and other local dishes may be ordered. Seafood and tropical fruits are good. Continental food is served at the best hotels and clubs.

GAMBLING . . . Public gambling is prohibited by law. There is a national lottery twice a month.

LANGUAGE . . . The Spanish language is official, but you'll have no trouble being understood when speaking English.

LAUNDRY AND DRY CLEANING . . . There are many laundry and dry-cleaning establishments in San Salvador.

LIQUOR . . . All kinds of liquors are available and at very reasonable rates. Scotch whisky can be purchased for as little as $5.00 per bottle. Local liquors are of good quality.

MEDICAL FACILITIES . . . Doctors and specialists, many of them graduates of United States and European universities, are available.

MOTION PICTURES . . . American, Mexican, Argentine and European films are shown in the local theaters. Recommended theaters are the *Caribe, Central, Regis, Avenida* and *Apolo.*

MUSIC . . . American, European, Mexican, Cuban and Argentine music, all popular. Marimba music can be enjoyed, but the dance orchestras are composed mainly of American-type instruments. Serenades are still a custom.

NIGHT CLUBS . . . There's *Chalo's* and the *Gran Mirador,* situated in the hills overlooking the city. Dining and dancing Friday and Saturday nights. No floor shows.

PHOTOGRAPHY . . . Black-and-white still and movie film, color film, cameras and practically all other photo equipment available at the numerous photo-supply shops in San Salvador. V. Crisonino, Salvador Photo Supply, Calle Delgado No. 21, is one of many.

RELIGION . . . Mostly Catholic, but all denominations are represented.

RESTAURANTS AND BARS . . . Your best bets are the main hotels and clubs, where almost any type of drink or food can be had. The *Siete Mares* in San Benito and the *Monterey* are recommended.

SHOPS AND STORES . . . The better class of shops covers a radius of about six square blocks. Also try shops in the Caribe Building, Silva's Building, the hotels and airport. The Public Market is good for local goods and souvenirs.

SPECTATOR SPORTS . . . Soccer games (the national sport) are held nearly every Sunday and holiday at the National Stadium. Basketball during winter season only. There's cockfighting, too.

SPORTS... Deep-sea fishing can be enjoyed off the coast, also at the Estero de Jaltepeque and in the Gulf of Fonseca, off the port of La Union. Sailing along the wide channels of the Estero de Jaltepeque and Jiquilisco, the visitor is fascinated by the vistas of lush tropical vegetation, quiet waters, roaring surf and breathtaking sunsets. Surf bathing at the various beaches along the Litoral or coastal highway is another attraction.

TIME... Same as United States Central Standard Time.

TIPPING... Slightly less than in the United States.

TRANSPORTATION... Taxis may be hired for tours and several agencies offer guided tours. Car hires are also available. Avoid buses during rush hours.

WATER... Hotels serve bottled water and there are soft drinks.

WHAT TO BUY... Native handcrafts, hand-woven textiles, pottery, native dolls, leather goods, blankets and jewelry.

WHAT TO WEAR... Sports clothes are everyday wear. Nights are cool enough for worsteds. Topcoats not necessary at all. Hats should be lightweight felt or palm. A raincoat for May to October.

WHERE TO GO—SIGHTSEEING...

San Salvador... Is an important commercial center, being the third largest exporter of coffee. It is a growing city and has been modernized because fires have destroyed some of the principal buildings. Several old churches such as "La Merced" remain. A trip to the hills overlooking the city, called Planes de Renderos, where various restaurants are located, is worth while in order to get an "aerial" view of the city. Balboa Park, with its "Devils Door" vantage point, crowns the summit. Tours of the city and of the various outlying places of interest are available. Because of the country's dense population, on these tours you'll find the land tilled even on the volcano slopes. Santa Ana, second largest city, is a coffee center. The coastal highway also offers interest.

Izalco... Is a 6,000-foot volcano near the old colonial city of Sonsonate, about 40 miles from San Salvador. Of the 14 volcanoes which exceed 3,000 feet in height, Izalco is the country's most famous, pouring out flame, smoke and lava with clock-like regularity every 8 minutes. Often called "Lighthouse of the Pacific," its fires serve as a beacon to navigators in the Pacific, 25 miles away. A few remnants of the vanished aboriginal race may still be found in the villages near here. The best view is from Cerro Verde mountain top.

Panchimalco... Beyond Planes de Renderos is the Indian town of Panchimalco. Low adobe houses with tile or thatched roofs, irregular streets paved with uneven blocks of stone, and an old colonial church have attracted tourists by their peaceful charm. The inhabitants, the Panchos, preserve their ancient customs. The women wear ample blouses, wide, long skirts made from material woven on their primitive looms. On their heads they wear bright-colored shawls and adorn their necks with red and blue necklaces decorated with old Spanish silver coins. The men wear simple cotton dress and palm hats.

El Boqueron... The crater of the Volcano of San Salvador, 6,333

All types of merchandise are sold by street vendors in San Salvador, capital of El Salvador.

One of the most beautiful places in El Salvador is Lake Coatepeque, popular resort area. Across the lake is the Santa Ana volcano.

feet high, may be reached from Santa Tecla. The crater of the volcano is a mile wide and a half mile deep. At the bottom there is a smaller cone left by the eruption of 1917. From the northern edge a petrified stream of lava stretches for many miles down a slope, toward Quezaltepeque. The view from the crater is very impressive; the cities of Santa Tecla and San Salvador lie below and farther off.

Lake Ilopango ... Is 10 miles from San Salvador and easily reached by an excellent paved road. Of volcanic origin, this beautiful lake 10 miles long is the favorite resort of the Salvadoreans. There's a modern park at Apulo, with restaurants, bathing houses and pier.

Lake Coatepeque ... One hour's ride from San Salvador is one of the most beautiful lakes in Central America. There are good hotels and restaurants. The shores are lined by beautiful private residences. The waters are highly medicinal and compare favorably with those of Vichy. No trip to El Salvador can be complete without a visit here.

Other places to visit include the National Parks of Atecozol and Ichanmichen, Apastepeque Lake and the Cerro de Las Pavas which you reach through a sixteenth century village, Cojutepeque.

SOURCES OF FURTHER INFORMATION ... There is a National Tourist Bureau at Calle Rubén Darío No. 55, San Salvador. Pan American's local office is in the Edificio Dueñas. In New York the El Salvador Consulate is at 55 W. 42nd St.

GUATEMALA

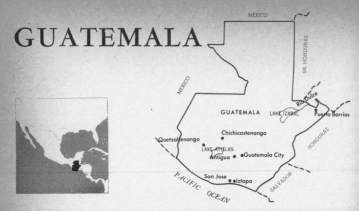

WEATHER IN GUATEMALA CITY—Lat. N14°37'—Alt. 4,850'

	JAN.	FEB.	MAR.	APR.	MAY	JUNE	JULY	AUG.	SEPT.	OCT.	NOV.	DEC.
Average Temp.	61.3	62.8	65.7	66.2	68.0	66.2	65.8	66.0	65.7	64.8	62.8	61.3
In. of Rain	0.3	0.2	0.5	1.3	5.6	11.5	8.0	8.0	9.2	6.7	0.9	0.2

LOCATION ... South and east of Mexico, Guatemala is the most northern country in Central America.

CHARACTERISTICS ... Guatemala is for the traveler who is seeking atmosphere rather than gay night life, local color rather than chic resorts. Part of Guatemala's charm is its unspoiled native life. Guatemala City has been rebuilt since the last earthquake in 1917; it is a small, clean city with a cosmopolitan air. Guatemalans are friendly and glad to help the visitor. They are a quiet-spoken, well-educated, proud and patriotic people.

POPULATION ... Approximately 3,500,000, or about the same as Chicago.

SIZE ... 42,456 square miles, similar to the area of Tennessee.

CAPITAL ... Guatemala City, with roughly 300,000 inhabitants, is about the size of San Diego.

GOVERNMENT ... A republic, the Government is divided into three bodies: executive, legislative and judicial. The executive is represented by the President and ten Cabinet Ministers, the legislative by one Congress composed of 66 members representing 22 states (called *Departamentos*). Each state has a Governor appointed by the President.

HOW TO GET THERE ... By Pan American Clipper, 4½ hours from New Orleans; 6 hours from Miami, via Havana; 2¾ hours from Mexico City; 8½ hours from Los Angeles. From Houston, 2¾ hours to Mexico City where connections are made for Guatemala.

From New York, about 7¼ hours to Mexico City, 2¾ more to Guatemala. By ship 3 days from New Orleans to the Guatemalan port of Puerto Barrios.

ACCOMMODATIONS... There are good hotels in Guatemala City and throughout the highlands. Except where noted rates below are single, American Plan and apply the year around. First-class hotels include: the *Palace* (European Plan $7 to $9), *Pan American* ($12 to $14), the *Maya Excelsior* ($11 to $14) and the *San Carlos, Hotel Lima* ($9 single, $12 double European Plan; $5 more each American Plan). Others in order of merit are the *Plaza* ($10 to $12), *Colonial, Gran Continental*. There are a number of good pensions ($3.50 to $5) including *Casa Shaw, Chez Bruna* and *Fernandez*.

ARTS... Indian crafts and weaving. Many modern cultural groups in music, ceramics and painting. Guatemala City has fine museums, art academies, and exposition centers.

BALLET... Although there is no set season, the Ballet "Guatemala" and foreign groups perform from time to time in the capital.

BANKS... In Guatemala City there are the Bank of London and South America, Ltd.; Banco Agricola Mercantil; Credito Hipotecario Nacional; Banco de Occidente; Bank of America; Banco Agrario Nacional Banco Inmobiliano; Banco de Comercio é Industria; and Banco del Agro.

CALENDAR OF HOLIDAYS... Official holidays: January 1; Thursday and Friday of Holy Week; May 1; July 3; August 15; September 15 (Independence Day); October 20; and Christmas Day. There is a long roster of fiesta days; some of them are: March 19 at San José; Holy Week celebrated throughout the country in April; July 25 at Santiago de Atitlán; July 28–31 at Momostenango; August 14–16 at Guatemala City; November 1 and 2 throughout the Republic; December 8–12 at Escuintla; December 17–21 at Chichicastenango.

CIGARETTES AND TOBACCO... American cigarettes of any popular brand are available but generally cost more than local cigarettes such as Victor, Club, Raleigh, Fleetwood and Altenses. Only 3½ ounces of tobacco in any form are allowed to be brought into the country.

CLIMATE... It is almost always balmy and pleasant, although there is a "showers" season and a dry season. See chart on page 328 for Guatemala City temperatures. In the highlands the days are warm, the nights cool.

CLUBS... Guatemala Country Club, Mayan Golf Club, American Club, Italian Club, Alejandro Von Humboldt (German), Lions Club, Rotary Club, Tennis Club and Guatemala Club. Visitors' cards can be arranged through your travel agent.

COMMON COURTESIES AND LOCAL CUSTOMS... Since, as mentioned before, Guatemalans are quiet spoken and well bred, loudness in speech and manners and exaggerated dress are frowned upon. Men should always wear a jacket in restaurants and clubs.

COMMUNICATIONS... Local dial telephone service in Guatemala City. Long-distance service to all points in the interior of the

Republic through local public service and international calls through Tropical Radio and Telegraph service and All America Cables. Radiograms to all parts of the world. Postal cards by airmail carry 5 cents postage; 6 cents for ½ oz. letters.

CURRENCY . . . The monetary unit is the quetzal, which is divided into 100 cents and is at par with the United States dollar with similar coin and bill denominations.

CUSTOMS REGULATIONS AND DOCUMENTS REQUIRED FOR UNITED STATES CITIZENS . . . Tourist cards (dated within 60 days before arrival) may be obtained through all Guatemalan consulates and some offices of PAA, especially gateways (coastal cities), as well as through some travel agents. Cards cost $2 U. S. currency. Only documentary proof of citizenship and age are necessary to obtain them. All travelers must be in possession of smallpox vaccination certificates. A logical amount and class of photographic equipment is allowed. Customs officials are instructed to conduct inspection of baggage of visitors very lightly. Liquor and tobacco are restricted to 1 bottle and 3½ oz., respectively.

DRUG STORES . . . No soda fountain, but both European and U.S. pharmaceuticals and cosmetic products. French perfumes may be purchased freely at reasonable rates.

ELECTRIC CURRENT . . . In Guatemala City and throughout the tourist centers, it is 110 volts, A.C.

FAUNA . . . Deer, wild boar, mountain puma, monkey, alligator, tapir, wild turkey, duck, crane. Guatemala's national bird is the quetzal, a rare species with beautiful feathers. The country is also well known for its variety of humming birds.

FLORA . . . Climatic conditions make Guatemala an ideal spot for an almost unlimited variety of flowers, such as the native orchid and hydrangea, hibiscus, violet and rose. A white orchid called *monja blanca* (white nun) is indigenous to the country, and is Guatemala's national flower.

FOOD . . . Most restaurants serve Continental food, others specialize in native dishes. Here are some you may want to try: *Gallo en chica, enchiladas, chiles rellenos, chojin, tamales, rellenitos de platano* and, of course, Guatemalan coffee, one of the best. Pasteurized milk is served in Guatemala City; however, it may be wiser for the traveler to drink it boiled only.

GAMBLING . . . Unlawful. National lotteries, bingo games. Private betting at cockfights and horse races is overlooked.

LANGUAGE . . . Spanish is the official language, but you will have no trouble being understood when speaking English.

LAUNDRY AND DRY CLEANING . . . Dry-cleaning establishments and hotels where you can get practically anything done—double tariff for rush orders—within 24 hours.

LIQUOR . . . Chief native liquors are rum *Amaja* and rum *Coloso*. They sell for about $2.50 a bottle. Popular U.S. drinks are available from 60 cents to 90 cents. Hotel bars are open mostly between 10:00 A.M. to 9:00 P.M.; others until midnight, a few until 2:00 A.M.

MEDICAL FACILITIES ... Practically all doctors speak English, and specialists exist in almost all phases of medicine. Most of the doctors and surgeons are ex-interns from famous institutions in the United States such as the Mayo Clinic, Johns Hopkins and others.

MOTION PICTURES ... U.S., British, Italian, French, Mexican and Argentinean films are shown by most movie houses. In the center of town are the *Lux, Capitol, Palace, Fox, Roxi, Capri, Cali* and *Paris.* In the residential district the *Reforma,* a plush, up-to-date theater. All foreign films have Spanish titles.

MUSIC ... Guatemala originated and is noted for marimba instruments. Its native dance is the *son,* which is danced during all celebrations. In Guatemala City marimba music may be heard nightly at *El Gallito's* and *Pierrot's.* Band music is played weekly at Central Park; the Guatemala Symphony Orchestra performs several times a year under local and guest directors.

NIGHT CLUBS AND CABARETS ... There isn't much night life in the capital; however, the few night spots are located in the downtown district. *Pigalle* (floor show), *El Gallito* and *Pierrot* (local color), *Choco's Bar, Bar Robles, Bouganville, Maracas, Giani's Monterrey.*

PHOTOGRAPHY ... Black-and-white and color film, stills and movies are available at Alvarez, Andreu, Biener, Biener-Tabush, Legrand, Muñoz and Serra. All of them develop still film and Andreu's develops color and black-and-white movies.

RELIGION ... The country is Catholic; however, Protestant sects such as Presbyterian, Seventh Day Adventists, Episcopalian, Lutheran, Church of England, and Baptist are represented. There is a synagogue. Most of the Protestant sects have services in English, the Lutherans in German.

RESTAURANTS ... Besides the dining rooms of Guatemala City's first class hotels listed before, *El Patio* and *La Casita* serve Continental food; *Triana* and *Las Casuelas* specialize in dishes from Spain; *Sans Souci* and *El Gallito* feature local dishes; *Altuna* has good sea food and Italian delicacies. All of these are centrally located. Halfway between the capital and the southern suburbs is *Las Palmas,* with exquisite Italian and Continental dishes, and *Trocadero,* specializing in sea foods, and farther out is *El Intimo* with à la carte service. The excellent *Chung King* and *Fu Lu* serve Chinese food. There are fine French pastry shops such as *Simon, Jensen's, Palace Bonbonniere* and *Austria,* where one may enjoy coffee, tea, chocolate and any soft drinks. Snacks may be had at *Pecos Bill, Reforma, Cafeteria Robles, Satelite, Cafeteria Plaza* and at any of the many hot-dog stands. Restaurants are not expensive. A dinner at one of the best (*El Patio, La Casita*) will cost from $2.50 to $3. Native dinners range from 80 cents to about $1.25.

SHOPS AND STORES ... Shopping district in the capital is along 6th Avenue; on 12th Street and 8th Street, as well as on 9th, 10th and 11th Streets. Stores generally open from 8:30 A.M. to 12:30 noon and from 2:30 P.M. to 6:30 P.M. Native curio shops are open until

8:00 P.M. Some of the main stores are: La Paquetería, La Ciudad de Paris, La Perla, La Marquesa, El Paje, Fru-Fru, El Cairo, Lazaro. These stores carry U.S. and European merchandise. Curio shops are: Maya-tex on 7th Avenue at 9th Street; Robbie's, at 6th Avenue, No. 9–61; Guatelandia, at 8th Avenue, No. 8–24; Mildred's, at the San Carlos Gran Hotel; souvenir shop at the Pan American Hotel; La Regional and several others at Central Market; and Rigalt's, Nelly's, La Dama and Regina Shop on 12th Street between 4th and 5th Avenues. Also Handtex, 12th Street and 16th Avenue; Domus, 12th Street 3–53, and Cecile's, 7th Street 3–67.

SPECTATOR SPORTS . . . Soccer and basketball, both local and international games every Sunday and occasionally weekdays, held at the capital's Olympic Stadium and Gymnasium, located at the Olympic City on 7th Avenue Colonia Lima; baseball at the Olympic Field, situated at Minerva Park at the end of Avenue Simeon Cañas.

SPORTS . . . Golf, tennis, swimming, bowling, billiards. Sharpshooting and skeet at the Club de Caza, Tiro y Pesca. Fishing is good on both coasts, Puerto Barrios on the Atlantic and San José and Iztapa on the Pacific; boats and outboards may be hired by the hour and by the day; equipment should be procured in the city or brought from home. Hunting is plentiful: deer, pumas, pheasant, wild turkey, ducks, squab, quail, wild boar. Licenses for hunting arms are necessary; they may be obtained through hunting groups.

THEATERS . . . In Guatemala City occasional plays at *Teatro Universitario de Camara.* Plays are in Spanish. Other theaters, like the *Palace* and *Capitol,* have fewer performances.

TIME . . . Central Standard Time is observed throughout the year.

TIPPING . . . Tip for the same services you would at home, but slightly less.

TRANSPORTATION . . . Taxis abound in Guatemala City. Bus lines run in all directions covering practically the whole city. To travel inland you can use the services of a tour operator or hire a car, about $25 a day for trips outside the city. There are railroad and local airline services throughout the country.

WATER . . . Although purified, it may not be safe to the visitor unaccustomed to it. All hotels serve boiled water in their carafes. Popular U.S. soft drinks are also available.

WHAT TO BUY . . . Guatemala excels in colorful Indian weaving. Indian market and native curio shops offer a variety of these products. As an example, leather (hand-tooled) shoulder-strap bags cost from $3.50 to $6 in comparison with similar goods (imported from Guatemala) that sell in the United States for $24. Skirts in Mayan designs, shirts, blouses and sandals make wonderful and colorful sportswear.

WHAT TO WEAR . . . Medium-weight apparel, sportswear, light sweaters, walking shoes, topcoat and swimsuit are suggested. A light raincoat is advisable for travel during May to October and through the lowlands. A dark basic dress or suit is appropriate for evening.

WHERE TO GO—SIGHTSEEING . . .

In Chichicastenango, life centers around the colorful market place. In the background Indians burn incense on the steps of the Church of Santo Tomás.

Guatemala City ... In the capital take a look at the Church of Santo Domingo, which is whiter than white because milk and the white of eggs were mixed in the mortar to give it greater strength. The Presidential Palace of light green stone is interesting. A must for tourists is the relief map of the country found in Minerva Park, which gives you an excellent idea of the country. Many old churches escaped the 1917 earthquake, among them the Cathedral, which is interesting. The National Museum is of interest, too. The markets, particularly the big one at the Mercado Central behind the Cathedral, and Mercadito, or little market, are "must sees." Hayter Travel, Clark Tours and Eca Tours offer 4-, 5-, and 9-day tours which cover the Mayan highlands and Guatemala City and include Chichicastenango, Antigua and Lake Atitlán. Other tours include some of the out-of-the-way places such as a jungle trip and a visit to Rio Dulce and Lake Izabal. Using a tour operator is most convenient, but you can go on your own.

Chichicastenango is an interesting spot in Guatemala. There you will find the *Mayan Inn,* famous all through Central and South America. The food is wonderful, the setting unique. Spanish colonial and Indian art everywhere you look. Barefoot Indian boys are house servants. Strolling marimba players entertain you. Rates are about $8 to $14 per day, American Plan. A visit to the Indian market held Thursdays and Sundays is one of the main reasons for going.

Antigua is the former capital of the country. Some of the old buildings have survived. The market has good hand-wrought silver. Stay at *Rancho Nimajay, Posada Belém* or *Hotels Antigua* or *Aurora.* Palin, south of the capital, has a market under a Ceiba tree.

Lake Atitlán is 5,000 feet above sea level and is overlooked by three volcanoes. Hotels *Casa Contenta* and *Tzanjuyu* here are excellent. Indian villages ring the 85-mile shoreline. Other points of interest are: Quezaltenango, a mountain town with a cool, moderate climate. It has an interesting market and narrow streets. It is the country's second city. Puerto Barrios, chief port of the Caribbean, is a 200-mile train ride through the jungles from the capital.

SOURCES OF FURTHER INFORMATION ... The National Tourist Bureau at 6 Ave # 5-34 and the tour operators mentioned under WHERE TO GO have literature, maps and information. Pan American's office is on 6a Avenue, No. 12-12 (Tel. 2250 and 2251). In New York the Guatemala Consulate is at 30 Rockefeller Plaza.

HONDURAS

WEATHER IN TEGUCIGALPA—Lat. N14°6'—Alt. 3,200'

	JAN.	FEB.	MAR.	APR.	MAY	JUNE	JULY	AUG.	SEPT.	OCT.	NOV.	DEC.
Average Temp.	65°	71°	73°	74°	73°	75°	73°	73°	73°	70°	71°	66°
In. of Rain	0.18	0.05	0.29	0.97	5.90	5.00	6.76	6.53	7.76	3.55	1.26	1.31

LOCATION ... The Republic of Honduras lies between Guatemala and Nicaragua in the Central American strip, with coastlines on the Caribbean and Pacific. El Salvador is its neighbor to the southwest.

CHARACTERISTICS ... Honduras, most mountainous of the Central American countries, offers the vacationist adventure difficult to match in any other Latin American country today. In this little republic—which jumped from the ox cart to the airplane in one prodigious leap—sixteenth-century Spanish colonial atmosphere is superbly preserved. Here visitors can see the ruins of the ancient Maya city of Copan, which flourished about the time of Christ, and take a boat trip through a tropical jungle whose trees teem with brilliantly colored birds and hordes of chattering monkeys. All the larger cities of Honduras offer good hotel accommodations at a wide range in prices. Chief recreational pastimes include golf, tennis, hunting, swimming and fishing (both lake and deep sea). The people of Honduras are mostly Indian and *mestizo* (a combination of Spanish and Indian). They are friendly. You'll enjoy this tropical country off the beaten tourist track.

POPULATION ... 1,800,000 inhabitants.

SIZE ... Approximately 46,330 square miles.

CAPITAL ... Tegucigalpa, D.C. (Central District), with a population of 82,000. The neighboring city of Comayaguela has a population of 17,984. Altitude is 3,200 feet above sea level.

GOVERNMENT ... An independent republic.

HOW TO GET THERE ... By Pan American Clipper, only 9½ hours from New Orleans, 11 hours from Houston. Connections from San Francisco, Los Angeles and Miami, via Guatemala or San Salvador. By ship, 3 days from New Orleans.

ACCOMMODATIONS ... In Tegucigalpa, the best hotels are the *Lincoln,* about $9 single, American Plan, and *Prado,* $8 and up single, American Plan. More modest are the *Marichal, Boston, McArthur* and *Europa.* The *Savoy* is $5.00 and up single.

BANKS ... In Tegucigalpa, Banco Central de Honduras, Banco Nacional de Fomento, Banco Atlántica, Banco de Honduras; in Santa Rosa de Copan, Banco de Occidente. All of these banks correspond with United States banks and those in other parts of the world. Traveler's checks may be cashed and bought at any of those banks.

CALENDAR OF HOLIDAYS ... January 1; February 3, Honduras Virgin Day; May 1, Work Day; September 15, Independence Day; October 3, Birthday of Morazan, Central American hero; October 12, Columbus Day; December 25, Holy Thursday, Friday and Saturday preceding Easter. The Fair of Comayaguela opens every year from the 7th through the 24th of December.

CIGARETTES AND TOBACCO ... American cigarettes and tobacco are available; cigarettes cost 40 cents per pack. Local cigarettes, such as Crown, cost 25 cents, King Bees, 15 cents. These are manufactured by a branch of American Tobacco Company. Honduras is famous for its excellent tobacco from Copan, where fine cigars are manufactured.

CLIMATE ... Honduras has a tropical climate, but in Tegucigalpa there is a very pleasant climate throughout the year with the exception of March, April and May, when it gets warmer; however, the nights are always cooler. The climate on both the north and south coasts is always hot; it averages about 85 degrees and at times it goes up to 100 and 105 degrees in some places.

CLUBS ... Tegucigalpa Country Club, Casino Hondureño, Lions Club, Rotary Club, Tegucigalpa Golf Club, Club Tegucigalpa, Club Reforma, The Sky Room.

COMMUNICATIONS ... Honduras is served by All America Cables and by Tropical Radio and Telegraph Co., for cable, radio and radio-telephone service with the exterior. Local telephone and telegraph service is operated by the Honduras Government for interior communications. Airmail rate for postal cards and letters to the United States is 6 cents for every 5 grams.

CURRENCY ... The monetary unit is the lempira, and the current rate of exchange is 2 lempiras for $1, even though the official rate of exchange is 1.98 lempiras for selling dollars, and 2.02 lempiras for buying dollars.

CUSTOMS REGULATIONS AND DOCUMENTS REQUIRED FOR UNITED STATES CITIZENS ... Passport properly visaed is required, *or* a tourist card, which costs $3, may be obtained from any

Honduran Consul upon presentation of: a valid identification document such as a birth certificate, three (3) front-view photographs; valid smallpox vaccination certificate; round-trip or transportation beyond Honduras. Tourist cards are valid for thirty (30) days' stay, from date of entry into Honduras. One opened carton of cigarettes, 1 opened bottle of liquor may be brought in duty free.

DRUG STORES ... American products, as well as European and others, are available but are expensive. French perfumes may be purchased freely at reasonable prices.

ELECTRIC CURRENT ... The voltage in hotels in Tegucigalpa is 220 volts, 60 cycles, A.C. This is the voltage throughout the city. However, in other cities there is also 110 volts. Hotels will furnish transformers upon request to convert 220 to 110 volts.

FAUNA ... Among a variety of tropical animals, there are deer, jaguar, mountain lion or American puma, peccaries or wild pigs, wild turkey, monkey, alligator, tapir. Water fowl is abundant both on the north coast and Pacific coast lagoons, rivers, etc., especially from October to February. There are quail, whitewing pigeon, dove, parrot and many types of singing birds, such as *zorzal, jilguero, zensontle.* Opportunities for hunting are abundant.

FLORA ... There is a variety of flowers, among which are orchids of various types. A variety of hardwoods is available: mahogany, primavera, *guenacaste, carreto,* and many others. Honduras has enormous sources of timber, especially pine. Ordinary and tropical vegetation is found most anywhere in Honduras due to the variety of altitudes and climates.

FOOD ... Among the typical native foods there are *nacatamales, mondongo, tapado de carne salada, quesos blancos de Olancho y Choluteca, tortillas* and *enchiladas,* among others. Chili is not used as much as in Mexico and Guatemala. Restaurants and hotel dining rooms serve Continental food. Milk is available and good. Meals at the best hotels and restaurants range from $1 to $1.25 for breakfast, $1 to $2 for lunch or dinner.

GAMBLING ... There are no casinos, horse or dog racing; gambling is prohibited. However, during the Comayaguela Fair anybody can gamble from December 7 through December 24. The only legal gambling is the National Lottery, proceeds of which are used for charitable institutions.

LANGUAGE ... The official language is Spanish, but there is a large percentage of English-speaking people. Many Honduran people send their children to school in the United States. There are several American schools. The influence of large American companies established in the country for many years is causing the English language to be learned by all Hondurans.

LAUNDRY AND DRY CLEANING ... Laundry facilities cannot compare with those in the United States in either speed, quality or price. This applies also to dry cleaning. Although facilities are available, the service is fair and rather expensive. Hotels will take care of customers' laundry within 24 hours, at double tariff for rush orders.

LIQUOR . . . All kinds of fine liquors, both European and American, can be bought at lower prices than in the United States. Native liquors are *aguardiente* and *ron catracho.*

MEDICAL FACILITIES . . . Almost all doctors speak English. In Tegucigalpa there are the following hospitals: Viera, Centro Médico Hondureño; Sanatorio El Carmen; La Policlínica; Hospital San Felipe. In addition, the United Fruit Company has its own up-to-date hospitals at La Lima and Tela.

MOTION PICTURES . . . American movies are shown at *El Variedades* and *Clamer,* and Mexican films at *El Palace* and *Hispano.* Cinemascope at *Maduro.*

MUSIC . . . The distinctive music is the native marimba bands.

NIGHT CLUBS AND CABARETS . . . There is scarcely any night life in Tegucigalpa, but there is some at the *Terraza Club* of the Prado Hotel, the *Duncan Mayan Club,* and the *Reforma Club.*

PHOTOGRAPHY . . . Tourists can buy good photo equipment, black-and-white as well as color, still and movie film in Tegucigalpa and most of the north coast cities. American products are more expensive but European ones are cheaper here than in the United States. Film developing facilities are available within 24 hours. However, movie films have to be sent to the United States for developing.

RELIGION . . . Principal local religion is Catholic. However, there are a few churches for Protestant, Evangelist, and other denominations.

RESTAURANTS . . . Best restaurants in the capital are *El Chico* Club, very good; *McArthur,* for Spanish food; *Duncan Mayan* Restaurant; *The Grill; El Madrigal; Savoy* Restaurant, *El Carrusel,* and *Reforma* Restaurant.

SHOPS AND STORES . . . The better-class shops are to be found on Avenida Paz Barahona in Tegucigalpa. Fresh American groceries are available at Bazar Union, Linton's and La Surtidora. Baskets and pottery can be found at the Los Dolores market.

SPECTATOR SPORTS . . . Football (soccer), basketball and baseball.

SPORTS . . . Arrangements for golf and tennis can be made through the Pan American office or by contacting the president of the Tegucigalpa Golf Club. Information on how to make arrangements for hunting and fishing can also be obtained from Pan American.

TIME . . . Same as United States Central Standard Time.

TIPPING . . . Tip the same as you would in the United States.

TRANSPORTATION . . . Taxis or cars may be hired for tours around the country. Train service is available throughout the north coast. There is bus service, but it is very poor. Rates are reasonable. There is frequent scheduled air service throughout the country via SAHSA, a Pan American affiliate. Small planes may be chartered for three or four persons for special trips as well as larger planes for excursions.

WATER . . . Water is good and safe to drink. Water in Tegucigalpa and all other main cities comes from very high mountains. Bottled water from the Kist factory is available in Tegucigalpa.

WHAT TO BUY . . . Excellent Panamá hats, known as *sombreros de junco,* made in Santa Barbara, are among the best buys; also beautiful handbags made of same material as Panamá hats. Baskets, pottery, native crafts carved in beautiful, unusual hardwoods.

WHAT TO WEAR . . . Honduras, like all tropical countries, is informal, so take sports clothes—linen for north and south coasts, and tropical worsted, palm beach, light clothes for Tegucigalpa, except in December and January, when it gets cool, especially at night. No topcoat is ever necessary for men, but required sometimes for women. Men will need slacks, sports jackets. Dark suit desirable for evening, as well as dark daytime and evening dresses for women.

WHERE TO GO—SIGHTSEEING . . .

Tegucigalpa . . . Is a picturesque city where the colonial atmosphere is evident on every hand. Built on the side of Mount Pichaco, 3,200 feet above sea level, its streets run in all directions and at all angles and grades, culminating in odd little plazas at unexpected places.

Four of the city's churches and many of its pastel-colored stucco residences and business structures date back to colonial times. The President's palace is a fortress-like structure with towers and turrets facing the steep-banked Choluteca River.

Principal show places in the city include Morazan Plaza and Concordia Park. Bordering the former is an ancient cathedral, which is one of the handsomest and most graceful in Central America. Nearby is the National Museum, featuring an odd collection of living and stuffed animals, pottery and idols removed from the mounds at Copan.

Near Tegucigalpa is the old capital city of Comayaqua, founded in 1535. Twenty-five miles away by highway at Zamorano is the Pan American Agricultural School, which includes an outstanding collection of tropical plants and flowers.

Copan . . . Can be reached in little more than an hour by air. In the days of their glory, the temples, palaces and courts of Copan— capital of the first Maya Empire—sprawled over 15 square miles. Today many of these magnificent stone structures are intact and may be readily inspected. A quaint inn offers comfortable accommodations.

Several interesting tours are available through Copan Tours in the capital: An Introduction to Tegucigalpa, two days; Tegucigalpa and Zamorano (the famous agricultural school established by the United Fruit Company) three days; Comayagua (the ancient capital of Honduras which has been conserved in the tradition of the Conquistadores) and the Lowlands, three days; Ruins of Copan, three or five days tours.

SOURCES OF FURTHER INFORMATION . . . In Tegucigalpa inquire at Pan American's office, Avenida Colón and 4a Calle. In New York City the consulate is located at 17 Battery Place.

MEXICO

WEATHER IN MEXICO CITY—Lat. N19°26′—Alt. 7,349′

Temp.	JAN.	FEB.	MAR.	APR.	MAY	JUNE	JULY	AUG.	SEPT.	OCT.	NOV.	DEC.
Low	42°	44°	48°	52°	54°	55°	54°	54°	54°	50°	48°	43°
High	66°	70°	75°	78°	79°	76°	74°	74°	72°	70°	68°	65°
Average	54°	57°	62°	65°	67°	66°	64°	64°	63°	60°	58°	54°
Days of Rain	3	4	6	11	15	19	25	24	20	12	6	4

LOCATION ... Mexico lies between the United States and Central America, with coast lines on the Pacific Ocean, the Gulf of Mexico and the Caribbean. Mexico City is 1,560 air miles from Los Angeles, 1,275 air miles from Miami, 746 air miles from Houston.

CHARACTERISTICS ... Mexico, land of the ancient Aztecs, has a wide range of attractions for everyone: fabulous beaches and world-famous resorts ... modern cities flavored with the charm of Old Spain ... volcanoes, snow-capped mountains, blooming deserts ... thrilling bullfights, colorful fiestas ... exquisite shops, luxurious hotels, the gayest of night clubs. You'll find all these in Mexico. And you'll receive more than twelve pesos for one United States dollar!

POPULATION ... Estimated at 30,000,000—equal to about a sixth of the population of the United States.

SIZE ... 760,290 square miles, roughly a quarter of the area of the United States.

CAPITAL ... Mexico City, officially Mexico D.F. (Federal District), population estimated at 4,400,000, about the size of Chicago.

GOVERNMENT ... Mexico is a republic of 29 states, officially known as the United States of Mexico, and two territories (South Lower California and Quintana Roo) and a Federal District.

HOW TO GET THERE ... By Pan American or affiliate airlines,

Mexico City is 3 hours from Houston; 4¾ hours from Los Angeles; 2½ hours from Brownsville, Texas, via Tampico. By connecting air-lines through Houston, elapsed time to Mexico City is 6¾ hours from St. Louis; 9 hours from Washington D.C. Nonstop service from New York and Chicago, 6½ hours and 6 hours, respectively. Merida is 2½ hours from New Orleans and 3¾ hours from Miami via Havana. By train Mexico City is 3 days and 3 nights from New York, 2 days and 2 nights from St. Louis.

ACCOMMODATIONS . . . There are hotels of every type available. You can live luxuriously or modestly, depending upon your budget. Outside Mexico City there is little difference in price between the Class A and Class B hotels, but the difference in comfort can be great. Investigate carefully when making your reservations. Here are some of the good hotels (all European Plan) in Mexico City:

The *Reforma Intercontinental*, world-famed hotel on the fashionable Paseo de la Reforma, is convenient to the business district and sightseeing points of interest. Newly renovated by Intercontinental Hotels Corporation, it's modern throughout, uses only filtered artesian water, has new sanitary kitchens, excellent cuisine, informal coffee shop. Average rate $12 single, $14 double. Recent additions to the capital's impressive ultramodern hotels are the *Continental Hilton*, at Reforma y Insurgentes, the *Plaza Vista Hermosa* at Sullivan y Insurgentes, the *Bamer* and the brand new *Del Paseo* at Paseo Reforma and Napoles. Rates at all of these average $12 single, $14 double. *El Presidente* at Hamburg 135, also brand new, has rates of $14 single, $18 double. Rates at the *Alffer* at Independencia 59, $10 single, $12.50 double. The *Del Prado*, facing the Alameda, is a large hotel with murals by Diego Revera, Covarrubias and Montenegro. Coffee shops, dining room, bars, etc. Rates average $10 single, $12.50 double. The *Monte Casino* and the new *Premier* at Atenas 76 have average rates of $8 single, $10 double. The *Ritz*, well known as are other Ritz Hotels is at Avenida Madero 30. Murals by Covarrubias. Rates average $6 single, $9 double. The *Regis*, Avenida Juárez 77, has an excellent night club, *Capri Paolo* restaurant and *El Greco* bar. Rates average $6 single, $9 double. The *Prince*, Luis Moya 12, has good central location, bar and fine restaurant. Rates average $6 single, $8 double. The *Geneve*, Londres 130, is excellent. Rates are $4 single, $6 double. Also many fine smaller hotels, such as the *María Cristina, Cortés, Lincoln, Emporia, Majestic, Romfel* and *Francis*, with rates from about $5 single, $6 double.

ARTS . . . There is so much art in Mexico that it is difficult to decide what to see first. Musts are: the National Palace with frescoes by Diego Rivera; the Fine Arts Palace, with frescoes by Rivera, Orozco and Siqueiros; the Palace of Justice, with frescoes by Orozco and George Biddle; the National Museum of Anthropology, in which all the many cultures of Mexico are represented; the Central Art Gallery, which houses most of the Mexican moderns; the Ministry of Education, which contains sculptures, frescoes by Carlos Merida and Rivera, and a self-portrait by the latter. The Palace of Fine Arts houses a theater and a museum. The theater has a curtain of Tiffany glass depicting two extinct volcanoes. The Palace also houses El Museo Nacional de Artes Plásticas. The Museum of Flora and Fauna is filled with exotic specimens from all parts of the country. Galería Mexicana is devoted to the works of Rivera.

BALLET ... Visiting companies of ballet perform in Mexico occasionally. There is also good Mexican ballet several times a year. Opera is presented at the Palace of Fine Arts each spring.

BANKS ... There are hundreds of banks and branches throughout Mexico City. All major hotels have branch banks in their lobby. Banking hours are from 9:00 A.M. to 1:00 P.M., except Sunday and holidays. Most hotels and shops will change money at other hours. The National City Bank of New York, Uruguay e Isabel la Católica; Banco Nacional de México, S.A., Av. Isabel la Católica No. 44; Banco de Londres y Mexico, 16 de Septiembre y Bolívar; Banco de Mexico, 5 de Mayo y Motolinia; Banco de Comercio, V. Carranza 42.

CALENDAR OF HOLIDAYS ... There is scarcely a day in the year that there is not a fiesta in some province or town, but here is a list of national holidays celebrated by the entire country; New Year's Day; January 6, Day of Los Reyes Magos; February 5, anniversary of the establishment of the Constitution in 1857; Shrove Tuesday; celebrations like Mardi Gras; Easter week when most business houses and all Government offices are closed; March 21, Birthday of Benito Juárez; May 1, Labor Day; May 5, Mexican National Holiday celebrating victory over French at Puebla, 1862; September 16, *El Grito* or Independence Day; October 12, Columbus Day; November 1 and 2, All Saints and All Souls Days, the days of the dead; November 20, Anniversary of the Revolution of 1910; December 12, Guadalupe Day; December 16 to 25, the *Posadas* to celebrate Christmas.

CIGARETTES AND TOBACCO ... Mexican cigarettes and cigars are good and inexpensive. American cigarettes cost from 35 to 40 cents per pack here. Pipe tobacco, both American and English, and imported cigars are available but expensive.

CLIMATE ... Mexico City, situated at about 7,500 feet, has a wonderful springlike climate. Because of the altitude it is essential to take things slowly to avoid overfatigue. There are no sharply defined seasons, but there are light afternoon rains from June through October. Mornings are invariably sunny, even during the rainy season. Mexico City claims to have more sunshine than any other large city and it's an excellent spot for asthma sufferers.

CLUBS ... American, British, French, Rotary, Lions, University, Variety, Women's International, American Legion, Skal, YMCA, and YWCA. Cards are necessary for some and may be obtained from resident members or through a travel agency.

COMMON COURTESIES AND LOCAL CUSTOMS ... Bargaining is accepted practice in the markets and in small shops. The big stores have a one-price policy. Luncheon, served from one to three, is the big meal of the day. Drunks are regarded with intolerance. Women in slacks and shorts are not permitted on the streets of Mexico

City. Men should not remove their coats or ties. Women, unless they are in the heart of the city, should not be unescorted. Don't take pictures of people without asking permission. Everyone plays the national lottery. Residents call Mexico City merely "Mexico."

COMMUNICATIONS... Telephone, telegraph and cable services are available nearly everywhere, even in small cities. Airmail to the U.S. costs .50 centavos for each sixth of an ounce.

CURRENCY... The Mexican unit is the peso, designated by the dollar sign and worth about 8 cents in United States currency. Official rate is 12.50 pesos to the United States dollar. Banks and money exchangers may accept dollars at a slightly lower rate.

CUSTOMS REGULATIONS AND DOCUMENTS REQUIRED FOR UNITED STATES CITIZENS... Tourists are permitted to bring in anything for personal use duty free. 2.2 lbs. tobacco (4 cartons cigarettes) 12 rolls of film, 3 quarts of liquor permitted duty free. Evidence of citizenship should be carried. If you have valuable articles of foreign make, cameras, etc., register them with the U.S. Customs before leaving the United States. There are no restrictions on importation or exportation of money except for gold, so don't buy jewelry containing gold coins. Radios and T.V. sets are restricted. They are registered and must be taken out on departure.

Tourist cards, valid for six months, costing $3, may be obtained from any Mexican Consulate or Tourist Commission office and from some Pan American offices. A multiple entry card, costing $5, is valid for various visits within six months. Passport, birth certificate or some other definite proof of citizenship is required. United States citizens as tourists may obtain their tourist cards upon arrival at the Mexican airport of entry. Smallpox vaccination certificate is necessary. Yellow fever and cholera certificates required if coming from an infected area.

DRUG STORES... In Mexico City, Sanborn's, Avenida Madero 4 and Reforma 45; Farmacía Juárez, Avenida Juárez 95; Farmacía Regis, Avenida Juárez 77, and dozens of others carry U.S. and European products. Small drug stores are to be found in or near all the better hotels.

ELECTRIC CURRENT... 110 volts, 50 cycle A.C. throughout most of the country.

FAUNA... Birds and animals native to Southwestern United States are found in Mexico. Parrots of many types, tapirs, honey bears and several varieties of monkeys are native to much of Mexico.

FLORA... Beautiful flowers and plants, spectacular flowering trees, cactus of all varieties, orchids of many kinds, and many exotic tropical plants abound.

FOOD... Tamales are, of course, known to everyone, but equally famous is *mole de guajolote*, turkey with a rich sauce. Tacos and *enchiladas* are made of meat or chicken rolled in *tortillas* (maize pancakes) and are delicious. Mexico abounds in fruits and vegetables. Indian dishes are found all over Mexico. Chile, *molé, tostadas* (toasted fried *tortillas* with chicken, beans and lettuce) are all Indian and good. Mexican beans (*frijoles*) appear in various dishes. Red snapper, Veracruz style, is a famous fish dish, sautéed with pimientos and spices. Fruits include a vast assortment of tropical types— avocados, bananas, pineapples, *zapotes,* pomegranates, guaves, limes and *mangos de Manila,* which are delicious. Many varieties of the above are unknown at home. Don't eat fruit unless you peel it yourself, and avoid raw vegetables. Try *higos rebanados* (delicious fresh sliced figs), *guacamole* (a mashed avocado salad) and of course, papaya, which you may or may not like. In Mexico City you can get any type of food you want. Milk for children. Meal times are later than in the United States. Luncheon is the main meal, served between 1:00 P.M. and 3:00 P.M. Dinner is late in the evening.

GAMBLING ... Not allowed. There is horse racing at the Hipódromo de las Americas in Mexico City every Tuesday, Thursday, Saturday and Sunday; from October to July. Pari-mutuels here and at jai-alai games. Betting on cockfights outside of Federal District.

LANGUAGE ... Spanish is the official language, but the tourist will have no trouble getting along in English; all the stores and hotels have English-speaking employees.

LAUNDRY AND DRY CLEANING ... Better hotels have their own plants and offer both special 24-hour service. There are other good plants throughout the city. Service outside the bigger cities is not recommended. Prices are about the same as in the United States.

LIQUOR ... Tequila and *pulque* are native drinks. Tequila, distilled mainly in Jalisco, is potent. Tourists should be cautious. *Pulque* is also potent and takes getting used to. *Mezcal* is still another native potion which is far from mild. Mexican beer is famous; Bohemia, Carta Blanca, XX and Corona are all good. Imported whiskies and brandies of nearly every brand are available but more expensive than in the United States. Native products are low in price.

MEDICAL FACILITIES ... English-speaking and American-trained doctors and dentists available, often as staff physicians in the best hotels. In Mexico City there is an American-British hospital (Calz. M. Escobedo 628), a French hospital and many Mexican institutions. If you need a doctor, consult your hotel or call the American hospital and ask them to recommend one.

MOTION PICTURES ... Mexican movie industry makes its own pictures. Hollywood and British films are usually with English sound, dubbed-in Spanish text. French and Italian movies are popular.

MUSIC ... The concert season is July and August. Most popular symphony orchestra is conducted by Carlos Chavez. In Mexico City concerts are held in the Fine Arts Palace. Orchestras of the National Conservatory of Music and National University give concerts throughout the year. There are also native *mariachi* bands, whose music is famous throughout the country.

NIGHT CLUBS AND CABARETS ... There are numerous clubs: *Capri,* Juárez 77, dancing and floor show; *El Patio,* Atenas No. 9, Latin American floor show; *Jacaranda,* Genova St. No. 54, *Chanteclair* in the Hotel Reforma are all excellent. Most of the top hotels have night clubs. Go to *El Eco,* Sullivan 43, for sophisticated jazz. For colorful, out-of-the-way spots, take a guide with you.

PHOTOGRAPHY ... All kinds of equipment are readily available. Prices are lower than in the United States on most articles, especially cameras. Color film may be developed in Mexico. American Photo Supply, Av. Madero 21; Foto Regis, Av. Juárez 80; Foto Rudiger, V. Carranza 11 are good places for equipment or film work.

RELIGION ... Mexico is a Catholic country. Some of the cathedrals are world famous and should be visited. Services in English are held at Christ Church Episcopal, Articulo 123 #134; Union Evangelical Church, Reforma 1870; Lutheran Church of the Good Shepherd, Palmas 1910; St. Patrick's Church (Catholic), Bondojito 248, Col. Tacubaya; First Church of Christ Scientist, #21 Dante, Col. Anzures.

RESTAURANTS ... Every possible type of food is to be found in Mexican restaurants. A la carte is, of course, more expensive. You choose your restaurants here, as you do at home, by what you want to spend. Here are some of the leading places in Mexico City: *Ambassadeurs,* Paseo de la Reforma 12 (swank and high priced); *Prendes,* 16 de Septiembre 12 (good European food, moderate); *La Cava,* Insurgentes 37 (excellent French food and steaks, lavishly decorated as an old French tavern, moderate); *Tibet-Hamz,* Avenida Juárez 64 (Chinese Restaurant specializing in Cantonese and Mexican National dishes, centrally located, nice atmosphere, moderate); *Chalet Suizo,* Niza 37 (very popular with tourists, specializes in Swiss and German food, moderate); *Quid,* Puebla 154 (very special); *Shirley's Restaurant,* Villalongin 139 (real American food, moderate); *Focolare,* Hamburgo 87 (swank and high priced); *Rivoli,* Hamburgo 123 (a gourmet's delight, high priced); *Jena,* Morelos 110 (deservedly famous, à la carte, expensive); *Chanteclair* in the Hotel Reforma; *Paolo,* Juárez 77 (Italian specialties, expensive, good); *Parador,* Calle de Niza 17 (Spanish specialties, expensive, good); *Sanborn's,* three locations: Del Prado Hotel Arcade and Paseo de la Reforma 45, the building of the United States Embassy, Madero 4 (United States dishes and Mexican, too). Other recommended restaurants are *Delmonico's,* Londres 87; *Mauna Loa,* Hamburgo 172; *Restaurant 1-2-3,* Liverpool 123; *Chipp's,* Genova 59; *Alex Cardini's,* Madrid 21, home of the famous Caesar Salad. All the top hotels have excellent cosmopolitan restaurants. Mexico City has many bars. Here are a few favorites: *La Cucaracha,* Gante 1; *El Colmenar,* Ejido y Eliseo; *Bar Jardin* in the Hotel Reforma. *Montenegro* and *Nicte-Ha* in Hotel Del Prado.

SHOPS AND STORES ... The parade of shops is endless. Mexico City's Avenida Madero is like the Rue de la Paix in Paris. Sanborn's is famous for textiles and handcrafts. Tillett's, on Paseo de la Reforma, has those wonderful handblocked prints. There are also good shops on or near 5 de Mayo, 16 de Septiembre, Niza and Insurgentes. Mexican jewelry of handmade silver can be bought everywhere. Among the good silver shops are Sanborn's, Calpini, Prieto, and Vendome. Perfumes are lower priced than at home. There are also good buys in quality leather and suede articles. Be sure to visit the markets. There is one in every district. Each one sells pottery, glassware, textiles, serapes and jewelry. The National Pawn Shop turns up a bargain now and then, too. It's a national institution worth a look. Mexican tinware and Mexican lacquer are to be found everywhere.

SPECTATOR SPORTS . . . Baseball; boxing and wrestling (Wednesday, Friday and Saturday in the Arena Coliseo or Arena Mexico); bullfights from October to March every Sunday at 4:00 P.M. Novice bullfights fill most of the months when the regular season is over. *Chareadas* or rodeos every Sunday morning at Rancho del Charro. Football (soccer) in season; horse racing from October to July, Tuesday, Thursday, Saturday and Sunday; jai alai, nightly.

SPORTS . . . Golf at Chapultepec Golf Club, Club Mexico and Churubusco Country Club. Cards can be arranged. (Inquire at your hotel or Travel Bureau.) Hiking is a good sport in Mexico. Hunting and fishing permits may be obtained at the Departamento Forestal y Caza, Edison 145, Mexico City, and the Secretaria de Marina, Azueta No. 9, respectively. Permits are needed for inland and deep-sea fishing. Polo at Polo Club de Mexico. Riding horses may be hired from several stables, called *pensiones.* Tennis may be played at the Reforma and Churubusco Country Clubs. Swimming is done in pools. Best of these are located on the Puebla road.

THEATERS . . . Vaudeville houses include the *Lírico,* the *Follies,* and the *Margo.* Other theaters featuring many plays by Mexican and foreign authors mostly in Spanish, are the *Iris* and *Ideal.* Two performances nightly, at 7:00 P.M. and 9:00 or 10:00 P.M. Tent shows, where you pay by the act, are a novelty and very informal and colorful.

TIME . . . Same as United States Central Standard Time except in northwest states where Mountain or Pacific Time applies.

TIPPING . . . Tip here as you would at home, 10 to 20 per cent. Overtipping gets you nowhere.

TRANSPORTATION . . . Taxis are plentiful and cruise all over the city. Empty taxis carry a sign reading *libre,* meaning free. Meters are now used on all Mexico City cabs. Pay what the meter shows, plus 50 centavos. Taxis from stands near hotels have the right to collect one peso surcharge instead of the 50 cents charged by *libres.* Fares are quite reasonable. Buses and streetcars serve the entire city. There is frequent bus service all over the country. Rates are very low. Drive-yourself cars may be hired but are not recommended because of different traffic rules and the need to speak Spanish.

WATER . . . Is potable in most large cities; elsewhere it is not. Plenty of good bottled water available. For distant trips take a bottle of chlorine tablets just in case.

WHAT TO BUY . . . This depends on what you want to spend, what takes your eye and what you can't live without. Silver is, of course, a staple product. Careful shopping will turn up the unusual: Mexican glassware, pottery, handwoven textiles, lacquers, native baskets, fine leather goods and handcrafts of all types. If you go on side tours, various spots are famous for certain things, Taxco for silver, for instance, and beautiful tinware; Oaxaca for pottery and serapes, gold filigree and black pottery; Guadalajara for handblown glass and pottery. Each state has its own style of handcrafts. Perfumes are cheaper than in the United States, but patronize the stores, not street vendors. Take purchases through U.S. Customs yourself rather than have them sent by the store.

WHAT TO WEAR ... Mexico City is very dressy. Black street dresses are fashionable. Dress here as you would in any large United States city. But never, never wear slacks or shorts in public places or on the street. High altitude makes for cool nights and some cool days. Bring a topcoat, raincoat. For coastal resorts, plenty of cotton frocks, sports clothes, bathing suits and pastel silks. Good walking shoes are a must. As there is little central heating, a warm robe is needed in winter. Bring dark glasses. Evening clothes depend upon you and the kind of gaiety you plan, but are not necessary in Mexico City night spots. Sweaters come in handy. Men should take seersucker or linen jackets and suits. Wool suits for Mexico City, light topcoat, swimming trunks, raincoat, bathrobe, sports shirts and slacks.

WHERE TO GO—SIGHTSEEING ...

There is so much to see in Mexico that you have to take your choice unless you have a lot of time. Guides are available and the government requires all *bona fide* guides to be licensed. Don't take chances; hire them through hotels or tourist bureaus.

Mexico City ... The museums are mentioned under ARTS. La Catedral on the Zócalo is the oldest church on the American continent; Chapultepec, a beautiful forest park with a castle on a hill, dates from pre-conquest times. It contains a zoo and a lake; there are band concerts, promenades and wide, shady walks. The Franciscan Monastery at Churubusco is worth a trip. There are many short one-day trips from Mexico City. Among them consider: Sanctuary of the Virgin in La Villa de Guadalupe, patron saint of Mexico, accessible by trolley and bus; the Pyramids at San Juan Teotihuacan, and ruins of a sacred city. (This is about 30 miles from Mexico City.) Xochimilco floating gardens and flowery canals; beautiful church and monastery. City tour, including Chapultepec Castle, National Palace, museums and residential district, costs about $5 per person; Shrine of Guadalupe, Pyramids and Acolman Monastery tour costs about $6.50; one-day tour to Cuernavaca and Taxco, including lunch, costs about $13; two-day tour, including hotels and meals in Taxco, costs about $23 per person. See also snow-covered Popocatepetl, an easy car trip through interesting Amecameca to the 13,000 foot level.

Cuernavaca ... 46 miles from Mexico City by a new super highway. A fashionable resort once favored by Cortés, Maximilian and Carlota. See Municipal Palace with Rivera murals donated by Dwight Morrow, Borda Gardens. There are pyramids, lakes, cathedrals, quaint streets, wonderful old houses, good shops. There are many good hotels, American Plan. Many have gardens, swimming pools, bars.

Taxco ... 101 miles from Mexico City. Beautiful, picturesque town, surrounded by hills. Several first-class hotels and bars. *De La*

The Palacio de Bellas Artes contains the national theater and galleries of some of Mexico's best art. The Mexican Symphony Orchestra gives concerts here, too.

Only an hour by plane from Mexico City is Acapulco, with magnificent views of the rugged Pacific coastline. These tourists are on the terrace of the Mirador Hotel.

You'll be fascinated by the remarkably preserved ruins of ancient Mayan civilization, such as these at Chichen-Itza near Merida, Mexico.

Borda, Victoria, Posada de la Mission and *Rancho Telva* (under Wells Fargo management). Rates start at 180 pesos double, American Plan. *Santa Prisca* and *Los Arcos* start at about 130 pesos double, American Plan. Paco's Bar and Berta's are popular. Streets are cobbled, houses have overhanging balconies. This is the silver center. Sunday is Indian market day, and Mexican tinware abounds.

Acapulco ... 282 miles from Mexico City by road, about 60 minutes by plane. Magnificently beautiful coastal resort on the Pacific. The oval bay is surrounded by mountains and the scenery is fantastic. Hotels are numerous and range from super de luxe to modest. Newest are *El Presidente, Elcano, Las Brisas* with rates of about 400 pesos double, European Plan. *Hotel Pierre Marquez,* located on Revolcadero Beach, 12 miles from the city, is very swank. European Plan rates are about 250 pesos single, 300 up, double. There's a good coffee shop and dining room. The *Prado-Americas, Hotel Flamingos, Majestic, El Mirador, Caleta, Club de Pesca* and *Palacio Tropical* all start at about 320 pesos double, American Plan. Many lower-priced hotels: the *Bahia, La Riviera, Papagayo, Del Monte, Noa-Noa, La Quebrada Panamericano, La Playa* and *Las Hamacas.* Swim at Caleta in the morning, at Los Hornos Beach in the afternoon; see the spectacular diver at the La Perla Club. Hotels arrange fishing and hunting. Shops are filled with handcrafts.

Guadalajara ... Second city of Mexico, was founded in 1530, is 5,248 feet above sea level and has a fine year-around climate. Good hotels such as the *Fenix, Del Parque, Gran* and *Morales,* charge from 50 to 80 pesos double, European Plan. There's lots to see here. Nearby are Tlaquepaque, famous for pottery and mariachi music, Lake Chapala and the art colony of Ajijic, and the small town of Tequila where the native drink is made. There are many good buys in glass, ceramics and leather. See the cathedral and the state museum. Guadalajara is only 1¾ hours by plane from Mexico City, with flights daily.

Oaxaca ... 330 miles from Mexico City, less than two hours by air. Very old, pre-Spanish city with year-round pleasant climate. Located in beautiful semi tropical valley near jungle and mountains. Several good hotels: *Marques del Valle, Monte Alban, Margarita, Oaxaca Courts,* with cottages, swimming pools. Rates average 150 pesos double, American Plan. See the archaeological site nearby at Monte Alban; the ruins at Mitla, 45 minutes away; the church of San Felipe Neri with Churrigueresque altars; the Cathedral; the Church of Santo Domingo with its genealogical tree of the Virgin; La Soledad with the famous shrine of the Virgin. City market is picturesque, and on Saturday natives from surrounding villages come to buy. Serapes, black glazed pottery, blankets, thin woven-straw mats, obsidian and jade idols are outstanding here. Hunting is excellent.

Yucatán ... 2½ hours by air from Mexico City, on the Gulf of Mexico. This is where the great Maya civilization flourished. All social classes speak the Mayan language, and native men and women always dress in white. Women wear their hair in coiled braids piled on the head and tied with colored ribbon. The ruins of Chichen-Itza,

A good place to make your headquarters in Mexico City is the Hotel Reforma Intercontinental, right in the center of all the activity that makes Mexico interesting.

Uxmal and Izamal are accessible from Merida, the capital of the state of Yucatán. Merida has several good hotels, the *Merida,* the *Colón,* the *Montejo, Gran Hotel, Caribe* and *Reforma.* Some have air-conditioned rooms. Rates 50 pesos up double, European Plan.

Chichen-Itza is an archaeological wonder. The ruins of the once-great Maya city are fabulous. The Temple of the Warriors, the Round Tower, the Great Temple of Kukulkan all testify to the remarkable culture and progress of the Maya civilization.

The ruins of Uxmal, 58 miles south of Merida, are reached by bus or taxi. The Nunnery, the Governor's Palace, the House of the Prophet, a pyramid surmounted by two temples, are marvelous to see. Izmal is older than Chichen-Itza but is less frequently visited.

The weather in Yucatán is hot and humid. Take summer clothes. It's advisable to take along a pair of sun glasses, for the light is blinding. Never walk in the sun bareheaded. Yucatán is a hunter's paradise. It is filled with pheasant, deer, wild turkey and tropical game. You can hunt alligators too, if you feel like it. It is possible to visit other Mayan ruins from Merida, but special arrangements are necessary. Kabah, Sayil, and Labna in the Yucatán jungle are a trip for the hardy.

SOURCES OF FURTHER INFORMATION ... The Mexican Tourist Commission, Avenida Juárez 89, Mexico City, will upon request supply free maps, folders, etc. This government bureau has offices in New York, Chicago, New Orleans, Miami, San Antonio, Houston, Los Angeles and San Diego. The Mexican Tourist Association, Balderas 36, will also supply free literature on tourist attractions.

Tickets for bullfights, jai alai, etc., may be obtained easiest through travel bureaus by paying a ticket-broker's fee. There are dozens including Cooks and American Express. Pan American's office (Tel. 46–46–60) is at Paseo Reforma 35, next to the U.S. Embassy (Tel. 46–94–00).

A good English newspaper, the *News,* is published daily. The *Daily Bulletin, This Week* and *The Gazer* are free tourist publications.

NICARAGUA

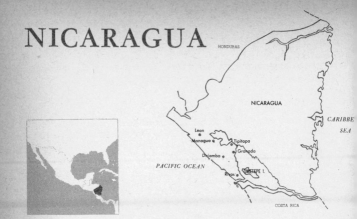

WEATHER IN MANAGUA—Lat. N12°8′

	JAN.	FEB.	MAR.	APR.	MAY	JUNE	JULY	AUG.	SEPT.	OCT.	NOV.	DEC.
Average Temp.	81°	82°	83°	86°	86°	82°	82°	83°	82°	82°	82°	80°
In. of Rain	0.12	0.02	0.02	0.50	5.64	8.24	5.11	4.74	8.38	11.58	1.70	0.41

LOCATION ... In the heart of Central America, bordered on the north by Honduras, on the south by Costa Rica, on the east by the Atlantic Ocean and on the west by the Pacific Ocean.

CHARACTERISTICS ... Land of lakes and volcanoes, Nicaragua gives its aerial visitors a breath-taking introduction to its spectacular scenery with a spine-tingling view of some of the 20-odd volcanoes that line the western side of the largest Central American republic. Some of the volcanoes spout clouds of steam and smoking ash, others cradle sky-blue or peacock-green lakes in their craters. While black, congealed lava makes many of the peaks a forbidding spectacle, a luxuriant green mantle of tropical growth makes others a delight to see. Nicaragua is also a land of broad lowlands, matted by rain forests and laced with swift-flowing rivers. But only the adventure-some explore this sparsely populated, little-developed region in the east. Most visitors head for the Pacific coastal plain, with its back-drop of volcanoes, where the bulk of the population, the principal cities, resorts and lakes are concentrated. The Nicaraguans are noted for their friendliness. They also go in for many fiestas.

POPULATION ... The inhabitants of the country number approximately 1,600,000.

SIZE ... 57,145 square miles, about the same size as Illinois.

CAPITAL ... Managua, with 152,000 inhabitants.

GOVERNMENT ... A republic.

HOW TO GET THERE ... By PAA Clipper from Los Angeles, via Guatemala, in approximately 11¼ hours; from San Francisco, 13¾ hours; from New Orleans, 10¾ hours; from Miami 3¾ hours; and also from Panamá, 2¾ hours. By ship 12 days from New York.

ACCOMMODATIONS ... In Managua: *Gran Hotel* and *Lido Palace Hotel* are the most frequently visited. Both have their own swimming pools. Rates about $10 and up American Plan. Other hotels: *Hotel Nicaragua, Estrella, Hotel Majestic* in Diriamba; *Santa Maria Ostuma*, a mountain hotel, 81 miles from Managua; the *Hotel Barlovento*, located in San Juan del Sur, a beach resort on the Pacific coast near the Costa Rican border. Approximately 2½-hour drive from Managua.

BANKS ... Banco Nacional de Nicaragua, Bank of London and South America, Ltd., Galley and Dagnal, Banco Hipotecario, Banco Tefel, Banco Nicaraguenie, Banco de America. Traveler's checks may be cashed anywhere.

CALENDAR OF HOLIDAYS ... There is a long roster of fiesta days. The most important are January 12 to 16, Fiesta Señor de Esquispulas, at Tipitapa, 14 miles from Managua; January 20, San Sebastian, at Diriamba, 25 miles from Managua; Holy Week, during which all business houses are closed and almost the entire population goes to the many beaches on the Pacific coast; May 1, Fiesta del Trabajo; May 30, Mother's Day; July 4; July 14, Bastille Day; August 1 to 10, Santo Domingo de Guzmán, celebrated in Managua with bullfighting, cockfighting and public demonstrations. (On the first day of this fiesta, Santo Domingo de Guzmán is brought from "Las Sierras." Hundreds of Managua inhabitants parade on horseback. On the last day, Santo Domingo de Guzmán is taken back to the Sierras in the same manner. It is the belief of the Indians that if Santo Domingo de Guzmán is not taken back to his church in "Las Sierras," he will disappear in Managua and will be found in his church.) September 14, Batalla de San Jacinto (Nicaraguan troops defeated the famous American Filibusters headed by William Walker); September 15, Dia de la Independencia; November 29 to December 7, La Purisima, celebrated in the whole country in honor of Virgin Mary; December 25, Christmas.

CIGARETTES ... American cigarettes are available; however, the local brands are quite satisfactory and are available for approximately 25 cents per pack.

CLIMATE ... Nicaragua, like other countries in Central America, has two seasons: the rainy and the dry season. Both have their advantages—the rainy season is warm but fresh, the dry season is cool but very dry. The best time to visit is December to May.

CLUBS ... Club Terraza, Club Managua, Club Internacional, French Club, Nejapa Country Club, Rotary, Lions International, Club España. There are other small clubs, restricted to members.

COMMUNICATIONS ... Nicaragua is served by All America Cables and Tropical Radio for both phone calls and telegraph messages to foreign points. The Government owns Radio Nacional, which provides communications to points within the country and also international communications.

CURRENCY ... The monetary unit is the cordoba. The rate of exchange is C.7.00 to $1 but market or street rate varies depending upon demand.

CUSTOMS REGULATIONS AND DOCUMENTS REQUIRED FOR UNITED STATES CITIZENS ... Passengers may bring up to $100 worth of new personal effects, 1 carton of cigarettes, 1 bottle of liquor, duty free. You will need a passport, visa, sufficient funds, smallpox vaccination certificate and police certificate. Citizens born in Continental U.S. may enter with a tourist card. Contact the Nicaraguan Consulate for information.

DRUG STORES ... All American drug products available, and many excellent locally manufactured items. Also imported drugs, perfumes and cosmetics.

ELECTRIC CURRENT ... Electric current is alternating and is rated at 110 volts. However, during peak hours the voltage drops off substantially.

FAUNA ... Deer, wild turkeys, wild ducks, and other tropical animals and birds.

FLORA ... Carnations, dahlias, orchids, roses, gardenias, and a great variety of tropical vegetation.

FOOD ... Nicaragua takes pride in its tropical dishes. All kinds of Latin foods are served; American dishes may be obtained on request. Food generally is inexpensive and meat very good.

GAMBLING ... There is an official Government lottery and all the profits are for the hospitals. On certain fiesta days, gambling, i.e., roulette wheels, is permitted.

LANGUAGE ... Spanish is the official language, but due to settlement of many English, German, Chinese, and French, almost any language is spoken.

LAUNDRY AND DRY CLEANING ... All hotels furnish 24-hour service for laundry and dry cleaning at reasonable prices.

LIQUOR ... All kinds of imported liquors are available. There are several locally made rums.

MEDICAL FACILITIES ... Most of the doctors in this area have been educated in the United States or Europe, and speak Spanish, English and one other language. There are two hospitals in Managua: the Hospital General and the Baptist Hospital.

MOTION PICTURES ... There are many motion picture theaters from the finest, air-conditioned houses to the outside unroofed theaters. Prices range from 35 cents to 90 cents.

MUSIC ... Both American and Latin American music is played in all clubs.

NIGHT CLUBS AND CABARETS ... There are many small clubs and cabarets. Saturday night is especially lively.

PHOTOGRAPHY ... Black-and-white film can be purchased and processed in Managua, but it is recommended that processing be done elsewhere due to the poor quality of the work here.

RELIGION... The country is Catholic, but other sects are represented.

RESTAURANTS AND BARS... There are several excellent restaurants in the center of town, such as *Bonbonniere, El Patio, La Colmena, Salon Vargas, Gambrinus, Guadalajara, Ambassador,* and the *Versailles.*

SHOPS AND STORES... Most of the stores in Managua are located on Avenida Roosevelt and Calle Central, where you will find American merchandise of all kinds. Nicaragua is famous for hand work and filigree gold jewelry at reasonable prices.

SPECTATOR SPORTS... Baseball, basketball, and cockfights are the outstanding sports. Also bullfighting (they don't kill the bull). Managua has the most modern and largest stadium in Central America, with a seating capacity of 40,000. At present, there are 162 baseball teams in Nicaragua.

SPORTS... Deep-sea fishing, sailing on the lakes, swimming, hunting, golf, tennis.

TIME... Same as United States Central Standard Time.

TIPPING... About the same as home.

TRANSPORTATION... Taxis. Cars may be hired for tours around the country. Bus trips also available.

WATER... Most hotels serve boiled water containing chlorine. Bottled water is also available, and soft drinks made with purified water.

WHAT TO BUY... Native handicrafts, alligator goods, hand-embroidered articles, hammocks, guitars, shoes (very fine shoes are hand made in Nicaragua).

WHAT TO WEAR... Sports clothes and all kinds of light clothing, as Nicaragua has predominantly a tropical climate.

WHERE TO GO—SIGHTSEEING...

Managua... The capital, Managua, is 28 miles from the Pacific. It rises gradually from the shores of Lake Managua and its red tile roofs and pastel-colored buildings give it a pleasant effect of freshness. The Nicaraguan capital is a new city. In 1931 an earthquake followed by a fire destroyed a large part of it; all new structures have been kept to one or two stories.

The best way to see the city is to start at Central Park near the lake front. Across the street is the park dedicated to Rubén Darío, Nicaragua's immortal poet. In this vicinity tourists may visit the capitol (called the National Palace), the city hall (known as the Palace of the National District), and the new cathedral. In Parque Darío is the splendid monument dedicated to the poet. On the east side of this park is the fashionable Club Managua.

For an interesting tour of the city, hire a car and drive past the President's residence, built in Moorish style on a hill overlooking Lake Tiscapa in the crater of an extinct volcano. A stop should be made at Piedrecitas Park, loveliest spot in the capital. Here are gardens and terraces where one may order a cool drink and enjoy a magnificent view of three lakes—Asososca, Managua and Jiloa—with bald, smoking Mt. Momotombo in the distance.

In the southwestern section of Managua is one of the city's most unusual sights. There are the footprints of people and animals made 2,000 to 5,000 years ago, according to foremost authorities. At some undetermined era they fled westward from a volcanic disturbance, leaving their footprints in a mudflow which later solidified.

From Managua, the tourist can make many interesting excursions. Motor launches may be rented for trips around Lake Managua. A pleasant drive is that to Tipitapa, a spa on Lake Managua, 14 miles from the capital. Here are hot springs, a comfortable hotel, casino, bathhouses and a swimming pool. The town is also famous for its fish dinners.

Granada . . . Nicaragua's oldest city; may be reached either by car or railroad from the capital. Situated at the northwest end of Lake Nicaragua, 30 miles from Managua, Granada was founded by the Spanish conquistadores in 1524. Today it is still a charming and leisurely old town with many Spanish landmarks. Sharing the streets with modern cars, are horse-drawn carriages and yokes of oxen drawing high-wheeled carts.

Lake Nicaragua is 100 miles long, 45 miles wide, and dotted with islands. One, Ometepe, is crowned by two high volcano peaks. The lake is the only one in the world where sharks, sawfish and tarpon may be found in fresh water. Historians believe that ages ago Lake Nicaragua formed part of a Pacific Ocean bay, then during one of the volcanic eruptions the entrance to the bay was closed. Thus the saltwater fish were trapped, and as fresh-water streams gradually diluted the salt, they adapted themselves to the change and survived.

Fifty miles north of Managua is **Leon,** a seventeenth-century Spanish city, which has one of the largest and oldest cathedrals in Central America. It was built in the eighteenth century and contains the tomb of the poet Rubén Darío. The University of Leon graduated students before the landing of the Pilgrim Fathers at Plymouth Rock. A short distance from Leon is the beach resort of Poneloya on the Pacific, with broad sand beaches and good hotels. Ideal for tourists.

A ride on the Inter-American highway takes you as far as the Costa Rican border, going through the coffee plantations and the city of Diriamba, where you will find the modern *Hotel Majestic,* located at an altitude of 3,000 feet above sea level. There are many nice beaches on the Pacific Coast, connected by good roads. Among them are San Juan del Sur; Casares, Boquita, Masachapa, Poneloya and Zapote.

The gold mining district may be visited and is accessible by air.

SOURCES OF FURTHER INFORMATION . . . The principal source is the Pan American office in the Gran Hotel, in the center of Managua, where tourist information and travel to the interior are available.

In New York, The Nicaragua Consulate is located at 1270 Ave. of the Americas.

PANAMA
AND THE
CANAL ZONE

WEATHER IN PANAMA CITY—Lat. N8°57'—Alt. 40'

Temp.	JAN.	FEB.	MAR.	APR.	MAY	JUNE	JULY	AUG.	SEPT.	OCT.	NOV.	DEC.
Low	78°	79°	79°	80°	78°	78°	79°	78°	78°	77°	77°	78°
High	80°	81°	83°	84°	82°	80°	81°	81°	80°	79°	79°	80°
Average	79°	80°	81°	82°	80°	79°	80°	80°	79°	78°	78°	79°
Days of Rain	.9	.9	.6	2.8	7.8	8.2	7.2	7.8	7.9	10.1	10.1	4.2

LOCATION ... The Isthmus of Panamá is geographically situated between Costa Rica in Central America and Colombia in South America. At its narrowest point, 50 miles wide, the Atlantic and Pacific Oceans are united by the world-famous Panamá Canal.

CHARACTERISTICS ... Here is a wonderful combination of old-world charm and modern comfort. The natural friendliness of its people, their gaiety and hospitality make Panamá a place to be visited and enjoyed. It is a paradise for sportsmen. Big-game fishing is famous here and hunting is excellent in the interior. There are luxury hotels and good beaches where swimming is delightful. Tourists are an old story in this colorful little country; they are very welcome.

POPULATION ... Estimated over 1,000,000, the size of Buffalo, New York.

SIZE ... 28,753 square miles.

CAPITAL ... Panamá City, population 234,610.

GOVERNMENT ... Panamá is an independent Republic of 9 provinces, except for the 10-mile-wide strip of land surrounding the Panamá Canal, land-leased to the U.S. Government and under its jurisdiction.

HOW TO GET THERE ... By Clipper from Miami, 4 hours; from New Orleans on nonstop service, 6 hours; from Houston 14½ hours via Mexico City. From Los Angeles 14 hours. By National-PAA-Panagra interchange 9½ hours from New York. By ship, about 5 days.

ACCOMMODATIONS ... The hotels are all run on the European Plan. The lavish *El Panamá Hilton,* situated in the residential section of Panamá, is the best. It is one of the most spectacular buildings of its kind. Studio-style bedrooms with private terrace are ultra-modern in design for beauty and comfort even in summer. Air-conditioned rooms are also available. Public rooms are air-conditioned, and featured are an outdoor patio, swimming pool, cabaña and tennis club, putting green, roof garden and dancing, gaming casino. Rates are $10 up, $15 up double (slightly higher Jan. to April). Also available are suites, from $20 to $24 single and from $25 to $29 up, double. The *Hotel International,* also quite new, has air-conditioned rooms and roof garden and is located in the downtown area; rates here are $8 up with private bath. The *Roosevelt, Colombia,* and the *Tropicana,* also in the downtown area, are well recommended and less expensive.

ARTS ... The Panamá Museum in Panamá City contains a representative collection of native arts and crafts that have been influenced by Spanish and ancient Inca civilization. Fortunately, Panamá crafts have escaped being over-commercialized. You will see fine examples of Panamanian taste and imagination in the art of these people.

BALLET ... The Escuela Nacional de Ballet and the Escuela de Ballet Gladys Heurtematte, just being developed, occasionally present ballets at the Nacional Theater. *El Tamborito,* the national dance, is colorful and enchanting. The folk dances may be seen particularly during the 4-day Pre-Lenten Carnival period. Dancers wear the *pollera,* the national costume jewels that are old family heirlooms.

BANKS ... In Panamá City, the National Bank of the Republic of Panamá, the Panamá Trust Co., the Chase Manhattan Bank of New York, the First National City Bank of New York; these last two have branch offices in Balboa, C.Z., and Colón, R.P.

CALENDAR OF HOLIDAYS ... Carnival Time, 4 days of fiestas before Ash Wednesday; New Year's Day; March 1, Constitution Day; May 1, Labor Day; November 3, Independence from Colombia; November 28, Independence from Spain; December 8, Mother's Day; Christmas Day.

CIGARETTES AND TOBACCO ... Practically all cigarettes here are American brands. A package of cigarettes costs 30 cents. There are a 15-cent and a 20-cent brand of Panamanian cigarette, the latter similar to American brands. Duty-free allowance 200 cigarettes.

CLIMATE ... The temperature of tropical Panamá is remarkable for its uniformity throughout the year. The average temperature is about 80 degrees. Noon is the hottest part of the day. Most of the stores close for a 2-hour lunch period. .Except for rainy October, Panamá is a pleasant place for visitors the year around, although it is at its best during the driest months, January through April.

CLUBS ... The Union Club and Golf Club in Panamá City extend cards to visitors through the courtesy of their members. The same goes for the Strangers Club in Colón. There is also the Rotary International of Panamá and Lions International. Beer garden clubs, the Rancho and the Atlas, are open to the public.

COMMON COURTESIES AND LOCAL CUSTOMS...Like all Latins, Panamanians are friendly and courteous to strangers. The afternoon nap is a well-established custom.

COMMUNICATIONS...There are telephone, telegraph and cable facilities in all major centers. All American Cables. Local service is good. Airmail rate between Panamá and the States is 10 cents a half ounce.

CURRENCY...The monetary unit is the Balboa, on a par with United States currency.

CUSTOMS REGULATIONS AND DOCUMENTS REQUIRED FOR UNITED STATES CITIZENS...The Tourist Card ($1) is sold at transportation offices through the United States port of embarkation. Carry proof of citizenship for re-entry to the United States.

Smallpox vaccination certificate and transportation beyond Panamá required for tourist card and admission into Panamá. Cholera and yellow fever certificate required if coming from infected area.

DRUG STORES...Well-stocked drug stores everywhere.

FAUNA...The central jungles of Panamá are full of rare birds and wild tropical game. There are jaguar, puma, tigrillo, ocelot, mule, deer, wild boar, peccary and the *conejo pintado* (painted rabbit). The fowl include wild turkey, quail, partridge and pigeon. The name "Panamá" means abundance of fish. Panamanian waters off both shores offer all sorts of deep-sea, big-game fish. There are giant tarpon, marlin and sailfish, to mention a few. The mountain streams of Panamá have some of the best trout in Central America.

FLORA...The rich tropical vegetation and bizarre flowers of Panamá are often breath-taking in their beauty. Orchids grow in profusion all over the countryside. The majestic palms are everywhere, especially along the superb beaches. If you go up into the highlands, you'll see the huge coffee plantations of Panamá's large coffee industry. The entire Panamanian landscape is a riot of color.

FOOD...American, French or Spanish cookery can be had in all restaurants and hotels. You will also enjoy the Panamanian food. Try a delicious *sancocho,* chicken soup with vegetables, the Panamanian tamales, which the natives boast are the best in Central America. *Arroz con pollo,* a universal dish in Latin America, is delicious made in the Panamanian manner. *Patacones de platano verde,* or fried plantains, are a cocktail-hour delicacy. Meals are about the same price as in the United States.

GAMBLING...The National Lottery is universally popular. Drawings every Sunday at 11:00 A.M. Pari-mutuel betting every Saturday, Sunday and holiday at the new José Antonio Remon Race Track. A gaming room is open nightly on El Panamá Hilton Hotel roof.

LANGUAGE...The official language is Spanish, but almost everybody speaks English too.

LAUNDRY AND DRY CLEANING...Available on a 24-hour service at El Panamá or outside establishments.

LIQUOR...All the regular brands are available in Panamá at prices lower than in the States. Panamanian beer is excellent.

MEDICAL FACILITIES ... American-trained English-speaking doctors are available in Panamá's modern hospitals and clinics. Your hotel will help you if you need one. The Republic takes great pride in its high health standards.

MOTION PICTURES ... First-run American pictures are shown at the *Lux, Bella Vista* and *Central* theaters, which are the best. There's also a new drive-in theater. All pictures are in English with Spanish titles. There are showings also of Spanish, French and Italian films. *El Presidente* is the most popular for Spanish-speaking pictures, made mostly in Mexico or Argentina.

MUSIC ... You'll hear all kinds of music all the time you are in Panamá. The combination of native music and the influence of jazz has given an individual slant to the Panamanian type of Latin music with its several kinds of drums for *El Tamborito,* Panamá's famous national dance.

NIGHT LIFE AND CAFES ... Panamá City is a gay all-night town. Most hotels have music and dancing. Especially nice is the Bella Vista Roof at *El Panamá Hilton.* For late-evening dancing and drinking, also try *No Me Digas* and *Maxims.* Other spots include *O.K., Amigo,* and *Catalina.* The *Happyland,* a rather slapstick atmosphere, but fun, has a floor show. A moonlight drive through the ruins of old Panamá is a nice way to spend an evening. There are a variety of beer gardens that are fine for quiet drinking and eating, *Jardin el Rancho,* the *Jardin Sky Chef* and the *Atlas Club* are good.

RESTAURANTS ... Panamá City's best restaurants are the *Sky Chef* in the former Balboa Beer Garden and *El Rancho.* Wonderful food and drink are served under the stars. There's good food in the hotel dining rooms, both native and American cooking. Try *El Oriente* for Chinese food. The *Atlas Club* is a good place to dine. Meals in Panama cost about the same as they do at home.

SHOPS AND STORES ... Central Avenue is the great shopping center in Panamá City. Good shops include: French Bazaar, American Bazaar, Motta's, Novedades Antonio, Quinta Avenida, Maduro and Dagmar's. Fastlich jewelry store and International Jewelry Store. Hotel El Panamá arcade. Shaw's for chinaware and ceramics. Leading Oriental store: Salomon's.

SPECTATOR SPORTS ... Horse racing, Saturday, Sundays and holidays at the new José Antonio Remon Race Track, with Club-house available to tourists; baseball and the unique annual fishing rodeo that is increasingly popular with the world's best fishermen. Basketball is becoming very popular. Swimming races and golf tournaments draw crowds, too. Bull fighting during dry season.

SPORTS ... The fishing is marvelous, both in the sea and in the trout streams in the mountains. Exciting big-game fishing for marlin, tuna, dolphin, pompano and mackerel can be done at various seasons of the year. Boats complete with bait, tackle, food, and crew are available at reasonable rates on a 24-hour or less basis. The best trout streams can be found in Chiriquí, the central province of Panamá. The interior is a hunter's wonderland. The mountain jungles abound with big game and wild fowl. Jaguar, puma, tigrillo and ocelot, mule deer, tapir and wild hog are among the principal animals. The fowl include wild duck, turkey, partridge and some quail. There are guides, horses, and all varieties of camping equipment for hire. There is open season all year round for both hunting and fishing. Panamá's beaches are beautiful and the waters of the Pacific and Atlantic oceans offer wonderful swimming and sailing. Panamá has fine golf courses, too. The Panamá Golf Club in Panamá City has an exceptionally fine course that is available to tourists. The Rey Island Club, a floating inn for sports fishermen, is operated by El Panamá in Piñas Bay, in the heart of big game waters.

TIME ... Same as United States Eastern Standard Time.

TIPPING ... The 10 per cent rule applies here on all tipping. Tipping runs pretty much as it would at home.

TRANSPORTATION ... There are cabs and cars for hire in Panamá City and other large towns at reasonable rates. There is good air service, also bus and railway systems.

WATER ... The water is uniformly excellent in all but the most primitive villages. Water bottles and chlorine tablets should be part of your hunting equipment.

WHAT TO BUY ... Panamá hats are good. Leather goods, especially alligator skins, cameras and Swiss watches are other top buys. French perfume, English and Swedish china, Peruvian silver, Colombian emeralds, textiles of all kinds. Chinese silks and rugs, English woolens and cashmeres and Italian and Irish linens are all good buys. The cities of Panamá and Colón are very fine shopping centers. You may have "liquor in bond" delivered to your plane, tax free or buy it at airport.

WHAT TO WEAR ... Lightweight, comfortable clothes are essential in Panamá. Cool cotton and linen clothes during the day and lightweight black at night for women. Linen and seersucker suits for men. Formal clothes are worn for evening in the more lavish night spots. Have them cool and colorful. White jackets for men. It is advisable to bring along a lightweight raincoat. The nights are cooler in the mountains and you will need a lightweight topcoat.

WHERE TO GO SIGHTSEEING ...

Panamá City ... Panamá City, like the entire Republic, is an interesting mixture of old Spanish culture and Western Hemisphere civilization with overtones of native Indian culture. The city is divided into three parts: the present city, Old Panamá (destroyed by the famous pirate Morgan in 1671), and the beautiful residential sections. Your sightseeing trips should include the San Francisco and the Cathedral, the largest churches in Panamá City, facing on the Plaza Catedral, and the Church of San José, with its famous Altar of Gold saved from the original church in Old Panamá City. The native market place is bustling and colorful. Here, native fishing boats bring their daily catch to be sold. See also the Presidencia, home of Panamá's presidents. The patios are very beautiful; plumed egrets wander through them. Bolívar Plaza contains a handsome monument of

Simón Bolívar, one of Latin America's greatest heroes. Walking along Las Bovedas Promenade you'll have a glorious view of the Bay of Panamá. The Palace of Justice, a fine example of Spanish colonial architecture, faces the Promenade. The Church of Santo Domingo on Calle 3A has the famous Flat Arch.

The King's Bridge is the first thing to see in Old Panamá. It marks the boundary of the old city. The best place to start your tour of the ruins is the plaza in front of the old cathedral. Stone pillars mark the site of the first administration building. Going toward the sea you will come to the great arch that was part of the original San José Church that housed the Golden Altar.

Colón and the Canal Zone... No one going to Panamá should miss seeing the Canal Zone and the Panamá Canal. One is able to watch the giant locks in action and the entire engineering masterpiece perform. Coming from Panamá City, you first reach the town of Balboa, headquarters of the Zone. The Administration Building has interesting murals depicting the history of the canal. The Orchid Gardens in Balboa are breathtakingly lovely. Ancon is the residential district.

On the Atlantic side, there are the twin cities of Cristobal and Colón. Cristobal is in the Canal Zone and Colón is in the Republic of Panamá. Cristobal is primarily a port city full of the colorful mixture of sailors of the nations of the world. Colón is a very cosmopolitan city. The night life is very gay. Try to visit the famous *Strangers Club*. Marvelous food can be had at the excellent Hotel *Washington*, run by the Government. *Bilgray's Tropic* is also good.

Portobello... Near Colón, Portobello, the old fortress city, is an important sight to see. The "King's Treasures," gathered from Peru and Colombia, were stored here. The fort was used to ward off the attacks of the pirates in the early days of Spanish conquest. There are daily tours through these interesting historical ruins.

Taboga... The Island of Flowers is one of the loveliest resorts in Panamanian waters. The fishing and swimming here are very fine. The *Hotel Paraiso La Restinga* offers cool and pleasant accommodations at reasonable prices and interesting sightseeing nearby.

The Chiriquí Highlands... Chiriquí Province, bordering on the Republic of Costa Rica, is the coffee and sugar district of Panamá. There's good hunting for wild game. Trout fishing in the streams of 11,000-foot El Volcan is the very best. There are guides and accommodations available at reasonable prices. Go by air, stay at the *Nacional* in David, or at the *Hotel Panamonte* at Bouquete.

The San Blas Islands... Are a group of islands off the Atlantic coast where the colorful Cuna Indians live. The blue of the sea and the vivid costumes are a fantasy in colors. Indian women wear earrings and nose rings. Go by boat or plane.

SOURCES OF FURTHER INFORMATION... There is a Panamá National Tourist Commission in Panamá City. Pan American's office is Calle "L" #5, Panamá City, R.P. The Public Relations Office of the Hotel El Panamá is also at your service.

ARGENTINA

WEATHER IN BUENOS AIRES—Lat. S34°16′—Alt. 45′

Temp.	JAN.	FEB.	MAR.	APR.	MAY	JUNE	JULY	AUG.	SEPT.	OCT.	NOV.	DEC.
Low	63°	62°	59°	53°	46°	41°	42°	43°	46°	50°	55°	60°
High	85°	84°	78°	72°	64°	58°	57°	59°	63°	69°	75°	82°
Average	74°	73°	69°	63°	55°	50°	50°	51°	55°	60°	65°	71°
Days of Rain	7	6	7	8	7	7	8	9	8	9	9	8

LOCATION . . . Argentina fills the southern point of South America except for the thin strip of Chile along the western border. It extends for 2,300 miles from Bolivia to Tierra del Fuego between Parallels 22° and 55°, almost the distance across the whole United States.

CHARACTERISTICS . . . "B.A." is a modern city as cosmopolitan as any in the world. The theaters, shops, hotels, subways, and public buildings are the last word in progress. You will do the same things here that you would do in New York, London or Paris. You will dress in the same way, too. There is much that is strange, much that is new and exciting. But keep in mind that the Argentinians, and particularly the Porteños, as residents of Buenos Aires are called, are sophisticated people not in any sense to be considered or treated as "natives."

POPULATION . . . 20,100,000—about equal to the population of New York State and Iowa.

SIZE . . . About 1,072,745 square miles, approximately a third the size of the United States.

CAPITAL . . . Buenos Aires, the largest city of Latin America, with a population of about 3,775,000. Greater Buenos Aires has a population of 5,900,000.

GOVERNMENT . . . Argentina is a republic, with a constitution similar to that of the United States.

HOW TO GET THERE . . . By Pan American's de luxe through-plane service to Buenos Aires via the east coast of South America,

25⅓ hours from New York. By National, Pan American and Panagra with no change of plane down the west coast 22¾ hours from New York via Washington and Miami. By ship 19 days from New York or New Orleans.

ACCOMMODATIONS ... In Buenos Aires, the *Plaza,* on the Plaza San Martín, has top rating among North Americans. It is modern and beautifully run. Much of the social life of the city revolves around it. Rates $6 to $7 single, $8 to $11 double with bath, European Plan, plus service charge of 24 per cent.

The *Alvear Palace* on the Avenida Alvear also has an excellent reputation. The rates are less than at the *Plaza.* Even less expensive are the *Continental,* in the business district, the *Lancaster,* accessible to the shopping district, the *City, Claridge, California* and many others. All of these hotels cater to an international clientele. Because of the hotel shortage, make reservations well in advance. There are various apartment hotels if you plan to stay for a longer time. You may also find comfortable accommodations in the various boarding houses which abound. The best way to find these is through advertisements in the local English newspapers.

ARTS ... Buenos Aires' National Museum of Fine Arts at Avenida Libertador General San Martín 1578 (open daily except Mondays) is the largest and most important museum in the country. It contains not only paintings and sculptures of world masters, but also works of native Argentinian painters and sculptors. Also worth seeing are the Museum of Decorative Arts at Avenida Libertador General San Martín 1902 (open from Tuesday through Sunday), notable for its paintings, tapestries and antiques. The Museum of Spanish-American Art, Isaac Fernández Blanco, at Suipacha 1422 (open from Wednesday to Sunday), is a lovely reproduction of a colonial house and has an interesting collection of old silver, costumes and antiques. The Municipal Museum of Fine Arts is at Avenida Libertador General San Martín 2373. There are also a number of private art galleries, including Wildenstein, which have interesting exhibitions.

BALLET ... There is a local ballet company which, during the season (May to September), performs at Buenos Aires' famous *Teatro Colón.* There is a short ballet season before and after the grand season, too. In addition to native artists many world-famous dancers appear in Buenos Aires during the season.

BANKS ... In Buenos Aires, the National City Bank of New York, Bartolome, Mitre and San Martín; First National Bank of Boston, Diagonal Noter and Florida; the Royal Bank of Canada, Banco de la Nación, the Central Bank, similar to our Federal Reserve.

CALENDAR OF HOLIDAYS ... The officially recognized holidays are: January 1, New Year's Day; January 6, Dia de Reyes; two Carnival Days; Thursday before Good Friday; Good Friday; May 1, Labor Day; May 25, National Anniversary of the Cabildo; Abierto of 1810; Corpus Christi; June 20, Flag Day; July 9, Independence Day; August 15, Assumption of the Blessed Virgin; August 17, Anniversary of San Martín's death; October 12, Columbus Day; November 1, All

Saints Day; December 8, Feast of the Immaculate Conception; Christmas Day.

CIGARETTES AND TOBACCO ... American cigarettes are hard to find and cost around 55 cents U.S. per pack. Bring in all you're allowed; *see* CUSTOMS REGULATIONS. American pipe tobacco is also hard to obtain.

CLIMATE ... Buenos Aires has a mild climate. The seasons are reversed, of course. Winter begins in June and summer in December. The warmest months are January and February. It seldom freezes and never snows in winter, but it is chilly. There is no rainy season. All in all, October to December is the ideal time to visit Argentina.

CLUBS ... In Buenos Aires, the American Club, Viamonte 1133 (guest cards can be arranged; inquire of Pan American locally); the American Women's Club, Paraguay 755 (visitors are welcome); English Club, Avenida 25 de Mayo 586; Automobile Club, Avenida Alvear 2759; Rotary International, Florida 229; Strangers Club, Bartolome Mitre 430; Y.M.C.A., Reconquista 439; Y.W.C.A., Tucumán 844; Lions. For sports clubs *see* SPORTS.

COMMON COURTESIES AND LOCAL CUSTOMS ... Office hours in Buenos Aires are from 9:00 to 12:00 and 2:00 to 6:00. Street doors to apartment houses are locked after 9:00 P.M. Cocktail parties are from 7:00 to 9:00. The dinner hour is from 9:00 on. It is appropriate to send flowers to your hostess after a dinner. Send them the day of the party if it's a dance or a large affair. Everyone goes to tea rooms in Buenos Aires. Argentineans usually dine and entertain in their homes.

COMMUNICATIONS ... There are six telegraph companies. Teléfonos del Estado has direct international radio phone circuits to the United States and Europe. All American Cables also operates here. Overseas calls made from all phones. Daily airmail service.

CURRENCY ... The monetary unit is the peso written with the $ and worth approximately 60 pesos per U.S. $1.00. Money can be changed in banks, exchange houses, hotels and travel agencies without restrictions.

CUSTOMS REGULATIONS AND DOCUMENTS NEEDED FOR UNITED STATES CITIZENS ... All articles for personal use are duty free. Permits needed for typewriters, portable radios, cameras. Be sure to declare them. One hundred cigarettes, 25 cigars may be brought in duty free. Duty must be paid on new articles for personal use. For visits up to three months, tourists need only a passport and a vaccination certificate. On application, visit may be extended for three months. Tourists may take as baggage when leaving the country leather articles (including shoes) and fabrics up to a value of 5,000 pesos (300 U.S. dollars) exempt from export permit.

DRUG STORES ... Argentine drug stores, or *farmacías,* sell drugs and toilet articles only. One of the largest drug stores in the world is Franco Inglesa at Florida and Sarmiento, Buenos Aires. There are many others in every district, which alternate staying open all night. You can get anything you want and most of them deliver.

ELECTRIC CURRENT ... 220 volts, 50 cycles, A.C. European Continental-type plugs needed.

FAUNA ... Varied and abundant. Tourists can bring hunting and fishing equipment. Dove, duck and partridge hunting are good. Wild game like puma, jaguar and some deer are found in the mountains. Vicuña, smaller than the llama, provides wool for scarves, sweaters and ponchos; very warm. Fishing is excellent; lake-region trout and salmon are superb. Dorado, a river species and without doubt the fightingest fish in the world, is found in the Paraná River. National bird is the *hornero* (oven bird), small and gray; makes its own home of mud and straw with curving entrance which protects it from wind and rain; greatly admired and respected by Argentineans. In contrast to this little bird is the tremendous condor, inhabiting the lofty Andean peaks.

FLORA ... Argentina lies in three climatic zones, therefore its flora is varied. Jungle and forests lie to the north; *quebracho* wood, hard as steel, is abundant. National flower is the *Ceibo*, reddish bud of the Ceiba tree. Flower vendors have open-air shops along Buenos Aires' principal thoroughfares. Fruits are abundant; grape country is Mendoza, a famous wine-producing region. The Botanical and Zoölogical Gardens at Palermo are rated among the best in the world.

FOOD ... Steak, steak, steak is the thing most North Americans remember. It is wonderful and inexpensive. But it is not the only food in the Argentine. So after you've had your fill try some of the more exotic dishes, such as the *empanada*, a sort of meat pie eaten with the fingers. Some of these contain raisins, a hard-boiled egg and olives. *Chorizo* is a highly spiced version of the hot dog and worth a try. *Paella*, rice with chicken, is excellent. *Puchero de gallina*, chicken, sausages, corn, potatoes, and squash cooked together, is a fine dish. If you can't get away from steak, try *bife a caballo*, or steak on horseback. This is a steak with two fried eggs. *Dulce de leche* is a famous dessert, milk and jam served on thin pancakes. Milk is available everywhere and safe to drink.

GAMBLING ... Horse racing at Palermo and San Isidro with pari-mutuels. There are lotteries very week. The Christmas lottery is the biggest. Gambling other than at authorized casinos is forbidden. There are casinos in Mar del Plata, Necochea, Miramar and Mendoza.

LANGUAGE ... Spanish with variations of pronunciation and vocabulary rather than pure Castilian. However, English is spoken to a considerable extent.

LAUNDRY AND CLEANING ... These are excellent. Among the dry cleaners in Buenos Aires: Sandoz, Avenida Libertador General San Martín 3556; Casa Alvarez, Piedras 1080. Laundries include: Aseo Billinghurst, Billinghurst 1560; Del Norte, Cavia 3581; Franco-Argentino, Ceriño 3373. Velco, Luís Maria Campos 201, has a special service for tourists—laundry and dry cleaning in 8 hours.

LIQUOR ... Scotch and other imported liquors (good Scotch, that is) are more expensive here than in the United States. Argentina produces a lot of wine, most of it good, some of it very good. Among those recommended are: Bianchi Cabernet, Casa de Piedra, Fond du Cave, Norton, San Felipe. Good domestic champagnes cost about 30 or 40 pesos. Try Federico de Alvear or Monitor. There is good local beer, too. American cocktails are served by name in all bars, but a martini is called a San Martín.

MEDICAL FACILITIES ... There is an excellent British Hospital in Buenos Aires at Pedriel 74. There are also many private clinics or nursing homes. The Little Company of Mary, Avenida Libertador General San Martín 2676, has English-speaking sisters as nurses. There are many excellent doctors and dentists.

MOTION PICTURES ... The big movie houses in Buenos Aires show American films with Spanish subtitles. There are also English, French and Italian pictures. Performances are at 4:00, 6:00, 8:00 and 10:00 o'clock. The big houses are around the Avenida Corrientes and Lavalle, which corresponds in a manner to Broadway. *Metro, Opera, Gran Rex, Broadway* and *Normandie* are modern American-style, air-conditioned houses. For newsreels and shorts go to *Porteño, Novedades* or *Rotary*. Prices are about 25 cents.

MUSIC ... The *Teatro Colón* is said to be the largest opera house in the world. It is the pride of Argentina. The season starts May 25 with a gala performance attended by the President and his cabinet. The theater has a National Symphony Orchestra of 100 pieces and its own opera and ballet company. Internationally famous conductors, singers and dancers appear. Dress is a must on gala nights. There is a summer season from January to March in the outdoor theater *Anfiteatro Municipal* at Parque Centenario. There are three other symphony orchestras which are heard frequently during this time. It is interesting that during the opera season the French and Italian operas are presented first, the German favorites toward the end of the season.

Other types of music include the native Argentinian folk music, which is basically Spanish. There is much serious music, too, with a folklore background, which is played in this country. There are several native ballets, also, with folklore background. Then there is the typical Argentine music, including the tango. Tango orchestras are numerous and popular.

NIGHT CLUBS AND CABARETS ... Buenos Aires is a gay city and a big one, so you may find almost any kind of night life you prefer. There are dance halls, small boites, large brassy spots. The better spots include: *Gong,* Córdoba 630, with American and tango bands, always filled with smart Argentinians and Americans. *Tabarís,* Corrientes 829, popular with tourists. *Embassy Casino,* Suipacha 751, very swank, good music, fine floor show. Don't overlook some of the folklore spots, such as the *Mi Rincón,* Cerrito 1050, *Achalay Huasi,* Esmeralda 1040 and *La Querencia,* Av. de Mayo 870 with typical Argentinian music and dances.

PHOTOGRAPHY ... Black-and-white and color film frequently cannot be purchased here. Very often only European films are available. Color films cannot be developed here. Other types, yes. Quality of work, good. All types of American and European cameras can be purchased at high prices. There are many good photo shops on Florida Street and Kodak Argentina, Ltd., Alsina 951.

RELIGION ... The religion of the country is Roman Catholic, but there are churches of all denominations to be found. American Church (Methodist Episcopal), Corrientes 718; Anglican, St. John's Pro-Cathedral, 25 de Mayo 282; Scottish Presbyterian, Perú 352; Christian Science, Ayacucho 349 and Sargento Cabral 847; United Lutheran, Cuenca, 3285; Baptist, Bolaños 262; Disciples of Christ, F. Lacroze 2985; Seventh Day Adventist, Uriarte 2429; Mormon, V. del Pino 2120; Orthodox Church, Brasil 312; and Israelitic Synagogue, Libertad 785.

RESTAURANTS AND BARS ... The hotels all serve good food. The *Plaza Grill* is famous for its pepper steaks. *La Cabaña,* Calle Entre Ríos 431, has wonderful steaks cooked on an open grill, particularly baby beef. The *Shorthorn Grill,* Corrientes 634, and *Amerios* at Sarmiento 1251, are also famous for steaks. *El Pescadito,* Pedro de Mendoza 1475, is in La Boca, or the Italian quarter, by the docks, and is a tavernlike spot which serves fine fish. In Buenos Aires there is what is called the *bodegón,* or corner restaurant, which is comparable to that little out-of-the-way spot at home that you and a few others know about. Sometimes they are good; sometimes terrible. Worth a try if you come across one you think you might like. *Chez Tatave,* at Tres Sargentos, has good French cuisine with atmosphere. Try *Au Bec Fin,* at Arenales for fine international food. For dining and dancing in the American manner, try *Amerio's,* Calle Sarmiento 1251. *Hosteria del Caballito Blanco,* Charcas 479; *Harrod's,* Florida 877 and *Coraggio,* Entre Rios 662, for good food at low prices, and singing waiters.

There are hundreds of bars in the city, but take note of the *Plaza, City* and the *California Hotel Frisco Bar.* All the hotels have cocktail lounges, too. The confitería, or tea room, occupies a unique place in Buenos Aires. Unlike our tea rooms, these are very smart and are frequented by the very best of Argentinian society. Tea time (4:30 P.M.) is the fashionable hour. They combine the best features of our cocktail lounge, soda fountains and tea rooms. A visit is a must. *Confiteria Gran Rex, Del Molino, Los Dos Chinos* and *Ideal* are tops.

SHOPS AND STORES ... The big stores are open from 9:00 A.M. to 7:00 P.M. Some of the smaller ones are apt to close two or three hours for lunch. Shopping is an event of importance in Buenos Aires. In fact, the main shopping center, Florida, is closed to any but foot traffic for most of the day. The shops in the Argentine capital are among the finest in the world. Some of them are along Avenida Santa Fé. The two largest department stores are Harrod's and Gath and Chaves. For good dress materials and tailored suits visit any one of a number of fine shops, such as Warrington's, Rhoder's and Manchester's. For luggage and leather goods, Pisk, Mayorga, Mattaldi, López & Cía and Kelly's. For handmade shoes, Ricardo, Lopez Taibo, Guante. For some interesting records of "camp" or gaucho music similar to our Western songs, go to Casa América, Lottermoser or Rasmussen. The city is a center for jewels and silver. Inexpensive alligator bags and suede coats are available all over town.

SPECTATOR SPORTS ... Horse racing at Palermo and San Isidro. At Palermo the grandstand seats 30,000; at San Isidro it seats 50,000. Polo matches are played at Hurlingham and at Las Tortugas Country Club and Palermo. Soccer is the national game. Matches at River Plate Stadium, which seats 100,000 people. *Pato,* a sort of basketball on horseback, is dangerous and exciting. Horse shows are the important social event at Club Hípico Argentino and at the Exposicion Rural in August. Boxing and wrestling matches at Luna Park.

SPORTS ... There are many excellent golf courses at the clubs. You need a guest card which can be arranged through an introduction. (Inquire at local Pan American office.) The clubs include: the San Isidro, the San Andrés, the Hurlingham, the Hindú and Campos Argentinos de Golf. Tennis is played at Hurlingham, the Lawn Tennis Club of Buenos Aires, the Lawn Tennis Club Argentino. Cards are needed. There are public courts at Palermo. Horseback riding is popular and there are miles and miles of bridle paths in Palermo Park. Horses may be rented from Rustici's, among other stables. The country clubs all have swimming pools. Rowing is one of the favorite sports. At El Tigre, some 45 minutes from the capital, there are many boating clubs. There are also several sailing and yacht clubs for which cards may be arranged. (Inquire at Pan American office in Buenos Aires.) Fishing usually means a trip somewhere, to San Martín de los Andes, Nahuel Huapi, Traful, or Sierra de la Ventana, all of which are overnight trips at least. For dorado fishing you go up the Paraná River some 36 hours away. Ski season at Bariloche is July-October.

THEATERS ... Evening performances start about 10:00 P.M. But there is a before-dinner performance, called "Vermouth," on Saturdays at 6:00 P.M. The principal theaters are *Nacional Cervantes, Patagonia, Ateneo* and *Liceo,* with varied repertories of modern and classic plays. At the *Maipo* you'll see slapstick and girls. At the *Odéon* visiting French companies perform.

There are also many so-called experimental amateur theaters, some of very high standard, like *Los Independientes, Teatro del Pueblo* and *Máscara.*

TIME ... Two hours later than United States Eastern Standard Time.

TIPPING ... Tipping has been ostensibly abolished by law in restaurants. A service charge is added to your hotel and restaurant bills. It is however customary to tip approximately 10%.

TRANSPORTATION ... Taxis cruise the streets constantly, are identifiable by red license plates and red signals on meters. They are cheap but hard to get during the luncheon interval and at the end of the business day. Buenos Aires has five subway lines, which are closed between 1:00 and 5:00 A.M. Streetcars are plentiful, but slow. There are buses which are comfortable and large, and buses which are uncomfortable and slow. Also many trolley buses. Cars, with chauffeur, can be easily hired for about 75 cents an hour in Greater Buenos Aires.

WHAT TO BUY... Alligator bags and other articles made of alligator leather are much cheaper here than at home. A good bag can be bought for $25. Handmade shoes are less expensive in Argentina, too. Furs are excellent. A nutria coat costs much less than in the U.S., as do steamer rugs and ponchos made of vicuña and guanaco fur. The antique shops sometimes turn up a bargain. *Bombachas,* the baggy trousers worn by gauchos, are fun to bring home. Most popular souvenir is the *mate* used for drinking *yerba mate* and the *bombilla,* or silver tube, that goes with it. Don't be tempted by aigrettes, birds of paradise or ostrich. You can't bring them through our customs. Kid gloves are a good buy. Hand-embroidered blouses are excellent. Antelope jackets and sleeveless pullovers are also good values.

WHAT TO WEAR... Dress in Buenos Aires exactly as you would in any large city. In their winter you'll need a fur coat or a winter wool coat, suits, afternoon dresses. In their summer, linens and cottons, sheer dark crepes. Evening clothes, of course, if you are going to be social. You dress for the opera galas, not for the theater. Men dress conservatively in Buenos Aires, so dress as you would in a city at home. Argentinian men *always* wear a coat in Buenos Aires, even in midsummer. You may wear slacks and a sports jacket if you like. Light suits are correct in summer. Take a topcoat and a heavier coat in winter. Dinner clothes if you plan to go out much. Keep in mind that the farther south you go in Argentina, the colder it gets; the farther north, the warmer, but keep the reversed seasons in mind.

WHERE TO GO—SIGHTSEEING...

Buenos Aires... The Calle Florida is the main shopping street, Avenida Corrientes is the Broadway. The Avenida 9 de Julio is said to be the widest avenue in the world. It has five lanes for traffic, separated by grass plots, and parking space underneath for 1,000 cars. One of the best ways to see the city is by taxi or hired car. Here are some suggested rides: out the Avenida Alvear to Palermo Park, from the Plaza de Mayo to Plaza Congreso, then along the Avenida General Paz. La Costanera is a drive along the waterfront. Palermo Park has everything: a rose garden, a race course, miles and miles of beautiful walks, drives, and path. Hire a horse-drawn coach and see it. There are few old buildings in the capital, as it is essentially a modern, rebuilt city. There are some interesting old churches. The quarter of the city known as La Boca is atmospheric, mostly Italian and by the waterfront. Interesting if you like local color. Take a look at Casa Rosada, the pink house occupied by the President of the Republic. The Hall of Congress is worth seeing, too. Among the old churches visit Nuestra Señora de la Merced (Our Lady of Mercy), the Cathedral on Plaza de Mayo, Santo Domingo and Nuestra Señora de Pilar. El Tigre, the delta of the Paraná River, is about 45 minutes from the capital and is the favorite nearby resort.

Museums: In addition to the various museums listed under ARTS, the *National Historical Museum,* Defensa 1600 (open Sundays, Thurs-

On the border between Chile and Argentina stands the famous statue of "Christ of the Andes."

days and holidays), is worth seeing for its exhibitions of historic flags, uniforms, documents and arms from the period of Argentine struggle for independence. Also very interesting is the *Argentine Museum of National Sciences, Bernardino Rivadavia,* at Calles Campichuelo and Dr. Angel Gallardo (open Tuesdays, Fridays and Sundays), and the *Ethnographic Museum,* Moreno 350 (open Thursdays and Sundays).

Lujan is a typical camp town about an hour and a half out of the city. There is a magnificent Gothic cathedral, where pilgrims flock each year. The Virgin of Lujan is the patron sait of Argentina. There is also a famous museum, the Cabildo, which is an old town hall preserved from colonial times.

La Plata, about an hour's trip from Buenos Aires, is the university city of Argentina. The Natural History Museum has a wonderful collection of prehistoric animals. The city also has a fine race track.

Mar del Plata, on the Atlantic Ocean, about 250 miles from the capital, is Argentina's leading beach resort. Here is the famous *Casino,* the largest in the world, next to the luxurious *Hotel Provincial.* There are many beaches here. Cabañas may be rented at Bristol Beach. St. James Beach is filled with private clubs. There are about 250 hotels at the resort. The *Riviera* is open the year round; the others during the season. Among the tops are: the *Horizonte,* the *Hermitage,* the *Tourbillon,* the *Nogaró,* the *Royal.* Apartments may be rented, too. Fishing is fine here and the seafood is famous. From Mar del Plata you can make trips to the estancias at Chapadmalal and Ojo de Agua, where two of the famous breeds of Argentine race horses originated. Necochea, south of Mar del Plata, is the second largest beach resort. Still further away is Tandil in the hills, a favorite summer resort.

Buenos Aires' "Ninth of July" Avenue (said to be the widest in the world) and the Obelisk, which commemorate the 400th anniversary of the founding of the City of Buenos Aires.

Plaza del Congreso in Buenos Aires, Argentina.

Nahuel Huapi National Park offers wonderful vacation opportunities and good facilities, such as Hotel Llao Llao, sourrounded by 12,000-foot peaks.

Iguassú Falls on the Brazilian border, about 1,300 miles from the capital, 6½ hours by plane or 6 days by boat, is one of the most magnificent sights in the world. The falls are greater than Niagara or Victoria Falls. The season here is May to November. *Hotel Cataratas* is the place to stay.

Argentine-Chilean Lake District . . . Go by plane in only 4½ hours to (San Carlos de) Bariloche, which looks like a Swiss village and in fact was originally settled by the Swiss. This is in Nahuel Huapi National Park, which has several distinct regions. The popular spot is Lake Nahuel Huapi where there are two excellent Government-operated hotels, the *Llao-Llao* (pronounced yao-yao), the *Tunquelen;* and other small hotels around the lake. The lake is at an altitude of 2,000 feet and is surrounded by mountains which point some 12,000 feet upward. During the winter season (July to October) there is excellent skiing and the *Cathedral Hotel* provides first class lodging. Game is protected, but you may get a permit to shoot wild boar. Fishing is wonderful at Lake Traful, 4 hours from Bariloche. You can climb the peaks, too. *Club Andino Bariloche* arranges things and furnishes guides. The hotel is excellent, the food very good. Take the boat trip (motor launch) to Puerto Blest at the end of a 10-mile fjord. You pass Cascada Blanca, a huge waterfall from the great glaciers. From Puerto Blest you can go to Puerto Alegre on the Chilean border and continue into Chile or return to Bariloche and Buenos Aires. If you go on into the Chilean lake regions, you will cross the border at Puerto Alegre. In Chile head for Lake Todos Los Santos as far as Villarica Lake. Here you stay at Pucon at the *Pucon Hotel,* where there is a golf course, good salmon fishing and swimming. For further information on Chilean lake region, *see* CHILE.

Other Side Trips . . . While in Argentina you should visit Mendoza, Argentina's great wine center; Córdoba, South America's second oldest city, now becoming modernized, and Salta, still a quiet, lovely Spanish Colonial city.

SOURCES OF FURTHER INFORMATION . . . Pan American has a tourist corner, offices at Avenida Rogue Saenz Pena 788 and at the Plaza Hotel. Two English-language newspapers, *The Buenos Aires Herald* and *The Standard* are published in Buenos Aires. In New York, the Argentine Travel Bureau is located at 299 Madison Avenue.

BOLIVIA

WEATHER IN LA PAZ—Lat. S16°29'—Alt. 12,200'

Temp.	JAN.	FEB.	MAR.	APR.	MAY	JUNE	JULY	AUG.	SEPT.	OCT.	NOV.	DEC.
Low	43°	43°	42°	40°	35°	36°	34°	35°	38°	40°	42°	43°
High	64°	64°	64°	66°	66°	60°	61°	62°	62°	65°	67°	64°
Average	54°	54°	53°	53°	51°	49°	48°	49°	50°	53°	55°	54°
Days of Rain	25	16	15	7	1	6	1	6	12	11	10	24

LOCATION ... Bolivia is the only country in South America, except Paraguay, without a seacoast. While much of the country consists of low plains which are humid and hot, the western section, where the principal cities are located, is a large 12,000 ft. plateau.

CHARACTERISTICS ... La Paz, highest capital in the world, is over 12,000 feet above sea level. The city itself is in the bottom of a deep, narrow gulley entirely surrounded by mountains. It is a city of steep streets with houses built on inclined surfaces. The airport is on a plateau high above the city. The plateau is studded with snowy peaks that reach another 6,000 feet into the sky.

POPULATION ... Estimated 3,922,000 in 1950, the population is about the same as that of Chicago and Tacoma combined.

SIZE ... Estimated 424,162 square miles, about the size of Texas and California combined.

CAPITAL ... La Paz, with about 350,000 inhabitants, slightly larger than Rochester, New York. Cochabamba's population is 120,000.

GOVERNMENT ... A republic with a President, Senate and a House of Deputies.

HOW TO GET THERE ... By National, Pan American and Panagra interchange to La Paz, 20 hours (elapsed time) from New York via Washington and Miami. By Panagra 3½ hours from Lima, Peru. Cochabamba is an hour's flying time from La Paz. By ship from New York, 14 days to Mollendo, Peru; then about 46 hours by rail and Lake Titicaca steamer to La Paz.

ACCOMMODATIONS ... Best hotels are the *Crillon,* the *Copacabana* and *Sucre Palace,* where rates start at about $5 single, European Plan. It is advisable to get confirmed reservations in advance. There are other more modest hotels and also several pensions.

ARTS ... The *Tiahuanaco Museum* houses a significant collection of pre-Inca relics and is well worth a visit. Check for hours.

BALLET ... There is no local ballet company, but occasionally visiting troupes stop here.

BANKS ... Banco Central de Bolivia; Banco Mercantil, Banco Boliviano Americano; Banco Nacional de Bolivia; Banco Popular del Peru; Banco Popular Colombo Boliviano; Banco Commercial e Industrial, Banco de la Nación Argentina.

CALENDAR OF HOLIDAYS ... New Year's Day; Carnival in February; Easter; May 1, Labor Day; Corpus Christi in June; August 5, 6, 7, Festival on Lake Titicaca; October 12, Anniversary of the Discovery of America; November 1, 2, All Saints Day; Christmas Day; various local holidays.

CIGARETTES AND CIGARS ... American cigarettes are available in a few places. The tourist may bring 100 cigarettes or 20 cigars.

CLIMATE ... Some foreigners find the high altitude difficult for the first few days. They are advised to walk as little as possible and to hire cabs for any destination. Just take it easy until you are acclimated. The weather is cool all year around and cold in winter, but sunny most days. Even in summer you need blankets at night.

CLUBS ... Anglo-American Club, Automóvil Club Boliviano, Club "La Paz" (Social Club), Club Hípico "Los Sargentos" in Obrajes, La Paz Tennis Club in Calacoto, La Paz Golf Club in Mallasilla, Club de Golf "Los Pinos" in Calacoto, Club Andino Boliviano in Chacaltaya, Rotary Club, Lions Club, Club de Caza y Pesca in Mallasilla, Yacht Club in Huatajata on Lake Titicaca, Círculo de la Union, Círculo Peruano. Guest cards may be arranged through the Panagra Office.

COMMUNICATIONS ... All America Cables, Calle Socabaya; Western Union, Avenida Mariscal Santa Cruz; CIRBOL (International Cable and Telephone communications) Avenida Camacho Esq. Ayacucho and local communication companies.

CURRENCY ... The Boliviano is the unit of exchange and the rate varies.

CUSTOMS REGULATIONS AND DOCUMENTS REQUIRED FOR UNITED STATES CITIZENS ... Passport and tourist card, but no visa for tourist visits up to 90 days. Good health. Inquire of Pan Am about business travelers' requirements. Personal effects such as cameras and typewriters are allowed, but must be declared when entering. For all other articles, passengers must secure special permission. One bottle of liquor allowed duty free. *See also* CIGARETTES.

DRUG STORES ... Almost all have American products. Many good German and Swiss drugs are available.

ELECTRIC CURRENT ... Generally 110 volts, 50 cycles, A.C.:

220 volts, A.C., is also available. Hotels are generally adapted for U.S.-type plugs.

FAUNA . . . Many species of fish. Fresh-water fishing is excellent. Many small animals are found in Bolivian forests, including wolves, tigers, bears, crocodiles, caimanes. There are also many kinds of game birds.

FLORA . . . The vegetation of the valleys of Bolivia is very beautiful. There are virgin forests in the Orient of Bolivia.

FOOD . . . Truly native food is highly seasoned with a really hot pepper. Among favorite dishes are *chuño; Empanadas,* native meat pies; *plato paceño,* corn, potatoes, cheese and beans. Fish is served well, and try *picantes,* bits of chicken cooked in pungent sauce. You can find more cosmopolitan food in the hotels and some of the restaurants.

LANGUAGE . . . Spanish; but in the better hotels, restaurants and shops, English is spoken and understood.

LAUNDRY AND DRY CLEANING . . . Pamba is the best, where all clothes can be very well cleaned or dyed.

LIQUOR . . . Most liquors are expensive because of the import duty. Local beer is good.

MEDICAL FACILITIES . . . The American Clinic is one of the best, with a North American director. There's also the Clínica Santa-Isabel and Clínica Muller.

MOTION PICTURES . . . *Municipal Theater, Cine 6 De Agosto, Monje Campero, Tesla, Cine La Paz,* and others.

MUSIC . . . Famous musicians can be sometimes heard in the local theaters. There is the Bolivian Symphonic Orchestra. Also on some holidays you can hear native music in the stadiums or public places.

NIGHT CLUBS AND CABARETS . . . Most popular with tourists are the *Altri Tempi* at Sopocachi, *Gallo de Oro* (Golden Cock) at Obrajes, *Sans Souci* at Calle Aspiazu, *El Corso* (modest) and *La Taberneta* among others. The Hotel Crillon also has a cocktail lounge, dining and dancing.

PHOTOGRAPHY . . . Black-and-white still film as well as color film are generally difficult to locate, so bring your own supply. Cameras and equipment are not available in local shops. Developing facilities, limited to black-and-white still film, are of good quality. Kodak is at Casa Kavlin, Calle Potosi 259–263, La Paz and in all principal cities. *Note:* All visitors receive a declaration to cover their cameras when they enter Bolivia. This declaration must be kept and presented to the Customs inspector to allow such visitors to depart with their cameras.

RELIGION . . . There are many Catholic churches. Churches of other denominations include the Seventh Day Mission, Protestant, Emmanuel, Hebrew, Nazarenes and Jehova's Witnesses.

RESTAURANTS . . . *Maly, Galley* and *La Casserole, Daiquiri* (good parrilladas), *El Topolino, Pasavoga, El Milano, Casa Argentina* and others for good "picantes" and Bolivian specialties.

SHOPS AND STORES... The shopping center is the Calle Comercio, La Paz. Shops offer vicuña coats, alpaca, gold and silver jewelry, filigree work, porcelain. The Central Market is held daily, but the Sunday market on the Plaza San Francisco is the most colorful. The markets are run by native women who wear those fantastic derby hats. Calle Sagarnaga is the Street of the Indians, and here everything imaginable is for sale. Everywhere you will find Ekeko, the Indian god of good luck. He comes in plaster and silver with a load of household items on his back and a bright knitted cap.

SPECTATOR SPORTS... Soccer, football and basketball are played in the stadium at Miraflores.

SPORTS... There are fine trout streams. Lake-trout fishing here is gaining world renown for some of the world's biggest rainbows; the record is 37 pounds. Skiing is excellent near La Paz, but over 17,000 feet above sea level. There is a new golf course, Mallasilla Golf Club, with grass greens and fairways, about one-half hour from downtown La Paz. Tennis is popular. Hunting and shooting are good in the Yungas and near Cochabamba. There is big-game hunting in the wilds of Eastern Bolivia (twice weekly air service to Concepción).

TIME... One hour later than United States Eastern Standard Time.

TIPPING... No tipping for taxis. To porters, Bs 500 per each bag. Messenger boys, Bs 200. There is 10 per cent for the service charge added to your hotel bill.

TOURIST TAXES... Applicable only to air transportation, equivalent to 13 per cent of transportation cost within the country.

TRANSPORTATION... There are plenty of taxis around La Paz and they are inexpensive. There are several lines of buses between the central city and outlying areas, but they are crowded and unpleasant. Autocarriles are a form of bus.

WATER... It is advisable to drink bottled water throughout Bolivia.

WHAT TO BUY... Vicuña coats and rugs, alpaca, gold and silver jewelry, especially the jointed silver fish, Porcelain, handloomed blankets and rag dolls in native costumes, gold filigree, the little god Ekeko, colored shawls and woven hats.

WHAT TO WEAR... In La Paz it is cool in the morning and the late afternoon. Take suits and dresses such as those worn in the United States in the fall. A topcoat is an absolute must. And it is wise to take a topcoat when starting out for a day's trip. The mercury is temperamental in this city in the Andes and takes frequent and unexpected dives, so have a warm bathrobe, bedroom slippers. A hot-water bottle is a good idea, too. The same rules of dress apply to men: wool suits, topcoats, sweaters.

WHERE TO GO—SIGHTSEEING...

La Paz... In and around La Paz the Indian market is a must. The cathedral is one of the largest churches in all South America. A trip around the city is interesting (each section represents a stage of history) to see its various architectures. You don't have to go anywhere to see snow-capped Illimani, the mountain which towers over the city. From Monticulo, a small park in residential La Paz, you get a magnificent view of the city. The Prado with its promenade is the pride of the city. Visit the Tiahuanaco Museum, (*see* ARTS) and the old Spanish San Francisco church.

Cochabamba...Is a popular resort city and center for foreign oil companies. It is located in a garden valley, one of the most fertile spots in the country. Indian traffic cops stand on raised platforms at street intersections, wearing bulging trousers and *kepis*. The old Spanish houses have overhanging tiled eaves. Hotels include the *Capitol*, the *Gran Hotel Cochabamba*, with swimming pool, tennis courts, the *Beverley* also with swimming pool, the *Colón* and the Ambassador. Cochabamba was the home of the late Simon Patiño, the Tin King of Bolivia. He built *Los Portales*, a palace with solid copper roof, near the edge of the city, now a museum. El Cortijo is a lovely spot, with excellent bar and restaurant, swimming pool and tennis courts. Fifteen miles from the city is Pairumani, the Palacio estate of 5,000 acres, with model farms, gardens, and a magnificent house. The shopping center of Cochabamba is comparable to that of La Paz. The Indian market is especially interesting. The magnificent climate here is the main feature. From La Coronilla, a small mountain, you have a wonderful view of the town with its red-tile roofs.

Copacabana...This is a famous shrine visited every August by pilgrims from all parts of the country. Its main feature is the church that has the Virgin of Copacabana which was carved in the sixteenth century. There is a hotel operated by the Government and one run by Companía Hotelera Boliviana. The *Club Princesa* is the place to go here. Drinks served; dinner at night. Ask for *ananas con rum,* a tropical concoction of lush pineaple juice and medium-brown rum.

Copacabana is 3 hours or so from La Paz on Lake Titicaca, the world's highest lake. Spend the night there; see the sun rise across those strange waters, straw boats, wild ducks and geese.

Santa Cruz...This very old 16th century city is virtually isolated from our world. Reached only by air, it is a handy overnight stop, flying over spectacular country between Lima and Rio de Janeiro. The climate is semi-tropical with marvelous citrus fruits, pineapple. Famous for its light, jolly people. Spend Carnival here.

Sucre...the former, and still official, capital of Bolivia is known as the white city because all its churches have white towers. It has an old university, interesting buildings and an air of quiet charm.

Potosí...The city whose silver gave the Spanish conquerors fame and glory. In the 16th Century, it was densely populated. Notable for its colonial churches and buildings, old paintings.

The Yungas are deep, narrow tropical valleys descending sharply from the high plateau. The climate is subtropical. The drive (5 hours from La Paz) gives you a close-up view of Indian farms and villages.

SOURCES OF FURTHER INFORMATION...There are several good travel agents. Grace y Cía (Bolivia) at Mercado 1085 (Tel. 12100–12106) and a tourist office at Avenida 16 de Julio No.

BRAZIL

WEATHER IN RIO DE JANEIRO—Lat. S22°54'—Alt. 30'

Temp.	JAN.	FEB.	MAR.	APR.	MAY	JUNE	JULY	AUG.	SEPT.	OCT.	NOV.	DEC.
Low	74°	76°	75°	73°	69°	67°	65°	66°	66°	69°	71°	73°
High	82°	83°	81°	81°	75°	74°	73°	73°	74°	75°	78°	81°
Average	78°	80°	78°	77°	72°	71°	69°	70°	70°	72°	75°	77°
Days of Rain	13	11	12	10	10	7	6	7	11	12	12	14

LOCATION ... This huge country, covering half of South America, occupies the east-central section of the continent and includes several climatic regions—the tropical Amazon basin near the equator, the sub-tropical central section, and the temperate climate of the mountainous regions facing the southern coast.

CHARACTERISTICS ... Rio de Janeiro is a city of beauty, of white buildings, mosaic walks, blue, blue water, purple mountains. It is a city of gaiety, a carnival city, ready to amuse you. Its Copacabana Beach and its hotels are world famous. You can have fun in Rio. The hotels are superb, the scenery fabulous. São Paulo is the fast-growing industrial center where tourists are treated wonderfully.

POPULATION ... Estimated approximately 63,000,000, roughly a third of the United States population.

SIZE ... 3,287,195 square miles, slightly larger than the United States.

CAPITAL ... Rio de Janeiro. The metropolitan area population of Rio is just over 3,000,000, of São Paulo 3,200,000, larger than Philadelphia proper.

GOVERNMENT ... A federation of 21 States, one Federal District and 4 Territories, with a President, a Federal Senate and a Chamber of Deputies.

HOW TO GET THERE ... By Pan American Clipper 18 hours from New York to Rio, an hour more to São Paulo. By ship from New York, about 11 days. Panair do Brasil airline provides local air service within the country.

ACCOMMODATIONS ... Rio de Janeiro has many excellent, well-staffed hotels. On Copacabana Beach, the *Copacabana Palace, Trocadero, Excelsior, Miramar* and *California* all enjoy a magnificent view of the ocean. The *Copacabana Palace* has a swimming pool and night club. The *Excelsior* and *Miramar* have excellent restaurants. The "Stadium" in the *Excelsior* is very popular for late dinner and dancing. The *Gloria,* closer to town, is the best of the older hotels, and has been thoroughly modernized. The view of Rio's harbor from the *Gloria* is magnificent. It has a swimming pool and one of Rio's most popular night clubs. The better hotels located in the city are the *Serrador, Ambassador* and *San Francisco.* Most luxurious hotels in São Paulo are the *Jaraguá* and *Othon Palace.* Rates from $7.00. Other good hotels are the *Lord Excelsior* and *Esplanda.*

ARTS ... The Museum of the Indian, located in front of Gate No. 15 of the Maracaña Stadium, is the newest and most modern museum in Rio. It consists of a series of expositions, agreeably organized about different themes of the life of Brazilian Indians. The National Museum in Rio's Quinta da Boa Vista Park, one of the oldest in Brazil and once the residence of Dom Pedro I and Dom Pedro II, has interesting collections of mineralogy and ethnography. Natural Historic Museum, on Praça Marechal Ancora, has a superb collection of historical objects, silver, porcelain, paintings, etc. National Museum of Fine Arts, Avenida Rio Branco, houses collections of old paintings and sculpture and also has a gallery showing contemporary artists. The Museum of Modern Art exhibits modern painting and sculpture. Museum of Historical and Geographical Institute, Praça Mahatma Gandhi, has interesting collections from the period of the monarchy. In São Paulo see the Ipiranga Museum for historical objects, and the excellent Museum of Modern Art.

BALLET ... Foreign and local ballet companies appear at the Teatro Municipal during the winter season (May to August).

BANKS ... In Rio: National City Bank of New York, First National Bank of Boston, Royal Bank of Canada, all on Avenida Rio Branco; American Express Co., Rua Mexico 74. All these banks are also in São Paulo.

CALENDAR OF HOLIDAYS ... New Year's Day; Easter; Tiradentes; May 1, International Labor Day; May 30, Corpus Christi; June 29, St. Peter's Day; September 7, Independence Day; November 1 and 2, All Saints and All Souls Days; November 15, Republic Day; Christmas.

The Carnival in Rio is one of the gayest in the world. All business stops for three days. There are costume balls, among them the famous Copacabana Palace and Municipal Theatre Ball. There are also galas at clubs, and private homes, dancing in the streets, lavish costumes, fireworks, music, pretty girls and everything it takes to make a carnival. It is always held just before Lent.

CIGARETTES AND TOBACCO ... Brazilian cigars are among the world's finest mild cigars. Suerdick Co. makes the best. American cigarettes are available.

CLIMATE . . . It's always summer in Rio. During the winter season, June to September, the nights are quite cool and there is an occasional cool day. But temperatures below 50 degrees are almost unknown. It's often very hot in Rio's summer. São Paulo is 2,500 feet above sea level with an equable climate. Local winter and spring are the best times to visit.

CLUBS . . . In Rio: A.B.I. Brazilian Press Association (no cards needed) has a separate section for non-member guests; American Chamber of Commerce and American Society at Av. Rio Branco, 80, 19th floor; American Club, Ave. Rio Branco, 80, 20th floor, is an American Businessmen's Luncheon Club, excellent food and bar service; University Club (for graduates and students of North American Universities), Avenida Graça Aranha, 182; American Legion, Avenida Graça Aranha, 182; Y.M.C.A. and Y.W.C.A.; Rotary Club, Avenida Nilo Peçanha, and Lions Club. For golf and yacht club, *see* SPORTS. Principal clubs in São Paulo are the Automobile (businessmen's luncheon) Club, Jockey Club for lunch and the Scandinavian Club (cards needed at all three).

COMMON COURTESIES AND LOCAL CUSTOMS . . . Beware of the traffic—South Americans drive with more abandon than we do. The dinner hour is from 8:00 to 10:00 P.M. Cocktails are at 6:00. Local businessmen stop between appointments for a cafezinho (demitasse) at one of the innumerable cafés.

COMMUNICATIONS . . . Long-distance telephone; Radio Internacional-Radional; telegrams and radiograms and cables. In Rio: All America Cables is at Avenida Rio Branco; Radio Internacional, Avenida Almirante Barroso; Radiobras, Avenida Rio Branco (for long distance, dial 01); Western Telegraph Co., Rua Candelaria; airmail. São Paulo has the same facilities.

CURRENCY . . . The monetary unit is the cruzeiro, worth about 7 cents. You get best value in exchange at the cambios (money exchange shops). The rate fluctuates widely.

CUSTOMS REGULATIONS AND DOCUMENTS REQUIRED FOR UNITED STATES CITIZENS . . . You may bring in: liquor, cameras, cigarettes in limited quantities. You need passport, vaccination certificate, tourist card issued by carrier, two passport photos.

DRUG STORES . . . No soda fountains but most drugs.

ELECTRIC CURRENT . . . 110–120 volts, 50 cycles, A.C.

FAUNA . . . Rich and varied in species of birds and wild animals.

FLORA . . . Orchids; Bougainvillea; 100,000 different species of plants and trees can be seen at the Botanical Gardens.

FOOD . . . Naturally coffee is plentiful, for Brazil is the world's largest producer of coffee. All the hotels serve international food if you don't want to sample the native dishes. If you do, however, try feijoada, made of meat, black beans and rice, cooked separately and spiced with herbs. The Brazilians do well by fish of all sorts. If you like hot food try Vatapá, a fish porridge which contains several varieties of fish and shrimp mixed with local vegetable oil called Dendê, then sprinkled with pepper and paprika, served very hot. Try camaroes a la Grec (shrimps on a spit) at the Copacabana. Local beef dishes are superb. Try churrasco, grilled filet of beef with onions and peppers. The Brazilian Creole dishes are magnificent.

GAMBLING ... The casinos in Rio were shut down a few years ago. But there is racing at the Jockey Club track on Saturday and Sunday with pari-mutuel betting.

LANGUAGE ... Portuguese. English is understood in tourist centers.

LAUNDRY AND DRY CLEANING ... Can be arranged through your hotel. Two-day delivery if requested.

LIQUOR ... Excellent native wines. Best wines served with native dishes are fine white Portuguese. There are good Brazilian rum and gin. Scotch and other imported liquors are expensive. Brazilian beer is fine and costs about 15 cents a quart. "Pilsen Extra" and "Brahma Extra" are recommended. Draft beer is called Chopp.

MEDICAL FACILITIES ... Hospital Dos Estrangeiros, Rua Passagem 188, Rio, is staffed with English-speaking doctors and nurses as is the Hospital Samaritano, Rua Conselheiro Brotero 1486 in São Paulo.

MOTION PICTURES ... There are many fine cinema houses Fairly new Hollywood movies are shown in the big ones.

MUSIC ... The *Teatro Municipal* in Rio is the mecca of music lovers who from June to September hear world-famous singers and conductors. Villa-Lobos, the composer, is a Brazilian. Brazilian folk songs and chants are famous. There is a National Symphony Orchestra. Fine concerts are given at the National School of Music. The samba is Brazilian. São Paulo offers fine concerts and Italian opera.

NIGHT CLUBS ... In Rio *Sacha's* is swankiest Copacabana Beach *Boite*. It is expensive but nice. Excellent food and soft music for dancing. *Au Bon Gourmet,* is a charming first-class night club. The better known hotel night clubs are the *Studium* in the *Excelsior Hotel,* the *Midnight Room* in the *Copacabana,* the *Beguin* in the *Gloria Hotel,* and the *Night and Day* in the *Serrador Hotel,* the latter with excellent Brazilian floor show. The *Studium* offers dining and dancing with no cover or minimum charge. Others feature dancing and entertainment usually with a moderate cover or minimum charge. For those who like their drinks in a quiet atmosphere, there are countless small, intimate bars with low lights and soft music. Some of the better known are the *Scotch Bar, Club 36, Michell's, Little Club, Baccarat* and *Maxim's.* Leading São Paulo night clubs are the *African Boite* and *Boite Oasis,* both with floor shows, both expensive. More reasonable is the *Studium* in the Jaragua Hotel, 8th floor, with good music and atmosphere. The *Jardim de Inverno Fasano* offers very good food and music.

PHOTOGRAPHY ... There are Kodak dealers in all major cities. In Rio at Campo de São Cristóvão, 268. In São Paulo at Av. Brigadeiro Luîs Antônio, 453.

RELIGION ... In Rio: Union Church, Protestant nondenominational, Rua Paula Freitas, 99. Our Lady of Mercy Chapel, for Eng-

lish-speaking Catholics, Rua Visconde de Caravelas. Jewish Synagogue, Rua Tenente Possolo. Christ Church (Anglican), Rua Real
Grandeza. First Church of Christ Scientist, Av. Churchill. São Paulo,
while principally Roman Catholic, has most denominations represented.

RESTAURANTS... Most of the hotel restaurants are good. In
Rio the *Copacabana Palace Bife de Ouro* and *Excelsior* restaurants
are considered the finest. Restaurants specializing in French cuisine are
very popular in Rio. *La Crémaillère* and *Le Bec Fin* are the best.
For those who like Italian food, *Al Pappagallo* and *Cantina Sorrento*
are well recommended. The *Albamar* serves wonderful seafood Brazilian style. For native dishes, *Cabeça Chata* and *Bode Preto*. *Churra-
scaria Gaucha* and *Recreio* for barbecued meat. *Restaurant Mesbla*
serves fine food and offers a magnificent view of Sugar Loaf and the
famous Rio harbor. The *Vendome* offers excellent French cuisine. The
better hotel restaurants in the city are the *Gloria, Ambassador* and
Serrador. The *Santos Dumont Airport Restaurant* is convenient and
good. For suggestions on various Brazilian food specialties to try at
restaurants see the section FOOD above.

In São Paulo the best restaurants are *Cassarole, La Popote* and
Freddy for French cuisine and atmosphere. *A Baiuca*, international
cuisine. *Cantina Piemontese,* Italian food. *Excelsior* on the 23rd floor
of the Hotel Excelsior (50 choices for U.S.$ 1.50) including a huge
Smorgasbord. *Zillerthal* for German Eisbein und Sauerkraut, Wiener
Schnitzel. *Cá D'Oro* for international cuisine, nice atmosphere. The
Airport Restaurant is very good.

SHOPS AND STORES... In Rio: H. Stern, Av. Rio Branco, 173,
Amsterdam, Rua Mexico, 41, Michael, Av. Copacabana, 542, and
Maximino, Rua Santa Clara, 27–B, for set and unset precious and
semi-precious stones. Casa Hugo, Rua Buenos Aires, 91, and Zitrin,
Rua Buenos Aires, 110, for souvenirs and curios; Casa Anglo-Ameri-
cana, Rua da Assembleia, 73, antiques and Portuguese silver; Casa
Imperial, Rua da Assembleia, 73, antiques and Portuguese silver;
Casa Imperial, Rua Gonçalves Dias 56, for lingerie and wonderful
handmade blouses; Henrique Liberal and Cia, excellent antiques and
wood carvings; Casa Sloper, Rua Uruguaiana and Mesbla, Rua do
Passeio 42, are the best department stores in the city. Perfumarias
Carneiro, Rua do Ouvidor, 103, and Casa Hermanny, Rua Gonçalves
Dias, 50, are best for French perfumes. Don't be tempted by street
peddlers of perfumes or stones. For other suggestions *see* WHAT TO
BUY below.

Shops and stores in São Paulo include the Mappin Stores, Mesbla,
Sears Roebuck, Casa Sloper and several other good stores. Rua Barão
de Itapetininga is the main shopping street. R. Simon & Cia. Ltda., at
Praça da Republica, 146, and H. Stean, at Praça de Republica, 242,
for Brazilian precious stones and handmade jewelry.

SPECTATOR SPORTS... Soccer is Brazil's most important sport.
Around Rio, horse races at the Jockey Club (Thursdays, Saturdays
and Sundays). The races are important in the social life of Rio. The

Grande Premio Brasil race in August draws everyone who is anyone. Soccer at Municipal Stadium. Boxing matches at Municipal Stadium. International tennis matches. In São Paulo soccer is played on Sundays at the Pacaembu Stadium (70,000 capacity), horse races at the Jockey Club on Saturdays and Sundays.

SPORTS ... In Rio golf at Gavea Golf and Country Club in the midst of orchid-bearing trees, sensational scenery, card necessary. Itanhangá Golf Club at Lake Jacarepaguá is another scenic marvel; good course, card necessary. The Yacht Club of Rio de Janeiro on Avenida Pasteur is the best in town. This club is host to the Buenos Aires-Rio annual yacht ocean race. Nice restaurant, good drinks. Card necessary. Sociedade Hípica Brasileira for horseback riding, card necessary. There is fine salt and fresh-water fishing around Rio. In the highland lakes there are plenty of fish to be caught. Hunting is good in the interior—boar, duck, alligator and onça (Brazilian tiger). Hunting parties very difficult to arrange. The Rio Country Club has a swimming pool and tennis courts, card needed. Swimming, of course, is a national sport. If you want to climb mountains, you can do it right in Rio. There's golf at the São Paulo Golf Club (card necessary), underwater fishing at Ubatuba near Santos, numerous tennis clubs (cards necessary).

THEATERS ... There are several theaters in Rio. During their winter you see foreign companies as well as local ones. Most of the plays are in Portuguese, but even if you don't understand it, you'll enjoy the experience. For those who enjoy musical reviews *type français* there is usually a good show at the *Recreio*. Times of performances 8:00 P.M. and 10:00 P.M., except Mondays. In São Paulo performances start at 9:00 P.M. and are in Portuguese except for those of foreign companies.

TIME ... Two hours later than United States Eastern Standard Time.

TIPPING ... A service charge of 10 per cent is added to your hotel bills. It is usual to tip 10 per cent in addition. When taking a cab, tip about 10 to 15 per cent.

TRANSPORTATION ... Taxis cruise the city. All have red license plates. You can phone the nearest taxi stand for a cab. Community taxis, called *Lotação*, carry 8 to 20 passengers and charge about 5 cents each. Some follow regular routes marked on their windshields.

Carry small denomination cruzeiro notes because you can't get change for the larger ones when using taxis.

Buses and streetcars operate along Copacabana section and throughout the city. During rush hours they are very crowded.

WATER ... It is advisable to drink only bottled water. *Agua Lindoya* is non-carbonated; *Agua Magneziana* is mildly carbonated and *Agua Caxambu* is highly carbonated. All are good.

WHAT TO BUY ... The best buys in Brazil are the precious and semi-precious stones. Topazes, amethysts, aquamarines and tourmalines are the more popular stones. Alligator bags and other leather goods are cheaper here than at home. French-type perfume is cheap, but do not patronize street peddlers. Wood carvings, antique silver, hand-made lingerie and blouses are all good buys here. Note: Shipping packages out of Brazil is complicated and expensive.

WHAT TO WEAR... Women will want lightweight spring or summer clothes, plenty of beach wear. A great deal of black is worn in Rio during the winter, especially evenings, so some good little black dresses will come in handy. Hats and jewels are worn after six. Fur jackets and stoles are seen in the evening. A lightweight woolen suit is always nice to have along. Slacks and a topcoat may come in handy. Evening and dinner clothes for the season. Men will want linen suits, lightweight wool suits, beach wear, dinner clothes, if you are there during the Brazilian social season, June through September. Highly recommended are seersucker suits or wrinkle-proof synthetics for men during Brazilian summers, heavier suits for winter. Keep sports clothes on the conservative side.

WHERE TO GO—SIGHTSEEING...

Rio de Janeiro... Rio is full of things to see. You can scarcely miss the magnificent Copacabana Beach section with its serpentine mosaic walk famed the world over. Neither can you miss Sugar Loaf Mountain and Corcovado (Hunchback Mountain) which tower over the city. Sugar Loaf is a huge granite cone at the entrance of the bay. Take the cable car to Sugar Loaf and a funicular to Corcovado. The summit of Corcovado is crowned by the famed statue of Christ the Redeemer. The views from these two spots are fabulous. Visit the Gavea district by car; it affords some of the most beautiful scenery anywhere. This is where the race track is, too. Among the many churches, be sure to see the Church of Nossa Senhora da Gloria do Outeiro with its Bible scenes in blue tile. The São Bento Monastery is interesting, but only men are allowed in the cloisters. The Guanabara Palace, the residence of the President (now the municipality), is at Rua Pinheiro Machado, was once the residence of Princess Izabel. The São Joaquin Palace, Praça de Gloria, is the official residence of the Archbishop.

The largest park in Rio is the Quinta da Boa Vista, containing the National Museum, once the residence of two emperors. It has zoological gardens, a small tropical-fish aquarium. Botanical Gardens are situated near Lake Rodrigo de Freitas and the Jockey Club. Here is a great avenue of palms 2,200 feet long. Tijuca Forest is fine for a day's excursion.

A trip to Paquetá, an island at the far end of the bay, is a delight. You may hike, cycle or hire a carriage for a drive from one end of the island to the other. There is a ferry trip from Praça 15 de Novembro and a shorter ferry ride to Niteroi, a picturesque town across the bay, which is the residential section for the English colony. There are pleasant beaches at Icarai and Imbui for a quiet day's jaunt.

Petropolis... Is the leading summer resort in Brazil. It is about an hour's ride from the capital and boasts one of the finest resort hotels

Rio de Janeiro's world-famous Copacabana Beach is flanked by luxury hotels and purple mountains.

From the top of Sugar Loaf Mountain, rising over 1,300 feet from the sea, you get a magnificent panorama of Rio de Janeiro, capital of Brazil.

in the world: *Hotel Quitandinha*, decorated by Dorothy Draper. It is set in the middle of fantastic tropical scenery, including orchid-draped trees on the edge of a lake. The hotel is the last word in modernity and swank. There are 20-foot bird cages, indoor Roman pools, a theater, a marble entrance hall and almost anything else you can imagine. English is just one of the languages spoken. The food is good and the rates not exorbitant. Here you can swim, ride, boat, play tennis or dance. The President has a suite there. Nearby is the royal palace built by the last Emperor of Brazil, Dom Pedro II. The palace is now the Imperial Museum. You may see the royal jewels Thursdays and Sundays.

Another popular resort nearby is Therezopolis, which is about 3 hours from Rio. Best hotels there are *Fazenda da Paz* and *Pensão Pinheiros*.

São Paulo ... South of Rio is São Paulo, the great industrial city of Brazil. It can be reached in one hour by air, or seven hours by bus. The trip by train is overnight. Travel agents will arrange sightseeing tours, and you'll be fascinated with all the new, beautifully modern buildings. The famous Snake Institute Butantan is worthy of a visit. Also interesting is the permanent industrial exhibition at Parque Ibirapuera. See under each paragraph heading beginning page 378, for details on São Paulo.

Santos . . . Only an hour south of São Paulo is Santos, the world's largest coffee port. This is a resort center with beaches and excursions to nearby mountains. The *Parque Balneario* and the *Atlantic* are good hotels. See the orchidarium and Guarujá across the bay. The drive or cograil trip from São Paulo to Santos is exciting and interesting. Buses run very frequently between the two points; the ride takes about one hour.

Iguassú Falls . . . On the Argentine border is one of the sights of the world. They can be reached in about five hours by plane from São Paulo. Larger than Niagara, they are two and a half miles wide. Eight miles away are the falls of Sete Quedas (more on Iguassú Falls in section on ARGENTINA).

Belem . . . the capital city of the State of Pará is at the mouth of the Amazon, way north of Rio. It has a fine hotel, the *Hotel Grande*, which is immaculate and has good food (operated by Intercontinental Hotels Corporation).

Manaus . . . For the adventurous, looking for something different off the tourist path, there are frequent flights from Rio and Belem via Panair do Brasil to Manaus, 1,000 miles up the Amazon in the heart of the jungle. The center of the rubber boom of 50 years ago, Manaus has a fabulous history. You can take river trips, fish for *tucunaré*, one of the world's great game fish, and buy an alligator hide or jaguar skin for a very few dollars. The *Hotel Amazonas* is new and modern, with some rooms air-conditioned. Rates are about $23 double, American Plan. Sightseeing and fishing are organized by the *Hotel Amazonas* on moderate rates.

Salvador . . . Salvador (formerly Bahia) is the royal capital port and the fourth largest city in Brazil. Here the new *Hotel da Bahia* is the best. The market, native costumes, colonial buildings, fabulous beaches, rainbow-tinted houses make it well worth a visit.

Brasilia . . . The new capital city, is rising on a high plateau some 580 miles northwest of Rio de Janeiro. Started in May 1957, Brasilia already boasts a magnificent presidential palace, the "Palace of Dawn," and a fine new, 400-room *Brasilia Palace Hotel*. Over 35,000 people are now living in or near the site; most of them are actively participating in one or more of the building projects which will enable Brasilia to become the nation's federal capital by April 1960—as under current law it must.

SOURCES OF FURTHER INFORMATION . . . The local tourist commission office at Rua Mexico 104 in the Brazilian Newspaper Association Building has folders, maps, lists of events. The *Brazil Herald* is an English-language newspaper. The Pan American office is at Avenida Presidente Wilson, No. 165A (Tel. 52–8070) in Rio, at Avenida Ipiranga, 95 (Tel. 36–0191) in São Paulo. In New York the Brazilian Government Trade Bureau is at 551 Fifth Avenue.

BRITISH GUIANA

WEATHER IN GEORGETOWN—Lat. N6°49'—Alt. below sea level

Temp.	JAN.	FEB.	MAR.	APR.	MAY	JUNE	JULY	AUG.	SEPT.	OCT.	NOV.	DEC.
Low	74°	74°	75°	76°	75°	75°	75°	75°	76°	76°	75°	75°
High	84°	83°	85°	85°	85°	85°	85°	86°	87°	87°	86°	84°
Average	79°	79°	80°	80°	80°	80°	80°	81°	82°	82°	81°	80°
Days of Rain	20	17	19	17	23	25	24	17	8	7	13	22

LOCATION ... British Guiana lies along the northeast shoulder of South America between Venezuela and Surinam.

CHARACTERISTICS ... For vacationists who like to get off the beaten track, British Guiana offers picturesque towns, strange peoples and odd customs, spectacular scenery and untamed jungles; and in the center of the country is one of the wonders of the world, Kaieteur Falls, five times higher than Niagara. Sometimes called the "land of six peoples"—Africans, Amer-Indians, Chinese, East Indians, Portuguese and other Europeans—British Guiana has a reputation for overwhelming hospitality shared by all.

POPULATION ... 500,000 inhabitants, 90 per cent of whom live on the flat coastal belt. Owing, among other things, to improved health conditions, the population is expected to double in the next decade.

SIZE ... 83,000 square miles, about the size of Great Britain.

CAPITAL ... Georgetown, "The Garden City of South America," population 91,529.

GOVERNMENT ... Partly elected, partly nominated.

HOW TO GET THERE ... By Pan American Clipper 15 hours from New York via San Juan, 1¾ hours from Port-of-Spain.

ACCOMMODATIONS ... In Georgetown, the *Park Hotel, Hotel Tower, Palm Court Hotel,* all on Main Street and the *Woodbine Hotel,*

Newmarket Street. All charge from $4.50 to $15.50 per day, which includes all meals.

CURRENCY ... The B.W.I. or British Caribbean dollar, worth about 58 cents in United States currency. £1 equals $4.80 in B.W.I. currency. The coins are 1, 2, 5, 10, 25, and 50 cents. Currency notes are in $1, $2, $5, $10, $20 and $100 denominations (all British West Indian).

CUSTOMS REGULATIONS AND DOCUMENTS REQUIRED FOR UNITED STATES CITIZENS ... Passengers are required to make only an oral declaration. Passports are not required of any Canadian or American citizen who satisfies a member of the Immigration Service that he is a Canadian citizen, or citizen of the United States of America, as the case may be; that he is in possession of a return ticket; and that he intends to remain in the Colony for a period not exceeding 3 months from date of his entry.

RESTAURANTS AND BARS ... All the hotels in Georgetown have restaurant services and are equipped with bars. For European and Chinese dishes try the *New City Restaurant;* for soda fountain snacks, local, European and other dishes, the *Brown Betty Restaurant;* for bar and snacks, the *Cactus Club* and *Palm Court.*

WHERE TO GO—SIGHTSEEING ...

Georgetown ... Georgetown is a garden city with many sights of interest. It lies at the mouth of the Demerara River and extends for 2 miles along the river front. It has excellent roads, wide and straight, and shady, tree-lined avenues. A visit to the Botanical Gardens is of first importance, quiet, cool and beautiful, a wonderland of tropical verdure, the plant population ranging from exquisite tropical flowers to experimental rice fields, the famous victoria regia, lotus lilies and graceful palms. The Zoological Park in the Botanic Gardens contains a collection of local fauna set in picturesque surroundings.

Kaieteur Falls ... The fabulous Kaieteur Falls, with a sheer drop of 741 ft., is one of the world's highest "bridal" falls. If you leave Georgetown at 9:30 A.M., the falls can be reached in a delightful hour's flight over the jungle and up the gorge of the Potaro River. A short walk to the brink of the falls for a picnic lunch and a view of the falls from various vantage points is a memorable experience. A plane which carries six passengers (for $57.50 B.W.I. each) can be chartered through the British Guiana Tourist Committee, but as this service is not run on a regular schedule, the Committee must be informed before the arrival of prospective visitors.

SOURCES OF FURTHER INFORMATION ... There is a British Guiana Tourist Committee and the government information services in Georgetown. Booker Shipping (Demerara), Ltd., at 49–53 Water Street, are agents for Pan American in Georgetown. In New York contact the British Guiana Tourist Committee, c/o John H. Hunter and Sons, Inc., Representatives, 39 Pearl Street.

CHILE

WEATHER IN SANTIAGO—Lat. 33°27′—Alt. 1800′

Temp.	JAN.	FEB.	MAR.	APR.	MAY	JUNE	JULY	AUG.	SEPT.	OCT.	NOV.	DEC.
Low	52°	52°	50°	46°	47°	42°	43°	43°	43°	48°	49°	53°
High	83°	83°	84°	72°	68°	58°	59°	61°	66°	74°	79°	84°
Average	67°	66°	64°	56°	55°	47°	48°	51°	54°	60°	63°	66°
Days of Rain	0	0	1	1	10	12	11	9	3	1	1	0

LOCATION ... A narrow strip between the Andes and the South Pacific, Chile extends from Peru 2,600 miles along the west coast of South America—farther than from New York to Los Angeles.

CHARACTERISTICS ... The capital of Chile has a different atmosphere from most of the capitals in its sister countries. Somehow it is less Latin. Many of the people have English, Irish or German ancestry. You will see many blond people who speak only Spanish but look as though they should speak English. Santiago itself is beautifully located on a high plain. The Mapocho River runs through the city; the peaks of the Andes are to the east. Commanding the city is Cerro San Cristobal, whose terraced slopes rise high above the town. The city is modern and there are few old buildings.

POPULATION ... Estimated 6,800,000 in 1950, the population of Chicago and Philadelphia together.

SIZE ... 286,396 square miles, a larger total area than Texas, but most of the country is barely 100 miles wide.

CAPITAL ... Santiago, the fourth largest city of South America with a population of approximately 1,800,000. Larger than Baltimore.

GOVERNMENT ... A Republic with a President and National Congress elected by universal suffrage.

HOW TO GET THERE ... By National, Pan American and Panagra without change of plane down the west coast of South America, 16 hours (elapsed time) from New York, 10 hours from Miami. Stopovers if you wish en route. By Pan American Clipper

down the east coast; 22¾ hours to Buenos Aires from New York.
Then by Panagra, Santiago is 2¾ hours from Buenos Aires. From the
United States West Coast, flights for South America connect at Miami
or Panamá City. By ship about 18 days from New York to Valparaiso
and about 30 days from the United States West Coast.

ACCOMMODATIONS ... Hotels in Santiago are marvelous,
have good food and smart European-style service. The *Carrera*, operated by Intercontinental Hotels, is a fine 17-story hotel with
roof-top swimming pool and garden. It is one of the finest on the
continent. Rates are about $8.50 single, $11 double, European Plan.
Other first-class hotels in Santiago are the *Crillón* and the *Panamericano*—rates slightly lower than the Hotel Carrera. First-class but not
deluxe are the *Ritz, Savoy, City, Kent* and *Santa Lucía*.

ARTS ... The Museum of Natural History, the Museum of Fine
Arts, the National Library, claimed to be the largest on the continent.

BALLET ... There is a native ballet company which performs at
the Teatro Municipal. Visiting ballet companies appear occasionally.

BANKS ... First National City Bank of New York, Bank of
London and South America Ltd.

CALENDAR OF HOLIDAYS ... May 1, Labor Day; May 21,
Patriotic Day; September 18 and 19, Independence Day; October 12,
Discovery of America; November 1, Religious Day; December 8,
Immaculate Conception; Christmas; and several other religious feasts.

CIGARETTES ... American cigarettes are not available. Best
local cigarettes are *Liberty, Capstan*.

CLIMATE ... The name of the country is derived from an Indian
name meaning "cold." Santiago, however, is mild the year round.
The climate is similar to that of Southern California. It grows colder
as you go south, warmer toward the north. Their summer season is
our winter. Altitude of Santiago is 1,800 feet.

CLUBS ... Cards may be arranged for most of the Santiago clubs
through members or if you are a member of a comparable club at
home. Club de la Unión is famous and very good. Their restaurant
and cellar are marvelous; Club Hípico is exclusive and swank; Los
Leones Golf Club; The Prince of Wales Club for golf; the Polo Club
has tennis courts and swimming pool. Others include Stade Française,
Estadio Italiano, Estadio Español, Lions, Rotary.

COMMON COURTESIES AND LOCAL CUSTOMS ... The
chaperone is a thing of the past in Chile. The dinner hour is late,
after nine. Tea around five is a local custom. Cocktail parties begin
around seven. If invited for dinner to a Chilean home you may
be from a half hour to an hour late unless your host says "English
time."

Many young Chileans are at one time or another members of the
fire department. When a siren sounds men leave anything they are
doing, and rush to the fire.

COMMUNICATIONS ... West Coast Cables, All America
Cables, long-distance telephone.

CURRENCY ... The monetary unit is the peso, written with the

$ and worth about one tenth of a cent. The rate of exchange is about 1,100 pesos to the dollar but varies frequently.

CUSTOMS REGULATIONS AND DOCUMENTS REQUIRED FOR UNITED STATES CITIZENS ... Passport, vaccination certificate, health certificate are required. No visa required for U.S. tourists for visits up to three months. You may bring in all articles of personal use. No restrictions on cameras and small restrictions on liquor (about 2 bottles per person). Two cartons of cigarettes and 2 tins of tobacco allowed duty free.

DRUG STORES ... A few United States products are available in local drug stores.

ELECTRIC CURRENT ... 220 volts, A.C.

FLORA ... Flowers are abundant; a great variation in all the length of the territory. There are some exclusively national specimens in the south, where you will find unexplored woods. *Copihue,* beautiful specimen of Chilean flora, is the national flower.

FOOD ... Seafood is famous in Chile; their lobster dishes are wonderful. Try *caldillo de congrio,* a fish soup, shrimp called *camarones,* an excellent variety of baby crayfish called *langostinos* and crab called *jaibas. Chupe de Mariscos* is a superb shellfish plate. *Chupe de locos* is a scallop soup. *Congrio* and *corvina* are delicious. There is, of course, excellent inexpensive beef here, too. The national dishes are in the highly spiced category. Desserts are cool and imaginative, pineapple with champagne, for instance.

GAMBLING ... Racing at Club Hípico with pari-mutuels on Sunday, and at the Hipódromo de Chile; gambling casino at Viña del Mar (September 15–March 15).

LANGUAGE ... Spanish, of course, is the official language, but the majority of the people in tourist centers speak and understand English.

LAUNDRY AND DRY CLEANING ... Hotels will furnish the information required and some of them have their own service. Two good dry-cleaning companies in Santiago are Lavatex Lavandería Manchester and Sandrico, which will give you 24-hour service for a 50 per cent surcharge. The ordinary service is 5 days, for suits and shirts.

LIQUOR ... The native wines are the thing to buy and drink. Tops are *Santa Carolina,* a white wine, *Tarapaca, Zavala* and *Tocornal* in the burgundy class. Some Chilean Rieslings are well-known in the States and there are many more brands available. *Viña Undurraga* wines are also good. Chilean champagnes are dry and splendid. All the wines are inexpensive.

MEDICAL FACILITIES ... There are several hospitals, and English-speaking doctors are available in most of them. Two of the good ones in Santiago are Clínica Santa Maria and Clínica Alemana.

MOTION PICTURES ... About all of the films shown in the States are shown in the Santiago theaters with only the difference of having titles in Spanish. The best theaters are: the *Windsor, Metro, Bandera, Central, Plaza, Astor, Pacífico* and the *Rex,* which is the most modern. If you care to see pictures in Spanish, you can go to the *Teatro Santiago*.

MUSIC . . . There are concerts at Santiago's Teatro Municipal with native conductors and frequently big-name guest conductors from the United States and Europe. Guitar music is a staple of the country.

NIGHT CLUBS, CABARETS . . . The *Boite* in the *Hotel Carrera* is very swank as are the *Tap Room* and *Waldorf*. Others in Santiago are *Goyescas* and *Charles, El Sarao,* which is an old colonial farmhouse, *Las Brujas* and *Las Perdices,* all a half hour from center of town.

PHOTOGRAPHY . . . Supplies available at Kodak Chilena Ltd. Alonso Ovalle 1188.

RELIGION . . . Chile is a Roman Catholic country. There are other churches however.

RESTAURANTS AND BARS . . . Food in Chile is marvelous and cheap. In Santiago the hotels *Carrera* and *Crillón* have excellent Continental food. The *Danubio Azul* (Chathan Club) gives first-class service and specializes in Chinese food, music in the patio in summer; English is spoken at *El Parron,* famous for meat and mixed grills, Chilean dishes. It also has an outdoor patio. In summer try the uptown *Castillo Fornoni* for dinner. The *Waldorf* has American and French cuisine, a good orchestra. The *Mandarin* serves continental food, dinner dancing. *El Sarao* is an old Chilean inn 20 minutes' drive from the center of the city. Try also *Nuria* and *El Escorial* which serve continental dishes.

SHOPS AND STORES . . . Among the best stores in Santiago are Los Gobelinos, Falabella, Almacenes Paris, Casa García, Rosenblitt, Casa Muzard, Flano and Ville de Nice. Stores are closed Saturday afternoons and all the feast days: during the week, they are open from 9:30 to 1:00 and 3:00 to 7:00.

SPECTATOR SPORTS . . . Around Santiago there is racing on Sundays and feast days at the Club Hípico and Hipódromo de Chile. Pari-mutuel betting, of course. There is racing in season at Valparaiso, too. Here the Derby, a big social event, is held. Soccer is a favorite sport and there are matches throughout the season. There are ski tournaments in the Chilean Andes and in the ski resorts near Santiago.

SPORTS . . . This is the one country in South America where sports take precedence over almost everything else, including sightseeing.

Skiing . . . Only two hours by car from Santiago are Lagunillas and Farellones, ski centers popular with Chileans. Both places have ski lodges, or *refugios*. There are ski runs, practice slopes and lifts.

Portillo is the ski center of the country. Special ski trains run from Santiago. Here is the new *Hotel Portillo,* which is an eight-story building, including a movie theater, night club, central heating and a hospital. At Portillo there are magnificent trails, tows, chair lifts and a 9-mile ski run. Some of the top instructors in the world are on hand during the July-October season. There is skiing, too, in the Chilean lake region at Llaima.

Fishing . . . Iquique in the north of Chile is considered the world's finest fishing ground for broadbill swordfish (*albacora*), striped marlin, yellowfin tuna and oceanic bonito. Best season, March through August. If you prefer fresh water angling, the streams and lakes are full of trout. Best season, October 15 to April 15.

Other Sports . . . Favorite sport of the Santiago social set is wild-dove shooting near Santiago. Tennis, golf, riding, and swimming are all possible in and around Santiago. The Prince of Wales Country Club and Los Leones Golf Club have fine golf courses. Cards are needed. The Polo Club has tennis courts and a swimming pool.

THEATERS . . . In Santiago the *Atelier*, the *Petit Rex,* the *Satch,* the *Imperio* and the *Municipal,* which also has musical performances. All plays are in Spanish.

TIME . . . One hour later than U.S. Eastern Standard Time.

TIPPING . . . There is a 10 per cent service charged added by law to hotel bills. Tip bellboys, hat-check girls, washroom attendants a few pesos. It is not customary to tip cab drivers.

TOURIST TAXES . . . There is an 11 per cent Government tax in addition to the 11½ per cent service charge to be paid at hotels and different resorts, payable according to your bill.

TRANSPORTATION . . . Taxis are plentiful and reasonable.

WATER . . . It is advisable to drink bottled water. Puyehue, bottled at the resort of that name, is one of the best.

WHAT TO BUY . . . Shopping is not the major sport here, but handcrafts are the thing to buy. Black pottery jars can be bought at The Market. Hand-wrought copper trays and candlesticks. *Choapinos,* soft-napped wool rugs, are handsome. The Chilean wines are wonderful and cheap.

WHAT TO WEAR . . . Depends a great deal upon where you are planning to go in Chile and at what time of year. It is colder toward the south; warmer toward the north.

For skiing in the Chilean Andes, June-September, you'll wear the same kind of ski togs you would in Switzerland or in the United States. Santiago has climate similar to that of Southern California. It never gets very hot or very cold. Wear the same sort of thing you would at home in spring. A fur jacket and topcoat come in handy.

Cocktail parties are dressy, so pack afternoon dress and your newest and gayest hat. The hats of Chilean women are world famous. Flowers and feathers preferred.

Men can wear sports jackets and slacks in town, but regular business suits are more appropriate. A topcoat is a necessity. Evening clothes are not necessary as dark suits are the accepted dinner attire.

WHERE TO GO—SIGHTSEEING . . .

Santiago . . . Santiago is a beautiful modern city surrounded by snow-capped mountains. You will get the best view of it from Santa Lucia Park, a picturesque hill covered with terraces, gardens and walks high in the middle of the city. The first Spanish fort in Chile, it is open to the public from 7:00 A.M. till midnight, and can be reached by car. There are gardens and a small museum. Cerro San Cristobal rises about 1,000 feet above the city. You can lunch here at the *Restaurant Casino*. There is a funicular to the summit, from which you get a magnificent view. The road to the top is lined with gardens and promenades. Be sure to include a visit to Government House, *La Moneda,* the residence of the President; well worth seeing. The beautiful Avenida O'Higgins, best known as the Alameda, is the widest and longest street in the city, with walks in the center.

Try to get invited to a *fundo,* or farm, for a sample of Chilean life, where your host may stage a rodeo for you. Chilean rodeos are different from American ones. You should try to see one if you are around in November or December. The cowboys, called *huasos,* play guitars and the songs are very similar to our Western ones. The national dance of Chile, the *cueca,* is danced to guitar music.

Viña Del Mar . . . Literally Vineyard of the Sea, Viña is delightful, reminiscent of Nice, Monte Carlo, Juan-les-Pins, or Soller in Mallorca. Drive both ways by car to see more and stop for interesting meals. Best way is to hire a car in Santiago, go via Valparaiso over two coastal ridges, Barriga and Zapata. Return via Casablanca, Cartagena and other seaside resorts. You can get there by train in 3 hours. The season for Viña del Mar is Chilean summer, December to March.

For gambling visit the Casino where roulette and *punto y banca* are played from September 18 to March 15. Excellent cabaret, orchestras play jazz and *típica.* Also very good restaurant. On weeks ends or holidays reserve tables for dining room or cabaret.

The modern *Mirimar Hotel* overlooks the Pacific Ocean and beach and has one of the best kitchens in Chile. The *Hotel San Martín* is new and well located.

The *O'Higgins Hotel,* named after General Bernardo O'Higgins, Chile's George Washington, is older, grander. Both high cuisine and Creole dishes. Cozy fireplace in the grill.

The above-mentioned hotels have the best food in Viña. However, on the dramatic sea drive northward there are small charming restaurants in lovely little places like Concon. En route to Concon, try *Los Lilenes* for seafood either inside or on open-air terraces.

The Municipal Casino also has a good restaurant, worth visiting just to see the thousands of people at the gaming tables. The *Cap Ducal,* located by the Estero in front of the Casino, also serves excellent meals.

Restaurant *La Virreina's* window bears the inscription: *Cocteles y aperitivos.* It's the fashionable spot to meet in late morning for eye-openers. Order a *vaina,* local eggnog, or a Spanish *anís* and soda.

There are races every Saturday during summer at the Sporting Club and good golf at the Granadilla Country Club. Viña del Mar is extremely smart. Wear your newest clothes. Rates at hotels range from $6.50 a day, European Plan.

Chilean Lake Country . . . The Chilean Lake country is one of the most picturesque lake regions anywhere. It's a land of magnificent scenery and fine sports. You can tour the Lake Country by train, bus, and boat . . . traveling south from Santiago. Pucon is probably your first stop on a typical itinerary. It is on Lake Villarrica, which offers

The Chilean Army band plays on steps of the promenade across from the fine Hotel Carrera in Santiago.

incredibly good rainbow- and brown-trout fishing. Villarrica volcano 9,000 feet high, is nearby. The *Hotel Pucon,* here, is fine.

Traveling on by train or aerotaxi you reach Osorno—one of the most beautiful towns and volcanos on your route. It rises in a perfect cone on the edge of a placid lake. Best hotel is the *Burnier,* quite moderate in price.

Leave Osorno by bus and drive to Enseñada through scenery very much like that of the blue-grass region of Kentucky, or to Puerto Varas, where you journey by launch to Enseñada across Lake Llanquihue (pronounced "Yankee way").

From Enseñada, you have an hour's bus ride to Petrohue where a small steamer awaits you for a beautiful trip across Lake Todos los Santos. You arrive at Peulla and spend the night in a comfortable hotel patterned after a Swiss chalet. While here you can take day excursions to Cabatue and Rio Blanco. You clear customs at Peulla and shortly after leaving by bus, you arrive at Casa Pangue, and enter Argentina.

If you enter Chile from Argentina, go by way of Bariloche and enter the Lake Country at Peulla. Go by boat to Villarrica, where the scenery is as fine as the fishing or skiing. The trees, the forests, the fjords, the snow-capped mountains, the crystal lakes, the views, the fishing, the magnificence of the scenery will entrance you. In Villarrica stay at the *Hotel Antumalal* which has a beautiful golf course and facilities for water skiing. You should really have two weeks to devote to this lake trip. For more on the Lake Country, *see* page 372, also Travel Tip 15 in the front of this book.

SOURCES OF FURTHER INFORMATION ... Panagra is represented by Grace y Cía in Santiago. There are offices at the Hotel Carrera (Tel. 82011) and at Morande 315 (Tel. 81961). The Chilean Consulate General in New York is at 61 Broadway.

COLOMBIA

WEATHER IN BOGOTA—Lat. N4°36′—Alt. 8,500′

Temp.	JAN.	FEB.	MAR.	APR.	MAY	JUNE	JULY	AUG.	SEPT.	OCT.	NOV.	DEC.
Low	45°	45°	46°	50°	50°	49°	48°	48°	46°	48°	48°	46°
High	71°	70°	71°	68°	67°	67°	67°	67°	67°	68°	68°	69°
Average	58°	57°	58°	59°	58°	58°	57°	57°	57°	58°	58°	57°
In. of Rain	2.14	1.12	2.93	4.03	4.08	2.65	1.86	1.28	2.60	6.33	7.20	3.83

LOCATION ... Colombia lies at the northern end of the Andes, with Panama on the west, Venezuela and Brazil on the east and Ecuador and Peru on the south. It is the only country in South America that fronts both the Atlantic and Pacific Oceans.

CHARACTERISTICS ... Colombia is very Spanish in its culture and traditions. This can be seen in its churches, its old public buildings, and in its mountain towns. Bogotá, the capital, has often been called the Athens of America because it has been a cultural center since the time of the Spanish Viceroys.

The principal thoroughfares of Bogotá are Carrera 7a, Carrera 10a, Carrera 13 and Avenida Caracas stretching for about 90 blocks. The main shopping center is on Carrera 7a between Calles 10 and 25. In this area too are the fine hotels, clubs and theaters of the city. The national flower of Colombia is the orchid. It grows everywhere, but it is one of the sights of Medellin. Colombia is a country of infinite variety, from skiing in Manizales to jungle hunting and fishing in Leticia.

POPULATION ... Estimated at 14,000,000, the country has about as many inhabitants as Canada.

SIZE ... 495,519 square miles, slightly larger than Texas and California combined.

CAPITAL ... Bogotá, with a population of over 1,000,000, is the size of the Kansas City metropolitan area.

GOVERNMENT ... A republic governed by a President.

HOW TO GET THERE . . . By Avianca New York-Bogotá 10 hours; Panamá-Medellín-Bogotá 3¼ hours; Caracas-Bogotá 3½ hours; Quito-Bogotá 2 hours; by Pan American Miami-Barranquilla 5½ hours; Panamá-Barranquilla 1¾ hours; Caracas-Barranquilla 2½ hours; by Umca Panamá-Medellín 2 hours; by Panagra Panamá-Cali 2 hours; Quito-Cali 1¼ hours.

ACCOMMODATIONS . . . Newest and best in Bogotá is the *Hotel Tequendama,* which, like all Intercontinental Hotels, is well planned, beautifully equipped, and operated by American standards. It has studio-type rooms with a view of the mountains and city. Singles about $7, doubles $8.00 to $11. The leading hotel in town, it is a convention headquarters, and the first choice of international society. 100 per cent air-conditioned. The *Hotel Continental* is also good. Among others are *Hotel Granada, Hotel San Francisco, Residencias Santa Fé.*

ARTS . . . A "must" for the tourist is the *Quinta de Bolivar,* which was given to the Libertador, Simon Bolivar, by the first vice-president of Colombia in 1820. It is a perfect example of Spanish colonial architecture. Also of interest is the Museum of Colonial Art located in front of the Palacio San Carlos, the actual residence of the President of the Republic. This museum contains Spanish colonial painting, sculpture and furniture. In a special vault of the Banco de la República is the Gold Museum, a collection of 7,000 pieces of jewelry and amulets made by primitive Indian tribes living in Colombia before the Spanish Conquest. The National Museum is devoted to archaeology and the history of the country.

BALLET . . . Visiting ballet groups appear frequently. There are several ballet academies in Bogotá.

BANKS . . . The Banco de la República, Banco de Colombia, Banco de Bogotá, Banco Popular, National City Bank of New York, Royal Bank of Canada, Bank of London and South America.

CALENDAR OF HOLIDAYS . . . January 6, Epiphany; March 19, San José, Holy Week; May 1, Labor Day; Ascension; Corpus Christi; June 29, San Pedro, San Paulo; July 20, Independence Day; August 7, Battle of Boyacá; August 15, Asunción de Nuestra Señora; October 12, Columbus Day; November 1, All Saints Day; November 11, Independence of Cartagena; December 8, Immaculate Conception; Christmas and New Year's Day.

CIGARETTES AND TOBACCO . . . All American brands of cigarettes and tobacco. Cigarettes are about 25 cents U.S. per package. There is also a variety of local cigarettes, cigars and tobacco at much lower prices. All very good.

CLIMATE . . . Bogotá has an altitude of 8,500 feet. The city is cool throughout the year, similar to spring in the United States.

CLUBS . . . In Bogotá, the Jockey Club, Gun Club, Anglo-American Club, Club Médico, Lawyers' Club. The Lions and Rotary meet at the Hotel Tequendama. Country clubs are the Bogotá Country Club, Los Lagartos, San Andres Golf Club, Military Club.

COMMON COURTESIES AND CUSTOMS . . . A mixture of Spanish, European and American. Dinner can be as late as 10:30.

Colombia society enjoys visiting the hotels and night clubs for dining and dancing.

COMMUNICATIONS ... All America Cables for overseas cables; radiograms through National Government Radio; Marconi; long-distance telephone service to U.S., Canada and Europe.

CURRENCY ... The monetary unit is the peso written with a dollar sign. Colombia pesos are equal to about eight to the dollar at free market rate (but subject to fluctuations).

CUSTOMS REGULATIONS AND DOCUMENTS REQUIRED FOR UNITED STATES CITIZENS ... Tourists may obtain a Tourist Card, good for 90 days, and several entries. Passport not required. Smallpox vaccination certificate. Yellow fever certificate on return if you visited places other than Bogotá, Barranquilla, and Cartagena. You may bring in, duty-free, 200 cigarettes or 50 cigars, and a bottle of liquor for personal use.

DRUG STORES ... Everywhere. All U.S. products available.

ELECTRIC CURRENT ... Current is 150 volts A.C., 60 cycle except at the Hotel Tequendama, which has been completely converted to 110 volts, A.C. Transformers should be 110-150 volt, A.C., 60 cycle with regular U.S. flat-prong plugs.

FAUNA ... Colombia is filled with wild life. Jaguars, pumas, panthers, tapirs, armadillos, partridge and a great variety of exotic birds are waiting for the hunter, but arrangements should be made in advance. Excellent fishing on the sea coast.

FLORA ... Every variety of tropical flower, particularly orchids in Medellín.

FOOD ... Native dishes, such as *ajiaco, puchero, sancocho, ternera a la llanera,* are highly spiced and marvelous. Try a Colombian *piquete,* which is a popular Colombian meal combining potatoes, *platanos,* meat, *yuca,* and *ají,* a very highly seasoned sauce. Restaurants and hotels in Bogotá serve more international food than those in any other city in South America.

LANGUAGE ... Spanish is the universal language, but English and French are widely spoken. The traveler from the United States has no trouble making himself understood.

LAUNDRY AND DRY CLEANING ... Available in every section of the city. Twenty-four-hour service at the Hotel Tequendama.

LIQUOR ... In every bar and restaurant the popular drink is Scotch, but try the native drink, *aguardiente,* a fiery liquor. All liquors are available, but expensive. Ron Caldas, a rum made in Manizales, is excellent and comparable to Jamaica rum.

MEDICAL FACILITIES ... There are many English-speaking doctors and nurses who have had U.S. training and experience.

MOTION PICTURES ... There are large, comfortable movies houses. Largest in Bogotá are the *Teatro Colombia,* the *Coliseo,* the *Cid,* and the *Olympia.* Most of the movie theaters in town are good, however. M-G-M has a chain. The open-air theater, *La Media Torta,* located near the Quinta de Bolívar, presents free plays, musical shows, and native dances almost every Sunday.

MUSIC . . . Bogotá has a conservatory of music and a National Orchestra. Bands play Sunday mornings in the Parque Independencia. Famous artists from all over the world sometimes perform at the traditional *Teatro de Colón*.

NIGHT CLUBS AND CABARETS . . . Bogotá society prefers the *Monserrate Room* at the *Hotel Tequendama* and the *Grill Europa*. Others are the *Casbah, Grill Colombia, Leon's, Sahara, Grill Waldorf*, and *La Pampa*.

PHOTOGRAPHY . . . Supplies available at Kodak Colombiana Ltd., Carrera 13, No. 18–66, Bogotá, and in other major cities.

RELIGION . . . Colombia is a Catholic country and has 17 cathedrals. In Bogotá the Protestant Church attended by the English-speaking colony is the Union Church on Calle 24 No. 5–43; St. Alban's, the Episcopal Church, on Calle 69 near Carrera 7. English-speaking Catholic services also available.

RESTAURANTS . . . The food at the top hotels is excellent. A continental cuisine is featured at the *Monserrate* and *Grill Europa*, noted above. They have cocktail lounges too. *Gran Vatel* is a first-class restaurant serving Belgian and French dishes. *Temel* is noted for seafood and steaks. Also try *Mesón de Indias* for Spanish dishes, *Koster* and *Cyrus* for French, *La Pampa* for Argentinian, and the *Sahara* for French-Arabic. The private clubs also serve good food. *See* CLUBS.

SHOPS AND STORES . . . Shopping center of Bogotá is Carrera 7a, which is also the commercial center of the city. Some of the many good shops are: Valdiri, Sandra, Picadilly, Almacén Bogotá, Jennie, Camacho Roldan, Gregory, Salon Margarita, and Daniel's. Sear's has two branches in Bogotá and is the largest department store in the city. Many shops offer jewelry, silver and other items at much less than prices at home.

SPECTATOR SPORTS . . . In Bogotá horse racing Sundays at the *Hipodromo,* pari-mutuel betting as in the U.S. Bullfights Sundays February to March at the *Plaza Santamaria*. Polo matches at the Polo Club at Bogotá, Polo Club de Santa Fe. Soccer is the national sport. Baseball is played in Barranquilla and Cartagena. Cock fighting is popular.

SPORTS . . . There are many golf courses in Bogotá, among them the Bogotá Country Club (cards required, two 18-hole courses), Los Lagartos, and San Andres. Tennis courts at all three clubs. Two of the country clubs have pools. The Aero Club de Colombia, located in Suba (15 miles out of Bogotá), has a fleet of Cessnas for hire. Hunting and fishing expeditions to various parts of the country can be arranged. There is excellent duck shooting. Good marlin fishing is to be found at Barranquilla. Lake Tota, about 160 miles from the capital, in the mountains, offers the best trout fishing in Colombia.

THEATRES . . . The *Colón* is the opera and concert house; the *Colombia* also has stage shows from time to time.

TIME . . . Same as United States Eastern Standard Time.

TIPPING ... Usually 10 per cent.

TRANSPORTATION ... There are many taxi fleets and cars for hire; they are very cheap. Aerotaxi (affiliate of Avianca) has air service to areas otherwise difficult to reach. Helicopter service is also available through Helicol (Helicopteros Nacionales de Colombia, another Avianca affiliate).

WATER ... Safe in all the big cities.

WHAT TO BUY ... Bogotá is the world center for the best emeralds (Bauer, Kling, and Kraus are the leading jewelry shops). There is the usual handwrought silver, Indian rugs, blankets, arrows, hats and pottery. The figurines sculptured from crude rubber and tinted are unusual; these are available in Cartagena.

WHAT TO WEAR ... For Bogotá women will need lightweight wool suits and dresses, sweaters and skirts, and fur jacket or topcoat. For the coastal cities lightweight clothes, of course. A raincoat is recommended wherever you go. Men need a topcoat and light wool suits for Bogotá. Summer sports clothes for the coastal cities.

WHERE TO GO—SIGHTSEEING ...

Bogotá ... There are many old Colonial buildings in Bogotá dating from the pre-Bolivar era. The Palace of San Carlos, where the Libertador once lived, now the President's home. Also the Teatro de Colón and the churches of La Veracruz, San Ignacio, San Agustin, La Tercera, San Diego, and San Francisco. All of these are very old. There are at least 60 churches in the city. The cathedral on the Plaza de Bolivar was originally built in 1572. Also don't fail to see the Quinta de Bolivar. Bogotá's seats of learning are many. You should see the University City, the Universidad de los Andes, the Gimnasio Moderno, and the Colegio Nacional de San Bartolomé, founded in 1604. Near the capital is Monserrate, a peak that may be ascended by funicular or cable car. There is a famous chapel on the summit. The Salto de Tequendama is a spectacular waterfall 13 miles from the city. It was an Indian shrine, and there are many legends connected with it. There's an inn nearby. Las Salinas de Zipaquirá, 30 miles from the city, are salt mines which are also spectacular. Entering through a portal, one can drive for three miles underground. At the end of the largest gallery is a full-sized cathedral. By car or horseback go on to Laguna de Guatavita, 35 miles from the capital, a lagoon rimmed by high mountains, which was held sacred by the ancient Chibchas.

Barranquilla ... A chief seaport, it is a bright modern city near the mouth of the Magdalena River, one of the greater waterways of the Western Hemisphere. It is a place of contrasts—of streamlined cars and boys riding burros, of a native dance known as *la cumbia* and modern jazz. It gets cooler from November to March. Best hotel in the city is the *Hotel El Prado,* with many air-conditioned rooms. The *Hotel Pradomar,* at the seaside resort 20 minutes away, is also good. The country clubs have fine golf courses, tennis courts and swimming pools. Wonderful deep-sea fishing nearby.

Cartagena ... is a wonderful old walled city which lies on a

The centrally heated new Hotel Tequendama (left) with every modern convenience for your stay in Bogotá, Colombia.

sandy peninsula. There are many interesting old buildings and fortifications dating from the sixteenth century. There is good swimming at Boca Grande Beach. The *Hotel del Caribe,* located on this beach, has a casino. Also the *Hotel San Felipe* located in the city is good.

Cali ... is a city in the rich Cauca Valley with altitude of 3,000 feet and, pleasant year-round climate. There are eight parks, and the Cali River cuts through the city. Cali is surrounded by sugar plantations. Close to the city is the Estancia La Maria, locale of the famous book, *La Maria,* by Jorge Isaacs. The *Alferez Real* and the *Hotel Menendez* are on the Cali River; another good hotel is the *Aristi.* The *Club Campestre de Cali* is an ancient hacienda with incredibly green surrounding country. It's the social center of the city and an extraordinary place. *Club San Fernando* is also very good. The 300-year-old *Hacienda Cañas Gordas* is beautifully preserved. Six miles from Cali, this is a "must." Visitors are welcome. Two good restaurants are *Hosteria Madrid* and *Don Carlos.*

Medellin ... Famous for its orchids, it is situated about 150 miles northwest of Bogotá. It has the climate of late spring and is a garden spot. It is an air-route junction and an industrial center of the country. The *Nutibara* is the leading hotel and compares with the best. The *Medellin Country Club* has excellent food and rooms, golf course, tennis courts and swimming pool. There are many interesting excursions available out of Medellin, such as the orchid plantation of Sra. Bertha Hernandez de Ospina, a trip to Santa Elena up in the mountains and to *El Boqueron,* a mountaintop restaurant.

Manizales ... Has the largest cathedral in the country. One hour from Bogotá by air, it is a photographer's paradise. The city has an altitude of 7,000 feet, and nearby at Nevado del Ruiz at 15,000 feet there is year-round skiing with ski lift and ski lodge. Manizales produces the best coffee in Colombia. The people are extremely hospitable. Every tourist is welcomed with a free bottle of Ron Caldas.

SOURCES OF FURTHER INFORMATION ... National Tourist Offices in all principal cities. Pan Am offices at Carrera 10, No. 24–41, Bogotá (Tel. 420–720); Carrera 45, No. 34–20, Barranquilla (Tel. 11610). Panagra's at Carrera 10a, Seguros Bolivar Building, Bogotá (Tel. 411128). Colombian Consulate at 444 Madison Ave., New York.

ECUADOR

LOCATION ... Ecuador is on the northwest coast of South America between Colombia and Peru, occupies a region where the Andes split into two ranges, and divide the country into three regions: the inter-Andean valleys or "sierra," producers of cereals, potatoes, fruits and pastures; the "costa" or litoral, with great plantations of coffee, cocoa and banana (Ecuador is the first banana exporter in the world); and the east low plains—where the fabulous Amazon jungle begins. Quito, the capital, is less than 3½ hours by air from Panamá. The Galapagos Islands, famous for their giant tortoises, are a part of Ecuador, 3 hours by air west. These islands have a wonderful climate, are primitive and as yet undiscovered by tourists.

CHARACTERISTICS ... In Quito the sun rises at about 6:00 A.M. every morning because the city is on the equator. Quaintly beautiful, the city is filled with wonderful Spanish colonial architecture and art. Its streets are colorful and some of them are steep. The country descends from the grandeur of the Andes to the tropical city and busy port of Guayaquil (over 420,000 inhabitants on the Guayas river. Ecuador is a miniature world: sea, beaches, desert and jungles; snow-capped mountains, pastures and valleys. For wonderful scenery, a taste of ancient civilization, a touch of deep-sea fishing, try Ecuador, where North Americans are extremely welcome.

POPULATION ... 4,086,000, about half that of Texas.

SIZE ... 106,507 square miles, about the size of Colorado.

CAPITAL ... Quito, a city of 285,000, slightly larger than Omaha, Nebraska.

GOVERNMENT . . . A Republic of 18 provinces and one insular territory, with a President, Vice President, Senate and Chamber of Deputies.

HOW TO GET THERE . . . On the interchange flight of National, Pan American and Panagra, New York to Quito is 14¾ hours, to Guayaquil 13½ hours. From Miami to Quito the time is 9½ hours, 7¾ hours to Guayaquil. Flying time between Quito and Guayaquil is only 50 minutes. By ship about 9 days from New York to Guayaquil.

ACCOMMODATIONS . . . The *Humboldt Capitol* is the best hotel in Quito. Centrally located, it enjoys a particularly comfortable and attractive atmosphere. Rates $11.00 double and $8.00 single, European Plan (without meals). All rooms with bath and central heating. The *Colón,* 10 minutes to the center of town, has a friendly, pleasant ambient. Excellent food. Rates: run from $7 to $9.20 double and $3.50 to $5.80 single, European Plan, including American-type breakfast. Also American Plan (with all meals). The *Embajador,* 12 minutes to the center of town, has comfortable rooms, all with private bath. Rates: $8.00 double, $4.50 single, European Plan. The *Majestic* and the *Crillón* are commercial hotels in the center of town. Rates run from $5.00 double and $3.00 single, European Plan. *Residence Lutetia* is a comfortable and very clean boarding house. Rates (including meals) run from $12.00 double; $7.00 single; $125.00 a month. By the end of 1959 the new and very modern *Hotel Atahualpa,* run by Americans, is due to open.

ARTS . . . Quito, during colonial times, was the art center of South America. There are churches and museums containing century-old paintings and scultpures. Quito's magnificent churches like La Compañía, San Francisco, La Merced, San Augustín, etc., with altars carved like lace, famous old paintings and sculptures—sparkling baroque jewels of the Moorish art—are wonders without equal elsewhere in the Southern Hemisphere.

The Museum of Colonial Art exhibits a fine collection of Ecuadorian paintings and sculptures of the last four centuries. The Franciscan Museum and the Museum of the Monastery of Santo Domingo have a valuable collection of colonial religious art.

The Casa de la Cultura Ecuadoriana has a gallery of antique and modern Ecuadorian art and a museum of musical instruments, the Museo Musical Traversari, one of the most complete in the world.

BANKS . . . Banco Central del Ecuador, Banco del Pichincha, La Previsora, Banco de Abasto, Banco de Préstamos, Banco Popular and Banco de Londres y América del Sur. *See under* CURRENCY.

CALENDAR OF HOLIDAYS . . . New Year's Day; 2-day carnival on Monday and Tuesday preceding Lent; Maundy Thursday and Good Friday; May 1, International Labor Day; May 24, Battle of Pichincha; July 24, Bolívar's Birthday; August 10, Ecuador's Independence Day; October 9, Anniversary of Guayaquil; October 12, Day of Columbus; November 1, All Saints Day; November 3, Anniversary of Cuenca; December 6, Foundation of Quito; and Christmas Day.

CIGARETTES AND TOBACCO ... All American brands of cigarettes are available at 30¢ a pack. 50 cigars, 300 cigarettes, 7 ounces pipe tobacco admitted duty free. There is a variety of local cigarettes. American pipe tobacco is also sold.

CLIMATE ... Don't think of Ecuador as a hot country. The coast is tropical, but the sierra with its snow-capped mountains is cool. Quito is called the City of Eternal Spring, but it is apt to be a little colder than spring as we think of it. June to October (the dry season time) is the best to visit Quito or Guayaquil.

CLUBS ... The Quito Tennis y Golf Club for bridge and other card games. Rotary and Lions. Cards may be arranged. For golf and tennis, *see* SPORTS.

COMMON COURTESIES AND CUSTOMS ... Bargaining is accepted practice in small shops or with street vendors. Women in slacks are not seen on the streets. Office hours in Quito are from 8:30 A.M. to 12 noon, and 2:00 to 6:00 P.M. Afternoon tea is ritual in Quito's social life. Cocktail parties begin around 6:30 P.M. The dinner hour is between 8:00 and 10:00 P.M.

COMMUNICATIONS ... All America Cables and Radio Inc. and Radio Internacional del Ecuador. Airmail rates to American countries: letters 12 cents (2 sucres, Ecuadorian currency); postcards, 7 cents (1.20 sucres, Ecuadorian currency).

CURRENCY ... The monetary unit of Ecuador is the sucre, divided into 100 cents. It is worth about 6 U.S. cents. Banks, travel agencies or money-exchange houses will exchange at the rate fixed by the Central Bank of Ecuador. Principal exchange houses are: Rodrigo Paz, Pasaje Royal; Egcasa, Venezuela 738; La Bolsa, Venezuela 927; M.M. Jaramillo, A., Mejía 401; Carlos Musello, Venezuela 727; and Tambaco, Chile 1058.

CUSTOMS REGULATIONS AND DOCUMENTS REQUIRED FOR UNITED STATES CITIZENS ... No restriction on currency, cameras or films, 1 liter liquor, 300 cigarettes, or 50 cigars, or 7 ozs. pipe tobacco admitted duty free. No visa required, only tourist card issued by air carrier, with photo attached (fee $1.00); certificates of smallpox vaccination and health certificate stating that you have no contagious or incurable disease; 2 front-view photos. Business travelers should check regulations about bringing in samples.

DRUG STORES ... There are modern stores where most United States and European medicines are sold. However, bring your own special prescriptions, already filled, with you.

ELECTRIC CURRENT ... 110 volts, A.C., is the standard voltage in Ecuador, as in the United States. Regular American-type plugs.

FAUNA ... The most imposing is the condor, the giant bird that lives in the highest altitudes of the Andes. Birds of fantastic plumages—from the small hummingbird to the large-beaked *huacamayos* —can be found in the mountains. There are also herons, flamingos, ibis. In other zones of Ecuador there are monkeys, pumas, wildcats, bears, tapirs, deer, alligators. The waters of Ecuador are rich in many types of fish.

FLORA ... Among the native species the most important are: the cinchona tree (quinine), kapok tree, balsa tree, guayacan tree, fan-palm tree. *Naranjilla* is a fruit grown only in Ecuador.

FOOD ... Typcal native dishes are well spiced and fairly exotic for the American palate. Try *llapingachos*—fried mashed potatoes with cheese—or *locro,* a stew soup of potatoes and cheese, either of the two with an avocado on top. *Humitas* are tamales made of sweet corn, more delicate than the Mexican type. If you are in a bar at noon, try *ceviche de corvina* or *ceviche de langostinos* or *cocktail de camarones.* They are native dishes; hot, but very good with a glass of beer. Try *naranjillada,* a fruit-juice drink. Pasteurized milk is available in bottles. Wine is expensive here. Food prices in restaurants are lower than in the United States; meals run from $2 up. *See* LIQUOR.

GAMBLING ... Horse racing with pari-mutuel betting (*See under* SPECTATOR SPORTS.) There is a weekly national lottery. Also a casino at the beach resort Playas, near Guayaquil.

LANGUAGE ... Spanish, although English is spoken and understood in the tourist centers, hotels and better shops.

LAUNDRY AND DRY CLEANING ... La Química, Luxor and Iris are among the best in Quito. 24-hour service, good quality, prices below those in the United States. Your laundry can always be arranged for through your hotel.

LIQUOR ... Pilsener and Victoria are two native beers famous throughout South America. American drinks (about 70 cents) are available in hotels and restaurants, as are French and Chilean wines, but they are expensive.

MEDICAL FACILITIES ... Hospital Vozandes (The Rimmer Memorial Hospital) Tel. 33044; Clínica Santa Cecilia, Tel. 30244; Clínica Pichincha, Tel. 32641; Clínica del Niño (for children only), Tel. 30847; and Isidro Ayora Maternity, Tel. 31502, are modern hospitals and have English-speaking doctors.

MOTION PICTURES ... All movie houses in Quito show American films with titles in Spanish. The best theaters are: *Bolívar, Atahualpa, Pichincha* and *Alhambra,* in the center of town; *Teatro Universitario, Colón* and *Capitol* in the residential zone.

MUSIC ... *Pasillo, San Juanito, Albazo* and *Yaraví* are the native dances. Military bands give Sunday- and Thursday-evening concerts in the principal squares. Internationally famous artists play at the Sucre Theater in Quito.

NIGHT CLUBS AND CABARETS ... Quito is not much of a night-club town. Most important are *Bagatelle, Pigalle* and *Henry's* (in the residential zone); and *Le Toucan* (out of town). Prices are about 20 per cent above those in the U.S.

PHOTOGRAPHY ... Black-and-white and color still and movie film are available as well as cameras and photo equipment. Prices slightly higher than in the United States. Developing of still films takes 24 hours. Color film can also be developed locally.

RELIGION ... Ecuador is a Catholic country. Quito has about

60 churches. There are also Protestant (several denominations) churches, Witness of Jehová and Jewish synagogues.

RESTAURANTS . . . *Hotel Colón* has the best food in Quito, Calle Tamayo 233 (Tel. 31401), *Normandy* is excellent for French and international cuisine, Tarqui 257 (Tel. 33154). *Hotel Humboldt* also has a good restaurant on the top floor. All these places can prepare a fabulous typical Ecuadorian luncheon or dinner, but you must order by telephone, two or three hours ahead of time. For Italian food, try *Rincón de Sicilia,* Ave. 10 de Agosto 971 (Tel. 30678). Prices in restaurants listed above run from $2 or $3 for a complete meal with beer, considerably more with wine.

SHOPS AND STORES . . . Shopping center in Quito is on Venezuela and Guayaquil streets. You must see "Fábrica AKIOS," Gorívar 326 (Barrio Obrero), which has a varied stock of typical women's wear and many local curiosities. Folklore (Av. Colón 274) makes very fine handwoven rugs. *Silver shops:* Hamilton, Chile 1065; Joyería Cisneros, Venezuela 918 are the best; *Curios and Antique Shops:* Galerías Metro, Chile 1072; Turismo Recalde, Chile 1056; Galerías Bolívar, Espejo Street (one block from the Humboldt Hotel inside the lobby of Teatro Bolívar); and Diamond Club, Venezuela 858 (interior). *Book Shops:* (books in English), Librería Científica, Venezuela 645; Su Librería, Chile 1160 (Portal Arzobispal); and Librería Selecciones, Venezuela 589. Shops are open from 8:30 A.M. to 12:30 P.M. and from 2:00 to 6:30 P.M.

SPECTATOR SPORTS . . . Horse racing on Sunday at Quito's Hipódromo La Carolina and Hipódromo Santa Cecilia in Guayaquil. Pari-mutuel betting, 30 cents (5 sucres) a ticket. Polo matches are played in Quito, Guayaquil and Riobamba. In Quito and in several towns at the uplands a local sport called *Pelota de Guante* (glove ball) is played on Saturday afternoons and Sunday at Estadio Mejía (Mejía College's sport ground). No admission ticket. Ask a player to allow you to pick up the *guante* (bat) and/or the ball; considering their heavy weight you will marvel at their skill. Soccer and basketball are very popular sports. Soccer is played Saturday afternoons and Sunday mornings at Estadio Olímpico Municipal, Estadio de la Concentración Deportiva and Estadio Universitario. For basketball and indoor sports: Coliseo and Plaza Arenas.

SPORTS . . . The Quito Tennis y Golf Club is a de luxe country club in Quito, on the way to the airport, 15 minutes from town. It has a good golf course, tennis courts and a lovely indoor swimming pool. Cards can be arranged. Near Quito are thermal swimming pools at Alangasí, Tingo and Cununyacu. For hunting wild game, arrangements may be made through local travel agencies. In Guayaquil, the Golf Club, Tennis Club and Yachting Club are equally fine. Here fishing is varied and abundant. There is big-game fishing for bonito and marlin on the coast at Playas, Salinas, and farther north, at Manta.

THEATERS . . . Principal theater in Quito is *Teatro Sucre*. Plays in Spanish only. Also concerts and ballet.

TIME . . . Same as United States Eastern Standard Time.

TIPPING . . . In hotels and restaurants tip 10 per cent. To porters 5 sucres (30 cents) for all luggage. No tips for taxi drivers.

TRANSPORTATION . . . Taxis are available everywhere in Quito. Fare from downtown to the residential zone, or vice versa, is 30 cents (5 sucres). Buses are always crowded. *Colectivos* (station wagons) offer fairly good service, fare 6 cents (1 sucre). Auto rental with driver $1.20 (20 sucres) per hour in the city. The rate between airport and the city is $0.60 (10 sucres) per person or $1.80 (30 sucres) private car. Prices should be settled in advance. Cars may be hired for about $12 (200 sucres) per day. For schedules of trains or special trips by car outside the cities, see a travel agency.

WATER . . . Bottled water is advised. Güitig Imperial and Mercedes are the best.

WHAT TO BUY . . . Panamá hats are the best buy in Ecuador. Properly called Montecristi, they are woven here, and not, as you might think, in Panamá. Montecristi and Jipijapa hats, famous the world over, may be bought for $14 to $60 but it is recommended to be advised by an expert or a travel-agency guide. Beautiful antique-silver Indian ornaments. Indian costumes, hand-carved wooden chests, handbags and cigarette cases woven of palm fiber. Native rugs, shawls and tweeds woven by Indians, beautiful and colorful native embroideries and pottery, all kinds of articles, such as bookends, plates, salad bowls, made out of shiny Guayacan wood.

WHAT TO WEAR . . . Quito is cool (see chart page 402). For women woolen suits and dresses with fur jacket or topcoat. Men need woolen suits and topcoats. For places on the coast of Ecuador like Guayaquil and Playas, you'll need tropical clothes and swimming gear.

WHERE TO GO—SIGHTSEEING . . .

Quito . . . There is a lot to see in the capital itself. Quito is full of excellent examples of colonial art. Any of its churches is rewarding to the tourist. The Church of San Francisco is famous for its art treasures and cloisters. Women may not enter the cloisters without permission. La Compañía, the church of the Jesuits, was built by Mohammedan workmen. All the churches have magnificent displays of gold, silver and jewels, exquisitely carved altars and vaulted ceilings brilliant with gold leaf. The Church of La Merced and the Chapel of the Virgin of the Rosary in the Church of Santo Domingo must be seen. Don't miss Quito's museums. *See* ARTS.

Quito is a city of steep streets, white houses and red-tiled roofs. Climb Panecillo (The Little Loaf of Bread) for a breath-taking view of the city. Walk through La Ronda street—one of the most typical in town—and go to Paseo Escénico (Scenic View) in the residential zone. In the Chillos Valley, about 1 hour away from Quito by car, are the thermal swimming pools of Alangasí and Tingo. Sightseeing tours: City tour (2½ hours); Equatorial Monument tour (2½ hours); Valley of Chillos tour (3 hours). Rates $5 to $7 for each of two persons.

Side Trips . . . The Indian Fair at Saquisilí, on Thursdays only, is an interesting sight. The trip takes you by the snow-capped volcano of Cotopaxi. Saquistilí is 1 hour and 45 minutes from Quito by car; the tour takes the whole day. A 2-day trip by car to Otavalo for the early Saturday Indian Fair, one of the largest in Ecuador, is fun. The Otavalo Indians weave wonderful woolen cloth that is not unlike Scotch tweed. Ambato, known as the garden city of Ecuador, is in the interior on the way to Baños, where the Amazon jungle starts. Baños is something of a summer resort and a spa; the climate is temperate. There are small, but comfortable and clean, hotels with good food. Santo Domingo is a little village of the Colorado Indians. They paint their bodies red and comb their hair in a way that resembles a helmet. Very interesting to tourists. The tour takes 2 days and it's better to go on Sundays. All these trips must be arranged in Quito through a travel agency.

Guayaquil... The rail journey from Quito to this city descends from the Andes into the heart of the jungle. Guayaquil lies about 60 miles from the ocean on the Rio Guayas and has a pleasant tropical climate with an average temperature of 80 degrees. Hyacinths float on the river, which teems with boats and ships. Guayaquil is the principal port of Ecuador and important commercial city.

The *Humboldt International Hotel,* on the waterfront of the River Guayas, is new and up to the most modern standards. Each room has a private balcony either facing the river or overlooking a beautiful swimming pool. The dining terrace also offers a view of the river. Rates $8.00 single, $11.00 double, European Plan. The *Hotel Metropolitano* is also good; the rooms are comfortable, the food good. There are a bar and ice-water machines on each floor, swimming pool on the roof. The *Hotel Continental* and *Hotel Palace* are modern and comfortable. Excellent food. Other hotels are the *Majestic* and *Crillón.* There are several good restaurants, including *Salón Rex, La Dulzura, Fortich* and *Melba,* luxurious soda fountain. There are a yacht club, a golf club, and an excellent tennis club. Cards are needed for all of these. (Inquire at your hotel.)

Playas... Is the beach resort of the country, an hour and a half from Guayaquil. Here the *Hotel Humboldt* is modern. You may swim in the sea or in a pool. Everything is modern and the food excellent. Rates from $12.50 to $25 double, American Plan. There is a good deep-sea fishing in the Humboldt current.

Cuenca... Only an hour from Guayaquil by Panagra service, was founded in 1557; still is genuinely colonial and located on a beautiful flowery plain, 8,468 feet in the Andes. Cobbled streets. Old buildings with lavish use of marble. Murals are painted on patio walls in private homes, often with old Spanish proverbs inscribed. Here you can see the world-famous panamá hats made of toquilla straw. Be there on a Thursday for the Fair.

SOURCES OF FURTHER INFORMATION... In Quito, Metropolitan Touring, Benalcazar 699 (Tel. 10184), Ecuadorian Tours, Espojo 933 (Tel. 12305), Tambaco Turismo, Chile 1060 (Tel. 10643), and Agencia Renato Pérez, Venezuela 955 (Tel. 10372) are travel agencies which have folders and maps and will provide tourist guides. In New York the Ecuadorian Consulate is at 30 Rockefeller Plaza.

FRENCH GUIANA

WEATHER IN CAYENNE—Lat. N4°50'—Alt. 25'

Temp.	JAN.	FEB.	MAR.	APR.	MAY	JUNE	JULY	AUG.	SEPT.	OCT.	NOV.	DEC.
Low	75°	75°	75°	77°	75°	75°	73°	75°	73°	75°	77°	75
High	84°	84°	84°	84°	84°	84°	86°	88°	90°	90°	88°	84°
Average	80°	80°	80°	81°	80°	80°	80°	82°	82°	83°	82°	80°
Days of Rain	25	23	19	18	27	24	18	9	2	6	8	27

LOCATION ... French Guiana is situated on the northeast coast of South America between Dutch Guiana and Brazil.

CHARACTERISTICS ... Wild and primitive, French Guiana is a backward country, unspoiled by modern trends and the least explored of the three Guianas, but known around the world for its formerly infamous Devil's Island Penal Colony, now deactivated. The country is rich in unexploited minerals and hardwood timbers.

In Cayenne the visitor sees carts drawn by water buffalo, trees loaded with wild orchids; a trip up-river in a motor-powered dugout canoe reveals the lush jungle with its multi-colored birds and butterflies.

POPULATION ... 23,308, of whom 13,348 reside in Cayenne according to the 1957 census.

SIZE ... The country has an area of 35,135 square miles and a coastline of 200 miles.

CAPITAL ... Cayenne, located at the mouth of the Cayenne River, whose population is composed of the native Guyanese and numerous French governmental employees and Chinese.

GOVERNMENT ... French Guiana is now a Department of France over which a Prefect named by the French ministry presides.

HOW TO GET THERE ... By PAA Clipper, 18½ hours from New York, with stops at San Juan, Port-of-Spain, Trinidad, and British and Dutch Guiana.

ACCOMMODATIONS ... There's an excellent new *Hotel Montabo* located five minutes' drive from the center of Cayenne. It's on top of Montabo Hill about 200 feet above the sea, with a view of Devil's Island to the northwest. The hotel has 30 rooms, each with bath and twin beds. Food and service are very good. Rates from $6; meals average about $5 daily. The restaurant and bar at the *Rochambeau Field Guest House* are open but guest rooms and swimming pool are not completed.

CURRENCY ... The monetary unit is the French franc. Official rate, 420 to 1 U.S. American dollars are accepted at current exchange rate.

CUSTOMS REGULATIONS AND DOCUMENTS REQUIRED FOR UNITED STATES CITIZENS ... United States citizens must have a valid passport, yellow fever inoculation. For return to the United States you must have a smallpox vaccination certificate.

WHERE TO GO—SIGHTSEEING

Cayenne ... In the center of town is the Place des Palmistes, which beckons to the visitor in the heat of the day. It is a park of green grass, cool and inviting, with giant palms overhead. A stroll through the palm-lined walks reveals well-kept tennis courts. To the north the visitor may see the official residence of the Prefect which was built by the Jesuits, the hospital and offices of the Principal public services. To the east are the Sports Stadium and the Botanical Gardens.

A taxi can be hired which will carry the visitor to see the summer homes along the beach. On the grounds of the Prefect's beach home are beautiful birds in huge cages, tigers, monkeys, deer, etc. Another tour will take the visitor through the jungle where trees and foliage are so dense that the sun never penetrates, where bamboo grows in huge clumps that form an archway over the road.

A trip up-river is well worth taking, although it is not usually possible to return the same day. Unless one likes "roughing it," better not attempt a river journey—but for those with a zeal for adventure, by all means, don't miss it!

Devil's Island ... Off the coast of French Guiana is a rocky, palm-covered little tropical island that one day may become a delightful tourist resort with a fascinating appeal all its own. It is Ile au Diable —Devil's Island.

The Iles de Salut—of which Devil's Island is one—are situated 6 miles off the Guiana coast, and are one of the sights pointed out to passengers by captains of Clipper flights to Cayenne.

SOURCES OF FURTHER INFORMATION ... J. Ste. Claire 6, Avenue du General de Gaulle, are agents for Pan American in Cayenne. In New York contact the French Government Tourist Office, 610 Fifth Avenue.

PARAGUAY

WEATHER IN ASUNCION—Lat. S25°16′—Alt. 253′

	JAN.	FEB.	MAR.	APR.	MAY	JUNE	JULY	AUG.	SEPT.	OCT.	NOV.	DEC.
Average Temp.	80°	80°	78°	72°	67°	63°	64°	66°	70°	72°	76°	80°
In. of Rain	5.4	5.1	4.2	5.1	4.6	2.8	2.2	1.6	3.1	5.5	5.8	6.2

LOCATION ... An inland country, Paraguay is crowded between Argentina, Brazil and Bolivia in central South America.

CHARACTERISTICS ... Paraguay is a bit off the beaten track. It is not for the tourist who wants to find everything comparable to things at home. But it is definitely for those who like the colorful, the picturesque and a spot not overrun by tourists. Asunción, the capital, is a port on a river, in which the native women wash their clothes and beat them on stones.

POPULATION ... Estimated 1,405,627 in 1950, the population approximates that of Baltimore and Rochester, New York, combined.

SIZE ... About 150,500 square miles, slightly bigger than Montana.

CAPITAL ... Asunción, a city of 205,605, roughly the size of Bridgeport, Connecticut.

GOVERNMENT ... A republic with a President, Congress and Council of State.

HOW TO GET THERE ... By Panair do Brasil—5¼ hours flying time from Rio de Janeiro, 3 hours from Buenos Aires. By ship from New York, about 19 days to Buenos Aires, then 4 days by river steamer.

ACCOMMODATIONS ... Although the city of Asunción has no running water, the *Gran Hotel del Paraguay,* as well as all the other first-class hotels and most good residences, have their own artesian wells with hot and cold running water in modern bathrooms. The Gran Hotel was once the residence of Lopez, paramour of Eliza Lynch, who practically held court there. The murals in the hotel dining room, which were once her private theater, are strange and provocative. There are two other hotels in the city: the *Asunción Palace,* which is new, and the *Colonial,* which is old.

CUSTOMS REGULATIONS AND DOCUMENTS REQUIRED FOR UNITED STATES CITIZENS ... Passport, visa, smallpox certificate and police certificate required.

WHERE TO GO—SIGHTSEEING. ...

Asunción ... There is a new modern bank building in the city, which stands like a white symbol. The streets in front of it are thronged with natives on donkeys. A familiar sight are shawl-wrapped native women, carrying black umbrellas, riding sidesaddle on donkeys. The older buildings have more than a touch of the Italian about them, for the elder Lopez imported an Italian architect who designed the palace and the Pantheon, which is modeled on Napoleon's tomb. It contains the coffins of Lopez, two Paraguayan unknown soldiers and other national heroes. The shopping center is Calle Palma, where merchandise brought by steamer from Buenos Aires is for sale.

The ladies of Asunción go hatless, wear white gloves, bags and shoes, and gather for tea each afternoon at one of the tearooms which dot all South America. There is an excellent restaurant, the *Terraza Caballero,* overlooking the bay on the Paraguay River. Try a cocktail made of *cana,* native rum. There are some fine private clubs for which you will need a card. The *Club Centenario* and the *Club Union* are the best. Roulette and baccarat are played at Club Union and at El Casino.

Paraguay lace is world famous and it is made chiefly in the village of Itaugua. This lace is sold at hotels in Asunción and at the airport.

In all Paraguay, there are only about 40,000 Indians. A few of them can be seen in a reservation, near Asunción, which is kept by a Sociedad de Protección al Indio. Some of these Indians can also be seen in the city, from time to time, trying to sell souvenirs. Guided tours to the reservation, or *campo,* are conducted by a local tourist agency. Paraguay has no racial problem. The Guaraní Indians, who populated this country, were completely absorbed by the Spaniards, who took the Indian dialect, the Guaraní, and developed it into a full, rich language, which is now spoken by practically every Paraguayan. Thus, Paraguay became a bilingual country. Spanish is the official language, but in the country, Guaraní is used more.

San Bernardino ... The only city outside of the capital which caters to tourists is San Bernardino, on a lake 2 hours away by car. The lake, called Ypacarai, is shallow and is easily heated by the summer sun. San Bernardino is the Paraguayan summer resort. During the hottest season (December through February), the little place is alive with young, gay people from Asunción's society. There is the *Hotel del Playa,* and a really swank club: *Club Náutico San Bernardino.*

PERU

WEATHER IN LIMA—Lat. S12°03'—Alt. 501'

Temp.	JAN.	FEB.	MAR.	APR.	MAY	JUNE	JULY	AUG.	SEPT.	OCT.	NOV.	DEC.
Low	63°	65°	64°	62°	58°	57°	56°	56°	56°	57°	60°	63°
High	81°	83°	84°	80°	76°	70°	67°	67°	69°	69°	74°	79°
Average	72°	74°	74°	71°	67°	64°	62°	62°	63°	63°	67°	71°

LOCATION ... Peru, on the west coast of South America along the Pacific, contains some of the highest peaks of the Andes.

CHARACTERISTICS ... Peru is one of the most astonishing countries in the world. Archaeologists have still not fathomed the mysteries of the civilizations once here which go back to prehistoric times. The magnificent Inca ruins at Cuzco and Machu Picchu are awe-inspiring. Today the outstanding feature of Peru is the blending of its Indian and colonial past with its twentieth-century present. Peruvians are among the most traditional and conservative people in South America, but with it all, extremely sophisticated. The women are ultra chic. The Indians are colorful.

POPULATION ... Estimated 10,000,000; the population is about equal to that of Chicago, Philadelphia and Los Angeles combined.

SIZE ... Roughly the shape of California, Peru is three times larger—482,258 square miles.

CAPITAL ... Lima, a city of 1,050,000, is larger than Baltimore.

GOVERNMENT ... A republic with a President, assisted by a cabinet, and two legislative chambers.

HOW TO GET THERE ... By de luxe through-plane service 11 hours from Miami; 16¾ hours from New York.

ACCOMMODATIONS ... The *Gran Hotel Bolivar,* Plaza San Martín, is famous and good. It has everything, including a nightclub. Rates range from about $7.50 single, and from about $11.50 double, European Plan, plus 10% service charge and 6½% tax. For modified

American Plan (breakfast and one other meal) add about $3; all meals about $6. Represented by Intercontinental Hotels. The *Crillón* is air-conditioned, spotless and modern with all facilities. Turkish baths. Grill serves excellent European food of all kinds, smorgasbord featured. Rates $6 up single, $8.50 up double, European Plan. The *Hotel Maury* is located one block from the Plaza de Armas. Formerly an old-fashioned and picturesque hotel, it has been reconstructed in modern style. Rates are from $5 single and $9 double, European Plan. Other hotels include the *Hotel Savoy*, *Hotel Alcazar*, and *Hotel Continental*, which has a night club. Rates start at about $6 a day, European Plan. There are also the *Claridge Apartments* where rates are from $4 up, American Plan.

The *Lima Country Club* is in San Isidro, a five-mile taxi ride from the city. This is one of the finest places to stay in Peru, with tennis courts, swimming pools near the golf course. Rates are from $10, plus taxes, European Plan. Lovely view, quiet, good food, wine, service. American tourists can obtain guest privileges. The numerous pensions offer comfortable accommodations at modest rates. These pensions are usually charming villas with gardens and many servants to take care of you. Rates run from about $30 a week, including meals. Both hotels and first-class pensions are heavily booked during the season—December to April. Reservations should be made well in advance.

ARTS... National Museum of Archaeology (Inca Museum) in a Lima suburb houses a fabulous collection of specimens of Inca and pre-Inca cultures. Open every day 10–12 and 3–6. The Pinacoteca Municipal Merino is devoted to the works of Peruvian artists. The "Museum of the Republic" (colonial) houses colonial collections of Lima. To see the finest examples of modern native craftsmanship, a trip to Truman Bailey's workshop in Miraflores, a suburb of Lima, is recommended. Mr. Bailey, an American artist, has revived many of the old pre-Columbian designs and crafts. The Quinta de Presa, now a museum, is a villa with many relics of La Perricholi, the actress whose story is told in Thornton Wilder's *Bridge of San Luis Rey*.

BANKS... In Lima, First National City Bank of New York, Royal Bank of Canada, Banco de Credito, Banco Popular de Peru, International Bank of Peru, Banco Comercial de Peru, Banco Continental, Banco de Londres y America del Sud, Banco de Lima, Banco Union, Banco Wiese and Banco Gibson.

CALENDAR OF HOLIDAYS... New Year's Day; Holy Week, which consists of Thursday and Friday before Easter; May 1, Labor Day; June 8, Corpus Christi; June 29, St. Peter, St. Paul; July 28, 29, 30, Independence of Peru; August 30, Santa Rosa de Lima; October 12, Day of Columbus; November 1, All Saints Day; November 27, Battle of Tarapaca; December 8, Immaculate Conception; Christmas Day. June 24, Amancaes in Lima, Indian Day holiday celebration; June 24, Inti-Raymi in Cuzco, Indian Day celebration to ancient Sun God. For Cuzco plane and hotel reservation required well in advance. Holy Monday, a week before Easter Sunday, religious festival of "Our Lord of Earthquakes," in Cuzco.

CIGARETTES, PIPES AND TOBACCO ... Popular brands of cigarettes are available in Lima at about $4.00 a carton. A passenger may bring in 200 cigarettes, 25 cigars or 2 tins of tobacco.

CLIMATE ... Spring begins in September. Summer starts in December. It hardly ever rains, but in winter there are heavy overcasts. Cold, damp weather prevails April through September. The Humboldt current off the coast keeps it from ever becoming unbearably hot. January through April is the ideal season in Lima.

CLUBS ... Lima's clubs are delightful. Guest cards are required and can be requested through members only. There are the Club Phoenix, Country Club mentioned before, Lions and Rotary Clubs. *See* SPORTS.

COMMON COURTESIES AND LOCAL CUSTOMS ... Lima is proud of its traditions and conserves many old customs. Life goes on at a comparatively leisurely pace and social activities are often on the formal side. Tea, from 5:30 to 7:00, is an important daily event. Cocktail parties usually begin about 7:30 and the dinner hour is from 9:00 on. In the summer, stores and offices are closed for three and a half hours at noon, to give everyone an opportunity to go to the beach, and in the winter are closed for two hours for lunch.

Everyone plays the lotteries here. Do not address taxi drivers, waiters or other servants familiarly. Peruvians are very formal, very polite; they resent casualness. As in most Latin American countries, both men and women shake hands on meeting and on saying goodbye.

COMMUNICATIONS ... Telephones (long distance); West Coast Cable and All America Cables and Radio; airmail.

CURRENCY ... The sol is the monetary unit of Peru. It is worth about 4 cents. Dollars may be exchanged freely at banks or money exchange houses.

CUSTOMS REGULATIONS AND DOCUMENTS REQUIRED FOR UNITED STATES CITIZENS ... Valid passport; tourist card (fee $2.00) good for 90 days, or a visa free of charge. You will need a smallpox vaccination certificate, return ticket.

DRUG STORES ... Along Jirón de Unión, Lima's main shopping street, there are many drug stores including Antigua Botica Francesa, Botica Inglesa. On Calle del Correo, Botica del Correo (in front of the Post Office). Botica El Inca (Plaza San Martín). Most well-known American products available here.

ELECTRIC CURRENT ... 220 volts, A.C., 60 cycles. U.S. appliances can be used only with transformers or resistor cords.

FAUNA ... The llama, indispensable beast of the highlands, is the most notable animal in Peru. Vicuña, mountain lions and condors in the sierra, and all sorts of animals such as tigers, snakes, alligators, monkeys, sloths, etc., as well as the greatest variety of birds in the jungle region of the interior. There are organized tours to the jungle.

FLORA ... All kinds of flowers (orchids, roses, geraniums, violets, cactus, etc.).

FOOD ... Excellent meals can be had in Peru. The cuisine here is more interesting than any other in Latin America. Peruvian seafood from the cold, teeming waters of the Humboldt current is exceptional. *Cebiche* is raw fish marinated in lemon juice and served with onions and hot peppers; delicious. *Corvina* (sea bass) is prepared in many ways. One of the most interesting local dishes is *anticuchos*, squares of beef heart (corvina and shrimp are also used) on skewers broiled over charcoal, served with hot sauce. Hot chili pepper (*aji*) is widely used as seasoning. *Camarones* are big, sweet freshwater shrimp.

Fruits including pineapple, papaya and chirimoya, are varied and excellent. Avocados (*paltas*) are plentiful. Many Chinese restaurants. *Pachamanca* is a local feast, consisting of chickens, pork, sweet potatoes, corn and yucca cooked in a pit over hot stones. Corn originated in Peru and there are hundreds of varieties. *Chicha morada* is a soft drink made from purple corn. Excellent bottled milk is available in Lima, but be sure to ask for *Maranga* or *Plusa,* and have it served directly from the bottle.

GAMBLING ... Everyone here plays the various lotteries, but tourists are warned to watch drawing dates. There is horse racing Saturdays, Sundays and holidays from April to December at the Hipódromo de San Felipe. Cockfighting Saturdays, Sundays and Mondays starting at 7:00 P.M. in Coliseo Sandia.

LANGUAGE ... Spanish, of course, but English is spoken and understood in the hotels, shops and other places you will frequent.

LAUNDRY AND DRY CLEANING ... American Dry Cleaners (Conquistadores 655, San Isidro); Lima Dry Cleaners (Avenida Petit Thouars 31st block); Giesman (Huallaga 918); Hotel Bolívar Dry Cleaning. All of these take from 24 hours to three days and give good results. Invisible darning Calle Urrutia 758 or Carabaya 1027.

LIQUOR ... *Pisco,* a native grape brandy, is inexpensive and served in a variety of drinks. Most popular is the pisco sour, made with lemon juice and given a frothy topping of egg white. Good beer is brewed in Peru. All well-known cocktails and brands of liquor are obtainable at about the same cost as in the United States. Excellent local wines including champagne are available.

MEDICAL FACILITIES ... Anglo-American Hospital in San Isidro, also Clínica Loayza, Clínica Lozada (English spoken). If you need a doctor, inquire at Pan American or at your hotel.

MOTION PICTURES ... Latest American movies are shown in Lima. Best movie theater costs about 50 cents. Principal theaters are the *Tacna* on Avenida Tacna, the *Metro* on Plaza San Martín, *Colón* on Plaza San Martín, the *Excelsior* and *Biarritz* on Jirón Unión; *Le Paris,* on Avenida Nicolás de Piérola; *Teatro Central* on Jirón Ica. Most of the pictures are in English.

MUSIC ... The National Symphony Orchestra plays at the outdoor auditorium of the Campo de Marte on Sundays during their summer, at the Municipal Theatre in winter. Visiting artists perform in Lima too. The "Entre Nous" cultural institution presents Peruvian folklore programs of music and dancing in native costumes every Thursday at 7:00 P.M.

NIGHT CLUBS AND CABARETS ... Most important include

Hotel Bolívar Grill; Embassy, tea dancing every evening 7:00 to 9:00 P.M. (Plaza San Martín); the *Negro-Negro* (Plaza San Martín); *Hotel Continental* roof garden and night club. But Lima is not much of a night-club town.

PHOTOGRAPHY...All types of films are available in Lima at prices about 50 per cent above those in the United States.

RELIGION...Peru, of course, is Catholic and there are many magnificent churches. Most important is the Cathedral on the Plaza de Armas (what is said to be Pizarro's body can be seen in a glass coffin in the right nave of the cathedral). La Merced on Jirón Unión, San Agustín on Plateros de San Agustín, Santo Domingo on Santo Domingo Street, and St. Francis church with catacombs. There is, however, freedom of worship.

RESTAURANTS...Lima citizens like their food highly seasoned, and if you like yours that way, we suggest the *Pildorin* and *La Toscana* restaurants for authentic Peruvian dishes. The *Bolívar, Crillón,* and *Maury* hotels have good restaurants. Other restaurants in downtown Lima you will enjoy are—*Le Pavillon* and *La Corsiea,* specializing in French cuisine; and *Club 91* (Italian), the best de luxe restaurant in town; *Chez Victor, Tony's* (German style), *Granada* and *Aragón* (Spanish), *Kuo Wa* (Chinese). For the visitors who want to taste the real Spanish-Colonial atmosphere with delicious food and excellent drinks, the *Trece Monedas* is a must. In the suburbs you will like *Chez Andres* and *Giannino's* in Miraflores and *La Marseillaise* on the beach at Herradura (November-April). Also at Herradura is the *S.O.S. Restaurant,* serving excellent food in attractive surroundings. No visit to Lima is complete without a drive up the side of the Andes, 20 miles from Lima, to the *Granja Azul,* one of the most interesting settings on the west coast, for spring chicken spit-roasted— all you can eat for $3, also steaks and crêpes Suzette. *Crem Rica,* a chain of sandwich and soda fountain type restaurants, has one on Jirón Unión. This and *Mauricios* serve excellent inexpensive meals.

The average price at most of the restaurants listed above is about $2 for luncheon and $3 for complete dinner with beer, but not with wine. The *Club 91* and *Pavillon* are more expensive, but worth it for atmosphere and quality of food.

SHOPS AND STORES...Lima's main shopping thoroughfare is the Jirón Unión. It starts at the Plaza San Martín. The main store for men and women is Oeschle's on the Plaza de Armas. It is lined with silver shops, big and little, full of bargains in tea sets, jewelry and almost anything else you can think of that comes in silver. Well-known silver shops are Welsch, Kohler, Siam, Murgia, Piaget; visit Lima's major silverwork plant, the Camusso factory on Avenida Colonial. For leather goods: Pedro D. Díaz on Jirón Unión. For men, Crevani and Cambana on Jirón Unión. For antiques and Incaic curiosities, The Tourist Shop, an upstairs shop on Unión 892, has a fascinating collection of Indian costumes, gold and silver jewelry, alpaca slippers and rugs and hand tooled leather coffee tables, authentic pre-Inca pottery (reproductions too). Also, Casa Mas, and

Old Cuzco on Jirón Unión. Fluffy llama slippers, fur rugs and all sorts of souvenirs are for sale in two or three little shops on Unión close to the Plaza San Martín. Take a look at the big pottery factory on the road to Callao for unusual gifts.

SPECTATOR SPORTS ... You can find almost any kind of sport you want. Horse racing Saturdays, Sundays and holidays at the attractive Hipódromo. The "polla," a horse racing pool, rivals the lottery in popularity. There are bullfights most of the year in Lima, but the real season is October to December.

Cockfighting at the Coliseo de Sandia on Saturdays, Sundays and Mondays. There are automobile races, fencing, yacht races, cricket matches, bicycle races. Boxing matches at Luna Park. Soccer at the Estadio Nacional. Basketball and baseball are popular. Horse shows at the Club Hípico Peruano. Polo matches at the Polo Club.

SPORTS ... There is excellent swimming and bathing along the coast at the many beach resorts. At the Herradura beach little cabañas may be rented by the hour, also at some of the other beaches such as Lobo del Mar. Surfboarding in the Hawaiian manner is popular at the Waikiki Club on special invitation. Swimming in summer only, December to March.

The Lima Golf Club and the Los Incas Club offer excellent golfing facilities. Visitors must obtain guest card from a member. Greens fees are in the $2 to $3 range. In San Isidro (a suburb) there is a bowling club. The Lawn Tennis Club also has facilities for swimming and other sports besides tennis; serves food.

Peru offers some of the world's finest deep-sea fishing at Cabo Blanco (Talara), and fine rainbow-trout fishing in the rivers flowing into Lake Titicaca. Facilities are limited, and information should be obtained in advance of your trip. Panagra's Traffic and Sales office in the Hotel Bolívar, Lima, will assist you.

THEATERS ... The theater is important in Lima. There are many legitimate and musical productions. There are usually performances at 6:45 and 9:45, matinees at 3:45. *Teatro Municipal* and *Teatro Segura* are the two most important theaters.

TIME ... Same as United States Eastern Standard Time.

TIPPING ... A 10 per cent service charge plus 6½% tax is added to your bill at most hotels, but leave another 10 per cent tip. Where no service charge is added, leave about 15 per cent tip. No tipping is expected by taxi drivers.

TRANSPORTATION ... Taxis are plentiful and inexpensive. The official rate for a taxi trip anywhere in the central part of Lima is 5 soles per cab, not per person. The rate from Lima to San Isidro is 10 soles and to Miraflores 12 soles, with all rates doubled after midnight. The official rate per hour is from 40 to 50 soles, depending on the type of cab and where the cab is to be used. Agree on rate with driver in advance. Cars may be hired for about $15 per day. There are many buses but they are usually crowded. There are street-car lines which go to nearby resorts.

WATER ... It is best not to drink the water in Peru. Bottled waters: Viso, San Antonio and San Mateo. If you want non-carbonated water specify *"sin gas."* Also Coca-Cola, Pepsi-Cola, Crush, Sparkling Orange.

WHAT TO BUY ... Silver, of course. Jewelry, tea sets, antique silver all cost far less than at home. Indian textiles hand loomed and hand spun. Peruvian Indian costumes, llama and alpaca slippers, rugs, etc. Dolls dressed in Indian costumes are a tourist favorite. Lima's market on the Jirón Ucayali is one of the sights of the city. The better shops have fixed prices, but in the market bargaining is accepted practice; don't pay the first price asked.

WHAT TO WEAR ... Take lightweight clothing to Peru—suitable for spring and autumn in the States, unless you intend to go into the mountains, in which case you will also need woolens and tweeds. Tropical clothing is not practical except in Peruvian summer (U.S. winter). Lima is sophisticated and formal. It is a city of traditions.

WHERE TO GO—SIGHTSEEING ...

Lima ... There is a lot to see in the city of Lima. Lima's Plaza de Armas is one of the most historic spots in South America.

The room where the trials of the dreaded Inquisition took place can be visited on the Plaza de Bolívar. Oldest university in the Americas (founded 1551), the University of San Marcos, is located near the Plaza San Martín. Avenida Arequipa, a long, shaded boulevard, leads to Miraflores and San Isidro.

The Chosica Valley, an hour's drive east from Lima, has sunshine the year round and has hotels on the Rimac River, pleasant stops for luncheon or tea. Ancón is a summer beach resort about twenty-five miles on the Pan American Highway north of Lima, also the site of interesting archeological discoveries believed to be 2,000 years old. Visit the nearby artificial satellite observatory.

Callao ... is the port of Lima, about seven miles from the city, reached by streetcar or taxi. In early morning or late afternoon the pier is busy with fishing boats. The famous guano islands can be seen offshore. The Real Felipe Fortress is now a military museum.

Cuzco ... The city, the ancient capital of the Incas, is 11,444 feet above sea level. The city is a mixture of Spanish and Inca civilizations. The Cathedral on the Plaza de Armas is the most interesting of the many churches in the city. The altar is of silver, and there is a dragon carved from a single emerald. Cuzco is two hours by air from Lima. The *Hotel Cuzco* here is excellent.

Machu Picchu ... Is probably the most awe-inspiring sight in South America, an absolute must on any trip to the southern continent. A mountain-top sanctuary used by the Inca rulers in times of distress, it was so well hidden that its existence was hardly dreamed of until its discovery in 1911 by Hiram Bingham, one-time Senator from Connecticut. There are magnificent ruins with temples, houses, a cemetery. A strangely cut stone altar, where the priests "tied the sun" at the times of the equinoxes, overlooks the beautiful Sacred Valley. Three hours by train from Cuzco. Minimum time for Cuzco-Machu Picchu trip is three days. Nearby towns are interesting too.

Pachacamac . . . About twenty miles south of Lima are pre-Inca ruins such as the Temple of the Creator-God which predates by a long, long time the Inca Temple to the Sun which was erected near it. Allow about three hours for this trip. Go by guided tour.

Huancayo . . . Can be reached by a spectacular rail trip over the highest standard-gauge railway in the world, 15,805 ft. Excellent tourist hotel. Purchase rail ticket Friday, $7.00 round trip, leave Saturday, return Monday. Oxygen is carried for passengers who may need it. Huancayo is an ancient Inca center. Every Sunday the Indians crowd the streets with their wares. They utter almost no sound. The silence is the striking thing about the market.

Puno . . . On the shores of Lake Titicaca, the highest lake in the world, is just across from Bolivia. Overnight steamers make the run at least twice a week. Train-boat connection from La Paz Wednesday and Friday arriving Cuzco the following day. From Cuzco to La Paz, train-boat connection Monday and Wednesday, arriving La Paz the following day. Approximately $18.00 one way. The lake itself is well worth seeing and there is the good *Hotel Puno*. The uncountable number of ancient Indian agricultural terraces is amazing.

Paracas . . . An easy 3-hour drive from Lima on the Panamerican Highway. Summer resort. Modern *Hotel Paracas* has swimming pools.

Arequipa . . . Peru's second city, lies in the shadow of cone-shaped volcano, El Misti. It is called the "white city" because most of the buildings are made of a white volcanic stone, and has many interesting houses and churches dating from colonial times. One of Arequipa's chief claims to fame is its dry climate with sunshine practically all the time. Llamas wander the streets. At 7,500 feet above sea level, Arequipa is an ideal stopping point to get accustomed to the altitude before continuing to La Paz or Cuzco. The *Hotel Arequipa* here, one of the Peruvian national chain, is excellent. Arequipa is 2½ hours by air south of Lima. There's train service from Arequipa to Cuzco or La Paz via Puno.

Trujillo . . . Northwest 315 miles from Lima is Trujillo, a typical Spanish colonial city. The *Hotel Trujillo* is good and there are others, including the *Jacobs*, the *Grau* and the *Libertad*. There are many ruins nearby, most of them dating back to the Chimus, a pre-Inca race.

Talara . . . An oil center on the northern coast of Peru, is becoming an important game fishing center. The *Cabo Blanco Fishing Club*, a private organization, has facilities at Cabo Blanco, about forty miles from Talara. The only hotel in Talara is the *Royal*.

Tingo Maria . . . Reached by air from Lima, is one of the most comfortable places to see the Amazon jungle. There is an excellent government hotel.

SOURCES OF INFORMATION . . . For information on sightseeing tours, tickets or immigration matters contact PAA's affiliate, Panagra, in the Hotel Bolívar (Tel. 75–100). A "Tourist Corner" in this office is especially designed to furnish the visitor all information on sightseeing, trips to the interior, shopping, etc.

In New York, the Peru Consulate, is at 10 Rockefeller Plaza.

SURINAM

WEATHER IN PARAMARIBO—Lat. N5°50′

	JAN.	FEB.	MAR.	APR.	MAY	JUNE	JULY	AUG.	SEPT.	OCT.	NOV.	DEC.
Average Temp.	79°	80°	80°	80°	80°	80°	80°	82°	83°	83°	82°	80°
In. of Rain	8.4	6.3	6.7	9.0	12.3	12.0	8.2	6.3	3.0	3.0	4.7	8.4

LOCATION ... Surinam (or, as it formerly was called, Dutch Guiana) lies along the northeastern coast of South America, between British and French Guiana and north of Brazil.

CHARACTERISTICS ... Development of natural resources is the chief concern of Surinam. The traveler with an eye for unusual places will find great delight in Paramaribo, the surprisingly cosmopolitan capital of this wild and primitive land.

Surinam is only faintly tourist conscious, but visitors are cordially welcomed, Government officials are cooperative, and friendly citizens provide a ready pipeline for information on such events as Javanese birthday parties, Hindu weddings and Creole processions, or *winti* dances, which may be of interest to the visitor.

POPULATION ... The country has approximately 210,000 inhabitants, including 3,700 Amerindians, the race which predates the discovery of the country by Spaniards. There are also bush Negroes, Creoles, Indians, Indonesians, Chinese and 2,500 Europeans.

SIZE ... 54,300 square miles, slightly larger than North Carolina.

CAPITAL ... Paramaribo, on the Surinam River, with approximately 100,000 inhabitants.

GOVERNMENT ... Part of the Kingdom of the Netherlands; since 1949 the country has had its own responsible Government of 9 ministers and a House of Representatives of 21 members, which are elected by popular vote.

HOW TO GET THERE . . . By Pan American Clipper from New York via San Juan, Antigua, Bridgetown, Trinidad and Georgetown, through-plane service 16 hours. From San Juan about 8½ hours.

ACCOMMODATIONS . . . The few hotels in Paramaribo have pleasant, spacious rooms (a necessity in the tropics), some with private bath or shower and air-conditioning. Good food and polite service you'll find everywhere. The *Hotel Vervuuert* is the leading hotel, with cocktail lounge and roof garden. The others are the *Palace Hotel* with air-conditioned cocktail lounge, *Pension Alexandra, Pension Kersten, Hotel Lashley,* and *Pension Central.* The prices vary from about $5.50 to $13, American Plan. In the districts you'll find Governmental *pasanggrahams* (boarding houses), clean and spacious, with good food. Prices, meals included, about $5 a day.

CURRENCY . . . The monetary unit is the guilder (Surinam guilder), 100 cents to the guilder; the value is about 50 cents U.S.

CUSTOMS REGULATIONS AND DOCUMENTS REQUIRED FOR UNITED STATES CITIZENS . . . American passports or proof of U.S. citizenship; return or through ticket; smallpox vaccination. Permits for any sort of shotgun are needed.

WHERE TO GO—SIGHTSEEING . . .

Paramaribo . . . Paramaribo has a cosmopolitan air despite the fact that within the proverbial stone's throw there is dense tropical jungle where native Indians still hunt with poisoned arrows and bush Negroes still practice ceremonial rites of their African tribal ancestors, maintain their own jungle villages and wear only loin cloths.

Paramaribo's heterogeneous population includes, in addition to Negroes, Indians and Creoles, Javanese as comely as those of Bali, Hindus with the same culture and customs as those of India, and Chinese with their Oriental ways. Yet in appearance the city is thoroughly Dutch—a true bit of Holland transplanted to South America.

The city's marketplace is a riot of color, dominated by the *Kotto Missie,* or native marketwoman, who is noted for her great dignity.

Government Square is the center around which life in Paramaribo revolves. Adjacent to the square are the Governor's House and other Government buildings; the beautiful Park Club; the city's principal business district; and the river waterfront, serving alike ocean-going steamers, river boats and dugout canoes used to transport produce.

There are interesting sightseeing possibilities even for the transient visitors. In one day a real bush Negro village can be visited by car and launch; in one day you can reach an Amerindian dwelling by jeep; in one day it's even possible to see the town, go shopping, visit modern factories (plywood) and old plantations (citrus fruits) and have a look at the agricultural experimental station or botanical gardens. With two or three days you can take a jungle trip by steamer to the Moengo bauxite mines. Round trip fare, $30.

SOURCES OF FURTHER INFORMATION . . . In Paramaribo there's the Surinam Tourist Development Board and the Surinam Travel Bureau. The PAA office is at Keizerstraat 35.

URUGUAY

WEATHER IN MONTEVIDEO—Lat. S34°53′—Alt. 30′

Temp.	JAN.	FEB.	MAR.	APR.	MAY	JUNE	JULY	AUG.	SEPT.	OCT.	NOV.	DEC.
Low	62°	62°	60°	54°	49°	45°	44°	44°	47°	50°	54°	59°
High	83°	82°	78°	71°	66°	61°	59°	60°	64°	68°	74°	80°
Average	73°	72°	69°	62°	57°	53°	51°	52°	55°	59°	64°	69°

LOCATION ... Uruguay, the smallest of the South American countries, lies between Brazil and Argentina on the Atlantic coast. Montevideo is less than 150 miles from Buenos Aires.

CHARACTERISTICS ... This delightful little country is one of South America's famous playgrounds. Montevideo, the charming, gracious capital, is situated on the Rio de la Plata. A chain of beach resorts which extends for some 200 miles up the coast provides an unparalleled vacation land. Uruguay is famous for its excellent hotels, its casinos, its wide stretches of sandy beaches. Punta del Este is known as the Riviera of South America and is the gathering spot for wealthy South Americans who enjoy yachting, water skiing, gay night life (at the casinos), the luxury of the cabaña-dotted beaches, and the fine hotels.

POPULATION ... Estimated 2,500,000 in 1957, a third of it in Montevideo. Largest cities of interior are Salto (48,000) and Paysandú (50,000), both on the banks of the Uruguay River.

SIZE ... 72,172 square miles, about the size of North Dakota.

CAPITAL ... Montevideo, with a population of about 850,000, the size of St. Louis.

GOVERNMENT ... A Republic with a "pluripersonal executive," that is, instead of a President there is a Council of nine men. Otherwise, Uruguay's government is exactly like that of any other republic with advanced social legislation (Uruguay was called "the first welfare state").

HOW TO GET THERE ... By luxurious DC–7B Clipper service 24 hours (elapsed time) from New York. By ship from New Orleans or New York, 13 days.

ACCOMMODATIONS ... Best in Montevideo is the new air-conditioned *Victoria Plaza,* one of the Intercontinental Hotels. They've thought of everything for your comfort and convenience. Other Montevideo hotels downtown include the *Nogaró,* the *Alhambra,* the brand-new, low-priced *Crillon* and the *Residencial Uruguay.* On Ramirez Beach: *Parque Hotel,* which has a casino. On Pocitos Beach: the *Ermitage.* On Carrasco Beach, 12 miles up the coast: *Hotel Casino Carrasco* (open only during the season, December 8 to March 24), *Cottage Hotel.*

Hotels at Atlántida Beach, 35 miles up the coast: *Atlántida* and *Casino Golf Palace.* Also, small hostels, like *Chalet, Remanso, Mi Cielo, Los Angeles.* At Balneario Solís Beach, 62 miles up the coast: *Hotels Solís* and *Alción.*

At Piriápolis Beach, 72 miles up the coast: the big French-style *Argentino Hotel* and the small pension-like *Embassy, Juvencia, Rex, Italia, Atlántico, Perla, Rambla.* At La Paloma, center for salt- and fresh-water fishing, 160 miles up the coast: Hotel *Cabo Santa María.*

At nearby La Pedrera, *Hotel La Pedrera.*

At Punta del Este, a glamour spot 90 miles from the capital, the outstanding place is the *Cantegril Country Club,* one of the loveliest vacation spots in South America, and the *Victoria Plaza Annex.* For description and listing of other hotels here, *see* WHERE TO GO.

Rates at all of the above resort hotels range from about $4 at the smaller ones to $8 single, American Plan. At the *Victoria Plaza,* from $5 single, from $8 double, European Plan. *See under* TIPPING.

All over the interior of the country where no first-class hotels are available, the National Tourist Commission maintains a chain of *paradores,* or inns.

ARTS ... Museum of Fine Arts, at Park Rodó, contains works of Figari, Blanes and other outstanding Uruguayan painters. Historic Military Museum, at the top of the hill, overlooks Montevideo Harbor; Muncipal Museum of Fne Arts is at the Prado Park. At the many private galleries good paintings can be bought at bargain prices ($25 to $100).

BALLET ... There is the National Ballet Corps. European and American troupes come to Montevideo regularly.

BANKS ... Royal Bank of Canada, agent for American Express checks. Wagons-Lits/Cook for Cook's travelers checks. First National City Bank of New York also handles traveler's checks.

CALENDAR OF HOLIDAYS ... The Carnival held in Montevideo (usually in February) is gay and has a color and atmosphere all of its own. There's a colorful parade, music, dancing. There are masked balls, fiestas, and merrymaking everywhere you turn. *Semana Criolla* takes place in March. This is similar to a rodeo. The gauchos, or local cowboys, come from all over the country. They wear the traditional gaucho costume, which includes the *bombachas,* or full, baggy pants, the sign of the gaucho today. Exhibitions of riding, breaking of broncos, horse shows, are part of the show. Guitar playing is a gaucho accomplishment and their songs are similar to our Western folk songs. New Year's day is gala with displays of fireworks. Corpus Christi (in October) is the biggest Catholic celebration, with a parade down the main avenues. December 8 is Day of the Beaches, start of the summer season.

CIGARETTES, PIPES AND TOBACCO... American cigarettes are available at about 40 cents a pack, all brands of pipe tobacco, at correspondingly higher prices. The local "blond" cigarettes, made with American tobacco, are good. Local people prefer "black" cigarettes or roll their own. This practice is most common in the interior, where the gauchos sometimes use the corn husks instead of paper. It is quite an art to cut and dry the leaf, thin it out with a knife and crop it to the size of cigarette paper. Best local brands (blond, or *rubio*) are: *Master, Richmond, Union, Buffs, Poker, Nevada*. The best blacks, or *negros,* are: *La Paz* and *Republicana*. A pack of *rubios* of local manufacture costs one third of the American price; *negros* cost less than 10 U.S. cents a pack.

CLIMATE... Seasons in Uruguay are the opposite of ours. Their summer is our winter and vice versa. The season is December until March, usually considered the best time to visit Uruguay, although their autumn and spring are delightful too. It's exceedingly windy in the spring and children go to the beaches to fly kites. The climate is springlike, dry and invigorating; snow is unknown.

CLUBS... The Jockey Club has a fine restaurant, but tourists must be guests of members. Golf Club, Automóvil Club and Yacht Club are open to visitors. The Golf Club, with excellent food, is considered one of the best in Latin America. Rotary, Lions Club and Junior Chamber of Commerce.

COMMON COURTESIES AND LOCAL CUSTOMS... Dinner hour is very late, from 9:00 P.M. to 11:00 P.M. There is a central information number to dial in Montevideo "213," which informs you on train, airplane and bus schedules, weather reports, movie programs and anything else you might like to know about the city.

COMMUNICATIONS... All America Cables (with an office in the Victoria Plaza Hotel) and Western Telegraph Co.; long-distance telephone; airmail.

CURRENCY... Montevideo is a free market where all world currencies can be exchanged at the best available rates. The monetary unit is the peso, written with a $ sign and worth about 12 cents. Best exchange rate is obtainable at one of the *cambios,* or money-exchange stores such as Wagons-Lits/Cooks, Exprinter, COT, CEVI, Cambytur and others located all over Montevideo.

CUSTOMS REGULATIONS AND DOCUMENTS REQUIRED FOR UNITED STATES CITIZENS... Smallpox vaccination certificate and valid passport. Yellow fever and cholera certificate required if coming from infected areas. No visa. For short stays you may bring in 1 broken carton of cigarettes or 1 opened box of cigars or 3 small opened tins of tobacco, 1 camera.

DRUG STORES ... Drug stores are modern and stock most things you need, although items other than drugs must be bought at department stores or shops. Dialing "213" will tell you where the nearest drug store is located and what hours it is open.

ELECTRIC CURRENT ... Electric power in Uruguay is 220 volts, 50 cycles, A.C. Ordinary American plugs are used in the Hotel Victoria Plaza; in other hotels, adapters are necessary. Transformers for appliances using 110 volts are easily available.

FAUNA ... Pumas and jaguars are almost extinct now, but deer and boar exist in the western part of the country. Partridge, quail, parakeet and hares are plentiful. American ostriches may also be seen. Most interesting is the *hornero* (oven bird), who builds his sturdy two-room home (one for himself and wife, another for the eggs) of mud and straw, on roofs, telegraph poles and fences. He is loved as symbol of work and homemaking. Another interesting bird: the *Terutero* or *tero*, which is an expert at attracting the attention of trespassers to the place where his nest is *not* to be found; it is also a fine weatherman, announcing rain in advance.

FLORA ... Acacia, willow, pine, eucalyptus trees. Scarlet and white verbena brighten the prairies. Bougainvillaea and other semi-tropical flowers grow in profusion. Beautiful roses and carnations are plentiful in the spring and early summer, and are sold in the streets. Because of the spring wind Uruguay is a country of few trees. Local species are the *ombu* with soft wood that crumbles in your fingers and *ceibo* with wood as light as balsa and bright red flowers.

FOOD ... Beef is practically the national dish. You get steak such as you have never eaten, for very reasonable prices. Other specialties include barbecued pig, grilled chicken in wine, meat pie, grilled fish. Two good native dishes, are *carbonada* (a stew of meat, rice and, believe it or not, peaches, pears and raisins) and *parrillada* (assorted grilled meats). These are served at the Victoria Plaza. *Dulce de leche* (milk jam) is a local delicacy for dessert.

Mate, the South American tea, is the favorite drink. Native wines are excellent. The pastries are wonderful to look at and marvelous to eat. Leading hotels are the fashionable places to eat, and are excellent. There are many restaurants serving international food. Because of the large Italian population there are many fine Italian restaurants.

Sanitation standards are on a par with those in the United States. It's perfectly safe to drink the milk and water and to eat fresh fruits and salads.

GAMBLING ... There are many gaming casinos. The Park and Carrasco Hotels in Montevideo and the smart beach resorts have their own. There is horse racing Thursdays, Saturdays and Sundays at Hipódromo de Maroñas and Hipódromo de las Piedras with parimutuels. Uruguay has a national lottery like the one in Cuba.

LANGUAGE ... Spanish is the native tongue. But English and French are common.

LAUNDRY AND DRY CLEANING . . . Excellent. Laundry prices are lower than in the United States; dry cleaning, higher. The Victoria Plaza Hotel has its own laundry and dry-cleaning plant, offering 24-hour, first-class service.

LIQUOR . . . Local wines are fine and inexpensive; try Chablis Santa Rosa, San Borja, La Cruz, Mil Botellas, Pinot and Claret Cerros de San Juan, Fond de Cave and Faraut champagne. Local beer (made of barley) is delicious, more body and flavor than at home. Like cigarettes, beer can be either *rubia* or *negra,* depending on malt content; black beer is preferred in winter. *Malta* is a nourishing beverage for children, and the usual American soft drinks are also available. Local vermouths are good. Hard liquors of local manufacture include *caña* (a type of rum) and *grappa;* stay away from them. Scotch is about $10 a bottle; bourbon is practically unknown; French and Spanish cognac are relatively cheap. As you know, the practice of drinking wine with meals is very popular; no ice water is served unless you ask for it and explain carefully that you are actually planning to drink it.

MOTION PICTURES . . . Several excellent movie theaters showing American films and also French, English, Italian, Argentine, Mexican, Swedish, German, Russian, Japanese and other films, all in their original versions, with printed subtitles in Spanish. No stage shows. No popcorn.

MUSIC . . . Aside from symphony concerts (*see* THEATERS), there is little of musical interest. Popular music, tango, *milonga, vidalita,* and *Candombe,* a type of fast tango, is similar to that of Argentina.

During the Carnival, tourists have a chance to hear the *comparsas de negros* (most of them white boys in blackface) beating the real, authentic jungle drums. It is so phony that it has a charm of its own. In the summer, the Government sponsors native fiestas at the open-air theaters in the Parque Rodó and the Parque Rivera, where *pericón,* the stately and lovely old Uruguayan dance, may be enjoyed by the public. Also, during *Semana Criolla* (March), tourists can hear native songs and see native dances. Of course, all of these are similar to the Argentine folklore. Open-air symphony concerts are given, free, at Parque Rodó on Sunday mornings in summertime.

NIGHT CLUBS AND CABARETS . . . Night life does not flourish in Uruguay. What there is, centers around the casinos in the summer. *Victoria Plaza Hotel* is a popular spot for dinner music and dancing. Night clubs offering floor shows include *Intermezzo, Club de Paris, Do Re Mi.*

There are also "existentialist" bars and restaurants, where long-hair artists gather, to drink wine, eat cheese and bread, draw angular horses on the walls, and sing. It's more fun if you go after midnight. More conservative is *Chichilo's,* Italian restaurant (open only for dinner). It features a typical Neapolitan band; the musicians are Chichilo and his family, and everybody joins in the singing of canzonettas.

PHOTOGRAPHY . . . Black-and-white, still and movie film, of

American and European manufacture, is available; color films are sometimes in short supply. Cameras and all other equipment are also available, but no bargains are to be found. Film development and printing (including Ektachrome and Ansco color) are excellent; black-and-white films take 24 hours; color, 3 to 5 days; prices, moderate; quality of work, good.

RELIGION ... Cathedral at Plaza Matriz, Montevideo; many other Catholic churches in different parts of town and in all interior cities. Two Methodist churches, one Anglican, one Baptist, two Adventist, one German church, six synagogues.

RESTAURANTS ... You can find restaurants of all types in Montevideo. The *Victoria Plaza* has a first-class restaurant, serving native and American dishes in air-conditioned comfort. At *Chichilo's* (*see* NIGHT CLUBS) favorite dishes are caneloni, ravioli and all kinds of Italian pasta. A good dinner costs from $2 to $3. A couple can enjoy a whole evening at this place for $7, including tips to waiters and to orchestra for playing requested numbers. *Morini's* has fine steak (filet Chateaubriand and *entrecôte* are wonderful) and fish (*corvina a la parrilla*). A nice, traditional place, with sawdust on the floor, immaculate tablecloths and efficient service make up for the impression of decay you get seeing the place from the outside. *El Aguila* is a first-class restaurant, next to Teatro Solís; its dessert is famous (*gateau águila*) but so is everything that comes before. A dinner for two at any of these places will cost from 30 to 40 pesos ($3 to $4) including fine local wines. A recommended eating spot in Montevideo is the Golf Club, overlooking scenic Punta Carreta lighthouse, on the River Plata, is a five-minute ride from downtown. A specialty: *perdices en escabeche* (partridge boiled in olive oil, with spices). This is the most elegant place in town for lunch; preferred by businessmen and diplomats. Other first-class restaurants: *Automóvil Club, Ferrocarril, Hotel España, Forfait, Catari* (fine Italian pizza) *El Galeón, Exquisito* and *Hungaria* (Hungarian), *La Genovesa* (Spanish, despite its name), *Mario y Alberto, Chinese Lantern, Il Tevere, El Rincón, Sorrento*.

For typical Uruguayan dishes, aside from the *Victoria Plaza*, try *Forte Makale, Stradella* or *La Paloma*. The *Monterrey* is a typical small native spot with bar where *chivitos* (steak on a roll) are served.

SHOPS AND STORES ... Leading shops are: London Paris, Caubarrere, Tienda Inglesa, La Madrileña, Introzzi, Casa Soler, La Opera, Angenscheidt, Casa Rim, which are department stores. Specialty shops include: Bazar Colón for old silver, Montevideo leather factory near the Victoria Plaza and Pan American leather factory, on Plaza Independencia, Casa Schiavo for leather goods. Bargaining is not an accepted practice. The Sunday street fair is worth seeing and often has bargains. Stores are open from 8:30 to 12:00 noon and from 2:30 to 6:30 P.M.

SPECTATOR SPORTS ... Soccer, played in their fall and winter, is by far the most popular attraction; watching a game in the big (80,000 seats) Centenario Stadium is an experience. There's horse racing Thursdays, Saturdays and Sundays; *pelota vasca,* similar to jai alai; basketball, yacht races, golf and tennis tournaments.

SPORTS . . . Golf at Montevideo Club, which has a championship course. Hotel guests of the *Victoria Plaza, Parque,* and *Carrasco* granted guest cards. There are excellent courses at the beach resorts. Punta del Este has the Cantegril Country Club and Punta del Este Yacht Club. Cards may be arranged. (Inquire at your hotel.)

Fishing for dorado is one of the great sports of the country. Salto Grande (Great Falls) is a happy hunting ground for this colorful fish. There is a ranch-style guest house at Salto Grande.

Horseback riding is, of course, available; horses may be hired. Sailing and yachting are national sports. You may hire boats at beach resorts. Aquaplaning is possible if you have the skill. Tennis at all beach resorts and in Montevideo, too.

THEATERS . . . *Solís, Auditorio, Odeón, Sala Verdi.* Legitimate plays staged during winter season (United States summer months) by the *Comedia Nacional* (National Theater Company). Good Spanish, Argentine, Italian and French theater, ballet, opera and musical-comedy groups play Montevideo during winter season. Several good little-theater groups, including a theater in the round (*Teatro Circular*). Also, fine symphony concerts by the National Symphony Orchestra at the Auditorio, featuring world-famous conductors. Big shows and sports take place at the *Palacio Peñarol.*

TIME . . . Two hours later than U.S. Eastern Standard Time.

TIPPING . . . Hotels and most restaurants add a service charge varying from 15 to 22 per cent. Cab drivers should get about 10 per cent of the fare. Cafés have no service charge, so tip about 15 per cent. Movie ushers receive 20 centesimos, or less than a nickel.

TOURIST TAXES . . . There is a $2 (about 50 cents U.S.) landing tax on arrival at airport.

TRANSPORTATION . . . In Montevideo buses and trolley buses are plentiful but crowded. Taxis plentiful too and rates are low: 50 cents for a crosstown ride. Private cars are available for rent but at a minimum cost of $20 per day with limited mileage. Tours through travel agencies are recommended for sightseeing.

WATER . . . Perfectly safe to drink. Fine bottled mineral waters, *Salus* and *Matutine,* are also available.

WHAT TO BUY . . . Woolen goods are excellent and inexpensive. Amethyst, topaze and aquamarine stones are available at reasonable prices ($50 for a gold ring with large amethyst). Uruguayan specialties include: suede and *nonato* (unborn calfskin) bags, jackets, belts and other articles; also alligator bags, shoes, belts, billfolds. Prices are about the same as in Buenos Aires. Uruguayan nutria is the best in the world, with thicker, longer, softer hair and better color; a full-length coat costs from $250 to $350; a three-quarter coat from $150 to $250; a stole from $70 to $150. Furs can be bought in "blankets" (about 35 furs) to be styled at home. Price: $6 to $12 per fur. Another bargain: alparagatas and "ballerina" slippers, made of canvas with rubber soles, the most comfortable footwear for home and travel.

Souvenirs: silver mate cups and *bombillas*; knives with silver handle and sheath (price from $5 to $15); gaucho dolls (about $3); *boleadoras*, the stone balls wrapped in leather, used by gauchos to catch wild ostriches, *bombachas*, the baggy gaucho trouser, wide leather belts with pockets and silver knuckle. Colorful wool *ponchos* are an ideal gift for children.

WHAT TO WEAR ... During the season, their summer, you'll want the same type of summer clothes you would wear at home. For beach wear, the newest, smartest sports and beach togs are needed. You won't really need evening clothes, for life is informal, but some short dinner dresses in cotton or light color are appropriate. Take a light topcoat, a sweater or two. If you are in their wintertime, take clothes for an average fall day at home. Same requirements apply to men. Linen, cotton or lightweight wools for summer. Beach clothes, slacks, sports shirts. A topcoat. Life is very informal at Punta del Este and other summer resorts, where neckties are "banned."

WHERE TO GO—SIGHTSEEING ...

Montevideo ... Montevideo is a charming city, modeled to some extent on Paris. Its avenues are broad and tree-shaded. Plaza Independencia is surrounded by the sidewalk arcades. Montevideo is a café town and the streets are lined with sidewalk cafés filled with people drinking *café exprés*. There are numerous things to see in Montevideo itself, and many short excursions within city limits. See the Legislative Palace of Uruguayan marble and pink granite, topped with gold. The beautiful drive along the Rambla follows the beaches to Carrasco. The Planetarium in Park Pereira Rossell (home of the city zoo) is one of the most modern to be found anywhere.

The COT travel agency offers a wide choice of sightseeing tours to the summer resorts (Atlántida, Piriápolis, Punta del Este, La Paloma, La Coronilla) and to places in the interior, in comfortable buses, at very reasonable rates. (A full day's excursion to Punta del Este, including lunch and tea, costs only $5.) Rental of self-drive cars not advised: too expensive, too many restrictions.

From Montevideo to some 200 miles up the coast there is a chain of beaches and beach resorts, all of which are delightful, all worth seeing. An interesting three-day excursion is to La Coronilla on the Brazilian border. At Santa Teresa National Park, near the Brazilian border, there is a picturesque inn, *Parador San Miguel*.

Punta del Este ... The choice place here is the *Cantegril Country Club*. It is a delightful vacation spot which has been compared with Boca Raton in Florida. Cantegril is not a hotel, but a private club, where PAA passengers are welcome visitors. Guests rent lovely bungalows at a flat rate of about $20 per day. This includes lodging and meals for four persons. Minimum stay is two weeks. Sometimes during the local summer season, the bungalows are restricted to club members, so check with PAA. A new motel and *Cante Gril House*, a small hotel, are near the club.

Cantegril is also a residential area, where some of the finest homes in Punta del Este have been built. It boasts all kinds of sports activi-

Salto Grande (Great Falls) is one of the favorite areas for dorado fishing, a great sport of Uruguay.

The new Victoria Plaza, a social favorite in Montevideo, offers the finest of accommodations and a conveniently located center for all your vacation activities.

ties. It is the seat of the film festivals which attract to Uruguay some of the brightest movie stars from many countries. The Lido district has the largest and prettiest garden in Punta del Este.

The only hotel in Punta del Este of the large luxurious type is the Tudor-style *San Rafael Hotel,* facing the beach of the same name, which has a casino and night club. Rates are $8 to $10 American Plan. There's a government-operated casino and night club in the former Hotel Nogaro; open approximately December 15 to April 18.

Punta del Este has smaller and less expensive establishments, such as the charming *La Cigale,* which features French cooking, *Playa, Floreal* and many others, where a double room with meals costs $6 per person (plus the usual 22 per cent service charge). Newest hotel and restaurant here is the ultra modern *Victoria Plaza Annex.*

There are also tourist attractions in the interior of the country. Dorado fishing is the thing at Salto Grande in the Uruguay River (*see* SPORTS) and in the Rio Negro, near the Rincón del Bonete hydroelectric dam. Minas (80 miles north of Montevideo), with a Renaissance church and a fine little inn, *Parador Salus,* eight miles out of town (where food and lodging cost $4), is a quiet spot for fall vacations, as is the region of Colonia Suiza (80 miles west of Montevideo), an interesting place founded by Swiss colonizers. Try also to visit a ranch in the cattle country. Finest ocean fishing (shark, skate, black corvina) is found at La Coronilla, near Brazilian border. Several good inns here: *Parador La Coronilla, Costas del Mar, Oceania, El Pescador.*

SOURCES OF FURTHER INFORMATION ... The National Tourist Commission information bureau on the crossing of 18 de Julio and Agraciada Avenues, Montevideo; the Federación Uruguaya de Turismo, in the Victoria Plaza Hotel; Pan Am office, Palacio Salvo, Andes 1341–43, Plaza Independencia 848 (Tel. 8–9787). In New York, the Uruguay consulate is at 17 Battery Place.

VENEZUELA

WEATHER IN CARACAS—Lat. N10°30′—Alt. 3164′

Temp.	JAN.	FEB.	MAR.	APR.	MAY	JUNE	JULY	AUG.	SEPT.	OCT.	NOV.	DEC.
Low	56°	56°	57°	60°	62°	62°	61°	60°	61°	61°	60°	58°
High	75°	77°	78°	80°	80°	78°	77°	78°	79°	79°	77°	75°
Average	66°	67°	68°	70°	71°	70°	69°	69°	70°	70°	69°	67°
Days of Rain	6	2	3	4	9	14	15	15	13	12	13	10

LOCATION ... At the very top of South America, the coast of Venezuela is only about 10 miles from Trinidad.

CHARACTERISTICS ... Caracas, the birthplace of the great Liberator, Simón Bolívar, has a lot of authentic charm to offer the visitor. The city is a composite of modern and Spanish colonial architecture, but the intense building boom of the last 10 years has changed the face of the city so that its historical aspect is tending to disappear.

Its hotels vary from the simplest pension to the most modern. Its social and sporting clubs are magnificent. The city as a whole reflects the fact that it has become one of the wealthiest capitals in the world. There is lots to see and do and the fine climate makes it all very pleasant.

POPULATION ... Venezuela's growing population is now estimated at 6,000,000, nearing the total of Chicago and Los Angeles combined.

SIZE ... 352,150 square miles, as big as Texas plus Minnesota.

CAPITAL ... Caracas, a growing city of over 1,000,000.

GOVERNMENT ... By the new constitution of 1953 this country is now called the Republic of Venezuela and is a constitutional republic made up of one Federal District, 20 States and 2 Territories.

HOW TO GET THERE ... By Clipper nonstop, 7 hours from New York to Caracas. One-stop flights from Miami, 5½ hours. Caracas is 5¾ hours from Panamá, where connections are made with PAA flights from New Orleans, Houston, Brownsville, San Francisco and

Los Angeles, via Central America and Mexico. Less than 2 hours non-stop from Trinidad. By ship, about 5 days with stops, from New York.

ACCOMMODATIONS... In Caracas, the *Hotel Tamanaco,* with its superb view of the city, luxurious studio bedrooms, attractive night club *Naiguata,* extra large swimming pool, many shops, good bars and lounges, is a resort in itself. One of the best of the Intercontinental Hotel Corporation chain, it also makes a convenient headquarters for sightseeing or business appointments. The *Hotel Avila* is another luxury hotel. Others are *Ambassador, Comercio, El Conde, Mara, Potomac, Tiuna* and *Waldorf.* The Venezuelan Government has built a chain of hotels across the nation including the *Humboldt* atop Mt. Avila (7,000 ft.) in Caracas and the elaborate *Hotel Maracay* with golf course, swimming pool and movie theater at Maracay. Other hotels in this chain (CONAHOTU) are the *Bella Vista* at Porlamar on the Island of Margarita, and in the Venezuelan Andes the *Aguas Calientes,* the *Prado Rio,* the *Tama* and the *Trujillo.* Good hotels, many of them with air-conditioning, can be found throughout the nation. Most first-class hotels operate on the European Plan and rates begin about $10 single and $15 double.

ARTS... The Museum of Fine Arts has an excellent collection of historical paintings, especially by the national artist Michelena; Bolívar's Museum is an important national shrine with relics of the War of Independence.

BANKS... The First National City Bank of New York has a branch here, as well as the Royal Bank of Canada and the Anglo-South American Bank. Several important Venezuelan banks with U.S. connections, among them Banco Mercantil, Banco de Venezuela, Banco de Caracas and Banco Unión.

CALENDAR OF HOLIDAYS... Major holy days of the Roman Catholic Church. Other holidays include New Year's Day; Carnival Monday and Shrove Tuesday; June 24, Battle of Carabobo; July 5, Independence Day; July 24, Bolívar's birthday; October 12, Columbus Day; and November 1, All Saints Day.

CIGARETTES... American cigarettes are 60 cents a package.

CLIMATE... Caracas (altitude 3,164 feet) is springlike all year. Weather is perfect even in the rainy season, June to December. Venezuela has every kind of climate depending on the altitude.

CLUBS... Rotary and Lions Clubs are extremely active throughout Venezuela. Private clubs include the exclusive Caracas Country Club, the Valle Arriba Golf Club in Caracas and the Caraballeda Golf & Yacht Club on the coast. Club Paraíso and Club Venezuela are old social clubs patronized by the finest Venezuelan families. *See also* SPORTS.

COMMON COURTESIES AND LOCAL CUSTOMS... Caracas, because of its cool climate, has an unusual amount of formality. Shorts and sport shirts are not seen in the streets but are restricted to the beaches and country clubs. All of the best local restaurants and bars require men to wear coats. Dinner even in private houses is likely to be 8:30 to 9:00 P.M.—often much later.

COMMUNICATIONS...All America Cables. Radio telephone to United States and other countries. Radio International (Government station).

CURRENCY...The monetary unit is the bolívar, worth 30 cents in U.S. money, or, conversely, 3.35 bolívars make one dollar. The bolívar is divided into 100 centimos. There are no exchange restrictions. U.S. paper currency and traveler's checks may be easily changed at all hotels and at most tourist shops.

CUSTOMS REGULATIONS AND DOCUMENTS REQUIRED FOR UNITED STATES CITIZENS...For stays up to 36 hours, only proof of identity and onward transportation required. Otherwise passport and visa or tourist card for which you need proof of citizenship, smallpox vaccination certificate, letter of reference, four photos, and onward transportation. Only limited quantities of open bottles of liquor and cigarette packages permitted. No currency restrictions. Cameras may not be used from aircraft flying over territory nor may airports be filmed without prior permission.

DRUG STORES...Caracas, Maracaibo and other sizable towns have stores which carry United States toilet goods, patent medicines and staples. Prices higher than at home.

ELECTRIC CURRENT...In Caracas, 110 volts, 50 cycles, A.C. Elsewhere in Venezuela it is 110 volts, 60 cycles. Before importing electrical appliances one should check on the specific local condition.

FAUNA...The county is particularly rich in birds, from the smallest hummingbird to the huge herons and condors. In the extensive unexplored areas of the country there are many types of mammals and reptiles. Hunting for jaguars, crocodiles, tapirs and other wild game can be arranged.

FLORA...Within a short distance of Caracas there are forest areas, including 200,000-acre Rancho Grande National Park, that are alive with a variety of orchids and bromelias. Venezuela probably has the largest variety of tree species of any area of comparable size in the world.

FOOD...There are restaurants offering every style of cuisine. In Caracas, especially, one can find a host of international-type restaurants, as well as national cuisine. *Criollo* (native) dishes famous in Venezuela are *hallacas* (a type of tamale of corn, meat, eggs and olives, cooked in banana leaves). *Sancocho* is a stew of meats, chicken, roots and vegetables. Eating small oysters and clams with lemon juice is a custom to be found on all public beaches.

GAMBLING...There are no casinos but everybody plays the horses at the Hipódromo in Caracas on Saturdays, Sundays and national holidays. Try your luck at the "5 y 6", a six-horse parlay every Sunday with fabulous prizes. There are municipal and state lotteries several times weekly. Cockfighting may be seen in the country only a few miles out of Caracas.

LANGUAGE...Spanish is the official language but an increasing number of people understand English. Among nationals the common greeting is *"Qué hubo?"*

LAUNDRY AND DRY CLEANING . . . Good fast service in all hotels. Prices on par with or somewhat higher than in the United States.

LIQUOR . . . Some good native rums. *Ponche crema,* a not-too-potent cream eggnog; also may be bought by the bottle. Imported liquors are higher here than at home.

MEDICAL FACILITIES . . . Most hospitals are privately owned and operated. Many doctors are bi-lingual, with English probably the most common second language in use.

MOTION PICTURES . . . American films are shown everywhere in Venezuela, always with Spanish subtitles. Films from many nations are shown regularly, and, of the Spanish language films, those from Mexico are predominant. Movies are very popular and one can find some excellent theaters, including the *Boyaca, Broadway, Lido, Imperial, Paris, Radio City, Junin, Metropolitano, Rialto and San Bernardino.* Admission charges run about $1 to $1.50.

MUSIC . . . Just two blocks west of Plaza Henry Clay in Caracas is the *Municipal Theater,* a little old-fashioned but plushy opera house. First-class concerts, opera with visiting stars, good symphony concerts, too. The Venezuelan Symphony Orchestra gives frequent concerts which are generally free to the public. Open air concerts are given at the *Concha Acústica* (acoustic shell).

NIGHT CLUBS . . . The majority of the cabarets are new and entertainers are usually imported. Prices are high and it is best to investigate what one is likely to receive in the way of a check. The best known are the *Naiguatá* in the Hotel Tamanaco; *Pasapoga* on Avda. Urdaneta; *Ali Baba* on Avenida Andres Bello; *Bagdad* in San Bernardino. *Patio Andaluz, Le Mazot, Tony's* and *Hector's* are night spots without a floor show. A few miles out of Caracas on the Baruta road there is a French night club strangely called *Mi Vaca y Yo* with the unusual feature of a cow being made to walk through the dance floor every hour or so to remind the clients that milk is also available. There's also *Montmartre* in Baruta.

Hotel bars are open until 2:00 A.M., night clubs until 4:00 A.M. There are numerous bars which are the common man's club.

PHOTOGRAPHY . . . Black-and-white and colored movie and still films are available throughout Caracas. American and European cameras can also be purchased at prices which compare favorably with the U.S. Developing and printing of black-and-white film is done rapidly—24-hour service—at prices only a little higher than the U.S.; see addresses in telephone book. Ansco and Kodak ektachrome color film can be developed in 36 hours.

RELIGION . . . Venezuela is a Catholic country, but there is complete freedom in religious matters. There are churches of various denominations both in Caracas and in Maracaibo. The Caracas American Church is located at Avenida La Arboleda 54, El Bosque; English Church in Los Caobos.

RESTAURANTS . . . Among the many good ones to be found in Caracas are *Tony's, Hector's, Chicote, Monseigneur, La Crémaillère, Anatole, Tarzilandia, Tyrol, Centro Venezolano-Americano, Dragón*

Verde, El Palmer (Chinese), *El Patio, Bagdad Vert Galant, Casa Italia, The Steak House, Rincon Bavaria* and the dining rooms of the *Hotel Tamanaco, Hotel Avila* and *Hotel El Conde.* One of the most expensive is the exclusive *La Belle Epoque* in Colinas de Bello Monte.

SHOPS & STORES . . . Caracas has many shopping districts; one of the most popular is along the Avenida Sabana Grande. Store hours are usually 8 A.M. to 12 noon and 2 P.M. to 6 P.M. Stores of the department store type are VAM on Avenida Andres Bello, CORVET in Los Caobos and the Sears, Roebuck stores located at Bello Monte and San Martín in Caracas, as well as in Maracay, Puerto la Cruz, Barquisimeto, Maracaibo and Valencia.

SPECTATOR SPORTS . . . Horse racing every Saturday and Sunday in the Caracas Hipódromo. A huge new racing plant is currently under construction in El Valle just outside Caracas which is expected to be in operation before the end of 1959. Bullfights in the arenas in Caracas and Maracay are held on Sundays during the winter season, November through March. Baseball is the popular sport during the summer months and big-league players from the U.S. are to be seen with the various Venezuelan teams. Night games are well attended, but Sunday mornings are the most popular. In Caracas these games are played at the University City Stadium. Tennis is becoming an increasingly popular spectator sport with annual visits by champions from all over the world. Cock fighting is popular but more so in the interior towns of Venezuela.

SPORTS . . . Golf at the Caracas Country Club, Valle Arriba, Junko in Caracas, and at Caraballeda on the seacoast. Tennis at Altamira Club in Caracas and swimming at the Tamanaco, Casablanca and Paraíso. As all are strictly private clubs, special arrangements will be made for visiting tourists on a temporary basis, for use of certain of these facilities. Game hunting is available in the areas in the interior of the country and deep-sea fishing can be arranged at some of the boating clubs along the coast.

THEATERS . . . The *Teatro Municipal* and *Teatro Nacional* are in operation the year round with a variety of entertainment, including Spanish-speaking drama and comedy, opera, musical comedy, ballet and world-famous visiting artists. The Caracas Theater Club presents several works annually in the English language and the Caracas Sports Club presents a limited number of works each year.

TIME . . . One-half hour later than Eastern Standard Time. There is no daylight saving.

TIPPING . . . Most hotels add 10 per cent to their bills, but you are expected to tip individually those members of the staff assigned to your room or table. Average tip in restaurants is 15 per cent of the bill.

TOURIST TAXES . . . Aliens traveling on a passport with visa pay Bs. 20.- at entrance and Bs. 2.50 on exit. There is no entrance or exit tax for visitors with tourist cards.

TRANSPORTATION . . . Public transportation by bus, taxi or the share-the-ride taxis known as *"por puestos."* Taxis are plentiful and

Downtown Caracas, dominated by the twin buildings shown here, is the center of one of South America's busiest and most modern metropolises.

The huge pool from which one can view Caracas and the mountains beyond, is one of the many attractions of the Hotel Tamanaco.

operate 24 hours a day. Rates are not much higher than in any large city in the United States, although it is best to establish the fare before taking a long ride or tour. Inter-city bus service is fairly frequent and very good. Rental cars are available through Fiesta Cars Rentals.

WATER ... While the city water system has recently been modernized and has sanitary potable water, it is recommended that bottled water be used, particularly during a stay of short duration. Mineral waters from the United States are available in most restaurants and hotels. In the interior one should be particularly careful of the water found in the eating places and hotels. Travelers should restrict themselves to sealed bottled waters.

WHAT TO BUY ... Most articles of daily consumption in Venezuela are imported and shopping opportunities are limited. The duty on imported Swiss watches is much lower than in the United States. The best brands are those available in Caracas at prices much lower than those in the United States. For Rolex watches try Serpico and Laino. The jewelry stores in Caracas specialize in gold articles made of *cochano* gold, this being the pure gold that is still found in bottled in the Guayana country. The best available are at Panchita, Esq. Veroes with a branch in Sabana Grande and the two shops of Peters Brothers. Perhaps the most varied shopping is on the Isle of Margarita. There are natural pearls and a variety of mother-of-pearl articles, native hats, sandals, fine hammocks and other straw goods. Look into the handicraft shops the Ministerio de Fomento has opened in El Silencio in downtown Caracas, and at the Hotel Tamanaco, for examples of handmade souvenirs prepared in the interior by skilled artisans, and the handmade utensils made by the Indians of the Orinoco forest.

WHAT TO WEAR ... In Caracas summer wear the year around for daytime. This applies as well to the interior area of Venezuela, with the exception of places in the Andes Mountains, such as Merida and Trujillo. In the evening in Caracas fur jackets are worn and for almost all social occasions custom requires high-style, formal clothes. Coldest months are December through February.

WHERE TO GO—SIGHTSEEING ...

Caracas ... A well-constructed six-lane highway from the Maiquetia airport now carries the traveler into Caracas in about 20 minutes. Only a few years ago it was an hour and a half over a rather spectacular, sharp-turn road.

In the city of Caracas one finds drastic contrasts between the ultramodern styling and the old colonial architecture. Casa Natal, the house of Simón Bolívar's birth, is a fine example of the old Colonial. It is located near Plaza Bolívar, exactly in the center of old Caracas. Only a few blocks south of Plaza Bolívar is the Pantheon, site of the tomb of Bolívar. This is another example of graceful Colonial architecture, far different from the 20-story twin towers of the Civic Center Simón Bolívar.

For the most impressive sight of the city, take the cable car (*tele férico*) to the top of Mt. Avila, where you will find restaurants, bars, dancing and the luxurious Hotel Humboldt. A drive to see the Circular Militar and the Avenida de los Proceres, with its line of statues, monuments and well-arranged shrubs and flowers. Or a drive to the botanical gardens atop El Calvario. Throughout the city one finds dozens of plazas, and of interest to the North American visitor are the Plazas Henry Clay just north of the Santa Teresa Church and Plaza Washington in El Paraíso. University City, with its many buildings, large Medical Center and Hospital and two giant stadiums, is of interest to every visitor.

Maracay ... The drive from Caracas to Maracay over a newly constructed super-highway has cut the travel time to about one and a half hours. This drive is through the mountains and includes many scenic views of fruit, vegetable and sugar-cane farming. In Maracay the visitor will enjoy his stay at the *Hotel Maracay,* probably the most luxurious of the Conahotu chain of hotels. It has an 18-hole golf course, giant swimming pool and riding stables. The *Hotel Jardin* in Maracay is not a first-class hotel but is of considerable interest for the beautiful mosaic tiles and patio gardens inside the old Colonial structure. It was originally one of the many homes of the dictator Gomez. Only 60 miles from Maracay is the old Colonial town of Valencia. Today, Valencia is becoming an industrial center, with active manufacturing plants of world-famous tires, paints, plastics and cables. Good hotels in Valencia include the *Grand Hotel Valencia* and the *Hotel Carabobo.* Not far away is the Rain Forest and also nearby is the battlefield of Carabobo where the struggle for Venezuelan independence was won. A one-hour ride down the mountain to the sea brings one to the old port town of Puerto Cabello.

Maracaibo ... One hour and 20 minutes by air, to the west of Caracas, is the wealthy, fantastically fast-growing city of Maracaibo. Built on the shores of Lake Maracaibo, its activity fed by the more than 2 million barrels of oil pumped daily from its hundreds of wells drilled into the lake, it has a completely international population. In one of the most tropical climates, air-conditioning has changed the pattern of living in this area. Here one finds air-conditioned book stores, barber shops, theaters, restaurants, offices, and almost all hotels offer this pleasant retreat from warm weather. The *Hotel Del Lago,* of the Intercontinental Hotels Corporation group, offers everything the traveler needs. Good restaurant, pleasant bar and outstanding night club, swimming pool and conference rooms. Rates are from $13.50 single, from $18 double European Plan. Other good hotels are the *Detroit,* the *Fitzwater,* the *Shamrock,* the *Chama* and the *Hotel Peters.*

Orinoco River ... The Venezuelan Government operates modern twin Diesel steamers on the Orinoco, with comfortable cabins and adequate food and sleeping accommodations, on weekly schedules between Ciudad Bolívar and Puerto Ayacucho, at the beginning of the great rapids separating the lower Orinoco from the Upper River. This trip, which runs to between 5 and 6 days, permits one to see 600 miles of this virtually undeveloped river which is between 5 to 8 miles wide even after one has sailed more than a week above its mouth.

The new air-conditioned Hotel del Lago is a welcome oasis at Maracaibo, the oil center in Venezuela.

The fabulous Hotel Tamanaco in Caracas symbolizes the modern trend in Venezuela that is making the country very attractive to North American tourists.

The Middle Orinoco and the Venezuelan plains, Los Llanos, are famous for their cattle ranching and big-game hunting. If you have time, fly to Isla Margarita, less than 2 hours by air from Maiquetia airport, which is the principal source of oyster pearls in the whole of the Western Hemisphere. The island has a fascinating history, some of the most beautiful beaches in the world and facilities for all sorts of deep-sea fishing. The brand-new *Hotel Bellavista* here is excellent.

SOURCES OF FURTHER INFORMATION ... The *Caracas Daily Journal,* an English language newspaper that is sold throughout Venezuela, is a good source of information for movies, sports and local events. Politour in the Edificio Galipan will arrange tours and sightseeing. Avensa has a special tour to Canaima and other airs tours. The American Consulate is located in San Bernardino, near the Pan American Office, in Caracas. The PAA telephone is 55–81–01 in Caracas and the location is Puente Urupal on Avenida Urdaneta in San Bernardino. In New York the Venezuela Consulate General is at 600 Fifth Avenue.

Asia and the
Philippine Islands

BURMA

WEATHER IN RANGOON—Lat. N16°46'—Alt. 55'

	JAN.	FEB.	MAR.	APR.	MAY	JUNE	JULY	AUG.	SEPT.	OCT.	NOV.	DEC.
Average Temp.	72°	75°	85°	92°	84°	76°	75°	76°	78°	80°	75°	70°
Days of Rain	1	1	1	2	13	23	25	24	20	11	4	1

LOCATION ... Burma forms part of the Indo-China peninsula of Southeast Asia, 638 air miles southeast of Calcutta and 362 air miles northwest of Bangkok.

CHARACTERISTICS ... Burma is one of the most interesting and colorful independent republics in Asia. The people are of Tibeto-Mongolian stock, with brown, cheerful faces; they dress in bright, vivid attire. They are both hospitable to visitors and generous in spirit. Burma is a land of vast expanses of rice fields, and rich teak forests stretch up the hills. Burma is also known as the land of pagodas, where the dominant feature of any scene is the golden Buddhist pagoda. In this land of precious stones, rubies, jades and sapphires are of distinctive interest.

POPULATION ... Estimated 18,000,000; about the population of both Texas and California combined.

SIZE ... 261,789 square miles; nearly the size of Texas.

CAPITAL ... The city of Rangoon, situated on the Hliang, or Rangoon, River, is about 21 miles from the sea and is the main port of entry into the country by sea or air. There are no overland routes into Burma. Rangoon has a population of about 800,000.

GOVERNMENT ... A republic with a President, Parliament of two houses and a Cabinet headed by a Premier with 21 other Ministers. Until 1948, Burma had, for a century, formed a part of the British Empire.

HOW TO GET THERE ... Rangoon is a regular stop on Pan

American's Round-the-World routes. It is 2½ hours from Calcutta, 1¾ hours from Bangkok, approximately 50½ hours (elapsed time) from San Francisco, 38 hours from New York. Connections also available from other East Coast and West Coast cities. By ship to Rangoon from New York via Britain takes about 40 days.

ACCOMMODATIONS ... There are several hotels, but only one first-class hotel (by Far Eastern standards) in Rangoon, the *Strand*, operated by a British mercantile firm. It has excellent service. The hotel is located on Strand Road facing the harbor, close to the business and shopping area. American Plan, year around rate is $12 to $15. It is important to reserve rooms well in advance.

CLIMATE ... Like most other semitropical countries, Burma has only three seasons. The "hot season" from March to May is uncomfortable weather with temperatures reaching above 100 degrees at noon; during the "rainy season" from June to October, the weather is moderately cool, but the rain may stretch out into days; and the "cool season" from November to February has temperatures around the 70's. Humidity is high during the hot and rainy seasons; the best time to visit is during the cool season.

CLUBS ... Rotary.

CURRENCY ... The unit of Burmese currency is the kyat, which is divided into 100 pyas. The exchange value of the kyat is about 21 cents (U.S.) or K 4.76 to a U.S. dollar. The kyat is at par with the Indian rupee. Currency is controlled and exchange may be made only at the authorized banks.

CUSTOMS REGULATIONS AND DOCUMENTS REQUIRED FOR UNITED STATES CITIZENS ... Passport and visa required. Also health certificate, cholera (yellow fever if coming from infected area) and smallpox vaccination. Exit permits are required from those staying 10 or more days. Currency must be declared. Check on foreign currency restrictions. One still and one movie camera per person. Guns and a limited amount of ammunition are allowed into the country after all entry formalities have been complied with. Radios may be brought in after payment of duty. Travelers are also allowed to bring in or take out, duty free, 50 cigarettes, 25 cigars or ¼ pound tobacco, and 1 quart of liquor. Chinese-type articles are either prohibited or require a Certificate of Origin for entry into the United States. Consult the nearest U.S. Consul for latest requirements.

FOOD ... Burmese food is strikingly similar to Indian, Siamese and Malay food and consists of rice and curry. Curry dishes are generally meat or vegetables or a mixture, cooked with a liberal admixture of spices, pepper, onions and sesamum oil. Rice is the staple diet at all meals. Most hotels and restaurants serve Western food as well as Chinese and Indian dishes. The average cost of meals is about $2 for a person at high-class restaurants.

RESTAURANTS ... In Rangoon the *Strand Hotel* is the most popular Western-type restaurant. *Orient Hotel* on Sule Pagoda Road, *Chaun Hwa* on Sule Pagoda Road, *Hai Yuan* on University Ave. and *Nam Sin* on Prome Road (8 miles) provide excellent Chinese food, as does *Thamaing Restaurant* in Insein Road. Food is not expensive in Burma. Usual rates are not more than $2 per person.

WHAT TO WEAR ... For men, linen or any other light-material suits are recommended; for women, washable linen or cotton dresses. Rangoon is not a "dressy" place, but it is a good idea to bring your tropical "formals" along. Sun-glasses are indispensable. Light suits will do fine for any weather in Burma; raincoats are essential.

WHERE TO GO—SIGHTSEEING ...

Rangoon ... The capital of Burma, situated in the low hills about 24 miles from the sea, Rangoon is one of the most attractive cities in the East. It combines the mystery and religious charm of the East with all the modern facilities of the West. It is well laid out, with pleasant tree-lined streets, parks and gardens; there are two fine lakes, Royal Lake and Inya Lake, in the center of the city. The people are friendly and cheerful and highly attractive in their gay and colorful dress. Although conducted sightseeing tours are not available, jeep taxis or limousines may be hired at low rates for such a purpose, about $2 an hour for the vehicle. Here are the main sightseeing places in Rangoon:

Shwedagon Pagoda towers about 326 feet from the summit of a hill near the heart of the city and is a welcoming landmark that greets every traveler, by sea or air, to Burma. It is the largest pagoda of its kind in the world and every year attracts many Buddhist pilgrims from all over the world. It is the number-one place of sightseeing interest for tourists. Also in Rangoon is the picturesque Sule Pagoda, situated exactly in the heart of the city. A large reclining image of Buddha is in Pegu, about 50 miles east of Rangoon. It is over 150 feet in height.

Other attractions include the colorful bazaars bustling with activity; the cigar-rolling center where Burmese girls may be seen wrapping and rolling the tobacco leaf; umbrella shops, where skillful workers produce gorgeous umbrellas of silk and bamboo; workshops that produce silverwork or wood and ivory carvings; the National Museum; the State Library; and the State Institute of Fine Arts; Burmese costume drama, dancing, or puppet shows which can be seen frequently in the Burmese quarter of the city.

Burmese marriage ceremonies, the *Shinpyus* of young Burmese males when they are initiated into monkhood, and earring-boring ceremonies for young Burmese girls are other occasions of immense interest; the Rangoon Zoo and the occasional snake-kissing show, featuring the king cobra and the woman snake charmer; the busy port and teeming wharves; the campus of the University of Rangoon; the excellent race track; the religious buildings; all are interesting.

SOURCES OF FURTHER INFORMATION ... Feel free to inquire of Pan American's representative, c/o S. Huie and Company, at 186 Phayre Street, Rangoon, for tourist information. The Burma Consulate in New York is at 888 Madison Avenue.

CAMBODIA

LOCATION ... The Kingdom of Cambodia, formerly a part of French Indochina, is located on the Gulf of Thailand.

CHARACTERISTICS ... Cambodia is a picturesque country of rice paddies, sugar and rubber plantation, set against a background of ancient temples and monuments.

POPULATION ... Estimated at about 5 million.

CAPITAL ... Phnom-Penh, the only large city, with an estimated population of 450,000, on the "Tonlé Sap" river.

GOVERNMENT ... Cambodia is a Kingdom.

HOW TO GET THERE ... By Pan Am Clipper to Bangkok, Hong Kong or Saigon, then by connecting airlines to Phnom-Penh.

ACCOMMODATIONS ... First class hotel accommodations are limited. There is *Le Royal,* the small air-conditioned *Raja,* and the newer, partially air-conditioned *Sukhalay.* Among several restaurants try the *Kirirom,* the *Chanteclair* for French foods. Night life centers around *Le Cambodge.*

CUSTOMS REGULATIONS AND DOCUMENTS REQUIRED FOR UNITED STATES CITIZENS ... Passport and visa required. Also a smallpox vaccination, yellow fever and cholera if coming from an infected area. Visa applications should be made well in advance through Cambodian diplomatic offices.

WHAT TO SEE ... In Phnom-Penh, visit Jayavarman II Museum, the Cooperative Art Corporation and the Art School, with items for sale.

ANGKOR WAT ... Located at Siemreap, 262 miles west northwest of Saigon, on the air route between Saigon and Bangkok, the ruins of Angkor are by far the greatest tourist attraction in Cambodia. This architectural wonder of Angkor Wat (temple) and many other ornamental monuments, temples and palaces with 200-foot towers covering an area over 60 square miles was built by the Khmer warrier kings more than a thousand years ago. Hidden by jungle growth, the ruins were rediscovered only within the last century and are still in process of being restored. Siemreap is reached by air from Phnom-Penh in 1 hour. Here you can stay at the *Grand Hotel* or its annex, *Hotel De La Paix.* Single room, $5, double $9; Lunch/dinner: $3; Breakfast: $1. There are organized excursions at $6 per person and per day. Car with driver can be hired from the hotel at $30 a day.

SOURCES OF FURTHER INFORMATION ... Pan American address is care of Denis Frères Air Service, at 219 Terak Vithai Preah Bat Sisowath, Phnom-Penh, Cambodia.

HONG KONG

New Territories

Airport

KOWLOON PENINSULA

Victoria THE PEAK

HONG KONG

Aberdeen

BIG WAVE BAY

SHEK-O

THE LIDO RESORT REPULSE BAY

Macao I., Kwangtung Province—40 miles

WEATHER IN HONG KONG—Lat. N22°16'—Alt. 25'

Temp.	JAN.	FEB.	MAR.	APR.	MAY	JUNE	JULY	AUG.	SEPT.	OCT.	NOV.	DEC.
Low	56°	55°	60°	67°	73°	78°	78°	78°	77°	73°	65°	58°
High	64°	63°	67°	75°	81°	85°	87°	87°	85°	81°	74°	67°
Average	60°	59°	64°	71°	77°	82°	83°	83°	81°	77°	70°	63°
Days of Rain	6	8	11	12	16	21	19	17	14	8	6	5

LOCATION ... The British Crown Colony of Hong Kong comprises Hong Kong Island, Kowloon Peninsula and the New Territories in southeast China, about 90 miles south of Canton. Hong Kong is 700 air miles northwest of Manila. Its correct designation is "Hong Kong, British Crown Colony" or "Hong Kong, B.C.C." *not* China.

CHARACTERISTICS ... This British Crown Colony is one of the busiest ports in the Orient. It offers the traveler a chance to see an interesting and colorful Chinese city. The main body of the population is Cantonese (south China), the minority northern Chinese, Europeans, and Americans. Tourists are very welcome in Hong Kong. Macao, Colony of Portugal, easily accessible from Hong Kong, provides an interesting experience, too.

POPULATION ... Estimated 2,500,000.

SIZE ... The island of Hong Kong is 11 miles long with an area of 32 square miles. The total area of the colony is 391 square miles.

CAPITAL ... Victoria, often referred to as Hong Kong, with a population of about 365,000, slightly smaller than Portland, Oregon.

GOVERNMENT ... A British Crown Colony, the Queen represented by a Governor.

HOW TO GET THERE ... By Clipper from the United States West Coast via Honolulu about 52 hours (elapsed time), 3 hours from Manila, 4½ hours from Bangkok, 8¾ hours from Tokyo. Hong Kong is on Pan Am's Round-the-World Routes. By ship about 21 days from San Francisco.

ACCOMMODATIONS ... There are several fine hotels in Hong Kong, including: the *Peninsula*, the *Miramar* and the newly established, moderately priced *Astor, Carlton* and *Palm Court*. All are in Kowloon, all air conditioned; the *Gloucester* in Victoria, Central District; the *Repulse Bay* on the beach 20 minutes from Victoria; the *Winner House* and the *Sunning House* located on Hong Kong Island. Rates range from $5 to $10 single, $7 to $15 double. Suites from $12 to $20, all European Plan. Make your reservations in advance.

BANKS ... The First National City Bank of New York (only U.S. Bank in city), Hong Kong and Shanghai Banking Corp., Chartered Bank of India, Australia and China, Bank of Indo-China, Bank of East Asia, Netherlands Trading Society, National Handelsbank N.V. The American Express Co. also has a banking section.

CALENDAR OF HOLIDAYS ... The Chinese New Year (between January 15 and February 15) is a colorful event. Others include: January 1; Good Friday; Easter Monday; Whit Monday; Queen's Birthday (celebrated in June); summer holiday the first week day in July; summer holiday the first Monday in August; August 30, Liberation Day; Chinese Midautumn Festival Day in September; October 10, Foundation of the Republic of China; the day following Remembrance Sunday; Christmas Day; December 26.

CIGARETTES ... British and American cigarettes are readily available at prices no higher than in the United States.

CLIMATE ... The best season is from September 15 through March 1, the wet season is from April through June; the warm months are from the end of June through September.

CLUBS ... The Royal Hong Kong Club; Jockey Club; American Club; Rotary International; Junior Chamber of Commerce; Cricket Club; Ladies Recreation Club; Foreign Correspondent's Club; Sports Club. Cards may be arranged for most of these. (Inquire of Pan American locally.)

COMMUNICATIONS ... Cables to all parts of the world. Long distance telephone to U.S. and elsewhere.

CURRENCY ... The monetary unit is the Hong Kong dollar. The official rate of exchange is HK $5.80 to United States $1; however, all United States dollars are exchanged at the recognized open-market rate which fluctuates.

CUSTOMS REGULATIONS AND DOCUMENTS REQUIRED FOR UNITED STATES CITIZENS ... Passport and visas required. Smallpox vaccination, cholera inoculation for passengers from the Orient, India or Asia. Each passenger is allowed 200 cigarettes, or 25 cigars or 8 ounces of tobacco, and 1 quart bottle of liquor duty free. Chinese-type articles are either prohibited or require a Certificate of Origin for entry into the United States. Consult the nearest U.S. Consul for latest requirements.

DRUG STORES ... Chemists shops are numerous and have name-brand pharmaceuticals.

ELECTRIC CURRENT ... Voltage in Hong Kong is 220, A.C.; two-prong transformer plugs required.

FOOD... Excellent European and Chinese food are available in Hong Kong. No other city can offer such varieties combined with exquisite taste. The Chinese have been famous for centuries for their cooking, and their methods have been handed down from generation to generation. Some of their principal dishes are: fried rice, sweet-and-sour pork, sharkfin soup, birdnest soup, suckling pig, sweet almond cream, and hundreds more. Many northern delicacies such as Szechuan and Peking duck are available. Milk is safe to drink.

GAMBLING... Hong Kong has no casinos, but there is a wonderful race track at Happy Valley with pari-mutuel betting.

LANGUAGE... The official language is English, but the city is populated almost entirely by Chinese. Cantonese is heard mostly on the street. English, however, is readily understood in hotels, restaurants, and shops. In Chinese, Hong Kong means fragrant harbor.

LAUNDRY AND DRY CLEANING... Laundry is good. Dry cleaning is satisfactory but should be watched. Be sure your room-boy understands *clean* not *wash* if you want something dry cleaned.

LIQUOR... All drinks are available at moderate prices. Chinese prefer locally produced rice wine, which they drink warm.

MEDICAL FACILITIES... Excellent. The University of Hong Kong, Matilda Hospital, Queen Mary Hospital and St. Paul's Hospital all have excellent equipment. Both British and Chinese doctors.

MOTION· PICTURES... Numerous first-class air-conditioned theaters in the city show first-run American films. A few theaters show locally made Chinese films which would be of interest to tourists.

MUSIC... Native music can be heard at performances of Chinese opera, which runs constantly. Hong Kong has a choral group and a symphony orchestra composed of amateur musicians.

NIGHT CLUBS... *Champagne Room, Gaddi's, Paris, Maxim's, Paramount* and *Marco Polo Room;* all have excellent Filipino orchestras. Don't always expect a floor show.

PHOTOGRAPHY... All types of cameras and film are available. Kodak supplies are available at Edinburgh House.

RELIGION... Church of England and Roman Catholic churches; most American Protestant missions represented; Jewish synagogue.

RESTAURANTS... Some of the best are the *Parisian Grill,* French and Russian dishes; *Dairy Farm* for ice cream, sodas; *Jimmy's Kitchen* for steaks, and *Gingles,* American style; *Champagne Room,* with music; *Tai Tung* and *Kam Ling,* Cantonese style; *Mandarin Room, Goldfish, Princess Garden,* Peking style; and *Winter Garden* for Szechuan or Shanghai style. Continental food at *Gaddi's* and *Lido* or *Repulse Bay Hotel.* Others include *Café de Paris, Kowloon Restaurant, Maxim's.* Seafoods at floating restaurants in Aberdeen.

SHOPS AND STORES... Bargaining is a must everywhere you go whether in large stores or small corner shops catering to tourist trade. Chinese and Indian merchants enjoy it more than you do. You will find linens and embroidered articles on On Lan Street; carved camphorwood boxes, ivories on Queen's Road, East; silks, smoking jackets, lingeries, carved rosewood beads on Wyndham Street. You

The white pagoda overlooks the fine natural harbor that has made Hong Kong an important transshipment port and gateway between East and West.

can get wonderful bargains in British woolens from the importers and oriental clothing.

SPECTATOR SPORTS ... Horse racing, soccer, tennis.

SPORTS ... At the numerous beaches available, there's good swimming June through October, tennis (arrangements can be made for the use of courts at some clubs), golf by arrangement with the club.

THEATERS ... Chinese opera in Cantonese.

TIME ... 16 hours later than the United States Pacific Coast Time. Daylight Saving Time is observed April 15 through October 15.

TIPPING ... 10 or 15 per cent.

TRANSPORTATION ... Motor cars, rickshaws, tram cars, sedan chairs, buses, transport coolies, and lorries. Frequent and reliable ferry service between Kowloon and downtown Hong Kong.

WHAT TO BUY ... Because the port of Hong Kong is free of import duty on everything except liquor and tobacco, it is much cheaper to buy things here—French perfumes, clothing, items not prohibited. *See* CUSTOMS REGULATIONS and SHOPS and STORES.

WHAT TO WEAR ... For summer, clothing should be as light as possible. Sun shades and shady hats will be comfortable, too. A top coat may be required during the winter months.

WHERE TO GO—SIGHTSEEING ...

Hong Kong ... A visit to such districts as Sai Ying Pun and Wanchai is fascinating. Here are the "ladder streets," narrow lanes with steep flights of stairs and typically Chinese markets. On Cotton Street you can get bargains in woolen, cotton goods, real and artificial silk. There are curio dealers in this district, tailors, grocers and restaurants. There are open-air book shops where you see Chinese ranging from small tots looking at picture books to adults poring over books of learning. You should try to visit the Tiger Balm Garden and take a drive through the beautiful residential district. The reservoirs in Hong Kong are well worth seeing. The Government started the construction in 1851, the first in the colony.

Hong Kong has four very popular bathing beaches. Repulse Bay can be reached from Hong Kong in 20 minutes by car. The *Lido* on Repulse Bay Beach is also popular. Another beach resort is *Shek-O* in the old village of Dragon's Back Peninsula. Deep Water Bay and Big Wave Bay also have splendid bathing beaches. The fishing village of Aberdeen is one of the most picturesque places in Hong Kong. Interesting junks gather here by the hundreds. The natives here are descendants of the pirates who made Hong Kong dreaded by peaceful traders. Take a ride on the Peak Tram to the top of Hong Kong's peak. Visit also the Chinese temples and other historical sites in Hong Kong.

New Territories . . . Consist of 355 square miles leased from China on the mainland; terrace farming and typical Chinese villages afford an interesting drive which takes about 3½ hours including stops for pictures and lunch. Many of these points of sightseeing interest are covered in tours available from the numerous tour agencies.

Macao . . . Macao, Colony of Portugal is on the Peninsula of Chung Shan, Kwangtung. Macao is called the Monte Carlo of the Orient. Many tourists visit this city, which is a mixture of new and old Chinese, Portuguese, and Spanish. Daily boat service makes the trip in about 3 hours. Staterooms are available. The streets are lined by fine old trees and there are interesting gambling houses.

There are many points of interest to foreign visitors in this small colony: the Praya Grande, the grotto of the poet Camões, where there is a bronze bust of Portugal's immortal poet. It is believed that it was at this spot the poet was inspired to write some cantos of his well-known poem, "The Luisades." There are many Chinese temples to be seen here; beautiful gardens; the Guía Lighthouse, the oldest on the China Coast; the famous façade of the Cathedral of St. Paul, which is centuries old; Penha Hill; the Barrier Gate between this colony and the Chinese territory. Take in the Avenida Almeida Ribeiro, the main shopping center of Macao. Kwan Yin Tong, the Temple of the Goddess of Mercy, is where the first treaty between the United States and China was signed in 1844. Lin Fung Miu is another ancient Chinese temple, as well as the Ma Kok Miu, Temple of A-Ma, after whom Macao is named. (Macao was formerly known as A-Ma.) Other places of interest to see are: the yards for junks—all types are seen here, fishing junks, sampans and other wooden vessels; a trip to a match factory—the manufacture of matches is one of the important industries. There are some good hotels and restaurants here, such as the *Hotel Riviera*, the *Grand Hotel* and Restaurant, the *Central Hotel* and Restaurant, *Fa Siu Lau* (Laughing Buddha Restaurant, famous for roast pigeon), and *Nan Lau* Restaurant. The *Melco Club*, which is the Macao Electric Light Company's staff club is open to visitors. The Portuguese Inn (Portuguese food and atmosphere) is also good.

SOURCES FOR FURTHER INFORMATION . . . Feel free to call on the Pan American offices for information: Alexandra House (Tel. 37031) and Peninsula Hotel in Kowloon (Tel. 64005). 24-hour service at Clipper Information Center (Tel. 37031).

INDIA

WEATHER IN CALCUTTA—Lat. 22°30′—Alt. 85′

Temp.	JAN.	FEB.	MAR.	APR.	MAY	JUNE	JULY	AUG.	SEPT.	OCT.	NOV.	DEC.
Low	56°	60°	69°	76°	78°	79°	79°	79°	78°	75°	65°	56°
High	77°	82°	91°	95°	95°	91°	89°	88°	88°	87°	82°	77°
Average	67°	71°	80°	86°	87°	85°	84°	84°	83°	81°	74°	67°
Days of Rain	1	2	2	3	7	13	18	18	13	6	1	0

LOCATION ... The Republic of India is comprised of 20 States which include the former princely States.

CHARACTERISTICS ... This is a colorful country undergoing what amounts to a revolution in its social and economic life. Its fabulous temples, magnificent mosques, exotic bazaars and shops, its world-famous Taj Mahal are in themselves reason enough to visit India. Delhi, the Capital; Calcutta and Bombay, thriving industrial centers and major ports of India; Jaipur, the pink Capital of Rajasthan; the holy city of Benares; the ancient rock-cut caves of Ajanta and Ellora, and the temples of South India are some of the major tourist attractions of this fascinating land. The Indian Government is eager to have the outside world know more about the country.

POPULATION ... Estimated at 390,000,000 considerably more than twice that of the United States. The population is made up of many racial strains and constitutes one-seventh of the human race.

SIZE ... 1,269,640 square miles, a little more than half of the area of the United States.

CAPITAL ... New Delhi, which, together with Delhi City, has a population of nearly two million.

GOVERNMENT ... Republic framework with a Parliament (Council of States and House of the People). The Cabinet consists of a Prime Minister and Council of Ministers.

HOW TO GET THERE ... By Pan American Clipper, through-plane service from New York to Calcutta, 38½ hours (elapsed time); Delhi is 3 hours by air from Karachi, 3½ hours from Calcutta. By ship, 25 to 45 days.

ACCOMMODATIONS . . . In Calcutta there are three good hotels, the *Great Eastern,* the *Grand,* the *Spence's.* All have bars, restaurants and orchestras. Rates are about $8 single and $12 double excluding meals. Air-conditioned accommodations are somewhat higher. In the Delhi area there are seven good hotels, *Ashoka,* the *Imperial, Claridge's,* the *Janpath* and the *Ambassador* in New Delhi, and the *Cecil* and *Maiden's* in Delhi itself, the inclusive rates ranging from $8 single to $15 double. There are several good hotels in Bombay, the best being the *Taj Mahal Hotel,* the *Ambassador,* the *Ritz* and the *Greens Hotel.* Rates are $5 to $12 American Plan, single. Suites and air-conditioned rooms can also be had. These hotels provide good European cuisine as well as local dishes, and the water is safe to drink. They each have a cabaret and a permit room serving drinks to permit holders. (*See* LIQUOR)

ARTS . . . Some of the outstanding museums are the Indian Museum and the Victoria Memorial Museum in Calcutta; the National Museum, the Central Asian and Antiquities Museum and the National Art Gallery in New Delhi; the Prince of Wales Museum and the Jehangir Art Gallery in Bombay; the Government Museum in Madras.

BALLET . . . There is no ballet as we know it, but dancing occupies a unique place among the arts, combining action, song, melody, rhythm and harmony and is an integral part of Indian life, having both spiritual and social significance. There are four major schools of dancing in India: the classical Bharata Natyam of South India, the Kathakali of Kerala, the Kathak of North India and the Manipuri of Assam. The last three may be regarded as the counterpart of the ballet in the West. The folk ballet is entirely different. Some of the well-known troupes are the Indian National Theater, the Chitra Players, and the Students of Viswabharati (Santiniketan) and Kalakshetra, Madras.

BANKS . . . There are many banks in Calcutta, Bombay, Delhi and Madras, some of the important ones being the State Bank of India, the First National City Bank of New York, the Chartered Bank of India, Australia and China, Grindlay's Bank and Lloyd's Bank. Besides these there are the Bank of England, the Hong Kong and Shanghai Banking Corporation, and the Netherlands Trading Society in Calcutta, to name a few. There are foreign exchange booths at Dum Dum Airport, Calcutta, the Santa Cruz Airport, Bombay and Palam Airport, Delhi. Traveler's checks may be either purchased or cashed at the American Express or Thos. Cook's in Calcutta, Bombay and Madras or at all leading hotels.

CALENDAR OF HOLIDAYS . . . Hindu and Moslem festivals are governed by the lunar calendar, hence within a certain period their dates vary from year to year. January 26, Republic Day celebration; (March-April) Holi (Spring Festival); August 15, Independence Day; Muharram (Moslem holiday); (September-October) Dusserah; (October-November) Diwali (Festival of Lamps).

CIGARETTES AND TOBACCO . . . Cigarettes of Indian and British makes are plentiful. American brands are not available.

CLIMATE . . . Being a vast country, India has no uniform climate. In Calcutta, for example, the winter months (November-February) are moderately humid. The summer months (April-October) are quite warm and humid. Delhi experiences extremes of climate. In summer (mid-April to July) the temperature rises to about 110 degrees and it is hot and dusty; the rainy season (July, August and September) is warm and humid and the temperature ranges between 70 degrees and 90 degrees. In winter (mid-November to February) it is cold and bracing, the temperature at times touching 40 degrees or less. Delhi has a short spring (March to mid-April). The best time to visit Bombay is September to March, when temperatures are around 80 degrees. April and May are hot and June, July and August are the monsoon months of torrential rains.

CLUBS . . . Rotary Club in most major cities. Guest members are welcome. In Calcutta there are a number of good clubs, including the Calcutta, the Bengal, the Royal Calcutta Golf Club and an active Chamber of Commerce, which foreign businessmen like to visit. There is also an American Club, which meets once a month and is composed of the majority of the American community.

In Delhi, Delhi Gymkhana, the Chelmsford, Delhi Golf Club, National Sports Club of India (N.S.C.I.) and the Roshanara Club have arrangements for transient memberships. Bombay and Madras have also several European and Cosmopolitan Clubs.

COMMON COURTESIES AND LOCAL CUSTOMS . . . Visitors should take off their shoes before entering an Indian temple or Mosque. Otherwise behave as you would in your own religious house.

COMMUNICATIONS . . . There is a tele-communication system in India. Inter-city telephone calls may be made from larger cities, and radio telephone calls to the United States. Telegrams may be sent from the larger cities and railway stations.

CURRENCY . . . The monetary unit is the rupee, worth about 21 cents. It is divided into 100 naya paisa.

CUSTOMS REGULATIONS AND DOCUMENTS REQUIRED FOR UNITED STATES CITIZENS . . . Passport and visa are required. "Tourist visas" are recommended. Better obtain a tourist introduction card when you apply for your tourist visa, since tourists can enjoy many privileges not otherwise accorded to visitors. Inquire at the local Pan American Office about this. It is advisable to limit yourself to 200 cigarettes or 50 cigars or ¼ pound of tobacco, one regular size bottle of wine and ½ pint of spirits. There is no specific limit on cosmetics. There should, however, be no such single quantity as to invite suspicion of possible resale in India. Smallpox vaccination required and yellow fever and cholera certificates needed if coming from an infected area. See tip No. 6, Page 9.

DRUG STORES... Chemists, druggists or pharmacists can be found in the shopping and business centers and in most of the hotels. In large cities there is special night and Sunday service. Tourists should not expect to find, except occasionally, American products, especially cosmetics and toilet articles. Generally, any visitor requiring special medicines, vitamins, etc., should bring in enough to last him for his stay in India.

ELECTRIC CURRENT... In most areas, 220 volts, A.C. British type converter plugs required. Check at your hotel before using U.S. electrical appliances.

FAUNA... In its variety of wildlife few regions of the earth are as interesting as India. There are more than 500 species of animals. Typical are the wild elephant, tiger, panther, leopard, cheetah, *neelgai* (blue bull) bison, wild buffalo, rhinoceros, camel, sloth bear, wolf, fox, antelope, *sambhar*, gazelle, wild pig, monkey, and spotted, barking and swamp deer. There are zoological gardens in Delhi, Calcutta, Lucknow, Jaipur, Baroda, Bombay, Madras, Mysore and Trivandrum. Photographs of wildlife can be taken at the game sanctuaries in the states of Assam, Bombay, Madras, Mysore, Kerala and Uttar Pradesh. There is a large variety of birds, among which the peacock, *bulbul*, myna and the *sarus* crane are typical. As for game, pheasant, duck, partridge and geese are plentiful. Hunting excursions can be arranged.

FLORA... The better-known botanic gardens are in Calcutta, Darjeeling, Bombay, Poona, Octacamund, Coonoor, Bangalore, Madras and Trivandrum. Among the flowers, lotus, varieties of jasmine, orchid, rose lily, *champa, gulmohr* and laburnum are typical. The mango, banana, banyan, *neem, pipal,* cassia, tamarind, coconut, casuarina, sandalwood, rubber, teak, *sheesham,* bamboo, cinchona and eucalyptus are some of the tropical trees found in various areas.

FOOD... Some of the specialties are: in Calcutta *rossagolla* and *sandesh* (desserts); fish curry and rice; *shinghara* (meat or vegetable patties); in Delhi, *tanduri* chicken and *nan* (oven-baked chicken and bread); *rogan josh* and *paratha* or *chapatti* (mutton and wheat pancakes); *Pulao* or *biryani* and *korma* (rice and mutton curry); murge curry (spiced chicken); *kabab;* desserts—*sohan* and *halva, phirni falooda.*

LANGUAGE... Hindi is the national language, but English is commonly spoken. In dealing with managers and key personnel of hotels, you will encounter no difficulty when using English.

LAUNDRY AND DRY CLEANING... Laundries and dry cleaners are available. Domestic launderers (*dhobis*) pick up and deliver your laundry. Quick service is available in good hotels.

LIQUOR... In Calcutta and Delhi you can get several brands of liquor at considerably higher prices than at home, but in other places, especially Bombay and Madras, liquor permits must be obtained. Inquire at the Pan American office about this. No public drinking is permitted in Delhi, Bombay or Madras.

MEDICAL FACILITIES... Several good doctors and surgeons and hospitals and nursing homes. Inquire at your hotel.

MOTION PICTURES ... There are a number of movie theaters in Bombay, Madras, Calcutta and Delhi which are air-conditioned and comfortable. Both American and British films are shown.

MUSIC ... Indian music can be heard on All-India Radio. Performances by well-known musicians are held occasionally.

NIGHT CLUBS AND CABARETS ... Night clubs, as we know them, will not be found in India; however, many of the leading hotels have Western-style ballrooms and cabarets.

PHOTOGRAPHY ... India is wonderful for photography; clear light, variety in color and dress, beautiful scenery and ancient monuments provide an inexhaustible store of subjects for the camera. Two cameras, one of which may be a small movie camera, are allowed in duty free. Black-and-white and color films and facilities for developing are available in the big cities. While traveling by air in India, cameras must be placed in stowed baggage. A tourist can bring in 12 plates or 5 rolls of film with a camera and 2 reels of film with a small movie camera, duty free.

RELIGION ... Hindu, Moslem, and Sikh temples and churches of Catholic, Protestant and Buddhist denominations.

RESTAURANTS ... In addition to the hotel dining rooms and bars, the following are the recommended restaurants: In Calcutta: *Kwality, Firpo's, Nanking, Mocambo, Olympia;* in New Delhi, *Gaylords, Volga, Alps, Standard, Kwality, York, Nirula's, Embassy, Wenger's, Metry;* In Delhi, *Moti Mahal, Khyber;* in Bombay, *Rendezvous, Mokabar, Chetana* (vegetarian), *Gaylords, Volga, Napoli, Eros, Berry's, Bombelli's, Gourdon's, Chez Caroline, Rotisserie, Ambassador's Grill Room, Gul Mohar.*

SHOPS AND STORES ... In Calcutta, New Market, Bengal Home Industries Association; in New Delhi, Central Cottage Industries Emporium, Kashmir Government Arts Emporium and shops in Connaught Place, Janpath and Chandni Chowk.

SPECTATOR SPORTS ... The most popular games, borrowed from the West, are soccer, cricket, football and tennis. Important tournaments held in all large cities attract big crowds. Horse racing in Calcutta, Bombay, Delhi and Poona.

SPORTS ... Golf, tennis, badminton, soccer, hockey, polo, cricket, swimming, *shikar* (hunting—big-game hunting trips can be arranged) and fishing. Facilities are available at clubs for guests of members. For swimming there are some fine beaches in India and a few good pools in Calcutta, Delhi, Bombay and Madras.

TIME ... Indian Standard Time is 10½ hours later than United States Eastern Standard Time.

TIPPING ... At hotels which do not include a service charge, the usual tip is 10%. Taxi drivers are *not* tipped.

TRANSPORTATION ... Taxis and bus services. Bus services in India are not comparable with those in the States. Taxis are therefore recommended, preferably special unmetered taxis in Delhi, Bombay, Calcutta and Madras.

WATER ... Water in cities is reliable, but in general it is wise to drink only boiled or bottled water.

WHAT TO BUY . . . Silks, brocades, woven and printed textiles, jewelry, costume jewelry, ivory, woodwork (sandalwood, rosewood and walnut wood), articles made from horn, brass and copperware, silverware, *bidri* and other inlaid work, leather articles, lacquer work, toys, gold-and-silver-thread embroidery, lace, handbags, Jaipuri embroidered slippers. Government-controlled establishments, department stores and other well-known shops have fixed prices; bargaining is done in the smaller shops.

WHAT TO WEAR . . . Daytime dress is casual because of the high temperatures during all but the winter seasons. Seersucker, light cottons, dark or light linen—in short, washable fabrics. During the summer these are comfortable day or night. In winter, light tweed and flannel for Calcutta and heavy woolen clothing for Delhi is necessary. For the rainy season (mid-June to mid-October) be sure to bring a raincoat. In Bombay, light clothing is suitable the year round; Calcutta is quite formal so men may find a dinner jacket useful.

WHERE TO GO—SIGHTSEEING . . .

Calcutta . . . Long the capital of British India, Calcutta is still the commercial metropolis of modern India. It has a population of well over 5,000,000 and is a huge, sprawling, noisy city, teeming with life. The nerve center is Dalhousie Square, where tall, imposing buildings, Government offices and mercantile houses stand in a quadrangle around the placid waters of the reservoir. But the center of attraction is the famous Chowringhee, the beautiful wide avenue flanked on one side by shops, cinemas and fashionable restaurants, and on the other by the Maidan, which stretches as a vast expanse of green dotted with reservoirs, monuments and clusters of trees. Here are the playing fields where crowds gather to watch a football match. Here too are the Eden Gardens, famed as the cricketer's paradise.

Rising from the Maidan and overlooking the Chowringhee is the marble Victoria Memorial, built by the British. In its galleries are many objects of interest relating to British-Indian history, historical documents and paintings. The Hooghly, like the Thames, has lost some of its natural beauty due to the smoke of the factories that sprawl on its banks, but it is still appealing. Dakshineshwar Temple, where the great saint and yogi of the nineteenth century, Ramakrishna Paramahamsa, lived and Belur Math, the monastery founded by his great disciple, Swami Vivekanand, are both on the banks of this river. A little farther away are the Botanical Gardens, which are well worth a visit. Among the sights in these gardens is an ancient banyan tree which has so spread itself that several hundred people can sit in its shade. Connecting the two banks of the river is the new Howrah Bridge, the third largest cantilever bridge in the world.

Among other sights of interest are Fort William, built by Lord Clive in 1773; the Zoological Gardens; the Museum, the biggest in India; the Jain Temple, standing in a fascinating garden; and the Kalighat Temple, the oldest temple of Calcutta, which was there long before the city was founded. Trained guides are available at the

Government Tourist Office, 13 Old Court House Street. Several companies offer sightseeing tours.

Delhi ... Delhi's most ancient sites and monuments, dating from India's Epic Age, emphasize the dynamic change in modern India's way of life and thought. The city has continuously been the seat of Imperial power since the tenth century. Here, many cities have risen and fallen; only their ruins mark the site where they once stood. Old Delhi has many architectural masterpieces. The Red Fort, built 300 years ago, dominates the city and stands as a symbol of Mughal glory. Inside it are the relics of what was once the Imperial Palace of Shah Jahan, builder of the Taj Mahal. From the Fort to the Fatehpuri Mosque runs the Chandni Chowk, once famous as the richest street in the world. A little to the south towers the famous mosque, the Jama Masjid, one of the largest mosques in the world and one of the noblest buildings in India. South and southwest of the city are the Tomb of Humayun, built in the sixteenth century of red sandstone inlaid with white marble; the Cyclopean ruins of thirteenth-century Tughlakabad, the capital of warrior kings, with its massive fort and the founder's imposing tomb; and the Qutb Minar, dating from the twelfth century, another tower of victory, beautifully fashioned out of 700-year-old red sandstone, regarded as one of the most perfect towers of the world. Nearby is the famous rustproof Iron Pillar, dating from the fourth century A.D. Other points of interest are Isa Khan's tomb (fifteenth century in style); Nizamuddin, the burial place of saints, princes and poets for over three centuries; Nawab Safdar Jung's tomb, the last moghul monument of note (eighteenth century); Haus Khas, fascinating ruins of a once-important university, and a fourteenth-century water reservoir.

New Delhi ... with its symmetrical buildings, tree-lined avenues and spacious parks, is a planned city. It has a circular Parliament House and an imposing Central Secretariat, which stands at the approaches to the residence of the President of the Republic. On the right bank of the Yamuna is a hallowed spot—Rajghat, where the body of Mahatma Gandhi was cremated in 1948. The samadhi has become a national shrine. The modern Lakshmi Narayan Temple, opened by Mahatma Gandhi in 1937, and Jantar Mantar, an observatory with a unique set of 200-year-old-stone astronomical instruments, are also of interest. Trained guides are available at the Government of India Tourist Office at 88 Janpath.

Eastern India ... Santiniketan, 93 miles northwest of Calcutta, is the home of famous Viswa Bharati, the international university founded by the poet, Rabindranath Tagore. Darjeeling is a Himalayan hill station from which Mt. Kanchenjunga, the third highest peak in the world, and sometimes Mt. Everest, can be seen. Bhubaneswar, a city of ancient temples, is the new capital of Orissa. Nearby are the Jain and Buddhist rock-cut caves of Khandagiri and Udaygiri and Asoka's rock edict (second century B.C.) at Dhauli. Puri is well known for the Jagannath Temple and the annual car festival held in June or July. Fifty-one miles from Puri is Konarak, famous for the Sun Temple.

Nepal . . . The country of Nepal has recently become open for tourists. It offers such spectacular views as the all-in-one view of seven or eight of the highest mountains in the world and many other attractions. Khatmandu, the Capital of Nepal, can be reached by air from Calcutta, Patna and Delhi.

Northern India . . . South of Delhi, about 4 hours by road or rail through extremely interesting country, is Agra, the city of the Taj Mahal. Besides this fabulous edifice of extraordinary beauty, other important sights are the Agra Fort, Emperor Akbar's magnificent mausoleum at Sikandra, the tomb of Itmad-ud-Daulah and Dayal Bagh. Twenty-six miles from Agra on the way to Jaipur is Fatehpur Sikri, the abandoned Mughal capital city of palaces, which is in an excellent state of preservation. All of these date back to the sixteenth and seventeenth centuries. Benares (Varanasi), halfway between Delhi and Calcutta, is a Hindu pilgrim center. It is also the home of a famous university. About 6 miles from Benares is Sarnath, one of the great Buddhist centers, where the Buddha preached his first sermon. The pink city of Jaipur, an hour's flight from Delhi, is the capital of Rajasthan, in the heart of India's princely states. Colorful scenes, picturesque vistas of elegant buildings, dream-palace rooms, elephant and camel processions—it's a page out of an Eastern fairy tale. Amber, seven miles away, is a picturesque medieval capital containing many interesting architectural ruins.

About 150 miles northwest of New Delhi lies the much-publicized new capital of the Indian state of Punjab at Chandigarh. The first phase of this superbly designed city has risen out of the jungle at the foot of the Sivalikh range in only two years and represents the collaboration of some of the world's foremost architects, including Le Corbusier of France.

Kashmir . . . A tourist's paradise. The health resorts of Kashmir are among the most picturesque of the world. Pahalgam, in the center of the Liddar Valley, has excellent camping sites. Gulmarg, 8,700 feet above sea level, is the center of Kashmir's winter sports. Srinagar, the summer capital, like Venice, is built on the waterfront, on which float quaint houseboats designed and furnished for comfort and rest. Shikaras (light taxiboats) convey tourists over the lakes and bring vendors of daily necessities, curios and handicrafts, for which Kashmir is famous, to the houseboats. The beautiful terraced gardens, laid out in the sixteenth and seventeenth centuries by the great Mughals, are another attraction in this playground of the East. The permit to visit Kashmir can be obtained from the Director, Government of India Tourist Office, in Delhi, Bombay, Calcutta or Madras, or from the Ministry of Defence, New Delhi.

Southern India . . . Madras has a beautiful beach on the Bay of Bengal, a good museum and attractive public buildings. Thirty-seven miles from Madras is the seventh-century seaport of Mahabalipuram, famous for its seven rock-cut pagodas. Madurai to the south is noted for the great Meenakshi Temple. Octacamund is known as the "Queen of Hill Stations." The enchanting Brindavan Gardens are only 13 miles

What could be a more exciting adventure than a trip by elephant through the jungle of India. This party is enjoying a stop for lunch.

In New Delhi, the Lakshmi Narayan Temple, a modern blend of Eastern and Western styles of architecture, was opened by Mahatma Gandhi in 1937.

from Mysore. Nearby is Srirangapatnam, the former capital of Mysore State, with Tippu Sultan's fort, mosque, and palace. Belur and Halebid, about 120 miles west of Mysore, are famous for their elaborately sculptured temples. Hampi is the ruined capital of the mighty Vijayanagar Empire. Jog Falls is one of the highest waterfalls in the world. Trivandrum has a lovely beach, a famous art gallery and museum, and is well known for its ivory work. Ernakulam, across the harbor from Cochin, is famous for its backwaters, fringed by Hindu, Moslem, Christian and Jewish settlements. At the Periyar Game Sanctuary are wild animals in their natural surroundings. Kanya Kumari (Cape Comorin) is the southernmost tip of India, where the waters of the Arabian Sea, the Bay of Bengal, and the Indian Ocean meet.

Bombay... Known as Mumbai hundreds of years ago, this city on the Arabian Sea is called the Gateway to India. There is an actual gateway built on the waterfront to commemorate the visit of King George V and Queen Mary in 1911. It is now used for ceremonial landings and departures. The island of Bombay is one of the most important centers in India and is linked with the world by its modern harbor, the Santa Cruz airport, and good overseas communication. Since the division of India and Pakistan in 1947, when many Hindus moved from Pakistan, Bombay has grown rapidly to a population of four and one-half million. Reported to be the most cosmopolitan city in the East, Bombay has much appeal for the tourist. Places of interest include the Prince of Wales Museum, a stately, domed building with sections featuring arts, archaeology and natural history; the Jehangir Art Gallery; the Raja Bai Tower of the Bombay University Library, with a splendid view of the city; Marine Drive, in the modern residential area, leading to Malabar Hill, which faces the Arabian Sea. The view from here, popularly called "The Pearl Necklace," is magnificent—especially at night, when it reminds you of the French Riviera. The Hanging Gardens on the slopes of Malabar Hill are most attractive. The Terrace Garden is noted for its fine example of topiary art—the trees and shrubs have been trained and trimmed into the shapes of a variety of animals. The Mahalaxmi Temple, dedicated to Laxmi, goddess of wealth and plenty, is a popular place of Hindu pilgrimage. Near the temple is a Moslem shrine built 500 yards from the mainland on rocks which are completely submerged at high tide.

Other points of interest in Bombay: The Mahalaxmi Race Course, one of the finest in the East, where races are held on week-ends and holidays, from October to March; the Victoria Gardens with the Bombay Zoo, 20 minutes by car from the city; Crawford Market for fresh fruits, vegetables and fish on Dadabhoy Naorojee Road, with dozens of nearby shops selling everything from pots and pans to expensive jewelry; the Pherozshah Mehta Road and the Colaba Causeway, also shopping areas for Indian goods. Most shops have fixed prices, but bargaining goes on in pavement-shops. It is advisable to go out shopping with someone who knows the city.

Near Crawford Market is a fascinating part of Bombay, with Hindu and Jain temples and Moslem mosques in the midst of narrow lanes and teeming with people of varied origin—Parsees, Gujaratis, Maharashtrians, Tamils, Malayalis, Goans, Sikhs, Bengalis and others. Each retains his regional individuality of dress, language and customs.

SOURCES OF FURTHER INFORMATION . . . Government of India Tourist Offices are located in Calcutta, Delhi, Bombay, Madras, Agra, Varanasi (Benares), Jaipur, Darjeeling, Bangalore, Cochin, Aurangabad and Bhopal. Approved guides are also available at these offices. In New York the Government of India Tourist Office is located at 19 East 49th Street and in San Francisco at 685 Market Street. There are Pan American offices at 42 Choringhee Road, Calcutta (Tel. 442651), the Imperial Hotel, New Delhi (Tel. 48717, 48172), the Taj Mahal Hotel, Bombay (Tel. 35304).

INDONESIA

WEATHER IN JAKARTA—Lat. S6°10′—Alt. 25′

Temp.	JAN.	FEB.	MAR.	APR.	MAY	JUNE	JULY	AUG.	SEPT.	OCT.	NOV.	DEC.
Low	74°	74°	74°	75°	75°	74°	73°	73°	73°	74°	74°	74°
High	83°	83°	85°	86°	87°	86°	86°	87°	87°	87°	87°	85°
Average	79°	79°	80°	81°	81°	81°	80°	80°	80°	81°	81°	80°
Days of Rain	20	19	16	12	9	8	6	4	6	9	13	16

LOCATION ... This group of more than 3,000 islands extends along the Equator between Asia and Australia south of Malaya.

POPULATION ... Estimated at 80,000,000.

SIZE ... The islands are spread over an area as big as Europe, although the land area of 735,865 square miles is only about one-fifth its size.

GOVERNMENT ... A republic.

CAPITAL ... Jakarta, population about 3,000,000.

HOW TO GET THERE ... By Pan American Clipper, via Singapore, to Jakarta. Elapsed time counting stopovers about 65 hours from San Francisco.

ACCOMMODATIONS ... Hotels in Jakarta are very limited. The bigger hotels, such as *Transaera, Hotel des Indes* and the *Darma Nirmala* are often not available. People traveling alone may have to share rooms. Rates are $8 to $10 American Plan plus 10% service.

ARTS ... Don't miss visiting Jakarta's Museum, the finest of its kind in Southeast Asia—a wonderful ethnographical collection of arts and crafts from all the islands and old Chinese porcelains.

BALLET ... The world famous Balinese dances and ballet on special occasions.

BANKS ... The Chartered Bank. Nederlandsche Handel Maatschappi (Factory); Nederlandsche Handelsbank; Bank Indonesia; Escompto; Bank Negara Indonesia and Hong Kong & Sjanghai Bank. Cash travelers' checks at banks or hotels.

CIGARETTES AND TOBACCO...American brands, though expensive, are available.

CLIMATE...The East monsoon lasts from April to September. The West monsoon, which lasts from October to March, has more rainfall but it often comes as short tropical downpours.

CLUBS...Sports Clubs, Box Club and Wisma Nusantara are all private, but, if introduced, tourists may visit them.

COMMUNICATIONS...Telephone and cable communications are good. Airmail to the U.S.A., Rps. 3.50.

CURRENCY...The Indonesian Rupiah is the monetary unit. One United States dollar is worth Ind. Rps. 11.40.

CUSTOMS REGULATIONS AND DOCUMENTS REQUIRED FOR UNITED STATES CITIZENS...You will need a passport, visa and certificates for smallpox, cholera and typhoid. Duty-free allowances are: 200 cigarettes, 50 cigars or 500 grams of tobacco, 2 bottles of liquor, 10 Indonesian Rupiahs. Be sure your foreign currency is properly recorded to avoid difficulty in taking it out. You cannot reconvert from Rupiahs on leaving.

DRUG STORES...Only European type drug stores with very few and expensive American products.

ELECTRIC CURRENT...110-125 volts, 50 cycles, most places.

FAUNA...Varying with the island, there are tigers and panthers, elephants, single and twin-horned rhinoceros, monkeys, orangutans and gibbons, wild bear, the unique dwarf deer, crocodiles and giant lizards up to 9 feet long. Parrots, birds of paradise and the curious casuaris bird.

FLORA...Flowers grow in great profusion, notably the fragrant frangipani, scarlet hibiscus, many varieties of orchids; banyan trees, coconut and bamboo. The Botanical Gardens in Bogor are interesting.

FOOD...European, Indonesian and Chinese foods are served in the big restaurants. Native dishes include gado-gado (a mixture of all kinds of vegetables with peanut sauce and rÿsttafel). Mangoes, mangistans, papayas, bananas, pineapples and djeroeks (oranges) are among local fruits. Milk is available in the cities and safe to drink.

LANGUAGE...Indonesian is the national language, derived from Malay. English is spoken by hotel personnel and in the restaurants.

LAUNDRY AND DRY CLEANING...Readily available but quality and speed are not the best.

LIQUOR...In the big cities most foreign brands are available, but expensive. Bars are open from about 10:00 A.M. until midnight.

MEDICAL FACILITIES...No American hospitals, but fully equipped hospitals with good doctors and surgeons in all major cities.

PHOTOGRAPHY...Equipment and film are available, developing only fair.

RELIGION...The national religion is Islam although Buddhism and Brahmanism are still prevalent in some areas. Owing to the Dutch influence there are also many Catholics and Protestants.

RESTAURANTS...*Capitole Restaurant, Chez Mario, Ambassa-*

dor (air-conditioned), *Diplomat, Hotel des Indes, Nusantara, Airport Restaurant* are the best for European food. There are also good restaurants for Chinese food.

SHOPS AND STORES ... The main shopping centers are Nusantara and Pasar Baru. Downtown "Chinatown Glodok" is also attractive. Most shops stay open from 8:00 A.M. until noon and from 4:00 P.M. until sundown.

SPECTATOR SPORTS ... Football, tennis, badminton, swimming.

SPORTS ... Hockey, golf, yachting, hunting. *See* CLUBS.

TIPPING ... Only in hotels.

TRANSPORTATION ... Airline, rail, taxis and auto rentals.

WATER ... Water is safe to drink.

WHAT TO BUY ... Javanese and Balinese woodcarvings. Silverware and sarongs. Alligator and snakeskin goods, paintings.

WHAT TO WEAR ... One should wear very lightweight clothing.

WHERE TO GO—SIGHTSEEING ...

Bogor ... An hour's drive from Jakarta, has a famous botanical garden with hundreds of thousands of varieties of tropical vegetation. Thirty miles from Bogor is the Puntjak area (4,800 feet with invigorating climate). It's Jakarta's playground, studded with small hotels, restaurants and swimming pools.

Bandung ... The capital of West Java, a half hour by air from Jakarta, is one of the most delightful cities of the Far East (population 800,000), beautifully laid out on a high plateau surrounded by mountains covered with rice fields, chinchona and tea plantations and forests. The local people (Sundanese) are noted for their infectious gaiety and colorful dress. Visit one of the markets and see the remarkable building which houses the technical school of the University of Indonesia. Among the excellent hotels are the *Savoy Homan* and the *Preanger*. The 6,300-foot Tangkuban Prahu volcano is nearby.

Island of Bali ... "The Paradise of the Pacific," 3½ hours by air from Jakarta, this densely populated little island (the size of Delaware) has all the charm and spectacular beauty associated with it. The 10,000-foot Gunung Agung (Peak of Bali) is the island's Mt. Fuji. Mount Batur is the only active volcano. Bali-Hinduism, the important factor in the people's lives, is evident in their wide variety of colorful ceremonies and celebrations, and the omnipresent temples.

Djogjakarta (Djogja) and Solo ... Are the most typically "Javanese" cities of Java, known for their exquisite silverware and batik. Visit the magnificent Borobudur, one of the world's greatest Buddhist sanctuaries, twenty-four miles from Djogja. Two miles from Borobudur is the Mendut temple, which contains an indescribably beautiful statue of a seated Buddha, flanked by Boddhisatvas.

SOURCES OF FURTHER INFORMATION ... Maclaine, Watson and Co., N.V., agents for Pan American at the Hotel des Indes (Tel. Gambir 3745). Also the Nitour (National and International Tourist Agencies) at the Djalan Madjapahit Nr. 2.

In New York, the Indonesian Consulate at 5 East 68th Street.

JAPAN

WEATHER IN TOKYO—Lat. N35°42'—Alt. 30'

Temp.	JAN.	FEB.	MAR.	APR.	MAY	JUNE	JULY	AUG.	SEPT.	OCT.	NOV.	DEC.
Low	30°	31°	36°	47°	54°	63°	69°	72°	66°	54°	43°	33°
High	47°	47°	53°	63°	70°	76°	83°	85°	79°	69°	60°	51°
Average	39°	39°	45°	55°	62°	70°	76°	79°	73°	62°	52°	42°
Days of Rain	7	8	13	14	14	16	15	13	17	14	10	7

LOCATION ... Japan consists of 4 islands and over 500 small islets which lie in the North Pacific Ocean off the coast of China.

CHARACTERISTICS ... Japan is welcoming tourists, who have a wonderful opportunity to see the reconstruction of this war-torn country plus fascinating glimpses of Japanese culture, arts and architecture. Japan has always been a magnet for Americans for its customs and scenery. The people are eager for friendly relationships with the Western world. The Japanese Government is spending large sums of money developing and encouraging the already prosperous tourist industry. The trips permitted to tourists are packed with wonderful things to see and do.

POPULATION ... 92,000,000, according to the official statistics of October 1958, roughly half the population of the United States.

SIZE ... A narrow barrier 1,300 miles long, roughly the shape of California but slightly smaller in area (147,690 square miles). Few places in Japan are far removed from the mountains or the sea.

CAPITAL ... Tokyo, population 8,471,637.

GOVERNMENT ... a constitutional monarchy ruled over by an Emperor and a Cabinet. There is a Parliament of two chambers.

HOW TO GET THERE ... By Pan American Clipper from United States West Coast via Honolulu to Tokyo, about 24½ hours (elapsed time). Tokyo is on Pan American's Round-the-World Route. By ship the journey from the United States West Coast takes about 15 days.

ACCOMMODATIONS ... There are "Western style" hotels (which the average tourist will prefer) as well as some of Japanese style which are comfortable and good. In Tokyo there are the famous *Imperial Hotel,* the ultra-modern *Nikkatsu Hotel, Hotel Tokyo, Hotel Teito, Marunouchi Hotel, Tokyo Station Hotel* and the *Kokusai Kanko,* all located within a half-mile radius of the city's shopping center. The *Daiichi Hotel* and *Shiba Park Hotel* are just a few minutes' walk from it. Rates range from about $5 to $9 a day single, $9.50 to $12 double, European Plan. Be sure to have confirmed reservations on arrival.

ARTS ... Japanese art is too vast a subject to discuss in detail. Japanese paintings and sculptures are known the world over and the Japanese influence on Western painters has been enormous. The Japanese Art Academy in Tokyo holds an annual exhibit each year in the autumn. Nihon Bijutsu-in (Institute of Japanese Art) holds a private exhibition, as does the Nika-kai, or modern group. The Tokyo National Museum, which has branches in Nara and Kyoto, houses a wonderful collection of Japanese art, sculpture, carvings and other treasures of Japanese and Oriental culture. The Tokyo Metropolitan Art Gallery at Ueno is the principal and largest exhibition hall. The recently opened National Museum of Modern Art and the Bridgestone Art Gallery, with their year-round exhibitions, are conveniently situated in the heart of the shopping district. Numerous art exhibitions are held throughout the year at various locations, while group and one-man exhibitions are held at the city's leading department stores from time to time. Many national treasures and priceless works of art can be seen by the public at the temples and shrines in Japan, especially in the Kyoto-Nara district. Also interesting to see are the Meiji Memorial Picture Gallery in Meiji Park, with interesting paintings of historical events, and the Folkcraft Museum at Komaba, Tokyo, which has on exhibit an extensive collection of indigenous folkcraft. The Kamakura Museum of Modern Art at Kamakura, one hour by electric train from Tokyo, is visited by many.

BALLET ... There are several local ballet troupes which hold performances from time to time. Western ballet enjoys immense popularity among the Japanese. This has been further stimulated by the performances given here by visiting foreign artists.

BANKS ... In Tokyo, Bank of Japan, First National City Bank, Chase Manhattan Bank, Bank of America, Hong Kong and Shanghai Banking Corp., The Chartered Bank, Bank of Tokyo and Netherlands Trading Society.

CALENDAR OF HOLIDAYS ... Festivals are a part of the heart of Japan. Of national importance are: the Doll's Festival, March 3; the Boy's Festival, May 5; the Star Festival, July 7; the Shichi-go-san Festival, November 15. Other traditional events include: New Year's Celebration, January 1 to 3; Bean Throwing Ceremony, February 4; Floral Festival, April 8; the Feast of the Lanterns, honoring the dead, July 13 to 15.

CIGARETTES AND TOBACCO ... Some American brands of

cigarettes are available at about 35 cents a pack. Cigars are available in limited supply. Customs allow 200 cigarettes or 50 cigars or ½ lb. of tobacco.

CLIMATE ... The climate of Japan is similar to the Middle West in the United States, although it seldom gets either as hot or as cold. However, you'll need furs and heavy overcoats in winter and light clothes for summer. Japan is well worth a visit any time of the year, but spring and autumn are the best times.

CLUBS ... Rotary and Lions Clubs are very active in Japan and it is possible to attend in all the main cities.

COMMON COURTESIES AND LOCAL CUSTOMS ... There are many different customs in Japan. Automobile traffic keeps to the left. You must take your shoes off before entering a Japanese-style hotel, private home or temple. The Japanese never use soap in the bathtub. The custom is to lather themselves thoroughly, then rinse themselves, after which they enter the tub or big open bath, and soak themselves in the hot water.

COMMUNICATIONS ... Airmail, radio-telephone and international telegraph service.

CURRENCY ... The monetary unit is the yen. The rate of exchange is 360 yen to one United States dollar. Foreign currency is not legal tender in the stores or hotels, but can be readily exchanged at the banks for Japanese currency. No yen may be brought into or out of Japan but there is no limit on the amount of foreign currency that may be brought in. Only bank notes amounting to $50 or more must be declared on arrival. A maximum amount of yen equivalent to U.S. $100 may be converted back into foreign currency, provided it can be shown that the yen was acquired through proper channels. These conditions are subject to change, so check with your travel agent or the Pan American office.

CUSTOMS REGULATIONS AND DOCUMENTS REQUIRED FOR UNITED STATES CITIZENS ... Passport and except for visits of less than 72 hours, a visa. Vaccination certificate for smallpox for return to the United States. Cholera and typhus vaccination required of visitors from infected local areas. Chinese-type articles are either prohibited or require a Certificate of Origin for entry into the United States. Consult the nearest U.S. Consul for latest requirements. Regulations change frequently, so check with Pan American in advance.

DRUG STORES ... Aside from many Japanese drug stores, there are the fully stocked American Pharmacy and the Rexall Drug Co., both located in Tokyo, where you can obtain American products.

ELECTRIC CURRENT ... 100 volts, A.C., in local hotels and homes. There is no need to use special transformer plugs.

FAUNA ... Boar, deer, pheasant, quail, snipe, wild geese.

FLORA ... Cherry and plum blossoms, tea, persimmons, loquat, figs, and thousands of flowers including the lotus, wisteria, azalea, camellia, chrysanthemum (which forms the crest for the Imperial House). Japan is the land of flowers, and flower arrangement is taught to all its young girls. In Japan it is a high art, called *ikebana*. There are special *ikebana* classes for foreigners.

FOOD... Rice, as everyone knows, is the staple food. The Japanese cook this in a different manner than is generally done in the West, resulting in a much more glutinous, fragrant dish. Daintiness is the characteristic of a truly Japanese meal. Japanese cooks take great pride in having the table and the food look appetizing and attractive. Although it is possible to get Western food in all the cities, the main native dishes to try are *sukiyaki*, which is a sort of beef stew cooked at the table; *tempura*, which is fresh prawns deep-fried; and *chawanmushi*, which is chicken, pork and beef steamed with egg custard in a bowl. Fresh raw fish, broiled mushrooms, dried seaweed, bean curd are other native foods which are worth trying. Green tea is almost the national drink. *Kabayaki*, or broiled eels, is considered a great delicacy.

GAMBLING... There is horse racing (under Government control) from March to July and August to December. Tokyo's race track is the Fuchu race course in the suburbs. The Yodo race course at Kyoto is the next largest in the country. Bicycle racing, also under Government control, is a year-round attraction.

LANGUAGE... Generally speaking, tourists will find that they will have no language difficulty in traveling throughout Japan.

LAUNDRY AND DRY CLEANING... Good. Readily available and of good quality. Service is fast; where laundry is concerned, it is possible to get overnight service; dry cleaning takes about two days.

LIQUOR... *Sake*, a rice wine, is the national drink. Japanese beer is generally recognized to be as good as any other beer produced. Other spirits are readily obtainable at all the leading hotels, bars and restaurants. One bottle of liquor may be brought into Japan.

MEDICAL FACILITIES... There are several hospitals in Tokyo as well as fully qualified American and British doctors.

MOTION PICTURES... There are motion picture theaters which show American and European films besides the native productions, which run over 250 a year. The *Yuraku-za Hibiya Gekijo, Tokyo Gekijo, Marunouchi-Nikkatsu, Piccadilly Theater* are some of the important theaters in Tokyo showing pictures with original sound tracks. The *Imperial Theater* shows Cinerama films.

MUSIC... The Japanese are very much interested in all types of "Western" music. Five symphony orchestras, four of them in Tokyo, hold regular subscription concerts in season. The NHK Symphony Orchestra of the Japanese Broadcasting Corporation is especially popular. Choral groups give performances of religious works from time to time; instrumental and vocal recitals are daily occurrences. Frequent visits by foreign artists of international stature have enabled the Japanese to become acquainted with the highest present standards of artistry. The Fujiwara Opera Company, one of several, is the pioneer Japanese opera troupe and has appeared in the United States with its production of *Madame Butterfly*. Popular dances and jazz bands are numerous. Indigenous Japanese music, which is constructed on a tone scale different from that of Occidental music, may seem enigmatic to the average Westerner, but the skill of the instrumental performers may still be appreciated.

NIGHT CLUBS AND CABARETS... There are cafés and bars, but no night clubs as we know them. Some of the large hotels have dance floors and bands. And there are dance halls with Japanese taxi dancers. *Ochaya*, or tea houses, cater to hundreds of guests and the *geisha*, or professional entertainer, dances for the guests in what really amounts to a ritual dance.

PHOTOGRAPHY... Both black-and-white and color film are manufactured locally, while American brands may be obtained at leading stores. Prices for Japanese films are roughly equivalent to the film prices in America, but imported film may cost 30 to 40 per cent more. Black-and-white film processing service is available almost anywhere, many shops offering 24-hour service. The puzzling DPE sign hung out on many shops signifies that developing, printing and enlarging is done there.

RELIGION... There are about 24 Christian sects in Japan, including Roman Catholic, Presbyterian, Methodist, Episcopal and Congregational churches. The three major religions are Buddhism, Shintoism and Christianity.

RESTAURANTS... All major hotels have restaurants that serve international food. Besides these, the following are among the best in Tokyo: the *Tokyo Kaikan Prunier* for seafood, the *Suehiro Steak House, Grill Rossini* for steaks and chops, *Hana-cho, Sukiya-ro* for *sukiyaki* dinners, *Ten-ichi* for *tempura* dishes, *Sun-ya* for Chinese food. Prices vary widely, but in general range from about $3 to $5.

SHOPS AND STORES... Japan is a shopper's paradise. Ginza Street in Tokyo is the main shopping center. Principal and largest stores are: Mikimoto Pearl Store; Mitsukoshi, Matsuzakaya, Shirokiya, and Takashimaya, all department stores. There are, of course, many small shops.

SPECTATOR SPORTS... *Sumo,* Japanese wrestling, *judo* exhibits, baseball (tremendously popular—games are played at the stadium at Meiji Shrine grounds and the Korakuen Stadium), horse racing, swimming meets, football, tennis matches and archery. There are numerous annual meetings and tournaments.

SPORTS... There are golf, tennis, yachting, swimming, skiing, hunting, skating, fishing and bowling in various parts of the country.

THEATERS... Japan's native theatrical art is centuries old. The theater in Japan is divided into Noh, Kabuki and puppet drama. The Noh, originally a religious dance in the fourteenth century, developed into a highly stylized dramatic form dealing with historical and Buddhist subjects. It is the classical drama of Japan. The actors wear masks and elaborate costumes as they perform one of the 242 Noh plays which survive. There are six schools of Noh actors in Japan. The Kabuki—unlike the Noh, which was for the aristocracy—was for the people. Kabuki plays are similar to European dramas except that dialogue is accompanied by musical instruments or an orchestra, and all the women's roles are played by men. You can see Kabuki at the Kabuki Theater. An all-puppet theater, the Bunrakuza, is at Osaka. In season the Cherry Dance presentations at the theaters are worth seeing. There is modern Japanese theater, too; revues and light opera are popular and who could resist the Takarazuka Girls Troupe?

TIME . . . 17 hours later than United States Pacific Standard Time.

TIPPING . . . A bit less than at home. No tipping to taxi drivers.

TRANSPORTATION . . . There are modern tramways, streetcars, motor buses, and subways running through downtown Tokyo and Osaka. Suburban districts and nearby scenic spots are linked with the city by a network of high-speed electric trains. Taxis as well as cars for hire, are readily obtainable. Rates are approximately the same as those in the United States. The Japanese National Railways and Japan Air Lines operate throughout the country.

WATER . . . Generally speaking, the water of Japan is perfectly safe to drink, but it is recommended that visitors use their own judgment and act accordingly.

WHAT TO BUY . . . Tortoise shell from Nagasaki, porcelain and cloisonné from Nagoya, lacquerware from Kyoto, silk, cultured pearls, embroidered kimonos and obis, pottery, china, ceramics, Japanese prints and woodcuts, wonderful silk damasks and a host of other souvenirs and things which only the Japanese can make. Tourists in possession of a "Record of Cash in hand and Purchase of Commodities Tax Exempt for Export" form, which may be obtained on entry to Japan, may buy the following articles free of tax at shops designated by the local revenue offices: pearls and articles decorated with pearls; articles made of precious metal or metals; ivory and cloisonné ware; furs; cameras, including parts or accessories; binocular and monocular telescopes, including the carrying cases; articles used for room decoration; lighters and other smoking articles provided they are made of metal or lacquer work; ceramic ware; personal ornaments made of metal or lacquer work; woodblock prints; dolls.

WHAT TO WEAR . . . Let the season of the year determine this. Tokyo is roughly like Washington, D.C. Japan as a whole is like the Middle West. In winter you'll need furs, men will need overcoats. In spring, lighter weight clothes and in summer, cottons, light silks, sports clothes. Be sure to take a raincoat. You won't need evening clothes unless you are being entertained by very important diplomatic society.

WHERE TO GO—SIGHTSEEING . . .

Tokyo . . . Everything is so different, so novel, that just going out into the streets of Tokyo is a sightseeing tour in itself. You will want to see the Imperial Palace even though the inner enclosure is not open to the public. Walk or drive through Hibiya Park opposite the Imperial Hotel where the azaleas bloom in May and the chrysanthemums in November. In Shiba Park is the famous Zojo-ji Temple and 1,092 foot Tokyo Tower with television antenna and observation decks. The Palace Gardens, just a short distance from the temple, are quite lovely. Ueno Park, noted for its cherry blossoms, contains the

National Museum, the Zoological Gardens, the Metropolitan Art Gallery, the Imperial Library and a monument to General Grant, of all people. You will want to go shopping on Ginza Street, the main shopping thoroughfare. Sightseeing buses with English-speaking guides run twice daily and take you through the most fascinating and exciting parts of this metropolis.

Side Trips... There are packaged tours which cover the parts of Japan which are most interesting to foreign tourists. Starting at Tokyo you drive to Fuji-Hakone-Izu National Park and Atami Hot Springs Resort. You pass through Kamakura, which is the site of the shrine of the Great Buddha, or *Daibutsú*. You may climb inside the Buddha to shoulder level. A short distance from the Buddha is Hachiman Shrine, one of the oldest temples in Japan, located in a grove of cherry trees. If you are touring you will proceed to Hakone Mountains to the *Fujiya* Hotel, one of Japan's most elegant hotels at Miyanoshita, high in the mountains, or to the *Hakone Hotel* on the shores of Lake Hakone, from there on to Atami over the Ten Province Pass, from which you will get a wonderful view of Mt. Fujiyama. The *Atami Hotel* is good here.

The third day of the tour takes you by train to Kyoto, known as the "classic" city of Japan. The fabulous shrines and temples, "Teapot Lane," the many bazaars and shops are famous. The *Miyako Hotel* overlooks the city from a hill. The *Kyoto Station Hotel* is located squarely in the city's shopping district. You will visit the grounds of the old Imperial Palace and the Higashi-Hongan-ji, one of the most elaborate Buddhist Temples in the country. Heian Shrine in Okazaki Park is a famous Shinto shrine set in the midst of formal gardens. Once a year, this is the site of festivals, and endless processions of Shintoist, dressed in costumes depicting various periods in history pay homage there. On the fifth day, you leave Kyoto for Nara, which is considered the cradle of Japanese art and culture. Here is the *Shoso-in*, whose treasures are displayed very occasionally in Tokyo. Here, too, are wonderful examples of early Japanese architecture, the *Todaiji Temple* with its Hall of the Great Buddha, largest wooden structure in the world, housing the Great Buddha, which is over 53 feet high; *Horyuji Temple*, built in 607 A.D. containing many art treasures over a thousand years old, and many other unusual sights attract the tourist. You will see Nara Park, where tame deer roam at will, and wander down the vermilion corridors of the *Kasuga Shrine*, founded in 768 A.D. The *Nara Hotel* is the place here.

From Nara, you go by electric train to Osaka, site of the annual spring International Music and Arts Festival, where Shin-saibashi, the city's shopping and amusement center, with its colorful bazaars, will enchant you. Osaka Castle, with walls formed of gigantic pieces of granite, and tiny bridges spanning the moat, is amazing. The Shitennoji Temple and the Temmangu Shrine are here and you'll find a theater, the Bunrakuza, devoted entirely to puppet shows. The *New Osaka Hotel, International Fair Hotel* and the *Osaka Grand Hotel* (double room with bath $10 and up) offer fine Western-style accom-

Geisha girls, such as these in traditional dress photographed in front of the Toji Pagoda, Kyoto, entertain tourists with ritual dances in Japanese tea houses.

A farm girl in peasant costume is photographed here in the garden of the old temple of Ohara in Kyoto.

In Honshu, about 70 miles southwest of Tokyo, Mt. Fuji, Japan's highest peak, rises 12,388 feet in an almost perfect cone.

modations. This tour takes about 5 days. But you can arrange to stay longer at any place you particularly like.

Another place of interest to go from Tokyo is Nikko, about 90 miles north of the capital. This is a mountain resort famous for its scenery and its 300-year-old Toshogu Shrine. The entire area is a national park. Just a few miles from Nikko at Lake Chuzenji are the Kegon Waterfalls. Here is the best trout fishing in Japan. There are good bathing and swimming, too. You will see the red-lacquered, crescent-shaped sacred bridge, which crosses the Daiya River. Here there is a five-storied pagoda considered to be the finest in Japan. The carvings of the world famous "Three Monkeys" are on the Sacred Stable beyond the Niomon Gate here. See also the Yomeimon Gate. The *Nikko-Kanaya Hotel* has a swimming pool and surprisingly enough, a skating rink.

You may go to Kobe, on the Inland Sea, 20 miles west of Osaka, a city which is backed by the Rokko Mountain Range. This city was in ruins after the war but is rapidly being rebuilt. Within half an hour of Kobe are the picturesque Nunobiki Waterfalls. You may drive to the summit of Mt. Rokko back of the city and play golf on an 18-hole golf course at the very top.

Take a train to Miyajima (Shrine Island), an excellent summer resort 12 miles southwest of Hiroshima, noted for its cherry blossoms and for its shrine built on supports running into the sea. The Main Shrine is connected with subsidiaries by galleries which stretch over the sea so that at high tide the Shrine seems to be afloat. Sacred dances are performed here by Shrine maidens. *Iwaso Inn* and *Kamefuku Inn* are the places to stay. You may, if you like, now go to Hiroshima, the atom-bombed city. There are guides available to take you on a conducted sightseeing tour.

You may also visit Nagoya, about 75 miles east of Kyoto, with its ruins of an ancient castle and a golden dolphin surmounting the donjon. Here is Atsuta Jingu, the second largest shrine in Japan. This is the center of Japanese porcelain-making, and the Noritake chinaware factory may be visited. This city is noted for its porcelain and cloisonné wares. The *Hotel New Nagoya* and *Nagoya Kanko Hotel* are the two most modern hotels. Japan's largest national shrine, Ise Jingu, is an hour and a half away by electric train. Gifu, about fifty minutes away by electric train, is famous for its cormorant fishing on the River Nagara. At Gifu there is the Western-style *Nagaragawa Hotel* on the very banks of the river, besides many fine Japanese inns. The places mentioned above are open to tourists. Trips range from 3 to 30 days.

SOURCES OF FURTHER INFORMATION ... In New York the Japan Tourist Association is at 45 Rockefeller Plaza, in San Francisco at 651 Market Street, and in Honolulu at 109 Kaiulani Ave., Honolulu 15. The Japan Travel Bureau has offices in New York, Los Angeles and in the Shin-Ohtemachi Bldg., Chiyoda-ku, Tokyo, as well as in many other Japanese cities. The Tokyo office of Pan American is in the Mitsubishi Shoji Building, Marunouchi, Chiyoda-ku. (Tel. 20–1021), across from the Central Railroad Station.

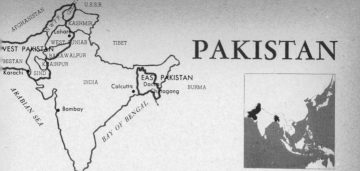

PAKISTAN

WEATHER IN KARACHI—Lat. N24°55′—Alt. 50′

Temp.	JAN.	FEB.	MAR.	APR.	MAY	JUNE	JULY	AUG.	SEPT.	OCT.	NOV.	DEC.
Low	58°	61°	68°	74°	79°	83°	81°	78°	77°	73°	67°	59°
High	76°	78°	82°	85°	89°	91°	88°	85°	86°	88°	85°	78°
Average	67°	70°	75°	80°	84°	87°	85°	82°	82°	81°	76°	69°
Days of Rain	1		1	1	0	0	1	2	2	1	0	0	1

LOCATION . . . Two widely spaced units comprise the new nation of Pakistan. East and West Pakistan are separated by approximately 1,000 miles of foreign territory, much the same as Alaska is separated from Continental United States. West Pakistan adjoins India, Iran, Afghanistan and the Chinese province of Sinkiang, whereas East Pakistan abuts the Republic of India, and Burma.

CHARACTERISTICS . . . While the name Pakistan is a new one, the land is both ancient and colorful. The terrain of East Pakistan is flat, covered with rivers, and very verdant. The landscape of West Pakistan is extremely varied, consisting of snow-capped hills and green valleys, with abundant food and fruit production. The latitude is similar to that of Southern California, as, except for the Himalayan region, is the terrain. You will find the people of Pakistan friendly and hospitable to visitors, especially Americans.

POPULATION . . . With a population of about 85,000,000 people, Pakistan is the fifth largest country in the world, numerically.

SIZE . . . About 364,737 square miles, which is larger than the combined areas of California, Oregon and Washington.

CAPITAL . . . Karachi, a well-planned, modern city, with over a million and a half population. Karachi is a big port and possesses one of the most up-to-date and busiest airports in Asia.

GOVERNMENT . . . A president and 11 ministers administer a federal form of government for both wings of the country. Governors seated at Lahore and Dacca are the chief representatives of the President in the provinces of West and East Pakistan.

HOW TO GET THERE ... By Pan American Clipper, about 29¾ hours elapsed time from New York. Karachi is on Pan American's Round-the-World route. By ship, about 23 days.

ACCOMMODATIONS ... Throughout Pakistan will be found a number of good hotels in most of the leading cities, such as Karachi, Lahore, Peshawar and Rawalpindi. In Karachi the following hotels are recommended: the *Metropole*, the *Beach Luxury*, the *Palace* and the *Columbus Hotel*. All of these hotels have orchestras and bars. Year around rates vary from $8 to $13 per day, American Plan.

ARTS ... National Museum, Karachi. The real center of art, however, is perhaps Lahore, where the Museum, Chunghtai's Studio, School of Modern Art and several other institutions have valuable collections.

BANKS ... There are numerous international banks in Karachi. Some of them are American Express Company, Lloyd's Bank, Bank of India, Chartered Bank of India, Australia and China and the Netherlands Trading Society. Exchange facilities are provided by the leading hotels.

CALENDAR OF HOLIDAYS ... March 23, Republic Day; Good Friday; April 26, Jumat-ul-Wida; May 2 and 3, Id-ul-Fitr; June 30, Bank Holiday; July 9 and 10, Id-ul-Azha (Festival of Sacrifice); August 6 and 7, Muharram; August 14, Pakistan Day; August 18, Janam Ashtami; September 11, Death Anniversay of Quaid-i-Azam; October 2, Dussehra; October 7, Id-e-Milad-un-Nabi (Prophet's Birthday); December 25, Christmas and Quaid-i-Azam's Birthday; December 31, Bank Holiday.

CIGARETTES AND TOBACCO ... Pakistan and British-named cigarettes and tobacco are plentiful, but American brands are somewhat more difficult to obtain. American cigarettes cost $5 a carton when available.

CLIMATE ... East Pakistan from November to mid-March is generally delightfully cool with low humidity and little rain. The rest of the year generally has higher humidity and temperatures. Mean temperature in cold months is 60 degrees and in the hot season 83 degrees. West Pakistan, except for the coastal strip of Sind, is subject to extremes from freezing night temperatures in January and February to the 70's in the daytime, making a very healthy winter climate. In summer, the days can be very hot, though the nights generally are cool. Karachi enjoys a pleasant climate with invigorating sea breezes except for months April, May, June and October.

CLUBS ... In Karachi, Sind Club, Rotary International Club, Lions Club International, Gymkhana, Boat Club and Race Club. Inquire locally.

COMMON COURTESIES AND CUSTOMS ... Shoes or sandals should be taken off before entering a mosque. Don't disapprove if men do not take off their Pakistani caps in social gatherings, as it is not customary to do so.

COMMUNICATIONS ... Direct radio-telegram and radio-telephone service with nearly the whole world is available. Airmail letter postage is Rs. 1-4-0, or about 25 cents, per half ounce to the United States

CURRENCY... The monetary unit is the Pakistani rupee, worth 21 cents United States per rupee. There are 16 annas in a rupee.

CUSTOMS REGULATIONS AND DOCUMENTS REQUIRED FOR UNITED STATES CITIZENS... A passport, properly visaed, is required. Certificates of smallpox vaccination and inoculation against cholera are required. Yellow fever inoculation certificate required if you are coming from a yellow fever area. Bona fide baggage of a passenger is exempt from duty when it accompanies the passenger. No duty is charged on 200 cigarettes and jewelry up to Rs 5,000 (about $1,000). There is no limitation on cosmetics and such things so long as they are within reasonable limits. Limit of £10 Sterling and Rs. 2,000 Pakistan currency.

DRUG STORES... American-type drug stores are not generally found in Pakistan. Chemists, druggists and pharmacists are found in all the shopping and business centers and in most of the hotels. American products are very scarce and very expensive.

ELECTRIC CURRENT... In Karachi, 220 volts, 50 cycles. Alternating and direct current are found in different parts of Pakistan.

FAUNA... The Zoo Gardens on Garden Road, near Karachi, present a picturesque scene.

FOOD... Pakistanis are fond of spicy but tasty food. There are numerous varieties of curries, *pulaos* (specially cooked meat and rice), and *kebabs* (fried and boiled meat), *shami kebab* (fried meat cakes). *Kofta* (meat balls) *murgh-i-mussalam* (stuffed fried chicken); and *shahi turke* (sweetbreads cooked in milk and honey) are a "must." Milk is available in Karachi but should be boiled.

LANGUAGE... English is used extensively in Government and generally in commerce and is also widely understood and spoken throughout Pakistan. Other languages widely used are Urdu, Bengali, Pushtu, Gujrati, Punjabi, Hindi and Baluchi.

LAUNDRY AND DRY CLEANING... Laundries and dry cleaners are available almost everywhere, but quality of work is poor. Home service is also easily obtained.

LIQUOR... In the main centers of Pakistan many foreign brands of liquor are available, but expensive. However, few Moslems drink, and it is the generally accepted custom among foreigners to abstain until sundown.

MEDICAL FACILITIES... Good doctors and surgeons. Fully equipped hospitals are to be found in all the leading cities. English is understood by hospital staffs. There is a good Seventh Day Adventist American hospital in Karachi. Holy Family Hospital run by American Medical Mission Sisters has hospitals in Karachi, Rawalpindi and Dacca.

MOTION PICTURES... There are a few movie theaters showing both American and English films. Two film studios are in operation in Lahore. The Ministry of Information and Broadcasting produces both cultural and documentary films for release at home and abroad.

MUSIC . . . Radio Pakistan, which is non-commercial, devotes a high proportion of its program hours to both the classical and folk music of Pakistan.

PHOTOGRAPHY . . . Photographic equipment, including cameras and still and movie film, black-and-white and color film, may be bought but not readily, and prices are higher than in America. Color and movie films are sent abroad for processing; 24-hour local service on black-and-white film. Inquire at your hotel or Pan American office for recommended camera stores.

NIGHT CLUBS AND CABARETS . . . Night clubs as we know them, are not found in Pakistan. However, all the leading hotels have Western-type barrooms and cabarets. The floor shows of the Beach, Luxury, Metropole, Palace and others are fair.

RELIGION . . . The majority of the people are Moslem. Others are Christian Hindus and Zoroastrians. Most faiths have established places of worship in Karachi and the principal cities of Pakistan. There is, of course, complete freedom of worship in Pakistan.

RESTAURANTS . . . The leading Karachi hotels have dining rooms. It is recommended that tourists dine at their hotel. *Shezan,* a new air-conditioned restaurant, is also recommended. Chinese restaurants are available for Chinese specialties.

SHOPS AND STORES . . . In Karachi the shops around the Metropole Hotel offer all varieties of goods. Elphinston Street is also a big shopping center. Prices on some items are high because of restricted imports.

SPECTATOR SPORTS . . . Hockey and football (soccer), are popular national games. Tournaments are held in the big cities. Cricket is also played in winter. Horse racing on the week ends in winter season in Karachi and Lahore with pari-mutuel betting.

SPORTS . . . Tennis facilities are available at clubs for members and their guests. There are numerous places for fishing and hunting Pakistan offers some of the finest deep-sea fishing found anywhere. Many clubs for football and hockey.

TIME . . . Time in Karachi and West Pakistan is 10 hours later than United States Eastern Standard Time. East Pakistan time is 11 hours later.

TIPPING . . . 10 per cent of the bill is the usual tip.

TRANSPORTATION . . . State-owned railroads in both West and East Pakistan and good air services provide access to most of the principal cities. Much of the track is 5'6" gauge, widest in use anywhere. For local transportation, taxis, buses, *tungas* (horse and carriage) and rented automobiles are available as are economical auto rickshaws and baby taxis.

WATER . . . Not safe to drink. Use special water flask in your hotel room for drinking and brushing teeth.

WHAT TO BUY . . . Ivory articles are admired for their beauty and delicacy; products of papier mâché and pieces of embroidery, brocades, fur caps, Baluchistan carpets, Sindhi glass-work and other hand-made goods. Visitors should see the sales and display centers at

About four hours by air from Karachi at Lahore is Pakistan's famous Badshahi (the Royal) Mosque, one of the largest in the world.

The Municipal Corporation Building on Bunder Road, a thoroughfare of Karachi, is representative of the local upward-reaching architecture.

Karachi Airport, at the leading hotels, at the Cottage Industry Center in Karachi; and similar centers in Dacca and Chittagong.

WHAT TO WEAR...In winter (October to April), tropical worsted; in summer, rayons, cotton and other washable fabrics. Winter nights sometimes become suddenly cold. A light topcoat should be taken along. Men can use summer-weight dinner jacket and black tie for evening functions. Women should bring white cotton formals.

WHERE TO GO—SIGHTSEEING...

Karachi...In Karachi sightseeing tours are limited, but you can get about the city by cab or *gharry* (a horse-drawn vehicle) the driver of which will act as your guide. About 3 miles from the town of Karachi is the Clifton Beach on the Arabian Sea. On moonlight nights the charm of the surroundings is increased many fold. A light topcoat should be taken along. Men can use summer-weight dinner jacket and black from Karachi is fertile Malir, which, with swimming pool and the *Grand Hotel,* offers a fine spot for relaxation. West of Karachi is the little island of Manora, which offers an excellent view of the city and interesting sights such as a pilot station, a lighthouse and a fishermen's camp that attract many visitors. From Manora westward, about 12 miles, is Cape Monz. Boat transportation and rental automobiles are available for these sightseeing trips.

Four and a half miles from Manora is Sandspit, accessible by boat up the creek, at this point separated from the sea by a narrow strip of beach. Spend a day there. Another such holiday resort is Hawk's Bay, about 12 miles from Karachi. Manghopir (11 miles north from Karachi), well-known shrine of a saint, is built on a rock and is famous for its hot sulphur springs. Children are especially interested in a tank that is full of crocodiles bred from two originally tamed by the saint. A trip to Bund Murad Khan is good for lovers of fish and sport. Another place worth visiting is Thatta, 64 miles from Karachi, full of historic ruins of Mogul and pre-Mogul period.

Lahore... Roughly 4 hours by air from Karachi, Lahore is the second largest city of Pakistan, with a population slightly over 1 million. It is the cultural and academic center of Pakistan, the location of over 40 colleges and institutions, including Punjab University. One of Lahore's great treasures is the exquisite Shalimar Gardens, a masterpiece of the great Mogul Emperor, Shah Jahan, who was also responsible for the Taj Mahal. The beautiful tomb of Jahangir, the father of Shah Jahan, is also well worth a visit.

The famous Badshahi (Royal) Mosque, one of the largest mosques in the world, is also located in Lahore. Among the many monuments of interest you'll see a plaque in the office of the *Civil and Military Gazette*, on the Mall, recording the fact that Rudyard Kipling once worked there. Kim's gun, Zam Zama, still stands outside the Museum where Kipling's father was curator.

Lahore is where Pakistan's film studios are, and it is the center for wrestling, a popular sport here. The city is at its best during the winter season, October to March.

Ancient Cities... Visitors should not miss seeing the archaeological excavations of Mohenjo-Daro in Sind and Harappa in the Indus Valley, in Punjab Province, dating to about 3,000 B.C., and other places of historical interest, such as Taxila in the Punjab and Bhambhore in Sind, and the famous Khyber Pass in the North.

East Pakistan... Principal places of interest: Sylhet is headquarters of the tea-growing area. Dacca, the capital, historically known for its silk and Dacca cotton muslin, has many historical monuments, including the Lal Bagh Fort, Bibi Pari's tomb, Bara Katra, Husani Dalan, Churihata Mosque, Satgumbad (seven domes) Mosque and Dhakeswari Temple, as well as modern structures and interesting museums. Places of archaeological interest include Mahasthan Garh, Rajshahi and Mainamati. The scenic Chittagong Hill Tracts is a region of picturesque towns, thick forest and wild animals and the quiet seaside resort, Cox's Bazaar.

SOURCES OF FURTHER INFORMATION ... There are several travel agencies in Karachi and a Pan American office in the Metropole Hotel (Tel. 50281). In Lahore contact the Public Relations Department of North Western Railways. Consulate General of Pakistan is located at 12 East 65th Street, New York.

PHILIPPINE ISLANDS

WEATHER IN MANILA—Lat. N14°36′—Alt. 25′

Temp.	JAN.	FEB.	MAR.	APR.	MAY	JUNE	JULY	AUG.	SEPT.	OCT.	NOV.	DEC.
Low	70°	71°	75°	75°	76°	76°	74°	75°	76°	75°	72°	71°
High	80°	81°	84°	87°	88°	87°	85°	85°	83°	84°	82°	81°
Average	75°	76°	80°	81°	82°	82°	80°	80°	80°	80°	77°	76°
Days of Rain	5	3	3	4	10	16	21	22	21	17	12	9

LOCATION ... This group of 7,109 islands (only 462 of which are larger than one square mile in area) lies in the Malay Archipelago. Borneo lies to the southwest and Formosa less than 100 miles to the north. Luzon is the largest of the islands.

CHARACTERISTICS ... Manila has practically recovered from the war and offers a welcome to tourists. The roads, highways and hotels are excellent. Beach resorts, within an hour's drive from the city, are splendid. English is generally spoken and the average American feels at home even though the scenery, the people and the customs are foreign. Winter is a fine time to visit the Philippines, for the sun shines constantly and the outdoor life is good.

POPULATION ... 23,122,200, of which 10,000,000 live on Luzon.

SIZE ... The total land area is 115,601 square miles, slightly larger than Arizona, but the islands are spread over an area as large as Mexico. Luzon, with 40,420 square miles, is the size of Kentucky.

CAPITAL ... Quezon City, a suburb of Manila, is now the official capital, although the seat of the national Government remains in Manila, which has a population of about 1,182,790, or approximately that of San Francisco.

GOVERNMENT ... Formerly a dependency of the United States, the Philippines are now a republic of 53 provinces with a President and a bicameral legislative body. The Philippines were granted their independence on July 4, 1946, by the President of the United States. There are 53 provinces and 28 cities in the Philippines.

HOW TO GET THERE ... By Pan American Clipper from San Francisco via Honolulu, about 37½ hours (elapsed time) to Manila. Hong Kong is 3 hours, Saigon is 4½ hours and Singapore is another 3 hours. By ship from San Francisco, 17 to 21 days.

ACCOMMODATIONS ... There are several excellent hotels in Manila: the *Manila Hotel,* which is right on Manila Bay, facing the Luneta (public park), the *Bay View Hotel* and *Swiss Inn* on Dewey Boulevard, *Filipinas Hotel,* facing Manila Bay, and the *Shellborne Hotel,* also facing the Luneta. Rates are $7 up.

ARTS ... The National Museum and the Art Gallery of the University of the Philippines offer interesting relics of weapons, art and costumes, and literature dating back several centuries. Exquisite Philippine handicraft is world-famous. Popular native industries are cigar manufacturing, shellcraft, *piña, jusi* and other textile weaving, wood carving, handmade silver filigrees, buntal hat making, making of snake and reptile belts, shoes and bags, and, of course, Philippine embroidery.

BALLET ... Ballet schools and public ballet performances are frequently held in Manila. Foreign ballet troupes perform regularly in Manila as well as in outlying cities.

BANKS ... The National City Bank of New York and Bank of America. Some of the larger local banks are the Philippine National Bank, the Bank of the Philippine Islands, the Philippine Trust Company, the Peoples Bank and Trust Company, the Prudential Bank, the Philippine Bank of Commerce. Other foreign banks are the Hong Kong and Shanghai Banking Corporation, the China Banking Corporation and the Chartered Bank of India, Australia and China. The Central Bank of the Philippines controls sale of foreign exchange. Hours of all banks are 9:00 A.M. to 2:30 P.M., Mondays through Fridays. Banks are closed on Saturdays, Sundays and on all official holidays.

CALENDAR OF HOLIDAYS ... New Year's Day; Maundy Thursday; Good Friday; May 1, Labor Day; July 4, Philippine Independence Day; August 26, First Cry of Balintawak, commemorating the commencement of the Philippine Revolution against Spain; November 1, All Saints Day; Thanksgiving Day, last Thursday of November; November 30, National Heroes Day; Christmas Day; and December 30, Rizal Day—Dr. José Rizal is the national hero. You will find that the Philippines celebrate the longest Christmas season— the Dawn Masses called *Misas de Aguinaldo* which start on December 16 (and every morning thereafter until *Misa de Gallo,* or Midnight Mass, December 24) and continue up to the Feast of the Three Kings, which falls on January 6.

CIGARETTES AND TOBACCOS ... All brands of American cigarettes are available. The Filipinos are now manufacturing comparatively good brands of blended cigarettes. Choice Corona cigars make ideal gifts to friends abroad. American cigarettes cost approximately 60 cents a package; a good brand of cigars will cost $4 a box. Monogrammed, Philippine mahogany gift boxes may also be made to order for a reasonable price.

CLIMATE ... The most pleasant season in Manila is around Christmas when the temperature is 75 to 80 degrees. The rainy season is from June to November; however, rains are generally interspersed with good sunny weather. April and May are warm months and sometimes uncomfortable for foreigners from cold countries; however, one may see gay fiestas, abundant flowers, weddings and various other interesting celebrations.

CLUBS ... There are many fashionable clubs in Manila, which include the Army and Navy Club just opposite the Manila Hotel, Club Filipino, the Elks Club, Yacht Club, the Casina Español, Manila Club, Wack Wack Country Club, the Manila Golf Club and the Manila Polo Club with all modern facilities for sports, recreations and social functions. Guest cards may be arranged with members.

COMMON COURTESIES AND LOCAL CUSTOMS ... Filipinos are noted for their hospitality, especially in the provinces. During the day, men generally dress informally with long- or short-sleeved shirts of cotton, silk or rayon, with plain or Hawaiian prints. Coats and ties are generally worn in offices, in exclusive hotels and night clubs in the evening. During the summer months and also throughout the year, the local version of evening apparel for men is the *barong Tagalog* made of piña cloth, derived from the pineapple fiber, or *jusi,* woven from silk and piña fiber. For strictly formal wear, the *barong Tagalog* is worn with tuxedo, black evening shoes.

COMMUNICATIONS ... Radio (RCA, Mackay), cable, transoceanic telephone facilities are available. Ordinary airmail to the United States is 40 cents for a minimum.

CURRENCY ... The monetary unit is the peso, valued at two pesos to an American dollar. Tourists may exchange their traveler's checks or dollars at the time of arrival at the airport or port with the Central Bank agents or with any authorized agent of the Central Bank of the Philippines while in Manila. The Manila Hotel and the Bay View Hotel are authorized agents of the Central Bank.

CUSTOMS REGULATIONS AND DOCUMENTS REQUIRED FOR UNITED STATES CITIZENS ... Valid passport and visa. Smallpox certificate (valid 3 years from date of issue). Tourists may bring in an unlimited amount of foreign currency, but it must be declared upon arrival. One hundred pesos in bills may also be brought in or out. Silver coins in excess of P5.00 ($2.50) are not allowed to be taken out of the country. The following will be allowed in duty free: wines and spirits, 1 quart; 300 cigarettes, 50 cigars or 2.2 lbs. of pipe tobacco; beverages, 1 quart; packaged tea, 2.2 lbs. No restrictions on cameras or films. Only military areas are banned from the photographer. Chinese-type articles are either prohibited or require a Certificate of Origin for entry into the United States. Consult the nearest U.S. Consul for latest requirements.

DRUG STORES ... Manila is literally dotted with drug stores, but the bigger ones are the Botica Boie on the Escolta, the shopping center of Manila. Dolor's Pharmacy, Metro Drug Store, Oro, Central, Occidental, Rubi, Quinta, Lexal Laboratories, Modern Pharmacal, Yucuanseh Drug Company and the Oceanic Commercial. All kinds of medicines and drugs are available.

ELECTRIC CURRENT ... Voltage in local hotels and everywhere in Manila is 220 volts, A.C. Standard-type transformers are necessary.

FAUNA ... The carabao, or water buffalo, is indigenous. There are several varieties of birds that are exported to the United States. Large shipments of monkeys are also shipped to U.S. zoos and research laboratories.

FLORA ... There is a wealth of fascinating plant life all over the Philippines. The flowers are beautiful; they are smaller but more fragrant than American flowers. In June and July you can get quantities of gardenias for practically nothing. The *sampaguita*, a small, white, multi-petaled and exceedingly fragrant flower, is the national flower. Orchids grow in abundance. The Vanda sanderiana species, or *waling-waling*, is the most famous of all Philippine orchids. This highly esteemed flower has large brown and purplish tinted blossoms which survive more than thirty days.

FOOD ... All kinds of food are abundant. Rice is the staple food. Native dishes include: *adobo* (a mixture of chicken, pork, and beef, and lots of garlic), *lechon* (a whole roasted pig), and *sinigang* (stewed fish or meat with vegetables). The mango is the best liked of all Philippine fruits and is available from May till late October. Good American, Spanish, Filipino, Chinese and European meals are available at $2 up. There is plenty of pasteurized milk produced by sanitary dairies.

GAMBLING ... The most popular form of gambling among Filipinos is cockfighting (two gamecocks fight with sharp leg spurs), which is held Sundays and holidays in the suburbs of Manila, and horse racing on Saturdays and Sundays at the San Lazaro and Santa Ana racetracks. Jai-alai is played nightly except on Sundays at the Jai-Alai Building on Taft Avenue, where one may find at the same time excellent music and food at its Sky Room and Keg Room.

LANGUAGE ... The Tagalog dialect, which is spoken in Manila and in the surrounding provinces, is the national language, better known as the Filipino language. English is taught from grade school up; the Filipino language is similarly taught as one subject. The Philippines hold the distinction of having the highest rate of literacy in the Far East. English is spoken and understood in any part of the Archipelago. *Mabuhay* is the Philippines' welcome to tourists and friends to the Philippine soil. It means "welcome," "long life," "farewell" or "good-by and Godspeed." Because the Philippines were under Spanish sovereignty for almost 400 years, Spanish culture and language are still dominant. (The Philippines were named after King

Philip II of Spain, who at the time of their discovery was the ruling monarch of that country.)

LAUNDRY AND DRY CLEANING...There are excellent laundries and dry-cleaning establishments, where work is done in a few hours. In a hotel, your roomboy will make the necessary arrangements. Rates are moderate.

LIQUOR...*Tuba*, a native drink, is made from the fermented juice of the palm. Philippine beer is exceedingly popular among Filipinos, alien residents and visitors alike. A great quantity of Philippine rum is also manufactured and exported. Philippine and imported liquors are always available. Hotel bars are open from eight in the morning to about twelve at night. Other bars are open later. The price of a drink of Scotch ranges from 75 cents to $1.25, depending on quality and the prestige of the establishment.

MEDICAL FACILITIES...There are numerous excellent public and private hospitals. A few American private hospitals are the Manila Sanitarium, Waterous Clinic, Mary Johnston Hospital, Manila Doctor's Hospital, and St. Luke's Hospital. There are also excellent Spanish and Chinese hospitals, whose medical staffs have been trained in the best American hospitals.

MOTION PICTURES...In Manila the *Ideal, Lyric, Capitol, Avenue, State, Galaxy, Odeon, Ever* and *Universal* are first-class air-conditioned theaters. There are also a great many second-class, air-conditioned theaters all over the city. These theaters show second-run films and double features. Movie theaters, or *cines* as they are commonly called, start at 8:30 in the morning. Last screening starts at about 9:00 in the evening. Hollywood, British, Italian and Spanish films are shown, although Hollywood films are the most popular. Foreign films with dialogue other than English or Spanish are shown with English subtitles.

MUSIC...The *kundiman* is a distinctive native music. This type of music has almost always a plaintive and amorous air. Several *kundimans* composed by great Filipino composers have won fame all over the world. Native *rondallas*, or string bands, are regularly heard over the radio. Filipinos are expert with the guitar and other stringed instruments. Excellent bands play nightly in many of the night clubs. The Manila Symphony Orchestra and the Filipino Youth Symphony periodically play concerts in school auditoriums. There's also the University of Philippines Symphony.

NIGHT CLUBS AND CABARETS...There are several night clubs in Manila. Among the most patronized are the Manila Hotel *Champagne Room, Jungle Bar,* the *Sky Room* in the Jai-Alai Building, the *Riviera* on Dewey Boulevard, and *Club Celebrity* in the Hotel Filipinas. These are all air conditioned. American bands, artists and other musical troupes often give performances in these night clubs. The *Metro Garden,* located near the piers, the *Sportsman,* the *Nautilus, Casa Marcos, Alberdi's* and the *Bayside* on Dewey Boulevard and *Di'Mark's* on Menlo Road are also popular.

PHOTOGRAPHY...Photo equipment, black-and-white and color film are available in Manila and other principal cities, but prices are much higher than in the United States. Developing and printing can be done within 24 hours.

RELIGION . . . While the country is predominantly Catholic, there are churches of all denominations, including the Philippine Independent Church and the Iglesia Ni Cristo, which are modified forms of Catholicism and Protestantism respectively. In Manila there are numerous American churches, such as the Central Church on San Luís Street, the Ellinwood Church on Wright Street, the Knox Memorial Church on Rizal Avenue, the Holy Trinity (Episcopal) on San Luís, and many others.

RESTAURANTS . . . In Manila the *Bulakena* Restaurant and the *Aristocrat* Restaurant on Dewey Boulevard specialize in native foods. *New Europe,* the *Keg Room,* the *Swiss Inn,* the *Petal* and *Bamboo Rooms* and *Moon Gate* at the Manila Hotel, the *Golden Lotus* at the Hotel Filipinas, *Bay View House* at the Bay View Hotel, *Café Indonesia* and *Boie's* on the Escolta serve Filipino, Spanish, American, Chinese, European and Indonesian foods. *Max's* on Dewey Boulevard and its main restaurant in Quezon City specialize in fried chicken and have delighted many tourists. The *D & E Restaurant* in Quezon City is also recommended. Prices in these eating places are not any higher than American prices.

SHOPS AND STORES . . . The principal shopping places in Manila are on the Escolta, Rizal Avenue, Dasmarinas, Quezon Boulevard, Carriedo and Echague. Native articles, especially souvenirs, are also available in native stores on the Escolta and in Ermita and Malate Districts. Most of the merchandise sold in the better stores is American. Stores are open from 8:00 A.M. to 12:00 noon and from 2:00 P.M. to 6:30 P.M. or later in the evenings. On Sunday the stores are open only in the morning. Prices are slightly higher than those in the States. Local products are inexpensive.

SPECTATOR SPORTS . . . Polo, baseball, soccer, basketball, boxing, yachting regattas. Baseball and basketball are now the most popular sports. Basketball games are held 12 months a year at the Rizal Coliseum. Tickets are sold at the game site or at a few better stores in Manila.

THEATERS . . . Amateur dramatic societies stage plays and operettas several times a year. Visiting opera companies and theatrical troupes give performances occasionally. The price of admission ranges from $2.50 to $10. While most of these plays are in English, Spanish is also used.

TIME . . . Manila is 16 hours later than United States Pacific Coast time and 13 hours later than United States Eastern Standard Time. Daylight Saving Time is not observed.

TRANSPORTATION . . . Good taxi service, buses, jeepneys, trains and steamer. There are over 72 daily inter-island air trips to all points of interest. Chauffeur-driven cars for hire are available for as low as $2 an hour in Manila or suburbs. Trips to outlying tourist spots in the provinces may be arranged.

The famous volcanic peak, Mt. Mayon, rises near the city of Legaspi.

WATER ... Water in Manila is excellent and safe to drink.

WHAT TO BUY ... Embroidery, buntal hats, delicate piña bags, handkerchiefs, bags, dining sets, rattan art, silver filigrees, linens, textiles, wood carvings, cigars, shellcraft, beautiful wooden salad bowls, canapé trays, fruit bowls and many other items.

WHAT TO WEAR ... Both men and women should take clothing of wrinkle-resistant materials. In the evenings at the clubs and best hotels, men wear black trousers and white sharkskin dinner jackets. Recommended materials for men and women are rayon, cotton, sharkskin, gabardine and other light materials. Bring sportswear, too.

WHERE TO GO—SIGHTSEEING ...

Manila ... In Manila you should see the Malacanan Palace, the official residence of the President of the Philippines; Santo Tómas, founded in 1611, one of the oldest universities in the world; Intramuros, the Spanish Walled City, now in ruins; Fort Santiago, an old dungeon built by the Spaniards and used by the Japanese as a prison and torture chamber; Rizal Stadium—Manila's sports center, and the new University of the Philippines at Quezon City. A short drive from Manila over an excellent highway is cool Tagaytay Ridge, overlooking beautiful Lake Taal. The Manila Hotel maintains a guest house at the ridge. On the way, at the church in Las Piñas, the famous Bamboo Organ, reputed to be the only one in the world.

Other interesting day trips from Manila include visits to the Balara Filters, Pagsanjan Falls, Clark Air Force base, the beautiful white sand beaches at Batangas and Bataan, historical Corregidor at the entrance to Manila, and the day cruise to the island of Mindoro.

One hour by air from Manila is Baguio, picturesque summer capital in the mountains. North of Baguio in Banaue one sees huge rice terraces carved from the mountainsides, a marvel of primitive engineering. If you have the time, you'll find it interesting to visit the Bicol provinces in southeastern Luzon and the southern islands of the Visayas, Mindanao and Sulu groups (2 hours by air from Manila).

SOURCES OF FURTHER INFORMATION ... The Philippine Tourist and Travel Association, with offices in the Shurdut Building, Intramuros, Manila, and at 153 Kearny Street, San Francisco. Pan Am office is at 204 Escolta (Tel. 31981). In New York, The Philippine Association, 527 Madison Avenue, can supply information.

SINGAPORE

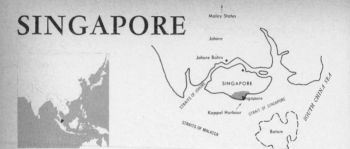

WEATHER IN SINGAPORE—Lat. N01°17′—Alt. 25′

Temp.	JAN.	FEB.	MAR.	APR.	MAY	JUNE	JULY	AUG.	SEPT.	OCT.	NOV.	DEC.
Low	73°	73°	74°	75°	75°	75°	75°	75°	75°	74°	74°	73°
High	86°	88°	89°	89°	89°	88°	88°	88°	88°	88°	87°	86°
Average	80°	81°	81°	82°	82°	82°	82°	82°	82°	81°	81°	80°
Days of Rain	16	11	14	15	14	14	13	14	13	16	18	19

LOCATION ... Singapore is an island in the South China Sea about a mile off the south end of the Malay Peninsula in Southeast Asia, 77 miles north of the equator. The City of Singapore is about 900 air miles south of Bangkok, and 1,400 miles southwest of Manila.

CHARACTERISTICS ... This Oriental City has always been a symbol of the color and romance to be found in the East. Its culture is native but all the overtones are European. It offers the best living conditions in Southeast Asia. The famed orchids are here and so are the Singapore slings. The hotels are comfortable, and there is plenty to do that is gay. Shops and bazaars are filled with fascinating things from surrounding countries.

POPULATION ... Approximately 1,500,000, of which about 80 per cent is Chinese.

SIZE ... 27 miles long and 14 miles wide, the Island with 286 sq. miles is about three times the area of our District of Columbia.

CAPITAL ... Singapore, with a million inhabitants approximates Buffalo, New York, in population.

GOVERNMENT ... Since April 1959 a self-governing state within the British Commonwealth. Foreign affairs vested in Britain. Head of state is known as the Yang-di-pertuan Negara. Governing head is the Prime Minister. Legislative body, the Assembly of fully elected members.

HOW TO GET THERE ... By Pan American Clipper, Singapore

is about 3½ hours flying time from Saigon. From San Francisco, the total elapsed time is 48 hours.

ACCOMMODATIONS ... Singapore hotels are comparable to the best anywhere. Recommended are the *Raffles, Cathay, Adelphi, Seaview, Princess, Biltimore* and *Ocean Park.* Rates are about $11 to $16 American Plan double. All the above hotels have air-conditioned bedrooms and dining halls. Make reservations well in advance.

ARTS ... The Malay Arts and Crafts Center has a collection of Malay silverwork, and rice-straw pictures on black satin (this is the best shop for native goods); the Raffles Museum has wonderful exhibits of the history, costumes and handicrafts of the people of Southeastern Asia and of its animal and bird life. While there is no art museum, weekly art exhibits are held in The Hall, which is provided by the British Council.

BANKS ... Among the many banks are the First National City Bank of New York, the Bank of America, the Chartered Bank, the Hong Kong and Shanghai Bank, to name just a few.

CALENDAR OF HOLIDAYS ... New Year's Day, Thaipusam (Indian) in January, Chinese New Year in February, Easter Monday, Hari Raya Puasa, Vesak Day (Ceylonese), Queen's Birthday, Bank Holiday June, Bank Holiday August, Hari Raya Hadji (Malay), Birthday of Prophet Muhammad (Malay), Deepavali (Indian), Christmas Day and the following day.

CIGARETTES AND TOBACCO ... English cigarettes (Players) are about 40 cents a pack. Most United States brands are available at 25 cents a pack.

CLIMATE ... Singapore has a fairly even temperature. It is very warm, and the humidity is very high; but the evenings are usually cool. There is no marked dry or wet season. May to October is the best time to visit.

CLUBS ... The Tanglin Club, the Royal Singapore Golf Club, the Island Golf Club, the Singapore Swimming Club, the Royal Singapore Yacht Club, the American Club and the Flying Club. Pan American Airways' representative will be glad to arrange guest cards to the American Club, Singapore Swimming Club. Rotary's here too.

COMMON COURTESIES AND LOCAL CUSTOMS ... The Malay is a stickler for etiquette. He serves and handles food only with his right hand (unless eating with a knife and fork). He is a modest person too. In greeting a Malay, do not shake hands or slap him on the shoulder. Aristocratic Malays never laugh and seldom even smile because they do not feel it is in good taste to show their emotions. Be conservative on sports clothes. Stick to solid colors and whites. Hawaiian sports shirts are not popular with the British and immediately identify the wearer as a tourist. This causes prices to spiral upward!

COMMUNICATIONS ... Government telephone service in the Colony and Federation. One can telephone the United States and practically everywhere else. Airmail postage to the United States is Straits dollars 1.10.

CURRENCY ... The Straits dollar written with a $ sign like U. S. currency, is the monetary unit. It is worth about 33 cents in United States currency. Money can be changed at any of the banks or hotels. Illegal money-changers will approach travelers on the streets in the business district. However, take note that in order for a foreigner to get an export permit for surface or unaccompanied shipments of purchases of Malayan products, he must obtain a receipt from the official money-changer or bank to prove to the export department that the goods exported were paid for by foreign currency changed legally. Contact the Pan American representative for assistance in arranging for export permits and foreign exchange clearance. It is illegal to take from the Colony any U.S. dollar notes in excess of what you brought in. NOTE: if you bring into the Colony U.S. currency in excess of $33, have the Customs officer make a note of the amount in your passport. This will allow you to take out your U.S. currency when you leave, as it is the only way to prove you brought it in. Traveler's checks and letters of credit are exempt from regulations governing foreign exchange.

CUSTOMS REGULATIONS AND DOCUMENTS REQUIRED FOR UNITED STATES CITIZENS ... Passport and health certificate (International type only) for smallpox required. Also yellow fever and cholera if coming from infected areas. You may bring in 200 cigarettes or 25 cigars or 8 oz. tobacco duty free. You may also bring in 1 quart each of malt liquor wine and spirits duty free. Processed (developed) movie films must be left in Customs Bond or pass the film censor. Chinese-type articles are either prohibited or require a Certificate of Origin for entry into the United States. Consult the nearest U.S. Consul for latest requirements.

DRUG STORES ... There are chemist shops with most United States toilet articles available. The downtown district has many such shops catering to drug needs.

ELECTRIC CURRENT ... This is a real problem to the traveler, as both alternating and direct current are available at 230 volts, depending on the specific area of the city. There are no fewer than 18 standard types of electrical plugs in current use—also depending on location and the whims of the Chinese contractors.

FAUNA ... In Singapore one finds quantities of tropical birds, fish and wild animals. Most notable are the talking Mynah bird and many species of monkeys.

FLORA ... Orchids and gladiolus grow profusely in Singapore and usually bloom three or four times a year.

FOOD ... Excellent Chinese foods are served in modern restaurants and certain native restaurants. Malay and Indian curries are tops. Favorite Malay dish is *satay*—barbecued kabob over charcoal. Milk is available and safe to drink. The water is excellent and safe. Coffee is poor by American standards (most Americans request Nescafé or other instant-type brands). The European restaurants, of which there are many, serve the best in all kinds of Western food— all moderately priced.

GAMBLING...The Singapore Turf Club has periodic meetings on the average of four to five times a year. Guest cards can be obtained to attend the races. There are no gambling casinos as such.

LANGUAGE...The official language is Malay—even the Chinese speak it. However, English is understood by all except a few cab drivers and porters.

LAUNDRY AND DRY CLEANING...This service is good but expensive. Be sure to emphasize what type of cleaning you want and when you want it back. All hotels have good service, though regular cleaning shops are better.

LIQUOR...There are no native drinks. Whisky is always "Scotch" although bourbon is available. A whisky and soda is called a *Stengah*—means half a "peg," or measure. Always ask for ice as the British rarely ice drinks. All bars close at midnight, though some clubs have later hours.

MEDICAL FACILITIES...United States Seventh Day Adventist Hospital is tops in Singapore. There are dozens of excellent British doctors in private practice. The General Hospital is the best equipped in the Far East and is expert in treating tropical diseases.

MOTION PICTURES...Most films are U.S. made. Chinese and Malay population prefer noisy action movies. Occasionally British films are shown. All have English sound tracks with Chinese subtitles. All theaters are air conditioned, clean and quite comfortable. Movies include the *Cathay, Capitol, Odeon, Pavilion, Rex* and *New Alhambra.*

MUSIC...The Chinese are more musical than the Malay. However, they stick to percussion instruments that are most often deafening. There are no concerts scheduled, although guest orchestras and conductors perform on occasion.

NIGHT CLUBS AND CABARETS...In amusement parks such as the Happy World, the Great World and the New World, you will find plenty of native cabarets. However, Europeans as a whole do not frequent them except on sightseeing occasions. Good places for dining and dancing are *Prince's Restaurant, Chicken Inn* in the Seaview Hotel, *Elizabethan Grill* in the Raffles Hotel, the *Capitol Restaurant, Cathay Restaurant,* and the *Singapore Airport Hotel.*

PHOTOGRAPHY...All kinds of film are available. Foreign cameras are inexpensive—especially German, Swiss, and Japanese imports which are duty free and tax free. Singapore has good processing—the best is the one-day service by the regular Kodak plant, 130 Robinson Road, Singapore.

RELIGION...There are churches of all denominations. The Wellesley Presbyterian Church has an American minister.

RESTAURANTS...*Princes* on Orchard Road, tops in food, featuring air-conditioned dining, dancing, lounge. *Adelphi Grill* in the Adelphi Hotel on Coleman Street, excellent food prepared by Swiss chefs, is also air conditioned—very popular. *Elizabethan Grill* in famed Raffles Hotel, excellent food, also air conditioned. The *Chicken*

Water taxis take you to points of interest along the river in Singapore. Across the bridge here is the Empress Palace

Inn on the sea in the Seaview Hotel; fried chicken in a basket, American style, with dancing to good music. Wonderful view. *Cathay Restaurant*, in famed Cathay Building, specializes in Chinese food, air-conditioned dining and dancing. The *Blue Room* in the Capitol Theater Building, best for Chinese food, also air conditioned. The above restaurants are the best in town. An average dinner will cost $5 U.S. per person.

SHOPS AND STORES ... Raffles Place in the center of town is the shopping district, but if you are seeking bargains and goods not available anywhere else in the world, all of Singapore is a good hunting ground.

SPECTATOR SPORTS ... Soccer, hockey, badminton, football and basketball. In 1949 the Thomas Cup was won by the Malayan badminton team. It was the first international cup open to world competition to be brought back to Malaya.

SPORTS ... Golf, tennis, fishing, swimming, yachting, sailing, badminton, squash.

TIME ... 15 hours and 20 minutes later than United States Pacific Coast Standard time.

TIPPING ... About the same as in the United States.

TRANSPORTATION ... Lots of taxis (about 15 cents a mile). The rickshaw was banned from Singapore in 1947 and has been replaced by the "trishaw," which is a bicycle fitted with a two-seater side car. Native women use these to go marketing. Not recommended, for they are dangerous. Inquire of PAA about car hire.

WATER ... The water is good for drinking.

WHAT TO BUY ... Helen Ling's for all kinds of Eastern art, Malayan-Javanese arts and curios; and C. K. Tang's for Chinese and Javanese woodwork, Bali heads. Malayan hand-worked silverware, jewelry and sarongs from Malayan Arts and Crafts Kiosk; Stamford Road for alligator and snakeskin goods; High Street for Indian saris; English silverware and crockery from Whiteaways, Robinsons and John Little's. B. P. de Silva for star sapphires, jade and other precious stones; Thaicraft for handwoven Siamese silk, stoles.

WHAT TO WEAR . . . Take a large quantity of light clothing because of the heat. Singapore is very smart; better take dinner clothes. Go easy on the Hawaiian "Aloha" shirts.

WHERE TO GO—SIGHTSEEING . . .

Singapore . . . There are many interesting sights and buildings to see in and around Singapore. A number of the places have been named for, and built in memory of, Sir Stamford Raffles, who rediscovered the island in 1819. Raffles Institute, which is next to Raffles Hotel, is a college which was founded in 1919 and named for him. The busy banking, shipping and commerce districts center around Raffles Place and Collyer Quay. The Post Office and Government offices are here too. You should go across the river to Empress Place and see the old Government Building and the Victoria Memorial Theater and Hall, which is Singapore's cultural center. The Singapore Court, the Municipal Building and old St. Andrew's Cathedral, built in 1862, are on St. Andrew's Road. Across from the "Padang" is the War Memorial, and if you go a little farther on, you can get a magnificent view of the sea and harbor. Two historic institutions located on Stamford Road are the Convent and St. Joseph's School, and the New Raffles Girls' School. Nearby is the Raffles Museum and Fort Canning Hill, where Sir Stamford Raffles lived, and where the garrison has been since Singapore was founded. Here, too, is the famed tomb of Iskander Shah, the last Malay ruler of Singapore in 1274, and the old European Cemetery.

Take a trip to the Sultan Mosque and Arab Street, which is the ancient Malay section of the city; the beautiful scenery at the McRitchie Reservoir and the jungle on Mandai Road. You'll want to get the wonderful view of the sea from the East Coast Road and to see the Chetty Temple on Tank Road and Chinese Buddhist Temple on Telok Ayer Street. The Botanic Gardens are well worth seeing, too. In 1877 the first Para rubber plants were grown successfully here, and later they formed the base of the rubber industry which has brought so much prosperity to Malaya. This is also the center of orchid growing.

Side Trips . . . Of special interest is the scenic drive to the State of Johore in the Federation of Malaya. Johore is only a 40-minute drive across Singapore Island. To get there one passes over the Causeway spanning the Straits of Johore. In Johore one may view the Sultan's zoo and mosque and on occasion obtain permission to visit the Palace. Mansfield & Co., Ltd. mentioned below offer a shopping tour, night life tour, and others on scenic beauty, local interest and temples, Singapore and Johore Bohru, coastal areas. Each takes about 3½ hours.

SOURCES OF FURTHER INFORMATION . . . Several tourist guide agencies in Singapore including American Express, Anglo-French Travel Bureau (Tel. 22560), and Mansfield & Co., Ltd., (Tel. 2412).

THAILAND
(SIAM)

LOCATION ... In the southeast corner of Asia between Burma on the west and Laos, Cambodia and Vietnam on the east.

CHARACTERISTICS ... Thailand is pronounced Tie-land. The people in the north and northeast are much fairer in color than those in the south. Thai rice is really the wealth of the country. Tourists will be impressed by the pleasantness and almost childlike cheerfulness of the Thai people. "The Land of Smiles" will best describe these pleasant people. "Mai Ben Rai," which means "never mind," is one of the Thai popular sayings.

POPULATION ... Estimated 22,000,000.

SIZE ... The area of Thailand is 198,455 sq. miles, which is about the size of the states of New York, Pennsylvania, Maryland, Virginia and North Carolina combined.

CAPITAL ... Bangkok, including the city of Thonburi, directly across the river, has a population of over 1½ million inhabitants.

HOW TO GET THERE ... By Clipper, Bangkok is 2¾ hours flying time from Hong Kong and approximately 40 hours eastbound from New York. By ship 50 to 60 days from New York.

ACCOMMODATIONS ... There are several good hotels (by Far-East standards) in Bangkok: largest and most modern is the air-conditioned *Erawan* with swimming pool and three dining rooms. It is the very best hotel in Thailand. *Oriental Hotel,* with its new Tower Wing, located on the river, *Trocadero Hotel* and Annex, and *Princess Hotel* are all in a central location and have most rooms air-conditioned. *Princess Hotel* has a swimming pool that is popular with tourists. The *Ratanakosindr Hotel* and the *Suriyanond Hotel* are located near the Grand Palace but are not in the main business area. Other hotels include the *Plaza, Grand Hotel, Metropole,* and *Pacific*.

ARTS... The National Museum in Bangkok has an extensive collection of sculpture, textiles and porcelains. Bangkok has some 350 Buddhist monasteries, many of which contain fine examples of Thai frescoes and sculpture. The two most important are the Chapel Royal or Wat Phra Keo in the old palace in which is housed the Emerald Buddha, and Wat Bencamabopit (Marble Temple).

BALLET... There is no ballet as we know it, but the world famous Royal Thai classical dancing is a must for tourists. It takes place at the Silpakorn Theatre November through May. Thai dancing may also be seen in various night clubs.

BANKS... The Bank of Thailand; Bank of America; Hong Kong Shanghai Bank; Bank of Ayuthia; the Chartered Bank of India, Australia and China; Bank of China; Banque de L'Indochine; Indian Overseas Bank, Ltd., Mercantile Bank of India, Ltd.; Nederlandsche Indische Handelsbank N. V. Traveler's checks may be cashed at banks or with licensed money changers and at many shops.

CALENDAR OF HOLIDAYS... There are thirteen official national holidays.

CIGARETTES AND TOBACCO... A few brands are available. Thai cigarettes are quite good.

CLIMATE... December, January and February are the best months to visit Thailand. It's hot but not humid during the day, and cool at night. March, April and May constitute the "hot season," June through October the monsoon season with torrential rains, and November through February the "cool season."

CLUBS... American Association, American Chamber of Commerce, American Women's Club, Rotary, Skol Club International and private clubs, which include the Royal Bangkok Sports Club, Polo and Riding Club, and the Turf Club.

COMMON COURTESIES AND LOCAL CUSTOMS... After you've been to Bangkok for a while you will learn how the Thais greet one another. It's a combination of placing the hands together as if in prayer while slightly bowing the head at the same time. The word "Sawasdi" means "hello."

COMMUNICATIONS... The telephone service will strain your patience. Have your hotel operator get you the local number you wish. Long-distance calls to the States are possible. Cable and radio service to all parts of the world is reliable. For the ordinary letter, air mail stamps cost 6 Ticals (approximately $.30).

CURRENCY... The local currency is the Tical (also called Baht), which is divided into 100 Satangs, worth about .05 or 20-21 to the U. S. dollar. The money market operates on a Free Market Exchange.

CUSTOMS REGULATIONS AND DOCUMENTS REQUIRED FOR UNITED STATES CITIZENS... You must have a passport and three extra photos. No visas for visits up to 90 days. Smallpox vaccination certificate required. Yellow fever and cholera inoculation if coming from infected areas. There is no malaria in the Bangkok area. Radios and TV sets require permits. You may bring in 100 cigarettes or 50 cigars and 1 bottle of liquor duty free. No more than $100 in U.S. currency, the rest in traveler's checks. Chinese-type articles are either prohibited or require a Certificate of Origin for entry into the United States. Consult the nearest U.S. Consul for latest requirements.

DRUG STORES...There are drug stores with the usual pharmaceuticals.

ELECTRIC CURRENT...Voltage 110, A.C., 50 cycle (220 A.C. in some hotels). The electric power is variable but improving. British-style plugs (round prong) are used for some electrical fixtures.

FAUNA...Tigers, serpents, crocodiles, bears, boars, deer (Asiatic varieties), rhinoceros, monkeys and gibbons, tapirs, porcupines, hares, leopards, sladang (wild cattle), wild dogs, elephants, big lizards, peacocks, parrots, myna birds and many other varieties of birds as well as domesticated and pet animals. Siamese cats, of course, including the Korat cats which are gray.

FLORA...Every variety of orchids, gardenias, hibiscus, and other exotic tropical plants; flame trees, teak forests, huge assortment of tropical fruits, namely, mangoes, rose apples, bananas (20 varieties), papaya, durians, oranges, pomeloes, and many varieties of very good but practically unnamable fruits.

FOOD...Chinese delicacies, such as bird's-nest soup and shark's-fin soup. Thai rice is considered the best in the world and Thai curries are excellent. Rice birds, *plakapong* (a large but delicate fish), superb prawns, are delicacies. There are also many restaurants that serve European foods (*see* RESTAURANTS).

GAMBLING...No organized gambling, except legal betting at the horse races, and government lottery held 5 times a month.

LANGUAGE...Thai (pronounced "Tie") is the national language. Personnel in the first-class hotels and shops understand some English, so don't worry about not speaking Thai.

LAUNDRY AND DRY CLEANING...Fine overnight laundry facilities. Dry cleaning is now available, but not the best.

LIQUOR...All the better known wines and spirits are available at bars and restaurants as well as in grocery stores. Try some *mekong* whisky made from rice, a local Thai product.

MEDICAL FACILITIES...The Bangkok Nursing Home, Bangkok Christian Hospital, Seventh Day Adventist Hospital, Red Cross Hospital, Chulalonghorn and Siritaj Hospital; Salyalak Clinic near Erawan Hotel. There are American- and European trained doctors.

MOTION PICTURES...Air-conditioned movie theaters showing pictures in English, mostly current American and British films.

MUSIC...Only in connection with dancing and drama, mentioned elsewhere, at the fights, and on radio and TV.

NIGHT CLUBS...European-type: *Bamboo Bar, Ambassador*

Club, Casanova Club, Key Note Club, Oasis. With hostesses: *Lido, L–85, Luna Club, Sani Chat Cay, Chez Eve, Champagne Room.*

PHOTOGRAPHY . . . Black-and-white and color film for stills and movies are available. Prices are high. Bring your own supply. Excellent film-developing facilities are available at a very low rate. Two-day service for black-and-white. Suggestions for photo purchases are Black and White Studio, New Road, opposite G. P. O., V. Lyluck, corner of Customs House Lane, New Road; Kodak (Borneo Co.) on Silom Road and Thai Photo Studio, corner Siphya Road.

RELIGION . . . The national religion of Thailand is Buddhism. There is a Protestant Episcopal church on Convent Road in Bangkok, the Protestant International Church, and there are numerous Roman Catholic churches in the City.

RESTAURANTS . . . *Erawan Hotel, Oriental Hotel, Trocadero Hotel, Princess Hotel, Hoi Tien Lau, Nick's Place, Casanova Club, Palms Restaurant* and *Key Note Club* and numerous very good Chinese ones. *Plaza Hotel* for Thai food.

SHOPS AND STORES . . . Hours same as in the United States; Chinese shops are open on Sunday. *See* WHAT TO BUY.

SPECTATOR SPORTS . . . Fish-fighting is practiced informally on Sundays but is considered illegal. Kite-flying contests are held on Sundays in the hot season on the Pramain Ground near the Royal Palace (March, April and May) and sponsored by the "Bang-Kok City Committee for Kite-Flying," a government department. Boxing with native music, a must, takes place Thursdays and Sundays at 5:00 P.M. In the Boxing Stadium, get ringside seats. There's also box-ing at Lumpini Stadium. Horse racing every Saturday afternoon at the Sports Club and Sunday at the Turf Club with pari-mutuel betting except during August and September. *Takraw* is one of the oldest Thai games. It is a kind of static soccer. The object of the game is for players, who form a circle, to send the hollow wicker ball across to one another by hitting it with any part of the body without its hitting the ground. *Takraw* may be seen all year round and is in the nature of a "pickup" game rather than an organized sport.

SPORTS . . . Fishing: There is a tremendous variety of fish in the rivers and the Gulf. Fishing trips can be arranged on the Menam Chao Phya River and in the Gulf of Thailand. There is fine duck shooting up the Menam Chao Phya and good rice-bird shooting in the rice paddies outside of Bangkok. Squash at the Sports Club. Tennis: There are both grass and clay courts as well as many private courts. Golf: There are courses at the Sports Club and the Turf Club, but guest cards are necessary. Swimming: There is a good modern pool at the Sports Club, Erawan and Princess Hotels in Bangkok and fine sea bathing in the Gulf of Thailand (*see* Hua Hin).

TIME . . . Twelve hours later than U.S. Eastern Standard Time.

TIPPING . . . Some hotels include 10% on the bill, but it is usual to add 10%. There is a 20% tax on hotel and restaurant bills.

TRANSPORTATION . . . Automobiles with a chauffeur may be hired at any hotel. Taxis are plentiful. *Samlors* ("pedicabs," i.e., rickshaws with a bicycle up front) are used by tourists and residents for short distances. Regular air service is available. Air rather than rail travel is recommended for trips to Singapore in view of Communist activities in Malaya.

WATER ... Drinking water out of taps is not recommended. Bottled water (*Polaris*) is available.

WHAT TO BUY ... There are many jewelers and silversmiths in Bangkok where fine semiprecious stones and antique jewelry, among other items, can be purchased. Try Ainslee on New Road, Zerner's at 68 Sathorn Road, Princess Hotel, Alex's on Oriental Avenue, Oriental Jeweler's in Oriental Lane, T. Seng in Bonmoh area and Jonny Siam. For very fine hand-woven silks and brocades try Amfarco in the Erawan and Oriental Hotels. Thai silk hand-weaving factory opposite the Trocadero Hotel and Thai Silk Company, Ltd., 430 Suriwongse Road. For made-to-measure dresses try Surapee, 518/8 Plernchitt Court near Erawan Hotel. Go to Thai Nakorn, Kwang Ann, E. Seng Chong, Pratib on New Road for Neilloware and silverware. Neilloware is a form of oxidized silver with inlaid and engraved designs. Nakorn Kasem is the antique dealer's area. Also, the Monogram Shops in Erawan and Trocadero Hotels for antiques. Crocodile and snakeskin bags, shoes, belts, and wallets at Crocodile Store on New Road. Bronze flatware with horn handles is also popular.

WHAT TO WEAR ... In Bangkok wear the same sort of clothes as you would in Nassau, Acapulco or Hong Kong. Lightweight suits, a light sports jacket and slacks for men; washable dresses for women. Bangkok is not a "dressy" place.

WHERE TO GO—SIGHTSEEING ...

Bangkok ... From a tourist's point of view, Bangkok is a unique city. It provides a vista of interesting sights, imposing and colorful temples and beautiful palaces. Bangkok is inter-linked by canals, called *klongs,* and the main river, called the Chao Phya. The floating market is the highlight of a visit to Thailand—go out at 7:00 A.M. by boat and come back at 10:00 A.M. The Temple of the Reclining Buddha (Wat Po) and the Temple of Dawn (Wat Arun), whose tower offers a fine view, are both interesting to see. *See also* ARTS. Other sightseeing possibilities include: boat trips on the river; the "thieves' market located in the Nakorn Kasem section of Bangkok; Pasteur Institute on Rama IV Road with its Snake Farm. Taxis are numerous and reliable guides are available.

Chiengmai ... The northern capital of Thailand is the second largest city in the country. Chiengmai is easily reached by air in about 3 hours by daily service from Bangkok, 20 hours by train. Tourists immediately will enjoy a complete change of scenery. While the surroundings of Bangkok are flat and extend into seemingly endless rice fields, Chiengmai has pleasantly hilly countryside and the famous teak forests. New hotels are being built there.

Hua Hin ... Thailand's best sea resort with a fine beach, good swimming, tennis, golf and sailing. The main season is from December

You'll be fascinated by the bizarre statues and temple architecture in Bangkok. Precious stones, gold and brightly colored tiles go into the elaborate designs of religious significance.

Charming Siamese girls in beautiful ornate costume do their intricate classical dances for tourists. The Siamese Classical Theater is a must in Bangkok.

to May. Hua Hin is about one hour by air from Bangkok, by express train in 6 hours and by road in 5 hours. There's a fairly good hotel.

Ayudhya ... The former capital of Thailand, founded in 1350, is noted for the ruins of its former palaces and temples, where a vast seated Buddha may be seen. Ayudhya (Ayuthia) can be reached by river from Bangkok in 6 hours and by road approximately 2 hours.

Lopburi ... The ruins of this very old city are located 100 miles north of Bangkok. Legend has it that Lopburi was founded in 468 A.D. as the town of Lavo by King Kalavarhadi. Under King Narai the Great, Lopburi became the capital of Siam. A Greek cabinboy, Constantin Phaulkon ("constant falcon") won the confidence and favor of the King to such an extent that he became what corresponded to the Premier. He induced the King to establish diplomatic relations with France, sending Siamese ambassadors to Louis XIV's court and receiving French ambassadors in Ayuthia and Lopburi. The "Constant Falcon" also persuaded the King to build forts and palaces and in the latter, though basically Cambodian in design, one can see in the ruins what may well have been an attempt to emulate the "Hall of Mirrors" at Versailles. The "Constant Falcon," with his zeal to convert the King to Christianity, was, with his master, overthrown by envious noblemen and lost his life in 1688. Lopburi may be reached by train in 8 hours, by river boat in about 10 hours or by car in 6 hours.

Angkor Wat, Cambodia ... Check with Pan American regarding the availability of tours by air to these fabulous ruins. See page 445.

SOURCES OF FURTHER INFORMATION ... Hotels and travel agents offer excellent guide service. Pan American is opposite the Trocadero Hotel (Tel. 32981) and at the Erawan Hotel. The Royal Thai Embassy is at 2940 Tracey Place, Washington 8, D.C.

VIETNAM

WEATHER IN SAIGON—Lat. N10°47′

Temp.	JAN.	FEB.	MAR.	APR.	MAY	JUNE	JULY	AUG.	SEPT.	OCT.	NOV.	DEC.
Low	64°	68°	68°	73°	74°	73°	73°	72°	73°	71°	68°	67°
High	93°	98°	98°	98°	97°	94°	94°	92°	92°	93°	92°	91°
Average	79°	83°	83°	86°	86°	84°	84°	82°	83°	82°	80°	79°
Days of Rain	3	4	2	8	21	27	25	24	22	15	14	12

LOCATION ... The Republic of Vietnam, one of the youngest republics in the world, is located in the extreme southeast corner of Asia, bordering the South China Sea. It was formerly a part of French Indochina. Saigon, its capital, is 681 air miles northeast of Singapore and 1,000 air miles southwest of Manila.

CHARACTERISTICS ... Saigon is one of the most attractive cities of the Orient, characterized by a combination of French and Oriental cultures and tastes. It has many fine buildings, wide, tree-lined boulevards, and sidewalk cafes in the French tradition. Adjoining is Cholon, the Chinese city and commerce center with all the appeal of the Orient.

POPULATION ... Estimated 22,000,000. Population of South Vietnam is approximately 11,000,000.

SIZE ... Overall size is 127,413 square miles including the northern portion which is administered by the Communist Vietminh.

CAPITAL ... Saigon is the capital of Vietnam; with its twin city of Cholon, it has a combined population of 2,000,000. The northern part of Vietnam, with its capital at Hanoi, is known as the Democratic People's Republic of North Vietnam.

GOVERNMENT ... Vietnam is a Republic, with a President, and a Constituent Assembly.

HOW TO GET THERE ... By Pan American Clipper, 4¼ hours from Manila and Hong Kong, 2½ hours from Singapore, 2 hours from Bangkok. For eastbound passengers, flights from Bangkok direct or via Phnom-Penh, Cambodia. Saigon may be easily included in the Round-the-World itinerary.

ACCOMMODATIONS... Best hotels in Saigon are the *Majestic,* the *Saigon Palace* and the *Continental Palace,* all located on Tu-Do Street in the main shopping section. Approximate rates are: Majestic, including light breakfast, and choice of lunch or dinner, from $8 to $11 single and $10 to $15 double. Saigon Palace, not including meals $7 to $9 single or double. Continental Palace, including light breakfast and choice of lunch or dinner $7 to $10 single and $9 to $11 double. The Majestic is completely air-conditioned; the Saigon Palace and the Continental have a limited number of air-conditioned rooms available at slightly higher rates.

CLIMATE... The climate is tropical with the average temperature shown on page 498. There are two seasons in Vietnam, the dry season from October to March and the rainy season from March to October. Visitors wishing to travel to remote areas or the mountain resort of Dalat, or the hunting areas, should plan to go during the dry season, although Saigon is suitable for visits at any time of the year.

CURRENCY... The monetary unit is the piastre, officially rated at 35 to one United States dollar. Visitors, however, may exchange their foreign currency at the airport at time of arrival, at the open market rate which varies between 70 and 75 piastres per dollar. Hotel rates noted above are quoted at the rate of 70 piastres to the dollar. There are several Exchange Control locations in Saigon where you may exchange foreign currency. The most convenient is located in the lobby of the Majestic Hotel.

CUSTOMS REGULATIONS AND DOCUMENTS REQUIRED FOR UNITED STATES CITIZENS... American citizens in possession of a passport, if traveling as tourists, are exempt from visas if their stay in Vietnam will not exceed one week. Smallpox vaccination, yellow fever and cholera inoculations are required if coming from infected area. Make visa applications, early through Vietnamese Legations. They require 4 to 6 weeks for processing. 400 cigarettes, one opened bottle of liquor may be brought in duty free. Passengers planning to visit the Hanoi area must have visas issued by the Democratic People's Republic.

WATER... Avoid drinking water that hasn't been boiled. Bottled drinks are available.

WHERE TO GO—SIGHTSEEING... If you have a week or so there are several interesting tours of Vietnam.

Dalat... Dalat is the popular mountain resort of Vietnam. It is located on the Langbian Plateau, at an elevation of 4,000 feet, in the Pays Montagnards du Sud. Fresh vegetables are grown here throughout the year. From December to March, Dalat supplies the area with the finest strawberries, which are usually served with whipped cream "*fraises chantilly.*" This mountainous area covered with spruce and pine, with swift and turbulant streams, is the popular big game hunting area of Vietnam where tiger, leopard, buffalo, and wild boar are found. In addition it has beautiful scenery and a good climate. Most of it is sparsely inhabited by the primitive hill tribe—the Moï. Accommodations are available at the *Dalat Palace Hotel*, a large government-operated hotel. Rates are about $5 a day, not including meals. There are also several smaller French-managed "bungalows" at higher rates, where delicious food is served.

Nhatrang...The village of Nhatrang is a popular beach resort lying on the shore of the South China Sea, a half-hour flight from Dalat. It may be included easily on a Dalat itinerary. This resort is popular for its white beach, its delicious seafood, and the boat trips that may be made to the small islands just off the coast.

When heat and rains prevail throughout the rest of Asia, from March to November, Nhatrang is at its popular best with clear days and fine transparent seas. (The rainy season at Nhatrang lasts from November to March). Hotel accommodations are difficult to obtain at all times of the year.

Hue...This city at the northern extremity of South Vietnam is the former capital of Annam and the site of colorful palaces and tombs of former emperors. Air Vietnam provides frequent flights to Hue, and quite often has week-end excursions at reasonable rates. Hotel accommodations are somewhat limited.

Angkor Wat...One of the great tourist attractions of the Orient, is easily reached by a number of flights weekly from Saigon to Siem-reap, the site of Angkor Wat. (For details refer to Cambodia section.)

Vientiane-Laos . . . There is daily transportation from Saigon to Vientiane, the capital of the kingdom of Laos, northwest of Vietnam. If you are planning to visit Vientiane or other cities in Laos, you must first obtain a visa through Laotian or French Consulates.

SOURCES OF FURTHER INFORMATION...Pan American's representative is located at 31 Duong Tu Do, Saigon, care of Denis Frères, General Agent.

This view is of only one part of the extensive area of Angkor Wat.

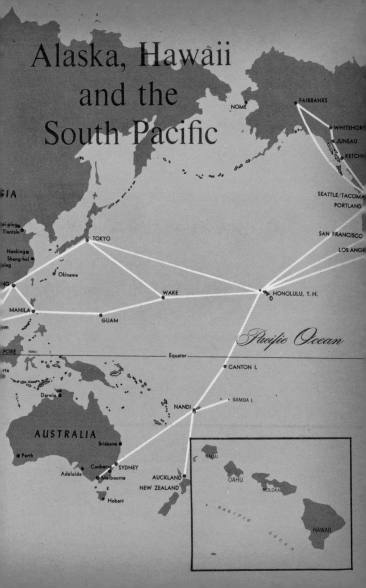

ALASKA

WEATHER IN JUNEAU—Lat. N58°18'—Alt. Approx. sea level

Temp.	JAN.	FEB.	MAR.	APR.	MAY	JUNE	JULY	AUG.	SEPT.	OCT.	NOV.	DEC.
Low	24°	26°	29°	34°	40°	46°	50°	49°	44°	38°	31°	27°
High	32°	35°	39°	47°	56°	62°	64°	62°	56°	48°	40°	34°
Average	28°	31°	34°	41°	48°	54°	57°	56°	50°	43°	36°	31°
Days of Rain	18	15	18	18	17	14	17	18	20	23	20	20

LOCATION ... Alaska, our 49th state, lies in the far northwest corner of the North American continent and includes the Aleutian Islands. The Alaska mainland is due north of Honolulu. The Aleutians extend as far west as New Zealand.

CHARACTERISTICS ... The name "Alaska" was derived from an Aleut word meaning "great land," and every inch of Alaska lives up to its name, with the highest mountains on the North American continent (Mt. McKinley, 20,300 feet) and rivers long and mighty (Yukon, 2,300 miles). It's a big and beautiful country from the steep-walled fjords of the southeast to the wide horizons of the Bering Sea coast. In the summer the sun shines 18 to 24 hours. In winter it's a Jack Frost wonderland awesomely illuminated by the Northern Lights. It's also a sportsmen's favorite, with big fish and big game.

POPULATION ... One of the fastest-growing regions under the American flag. Alaska's total population is 226,300, of which about 47,000 are military and about 35,000 are Indian, Aleut and Eskimo. Alaska's largest city is Anchorage, headquarters for the Alaska Defense Command, with a metropolitan population of 60,000. There are 12 cities in the territory with a population of more than 1,000 persons.

SIZE ... 586,400 square miles—more than twice the size of Texas.

CAPITAL ... Juneau, with a population of 5,956. Greater Juneau, however, has a population of 10,000.

GOVERNMENT ... Purchased in 1867 from Russia for $7,-

200,000, or less than two cents an acre, Alaska became an organized territory of the United States in 1912. On July 1, 1958, Congress passed a bill providing for the admittance of Alaska as the 49th state, and on January 3, 1959, the President signed the official proclamation of admittance. Alaska has a State Legislature composed of 20 senators and 40 representatives, which meets every two years.

HOW TO GET THERE ... By Pan American Clipper, nonstop service from Seattle to Fairbanks, 6 hours flying time; nonstop to Ketchikan, 2¾ hours, and from Ketchikan to Juneau, 1⅓ hours. From Fairbanks to Nome, 4 hours. Anchorage is 3 hours flying time beyond Juneau via Pacific Northern Airlines. By steamer it takes 2½ days to reach Ketchikan from Seattle; 3 days to Juneau, and 6 days to Fairbanks (via the Alaska Railroad). The Alaska Highway, now partially paved, is reached from points in the States through Alberta, Canada, or the newly constructed Hart Highway through British Columbia. It takes about a week to drive from Dawson Creek, B.C. (Milepost 0) to Fairbanks. There are excellent roads within Alaska itself.

ACCOMMODATIONS ... The *Baranof Hotel* in Juneau is one of the showplaces of Alaska; 96 rooms with private baths. Rates from $8. Coffee shop, private dining rooms, music nightly in the Bubble Room. In Anchorage the *Westward* is rated among the top hotels, with 160 rooms, $8 single with private bath. Cocktail Lounge and Coffee Shop. Top hotels in Fairbanks are the *Travelers Inn* (70 rooms with bath $11.50 and up single, $18 and up double) and the *Nordale* $5 and up single, $10 and up double. In Ketchikan, the *Ingersoll*, with 60 rooms from $5 single. All rates given are European Plan. Inns and motels are available at approximately the same rates.

ARTS ... In Juneau, the museum on the second floor of the Federal Building, and in Fairbanks, the University of Alaska museum on the campus, contain collections of Alaska Indian, Eskimo and Aleut artifacts.

BANKS ... In Juneau, the First National and B.M. Behrends. In Anchorage, the City Bank of Anchorage, First National Bank, and the National Bank of Alaska. In Fairbanks, the Alaska National Bank of Fairbanks and First National Bank of Fairbanks. In Ketchikan, Miners and Merchants Bank, and the First National Bank. Many places of business accept traveler's checks.

CALENDAR OF HOLIDAYS ... All national holidays are observed. The Fourth of July is celebrated throughout Alaska with pageants, parades and various demonstrations. In addition, there are Seward's Day on March 30, and Alaska Day, October 18. Opening days of the Salmon Derby in Juneau and Ketchikan are usually declared a civic holiday.

CIGARETTES AND TOBACCO ... Same prices and brands as in the rest of the United States.

CLIMATE ... Alaska is not a land of ice and snow. It is in the same latitudes as Norway, Sweden and Scotland. In the Arctic and in the area around Fairbanks, it is dry and cold with subzero temperatures in the winter, but quite warm and sunny during the summer months. Anchorage and the Kenai Peninsula area have weather comparable to the Midwestern states of the United States. The southern coastal areas are warmed by the Japanese currents. Although the temperatures are not extremely warm or cold, much rain falls the year around in these cities. The days of rain on the chart above are for southeastern Alaska only, and do not reflect the weather conditions in the interior. Best months to visit are May through October.

CLUBS . . . Rotary, Lions, Kiwanis, Elks, Moose, Eagles, Toastmasters, Toastmistress, Soroptomists, Quota, Business and Professional Women, and National League of American Penwomen, among others. Cards required for Elks, Moose and Eagles.

COMMUNICATIONS . . . Telegraph and telephone facilities to the other 48 states and elsewhere. Airmail rate is 6 cents per ounce.

CURRENCY . . . United States currency used throughout Alaska. In southeastern cities Canadian currency is generally accepted.

COMMON COURTESIES AND LOCAL CUSTOMS . . . You'll find the interests of the people very much like your own because Alaska has long been American to the core. You'll see familiar stores along Main Street, although civilization may appear to stop abruptly at city limits, because of the sparse population. An old timer is known as a *sourdough*, a tenderfoot is a *chechakho*.

DRUG STORES . . . All the usual products available in all drug stores.

FAUNA . . . Big game includes brown, black and grizzly bear, mountain goat and sheep, moose, deer and caribou. Other wildlife includes mink, beaver, marten, wolf and wolverine. Waterfowl are abundant. The beautiful Husky dog is used for transportation in the Arctic during the winter months. Many are house pets in other areas.

FLORA . . . Alaska is a blaze of color during the summer months with beautiful wildflowers and wild rosebushes. There are cultivated gardens in all of the towns and cities. A heavily wooded country, the principal trees are spruce, birch, hemlock, cedar, alders, cottonwood and mountain ash.

FOOD . . . Fish, crab and shrimp are among the best to be found anywhere. During the summer restaurants and hotel dining rooms serve freshly caught salmon and halibut. Various types of shrimp dishes are a specialty; tender, succulent crab is another of the northern treats. In Nome and Kotzebue reindeer is available. Almost all other foods are imported. Prices are slightly higher than in Seattle.

GAMBLING . . . Gambling is prohibited.

LANGUAGE . . . English is spoken throughout Alaska.

LAUNDRY AND DRY CLEANING . . . Same as at home.

LIQUOR . . . Same as in the rest of the United States.

MEDICAL FACILITIES . . . Excellent hospitals and clinics everywhere with staff physicians, surgeons and specialists, trained in the leading U.S. universities.

MOTION PICTURES . . . First-run pictures shown everywhere.

MUSIC . . . The Alaska Music Trail, a cooperative association in the major cities, sponsors the appearance of opera and concert artists during the winter season.

NIGHT CLUBS AND CABARETS...A variety of night clubs in the principal cities. Visiting U.S. bands and floor shows are featured.

PHOTOGRAPHY...Black-and-white still and movie film and color film are available throughout Alaska. Camera and other photo equipment available at drug stores and camera stores. Developing facilities are of the same standard as in the rest of the States. Prices slightly higher. Alaska is a photographer's paradise. To capture the beauty of the land it is recommended that color film be used.

RELIGION...Virtually all churches represented.

RESTAURANTS...Excellent restaurants and dining facilities are available. For the sportsman: most restaurants will cook freshly caught fish if requested. Full-course meals cost about the same as in the rest of the United States. Short orders slightly higher. Steaks are excellent in most of the better eating places.

SHOPS AND STORES...Modern, well-lighted, well-stocked establishments carrying all nationally advertised brands. Clothing stores carry a wide selection of both dress and outdoor clothing. Styles are current. Curio and gift shops feature native ivory, jade, black diamond, and various fur products, wood totems and leather wear, as well as native-made grass baskets and baleen baskets made of whalebone.

SPORTS...Fishing is Alaska's major sport, *see* WHERE TO GO. Golf is played at the Fairbanks Golf Club. Baseball, basketball and tennis are featured locally.

TIME...There are three time zones in Alaska. Juneau and southeastern Alaska observe Pacific Standard Time. Fairbanks and Anchorage are on Alaska Standard Time, 2 hours earlier than PST; Nome is on Bering Sea Time, 3 hours earlier than PST.

TIPPING...Same as in the rest of the United States.

TRANSPORTATION...Taxi firms, bus lines and limousine service in all of the principal cities. Car-rental services in Anchorage and Fairbanks only. In other cities cabs may be chartered from local cab companies for reasonable rates.

WATER...Excellent in all places.

WHAT TO BUY...Fur parkas, caps and gloves, wood and ivory carvings and jewelry, exquisite jade and black-diamond jewelry, totem poles, whalebone baskets and various other woven trays and baskets. Beautiful reindeer and other leather goods in hats, jackets, bags, shoes and clothing. Tanned salmon- and halibut-skin wallets and bags. Fur and leather moccasins and *mukluks* (Eskimo boots). Fur garments should be bought only from established firms. Cotton-print sourdough shirts in Alaska motif.

WHAT TO WEAR...Informality is the keynote in Alaska. The same weight and type of clothing as you would wear at home in spring and fall. Slacks are in order. Wool suits, tweeds, sweaters and rainwear are recommended. Dress clothes are not needed.

WHERE TO GO—SIGHTSEEING...

Juneau...In Alaska's beautiful capital city among the buildings of interest are the Territorial museum, Governor's Mansion and a number of interesting curio and leather shops. A 13-mile bus or taxi trip on Glacier Highway will take you to Mendenhall Glacier, a vast receding river of ice. (Price of round trip, $5.18.) In late July the Golden North Salmon Derby, a 3-day contest featuring prizes for big fish, attracts sportsmen from all over the United States. Information may be obtained from the Territorial Sportsmen Association, Juneau, Alaska. America's northernmost Catholic shrine, the Shrine of St. Theresa, is about 23 miles north of Juneau. No car rentals. Taxis may be chartered for reasonable rates.

Taku Lodge, a modern resort, is one of the scenic highlights of Alaska. About a half hour by air, or 3 hours by boat from Juneau, the Lodge features trout fishing and swimming in warm springs. Rates $18 a day American Plan. *Tougass Lodge* at Excursion inlet is 20 minutes by air from Juneau, also $18 per day.

Adjacent communities offer much of interest to the visitor. The charm of the old Russian days is still alive at **Sitka** where the old Cathedral of St. Michael, with its rich oil paintings and fabulous ikons, is located. A large collection of restored totems comprise the Sitka National Monument, open to visitors at no charge.

Mt. Edgecumbe, a United States Government education and medical center for native people, is across the bay one hour from Juneau by air.

Haines is 70 miles north of Juneau at Lynn Canal. It is the terminus of the Haines Highway. Is also reached by bus, air or motor boat. Excellent trout fishing. In the background is the scenic Chilkat range. The annual Fourth of July celebration and Strawberry Festival here features native Indian war dances. Stay at *Hotel Halsingland,* noted for its Swedish cuisine. Rates $4 to $7 double, European Plan.

Skagway retains the gold-rush atmosphere. Terminus of White Pass and Yukon narrow-gauge railroad. It is also reached by air or boat. From here there are tours to Lake Bennet and Carcross.

Anchorage, Alaska's largest city, is often called the Chicago of Alaska. It is the site of huge Army and Air Force bases where jet planes streak across the sky. It is constantly throbbing with activity. Connected by highway a short distance away is Palmer, a unique farming community which had its inception as a Government-sponsored cooperative. It will remind you of Vermont, with green fields and red barns.

Stellar attraction of the area is a visit to Mount McKinley's National Park, second in size to Yellowstone and habitat of wild animals and colorful birds. There are many beautiful lakes; excellent fishing can be found everywhere. *McKinley Park Hotel* is a beautiful, modern inn which accommodates 150. Park tours are available over the 90 miles of road within the reserve. For hikers and mountaineers Camp *Denali* offers limited facilities for the more adventurous. Tents for housekeeping, $10 per night double.

Katmai National Monument, on the far-flung Alaska Peninsula where volcanos dot the terrain, is another of the colorful trips avail-

Alaska's vastness and beauty achieve the ultimate at Mt. McKinley National Park. This view of Wonder Lake is in the area of 20,300-foot Mt. McKinley.

At Kotzebue, Alaska, 20 miles north of the Arctic Circle, Kotzebue Eskimos perform a native dance for visitors.

able from Anchorage. Accommodations and fishing camps are operated by Northern Consolidated Airlines. Large rainbow and grayling trout lakes are found at the various camps. Trips are $175 plus tax and up. Sightseeing flights are also available.

The romantic fur-seal islands in the Bering Sea can now be reached. Here 4 million seals and sea lions arrive annually to raise their young. Tours operated by Reeve Aleutian Airlines, $160 plus tax for 2-day round trip; meals and housing included.

Anchorage Fur Rendezvous is a week-long festival held in February and includes sports tournaments, ski contests, Eskimo pageants, parades and balls.

Fairbanks, heart of the gold-mining industry in the new state, is its second largest city. Here, too, are located two gigantic Air Force bases, where daily patrols leave for air duty over the North Pole. Points of interest include the huge Ester Creek gold operation where a hydraulic dredge works round the clock, a visit to the University of Alaska and its museum, and a trip to the University experimental farm. There are Husky dog kennels, a log-cabin town, and many unique restaurants and night clubs. Seasonal events in Fairbanks are: the Winter Carnival, a week-long pageant which includes the North American dog-racing derby, held in March; Golden Days, colorful celebration of discovery of gold, held in July; midnight baseball game on June 21, longest day.

A one-day trip down the Tanana River on a comfortable riverboat affords the visitor a glimpse into the past, with stops at Indian fishing camps and old burial grounds.

One of the most exciting trips out of Fairbanks is the 2-day all-expense tour with Wien Alaska Airlines to Kotzebue, on the Bering Sea and Nome (about $125). Eskimo dances, skin-boat rides, reindeer-steak dinners are all part of planned entertainment. En route you cross the International Date Line and see the East Cape of Siberia. There's auto sightseeing in Nome, and a visit with the King Island Eskimos, whom you can watch carving ivory under their skin boats called "oomiaks." Another excellent tour is to Barrow, largest Eskimo village, where you see whaling in season, huge arctic ice packs, primitive sod houses, and take a short trip to the farthest north village site of the continent, where visitors can dig for artifacts. At Barrow the sun stays above the horizon 82 consecutive days—41 before and after June 21.

You can fly or drive to the Yukon River (Circle City, 160 miles) past Circle Hot Springs.

Ketchikan is the first city of Alaska and an important seafood center and site of a new $54 million pulp mill.

For the sightseer there are many famous old Indian totems at Saxman Park, 2 miles out, and another series of Indian poles and houses is located at Mud Bright, about 11 miles from the city.

The Ketchikan Salmon Derby is held in early June and is the most spectacular event of the season. Prizes are awarded on a weekly basis; also for a seasonal derby. It is sponsored by the Ketchikan Chamber of Commerce. Information will be sent on request.

Bell Island Hot Springs Resort is an interesting spa 45 miles from Ketchikan with regular service, $6 by boat or $10 by plane. There are 15 furnished cabins with cooking facilities; rates from $30 per week. Meals are available at the main lodge for $6 a day. Fishing and mineral baths are the attractions.

Information on trout fishing, and the many excellent lakes is available from Ellis Air Lines, Ketchikan.

Kodiak is headquarters for the big-game hunter in search of a Kodiak bear, the world's largest carnivorous animal. Guides are available. In the town itself there are fish canneries and much lore of the old Russian days. Nearby is the Kodiak Naval Air Base.

SOURCES OF FURTHER INFORMATION ... The Alaska Visitors Association, Klein Building, Juneau, Alaska. Also local Chambers of Commerce. Pan American's offices in the Baranof Hotel (Tel. 106) Juneau, in the Nordale Hotel (Tel. 2118) Fairbanks and in the Ingersoll Hotel (Tel. 3131) Ketchikan.

AUSTRALIA

WEATHER IN SYDNEY—Lat. S33°52'—Alt. 138'

Temp.	JAN.	FEB.	MAR.	APR.	MAY	JUNE	JULY	AUG.	SEPT.	OCT.	NOV.	DEC.
Low	65°	65°	63°	51°	52°	48°	46°	47°	51°	56°	60°	63°
High	78°	78°	76°	71°	65°	61°	59°	63°	67°	71°	74°	77°
Average	72°	72°	70°	61°	59°	55°	53°	55°	59°	64°	67°	65°
Days of Rain	14	14	15	14	15	13	12	11	12	12	12	13

LOCATION ... Australia lies in the South Pacific in the temperate zone except for parts of the north which reach into the tropic zone. The Island of Tasmania, included in the Commonwealth, lies about 140 miles off the south coast.

CHARACTERISTICS ... This is the "sunshine continent," an open, smiling land of beautiful beaches, wonderful fishing, fine skiing and good golf. Australians spend most of their lives out-of-doors. They are marvelous sportsmen. Australians and Americans are alike in many ways. You'll find yourself quite at home "down under." There is, of course, no language barrier, although you will find some of their terms unfamiliar. Australia has something for everyone who enjoys new sights, new experiences. The cities are cosmopolitan, the roads good, the people hospitable. Much of Australia is wild and uncultivated, but the parts the average American tourist visits have most of the comforts of home with the advantage of being different.

POPULATION ... 10,000,000.

SIZE ... 2,974,576 square miles, approximately the area of the United States. Tasmania is slightly larger than West Virginia.

CAPITAL ... Canberra, a city of 36,000, about 200 miles southwest of Sydney.

GOVERNMENT ... A British commonwealth, Australia consists of six states (including Tasmania) which are self-governing on local matters, and the Capital Territory and the Northern Territory. The country as a whole is governed by a Federal Parliament and a Governor-General who represents the Queen.

HOW TO GET THERE . . . By Clipper via Honolulu, and the Fiji Islands, Sydney is 28¾ hours (elapsed time) from San Francisco and Los Angeles. Melbourne is about 2 hours longer on same flights. By ship about 21 days from the U.S. west coast.

ACCOMMODATIONS . . . Hotels in Sydney include: the *Australia*, 45 Castlereagh Street, rates about $14.50 double with bath; the *Carlton* and *Usher's* opposite the *Australia;* the very modern *Rex* in King's Cross area; *Hotel Pacific* at Manly on the Pacific about 7 miles from the city; *Astra Hotel* at Bondi Beach 7 miles away; *Glen Ascham* at Darling Point, ten minutes from town; the *Wentworth* on Lang Street, which is quiet and conservative. Rates at all these hotels are about $7 single, $14.50 double, with bath.

Hotels in Melbourne include: *Australia Hotel*, 266 Collins Street, modern and good, single with bath about $7; *Menzies Hotel*, 509 Bourke Street, about $9 per day single with bath; *Savoy Plaza Hotel,* 122 Spencer Street, $7 per day with bath; *Windsor Hotel,* Spring Street, is quiet and conservative, rates about $7.75 single with bath; the *Chevron*, 519 Kilda Road, is just outside the city about six minutes away, has tennis courts and swimming pool, attractive rooms from $8 a day. Just off the beach: *Prince of Wales Hotel,* well appointed. *The Federal,* Collins and King Streets, is a commercial-type hotel, $4 single, the *Oriental*, 41 Collins Street, conveniently near theaters and shops, $7 single. All of these, except the *Australia* and *Oriental,* include breakfast in prices quoted. Note that hotel reservations should be made well in advance, particularly during spring racing season from September to November.

ARTS . . . In Sydney, the National Art Gallery contains a good collection of Australian and foreign paintings and statuary. Australian Museum, College Street and Hyde Park, specializes in aboriginal life and natural history. Macquarie Galleries has exhibitions by leading Australian artists.

In Melbourne, the National Museum on Swanston Street carries a very fine selection of native crafts, as well as the stuffed and mounted "PharLap," the wonder horse. The National Art Gallery, Swanston Street, contains some of the finest works of art in the Southern Hemisphere. A noteworthy attraction in addition to the old masters is a collection of paintings by Australian artists.

BALLET . . . Touring American and European companies appear from time to time. There is a national company too, which tours the various states.

BANKS . . . There are a number of trading banks, all of which have branches throughout Australia. Traveler's checks can be cashed at any branch. Representatives of the Bank of New South Wales and the Commonwealth Trading Bank meet every incoming aircraft in order to convert overseas travelers' funds and cash traveler's checks, regardless of the arrival time of the aircraft. Other banks are Australian and New Zealand Bank; Commercial Bank of Australia; Commercial Banking Co. of Sydney; English, Scottish and Australian Bank, and the National Bank of Australia. Thos. Cook & Son is at 350 George Street in Sydney, 267 Collins Street in Melbourne. American Express is at 82 Elizabeth Street, Sydney.

CALENDAR OF HOLIDAYS ... New Year's Day; Good Friday; Easter Monday; Queen's Birthday (in June); January 26, Australia Day; Anzac Day, April 25; Labor Day, date varies in each State; Christmas Day; December 26, Boxing Day.

CIGARETTES AND TOBACCO ... *Philip Morris* are made in Australia, but if you prefer others bring them with you and pay duty (*see* CUSTOMS REGULATIONS). Most Australian cigarettes are the English type; pipe tobacco is very good.

CLIMATE ... Australian seasons are the reverse of ours; summer starts in December; autumn in March; winter in June; spring in September. Climates vary greatly within the continent. However, Australians go north for winter vacations, south in the summer. November through May is the ideal time to visit Australia.

CLUBS ... Sydney Turf Club; Lions; Rotary; Australia Jockey Club; American National Club. There are many private clubs for which guest cards may be arranged through members or via reciprocatory arrangements with other clubs throughout the world. Tourists must be sponsored by a member at The Athenaeum, Melbourne and Green Room, all on Collins Street; The Australian, William Street, and R.A.C.V., Queen Street. For sports clubs, *see* SPORTS.

COMMON COURTESIES AND LOCAL CUSTOMS ... Australians are rather like Americans in their habits. Except when attending official functions and balls, most Australians dress quite informally, as when in restaurants and hotels. Beachwear is the same as in the United States. Except in modern hotels, there is no central heating or air-conditioning.

COMMUNICATIONS ... Cable, radio and airmail service and Trans-Pacific telephone service. Airmail rates are: postal cards, one shilling; letters, two shillings per half ounce; airmail letters ten pence.

CURRENCY ... Monetary unit is the Australian pound, worth about $2.24. There are 20 shillings to the pound and 12 pennies to a shilling (1/-).

CUSTOMS REGULATIONS AND DOCUMENTS REQUIRED FOR UNITED STATES CITIZENS ... Passport and visa, two frontview photos. Vaccination certificate. Return passage or proof of sufficient funds. You may bring in duty free 400 cigarettes, or 80 cigars, or 1 lb. of tobacco, 3 quarts of liquor, unlimited foreign currency (except only £5 English Sterling allowed in, £25 (Aust.) out). No more allowed out than declared on entry. Exposed motion-picture film may be left in bond until departure to avoid censorship.

DRUG STORES ... Known as chemist's shops here. They carry pharmaceuticals, cosmetics and photo supplies and service. Most American pharmaceuticals and cosmetics, but no soda fountains. These are found in milk bars.

ELECTRIC CURRENT ... Voltage is 220–240 volts, some A.C. some D.C. Transformer plugs needed.

FAUNA ... The animals of Australia are known the world over. The kangaroo, koala, wallaby, platypus, anteater, and giant turtles. Among birds, count the fascinating kookaburra, which allegedly laughs instead of singing; the huge emu; the lyre-bird, which imitates its feathered colleagues; cockatoos and parrots; penguins; bower birds and love birds. All of these animals and birds won't be found around or in the cities, but are native to the country and may be seen in Sydney's Zoological Park or Melbourne's Zoological Gardens or at nearby fauna reserves such as the National Park.

FLORA ... New South Wales is famous for its vegetation. Distinctive to the section is the waratah, a rosette of red; the flannel flower, which has green-tipped white petals; the red Christmas bush. These and many others may be seen at Botanic Gardens. In Melbourne, a very fine selection of Australian flora is usually on display in the Botanic Gardens.

FOOD ... Australians are great meat eaters. Beef and lamb are very popular. There is also a plentiful supply of fish, together with most types of international foods. There is no shortage of food in this area. Prices in restaurants are quite reasonable by American standards. Pasteurized milk is available and is safe to drink.

GAMBLING ... No casinos, but there is frequent horse racing and dog racing at various courses with pari-mutuel (known as totalisators) and legal bookmakers.

LANGUAGE ... English.

LAUNDRY AND DRY CLEANING ... Laundry facilities compare favorably with the United States in speed, quality and price. Laundry and dry-cleaning facilities are also available in the better-class hotels.

LIQUOR ... Beer is inexpensive and the most popular drink. Good but stronger than ours. Whiskies, imported liqueurs, popular American cocktails are all readily available at prices about the same as at home, but no bourbon or rye available. Try Australian wines, especially still dinner wines. Hotel bars are open from 9:00 A.M. to 6:00 P.M. Drinks are available in restaurants and dining rooms until 10:00 P.M. in Melbourne. In Sydney, hours are 10:00 A.M. to 10:00 P.M., close from 6:30–7:30.

MEDICAL FACILITIES ... Medical facilities are comparable to those in the United States. Doctors and dentists are excellent.

MOTION PICTURES ... There are a number of theaters in both Sydney and Melbourne which show first-run Hollywood and British films, a few that show foreign films with English subtitles.

MUSIC ... The world-renowned Sydney Symphony Orchestra, headed by Dr. Nicolai Malko, gives concerts at Town Hall, Sydney, from early March till October, also open-air orchestral concerts. Visiting ballet companies, opera and concert singers appear at the Royal and at Town Hall.

Symphony and other concerts, as well as visiting artists from overseas, are also heard regularly in the Melbourne Town Hall. During the summer months Hollywood-Bowl-type performances are held in the Melbourne Botanic Gardens.

NIGHT CLUBS AND CABARETS ... There are many night spots in Sydney. Among them: *Prince's,* 42 Martin Place, which is allegedly the favorite of Café Society in Sydney. In Melbourne it's *Claridge's,* Toorak Road, South Yarra, *Blue Derby, St. Kilda* and *The Troika,* Hampton, with dinner and supper dancing to 2:00 A.M.

PHOTOGRAPHY ... Still and movie film, including color, is available at reasonable prices. Also a wide variety of cameras and accessories, mainly German brands. Kodak has its own laboratories and stores here (386 George St. in Sydney). Same-day developing service.

RELIGION ... In Sydney: St. Andrew's Cathedral (Anglican), George Street; St. Mary's Cathedral (Roman Catholic), College Street; St. Stephen's (Presbyterian), Macquarie Street; Wesley Chapel (Methodist), Castlereagh Street; Central Baptist Church, George Street; First Church of Christ Scientist, Forbes and Liverpool Streets; the Great Synagogue, Elizabeth Street.

In Melbourne: St. Paul's Cathedral (Church of England), Swanston and Flinders Streets; Baptist Church, Collins Street; Christian Science, St. Kilda, Kilda Road and Dorcas Street; Congregational, Latrobe Street; Jewish Synagogue, Toorak Road, South Yarra; Lutheran, 22 Parliament Place; Wesley Church (Methodist), 148 Lonsdale Street; Scots Church (Presbyterian), Collins and Russell Streets; St. Patrick's Cathedral (Roman Catholic), East Melbourne.

RESTAURANTS ... Luncheon and dinner hour are early by our standards. Some restaurants are licensed to sell hard liquor only until 10:00 P.M. So if you want to sit around all evening, pick your spot. Among the good places to eat in Sydney are the *Caprice* on the pier at Rose Bay; *Pruniers* and *Pruniers After Nine,* both at Double Bay; *Romano's* and *Prince's,* which have good food and smart clientele; the *Nanking* is in Chinatown and specializes in true Chinese foods. The *Elizabethan Inn,* in King's Cross, is just what it sounds like, a Tudorish sort of place which has an old English air about it; and the *Cahill* chain is reasonable and good.

In Melbourne, the best restaurants are *Molina's,* Bourke and Spring Streets; *Florentino* (Italian), Bourke Street; *Astoria* (Continental), Collins Place; the *Oxford Hotel,* Swanston Street, and the *Ritz* (Continental), Lonsdale Street. *Hotel Australia, Claridge's* and *Mario's,* dinner dancing nightly; Sunday night is well known at *Mario's,* when both waiters and professional artists appear in the floor show; Italian and French specialties here. *Maxim's* features international cuisine. Two medium-priced restaurants are the *Russell Collins,* corner of Russell and Collins Street, known for its floral decorations, and *Droussou's,* 243 Lonsdale Street, a cozy little Continental restaurant.

Dinner dancing nightly until 10:30 at *Menzies,* the *Australia, Chevron, Mario's* and *Oriental;* to 2 A.M. at *Claridge's, Blue Derby* and the

Troika; Friday and Saturday to 10:30 at *Savoy Plaza, Federal* and *Scotts*.

SHOPS AND STORES ... In Sydney, House of Curzon on Pitt Street features latest fashions from overseas; the Continental Bag Co., 11 Imperial Arcade, specializes in made-to-order lizard and crocodile bags and shoes; House of Prouds for opals, for which they are famous. For woolens and blankets, shop at David Jones, Ltd., Elizabeth Street, well known as "D.J.'s," which displays a fine array of both imported and local products and specializes in tweed clothing. Farmer and Co., George Street, caters to the well-dressed man. Grace Brothers of Broadway is one of the largest department stores.

Melbourne is well supplied with excellent shops and stores, the Myer Emporium being the biggest and most modern, which compares favorably with large American establishments. Georges, Collins Street, is a top woman's specialty store and rates high by any standards. This store carries large stocks of imported and local goods. There are many other stores, including Buckley and Nunn, Hicks Atkinson, Henry Buck Pty. Ltd., a first-class man's shop. In addition, there are lots of interesting, small shops in Melbourne's numerous arcades. Goods are not expensive.

SPECTATOR SPORTS ... Racing is the favorite sport in Sydney. There are four race courses in the metropolitan area: Randwick, which accommodates 100,000 people; Canterbury; Rosehill, which has a two-furlong stretch; Moorfield, 5 miles out, is the home of the favorites. Trotting races are held Saturday afternoons at Harold Park Race Course; Greyhound racing on Saturday nights. There is a tote at all courses and legal bookmakers, too. All tracks have restaurants and bars. Meets are held Saturdays and public holidays.

Cricket matches are played at Sydney Cricket Ground. Football is popular during their autumn and winter season. Tennis, of course, is the national pride. Matches are played at the Lawn Tennis Association courts at White City, Rushcutter's Bay. Boxing and wrestling matches at Rushcutter's Bay or Leichhardt Stadiums. Midget car and motorcycle racing at Sydney Sports Grounds. Yachting regattas at Sydney and its nearby coastal resorts. Golf tournaments at the various golf clubs. The Royal Sydney Golf Club at Rose Bay is world famous.

Horse racing is also the favored spectator sport in Melbourne. Races are held at least every Saturday. The principal courses are Flemington, Caulfield and Moonee Valley. The Flemington race course is so large that it has a straight six furlongs, for six-furlong races. All tracks have restaurants and bars, totes and bookmakers. During their winter months, Australian Rules Football attracts crowds of 20,000 to 80,000 spectators. Baseball and softball are also gaining popularity.

Visitors in Melbourne may also see top-ranking tennis stars in action at Kooyong at the end of November, when the Victorian Championships are played with entrants from all States. Boxing and wrestling matches are popular and are held on Friday nights at the West Melbourne Stadium. Cricket is regularly played at the Melbourne Cricket Ground and other ovals in the greater Melbourne area every Saturday during the summer months. From time to time test matches are played between Australia and overseas countries, such as England, South Africa and India.

SPORTS... There are many good municipal golf courses in Sydney at which visitors are welcome, or you may arrange for cards at the various private golf clubs. (Check with Pan American.) Royal Sydney Golf Club is the largest. Municipal courses at Moore Park, Randwick and Bondi. There are horses for hire and many bridle paths. Swimming is wonderful at the beaches to the north and south of the city. There are many indoor pools, too. Tennis may be played by visitors at many private tennis clubs upon application. There is game shooting during the open seasons. Inquire at the Tourist Bureau about this and about the new Prince Alfred Swimming Pool and Ice Skating rink. (Olympic hockey size, 185 by 85 feet.) Big-game fishing is a favorite sport in New South Wales. Marlin, swordfish, tuna and shark are plentiful. Inland streams are well stocked with trout and bass.

In and near Melbourne visitors may play golf on a number of fine public courses, one of the best being Yarra Bend National Park and Public Golf Course, a few miles from the city. They may also play on a private club course if they are introduced by members. Some of the better-known clubs are Metropolitan, Royal Melbourne, Commonwealth and Huntingdale. The St. Kilda Tennis Club opens its courts to the public, but visitors must be introduced by members at Kooyong courts. Private tennis courts are also available for hire. Horseback riding around the Botanic Gardens and Government House is pleasant.

Indoor swimming is available at the Melbourne City Baths, Swanston Street, Y.M.C.A., and Richmond Baths, where the water is heated. During Melbourne's summer months, you may swim at one of the nearby beach resorts, such as St. Kilda, Frankston, or, for those who like surfing, Portsea, which is 60 miles from Melbourne. Regular train and bus services operate to these resorts. Ice skating is available at St. Moritz, St. Kilda. Boating on the Yarra River is a pleasant pastime; boats may be hired at Macauley's new Boat Shed, day or evening. Squash courts are available for hire at Findlay's Health School, 279 Little Collins Street, Flinders Lane Squash Courts, 237 Flinders Lane, St. Kilda Courts (squash), Canterbury Road, St. Kilda. Fees are moderate.

THEATERS... In Sydney foreign companies usually appear at the *Empire.* The *Royal* features Australian companies in opera, ballet, musical comedies. The *Independent* has a repertory stock company under the direction of Doris Fitton. The *Tivoli* specializes in vaudeville and revues. Special drama and ballet performances occasionally.

In Melbourne, *Her Majesty's Theater,* Exhibition Street, shows all types of stage productions, from musical comedy to grand opera. The *Comedy Theater,* located at Exhibition Street, is well known for its first-class stage plays. The *Tivoli Theater,* Bourke Street, specializes in variety shows and stars both local and imported artists. There are also a number of little theaters in and around Melbourne, such as the *Union Theater* (University), *National Theater,* East Melbourne, opposite St. Patrick's Cathedral and the *Little Theater,* South Yarra.

TIME . . . Time in Sydney and Melbourne is 18 hours later than Pacific Coast Standard Time. There are three time zones within the country. No Daylight Saving Time.

TIPPING . . . Tip as you would at home, about 10 or 15 per cent.

TRANSPORTATION . . . There are electric trains, buses, trams and ferries. These last are important in Sydney, which is a harbor city. Cars such as the Holden, an Australian car made by General Motors, are for hire and are reasonable; traffic keeps to the left. There is a subway, too, known as the Underground, in Sydney.

WATER . . . Safe to drink, good tasting and very soft.

WHAT TO BUY . . . Australian woolens are the finest in the world. Blankets are a good buy. Crocodile and lizard bags and shoes are cheaper here.

WHAT TO WEAR . . . Depends entirely on when you go and where. Remember the Australian seasons are the reverse of ours. In their summer season, you will need beach clothes, sports attire and evening clothes. Formal dress is necessary only for official functions and gala balls. Dinner jackets, however, are popular when visiting night clubs and cabarets. For Melbourne, Sydney and the other large cities, dress as you would at home. Light-colored clothes are fine in summer. Medium or light-weight suits for women are always practical. Take a topcoat and raincoat. Men need slacks and sports jackets. White suits for the tropics, warmer clothes for other areas.

WHERE TO GO—SIGHTSEEING . . .

Sydney . . . Sydney, often called the Harbor City, is cosmopolitan and gay. Located on the coast of New South Wales, it is surrounded by beach resorts which stretch for hundreds of miles in each direction. It is a city of tall buildings, parks, tree-shaded streets. Its port is one of the world's busiest. Hyde Park, almost in the center of the city, is worth seeing. It contains war memorials, flower gardens and attractive walks. The Underground (subway) traverses its length. Very near by are the Botanic Gardens, on the edge of which stands the residence of the Governor of New South Wales. The gardens contain wonderful examples of Australian flora. At the Zoological Gardens, which are reached by ferry from Circular Quay or by electric tram over the famous Sydney Harbor Bridge, there is a fine assemblage of indigenous Australian animals which are shown in surroundings that resemble their native haunts. Centennial Park, reached by various electric tram lines, is enormous and has magnificent flower gardens and lakes. Visit Fort Denison, a little island in Farm Cove off Sydney Harbor, which was used to detain convicts. There are interesting relics to be seen there.

Bondi Beach, about a half hour from Sydney, is one of the most popular resorts on the coast. There are a Beach Pavilion, restaurants, swimming pool. Manly, another resort, is 7 miles to the northeast of Circular Quay, the main ferry station. It is reached by ferry in half an hour. Here there is fine surf bathing, a promenade and, on the bay side, a swimming pool. Cronulla, on the coast, is 17 miles away and has a fine beach and esplanade. Kurnell on Botany Bay is where Captain Cook landed. Coogee, Dee Why and Palm Beach are other beaches particularly well known.

The Blue Mountains, about 2 hours from Sydney, are well worth a trip. There is a 2-day planned tour from the city which takes you there or you may go on your own. The mountains range about 3,500 feet above sea level and fringe the Hawkesbury Basin. The scenery is magnificent and there are several towns with hotels for tourists. One of the sights is the Jenolan Caves, a series of limestone caverns lighted by electricity, giving an eerie and beautiful effect. There are guided tours daily. The *Jenolan Caves House* has good hotel accommodations convenient to the beautiful, unusual countryside. Near the caves is a bird and wildlife sanctuary which is well worth a visit. Katoomba is one of the main towns in the region. From there you may visit the Wentworth Falls and Leura Falls, all interesting. There are two National Parks within a comparatively short distance from Sydney, Kuring-gai Chase and Royal National Park. Each is a sanctuary for animal and bird life and each features indigenous flora. They are both worth seeing. Pay a visit to a sheep or cattle "station" (ranch), if possible.

Mt. Kosciusko . . . Not far from Sydney is Kosciusko National Park a mountain reserve in the Great Dividing Range. Here some of the world's best skiing is enjoyed from May to November. Six miles below the summit is the *Chalet,* an extraordinary-looking hotel made of checkered terra cotta with a round tower entrance. It has modern accommodations, central heating and other attributes, including a resident surgeon on hand for ski injuries. There are ski lifts nearby and daily classes under the auspices of the Kosciusko ski school. There is a good motor road from Jindabyne to the summit. Mt. Kosciusko is a summer resort, too. There are tennis courts, excellent trout fishing in the well-stocked streams, riding and mountain climbing.

Melbourne . . . Melbourne is popularly described as being like Boston in temperament and atmosphere. Its citizens are conservative and rather aloof. But once they know you, they are hospitable in the extreme. The city's streets are broad and airy. The center of the city is busy and crowded, but in the outlying sections there are beautiful gardens and parks. The city is situated on the Yarra River and from the river banks you get a lovely view of the skyline (sightseeing boats operate during Melbourne's summer months from Prince's Bridge). Collins Street is the pride of the town, a broad tree-lined street with shops, cafés and coffee houses. At the top of Collins Street is the Treasury Building, surrounded by the Treasury Gardens. An avenue of elms leads into Fitzroy Gardens, where you will see Captain Cook's cottage, miniature village, and the carved fairy tree. Enter from Spring Street or Wellington Parade. The Botanic Gardens to the southeast of the city feature the wonderful flowers for which this land is famous. Government House, residence of the State Governor, is near here. Take a trip to the zoo in Royal Park. There is a miniature railroad and an elephant ride for the children. You'll enjoy a drive along St. Kilda Road, a boulevard lined with triple rows of trees which runs from Prince's Bridge to St. Kilda, where you will find Luna Park, an amusement spot like Coney Island. There are restaurants, cinemas, skating rinks and roller coasters. At Village Belle, adjacent to the park, are night clubs and restaurants. Other points of interest include the Geological Museum, Gisborne Street; the Museum of Applied Science, next to the National Art Gallery, Swanston Street.

Less than an hour by electric train from Flinders Street Station and well worth while is the trip to Upper Fern Tree Gully with connecting bus to Olinda, Sassafras, Belgrave and Monbulk, resort towns which are noted for their beautiful fern gullies, forests and picturesque mountain walks. Readily accessible by train is Geelong, 45 miles from Melbourne, on Corio Bay. This progressive city is the gateway to Victoria's rich Western District. Two other interesting day trips well worth taking from Melbourne are to Ballarat, one of Victoria's leading provincial cities with beautiful gardens and statuary, and the Eureka Stockade; and to Bendigo, a charming provincial center in Northern Victoria.

Cowes (Phillip Island) is a delightful seaside resort noted for its remarkable mutton-bird rookeries, seal colony and koalas. Frankston is another popular seaside resort with panoramic views across the bay and pleasant inland walks. It's one hour from Flinders Street Station, Melbourne. Also take a day's trip to the favorite seaside resorts of Sorrento, Portsea, Flinders and Mornington, all on Mornington Peninsula; and Torquay, Anglesea and Lorne—all on the ocean.

Canberra... The federal capital of Australia is about 200 miles from Sydney. This is a modern city about 40 years old. It has pleasant gardens, and some beautiful buildings. The hotel here is the *Canberra*, $7.50 single, $11 double, with bath.

Brisbane... The capital of Queensland is a modern subtropical city with a population of 527,500. The hotels include *Lennons*, ($7.25 single, $11.50 double, with bath), the *Carlton*, the *Gresham* and the *National*. From Brisbane it is quite easy to visit Great Barrier Reef.

Great Barrier Reef... This great coral reef stretches for about 1,200 miles along the Queensland coast. It is reached by plane from Sydney in about 3 hours. Here you will find hundreds of small islands and coves almost completely unspoiled. There are plans for luxury hotels and resorts; one at Hayman Island has opened. But for the most part it is a paradise for fishermen, surf lovers and people who like to laze in the sun. At some points the reef is only about 20 miles from the mainland; at the widest it is 150 miles off. The most popular group of islands are the Whitsundays, south of Bowen, including Hayman Island, Lindeman Island, Day Dream Island. These are the "high" islands on the inner edge of the reef. The "low" islands such as Heron, Dunk and Green Island are part of the reef proper and are actually coral cays. At the Whitsundays, Lindeman is the first

Cruises and tours of all kinds are available to the vast vacation area of Great Barrier Reef. The group above is near Day Dream Island.

stopping place. Here is Mt. Olden, from which you can see for miles and miles. Day Dream nearby is a jungle paradise and the fishing for mackerel, bonito, snapper and swordfish is marvelous. Heron Island, about 300 miles north of Brisbane, is one of the most beautiful of the "low" islands. It has a magnificent beach, a green lagoon, wonderful trees and flowers. The sea here is clear; you can see the marine vegetation from an ordinary boat. All along the Great Barrier Reef you can take glass-bottom boats or motor launches along what the Australians call "the great canal." This is a magnificent vacation spot, a paradise for the sportsman and an escape for everyone tired of cities, night clubs and too many people. Even though many large hotels and night clubs are planned for this area, there is plenty of room, and people who want peace and quiet will still be able to find it.

Northern Territory ... Is really the world's "largest frontier." Here are the huge cattle ranches, the true wide-open spaces. Much of the territory is undeveloped, but year after year civilization encroaches a bit more. Darwin is the capital of Northern Territory. If you really want to see Australian aborigines in their native habitat, you must go into central Australia.

Adelaide ... The capital of South Australia, is in the center of sheep-and-cattle-grazing country. It is a well-planned city, with broad straight streets and avenues set at right angles. The city has been planned so that the beaches and hill resorts are no more than a half hour's trip from the capital. The three top hotels are *South Australian* (bed and breakfast, $5 per day), *Richmond* and *Ambassadors* (bed and breakfast, $4 and up per day).

Places of interest: Botanic Gardens, entrance from North Terrace, opposite East Terrace; Koala Bear Park in Parklands, between Walkerville car line and Zoological gardens; Torrens Lake, King William Street. Boats for hire. Bordered by Elder Park (south bank) and Memorial Drive (north bank). Suburban seaside resorts (within half an hour's journey by rail, tram or bus from the city) include Largs, Glenelg, Marino and Kingston Park (a National Pleasure Resort). Long stretches of clean, shelving sand and good bathing facilities are features of these modern seaside resorts.

Seven miles from Adelaide, in the Mount Lofty Ranges, and connected with the city by electric tram and bitumen road, is Morialta Falls Reserve, with a winding path which leads through magnificent mountain scenery to the waterfalls. Waterfall Gully, also in the Mount Lofty Ranges, is reached by following the Burnside tram line to the terminus, then about 3 miles along a winding road of exceptional beauty. Refreshments are obtainable at a kiosk. On Sundays and holidays buses run from the Burnside tram terminus to the Falls. The National Park abounds in shady gullies, magnificent trees and luxuriant foliage. Much of it has been preserved in its virgin state, but ample conveniences, such as refreshment rooms, cricket pitches, tennis courts, and golf links have been provided.

Tasmania . . . South of Melbourne is the heart-shaped island of Tasmania, smallest of the six Australian states. It is separated from the continent by 140 miles of the Bass Strait. A verdant, misty spot, it is rather like Ireland. Hobart, its capital, nestles in the shadow of Mt. Wellington, the summit of which is about twelve miles from the center of the city. The *Wrest Point Hotel* at Sandy Bay, Hobart, is excellent—rates about $7.50 a day single, including breakfast with private bath. There is also *Hadley's Hotel,* at similar rates. Hobart itself is a metropolis with theaters, shops, offices and factories. There are ferries and electric streetcars and trolley buses to the main suburbs. Among the attractions of Tasmania are the wildflowers in the spring. Mountain climbing, fishing, including trout fishing, and sailing are among the sports this island has to offer.

Tasmania has an excellent road system so you can tour the island in comfort by car or coach, or make your headquarters at a selected center and undertake from there day trips to many beauty spots. Tourist roads to the summits of mountains, easily accessible from Hobart and Launceston, give you impressive panoramic views. Here are two interesting trips:

Hobart to Launceston via East Coast (2 days): the East Coast provides a series of resorts of scenic interest. The tour covers 274 miles, with an overnight stop on the way. Leave Hobart via Hobart Bridge and pass by Cambridge and Sorell. Be sure to see the magnificent window in the century-old church at Buckland. Then, to Orford, Triabunna, and Swansea. During the afternoon proceed ·through

The Cathedral of St. Mary's is one of the many fine churches in Sydney. Almost all religious denominations are represented.

The beaches are excellent in Australia. This one is 60 miles from Brisbane, capital of Queensland.

Bicheno, St. Marys, and Scamander to St. Helens. From St. Helens the tour leaves the coastline and turns inland through Pyengana, Weldborough Pass, Derby, Branxholm, to Scottsdale and over Meredith's Siding to Launceston.

Hobart to Launceston via West Coast (2 days): this trip, almost in direct contrast to the East Coast, consists of bold, mountainous and forest scenery, commencing with the Derwent Valley and passing through Ouse. Tarraleah to the Hydro-Electric Works at Butler's Gorge. In the afternoon the tour continues along the West Coast Road, from which extensive panoramas of the beautiful ranges of mountains can be seen, on the way to Queenstown. Returning over the same road on the second day to Lake St. Clair, then via Bronte Park and Great Lake to Launceston.

Launceston . . . In the north of the State is Launceston, charmingly situated where the North and South Esk Rivers merge to form the River Tamar. This "garden city" is famous for its beautiful parks. Two of the top hotels are the *Brisbane* and the *Launceston*, both with rates of about $9 per day, both with bath.

Several large tracts of Tasmania have been reserved for pleasure purposes. The Mount Field National Park (about 40,000 acres), 50 miles from Hobart, includes Mount Field mountain range, with skiing and skating on the plateau. The scenery is superb. A still bigger national park is Cradle Mountain Lake St. Clair (about 525 square miles), where there are mountains, wild canyons, forests, waterfalls, and lakes galore. This reserve attracts hundreds of hikers annually. Limestone caves are another of Tasmania's attractions for sightseers. Caves have been discovered at several centers, the chief group being at Mole Creek, where caves known as King Solomon, Marakoopa, Baldock's and Scott's are located.

Perth . . . Capital of Western Australia, fringes the banks of the beautiful Swan River and enjoys the distinction of being Australia's sunniest capital. The Post Office and Commonwealth Bank in Forrest Place—a broad, though short, thoroughfare opposite the entrance to the Central Railway Station—are among the finest buildings in Australia and dominate the city's architecture. There are many others of striking architectural design.

Among the places of interest are the Art Gallery and Museum, Beaufort Street; Parliament House, Harvest Terrace; the Observatory, Havelock Street, the University of Western Australia and King's Park. King's Park, set aside in 1871, now comprises about 1,000 acres, most of which are in bushland state and grow a large variety of indigenous flora, which bloom profusely from August to November. There are good roads from which you get a magnificent panorama of Perth, the Swan River, and the Darling Ranges. The State War Memorial is here too. Within easy reach of the city are numerous ocean and river beaches available to visitors. Hotel accommodations are good at the *Esplanade* ($10 a day for room with bath and all meals); the *Palace* (about $5.25, room with bath and breakfast); and the *Adelphi* ($6.75, bed and breakfast).

SOURCES OF FURTHER INFORMATION . . . In Sydney the New South Wales Government Tourist Bureau will gladly supply information on attractions and activities of interest. Pan American's office is at Berger House, 82 Elizabeth St. (Tel. BW 2252).

In Melbourne the Victorian Government Tourists' Bureau provides information and makes arrangements for transportation, tours and hotels. Pioneer Tours offers bus tours. Both are on Collins Street. There are three daily newspapers with theater listings, sports events, etc. Pan Am's office is at 85 Collins Street (Tel. MF 6351).

In New York, Australian News and Information Bureau, 636 5th Avenue.

FIJI ISLANDS

WEATHER IN SUVA—Lat. S18°08′—Alt. Approx. sea level

Temp.	JAN.	FEB.	MAR.	APR.	MAY	JUNE	JULY	AUG.	SEPT.	OCT.	NOV.	DEC.
Low	74°	74°	74°	73°	71°	69°	68°	68°	69°	70°	71°	73°
High	86°	86°	86°	84°	82°	80°	79°	79°	80°	81°	83°	85°
Average	80°	80°	80°	79°	77°	75°	74°	74°	75°	76°	77°	79°
Days of Rain	21	19	24	20	17	14	10	12	14	14	16	17

LOCATION ... This group of about 322 islands, totaling over 7,000 square miles, lies in the South Pacific east of northern Australia. Suva, however, is nearly 2,000 air miles from Sydney in southern Australia.

CHARACTERISTICS ... All of Fiji is rather like a picture postal card. The colors are brilliant; the flowers vivid and ever present; even the uniforms of the Fijian police are picturesque. There are now more East Indians in Fiji than native Fijians and they add color to the scene. The local European community heartily welcomes visitors, as do the coconut planters on outlying islands. Prices are extremely low. All in all, it's a delightful dream spot with all the relaxed comforts and charms associated with South Sea islands.

POPULATION ... Estimated at 346,000, including nearly 8,000 Europeans.

SIZE ... 7,083 square miles. Viti Levu, the largest island, with 4,053 square miles, is smaller than Connecticut.

GOVERNMENT ... The islands in the group constitute the British Crown Colony of Fiji.

HOW TO GET THERE ... By Pan American Clipper from the United States West Coast via Honolulu about 27½ hours (elapsed time) to Nandi. Actually the time becomes a day later when you cross the International Date Line. Air service between Nandi and Suva by Fiji Airways. By ship, Suva is reached in about 14 days.

ACCOMMODATIONS ... There's a new, luxurious, air-conditioned hotel in Suva, the *Club Hotel*. Rates are $11 single, $21 double, $32 for suites, European Plan. The *Grand Pacific Hotel* is a lovely place on the harbor. Large and comfortable with verandas, it's British Colonial in atmosphere. Rates are $8 to $10, American Plan. Other hotels in Suva are the *Metropole, Garrick* and *Melbourne,* none with private baths, about $6 American Plan. Visitors may have to share double rooms during heavy tourist season, May to October, when you should reserve space well in advance. Away from town there are also several delightful hotels at the beach resorts; *see* WHERE TO GO.

CUSTOMS REGULATIONS AND DOCUMENTS REQUIRED FOR UNITED STATES CITIZENS ... Valid passport and vaccination certificate are required. Continuation or return ticket also required. 200 cigarettes, 25 cigars or 4 ounces of tobacco and 1 quart bottle of liquor for personal use are allowed, duty free. Passengers from the United States must declare any non-Fijian currency on arrival. Passengers must not leave the Colony with more United States currency than that declared on arrival. No restrictions on cameras, but all unexposed film must be declared. Excess may be left in bond.

WHAT TO WEAR ... Summer clothes are worn all the year round in Fiji by both men and women. During the winter a woolen cardigan is suggested. Formal dress is required only at certain functions, such as Masonic meetings, for men, and balls and dances, for women. Bring sunglasses, too.

WHERE TO GO—SIGHTSEEING ...

Suva ... There is a variety of tours available, ranging from one of an hour or so, which covers the high points of Suva, to a tour of several days, which includes all of Viti Levu and principal points of interest on outlying islands. There are also Harbor cruises. In Suva itself you will want to explore the central shopping areas, city markets, Walu Bay, Tamavua Heights, the Reservoir Lookout, Samabula, Lauthala Bay, Suva Point. A visit to the Colonial Sugar Mill at Nausori, 14 miles away, is also interesting. Even the Suva cemetery, with its brilliant colored croton trees, is interesting and different.

You should take a drive along Kings Road, which encircles the coast of the island to the north, and Queens Road, which bands it to the south. (The island is about 135 miles long.) On the north side you pass through Lautoka (*Lautoka Hotel*), starting place for the Blue Lagoon Cruise of the beautiful primitive Yasawa Islands, with interesting native villages, *kava* ceremonies and *mekes* (native dances). Farther along the road is Vatukoula, third largest town in Fiji, where one can visit the Vatukoula Gold Mines, one of the largest producers in the South Pacific. You drive for miles through sugar-cane country and cattle grazing areas.

On the south shore road you will see heavy tropical forests and the large pastoral areas of the Navua (River) flats with herds of grazing cattle. Korolevu, which is about midway between Nandi Airport and

Suva on the south shore road, is certainly the spot for anyone who is really serious about getting away from it all. There is an enchanting hotel with small native-type cabins (*bures*) right on the beach. Here you may stay for luncheon or for weeks. The swimming is excellent, the fishing marvelous, there are horses to ride and a wonderful deep-blue sea to look at. The price of all this peace and quiet is from $7.20 single, from $17 double, American Plan. Also popular is the *Beachcomber,* a ranch-type hotel nearer Suva. The facilities and low prices are about the same, the beach outstanding, but there's more activity in a pleasant, tropical sort of way.

On your island drives you will see picturesque South Sea villages, with thatched huts, palm-lined beaches, magnificent views of surf breaking on the coral reef. Along the roadside you'll see native Fijians with wiry bushy hair which practically stands on end, and children who wave to you happily. In the East Indian settlements you will find women wearing the traditional saris and some of the men wearing white turbans. The Fijians and East Indians live in separate communities, rarely intermingle, but manage to live peacefully.

The interesting weekly river and harbor tours include Lauthala Bay and Nukulau Island, for swimming, reef exploring and relaxing in a beautiful tropical setting. Costs are $5–$7.00.

Tribal dances take place only on special occasions and then are usually performed by natives from one of the smaller outlying islands. There are, on rare occasions, Fire Walking ceremonies on Mbengga Island, southwest of Suva, where Fijians baffle onlookers by treading barefoot over red-hot stones without apparent injury.

Tahiti ... This famous island is now readily accessible by air. There's a fortnightly overnight service in a 4-engine Solent flying boat to Papeete, Tahiti, via Aitukaki in the Cook Islands, or a weekly DC6B service to BoraBora, then by flying boat to Papeete.

SOURCES OF FURTHER INFORMATION ... The Fiji Visitors Bureau, situated opposite Suva's Town Hall building on Victoria Parade, has tickets for local events and information on tours, local sightseeing and cruises; literature in English on Fiji, maps of Suva, Viti Levu and the Fiji Islands. The Pan American Sales Office, Victoria Parade, can provide similar information.

A typical South Seas village, seen along the roads that lead around Viti Levu Island from Suva.

Coconut palms nod over the streets of Suva. Grand Pacific Hotel is in the foreground.

HAWAII

WEATHER IN HONOLULU—Lat. N21°18'—Alt. 25'

Temp.	JAN.	FEB.	MAR.	APR.	MAY	JUNE	JULY	AUG.	SEPT.	OCT.	NOV.	DEC.
Low	66°	66°	66°	68°	69°	72°	73°	73°	73°	72°	70°	68°
High	76°	76°	77°	78°	80°	82°	83°	84°	83°	82°	80°	78°
Average	71°	71°	72°	73°	75°	77°	78°	79°	78°	77°	75°	73°
Days of Rain	14	10	13	12	11	11	13	13	13	13	14	15

LOCATION ... The Hawaiian Islands lie approximately 2,090 miles southwest of San Francisco, a distance about equal to that between San Francisco and New York. Honolulu is about the same distance north of the equator as Havana, Cuba.

CHARACTERISTICS ... Wonderful beaches, tropical flowers, hula dancers and flower leis are part of the fiber of the Hawaiian Islands. Here you have the additional delight of being on home territory yet finding it as different as anything you have ever imagined. You can swim at the perfect beaches, luxuriate at wonderful hotels, go deep-sea fishing, learn to ride a surfboard, and enjoy the wonderful climate. It's a romantic spot, ideal for a vacation.

POPULATION ... 499,794, of which 230,485 live in Honolulu, a city almost as large as Miami.

SIZE ... The area of the island group is 6,441 square miles, of which the largest island, Hawaii, is over 4,000 square miles, approximately the size of Connecticut and Rhode Island together. Oahu is 40 miles long and 26 wide.

CAPITAL ... Honolulu

GOVERNMENT ... After a long history of desiring statehood dating back to 1903, Congress passed a bill providing for admittance of Hawaii as the 50th State, and on March 18, 1959, the President signed the official proclamation of admittance.

HOW TO GET THERE ... By Pan American Clipper from San Francisco, Los Angeles, Portland or Seattle. Flying time from San Francisco, 8¾ hours. By ship from San Francisco, 5 days.

ACCOMMODATIONS ... The *Royal Hawaiian* on Waikiki Beach, the best-known hotel in the Islands, has everything: dining terraces, dancing, entertainment, tennis courts. Rates about $16 to $30 double, American Plan (European Plan available). The *Halekulani,* also on the beach, is quiet and pleasant. Rates $10 to $32 double, European Plan. Other good hotels on Waikiki, all European Plan (with double rates quoted), include the *Moana,* under the same management as *Royal Hawaiian,* $8 to $16. The hotel rooms and cottages of Kaiser's huge Hawaiian Village are $10 to $40. There are a number of other excellent new hotels: The *Reef,* $8.50 to $50; the *Waikiki Biltmore,* $9 to $17; the *Princess Kaiulani,* $7.50 to $16; the *Surfrider,* $12 to $22; the *Waikikian,* $7 to $20. There are also many small hotels and apartment hotels which are available by the day, week or month. Rates given apply the year around; make reservations in advance.

ARTS ... Honolulu Academy of Arts contains interesting collections of Oriental and Western art, and special exhibitions of Pacificana and modern art. Bishop Museum houses one of the finest collections of Pacificana and crafts of the entire Pacific, birds, animals, famous feather work of the Hawaiians and historic relics. This is a must in Honolulu. Queen Emma Museum is the beautiful home of the former Queen and contains many collections of personal and household relics of the era in which she lived. Archives, next to Iolani Palace, contain important and valuable Hawaiian documents, relics and old photographs of early island history. Good source of reference on early culture, history and politics. The Iolani Palace throne room is interesting.

BALLET ... No ballet here, but there is always the hula. And it can be beautiful.

BANKS ... In Honolulu: American Security Bank; Bank of Hawaii; Bishop National Bank; Liberty Bank, Central Pacific Bank. These banks have many branches throughout the Islands.

CALENDAR OF HOLIDAYS ... New Year's Day; Chinese New Year, about a month later; Lei Day (May Day); June 11, Kamehameha Day; March 26, Prince Kuhio Day (Hawaii's first delegate to Congress); Flower Festival in September. Aloha Week in October or November is similar to Mardi Gras. Christmas Eve and Christmas Day.

CIGARETTES, TOBACCO ... Same as on the Mainland.

CLIMATE ... There are frequent but short showers. Like spring or early fall on the Mainland. Generally speaking, it's "short-sleeved" weather.

CLUBS ... Rotary, Lions, Y.M.C.A., Kiwanis, Junior Chamber of Commerce, American Legion, Soroptomist, Zonta, Altrusa. For golf and tennis clubs, *see* SPORTS.

COMMON COURTESIES AND LOCAL CUSTOMS ... You

will find that the Hawaiian people are extremely friendly and will go out of their way to make your stay enjoyable. Newcomers are called *Malihinis,* old timers, *Kamaainas* and warm friends, *Aikanes Aloha,* of course, in the traditional expression of greeting or farewell. Because of this highly relaxed, friendly way of life, you will undoubtedly find yourself becoming a "native" soon after your arrival. There is nothing that pleases the Hawaiians more. The Hawaiian lei is a very special thing. It can be made of any one of a number of native flowers, but each island has its own lei and every flower lei has a different meaning. Hawaiians refer to the rest of the United States as the Mainland.

COMMUNICATIONS ... RCA, Mackay, and Globe Wireless, telephone, radio and airmail.

CURRENCY ... Same as in the States.

DRUG STORES ... Many of them the same as on the Mainland.

ELECTRIC CURRENT ... Same as in most of the rest of the United States, 120 volts, A.C.

FLORA ... The Hawaiian Islands are a living flower show. Hibiscus blooms the year round. Bougainvillaea is everywhere, as is the famous night-blooming Cereus. The fabulous Bird of Paradise is guarded preciously when it blooms. Orchids are everywhere and are even sold in the dime stores. Hawaii's flowering trees are wonderful to see. The African tulip tree, the jacaranda, the shower trees, and Pride of India, the poinciana and many others are all indigenous to the Islands and add to their charm.

FOOD ... There are many restaurants and hotels where you can get international food. And, of course, there are wonderful Chinese and Japanese restaurants. The luau, which is a Hawaiian feast, features the Hawaiian dish *poi,* a paste made of the root of the taro plant. You must try it, along with the local fruits and juices, such as pineapple, papaya, guava nectar, passion fruit juice and papaya juice.

LAUNDRY AND DRY CLEANING ... Modern facilities same as on the Mainland.

LIQUOR ... All of the usual brands are available at regular prices. There are exotic local drinks with floating Vanda orchids, such as Moana Banyan Court Punch.

MEDICAL FACILITIES ... Same as on the Mainland.

MOTION PICTURES ... Same as on the Mainland.

MUSIC ... The Honolulu Symphony is the leading musical organization of the Islands. Members of the orchestra are working people who perform under the leadership of a competent director. Artist Series: visitors can enjoy good music presented by the finest visiting artists. Then there is the Hawaiian music so far iliar on the Mainland.

NIGHT CLUBS AND CABARETS ... There is a tremendous variety of night life in Hawaii, although the typical night club is in the minority. At most night clubs you can see a good hula and many places feature Tahitian and Samoan entertainment.

PHOTOGRAPHY ... All types of film and photo equipment are available throughout the Islands at the same price as on the Mainland. Film developing takes three or four days.

RELIGION . . . There are churches of all denominations.

RESTAURANTS . . . Top hotels all have several dining rooms and serve excellent food. One of the best-known and most popular restaurants is *Lau Yee Chai* in Waikiki. Its outdoor dance floor has a vertical rock garden and waterfall. The food is superb. There are a number of picturesque Japanese tea houses. Reservations should be made in advance. The *Tropics,* the *Broiler,* the *Tahitian Lanai* and the *Colonel's Plantation, Beef Steak* and *Coffee House* are popular. Be sure to attend a Hawaiian *luau,* a combination of the best native dishes and Polynesian entertainment. Some of the places which feature these are *Don the Beachcomber's* and *Queen's Surf* and the *Hawaiian Village. Luaus* are by reservation only. Among the best places for cocktails in the Waikiki area are: the *Royal Hawaiian Hotel, Captain Cook Bar* in the Surfrider, the *Bora Bora Bar* at Don the Beachcomber's, *Kamaaina Bar* at the Moana, the *Tiare Room Shell Bar* and *Ale Ale Kai Room* at the Hawaiian Village, the *House Without a Key* at the Halekulani, the *Gourmet,* the *Queen's Surf* and the bars of the new hotels.

SHOPS AND STORES . . . Honolulu is a wonderful place to buy Oriental wares, for Chinese *objets d'art* and other Chinese goods. The Watumull Stores in downtown Honolulu and Waikiki are good places to buy hand-blocked linens and other textiles, Hawaiian sportswear, carved Hawaiian woods and *lauhala* bags. *Lauhala* is the leaf of the pandanus tree, from which all sorts of novelties are made. At Waikiki as well as in downtown Honolulu there are many other good shops.

SPECTATOR SPORTS . . . Polo, wrestling, boxing, baseball, barefoot football.

SPORTS . . . Surfboard riding is the islands' pastime. Instructors can be hired by the hour. Water skiing is popular. Outrigger canoeing and catamaran (twin-hulled craft) sailing is also popular. You can charter boats to sail yourself or take one of the regular charter-boat trips. For deep-sea fishing, boats may be chartered; the fishing is sensational. You can learn to spear fish off the reefs. There are tennis courts open to the public at Ala Moana Park along the sea. Racquets may also be rented. You can hike in Hawaii's wonderful mountains by joining the Hawaiian Trail and Mountain Club. Hawaii's hunting includes pheasant, quail, pigs, deer and goats. Goat hunting is the only sport available the entire year. There are many bowling alleys. For those who prefer archery, targets are always standing in Kapiolani Park in Honolulu.

There are many good golf clubs. Your hotel manager can arrange a guest card for you. Walalae Golf Club is a championship course where the annual Hawaiian opens are held some years. Oahu Country Club is a private club used by many visitors who are invited to play by members. The Ala Wai in Waikiki and Pali are municipal courses.

THEATER . . . The Honolulu Community Theater offers a year-round program of stage plays.

TIME ... Two hours earlier than Pacific Standard Time.

TIPPING ... About the same as on the Mainland.

TRANSPORTATION ... Modern buses, taxis. Private cars can be rented easily. Frequent airline service between islands.

WATER ... Both water and milk are safe to drink.

WHAT TO BUY ... Hawaiian perfumes, native jams and jellies, textiles, coral jewelry, jades and Oriental goods. You may want to take home an *holoku,* the traditional Hawaiian gown with long train for formal wear, and a *muumuu,* which makes a fine house coat or hostess gown. Also Hawaiian wood crafts.

WHAT TO WEAR ... Sportswear is worn on many more occasions in Hawaii than on the Mainland. Cotton dresses for women, sports shirts and slacks for men. You'll need sweaters and topcoats for the higher altitudes of Hawaii and Kauai. Better take evening clothes along too. Dark glasses are a must.

WHERE TO GO—SIGHTSEEING ...

Honolulu ... Within Honolulu there are many attractions. Walking tours are popular. If you prefer the sea to the streets, there is a wide range of boat accommodations available. You can take one of the famous glassbottom-boat trips either day or night. You will want to see the Aloha Tower for a panoramic view of Honolulu Harbor and the city and hills of Honolulu. The Hawaiian Village in Ala Moana Park near the Ala Wai yacht channel and the sea is an exact replica of ancient Hawaiian homes. Also in Ala Moana Park you will see all sorts of sailing and fishing craft, interesting family groups picnicking, and the Kewalo basin fishing center. Iolani Palace, former royal palace of the Hawaiian monarchy, is now the seat of state government. A trip through the pineapple canneries is interesting; regular tours are conducted on canning days. The Honolulu fish markets are fascinating, located in an area of colorful Chinese stores; native fishermen sell octopus, squid, a tremendous variety of brilliant fish, and other seafoods. Also of great interest is Fisherman's Wharf, where the sampans that do most of Hawaii's deep-sea fishing gather. You will not want to miss seeing Upside-down Falls, a phenomenon that occurs when a heavy rain falls over the cliffs and is blown upward instead of falling downward. Take a waterfront tour along Ala Moana from the yacht harbor at the Ala Wai canal to Aloha Tower.

A must on your list should be a trip to Chinatown. Although the buildings are not so distinctive as those in San Francisco, the small apothecary, jade, food and other shops are well worth seeing. In addition to the abundance of exotic flowers to be seen everywhere, for flower lovers there are special hibiscus drives and walks along the streets of the lei makers. Also the Foster Gardens, which are public gardens containing all the flowers, trees and shrubs which grow throughout the tropics. Other Oahu Island attractions that can be included in a round-the-island tour by U-Drive car, taxi or special Gray Line tour or Trade Wind Tour Pali Cruiser are: a drive through a luxuriant forest to the famous Nuuanu Pali where from the lookout you get an impressive view; Pearl Harbor, now the home of the

Outrigger canoes of various sizes can be rented on Waikiki beach near the Moana Hotel, at left. Diamond Head looms in the background.

A luau, native-style feast, is an experience which visitors can enjoy, too, through arrangements with the Hawaii Visitors' Bureau and other organizations.

Pacific fleet; particularly interesting is the cruise on a yacht through Pearl Harbor; the Navy Yard, open to the public on Saturdays and Sundays (for United States citizens only). Diamond Head, a part of Honolulu and the city's greatest landmark, and Diamond Head Crater are at the eastern end of Waikiki.

Island of Hawaii... The Island of Hawaii, known as the "big island," is dominated by the spirit of Pele, the fire goddess who, it is said, causes the volcanoes Mauna Loa and Kilauea to erupt. Mauna Loa is the world's most active volcano and you will certainly want to see it. You will also want to go to Kilauea and Halemaumau, the fire pit thought to be Pele's home. Make your headquarters in the city of Hilo, the second-largest city in the Islands. The chief hotels are the *Hilo* and the *Naniloa,* both excellent. In the National Park section, about 25 miles from the city, is *Volcano House,* situated on the very edge of Kilauea's crater.

Among other things to see on Hawaii are Akaka Falls at the end of magnificent tropical gardens; Kalapana Beach, which has black sand churned from the lava of the volcano. Paradoxically, there is skiing in winter on the slopes of the volcano. Hunters shoot wild goats there. Visit Parker Ranch. There is the *Waimea Ranch Hotel* in the middle of the ranch, which is fine and comfortable. On the Kona coast of the island there is marvelous fishing. The charming *Kona Inn, Waiaka Lodge* and *Kona Palms* are headquarters for deep-sea fishermen.

Maui... On Maui there are inns and villages at various altitudes rising from sea level to the rim of Haleakala, the world's largest dormant volcano. The *Hotel Hana-Maui* at the eastern tip of the island is the last word in luxury, but there are others more moderate. The Crater is an extraordinary sight with its cinder cones rising thousands of feet. The cones are in brilliant colors as well as black. The unique Hawaiian flower, the silversword, grows near and around them. You may descend to the floor of the crater on horseback. The new *Maui Palms Hotel* in Wailuku is good.

Lahaina on the lee side of the island, is reached by the Lahaina-Wailuku Road, noted for its scenery. There you will see the biggest banyan tree in the Islands and the Church of the Holy Innocents, with a Hawaiian Madonna painted from a native model. While on Maui, try to see a *hukilau,* or community fishing party, at Hana. You may stay at the *Pioneer Inn.*

Kauai is known as the Garden Island because of its foliage. Captain Cook landed there. The *Kauai Inn* and *Coco Palms Lodge* at Lihue are modern and excellent. They are American Plan and have everything from swimming pools to Saturday-night hula shows. One of the largest sugar mills on the Islands is here. This is an island where you will do well to hire a U-Drive car or a private car, for you will have more fun and see more that way. Hanalei on Kauai is one of the finest beaches on the Islands. There are also on the lee side the Barking Sands, with five-foot coral and lava dunes. The sand, when rubbed, sounds like a dog barking.

There is the sliding bathtub, where falls spray down a natural chute into a fresh-water swimming pool. Here, too is the Wai Lua River, near the mouth of which is a hotel, very small and very good, the *Garden Island.* You may go by hired boat up a river filled with water hyacinths to the Fern Grotto, where ferns hang from the rocks.

Molokai... This island is almost completely unspoiled. There are ranches here and pineapple plantations. Wild deer roam all over the island and hunting is permissible. Some of the finest game fishing is to be found here. The *Seaside Inn,* a hotel by the beach facing the pineapple island of Lanai, offers relaxation.

SOURCES OF FURTHER INFORMATION... The Hawaii Visitors Bureau is located at 2051 Kalakaua Avenue (Waikiki). Pan American's offices are at Princess Kaiulani Shops, 2342 Kalakaya Ave., and in downtown Honolulu in the Alexander Young Hotel Building, 1021 Bishop Street (Tel. 86421).

NEW ZEALAND

WEATHER IN AUCKLAND—Lat. S36°53′—Alt. Approx. sea level

Temp.	JAN.	FEB.	MAR.	APR.	MAY	JUNE	JULY	AUG.	SEPT.	OCT.	NOV.	DEC.
Low	59°	60°	58°	55°	51°	48°	46°	47°	49°	51°	54°	57°
High	73°	74°	72°	68°	62°	59°	57°	58°	61°	63°	67°	70°
Average	66°	67°	65°	62°	55°	54°	52°	53°	55°	57°	61°	64°
Days of Rain	10	10	11	13	19	20	21	19	17	17	15	10

LOCATION ... New Zealand consists of two large islands (North Island and South Island) and numerous small islands, of which Stewart Island, just below South Island, and Chatham Island, 500 miles to the east, are the largest. Auckland is about 1,300 air miles east of Sydney, Australia, and about the same distance south of the Fiji Islands.

CHARACTERISTICS ... New Zealand is truly unique—a wonderland of scenery, a sportsman's paradise, and a delightful spot for a completely different vacation.

New Zealanders have much in common with Americans. On first acquaintance they appear reserved, but they are naturally friendly and hospitable. European New Zealanders live in harmony with native New Zealanders, the Maoris, whose arts and traditions have contributed much to the culture of the country.

POPULATION ... Estimated at 2,282,000—roughly the same population as Detroit. Auckland, the largest city (401,200 inhabitants), is about the size of Hartford, Connecticut.

SIZE ... 103,473 square miles; about the size of Colorado.

CAPITAL ... Wellington, population 231,500; the size of Sacramento, California.

GOVERNMENT ... A member of the British Commonwealth of Nations, New Zealand is politically independent and governed by its own Parliament. The Queen is represented by a Governor-general.

HOW TO GET THERE... By Clipper from San Francisco, Los Angeles, Seattle or Portland, to Auckland via Honolulu, Canton Island and the Fiji Islands. The elapsed time is about 30 hours from the Pacific Coast, 19 hours from Honolulu, or 7 hours from Fiji. By ship about 17 days from San Francisco.

ACCOMMODATIONS... There are no hotels of the super-deluxe class in New Zealand, but in most main tourist spots there are good, comfortable ones. Lodges provide excellent accommodations for sportsmen. Private bathrooms are limited and are not always available. Prices for food and accommodations are remarkably low and hotels are spotlessly clean. In Auckland the *Grand* on Princes Street is an old, established hotel with good service. The *Transtasman,* Eden Crescent, the *Star,* Albert Street, and the *Great Northern,* Queen Street, are modernized hotels with good service. Rates at all are American Plan, about $11 per day (private bathroom). The *Royal,* Victoria Street, and the *Waverley,* Customs Street, are the best of the medium-class hotels; good food, comfortable. Rates about $8 per day, American Plan. There are a number of less expensive hotels and attractive guest houses (unlicensed).

ARTS... The War Memorial Museum at Auckland contains one of the finest collections of Maori and Polynesian exhibits in the world. The Art Gallery features works by New Zealand artists. There are similar museums and art galleries in other cities.

BALLET... A local ballet company has been formed in Auckland. Visiting companies appear occasionally in local theaters.

BANKS... There are a number of trading banks, all of which have branches throughout New Zealand. Traveler's checks can be cashed at any branch. Representatives of the Bank of New Zealand meet every incoming aircraft in order to convert overseas travelers' funds, even when they arrive outside normal banking hours. Other banks are Bank of New South Wales, Australia and New Zealand Bank, Ltd., Commercial Bank of Australia, National Bank of New Zealand, and Thos. Cook & Son.

CALENDAR OF HOLIDAYS... Christmas Day; December 26, Boxing Day; January 2, New Year's Day; Anniversary Day (January 29 for Auckland); April 25, Anzac Day; Good Friday; Easter Monday; Queen's Birthday (early June); Labor Day (late October). There are special race meetings on the first four holidays mentioned, and in addition on Anniversary Day Auckland holds its famous yachting regatta. Stores are closed from 9:00 P.M. Friday to 9:00 A.M. Monday.

CIGARETTES AND TOBACCO... New Zealand cigarettes and tobacco are available; also English brands. No American cigarettes.

CLIMATE... North Island to the north of Auckland is moist and semi-tropical. Situated below the equator, it is warmer in the north and colder in the south. South Island is slightly cooler and higher. September to April is the ideal New Zealand season, as their seasons are the reverse of ours. July, August and September are best for winter sports. Because you are never far from the sea in New Zealand, the climate is moderate.

CLUBS ... Rotary International, Lions International, Overseas League, Victoria League, Royal Empire Society, Travel Club, English Speaking Union. (Admission to the racing or trotting clubs can sometimes be arranged. Inquire at your hotel.)

COMMON COURTESIES AND LOCAL CUSTOMS ... Tea is a ritual here, morning and afternoon. When you are invited to come to tea it probably means "supper." You drive on the left.

COMMUNICATIONS ... Radio telephones and cables to the United States. Airmail, of course.

CURRENCY ... The monetary unit is the New Zealand pound, worth about $2.80, the same as the British.

CUSTOMS REGULATIONS AND DOCUMENTS REQUIRED FOR UNITED STATES CITIZENS ... Passport and visa. Smallpox vaccination certificate, two passport-size photos. For one customs declaration 200 cigarettes may be brought in free of duty, or 50 cigars, or ½ lb. of tobacco. Also 1 quart of liquor. No revolvers, automatics or pistols allowed.

DRUG STORES ... No American-type drug stores. Pharmaceuticals and cosmetics are sold at chemists' shops.

ELECTRIC CURRENT ... In most city hotels, the voltage is 230 A.C., 50 cycles. A double-wound transformer is required to reduce the voltage for American appliances, but this will not work in all places.

FAUNA ... New Zealand is famous for its birds. Chief among them, and used as the emblem of the country, is the kiwi, which cannot fly. Other indigenous birds include the parakeet, long-tailed cuckoo, kingfisher, woodhen, kaka, pukeko. All rare and beautiful. The tuatara is a prehistoric reptile, sole survivor of the age of dinosaurs. Most of these native birds and tuataras can now be seen in captivity at the Auckland Zoological Gardens.

FLORA ... Flowers are fabulous. The *houhere* (lace-bark) with its masses of snow-white clusters blooms in the autumn and varies in height from 10 to 45 feet. The *kowhai* shrub with its pendulous yellow flowers grows forty feet high; *kaka's beak,* dainty and scarlet, is a beautiful thing, as is the climbing clematis and the red *rata.* The *pohutukawa,* the New Zealand Christmas tree, blooms along the coast in a profusion of red flowers during late December and early January. There are many other flowering shrubs as well as the mountain lily and edelweiss. *Totara, rimu* and the giant *kauri* are among native timbers. Imported Monterey pines from California have flourished to the extent that their products are now forming an important industry.

FOOD ... Seafood is good. Rock oysters are a delicacy in season. *Toheroas,* New Zealand clams, are popular but somewhat rare. Crayfish and whitebait abound. Trout and game are not sold commercially, but in sporting areas these dishes are served frequently. In general the food is nourishing and plentiful, even if it sometimes lacks the imagination of Continental cooking. Milk is plentiful and pasteurized. All food and meal prices are very reasonable.

GAMBLING . . . There is horse racing in and near Auckland with pari-mutuel betting. Almost any week end or holiday race meetings take place within easy distance of the larger towns. Bets can be placed on any race in New Zealand through the Totalisator Agency Board which has representative offices in all towns.

LANGUAGE . . . The language is English. Due to the number of troops stationed in New Zealand during the Second World War, American colloquialisms are readily understood, some adopted.

LAUNDRY AND DRY CLEANING . . . These services are available at leading hotels and are on a par with similar services in the United States, although perhaps not so speedy.

LIQUOR . . . Alcoholic beverages are sold only in licensed hotels and between the hours of 9:00 A.M. and 6:00 P.M. Scotch whisky, imported wines and liqueurs are available; beer and ale are plentiful. Guests living at licensed hotels are served up to 10:00 P.M.

MEDICAL FACILITIES . . . There are good hospitals and doctors.

MOTION PICTURES . . . Current American and British films are shown at theaters throughout the country.

MUSIC . . . There is a New Zealand National Symphony Orchestra, which tours the country regularly. Maori singing is very melodious and can be heard at concerts in Rotorua.

NIGHT CLUBS AND CABARETS . . . Night clubs do not figure a great deal in New Zealand's life, but there are a few. In Auckland, Restaurant *Sorrento* on One Tree Hill, dinner-dance with floor show, Wednesday and Saturday nights; *Kenley* Road House, Swanson, dinner-dance every evening (by reservation); *Town and Country Club*, dinner-dance week nights, except Monday and Friday; *Back of The Moon, Tirirangi* (by reservation). In Wellington the *Skyline*, dinner and dancing (by reservation).

PHOTOGRAPHY . . . Cameras and equipment are available but film is in short supply. Prices are higher than in the United States. Black-and-white stills can be developed in a day, color less than a week. Or you can take undeveloped film back home.

RELIGION . . . This is a Protestant country, but you will find all denominations represented. Baptist Tabernacle, Top Queen Street; Churches of Christ, Ponsonby Road; Church of England, Wellesley Street West; Congregational Church, Beresford Street; First Church of Christ Scientist, 116 Symonds Street; Jewish Synagogue, Princes Street; Methodist Church, Pitt Street; Presbyterian Church, Symonds Street; St. Patrick's Cathedral, Wyndham Street; Church of Jesus Christ of Latter Day Saints, Upper Queen Street.

RESTAURANTS . . . Excellent food is served at the *Gourmet* in Shortland Street, *La Boheme* in Wellesley Street and *Fagels* in Customs Street. Others recommended are *Hi-Diddle-Griddle, Domino Lounge, Trade Winds* and the *Blue Lagoon*.

SHOPS AND STORES . . . All types of stores are located in the cities and towns. Milne and Choyce, Ltd., Queen Street, Auckland, is one of the largest department stores in New Zealand. Manufactured goods are usually expensive, but woolen goods are superior and worth buying. There are a number of souvenir shops which specialize in Maori art work.

SPECTATOR SPORTS ... All cities and larger towns have racing and some trotting races. National sports are Rugby football in winter, cricket in summer. Tournament tennis and golf, women's basketball, soft ball, swimming meets, regattas, soccer football, wrestling and boxing matches. The biggest one-day yachting regatta in the world on January 29 at Auckland.

SPORTS ... All cities and towns, even small towns, have good golf courses. There is excellent skiing at Tongariro National Park, at Queenstown and in the Southern Alps. There are broad sandy beaches in the North and South Islands. There are miles of beaches stretching north and south of Auckland. On the West Coast, about thirty miles from Auckland, there is magnificent surf bathing in the Tasman Sea. There is yachting, sailing, boating of all sorts. This is the sportsman's heaven.

Fishing ... Many world-famous sportsmen claim that New Zealand's big game fishing and angling for trout is the best in the world. Before starting on a fishing tour of New Zealand, ask for the folder "New Lure for Anglers," for information on tackle and equipment.

Big Game Fishing ... Some of the best big game fishing in the world is found at Bay of Islands in the "northland" of North Auckland. It is here at Russell that the famous Bay of Islands Swordfish and Mako Shark Club has its headquarters. Zane Grey, the noted sportsman and writer, was among the first to discover and popularize the big-game fishing here. Black marlin, striped marlin, shark, kingfish, swordfish are all to be found here. Record-breaking is not unusual. There are a number of charter boats available with competent captains. Modern tackle is usually provided by the launchmaster. Best months are from mid-December through April. There are comfortable fishing lodges at the main areas. No license fee required.

Fishing in North Island ... The North Island is famous for the rainbow trout-fishing districts of Taupo, Tongariro and Rotorua. In some of these spots you can actually see the trout in great numbers. The Lake Taupo region is accessible from all parts of the Island. Since many streams feed this 25-mile-long lake, trout enter the lake from all sides. The famous Tongariro River is at the southern end. The *Tokaanu Hotel* and *Bridge Lodge* in Turangi provide accommodations for those who wish to fish the delta and lower pools of the Tongariro. Right by the lake is the new *Lake Hotel,* and the excellent *Wairakei* is nearby. Lake Taupo itself is a splendid spot to fish, particularly from February to April. But the Tongariro and other rivers are better from mid-February until the close of the season, when the fish are running upriver. There is wonderful fishing in the Rotorua district, too. The lakes are filled with rainbow trout, the best time being from November to early March. There are several excellent fishing camps as well as resort hotels in this area. In the Rotorua and Taupo districts the limit of take is 6 fish per day. Average weight is

4½ lb., and legal minimum 14 inches long. License fees are inexpensive.

Fishing in South Island ... Quinnat salmon and brown trout abound in the inland waters of the South Island. The streams in the Canterbury section between Christchurch and Timaru offer the best and easiest dry-fly fishing in the country. The Selwyn, Rakaia, Rangitata and Waihao Rivers are particularly good. The Selwyn lays claim to being one of the best brown-trout streams in the world. In the southern group of fishing waters, the Waiau is known for its Atlantic salmon and Quinnat salmon run, near the mouth of Waitaki. Lake Te Anau, largest of the South Island lakes, is the home of the Atlantic salmon. Best angling is at the lake outlet where the Waiau River leaves the lake. The Mataura River in this area has impressed many visiting trout fishermen by the fact that at certain times it literally "boils with fish." There are hotels and fishing lodges everywhere.

Hunting ... There is an unlimited number of deer to be hunted in New Zealand. Red, Fallow, Wapiti, Virginian, Sambur and Chamois may be stalked. The best season is New Zealand's autumn. You may also hunt wild pig. There is no license fee, but opportunities vary in different districts, so it is well to inquire in advance. Ducks, swan, pheasant and quail offer shooting possibilities, too. But there is a season and limit here. Usually the season is about four weeks in the autumn (March, April, May). All rifles brought into New Zealand must be registered with the Arms Officer of the Police Department on arrival. No revolvers, automatics or pistols allowed. For game, 12 and 14 gauge shotguns and .22 rifles are commonly used. For birds, double-barreled 12 gauge shotguns are popular.

THEATERS ... Visiting companies appear from time to time in Auckland, but as a rule most performances are presented by local companies. Don't expect anything very spectacular in this line.

TIME ... 20 hours later than United States Pacific Coast Time.

TIPPING ... Only for special services.

TRANSPORTATION ... Air services are good. Transport by motor coach is comfortable and reliable. Trains are not up to American standards. The most pleasant way of traveling through the country is by chauffeur-driven limousine. Auto rentals are also available. You can bring your own car in for six months or more if you take it out again at the end of your visit. For local use taxis are plentiful; also buses.

WATER ... You can safely drink the water.

WHAT TO BUY ... Woolens, blankets, English pipes. Maori carvings and dolls dressed in native Maori costumes. Paua-shell novelties.

WHAT TO WEAR ... This depends upon where you are going and what you are going to do. You'll need medium- and lightweight clothes for the North Island in their summer and heavier weight clothes in the winter. You will want beach clothes, raincoat, topcoat, slacks, sweaters and sports clothes. For walking through the Milford Track on South Island, you'll need boots and sports clothes and rucksack. (Rain capes and rucksacks are procurable at the Te Anau Hotel.)

For fishing you'll need whatever you always need. The same goes for skiing. In Auckland dress as you would in any medium-sized city at home. You won't need evening clothes particularly, but you certainly need a variety of sports clothes plus topcoat, sweaters and the like.

WHERE TO GO—SIGHTSEEING...

Auckland and Environs... Auckland was founded in 1840, so don't expect to find anything very old. But you will find a pleasant city located on two oceans, the Pacific and the Tasman Sea. Within the city itself there are 31 parks and reserves. Waitemata Harbor is famous the world over and there are beautiful beaches, which stretch to the north and south of the city. You will want to see the view of the city from One Tree Hill, an extinct volcano cone in Cornwall Park. There are, by the way, 65 extinct volcanoes in and around Auckland. Drive to Ellerslie Gardens, through the Kauri and Rimu forest to Titirangi and Atkinson Parks. Take a trip to the top of Mount Eden for another gorgeous view. The scenic drive in the Waitakere Ranges gives you a good idea of the New Zealand Bush. Waiheke Island, about 13 miles from the city in the Hauraki Gulf, has some wonderful beaches. The island is reached by ferry. Kawau Island, also in the Gulf, is about 30 miles away. There is a hotel there, the *Mansion House*. Take a sightseeing bus for the waterfront drive which goes to Mt. Eden, Tamaki Heights and Ellerslie Racecourse. Forty-five miles north of Auckland is Helensville, famous for its mineral hot springs.

Waitomo... No tour of North Islands is complete without a trip to Waitomo Caves, about 133 miles from Auckland. Here is the famous and unique Glow-worm Grotto. It must be viewed in silence for the glow-worms extinguish their lamps at the slightest sound. There are other beautiful caves here. The Cathedral, the Fairy Walk, the Crystal Palace are all lovely to see. There is a pleasant hotel here, too, the *Waitomo*.

Rotorua... Is in North Island, in the center of an area of thermal activity. There is everything here, boiling mud baths, spouting geysers, alkaline and sulphuric waters. The waters are famous for bathing and drinking. Rotorua is the center of Maori life. To visit New Zealand without having seen these New Zealanders is unthinkable. Whakare-warewa is a Maori village in which the Maoris live their own easy, pleasant lives in their carved and thatched huts. Maori carvings are wonderful. During the summer season Maori concerts are given at Rotorua. If you are fortunate enough to be there at that time, be sure to attend. Maori girls sing and do a dance reminiscent of the Hawaiian hula.

There are two-day trips of great interest which may be taken from Rotorua: the Waimangu (Government round trip) and the Rotorua-Okataina Trip. The first of these takes you to Earthquake Flats, site of a vanished lake, down the Waimangu Track, across two lakes to Lake Rotomahana. Cross the lake in a launch and walk to Lake Tarawera, which you cross by launch, to the buried village of Te Wairoa. Beyond are the Blue and Green Lakes. The Rotorua-Okataina trip takes you through six lakes, including picturesque and beautiful Lake Rotoiti.

Five miles from Lake Taupo there is the modern *Wairakei Hotel,* which is centrally heated by steam that is drawn from the nearby thermal area. The hotel has its own mineral swimming pool, golf course, tennis courts and bowling green. Trips are run several times each day to the Wairakei Valley thermal area which is spectacularly thrilling and easily accessible. Other sightseeing trips include the Karapiti Blowhole, called the "Safety Valve of New Zealand," Huka Falls; Aratiatia Rapids and Lake Taupo. Trout fishing is excellent here. See description under SPORTS.

Tongariro National Park and Egmont National Park ... There are two National Parks in the North Island that are well worth a visit if you have time. Tongariro National Park is in the center of the Island just south of Lake Taupo. There is a splendid modern hotel here, the *Château Tongariro*—a golf course, tennis courts, etc. Also wonderful fishing here in the mountain streams and some breathtaking scenery. You will see three volcanic cones, two of which erupt spectacularly but harmlessly from time to time. Much of this park is untouched forest. Egmont National Park, about 100 miles to the west of Tongariro, is dominated by snow-topped Mt. Egmont, which rises from the plains and is an extinct volcanic peak. Here, too, are a forest preserve and some interesting drives.

Wellington ... The capital (about 2 hours by air from Auckland) is built on steep hills overlooking a beautiful harbor. The hills may be climbed by cable cars and electric street-cars rather like those in San Francisco. The best hotels are the *Royal Oak,* the *St. George* and the *Waterloo*. There are interesting drives through the mountains which form a backbone for the capital and a good highway which follows the coastline north. There are, of course, all sorts of public buildings, a National Art Museum, Gallery and Dominion Museum, Alexander Turnbull Library, with unique Pacific literature collection, and the Botanical Gardens, to see in the city. A trip to Hutt Valley is worthwhile.

South Island ... The South Island has some of the most marvellous scenery in the world—high mountains, majestic fiords, wide plains, lovely lakes and unspoiled forests. Starting point is usually Christchurch (about 2 hours by air from Auckland), a graceful city with broad parks and lovely gardens. Hotels include the *United Services, Warners* and the *Clarendon*.

Mt. Cook ... Dominating the long chain of the Southern Alps is Mt. Cook (12,349 ft.), which towers over nearly a score of snow-clad peaks reaching 10,000 ft. There are accommodations at the newly built *Hermitage Lodge*. There are magnificent alpine views along the route from Christchurch.

Queenstown ... On a sheltered arm of S-shaped Lake Wakatipu. Hotels include *Eichardts,* the *White Star, O'Connell's Hotel* and *Fosters*. There are many sidetrips and launch excursions on the lake, and in winter nearby Coronet Peak is a popular skiing resort.

Lake Te Anau ... Second largest New Zealand lake, it has de-

The rolling country pictured here gives an idea of the scenery around Otehei Bay in New Zealand's popular Bay of Islands area.

Excursion launches take you all around the Bay of Islands for wonderful fishing and sightseeing. Shown here is the rock tunnel off Cape Brett, Pierce Island.

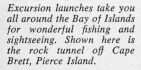

lightful fiords to explore by launch and its own special glow-worm cave. Nearby is lovely Lake Manapouri.

Milford Sound...Star of New Zealand's Fiordland is Milford Sound, reached through some of the world's finest forest and mountain scenery and through the ¾-mile-long Homer Tunnel, blasted through the solid rock of a mountain range. Milford Sound's rugged grandeur is often ranked with the fiords of Norway . . . sheer and bush-clad, the tall mountains drop straight down into the deep sea. Here, too, is the famous Milford Track, a 33-mile three-day walk often described as "The Loveliest Walk in the World." Hundreds walk it every year, but you need to be physically fit.

The Glaciers...On the West Coast of South Island the main tourist attractions are the Franz Josef and Fox Glaciers, which descend about 8,000 feet in eight miles into lowland forest less than 700 feet above sea-level. Visitors can reach these glaciers from a nearby tourist hotel, and there are daily guided excursions onto the ice itself. The West Coast is reached by railroad through the Otira

Tunnel, longest railroad tunnel (5½ miles) in the British Commonwealth, or by road through Arthur Pass or Lewis Pass.

Dunedin... Established by Scottish pioneers, is the nearest city to Queenstown. Hotels are *Wains,* the *City* and the *Grand.*

SOURCES OF FURTHER INFORMATION... In the United States, offices of the New Zealand Government Travel Commissioner at 153 Kearny Street, San Francisco 8, and at 630 Fifth Avenue, New York 20, will supply full information. In New Zealand, the New Zealand Government Tourist Bureau, 97 Queen Street, Auckland; Mercer Street, Wellington; Cathedral Square, Christchurch. Also the Tourist and Publicity Department 125 Lambton Quay, Wellington. The Public Relations Office, Achilles House, Customs Street (Tel. 31–825), specializes in services for Auckland visitors. Pan American's office is at Windsor House, 58-60 Queen Street, Auckland (Tel. 31–834).

From the Milford Hotel in the foreground there is a spectacular view across Milford Sound to the encircling mountains, and sharp crest of Mitre Peak (5,560 ft.).

At Whakarewarewa, Rotorua, Maori girls, dressed in Arawa costume, perform "canoe" poi in front of model whare. Warriors hold traditional Taiaha weapons.

Africa

BELGIAN CONGO

WEATHER IN LEOPOLDVILLE—Lat. S4°19'

Average Daytime Temp.	JAN.	FEB.	MAR.	APR.	MAY	JUNE	JULY	AUG.	SEPT.	OCT.	NOV.	DEC.
	79°	79°	79°	79°	77°	73°	70°	73°	77°	79°	77°	77°

LOCATION ... The Belgian Congo lies entirely within the tropics, mostly south of the Equator. It has only a narrow outlet to the sea at the mouth of the Congo River, separating the main part of the Portuguese province of Angola from the Cabinda Enclave, which forms the north boundary for a short distance.

CHARACTERISTICS ... The eastern part of the Belgian Congo known as the "Gem of Africa" is becoming increasingly popular with Americans and Europeans. Its scenery is most diverse. It includes active volcanoes, lakes, impenetrable forests, high plateaus and grassy meadows. The people are friendly. You are bound to find many attractions in their vast and beautiful country.

POPULATION ... The population of the Belgian Congo is composed of about 107,000 Europeans and 13,000,000 Negroes.

SIZE ... The area is estimated at 905,563 square miles, roughly one-third the area of the United States.

CAPITAL ... Leopoldville, with about 20,000 white and 400,000 native inhabitants. The native population lives in a native city and commutes from there for daily work to the European area.

GOVERNMENT ... The Belgian Congo is a Crown Colony governed by a Governor General reporting directly to the King of Belgium, except for the U.N. Trustee Territory of Ruanda Urundi.

HOW TO GET THERE ... Via Pan American World Airways in less than 27 hours elapsed time from New York. By ship about 14 days to Matadi, the seaport of the Belgian Congo.

ACCOMMODATIONS ... Recommendable hotels in Leopoldville are the *Memling* and the *Regina Hotel.* The daily rates are $5 to $7 single and $6 to $8 double, including breakfast, about $1.25 more for air-conditioned rooms. In Brazzaville, across the Congo River 20 minutes by ferryboat, is the *Relais Hotel,* a commendable hotel with excellent French cuisine. At Bukavu the *Royal Residence Hotel* and at Goma the *Hotel du Grand Lac* offer all the comforts of a first-class hotel in the United States. Rates from $6. Comfortable and clean guest houses are also available.

ARTS ... There is a museum of native arts in Leopoldville and a native crafts school of pottery in both Leopoldville and Brazzaville.

BANKS ... In Leopoldville, Banque Centrale, Banque du Congo Belge, Banque Belge d'Afrique, Societe Congolaise de Banque, Credit Congolais, Kredietbank, Banque Nationale pour le Commerce et l'Industrie, Banque de Paris et des Pays-Bas. Branch banks in other cities. Travelers checks are accepted in all banks and hotels.

CALENDAR OF HOLIDAYS ... In addition to red-letter Catholic holidays: July 1, declaration of the Congo as an independent state (it became a colony in 1908); July 21, Independence Day of Belgium; November 15, Dynasty's Day.

CIGARETTES AND TOBACCO ... Most American cigarettes and tobacco available. A package of American cigarettes costs about 24 cents. Good local brands are also produced.

CLIMATE ... The climate is hot and very humid in the western and central sections from November to May with frequent torrential rains. The dry season is most pronounced at the mouth of the Congo and on the Southern plateau (Elisabethville). June through September are the best months to visit the Belgian Congo because there is no rainfall during this period, and the evenings are always comfortably cool. For hunting, however, October through April are best, but check directly with a safari operator.

CLUBS ... The Golf Club, The Royal Cercle de Leo, and the Cercle Hippique (Riding Club) are on invitation basis only. There is also an American Men's Luncheon Club which meets every month. The Rotary, Lions, and Round Table are also represented. Two semi-private, open-air swimming pools are also available to the public.

COMMON COURTESIES AND LOCAL CUSTOMS ... This is a Belgian territory with European customs. It is customary to shake hands when you meet someone or say good-by. In better restaurants it is customary for men to wear coats and ties in the evenings in spite of the heat, but usually not during lunch.

COMMUNICATIONS ... Wireless cable and telephone connection via Brussels to the U.S. The airmail rate for postal cards and letters to the U.S. is 10 francs or 20 cents.

CURRENCY ... The official monetary unit is the Belgian Congo franc. One dollar equals 50 Belgian Congo francs.

CUSTOMS REGULATIONS AND DOCUMENTS REQUIRED FOR UNITED STATES CITIZENS ... Passport and visa. The internationally required yellow fever and smallpox certificates. Also a ticket for transportation out of the country. One opened bottle of liquor, a carton of cigarettes and non-professional camera allowed duty free.

DRUG STORES ... American drugs are available at high prices.

ELECTRIC CURRENT ... 220 volts A.C., throughout the Congo.

FAUNA ... The Eastern and Central part of the Belgian Congo abounds in all kinds of tropical birds and animals. The African gray parrot is found only in the Belgian Congo as are the small red buffalo, the tall kind of elephant and the Okapi.

FLORA ... The Belgian Congo is rich in all kinds of flowers. In the eastern mountainous part, roses and other flowers of the temperate climate are to be found. In the lower parts, the Bougainvillaea, hibiscus, the firetree (flamboyant) and the poinsettia are the most common ones. At Kisantu (70 miles from Leopoldville) there is an internationally famous botanic garden containing many varieties of orchids and unusual plants and flowers from all parts of the world. Government experimental gardens are to be found in many larger towns.

FOOD ... The moamba is a Congo specialty. It is a chicken or duck boiled in palm oil, with pili-pili, a very hot spice, and served with rice and boiled cassava leaves, or spinach. The variety of fruits is enormous: banana, tangerine, lemon, grapefruit, orange, pineapple, papayas, avocado, coeur de boeuf, mango, among others. Fresh milk is available in the Kivu and Katanga only, elsewhere condensed or powdered milk is used. Hardy souls might try a selected native cuisine of grasshoppers, toasted caterpillars and the staple manioc.

GAMBLING ... There is no gambling in the Belgian Congo.

LANGUAGE ... French is most widely used. Many speak Flemish, but English is fairly well understood and spoken by people in contact with tourists. There are over 60 native languages, four principal ones.

LAUNDRY AND DRY CLEANING ... Available but service is rather expensive and not very reliable. Drip-dry cotton and nylon clothing, which you can wash yourself, are most practical.

LIQUOR ... There are two local beer factories in Leopoldville with a good quality product. Coca-Cola, Pepsi-Cola and others have local bottling plants. Whisky and other spirits are available and lower priced than in the United States.

MEDICAL FACILITIES ... There are excellent doctors, dentists and good hospitals. The various Protestant missions have hospitals with modern equipment and outstanding doctors, "in the bush."

MOTION PICTURES ... The most important motion picture theaters at Leopoldville are: The Cinac, RAC, and the Palace. Most of the pictures are American productions with sound track in French.

NIGHT CLUBS ... There are no night clubs as such in Leopoldville. However, the air-conditioned *Manhattan Room* of the Hotel Regina is a cocktail lounge in the American style—dancing from 7:30 P.M. until the early hours. (*see* RESTAURANTS)

PHOTOGRAPHY ... All kinds of photographic equipment are

available in Leopoldville. Kodachrome film is also available. Ekta-chrome film is the only color film which can be developed locally.

RELIGION... The principal religion is Roman Catholic. How-ever, there are many American, Canadian, Swedish, English, and Danish Protestant missions scattered all over the Congo. A com-munity Protestant church and Sunday School is located in Leopoldville.

RESTAURANTS... The best restaurants in Leopoldville are the *Galiema, Deviniere* and *Grignotiere*. A la carte dinner is about $10 per person. Regular menus, if available, run from $2 to $5 for lunch and $4–$6 dinner. A good medium-priced restaurant is the *Restaurant du Zoo*. Out of town, at Djelo-Binza, is an excellent country restaurant combined with small night club, *The Borne*.

SHOPS AND STORES... There are several department stores in Leopoldville, the best being the PEK and Sedec. Shops are open from 8:00 to 12:00, and 3:00 to 6:00 o'clock. Almost all items are im-ported from Europe. A good gift shop is La Boutique de Leo.

SPECTATOR SPORTS... In November there is a tarpon-fishing contest at Moanda on the seacoast about 2 hours by air from Leopold-ville. The most outstanding horse shows of the Leopoldville Riding Club are in July. The biggest stadium in Africa, with 75,000 seats, is located in Leopoldville, and is used for all kinds of sports but chiefly for native football or soccer.

SPORTS... Hunting and fishing are the most suitable sports for tourists visiting the Congo. Travel agents in the United States can make arrangements. Check consulate regarding firearms permits.

THEATERS... European road companies and concert artists oc-casionally visit the larger cities and towns.

TIME... Leopoldville time is 6 hours later than United States Eastern Standard Time. Daylight Saving Time is not observed.

TIPPING... Tip all porters, doormen, waiters, etc., as custo-mary, but be guided also by the 5% service charge which is sometimes added to restaurant and hotel bills. For small services given by natives, tips should never exceed 5 to 10 francs, which is 10 to 20 cents. They definitely should not be calculated on a percentage basis.

TRANSPORTATION... In Leopoldville, from the airport to town, taxis can be used. The flat rate is 50 Belgian Congo francs ($1.00). Taxis to anywhere in the city, one block or twenty, cost minimum 45 B.C.F. ($.90). Taxis are rented, with driver, for about $10 per day. Drive-yourself rentals also about $10 but difficult to obtain for passing tourists. Bring International license. Sightseeing tours can be arranged.

WATER... Safe to drink in towns only. Imported and local bottled waters are available everywhere.

WHAT TO BUY... Ivory carvings and wood carvings are the most popular of the native arts. The widest choice is to be found in front of the Regina Hotel every evening. You should bargain with the natives and never pay more than half to ⅔ of the original asking price. Water color and oil paintings are hawked near every hotel. Some cost from 40¢ to 60¢.

WHAT TO WEAR ... You won't need elaborate tropical clothing but practical lightweight washable clothing and comfortable cool shoes. Bring some kind of a hat and sun glasses. Formal dress is customary only at parties in the evening throughout the year. Bring swimming suits since Leopoldville has two beautiful swimming pools. For trips into the jungle (or "bush" as it is known) check with your host or with PAA (in the Regina Hotel) as some special clothing is desirable depending on the time of year and places to be visited.

WHERE TO GO—SIGHTSEEING ...

Leopoldville ... There are a couple of itineraries you can follow in visiting the city. They cover the native market, (a "must" for color photographers—from 7 A.M. to 10 A.M. daily) the de Bock Park and the Zoological Garden, social home and sports center in the Native Quarter. A tour in the European Quarter should include the Museum of Native Life, St. Anne's Cathedral, King Albert Monument, Pioneers Monument and Stanley Monument. In Old Leopoldville are the navy yard, the old camp of Stanley, from whose time the discovery of the area dates. The road along the Congo gives you views of the Stanley Pool, the rapids, the Belvidere, the quay of the boats which cross the river to Brazzaville in French Equatorial Africa (about 20 minutes), Point Kalina and the Cristal Mountains. You can get a good view of the city from Mt. Leopold nearby. Aside from Brazzaville there are several nearby sightseeing trips that can be taken in about 3 days, which include the Inkisi Waterfalls at Zongo, the famous Inkisi Botanical Garden, the City of Kisantu (an educational center) and Thysville.

From Leopoldville you can take tours along the Congo by train, auto and boat to the principal points of sightseeing interest or include them in more extended itineraries, such as the grand Cape-to-Cairo tour. Most picturesque scenery in the Congo is in the Kivu region, with its volcanos, lakes, mountains and national parks. A trip of more than 1,000 miles in this scenic area is available by four-engine aircraft. Principal places of interest include Lake Kivu, called the "Jewel of Africa," where at Bukavu to the west you can see the famous 7-foot-tall Watussi natives and to the north the still-active Nyamalagira volcano, among others; the broad mountain-bordered plains of Albert National Park, where you see the great variety of wildlife at farther range but in greater numbers than at Kruger. (You can take a boat trip on Lake Edward in the park, too.) See the famous Ruwenzori Mountain range, called "Mountains of the Moon" (mountaineering available with guide); Ituri Forest (jungle, home of the pygmies), where you can go hunting in organized trips. Fishing is also excellent in many areas of the Belgian Congo.

SOURCES OF FURTHER INFORMATION ... The Belgian Congo Tourist Office. Office hours are 7:30–12 and 2–4:30. (Tel. 4096.) Address: P.O. Box 727. PanAm's Office is in the Regina Hotel in Leopoldville. Office hours are 8:00 to 12:00 noon and 2:00 to 5:00 P.M. (Tel. 3371 and 3372).

In New York, the Belgian Congo Tourist Bureau, 589 5th Avenue.

ETHIOPIA

Ethiopia is a mountainous land of 350,000 square miles, gateway to the big game hunting and oil country, in northeastern Africa, about 1¼ the size of Texas. Its rivers are the principal sources of the Nile. The vast majority of the thinly scattered population of 15 million are farmers and herdsmen. The climate varies from tropical to Alpine; the best time to visit is October to March. Addis Ababa, the capital (400,000 population) can be reached by Ethiopian Airlines from Frankfurt in 16 hours, from Athens in 13 hours. You need a passport and visa, smallpox and yellow fever certificates. There's a 6% tax on personal baggage. Duty-free imports are a half bottle of liquor, 50 cigars, 100 cigarettes or ½ lb. tobacco.

Best hotels in Addis Ababa are the *Ghion* and *Ras*. (The electric current is 220 volts, 60 cycle, A.C. with European type plugs.) Single room rates are U.S. $5 American Plan and up, meals about U.S. $1 each. (The Ethiopian dollar is worth U.S. $.40.) *Injera,* an unleavened bread, and *wot,* a highly seasoned stew, are among the native dishes. Chief native drinks are *tej* (mead) and *tella,* a home-brewed beer. American drinks are also available. Water is usually boiled and filtered. Bottled soda water is also available.

There are no night clubs, but the Imperial Body Guard Dance Band performs weekly at the *Ghion* and *Ras* hotels. Ethiopians love music.

Amharic is the national language among several others, although English is spoken and understood by many. The Ethiopians are a proud and aristocratic people, most of whom are of the Christian faith.

SIGHTSEEING . . . There are a number of tours of Addis Ababa which include a native mosque and the New Market, where you can buy hand-written bibles, old shields, swords and knives, silver ornaments and incense lamps quite cheaply; the Palace of Emperor Menelik II, and monument commemorating the "Massacre of Graziani"; Mount Entoto; various institutions such as the Haile Selassie I Theater. One-day excursions include a drive to Lake Gafarsa; the volcanic lakes at Bishoftu; the thermal baths and the sources of hot springs at Ambo; the town of Adama (Nazareth); the sugar plantation and re-finery at Wonji; and one-day trips to Addis Alem and Wolisso.

SOURCES OF FURTHER INFORMATION . . . Press and Information Department, P.O. Box 1364, Addis Ababa; Ethiopian Airlines, Addis Ababa (Tel. 3300). In New York the Ethiopian Consulate-General is at 270 Park Avenue.

GHANA

A coastline of waving palms, superb sandy beaches and exhilirating surf . . . a magnificent forest background . . . and in the north, rolling plains make this new member of the commonwealth of nations (it attained independence on March 6, 1957) an interesting setting for a holiday. Ghana is also a land of contrasts: of ancient castles built by early European traders who coined the name "Gold Coast" after the precious metal found there, and of modern buildings and growing cities. Above all, it is a land of light and laughter, of gaiety and courtesy, where a stranger is an honored guest.

Accra . . . A city of 150,000, is a regular stop on Pan American's African service, 20¾ hours elapsed time from New York. There are several good hotels. Most modern is the *Ambassador*—$8.40 single for bed and breakfast, $1.40 per person extra for air-conditioned rooms. Other hotels are the *Lisbon* at the airport, *Ringway*, *Avenida* and *Sea View*. The electricity in the hotels is 220 volts, 50 cycles, A.C. Restaurants are available only in the hotels and clubs. Lunch costs about $2, dinner $3. Both continental and English-style cooking are available. There is an abundance of local fruit, and food specialties include ground nut soup and palm nut soup. There is a local beer, and wines and most liquors are available at reasonable prices. The water is generally safe to drink in major cities. Bottled water is also available.

Cooler than many other tropical countries, the weather is hot enough for swimming but not too hot for sightseeing in the towns and villages. But avoid the rainy months of May, June and October in the South; August and September in the North.

To enter the country you will need a passport, visa, sufficient funds, and smallpox and yellow fever vaccination certificates. The Ghanaian pound interchangeable with sterling at par is used here, i.e., the pound is worth $2.80. You usually tip 6 pence to 1 shilling (7 to 14 cents) rather than on a percentage basis. The official language is English.

SOURCES OF FURTHER INFORMATION . . . Ghana Information Services, P.O. Box 745, Accra. Pan American's office at Ghana House, Post Office Square, P.O. Box 1119, Accra (Tel. 4198/4199). Ghana Information office at 605 Fifth Avenue, New York, N.Y.

LIBERIA

WEATHER IN FREETOWN (225 miles NW of Monrovia)—Lat. N12°8'

	JAN.	FEB.	MAR.	APR.	MAY	JUNE	JULY	AUG.	SEPT.	OCT.	NOV.	DEC.
Average Temp.	80°	81°	82°	82°	81°	79°	76°	77°	78°	79°	80°	81°
In. of Rain	.2	.1	.5	3.2	7.4	17.8	31.8	32.	27.8	11.4	5.7	.7

LIBERIA ... The Negro Republic Liberia, halfway down the west coast of Africa, about 3½ hours by Clipper from Dakar on the way to South Africa, was founded in 1821, by the American Colonization Society, which was organized in 1816 for the express purpose of helping freed slaves in the United States to return to Africa if they wished. This little country is a combination of modern Western efficiency and centuries-old African culture. Although only 310 miles from the equator, the climate is excellent. Tourists are welcome here and are treated with great friendliness and courtesy. The coastal area on the Atlantic Ocean has beautiful beaches and good fishing. Best time to visit is November-February, which avoids the rainy months.

Monrovia, the capital city of 25,000, was named after U.S. President James Monroe, who once headed the Society. Tourist accommodations are limited, but the air-conditioned *City Hotel,* a new hotel and restaurant in the center of Monrovia on Broad Street, is the best. The *Ambassador Hotel,* small but good, is on the beach, has a new swimming pool and excellent restaurant. The *Hotel Mesurado,* which also has a pool, is 2 miles from town on Bushrod Island, but furnishes free transportation at all times. The *French Hotel* in Monrovia is also recommended. Rates in all hotels range from $6 to $10. Both American and European food are served, and it's interesting to try the delicious dish, Country Chop, made from palm oil, rice, meat, and fruits.

The Pan American office is at 80 Broad Street. In New York, the Liberian Consulate is at 55 W 42nd St.

MOROCCO

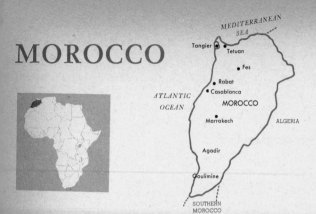

WEATHER IN CASABLANCA—Lat. N33°35'—Alt. 160'

Temp.	JAN.	FEB.	MAR.	APR.	MAY	JUNE	JULY	AUG.	SEPT.	OCT.	NOV.	DEC.
Low	44°	45°	48°	50°	60°	60°	64°	65°	62°	57°	51°	47°
High	62°	63°	66°	68°	72°	76°	80°	81°	80°	76°	69°	65°
Average	53°	54°	57°	59°	66°	68°	72°	73°	71°	67°	60°	56°
Days of Rain	8	8	9	8	5	2	0	0	2	7	8	6

LOCATION ... Morocco occupies the northwest corner of Africa, approximately at the same latitude as New York. The climate, however, is warmer due to the Gulf Stream; it is similar to that of Southern California. Casablanca is 369 air miles from Lisbon.

CHARACTERISTICS ... Morocco is fascinating for the tourist. Except for the new and modern cities, such as Casablanca, Tangier and Rabat, the country, especially in the south, has remained unchanged for centuries. The south, with its huge red *kasbahs* (forts), should be visited.

Marrakech, at the foot of the Atlas mountains, is world famous as is its *Mamounia Hotel* and the new Casino, open for gambling, during the season from November through May.

The Moroccan Tourist Office has built modern and comfortable living quarters at all interesting tourist spots.

POPULATION ... Estimated 9,000,000. The population of Casablanca, the biggest city in Morocco, is about 700,000—approximately the size of Pittsburgh.

SIZE ... About 160,000 square miles—about the area of California.

CAPITAL ... Although Casablanca is the largest city in Morocco, Rabat is the capital. The main residence of H.M. the Sultan is here as are all services of the Moroccan government.

GOVERNMENT ... H.M. the Sultan of Morocco is the supreme chief and governs the country. He is assisted by his son, the Crown Prince, and a government which is composed of approximately 15 Ministers.

HOW TO GET THERE ... By Pan American Clipper to Paris, then any connecting airline to Tangier or Casablanca, or by Clipper to Lisbon, then a short flight to Tangier and Casablanca. Via Paris, 13 hours; via Lisbon, 16 hours from New York. By ship, approximately 7 days from New York.

ACCOMMODATIONS ... In Casablanca, the newest and most modern hotel is *El Mansour,* situated in the business center of the town. De luxe service, all rooms with private bath, telephone, ice-cold drinking running water, air conditioning. Another famous hotel is the *Anfa,* where President Roosevelt and Sir Winston Churchill met in 1942. The Anfa Hotel is located on Anfa Hill, outside the city, but easily reached by bus or taxi. Other good hotels are: the *Noailles,* the *Transatlantique* and the de luxe *Marhaba.* In Marrakech, the *Mamounia* and the *Menara,* and in Rabat, *La tour Hassan,* are also de luxe hotels. Rates run from $5 to $10, European Plan.

ARTS ... The Musée des Arts Marocains in Casablanca shows samples of native crafts, pottery, copper works, rug weaving, gold and silver jewelry. Also remains of the Roman occupation of Morocco (statues, columns, potteries). There are other museums of Moroccan art in Rabat, Fes and Marrakech.

BALLET ... During the winter, the *Ballet de Paris,* and other visiting troupes perform at the Municipal Theater in Casablanca and in the principal cities of Morocco.

BANKS ... The Banque d'Etat du Maroc has a branch office in every town. Other important banks such as B.N.C.I., Credit Lyonnais, Credit Foncier, etc., have an office in every important town and are correspondents of many American banks.

CALENDAR OF HOLIDAYS ... New Year's Day; Easter and Easter Monday; May 1; May 8, V-Day; 40 days after Easter, Ascension Day; Whitsunday (Pentecost) and Monday; July 14, Bastille Day; August 15, Assumption Day; November 1, All Saints Day; November 11, Armistice Day; Christmas Day.

All Arab stores are closed during Moslem holidays; Jewish stores are closed during Jewish holidays, in addition to French holidays.

CIGARETTES AND TOBACCO ... American cigarettes available at 45 cents a pack. All French and English brands are available.

CLIMATE ... Along the shore, from Tangier down to Agadir, the climate is mild, not too cold in winter, not too hot in summer, similar to that of Southern California with about the same amount of rain. Inland, there are snowfalls in the Atlas Mountains in winter; it gets very hot in summer, especially at Marrakech and in the south, where the temperature can reach 130 degrees. Traveling in South Morocco is not recommended in the hot season, generally between June and the end of September.

CLUBS ... Automobile Club, Rotary Club, Club de l'Etrier, Golf Club de Fédala, Lions Club.

COMMON COURTESIES AND LOCAL CUSTOMS ... The Arabs do not drink wine but sweet mint tea and non-alcoholic beverages. Many Arab women are still veiled and do not sit at the same table as their guests. Friday is prayer day and many Arabs go to the Mosque on that day. The upper class of the population has approximately the same customs as in Western Europe.

COMMUNICATIONS ... Fair long-distance telephone and normal cable service. Airmail to the U.S. costs 55 francs per ounce.

CURRENCY ... In Morocco, the monetary unit is the Moroccan franc, equal to the French franc, with an official rate of 420 francs to the dollar. Money can be legally exchanged at the Banque d'Etat du Maroc, at the American Express offices, and in most hotels. In Tangier, all currencies are accepted at local daily rate and can be exchanged freely at all banks and exchange offices.

CUSTOMS REGULATIONS AND DOCUMENTS REQUIRED FOR UNITED STATES CITIZENS ... You may bring 1 carton of cigarettes, 25 cigars or 1 pound of tobacco in your luggage duty free. 1 opened bottle of liquor, only 10,000 French francs, no larger bills than $20. You need a passport, but no visa. Smallpox vaccination, cholera certificates if coming from infected area.

DRUG STORES ... All French drugs and a few American and English drugs are available in Morocco.

ELECTRIC CURRENT ... U.S. electric appliances can be utilized in Morocco merely by using a converter plug. This converter fits in the European electrical outlets and the U.S.-type cord can be plugged into the converter.

FAUNA ... Up in the Atlas Mountains wild boar. In the south, gazelle, Moroccan fox, hyena.

FLORA ... All European trees and plants, plus palm and date trees. Around the town of Agadir, in the south, grow the *argan* trees, to be found in only two places in the world: here and in Chile.

FOOD ... Famous French food available in all restaurants throughout the country. Native food can be eaten at certain restaurants (inquire at your hotel)—*see also* RESTAURANTS). Of course, the best native food to be had is when you are invited by a Moroccan family. The principal dishes are *mechoui* (whole roasted mutton), *pastilla* (salted pie containing mutton, eggs, pigeon, chicken, vegetables and typical Moroccan spices), *couscous* (semolina, mixed with mutton, chicken, all kinds of vegetables, hard peas and cooked raisins, in onion sauce). Moroccan pastries are excellent and sweet. Moroccans drink very hot, sweet mint tea with their meals. Their bread is round, flat, with very little crust, and is eaten warm.

GAMBLING ... There are two gambling places in Morocco, the Casino of Fédala and the Casino of Marrakech. Fédela is only 15 miles from Casablanca.

LANGUAGE ... The official language besides Arabic is French. But English is understood almost everywhere.

LAUNDRY AND DRY CLEANING . . . Good 24-hour service in the principal cities and good hotels. Unreliable in the small towns.

LIQUOR . . . All French and American drinks and wines available.

MEDICAL FACILITIES . . . No American hospital. Good municipal hospitals in all cities. Also very modern private hospitals with English-speaking doctors and nurses. Ask at your hotel.

MOTION PICTURES . . . Very rarely movies with English sound track and French subtitles. All newest American and French movies in French sound track versions. Very modern theaters.

MUSIC . . . The Orchestre Symphonique de Radio Maroc performs every two weeks at the Municipal Theater of Casablanca and at Rabat during the winter season. Visiting orchestras also give concerts of classical and jazz music.

NIGHT CLUBS AND CABARETS . . . In Casablanca, the *Rora*, Russian atmosphere. The *Guinguette*, the *Jardin d'Eté*, the *Embassy*, the *Montmartre*, the *Negresco*. All have floor shows. *Rora* and *Guinguette* have dinner dancing.

PHOTOGRAPHY . . . All kinds of camera and movie black-and-white and color films available in Casablanca and the principal cities of Morocco. Film developing in 24 hours. Work is good. Kodak-Pathé, S.A., is at 66, 68 Ave. de Generale Moinier, Casablanca; Casa Ros, Bv. Pasteur 8/14, Tangier; Sotaco, SA, 2, Rue de Statut, Tangier. Sunny Morocco is an ideal locale for color photography.

RELIGION . . . Moslem is the principal religion in Morocco; you find mosques everywhere. In every town, you also find Catholic and Protestant churches, and Jewish synagogues. In Casablanca the English church is located on Boulevard d'Anfa. There is also an English church in Tangier.

RESTAURANTS . . . In Casablanca, good restaurants are the *Cazenave*, *le Petit Poucet*, *l'El Mansour*, *le Marhaba*, *le Panoramique* on the top of the Anfa Hotel; *le Doge, Chez Maimaine* for French food. *Le Petit Rocher, la Mer, l'Amiraute* and *la Caravelle* along the shore for sea food. Russian specialties at the *Rora*. Spanish restaurants are the *Corrida, Las Delicias* and *le Celtique*. Prices run from $2.00 up.

SHOPS AND STORES . . . Moroccan branches of Galeries Lafayette of Paris, in principal cities of Morocco. In Casablanca, they are located at Place de France, in the business center of the town. Everything is available at a price slightly above that of France. Tangier is recommended for shopping. Being a free port, all kinds of goods from all over the world are available.

SPECTATOR SPORTS . . . Bullfights, horse, bicycle and motorcycle races during the winter. In autumn, Rallye Automobile du Maroc, followed by the International Automobile race of Morocco. Also, soccer, rugby, hockey, boxing, basket and volley ball. Tennis tournaments. Swimming meets in summer.

SPORTS . . . Golf at Casablanca, Fédala and Marrakech. Fishing up in the mountains and along the shore. Hunting during the season. A license is required for freshwater fishing and for hunting.

THEATERS ... All performances in French. At the *Municipal Theater* in Casablanca, the local opera troupe gives, during the season (November through May), all well-known operas, operettas and comic opera. Best troupes from France visit all the towns of Morocco.

TIME ... Greenwich Mean Time is observed in Morocco, 5 hours later than United States Eastern Standard Time.

TRANSPORTATION ... Plenty of taxis, most of them American make, and new. Watch the meter. Prices are doubled at night. Buses are available in all cities. Cars with or without chauffeurs can be hired at reasonable prices.

WATER ... Usually safe to drink; bottled water available.

WHAT TO BUY ... Native crafts, pottery, gold and silver jewelry, copper plates, hand-made rugs and carpets.

WHAT TO WEAR ... In summer, lightweight summer clothes. Swimming suits. In winter, warmer clothes but no furs. No dinner jacket needed.

WHERE TO GO—SIGHTSEEING ...

Casablanca ... Casablanca is a new and modern city built around what was a small Arab village, now the old Medina. It is very interesting to visit the old as well as the new Medina. The latter was built opposite the old town in the new Moorish style. Also to be seen is the Sultan's Palace; Anfa Hill, where the historic meeting of 1942 took place; the fine sand beaches and swimming pools along the shore, including Fédala, a lovely, small green city with a wonderful beach, 15 miles from Casablanca.

Side Trips ... Among the things to see in Morocco are the old typical towns and the south. Fes is the religious capital of Morocco and is the biggest Arab town in the country. It has a few hundred mosques, as well as museums, and Arab universities where students learn the Koran. Marrakech is the big southern town and the most picturesque. It is famous for its *Koutoubia* (the highest mosque in North Africa), its museums, its old Arab palaces and rich royal graves. In Marrakech there's the famous *Hotel Mamounia,* favorite vacation place of Sir Winston Churchill. The south of Morocco is wonderful, and tours can be easily arranged. The huge old *kasbahs* in the southern mountains have remained as they were centuries ago, unique and colorful. The principal spots to be seen are Taroudant, Tiznit, Tafraout, Zagora and the Dades and Todra valleys.

South of Tiznit is the town of Goulimine, where the blue people live, thus called because all men and women wear long blue veils which eventually color their skin. In the south you can also see the camel-mounted desert police. The seaports of Agadir, Mogador and Safi are most picturesque.

SOURCES OF FURTHER INFORMATION ... Transports Aeriens Intercontinentaux (TAI), 27 Ave. de l'Armee Royale, Casablanca, General Agents for Pan American. In New York The Moroccan Consulate is located at 342 Madison Ave.

SENEGAL

WEATHER IN DAKAR—Lat. N14°40'

Temp.	JAN.	FEB.	MAR.	APR.	MAY	JUNE	JULY	AUG.	SEPT.	OCT.	NOV.	DEC.
Low	62°	61°	63°	64°	66°	76°	78°	77°	76°	74°	71°	65°
High	73°	76°	75°	77°	77°	86°	87°	87°	86°	84°	81°	77°
Average	68°	69°	69°	71°	72°	81°	83°	82°	81°	79°	76°	71°
Days of Rain	0	0	0	0	0	1	10	14	15	14	1	0

LOCATION ... Senegal lies along the most westerly part of the coast of Africa. Its capital, Dakar, is the gateway to the group of new Republics that previously formed French West Africa.

CHARACTERISTICS ... This is a land of sunshine and of bright colors, a land of the old and the new. Dakar is fast transforming itself into a modern city with handsome buildings, spacious avenues. But only a few miles away in the wattle huts of the villages, the traditional African way of life continues with but little change.

POPULATION ... 2,270,000—of which 47,000 are Europeans.

SIZE ... 75,000 sq. miles, slightly smaller than South Dakota.

CAPITAL ... Dakar, with a population of about 300,000 (of which about 30,000 are Europeans).

GOVERNMENT ... Senegal, formerly a territory of French West Africa, opted in November 1958 to become an independent State, while remaining a member of the French Union. Its neighbors Mauritan, Soudan, the Ivory Coast, Niger, Dahomey and Upper Volta made similar decisions to become independent republics, all remaining nevertheless within the French Union. The other former territory of French West Africa, Guinea, when opting for independence, voted also to leave the French Union.

HOW TO GET THERE ... By Pan American Clipper, 21¼ hours from New York, 6 hours from Lisbon. By Panair do Brasil, 12 hours from Rio de Janeiro. By ship from New York, 10 days.

ACCOMMODATIONS ... The *Grand Hotel de N'Gor*, a new

hotel catering especially to the tourist trade, would be considered first class anywhere, and is outstanding for Africa. Situated 8 miles outside the city. Rates single $9 to $10; double $10 to $11. Also recommended, in the city, are the *Croix du Sud,* single from $8, double from $11; and the *Majestic,* from $6.50 to $10.50. Both the Croix du Sud and the Majestic are partially air-conditioned. Rates are European plan, year round.

CLIMATE . . . In Dakar the rainy season, or hivernage, months of July to October are hot and humid, and not recommended for a visit. Rest of the year is ideal vacation weather with warm, dry, sunny days and cool nights. Climate in the interior varies widely, but on the whole the winter months, December through May, are the best.

CUSTOMS REGULATIONS AND DOCUMENTS REQUIRED FOR UNITED STATES CITIZENS

. . . Passport, visa (obtainable from French Consulate of visitor's place of origin) and continuation or return ticket. Tourist visa for visits up to 8 days can be obtained upon arrival at Dakar. Yellow fever and smallpox certificates. 1,000 cigarettes, or 1 lb. tobacco, or 250 cigars allowed duty free.

RESTAURANTS . . . There are a number of first-class restaurants in Dakar, serving the best in French cuisine. Outstanding are the *Croix du Sud, Chez Marie Louise,* and the *Hotel N'Gor.* Lunch or dinner, with wine, runs about $5 to $6 per person. *Langouste* (crayfish) is a specialty. Filet steaks are excellent, but if you like them medium rare, ask for them fairly well done, or "*a point.*"

WHERE TO GO—SIGHTSEEING . . .

Dakar . . . See the native markets where the women in gaily colored costumes sell local produce, and where Moors from the northern deserts offer intricate silver work for sale. Nearby villages with wattle huts and palaver houses give glimpses of African tribal life.

Make sure to take a trip to Goree Island (about 20 minutes away by ferry), where slave traders imprisoned their victims before shipping them out of the country. There's an interesting museum here and a restaurant which serves good seafood.

Dakar is the jumping-off place for Timbuktoo, and if you are very ambitious you can visit the famed lost city of the deserts. But as yet there are no organized tours, and individual arrangements have to be made on the spot. Don't think of attempting this trip unless you have about 10 days to spare, and unless you are prepared to rough it. If you have two or three weeks free, then a trip on the Niger River by river steamer, with a side trip to Timbuktoo, is a wonderful experience. However take note that there are some months when due to low water level this service does not operate. A more comfortable trip would be to Conakry, capital of the republic of Guinea, one of the most attractive cities in Africa, and known as the "Pearl of the South." There is a good hotel, the *Hotel de France,* and frequent air services from Dakar (2 hours flight).

SOURCES OF FURTHER INFORMATION . . . The Syndicat d'Initiative et de Tourisme de l'A.O.F., 3, Avenue Roume, Dakar. The local Pan American office is in the Place Protet (Tel. 265–86).

UNION OF SOUTH AFRICA

WEATHER IN CAPE TOWN—Lat. S33°57′—Alt. 25′

Temp.	JAN.	FEB.	MAR.	APR.	MAY	JUNE	JULY	AUG.	SEPT.	OCT.	NOV.	DEC.
Low	60°	61°	59°	54°	51°	48°	47°	48°	50°	53°	55°	58°
High	80°	80°	78°	72°	67°	63°	62°	63°	66°	70°	74°	77°
Average	70°	70°	69°	63°	59°	56°	55°	56°	58°	62°	65°	68°
Days of Rain	4	4	4	7	10	12	11	11	9	7	6	5

LOCATION ... At the southern tip of Africa lies the Union of South Africa, comprising the provinces of Cape of Good Hope (Cape Province), Natal, Orange Free State and Transvaal, where Johannesburg is located.

CHARACTERISTICS ... Here is a land of contrasts, of wonderful tropical beaches, lush foliage, bright sunshine and high cool mountains, rugged terrain and endless stretches of veld. Brilliant flowers bloom in profusion along the South African coast. Cape Town and Durban are cosmopolitan and gay. There are good hotels, excellent swimming and fishing and all the fun you want. Inland, Johannesburg is an interesting city with a marvelous cool climate. Kruger National Park, the sanctuary for wild animals, is an unforgettable spot. So, for that matter, is all of South Africa, with its color, strangeness and allure.

POPULATION ... Estimated 14,418,000. Cape Town has 709,200 inhabitants, Johannesburg 1,030,200, and Durban 612,800.

SIZE ... 476,219 square miles, one-sixth the size of the United States.

CAPITAL ... Pretoria is the administrative capital; Cape Town, the legislative capital; Bloemfontein, the judicial capital.

GOVERNMENT ... A self-governing member of the British Commonwealth; a Governor-General represents the Queen.

HOW TO GET THERE . . . By Pan American Clipper 33 hours from New York to Johannesburg. By South African Airways, 3¼ hours from Johannesburg to Cape Town and 1¾ hours to Durban. By ship about 17 days from New York.

ACCOMMODATIONS . . . Among the tops in Johannesburg are the *Carlton*, Eloff Street; the *Waldorf*, Eloff Street; *Langham*, Kerk Street; *Criterion*, Jeppe Street; *Dawson's*, President Street; *Ambassador*, Pretoria Street; *Astor*, King George Street; *Skyline*, Twist Street, and the *Orange Grove* on Louis Botha Avenue. Rates range from $3 to $5 for bed and breakfast, $7 to $10 American Plan.

There are many excellent hotels in Cape Town and its suburbs; among them are the *Mount Nelson* at the top of Government Avenue, with magnificent views, and the *Grand*. Rates at top hotels about $6.50 to $9 single. In nearby Sea Point try the *Queens Hotel*, the *Arthur's Seat* and the *Clifton*. At Muizenberg on False Bay to the east, the *Balmoral*, *Marine* and the *St. James Hotel* which is extremely popular. There are pensions and boarding houses in Cape Town and its environs which are good, clean and reasonable.

ARTS . . . In Johannesburg the Art Gallery in Joubert Park contains a fine collection of European paintings. The Africana Museum in the Public Library tells the chronological history of South Africa.

In Cape Town the Michaelis collection of Dutch and Flemish paintings is housed in the Old Town House, which was built in 1755 and is an excellent background for the paintings. Visit the South African Museum filled with items of archaeological and ethnological interest. The National Art Gallery, off Government Avenue, contains fourteen galleries. Principal collections are the de Pass and Sir Abe Bailey exhibits. Koopmans-de Wet Museum contains a collection of Dutch colonial furniture, china and other nineteenth-century antiques.

BALLET . . . Local ballet groups include the Festival Ballet, the Theater Ballet and the Cape Town University Ballet Company. Overseas companies visit occasionally.

BANKS . . . Throughout the Union there are branches of Barclay's Bank, the Standard Bank, the Netherlands Bank, Volkskas Bank and the South African Reserve Bank. In Johannesburg, both First National City Bank and Chase Manhattan have banking offices.

CALENDAR OF HOLIDAYS . . . New Year's Day; April 6, Van Riebeeck Day; Good Friday; Easter Monday; Ascension Day; May 31, Union Day; 2nd Monday in July, Queen's Birthday; First Monday in September, Settlers Day; October 10, Kruger Day; December 16, Day of the Covenant; Christmas; and December 26, Boxing Day.

CIGARETTES, CIGARS AND TOBACCO . . . There are local brand cigarettes. English brands are available, but expensive.

CLIMATE . . . You can be comfortable visiting South Africa almost any time of the year. There are no extremes of climate and a high average of daily sunshine. The seasons being reversed, September is spring here, winter extends from May to August. The Cape has its rains during winter and the rest of the country during the summer. Except on the east coast in summer, there is little humidity.

CLUBS . . . Club life plays an important part in the social life of Johannesburg. There are many clubs which are glad to welcome visiting tourists to the city. Among the social clubs are the Rand, the New, the Union and the Automobile Club. For the ladies—the American Women's Club, Martha Washington Club and Rand Women's Club and the Vanguard. Visiting Rotarians are invited to phone the local Secretary (23-3376). Sports clubs include the Rand Flying Club, Royal Johannesburg Golf Club, Inanda Polo Club, Jockey Club and the Turf Club. The Transvaal Golf Union Club and Huddle Park Course are open to all. The Wanderers Club is one of the finest sports clubs and honorary membership can be arranged through Pan Am.

In Cape Town the Rotary Club, Cape Town City Club, Royal Cape Yacht Club, Zeekoe Vlei Yacht Club, Cape Hunt and Polo Club, Mountain Club of South Africa, Royal Cape Golf Club. The Cape Town Publicity Association in Adderley Street will be glad to give advice regarding temporary membership for visitors.

COMMON COURTESIES AND LOCAL CUSTOMS . . . The black people are pure-blooded aboriginals, usually of the Bantu race. Persons of mixed origin are referred to as colored. The word "native" refers to a black man, so when speaking to white people refer to them as just that. South Africans are famous for their hospitality. City dwellers are great tea drinkers and country people great coffee drinkers.

Another South African institution is the "sundowner party," which means getting together at the end of the day for drinks. Another pleasant custom is the *braaivleis* (pronounced "bry-flace"—a combination of the Afrikaans words *braai*—to roast, and *vleis*—meat). It is similar to our barbecue.

COMMUNICATIONS . . . There is telephone and cable service between South Africa and North America and London. Telegraph and cable offices in every village. Regular airmail services.

CURRENCY . . . The monetary unit is the South African pound worth $2.80, a very favorable rate for Americans. Money may be exchanged at banks, also at Thos. Cook & Sons and American Express.

CUSTOMS REGULATIONS AND DOCUMENTS REQUIRED FOR UNITED STATES CITIZENS . . . All goods must be declared. Cameras, field glasses, typewriters, etc., are duty free but must be declared. Open your carton of cigarettes. There is a duty on liquor. Passport and visa necessary. Proof of sufficient means and a return ticket, yellow fever and smallpox vaccination certificates are required.

DRUG STORES . . . Not as we know them. As in England they are called chemist's shops and sell only pharmaceuticals, of which there is a big variety. If you want a chocolate sundae, hamburger or hot dog, you'll get it at a milk bar, of which there are many.

ELECTRIC CURRENT . . . The current is 220–250 volts A.C. The cycles are 50, as opposed to 60 cycles in use in the United States. If you have an electric razor, you should bear this in mind. The British type of transformer plug is needed.

FAUNA . . . South Africa abounds in fabulous birds and beasts.

The best-known bird, of course, is the ostrich. In various areas of the Union you'll find secretary birds, pelicans, flamingos, purple-widow birds, red-eyed bulbuls, herons and many others.

FLORA ... If you are a flower lover you will find endless joy in the many botanical gardens and wildflower reserves. South Africans are by nature garden-lovers and in the suburbs you'll see some magnificent gardens surrounding delightful homes.

Thousands of flowers are to be seen during the spring months (September through November). The national flower of the Union is the Protea. Wild arum lilies, chincherinchees, with blooms that last for months, roses, dahlias, numerous types of erica—in fact, almost anything you can name is here. The silver leaf tree is indigenous and unique. In Natal you'll find some exotic tropical plants which do not flourish in harsher climes. Here you'll find guavas and avocados growing wild. Bougainvillaea grows in profusion as do camellias, cannas, acacia, wild cosmos and hundreds of other flowers. Jacaranda trees and flamboyants are numerous. In Cape Town the Kirstenbosch Botanic Gardens on the shady slopes of Table Mountain specialize in the study of native South African flora.

FOOD ... You will enjoy South Africa's national dishes, her excellent wines and brandies and wide variety of fruits. There's no problem about purity of the drinking water and no need to fear any unhappy results from eating the food, which is much the same as ours. South African lobster tails are a great delicacy and are served in many ways, such as cooked in butter, simmered, then served on buttered noodles or browned rice. Young fresh *mealies* (corn on the cob) is a popular dish. South Africans are great meat eaters and their steaks are particularly good. The locally homemade sausage called *boerewors* ("farm sausage") is excellent. Fish is plentiful and good. The variety of fruit is enormous—tangerine, lemon, fig, pineapple, pawpaw, avocado, melons, orange, apple, pear and some of the finest peaches. Rock oysters and crawfish are excellent. National dishes lean towards stews and *braaivleis* (barbecues). Milk is plentiful and safe.

GAMBLING ... No casinos. Horse racing in Cape Town, Johannesburg and Durban with pari-mutuel betting. Every weekend and almost every holiday meetings take place.

LANGUAGE ... The population is, in general, bilingual, speaking English and Afrikaans.

LAUNDRY AND DRY CLEANING ... Facilities are satisfactory and reasonably quick. Your hotel valet will attend to any requirements in this direction. Average price for dry cleaning a suit or dress is 85 cents. There are many dry-cleaning establishments.

LIQUOR ... South Africa makes good brandy, some good sweet wines and a fair sherry. The most popular drinks are beer, brandy and whisky, which are lower priced than in the United States. The whisky is Scotch; no bourbon is obtainable. South Africa has a local liqueur called *Van der Hum*, which is brandy-based and delicious.

Note that women are not allowed in public bars—they are welcome in private lounges in hotels. The bars are open from 10:00 A.M.

to 11:00 P.M. daily except Sundays, when you can get a drink only at your hotel.

MEDICAL FACILITIES ... There are excellent doctors and dentists. You may get free hospital treatment at any of the State hospitals. But there is a charge for special medical treatment. The Johannesburg General Hospital is the largest of its type in the Southern Hemisphere. In Cape Town the Groote Schuur Hospital and in Durban the Addington Hospital are up to date and efficient.

MOTION PICTURES ... There are many modern movie houses throughout the Union showing both British and American films and also some Continental ones. Of over 40 in Johannesburg the largest are the *Colosseum* and *Empire* in Commissioner Street, the *Metro* in Bree Street, the *20th Century* in President Street, and the *Monte Carlo* in Jeppe Street. These each seat about 3,000 people. In Cape Town the biggest are the *Colosseum* in St. George's Street, the *Alhambra* in Riebeeck Street, the *Metro* in St. George's Street, the *Van Riebeek* in Long Street. The *Broadway Theatre* on the Foreshore shows continental films. Durban's largest are the *Playhouse,* the *Metro,* the *20th Century* and the *Alhambra*—all in Smith Street. There are two performances daily at 2:15 P.M. and 8:00 P.M. on weekdays, three on Saturdays and none on Sundays. Seats may be reserved in advance.

MUSIC ... Some of the big cities have a municipal orchestra. There are ballet and opera performances seasonally. Guest performers visit the Union regularly from overseas. An *Eisteddfod,* or musical festival, is held annually in each province.

In Johannesburg interested visitors are invited to contact the Johannesburg Musical Society (33-6819) and the Johannesburg Philharmonic Society (23-1038).

NIGHT CLUBS AND CABARETS ... The clubs don't have floor shows, but in Johannesburg there is dancing nightly at the *Red Lantern,* the *Coconut Grove, Ciro's,* the *Sheraton,* the *du Barry,* the *Oxford,* the *Blue Gardenia,* the *Colony,* and the *Dorchester,* among others. In Cape Town, *Daryls* is good, and in Durban the *Cosmo* is very enjoyable.

PHOTOGRAPHY ... It's best to take with you all the film you'll need, although film is available. Also cameras and other photo equipment. Film-developing facilities are comparable with those at home.

RELIGION ... All principal religions are represented. Main places of worship in Johannesburg are the Anglican Cathedral, 56 de Villiers Street; St. George's Presbyterian Church, Noord Street; Irene Dutch Reformed Church, Plein Street; Central Congregational Church, Bree Street; Baptist Church, de Villiers Street; Central Methodist Church, Pritchard Street; Swedish Church, Hancock Street; Roman Catholic Pro-Cathedral, Kerk Street; Hebrew Synagogue, Wolmarans Street.

In Cape Town, among many others, there's an Anglican cathedral on Wale Street; a Dutch Reformed church on Adderley Street; St. Mary's Cathedral (Roman Catholic) on Roeland Street; Indian Mohammedan mosque, Long Street; a Methodist church in Greenmarket Square; a Lutheran church on Strand Street; a Presbyterian church on Somerset Road; a Christian Science church on Orange Street; a Jewish synagogue on Hatfield Street.

RESTAURANTS . . . The leading restaurants in Johannesburg include the *Carlton,* the *Criterion,* the *Waldorf, Dawson's,* the *Langham, Spaghi's,* the *Casino,* the *Quality Inn* with its oriental snuggery and *His Majesty's Cellar*—all in the center of the city and ranging in price from $2.50 to $3.50 for lunch and from $2.50 to $4.50 for dinner.

In Cape Town the best restaurants are the *Café Royal* and the *Grand Grill.* There's music at the less expensive *Waldorf.* A little farther from town are the excellent *Rossi's, Chiquito's,* the *Marine Buttery,* the *Vineyard,* the *Normandie,* and the *Palace Grill.*

SHOPS AND STORES . . . Stores are open from 8:30 A.M. to 5:30 P.M., Saturdays 8:30 A.M. to 1:00 P.M. The shopping streets in Johannesburg are Eloff, Joubert and Rissik Streets. On Eloff you'll find John Orr's; on Joubert Street there are Anstey's and Vanite (ladies), and on Rissik Street shop at Stuttafords. There are scores of other stores.

In Cape Town stores are open from 9 A.M to 5 P.M.; Saturdays 9 A.M. to 1 P.M. Among the better stores in Cape Town are Stuttafords and Garlicks.

SPECTATOR SPORTS . . . Horse racing in Johannesburg at Turffontein and Newmarket; in Durban at Greyville and Clairwood, and in Cape Town at Kenilworth. At Greyville on the first Saturday each July they run the "Durban July," one of the richest races held anywhere. You'll find cricket played all over the country in summer. Rugby is the national game and it is played in their winter. Soccer is popular and you'll find weekend matches in every city. Baseball is becoming popular with weekend games in Cape Town, Johannesburg, Durban and Port Elizabeth.

SPORTS . . . Swimming is magnificent all along the Union coast. There are dozens of golf courses throughout the country. There are tennis courts and many tennis clubs.

In and around Johannesburg there are about 18 golf clubs and two municipal courses, innumerable swimming pools and tennis. There is excellent black bass and trout fishing.

Tunny fishing near Cape Town is popular. You may angle for sole, silver fish, geelbek (Cape salmon), mullet, mackerel and many other varieties. For superb deep-sea fishing there is Hermanus, False Bay, Saldhana Bay. You fish for carp and bass on the Cape Flats lake. There are wonderful trout, bass and perch to be found in the lakes and streams in the Western Cape Province, which are within easy range of Cape Town. Licenses are required for fresh-water fishing.

There are occasions when you can ski during the winter months about 80 miles from Cape Town. Information on mountain climbing is available at the Mountain Club of South Africa, Yorkshire House, 38 Strand Street, Cape Town.

THEATERS . . . Visiting companies appear in the season (middle of May through September and also in December). In Cape Town there are several repertory groups which give performances at the

Labia, the *Little Theater,* and the *Hofmeyr.* Johannesburg theaters include *His Majesty's,* the *Reps, Brooke, Library* and the *Intimate.*

TIME . . . Seven hours later than Eastern Standard Time.

TIPPING . . . Tip for the same services as you would at home on about the same scale. There's no service charge on your bill.

TRANSPORTATION . . . Taxis are plentiful and not expensive. Outside of the municipal area you must set your price with the driver. All main cities have bus and tram services; cars are for hire at reasonable rates. This vast country is well served by rail and air services.

WATER . . . Safe to drink anywhere.

WHAT TO BUY . . . Native curios; spears; carvings; ostrich-skin bags; semi-precious South African stones; leather portraits; carved wooden animals; skins of African animals (antelope, snakes, leopards); carved ivory articles; *Karosses* (animal-skin blankets); stinkwood articles (brooches, trays, napkin rings, etc.); local pottery; tiles; wall plaques; beadwork; basketware; wooden earings. Best sources in Johannesburg are Sieradski's, the Gainsborough Galleries, Morris Davis and Ivy's; in Pretoria, Ivy's and in Cape Town Kottlers and Ivy's. In Durban the best place is in the native market.

WHAT TO WEAR . . . Remember that much of South Africa is plateauland, and that some parts lie at high altitudes. Johannesburg, for instance, has an altitude of nearly 6,000 feet, and during the winter months it can be cold in the early morning and after sunset. During the summer months women wear light dresses and the men lightweight suits. For the cold months light overcoats and woolen sweaters are necessary. A raincoat is necessary. At dances or other formal evening functions women wear long evening dresses and the men black or white dinner jackets, according to the season. For casual wear at holiday resorts, or for traveling, men wear slacks or shorts and shirts and women wear skirts or slacks and blouses.

WHERE TO GO—SIGHTSEEING . . .

Johannesburg . . . Is quite naturally called the Golden City. You mustn't miss a trip down a gold mine—a thrilling experience. You can go down 6,000 feet below the streets and find yourself at sea level. Conducted tours of the mines take place every Thursday morning. Application must be made to the Public Relations Department, Transvaal Chamber of Mines (Tel. 835-8211).

Another interesting sight is the dances performed by the native mine workers on Sunday mornings at the mine compounds. They are a genuine example of African talent. Visitors should get in touch with the Johannesburg Publicity Association (Tel. 23-2324) to arrange for mine-dance visits.

Another tour of interest is through a diamond-cutting factory, permission for which is obtained from the Master Diamond Cutters Association (Tel. 23-2760). From the top of Escom House, a 21-story building, round the corner from Pan American's office, you'll get a wonderful view of the city. Spend some time in the Herman Eckstein Park, where the Zoological gardens are situated. Don't miss a trip up to Northcliff where you get a sweeping view of the central Transvaal.

There are several tours of the city and suburbs which are worth taking and cost about $9 per 5-seater car. Don't miss a stroll through "The Wilds," a reserve devoted to native South African flora about 10 minutes from the city.

Near Johannesburg are many pleasant resorts with good boating and fishing. Black bass and trout fishing at Florida Lake is known throughout South Africa. Hartebeestpoort Dam, a lovely spot, is near Pretoria, about 40 miles from Johannesburg.

Pretoria . . . 30 miles north of Johannesburg, Pretoria is known as the "Flower of the Transvaal." In the late spring during Jacaranda Week when the trees bloom there is a festival and a contest to choose the Jacaranda Queen. There are some interesting buildings—the house from which Winston Churchill escaped in the Boer War; President Kruger's house; the Union Buildings and Gardens.

Good hotels include the *Assembly, Culemborg* and the *Union.* About 25 miles from Pretoria is the famous Premier Diamond Mine, where the Cullinan diamond was found in 1905.

Victoria Falls . . . One of the great wonders of the world, Victoria Falls, on the Zambesi River between Northern and Southern Rhodesia, is about 600 miles from Johannesburg. Discovered by Dr. Livingstone in 1855, they have become the mecca of tourists. At their greatest height they are about twice as high as Niagara and are more than a mile wide. The main falls are 273 feet high; the Rainbow Falls about 325. The volume of water in April is so great that mist and spray obscure the view. During June to October (the best time to visit) it is warm in the daytime and very cool at night, so take warm clothing along. Motor launches will take you up the river to Kandahar Island, the camp site of Livingstone. This is a full-day excursion and really fascinating. You pass Lodando Island, where occasionally hippopotami are to be seen and where crocodiles abound.

The luxurious *Victoria Falls Hotel* here has an open-air swimming pool, dancing, excellent food and comfortable rooms. Rates are about $6 single and up. There is a rest camp nearby.

Kimberley . . . This is a famous diamond-mining center in the Northern Cape about 300 miles from Johannesburg and 650 from Cape Town. You can get there by plane or rail. The Kimberley Diamond Mine is about a mile wide and is often referred to as "The Big Hole." This mine has been abandoned (shaft mining replaced open mining in the latter part of the nineteenth century), but special observation posts have been constructed so that visitors may see the amazing 450-foot hole. It is a sidewalk superintendent's paradise. There are, of course, active mines at Kimberley which may be visited. The dominating company, which arranges tours, is the de Beers Consolidated Mines, Ltd., founded by Cecil Rhodes and Barney Barnato. No uncut diamonds may be bought except from licensed dealers.

Kruger National Game Reserve . . . In the North Eastern Transvaal, along the border of Portuguese East Africa and just over 300 miles from Johannesburg, is the Kruger Game Reserve, some 200 miles long and from 30 to 60 miles wide. This is the world's most famous game sanctuary where all the wild animals of the African jungles—elephants, lions, giraffes, crossword-puzzle animals like the kudu, impalas, antelope, velvet monkeys and many many others—are to be seen from your car. The reserve is subtropical and the open season is May 29 to October 15. The southern area, however, is open all the year. Travel agencies will arrange inclusive tours if you wish or you may hire a car and drive yourself. It's about 7 hours' drive from Johannesburg and you need about a week to see the reserve thoroughly. There are 14 rest camps in the area where tourists may stay. Accommodations are comfortable with all modern conveniences. You are required to be in camp before sundown, so it is well to have a reservation. The largest and most luxurious camps are at Pretorius Kop and Skukuza, which accommodates 750 people.

From Johannesburg, the Pretorious Kop entrance (one of six) is the most convenient since the camp is only a few miles from the gate. From the Kop you will drive to Skukuza, passing the Hippo Pool en route. If you go north toward the Limpopo River (Kipling's gray, green, greasy Limpopo), you pass Letaba, a favorite spot for elephants, then to Shingwedzi, in the middle of the Mopani Forest. Plan if you can, to enter the reserve by one road and leave by another. Guides are not necessary as the roads are all well marked. Undersize cars are not advisable. The whole place is fabulous, a sort of never-never land you will not forget. The camera has replaced the gun and you have opportunities as nowhere else for photographing every type of animal from the safety of your car. African Car Hire and Springbok Safaris both operate excellent inclusive tours to the Kruger Reserve.

Cape Town . . . Cape Town is the parliamentary capital of the Union of South Africa. It is a magnificent scenic city sometimes compared with Naples because of its location on Table Bay with Table Mountain rising majestically behind the city. On either side of Table Mountain are the peaks of Devil's Peak and Lion's Head. Beyond Lion's Head a series of peaks known as the Twelve Apostles stretches toward Cape Point. It is possible to reach the top of Table Mountain by aerial railway and have a wonderful view of both the Atlantic and the Indian Oceans. The foliage and flowers which abound in the valleys and glens are magnificent.

Cape Town is a blend of the old and the new; narrow streets recalling Dutch colonial days; tall office buildings modern as tomorrow. Visit the Michaelis Collection of Flemish and Dutch paintings, the South African Museum with its fascinating "Post Office Stones," the National Art Gallery, the Houses of Parliament, which may be visited during recess, the Flower Market opposite the Post Office, the Castle whose foundations were laid in 1666. Stop in at the Municipal Botanic Gardens, which are open daily until sunset. These gardens occupy the seventeenth century site of the Dutch East India Company and contain magnificent specimens of trees and tropical plants. Take a 3-mile jaunt to the Aquarium, located at Sea Point, one of the dozens of delightful beach resorts within a 20-mile radius of Cape Town. Visit the Groote Schuur estate, the residence of the Prime Minister, which was left to the country by Cecil Rhodes. The residence is at Rondebosch, about 5 miles from town, and houses a fine collection of antiques. The Zoo is also at Rondebosch and so is the Rhodes Memorial.

Coastal suburbs stretch in each direction from Cape Town, some on the Atlantic Ocean and some on False Bay. The National Botanic Gardens at Kirstenbosch, on the eastern slopes of Table Mountain about 8 miles from the city, are famous. Admission to the Gardens is free. Groot Constantia, in Wynberg about 12 miles out of the city, is one of the few remaining old Cape houses in Dutch colonial-period style and is now a state museum. Be sure to take beautiful Marine Drive, which runs for 100 miles around the Cape Peninsula and includes Muizenberg, one of the most famous resorts in the country. The Cape Town Publicity Association will give you details of some wonderful drives in the vicinity of Cape Town with prices ranging from $5.60 to about $30 for a 5-seater car.

The Garden Route tour from Cape Town to Plettenberg Bay (300 miles) on the Indian Ocean is one of the most famous. Price about $85. The trip takes in the fabulous Cango Caves, visits an ostrich farm at Oudtshoorn, proceeds over Montague Pass to George and on to the "Wilderness," a lovely seaside resort.

Durban . . . You may go to Durban from Cape Town or Johannesburg either by motor coach, rail or plane. A crack train, the *Orange Express,* runs between Cape Town and Durban. This delightful coastal city, about 400 miles from Johannesburg on the east coast, has fine hotels, swimming, fishing, and a colorful population. The Indian and Native Markets are fascinating. There is a Zulu Reserve within 75 miles of the city to which motor trips are made. Durban itself has a Marine Parade and a residential section called the Berea, which is on a crest of hills.

Durban is a riot of color. Its sub-tropical climate makes its plant life luxurious. The wide streets are lined with flowering trees. This is a city of contrasts where the proud Zulu rickshaw boy, resplendent in skins and beads, carries Indian women dressed in exquisitely embroidered saris. There are some lovely drives, which range in price from about $9 to $30 per 5-seater car. Along the northern Natal coast are St. Lucia Bay and Richards Bay where there is wonderful surf and lake fishing. The Durban Country Club has a championship golf course. There is excellent horse racing here too. Hotels along the Marine Parade in Durban include the *Edward,* the *Marine, Claridge's, Edenroc,* the *Balmoral,* the *Cumberland,* the *Torquay,* and the *Majestic.* In the city, try the *Mayfair,* the *Caister* or the *Butterworth.* By all means take in the *Cafe de Paris* at Claridge's and the *Causerie* at the Edward on the beach front. There are many night spots in and around the city.

Royal Natal National Park . . . Is about half a day's run by car from Durban, a 20,000-acre reserve with magnificent scenery. Here are the Tugela River Falls, a game and flower sanctuary, and towering Mont Aux-Sources. There is an excellent hotel, the *Royal National Park Hostel* with swimming, riding, fishing and lots of beauty.

About 190 miles from Durban in the heart of Zululand is Hluhluwe (pronounced "Shloo-shloo-wee") where you see the rare white rhino, also plenty of black rhino, buffalo, impala, zebra, and other wild beasts. The views are wonderful, the foliage and flowers magnificent. There is an excellent rest camp with typical *Rondavel* huts. Bring your own food or purchase it en route. African servants will cook, if you like. Wear dark clothes; bright colors frighten the animals. Winter is the best time here. Two days are needed to make this tour.

The Drakensberg ... The mountain resorts of the Drakensberg Range bordering Natal and Orange Free State are popular tourist spots. There is some splendid and some very difficult mountain climbing here. The climate is fine—warm days and cool nights. The fishing is excellent; the hiking and riding magnificent. The hotels are modern, have swimming pools, cinemas, *braaivleis* (barbecues) and plenty of other entertainment. You may stay in a thatched *Rondavel,* or in the main hotel. Rates are about $4.50 a day and up.

SOURCES OF FURTHER INFORMATION ... The Johannesburg Publicity Association, Darragh House, corner of Plein and Hoek Streets (Tel. 23–2324) is an excellent organization which will go out of its way to help the tourist. Pan American's offices are at 517 Grand Parade Centre, Trafalgar Place (Tel. 22094) in Cape Town and 29 Loveday Street (Tel. 33–0723) in Johannesburg.

The Cape Town Visitors' Bureau in Adderley Street and the Durban Visitors' Bureau in West Street have available supplies of folders in English, city and country maps, information regarding local events, hotels, restaurants, tours, etc. In New York the South African Tourist Corporation at 610 Fifth Avenue has excellent travel information.

The characteristic African accommodations for tourists, called Rondavels, *are very handy for sightseeing around the Keurbooms River mouth and Plettenberg Bay on the Garden drive from Cape Town to Durban.*

INDEX